Senses, Sensors and Systems

A journey through the history of laboratory diagnosis

Senses, Sensors
and Systems

Contents

Preface

Man's efforts to unravel the causes of disease are as old as mankind itself. While the earliest healers naturally and necessarily focused on outward signs of ill health, the physicians of antiquity were already paying attention to body fluids. And if the methods of medieval uroscopy strike us today as more fanciful than useful, it is encouraging to note that by the late 17th century chemical and physical tests were available for demonstrating sugar and protein in urine. In the mid-18th century the Italian anatomist Giovanni Battista Morgagni (1682–1771) was still hunting for the causes of disease in the 'solid parts' of the body, yet a century later the Berlin physician Rudolf Virchow (1821–1902) was already ushering in the age of cellular pathology. In the 20th century it was the interior of the cell which increasingly became the centre of diagnostic interest, and in our own century researchers have begun delving into the mysteries of disease at the molecular level. Advances in biology, chemistry and technology have resulted in the powerful and reliable tools now used in laboratory medicine, tools that provide physicians with essential information for therapeutic decision-making. And as progress continues in molecular medicine, we can see entirely new possibilities on the horizon. Gene and protein analysis are making it possible to diagnose risk factors and disease susceptibilities before the onset of clinical disease, and they are also opening the way to treatments tailored more specifically to the needs of individual patients.

Senses, Sensors and Systems describes the (r)evolutionary changes that have taken place in diagnostic testing, tracing the developments which led from medieval uroscopy to today's lab-on-a-chip systems and point to yet more innovations to come. The book tells a story of discovery that few physicians, scientists, laboratory technicians or patients are very familiar with. The diagnostic options available in the past and present and some of the advances anticipated in the future are surveyed in depth and with a thematic breadth unmatched by other publications on the subject. In a masterly synthesis of historical and scientific information, the book shows how, over the centuries, theory experimentation, technical innovation and clinical experience have come together to create a medical specialty that benefits patients everywhere.

Prof. Lothar Thomas
Dept. of Laboratory Medicine
Northwest Hospital
Frankfurt am Main   August 2003

Introduction

One of the pleasantest ways of approaching a complex subject in science or medicine is by examining its history. This book offers you an opportunity to do just that. It takes the reader on a journey through the history of the diagnostic laboratory – a place the French physiologist Claude Bernard (1813–1878) once described as the 'inner sanctum of medicine' – and the tests that are (or once were) performed there. As with any tour, there are genuine points of interest that aren't on the itinerary and others that can only be visited briefly. But there will still be much to see. In their historical surveys, the authors – medical historians, scientists, physicians and science journalists from Europe, Japan and the United States – describe and explain many of the landmarks in the development of what is now commonly referred to as in vitro diagnostic testing. The book retraces the steps of the investigators who learned how to diagnose common, and in some cases still life-threatening, diseases by analysing body fluids such as urine or blood or, more recently, by analysing tissue samples. Diabetes, cardiovascular disease, cancer and major infectious diseases such as tuberculosis, AIDS and influenza are just a few examples of the conditions that can now be detected at an early stage thanks to the efforts of these pioneers. The authors also show how laboratory tests transformed medical practice by making it possible to diagnose pregnancy early, transfuse blood safely and detect coagulation disorders.

The earliest diagnoses were made using the unaided *senses,* for example by observing a urine sample for telltale signs of disease or tasting a patient's urine for the presence of sugar. Later a variety of instruments and *sensors* capable of extending the reach of the senses beyond their natural limits were added to the diagnostic armamentarium. The advent of the microscope, for example, led to the discovery of a new microworld and the pathogens that inhabit it. As understanding of the mechanisms of disease grew, diagnostic tests became more objective, and as a result have increasingly been performed by automated *systems* since the mid-20th century.

People have of course always played the leading in role in the diagnosis of disease. So it is only natural for this historical survey to place a special emphasis on introducing readers to the men and women whose investigations, discoveries and setbacks have contributed to the current state of clinical laboratory practice. Many of these pioneers set out to answer questions quite different from the ones they ultimately did answer. Advances in diagnostic methods have come about through a combination of hard work, intuition and chance. This last, it should noted, is not entirely random in science and medicine, but tends, as Louis Pasteur (1822–1895) once observed, 'to favour the prepared mind'. An effort was made to find out as much as possible about the physicians and scientists behind the achievements described here, though oddly it was often easier to find information on investigators who lived centuries ago than on their 20th-century counterparts. Also, the 20th and 21st centuries have witnessed an exponential increase in the number of medical publications, the majority of them authored by a team of investigators rather than by a single individual.

Test strips serve as visual signposts guiding the reader through the book. The colour scheme that has been selected is based on the colour changes seen in widely used diagnostic test strips and follows the sequence in which the strips were introduced. The material in the book is arranged both thematically and chronologically. Each chapter is devoted either to a particular medical specialty or to a major advance in laboratory testing. In addition to accounts of early practices and discoveries in ancient and medieval times, the chapters trace the explosive developments of the last 150 years, outline the current state of laboratory medicine and take a look ahead at some of the innovations on the horizon.

The chapters are grouped chronologically into four major sections. The first section focuses on the history of fields that date from before 1840 or grew out of significant work done prior to that year. The chapters in the second section cover developments that occurred after about the middle of the 19th century, as laboratory medicine was emerging as a new speciality. The third section examines the revolution that took place in the medical laboratory in the mid-20th century, when automation and immunoassays arrived on the scene and greatly increased the speed and accuracy of laboratory testing. The fourth and final section looks at the advances that have had an impact on laboratory diagnosis since 1983, the year the polymerase chain reaction was invented.

This book is intended not only to show how many difficulties and challenges had to be overcome for laboratory testing to get where it is today, but also to raise the reader's awareness of how many things simple laboratory tests are now able to tell us. Not only are in vitro diagnostic tests indispensable for making a correct diagnosis, but therapeutic decisions now often hinge on the results.

Another major aim in preparing this book was to keep it as reader-friendly as possible. Given the nature of the subject matter, striking a perfectly satisfactory balance between scientific precision and general readability was not always easy and in some places impossible.

I wish to express my sincere thanks to the authors and my colleagues; without their strong commitment to this project, it would never have been completed. I am equally grateful to the many experts who generously contributed their advice and views and who also provided many of the illustrations used in the book.

Sabine Päuser, PhD   Basel, August 2003

Fortune tellers, true observations and honest efforts

Le Medecin du Village

Johannes Büttner

This liquid, which commonly inspires men only with contempt and disgust, which is generally ranked amongst vile and repulsive matters, has become in the hands of chemists, a source of important discoveries, and is an object in the history of which we find the most singular disparity between the ideas which are generally formed of it in the world, and the valuable notion which the study of it affords to the physiologist, the physician and the philosopher.[1]

Antoine François [de] Fourcroy, 1755–1809

From matula to test strip

The history of urine examination

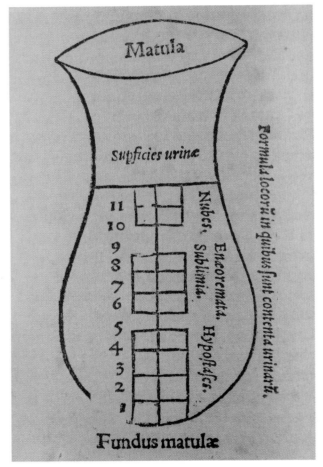

A urine flask, or matula. The flask has 12 divisions, grouped into zones for sediment, floating matter, clouds and the surface of the urine. Woodcut from De urinis libri VII by Joannes Aktuarios, 1529.

Since the beginnings of medicine, patients and physicians have paid special attention to human urine. References to its appearance in sickness and health have been found in writings in cuneiform script, Sanskrit, and Egyptian hieroglyphs. To find the first clear indications of what physicians hoped to learn by examining urine, however, one has to turn to the later medical literature of ancient Greece. In the properties of urine the medical practitioner saw signs pointing to hidden states or processes in the body. In the poetic phrase of an 18th century French encyclopedist, outward signs served 'as a torch to penetrate the dark interior of the healthy and the sick'.

From the writings of Hippocrates of Cos (c. 460–c. 375 BC), we know that the Greek physician carefully observed a whole range of signs before pronouncing on a patient's condition, the duration of the illness and the likelihood of a favourable or unfavourable outcome. Observable signs thus provided information primarily on the likely course of a disease, i. e. its prognosis. Diagnosis in today's sense did not yet exist, not least because the modern concept of disease would have been totally foreign to the physician of antiquity. For Hippocrates, disease was a state involving the whole patient, not a localised entity in its own right. Attention focused mainly on the pulse, while examination of the urine, or uroscopy, for the time being played a secondary role. The early Hippocratic writings refer mainly to the colour of urine and the *contenta*, i. e., the elements contained in the urine water, which were differentiated as cloud, floating matter and sediment. A typical passage from Hippocrates' *Prognostic*, a collection of teachings on the art of prognosis, reads:

> Clouds suspended in the urine are good when white but bad when black.[2]

While disease signs were initially identified by close observation alone, attempts were later made to fit them into an interpretive context. This required theories on the structure and function of the human body. The central theory in antiquity accounting for the workings of the human body was the humoral doctrine, which developed over time into the theory of the four humours (blood, phlegm, black bile and yellow bile) and received its definitive formulation in the works of the Greek physician Claudius Galen (AD 129 – c. 216), who later practised in Rome. The humours (Latin: *humores*), i. e. the fluids from which the body was thought to be composed, were assigned qualities (hot, wet, cold, dry). Health was seen as a state in which the humours were harmoniously balanced, while many diseases were attributed to a faulty mixture of humours, or dyscrasia.

Drawing on his own experiments in animals, Galen was also the first to develop physiological ideas about the function of the kidneys and the production of urine. He believed that blood was formed by a kind of boiling process in the liver from the chyme produced in the stomach. The liquid part of the blood, which the Greeks called 'whey' (by analogy with the watery part of milk) and which we now call 'serum', was thought to contain not only waste products from food and superfluous moisture, but also substances associated with disease. The kidneys excreted this liquid from the blood as urine. Galen wondered if this process was mechanical or the result of a special 'force'. Incidentally, *orós*, the Greek word for whey, later gave rise to the term *oúron*, or 'urine'. Given this theory of urine formation, it was natural to suppose that examining a person's urine would provide information about the condition of the humours in the blood. Galen's humoral theory

Physician studying a flask of urine brought by a young woman. Frontispiece from: Anatomia urinae galeno-spagyrica, *1658.*

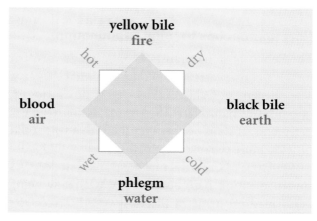

Schematic representation of Galen's humoral theory. The humours yellow bile, black bile, phlegm and blood are paired with the elements fire, earth, water and air. The qualities dry, cold, wet and hot are each shared by two humours.

was to remain the theoretical basis of urine examination until the beginning of the modern era.

Urine examination was developed further by physicians in Byzantium, such as Theophilos Protospatharios (7th century), and by physicians writing in Arabic, whether Muslim or, as in the case of Isaac Judaeus (Ishaq ibn Sulaiman al-Isra'ili) (880 – c. 955), Jewish. The signs observed in urine – colour, consistency (thin, thick) and *contenta* – were systematically derived from the assumed properties of the four humours. Intensely yellow urine, for example, pointed to a predominance of yellow bile, and hence to the liver. Theophilos' *On Urine* remained for many

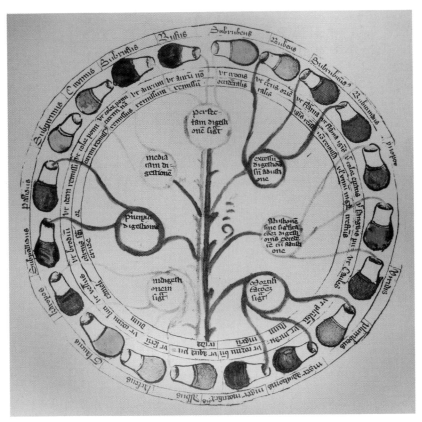

Urine colours. A colour chart from the Fasciculus Medicinae *of Johannes de Ketham (manuscript dating from 1400).*

centuries the best-known text on urine examination. After the invention of letterpress printing, it became part of the *Articella* ('Little Art'), the most important compendium of its time for medical students.

The matula

In the High Middle Ages it became customary to collect a patient's urine in a specially shaped glass vessel that permitted close inspection by the physician. This vessel was known by the Latin name *matula,* a word essentially meaning 'a container for liquids', but sometimes synonymous with 'chamber pot'. The matula was brought to the physician for examination in a bast basket, and frequently the physician did not see the patient at all.

The matula was the symbol of the medical profession in the Middle Ages, supplanting the snake-entwined staff of Aesculapius. This in itself is indicative of the high esteem that uroscopy attained in medieval medicine. The physician's assessment of urine colour was the distinctive medical act. Twenty or more shades of colour were distinguished, as descriptions in numerous old manuscripts attest. Over time, uroscopy evolved into an increasingly complicated art, replete with ever more speculative ele-

ments, including supposed affinities between parts of the urine flask and parts of the human body. Phenomena in the upper part of the flask, the clouds, were thought to be related to diseases of the head, for example, while the sediment was supposed to point to disorders in the lower regions of the body.

The most complete account of uroscopy, with theoretical speculations on its interpretation, was bequeathed to us by the Byzantine court physician Joannes Aktuarios, who lived in the 14th century. Byzantine and Arab uroscopy entered medieval western medicine in the 12th century, mainly by way of the Medical School of Salerno, which was instrumental in codifying the precepts of practical uroscopy, for example in *carmina,* or didactic poems, which were learnt by heart. The *Carmina de urinarum iudiciis* ('urine verdict songs'), by the Paris physician Gilles de Corbeil (1140–1224) are an example of this medical genre. The following hexameters by Corbeil offer an interpretation of clouds in the urine:

> Airy small cloud, a sign of panting breath,
> At the same time reveals the hot liver's infirmity.[3]

Uroscopy of this type was taught and practised for centuries, although it passed increasingly into lay hands. The 'water doctor' was already a well-known figure in the Middle Ages. In Shakespeare's *King Henry IV,* Sir John Falstaff is teased by his page:

> Falstaff: …what says the doctor to my water?
> Page: He said, sir, the water itself was a good healthy water; but, for the party that owed it, he might have more diseases than he knew for.[4]

Patients and physicians in the 16th century often complained that even 'the stupidest, most inexperienced rabble' practised urine inspection and deceived patients.[5] Uroscopy degenerated into uromancy, divination by studying urine.

New approaches to urine examination

The Renaissance naturalists were no longer content merely to observe urine and interpret what they saw. They began, as Galileo (1564–1642) put it, to ask questions of nature, in other words, to perform experiments. It soon occurred to them that this could provide more reliable diagnostic signs.

One type of experimental measurement deserves special mention here because it was already being performed on urine in the early Middle Ages: the determination of specific gravity (known today as specific density). From a text by the Arab scholar al-Khâzinî, who lived around 1120 in Mary in what is today Turkmenistan, we know of an instrument

Urine balance, c. 1600. Urine was measured in a metal can by filling the can to the brim, then poured into one of the balance pans and weighed with the weights at the top left.

The areometer of Pappus of Alexandria was described by al-Khâzinî around 1120. Left: a replica of Pappus' instrument; right: a modern areometer.

for measuring the specific gravity of liquids which the Greek mathematician Pappus (c. 300–350) is said to have invented in Alexandria. Al-Khâzinî described this instrument in such detail that it was possible to build a modern working replica. The instrument is based on the well-known principle of Archimedes (c. 287–212 BC), according to which the buoyancy of a body immersed in a liquid is equal to the weight of the liquid displaced. Pappus' instrument was known as an areometer, a name that refers to the 'empty space' between dissolved particles of a liquid. It was thus an instrument for measuring 'thinness'. Such devices are also called hydrometers. Al-Khâzinî measured the density of urine with great accuracy using this instrument and discussed the significance of the results for health.

Similarly, in a dialogue published around 1450 on experiments with scales, the Renaissance theologian and philosopher Nicholas of Cusa (1401–1464) proposed that the weights of blood and urine samples be measured, arguing that these differed in the healthy and sick and were therefore of great value to the physician.

From the 16th century onwards, weighing also formed part of the medical examination of urine in Europe. A treatise by Gerhard Dorn (fl. 1600), *The Anatomy of Urine*, describes the apparatus used for this procedure. However, the substances contained in the urine remained largely unknown, and attempts to explain the observed phenomena were still based on the humoral theory.

First chemical theory of disease

Striking out in a different direction, the physician Theophrastus Bombastus von Hohenheim (1493/4–1541), better known as Paracelsus, envisioned a new medicine based on alchemy. An advocate of chemical methods for investigating urine as well as in other areas of medical practice, he wrote: 'Therefore learn to separate and precipitate / if you want to be right in urine.'[6] He was referring to the chemical separation of the substances contained in urine. Paracelsus hoped that this would reveal signs hidden from the eye that could be used in the diagnosis of disease. Particularly noteworthy, even today, is his theory of 'tartaric diseases', which he believed were caused by the formation of solid, crystalline materials from unhealthy humours in the body. These materials he called '*tartarus*', deriving the term from the name for hell in Greek mythology. The term was meant to express both the 'falling', or precipitation, of certain substances to the bottom of a fluid and the agonising afflictions they caused, such as stones in the kidney and bladder, or the manifestations of gout. This was the first chemical theory of disease. The word 'tartar' later came to be used for the scale deposited

Urinary sediment crystals, from Robert Hooke's Micrographia *(1665). Hooke described these crystals as 'tartaric', i.e. as forms of the* tartarus *observed by Paracelsus.*

on the inside of wine barrels during fermentation. It also recurs in the works of Robert Hooke (1635–1703), who used it to describe the crystals he observed while studying urinary sediment under the microscope.

The pupils of Paracelsus attempted to create a chemistry-based medicine, or 'iatrochemistry', albeit with no lasting impact on medical practice. They used various methods to break down the substances contained in the human body and its excretions. Among the processes they copied from nature were putrefaction and fermentation. The art of the alchemists had refined the controlled use of fire in distillation. Paracelsus himself described the separation of urine into 'elements' by means of a distillation process. By observing urine – now in the retort instead of the matula – some of his pupils hoped to draw conclusions about the sites of disease in patients' bodies.

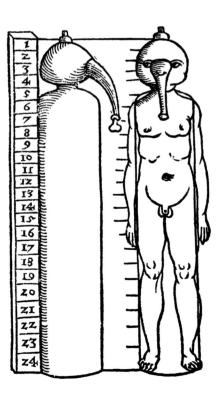

Two views of a urine retort, c. 1600. The retort is divided into zones corresponding to regions of the human body, as shown by the front view, superimposed on a human figure, on the right.

Early chemical investigations of urine

The first systematic attempts at analysing the chemical composition of urine were made by Jan Baptista van Helmont (1579–1644), who described himself as a *philosophus per ignem*, i. e. as a naturalist working with fire. Employing the distillation method, as others before him had done, he found various salts, one of which he identified as 'sea salt'. The discovery of phosphorus in urine by the alchemist Hennig Brand in the latter half of the 17th century was considered a scientific sensation. Urine contains salts of phosphoric acid, and Brand, after subjecting a large amount of urine to an elaborate alchemical process, had obtained a substance that glowed in the dark. We know today that the substance was elemental phosphorus and that the glow resulted from a process known as chemiluminescence. The strange glowing substance caused a considerable stir because it had originated in a living human body.

'Organic substances' come into view

Despite the crude methods employed at the time, it wasn't long before various pathological (i. e. disease-related) substances were discovered in urine. In 1695, for example, the Dutch physician Frederik Dekkers (1648–1720) precipitated a cheese- or serum-like substance by heating acidified urine. This substance, which behaved like egg white, occurred above all in patients with dropsy.

Distillation soon proved an unsuitable method of studying urine, as it emerged that substances occurring only in living organisms, and thus termed 'organic', were sensitive to heat. Finding ways of working with these sensitive substances took a rather longer, the first breakthroughs occurring in the late 18th century. In 1773 the French chemist Hilaire Martin Rouelle (1718–1779) succeeded in obtaining a 'soapy material' from urine by dissolving it out with spirits of wine (aqueous ethanol). Antoine François [de] Fourcroy (1755–1809) later named this soapy material *urée* (urea). The German-Swedish chemist Carl Wilhelm Scheele (1742–1786) achieved some notable successes with an experimental approach in which he isolated organic compounds in crystalline form by precipitation with 'reagents' and different types of solvents. In 1776 he found a substance which he named 'lithic acid', and which today we call uric acid, in bladder stones and in urine. The Englishman Matthew Dobson (1745–1784) obtained a sugar-like substance from diabetic urine. This explained the sweet taste of urine described by Thomas Willis (1621–1675) in diabetics. However, Dobson's method was too laborious for diagnosing diabetes.

Antoine François [de] Fourcroy *(1755–1809) made a successful switch to chemistry after studying medicine and was appointed professor of chemistry at the Royal Veterinary School in Alfort in 1783. A year later he was named professor of chemistry at the King's Garden, the forerunner of the Natural History Museum. Together with his assistant, Nicholas Louis Vauquelin (1763–1829), he performed numerous analyses of organic compounds. In 1789 he was active in the Revolution as a Jacobin. He was involved in compiling the people's complaints in the 'notebooks of grievances'. In 1793 he was elected as Jean-Paul Marat's successor to the National Convention, where he served on several committees. As a member of the Public Education Committee, he developed plans for modernising medical education. The newly founded faculties in Paris, Montpellier and Strasbourg were called Schools of Health, to distinguish them from the old medical faculties. In 1795 he was appointed to the Paris School as professor of medical chemistry and pharmacy. Napoleon I Bonaparte (1769–1821) made him a count in recognition of his services.*

Around the year 1800 the main components of urine were known: inorganic salts and a few organic substances such as urea, sugar and protein.

The pursuit of objectivity

The early 19th century witnessed far-reaching changes in medicine. Not only were medical discoveries now being made in a different way, but large hospitals were being built, providing a setting in which patients could be observed and compared in considerable numbers. Also, there were attempts at connecting observations in patients with autopsy findings – in other words, at linking clinical medicine with morbid anatomy. This entailed changes in the way patients and their excretions were examined. The goal was to develop objective methods. Increas-

ingly, observation using the senses was complemented by the use of instrumentation and, more particularly, by measurement. This made it possible to describe findings in the far more precise language of 'measure and number'. The concept of disease also changed. Diseases began to be described 'objectively', without reference to individual patients. The outward manifestations of illness became signs and symptoms: interdependent clinical findings which the physician had to piece together to arrive at a diagnosis and which themselves constituted integral and defining elements of the disease entities recognised by medicine. Medical science sought to explain these clinical findings in terms of cause and effect.

Urine as a marker of disease

In this climate of change, urine examination also acquired an entirely new significance. Around 1800 the presence of protein in urine was reported in a number of diseases, including malaria, gout, chlorosis (or green sickness, a form of iron-deficiency anemia in young women) and dropsy. At Guy's Hospital in London the physician Richard Bright (1789–1858) was investigating inflammation of the kidneys, which was very common at the time. He carried out extensive studies in a large number of affected patients, focusing in particular on albuminuria, the excretion of protein in urine. Bright had devised an ingeniously simple method for detecting urine protein: when heated in a teaspoon over a candle, urine coagulates if protein is present. In 1827, with the aid of autopsy evidence, he defined the three cardinal features of nephritis: dropsy, proteinuria and characteristic anatomical changes in both kidneys.[7] This was the first time that a urine finding had been included in the definition of a disease, and Bright's simple protein test became one of the most important urine tests in the medical armamentarium.

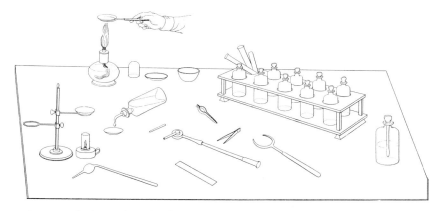

Apparatus for inspecting urine, from a book by Alexander Marcet. At the top left a sample is heated in a spoon over a spirit flame. Richard Bright, one of Marcet's students, used this technique to test urine for protein.

How do the kidneys make urine?

Over the course of 250 years, anatomists and physiologists have succeeded in elucidating the extraordinarily complex mechanism of urine production.

Although it had been accepted since the Middle Ages that urine is formed from blood in the kidney by a kind of filtration, a clearer picture of renal urine production only emerged in the 17th century. The first notable discovery was that by the Italian Lorenzo Bellini (1643–1704), who in 1662 found tubular structures in the kidneys that were filled with a salty liquid. Today 'Bellini's ducts' are known as renal tubules. Four years later, another Italian, Marcello Malpighi (1628–1694), published his famous work on the kidney, in which he described for the first time the clusters of microscopic blood vessels (glomeruli) which together with a surrounding capsule form the malpighian bodies (renal corpuscles). It was not until almost 200 years later, in 1842, that the connection between these structures was recognised by the Englishman William Bowman (1816–1892), who used the microscope to describe the structural units of the kidney responsible for urine production. In the same year the Leipzig physiologist Carl Ludwig (1816–1895) published his theory of urine production as a process of blood filtration. According to Ludwig, blood pressure forced water from the blood to pass through the vessel walls of the glomerulus, and a substantial proportion of the water was then reabsorbed from the renal tubules and thus retained by the body. In 1917 the American physiologist Arthur R. Cushny (1866–1926) presented the essentials of the current explanation of urine production, which, apart from the physical processes of filtration and water reabsorption, also postulated an 'active' reabsorption process for certain other substances that allows initially filtered substances, such as glucose, to be returned to the body. Eli Kennerly Marshall (1889–1966) and James L. Vickers (1899–1943) completed the picture in 1923 by proving that certain substances can also be discharged into the tubule directly from the blood, bypassing the glomerulus.

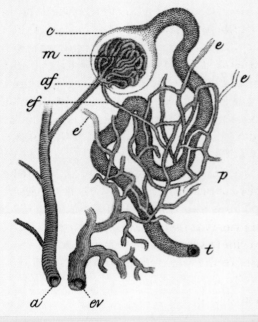

Human kidney glomerulus with renal tubule, arteries and veins, drawn by William Bowman (1842). The renal artery (**a**) carries blood to the kidney. A branch of the artery (**af**) enters the round structure (**m**) of the malpighian body (glomerulus), which is encased in the capsule (**c**) described by Bowman. Extending from the glomerulus are the tortuous Bellini tubules (**t**) which conduct the resulting urine away. Veins (**ef** and **ev**) transport blood away from the glomerulus.

Certain forms of nephritis continued to be known as Bright's disease until the second half of the 20th century.

In measure and number?

To be of any use in diagnosing and treating patients, chemical urinalysis had to be made simple. The search thus began for suitable reagents, i.e. for chemicals which, when mixed with urine, would produce a colour change, a precipitate or some other characteristic effect. Many chemical reagents for investigating urine were found during the course of the 19th century, and by the second half of the century they were available to physicians in bedside detection tests. Developing methods for the quantitative analysis of urine – i.e. for determining its constituents 'in measure and number' – proved a more formidable challenge. As early as 1808 Berzelius had performed a very thorough and exact quantitative analysis of the urine of a healthy man, which even 30 years later was regarded as unsurpassed in its accuracy. But it had taken him several months. Similarly, the 'laws governing the chemical composition of urine', which the American biochemist Otto Folin (1867–1934) enunciated some 100 years later, in 1905, based on many quantitative urinalyses in healthy subjects, were of little bedside help, since the methods used to derive them were too involved and time consuming to be widely practicable.

So what sort of urine examination could physicians of the time perform in their practices or in the hospital laboratory?

The view through the microscope

In the first decades of the 19th century physicians had learnt to use microscopes, which by then had become very powerful, for examining urine. The Dutchman Antoni van Leeuwenhoek (1632–1723) had studied urinary sediment with microscopes of his own construction and, in 1681, had found blood cells, which he called 'globular particles', in the urine of his horse after a hard ride. By the end of the 18th century familiarity with crystal structures was so advanced that microscopy of the urinary sediment promised clinical benefit. 'Blood and pus globules' (red and white blood cells) were also familiar as pathological components of the sediment. But it would be a long time – not until 40 years after the formulation of the cell theory in 1840 – before these materials were studied in greater detail. In 1842 the chemist Johann Franz Simon (1807–1843) described conspicuous structures in patient urine, which he called urinary cylinders. He correctly surmised that these cylinders in the urinary sediment were formed as 'casts' of the renal tubules from coagulating protein, cells and other material. This discovery was often erroneously ascribed to the pathologist Jacob Henle (1809–1885), who did not describe urinary casts until a year later.

It is worth noting here that at the end of the 19th century one of the first pieces of mechanical apparatus entered the medical laboratory. To accelerate sedimentation, the Swedish medical student Johann Theodor (Thor) Stenbeck (1864–1914) invented a simple hand-cranked centrifuge, which proved a significant advance not only in the examination of urine sediment.

Simple physical and chemical tests

Urine examination of course also included the physical measurement of density, which had been known since antiquity. But what about chemical methods? The Viennese chemist Johann Florian Heller (1813–1871), one of the fathers of clinical chemistry, strove – successfully – to place in the hands of 'the clinician and general practitioner … such methods of investigation as simple and easy to perform, yet as reliable, as possible.'[8] Some of Heller's tests continued to be used well into the 20th century, particularly in physicians' consulting rooms, just as Heller had intended. One example is Heller's 'ring test' for protein or albumin (the test did not differentiate albumin from other proteins), in which urine is layered over concentrated nitric acid in a liqueur glass. An annular precipitate forms in the presence of albumin. Because of the vessel employed, this test was known

Otto Folin *(1867–1934) was born to a poor tanner and midwife in the Swedish village of Åseda. After attending the village school, he emigrated to the United States at the age of 15 with the help of his elder brother. Following high school, he enrolled in chemistry at the University of Minnesota, later transferring to the newly founded University of Chicago, where he earned his PhD. His teachers included the physiologist Jacques Loeb (1859–1924), who helped Folin obtain post-doctoral training in Europe. Olof Hammarsten (1841–1932) in Uppsala and Ernst Leopold Salkowski (1844–1923) at the Berlin Institute of Pathology introduced him to the emerging fields of physiological and pathological chemistry. He came to his colleagues' attention by improving on a technically difficult method for measuring uric acid in urine. In 1900 he took over a research post at McLean Psychiatric Hospital in Waverley, Massachusetts, where he performed his pioneering studies on the composition of urine. In 1907 Folin was appointed professor of biochemistry at Harvard Medical School, and it was there, working with many of his students, that he systematically developed analytical methods for investigating blood and urine, thereby laying the foundations for modern clinical chemistry. Perhaps his most notable achievement was his use of colorimetry to create a complete 'system of blood analysis' suitable for use in the clinical laboratory. It came to be used worldwide. Shortly before his retirement, Folin fell ill and died. This portrait dates from shortly before his death. A Duboscq colorimeter is visible on his right.*

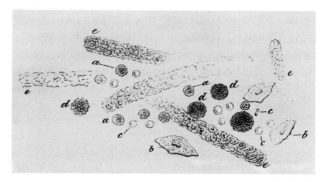

*Urinary casts depicted in an 1843 drawing by Johann Franz Simon, who first described them. The casts (**e**) arise in the renal tubules and consist of protein, cells and other materials from urine.*

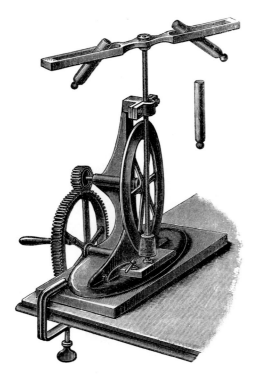

Thor Stenbeck's urine centrifuge: Urine is spun in tubes inserted into the centrifuge rotor. The sediment collects in the bulbous lower end of the tubes and can then be examined under the microscope.

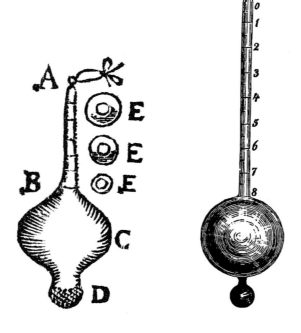

Areometers for measuring the specific gravity of urine. Left: hydrometrum urinae (urine hydrometer), with undefined graduations, described in 1727 by Johann Heinrich Methe in his medical dissertation. Centre: Heller urinometer from 1846 with Baumé units. Right: Schotten areometer from 1888, graduated in grams/millilitre.

in some hospitals as the 'liqueur or schnapps glass test'. For the detection of urine sugar, which by this time had been identified as glucose, the chemist Carl August Trommer (1806–1879) in 1841 described a later much-used test in which glucose is oxidised with a solution of blue cupric sulphate to produce a yellow or red precipitate.

In 1852, while studying human and animal metabolism, the chemist Justus [von] Liebig (1803–1873) developed a method for the quantitative analysis of urea and chloride in urine. In a letter to a friend he wrote of how

> the whole progress of physiology and pathology depends on such a method which could measure, and express in numbers, vital processes in health and disease.[9]

During the cholera epidemic in Munich Liebig's method was successfully employed to identify salt loss due to severe diarrhea and the accumulation of urea in the body. Yet because it required a fair amount of practice to master, it too was unsuited for use in the consulting room. Simple quantitative urine tests were soon on the scene, however. The French physician George Hubert Esbach (1843–1890), for example, devised a widely adopted technique in which protein was precipitated with a reagent in a graduated tube so that protein content could be read off from the markings. The introduction of two new analytical methods – polarimetry and the fermentation of glucose with yeast – met another important need by providing rapid quantitative tests to guide the treatment of diabetes.[10] In addition, a new item of equipment offered a significant improvement over the old uroscopists' highly subjective assessment of urine colour. In 1860 the physicist Gustav Robert Kirchhoff (1824–1887) and the chemist Robert Wilhelm Bunsen (1811–1899) invented the technique of spectral analysis for investi-

Johann Florian Heller *(1813–1871), a pharmacist's son, initially trained as a pharmacist before studying chemistry in Prague under Adolf Pleischl (1787–1867). During this period he also attended lectures in medicine, but did not receive any credits for this work because double degrees were not permitted in Prague at the time. When Pleischl was appointed to a professorship in Vienna in 1838, Heller, who had since obtained his doctorate, followed him there and began doing research in pathological chemistry in his apartment. He also gave courses in chemistry and later in physiological and pathological chemistry and microscopy for medical students. In 1847 he qualified as a lecturer in physiological and pathological chemistry. It was not until 1855 that he was officially appointed head of the pathological chemistry laboratory at Vienna General Hospital, a post he had held on a provisional basis since 1844. In 1855 the University of Jena awarded him an honorary doctorate of medicine.*

Heller's nitric acid test for protein (1842). Urine is poured on top of nitric acid in a glass. In the presence of protein, a white ring of precipitated protein forms at the zone of contact (Fig. 1).

Justus [von] Liebig *(1803–1873) left school at 14 to begin training as a pharmacist. Following an untimely explosion during a chemical experiment, he broke off his training to help his father, who was a purveyor of painters' supplies and common chemicals. Fortunately, though, he continued to be attracted to chemistry, and he returned to it as a student at the age of 17. Two years later he went to Paris on a scholarship from the Grand Duke, where he worked with the famous chemists Louis Jacques Thénard (1777–1857) and Joseph Louis Gay-Lussac (1778–1850). He was permitted to report his work on fulminic acid to the Paris Academy of Sciences, where he attracted the attention of Alexander von Humboldt (1769–1859), who was staying in Paris at the time. Humboldt recommended to the Grand Duke of Hesse that Liebig be appointed professor of chemistry at Giessen University. In Giessen Liebig built up a laboratory and academic department of chemistry that became world-famous and attracted students from all corners of the globe. Here he also made his major chemical discoveries and perfected the elementary analysis of organic substances. One key piece of Liebig's equipment was the 'five-bulb apparatus', which traps the carbon dioxide generated by combustion of an organic compound. Pins with a picture of the device were worn by Liebig's pupils as a kind of badge of recognition. Around 1840 Liebig began work on applying chemistry to the fields of plant and animal physiology. This led to his theories on crop fertilisation and what later became known as agrochemistry. In the course of chemical experiments on meat, he invented a 'meat extract' containing important human nutrients in a stable form. The extract was mass-produced by a factory in Uruguay, and remains available to this day. With his books, and especially his popularly written* Chemical Letters, *Liebig stimulated worldwide interest in chemistry.*

gating coloured light.[11] When observed with a spectroscope, coloured solutions such as urine or blood show the rainbow colours of the spectrum with dark extinctions ('bands') that are characteristic of dissolved pigments, such as blood and bile pigments.

A further quantitative measurement using light became common in the medical laboratory: the investigation of coloured solutions with a colorimeter. The coloured solution formed from blood serum or urine by certain reagents is compared with a reference solution, and a simple proportional calculation is then performed to determine the sample concentration from the reading and the concentration of the reference solution.

However, these chemical and physical tests were still too complicated for many physicians. Their introduction into medical practice thus remained hesitant, although kits containing the requisite apparatus and chemicals in little wooden boxes were on

Albuminimeter devised by George Hubert Esbach. Urine is filled to the mark U and the reagent (picric acid) is then added to the mark R. After swirling and being left to stand, the protein settles on the bottom. The protein concentration can be read off from the graduations.

sale by the second half of the 19th century. The Munich chemist and pharmacist Max [von] Pettenkofer (1818–1901), who later became the founder of hygienics, wrote in 1849 to his teacher Liebig:

> The reagent box now holds the self-same position that crocodile and basilisk were wont to occupy in the booths of the wandering Aesculaps. One has to have them, but they are good for nothing.[12]

Pettenkofer was alluding to the stuffed crocodiles and iguanas that hung from the ceiling in old apothecary shops.

For students of medicine, at least in Germany, a course on simple urine and blood tests – dubbed the 'pee course' by students – already formed part of the curriculum by the end of the 19th century. A large number of primers and textbooks were also available. In 1886, for example, Otto Seifert (1853–1933) and Friedrich [von] Müller (1858–1941) published their *Taschenbuch der Medicinisch-klinischen Diagnostik,* which had gone through 70 editions by 1975.

Finding the causes of disease

One distinctive feature of medicine in the second half of the 19th century was its search for causal 'theories' to explain the development and progression of disease. Around the middle of the century, thanks above all to Liebig, the concept of animal and human metabolism took hold, inspiring scores of

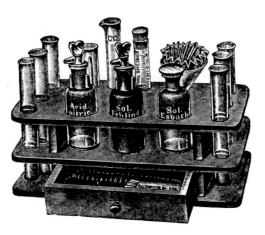

Urinalysis equipment produced by the Madaus company, probably in 1929. The stand contains the most important items for performing simple chemical analyses of urine.

researchers to conduct experiments of their own. One result was the discovery, by the general physician Friedrich Theodor Frerichs (1819–1885) and the chemist Georg Städeler (1821–1871), of the amino acids tyrosine and leucine in the urine of patients with acute yellow atrophy of the liver. They saw the excretion of these substances as evidence of a metabolic abnormality caused by this serious liver disease. Both amino acids are present in the healthy body, but are not excreted in the urine. They were identified by microscopic observation of their characteristic crystals.

The explanation that the French physiologist Claude Bernard (1813–1878) gave for the pathological excretion of glucose in the urine of diabetics also attracted much attention.

Over time, the chemical analysis of urine revealed a variety of rare substances that were difficult to classify. One such was alkapton, which the chemist Carl B. Detlev Boedeker (1815–1895) found in 1859 in a urine sample that had developed a striking dark discoloration on being exposed to air in an open vessel. The name derives from the observation that urine containing alkapton darkens especially rapidly on addition of an alkali. The abnormal urine component was identified as homogentisic acid, a metabolic product that cannot be broken down further and thus appears unchanged in the urine. The London clinician Archibald E. Garrod (1858–1936), who studied a number of cases of alkaptonuria in some detail around the turn of the century, found that this disorder occurred in people whose parents were close blood relatives. He made this observation at a time when the laws of inheritance formulated by the botanist Gregor Mendel (1822–1884) were being rediscovered. Garrod interpreted alkaptonuria, as well as another, similar disorder, cystinuria, the excretion of the amino acid cystine in the urine, and some additional diseases, as hereditary metabolic defects, for which he coined the term 'inborn errors of metabolism'. Many such genetic defects have since been identified, and the urine can be screened for some of them immediately after birth.

Detecting minerals by flame photometry

In the 20th century flame photometry – a refinement of Bunsen and Kirchhoff's spectral analysis – proved especially fruitful in opening up new possibilities for investigating 'minerals' in urine and blood samples. A particularly important application was in the measurement of the salts of alkali metals, such as sodium and potassium, and of alkaline-earth metals, such as calcium and magnesium, because their con-

After studying medicine in Göttingen and Berlin, **Friedrich Theodor [von] Frerichs** *(1819–1885) first worked as a physician in his native East Frisia, but returned in 1846 to Göttingen University, where he collaborated in particular with the chemist Friedrich Wöhler and the physiologist Rudolf Wagner (1805–1864) on animal metabolism. Frerichs quickly made a name for himself with a chapter he contributed on digestion to Wagner's* Handbuch der Physiologie. *In 1849 he became head of the Department of Medicine in Kiel; two years later he went to the University of Breslau. After Schönlein's resignation, Frerichs was appointed to his chair at Berlin's Charité Hospital. During his time at Kiel he wrote his well-regarded monograph on 'Bright's disease and its treatment'. In Breslau he worked on a large monograph on liver diseases, which appeared in 1861. Frerichs, who was ennobled by the Kaiser in 1884, was one of the most famous clinicians of his day.*

Anonymous caricature (pencil) of Kirchhoff (left) and Bunsen taking a walk. **Robert Wilhelm Bunsen** *(1811–1899) studied physics and chemistry in Göttingen, and after receiving his doctorate was enabled by a scholarship to undertake an extended study trip to Berlin, Vienna and Paris. In 1833 he became an untenured lecturer* (Privatdozent) *in Göttingen, later accepting a professorship at the Technical College in Kassel, where he succeeded the famous chemist Friedrich Wöhler (1800–1882). In 1839 he was called to Marburg and in 1851 to Breslau, where he met Gustav Robert Kirchhoff. When Bunsen was called to a professorship in Heidelberg one year later, he took pains to ensure that Kirchhoff joined him there as a physicist. A large new laboratory was built for Bunsen, which was soon illuminated with the new 'town gas'. We are indebted to him for multiple inventions and discoveries, including his methodical papers on gas analysis, photochemistry and spectral analysis. His publications on organic arsenic compounds, the cacodyl derivatives (the name alludes to their foul smell), were pioneering. He also invented many pieces of apparatus for the chemistry laboratory, including the Bunsen burner (inspired by the availability of town gas) and the grease-spot photometer. Bunsen was a character and very popular with his students. He was proud of his 'chemist's hands'. Whenever he touched the Bunsen burner flame during a lecture and the smell of burnt keratin permeated the room, he would say: 'See, gentlemen, at this point the flame is 2000 degrees.'*

Gustav Robert Kirchhoff *(1824–1887) was a physicist. After qualifying as a university lecturer in Berlin in 1848, he was appointed reader in 1850 at Breslau University, where he met Bunsen, whom he followed to Heidelberg in 1854. In 1875 he accepted a chair in Berlin. While still a student in Königsberg, Kirchhoff had described an important law of electricity. In Heidelberg he made his great discovery: the physical interpretation of the phenomena that occur during the emission and absorption of light by heated bodies. The starting point was the flame coloration of metal salts, which he had studied with Bunsen. Kirchhoff's work also paved the way for investigating the chemical composition of heavenly bodies with the spectroscope. In his eulogy at Kirchhoff's grave, August Wilhelm von Hofmann (1818–1892), founder and long-time president of the German Chemical Society, said that Kirchhoff had expanded the frontiers of human knowledge like few others in his century.*

Microscopic view of crystals of the amino acids tyrosine (needles in sheaves) and leucine (spheroids) in urinary sediment.

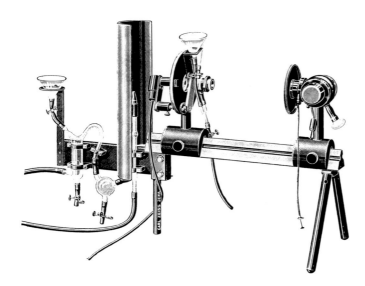

Schuhknecht and Waibel's flame photometer, manufactured by Carl Zeiss around 1941. The Bunsen burner can be seen inside its protective housing. Dilute urine was vaporised into the flame by the air inlet of the burner. The resulting flame coloration (yellow for sodium, red for potassium) was measured photometrically.

centrations in the living organism have to be held within narrow limits to ensure normal bodily function. The main method by which the healthy body controls the concentration of these substances is via excretion in urine. Quantification in urine and blood is therefore important to the physician. Even today, chemical analysis of these minerals remains difficult, requiring considerable skill. For this reason, flame-photometric measurement rapidly acquired great importance, especially in intensive care medicine. It involves blowing a finely dispersed sample of the test liquid, e.g. dilute urine, into the flame of a gas burner. The above elements show characteristic flame colorations, which are measured photometrically. Quantitative urinalysis of this kind can be performed in a matter of minutes.

Automation enters the lab

The second half of the 20th century saw a technical revolution in the clinical laboratory. Lab work became increasingly mechanised, as automated devices were introduced to perform chemical analyses of urine and blood. As a separate chapter is devoted to this topic, we will touch only briefly here on the birth of mechanised analysis. In 1957 the American biochemist Leonard Tucker Skeggs (1918–2002) described a new 'automatic instrument' for colorimetric analysis. This instrument automatically drew up a measured amount of test sample (serum or urine) and mixed it with the reagents. If necessary, the

mixture was heated. The resulting colour intensity was then measured in a photometer and the result recorded. Skeggs's 'Auto-Analyzer' was inspired in part by the growing problem of finding enough staff to perform chemical analyses manually. Today almost all analyses in medium- to high-volume laboratories are performed by automated systems.

Rapid tests

As early as the 19th century, amid efforts to promote chemical urinalysis to the medical community, there were a number of attempts at making urine tests quick and easy. Thus reagent tablets were developed that contained the mix and quantity of chemicals necessary for a single test. The tablet was dissolved in water and the urine sample added dropwise. The resulting colour was then compared with a colour chart. Similar products were also available for performing rough semi-quantitative estimates of various parameters, such as urinary glucose concentration. In the First World War military physicians urged the use of simple urine protein tests for the early diagnosis of the nephritis, which was common among soldiers at the time. Another important variant was the system of microchemical colour reactions developed by the Austrian chemist Fritz Feigl (1891–1971) to identify a number of substances by combining drops of reagent and sample on paper, a technique he called 'spot analysis'. These rapid tests did not, however, displace the techniques that had already been introduced into medical practices and hospitals using the standard laboratory equipment of the day.

After the Second World War pharmaceutical companies in the United States began to develop rapid diagnostics for urine testing. First off the mark was the Ames company with a tablet test for urinary glucose; the heat necessary for the reaction was generated by chemicals in the test tablet itself after the addition of urine. Clinitest from Ames was a big seller. Similar products entered the market in rapid succession until the 1950s, when a revolutionary new technology arrived on the scene.

The test strip revolution

Attempts to perform chemical tests with reagent-impregnated strips of paper date back to antiquity. Pliny the Elder (AD 23–79) described a test in which verdigris, which was used as a pigment, was examined for iron impurities using a papyrus strip soaked in gallnut juice which indicated iron by turning black. In the 17th century the chemist Robert Boyle (1627–1691) conducted detailed research on

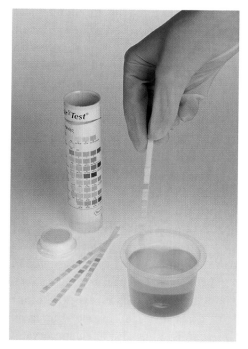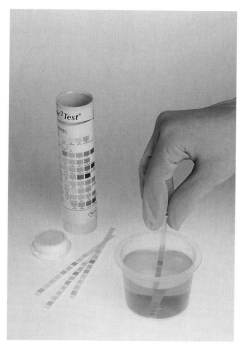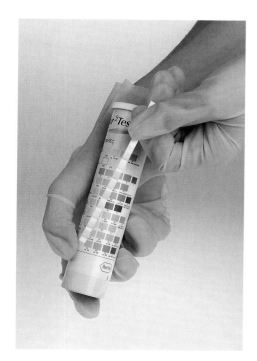

Multitest strips can simultaneously provide qualitative results for nine different urine parameters.

plant pigments and their ability to 'show something', i. e. to serve as indicators. He too used paper strips for this purpose, notably in his investigations of mineral waters.

In the 20th century test strips revolutionised and simplified urinalysis. A laboratory was no longer needed. Testing could be performed conveniently in the doctor's office, at the patient's bedside or virtually anyplace else. Indeed, patients could perform many of the tests themselves. Bunsen burners, test tubes and other laboratory equipment became superfluous. A reagent strip that every schoolchild is familiar with – and that provides a good example of the general principles involved – is litmus paper, which is used to distinguish acids and bases. Paper is impregnated with a dye or reagent solution. In the case of litmus paper, this is the violet pigment of a lichen found mainly in the Canary Islands. The paper with the dried pigment is produced in red or blue, and can be stored without difficulty. It is used by applying a drop of the test fluid to the paper and observing the colour change. Acids turn the paper red, bases turn it blue. When test strips were introduced into medicine, the technique was termed 'dry chemistry', although this is not quite correct as the chemical reactions in test strips take place in aqueous solution too, except that the water comes from the added sample, e.g. from urine. Reagent papers are known, incidentally, to have been widely used in Liebig's Giessen laboratory.

The test strip method was rapidly refined in the following decades. Soon multitest strips appeared on the market, making it possible to perform ten or more tests simultaneously with a single strip. At first, the test-tube methods standard at the time were simply transferred to the new paper strips, together with some of their drawbacks, such as poor specificity. Early strip-based tests for urinary glucose, for example, were just as apt to react with other substances in urine as the test-tube reagents were, thus giving false-positive results. Later-generation strips deployed ultraspecific enzymes as reagents, thereby reducing the number of false-positives. Enzyme detection is also the principle behind a test strip that identifies white blood cells (leukocytes) in a urine sample without the need for microscopy. Test strip technology took another major step forward when it moved beyond simple detection to quantification, for example of urinary glucose. The quantitative test strip is inserted into a special photometer that measures the colour intensity of the reaction zone on the strip.

A stroll through two and a half millennia

This brief historical survey shows how people have striven over the last two and a half thousand years to obtain information about diseases and their prognosis by observing and investigating human urine. It may come as a surprise that there were few changes of note between Late Antiquity and the Early Modern

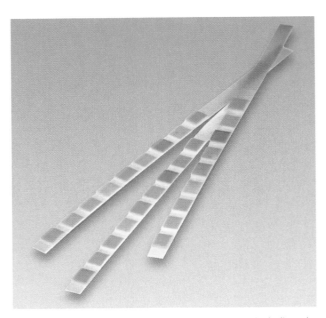

It is now possible to measure multiple parameters, including glucose, pH and ketones, with a single test strip.

period, i. e. from about 200 to 1500. For centuries 'uroscopy' in its myriad variations remained virtually unchallenged by other methods, primarily because of the dominance of Galen's teachings. Galen had formulated a theory of urine production which appeared convincing to his contemporaries and which continued to be accepted by subsequent generations until it was finally overturned by observations from alchemy, chemistry and, later, microscopy. For the medical practitioner, Galen's teachings long had the same authority as the works of Aristotle (384–322 BC) had in Scholastic philosophy.

With the growth of knowledge in physics and chemistry, uroscopy became increasingly experimental, particularly in the 19th century. But what exactly has the 'Scientific Method' contributed to urine examination as it is practiced today? The goal of identifying unequivocal diagnostic signs for a given disease has generally not been achieved. To be sure, there are certain urine findings that equate with a specific disease. In medicine these are termed 'pathognomonic', meaning 'indicative of disease'. In these cases, which are often genetic, substances are formed in the course of metabolism that do not occur in healthy individuals. The findings are therefore unequivocal. However, most findings have a variety of possible meanings, which is why it is often necessary to perform a number of tests and evaluate the results profile obtained.

Since the 19th century the other goal of the 'Scientific Method', namely to explain phenomena by uncovering causal relationships, has gradually been achieved in urology and nephrology, as investigators have expanded our understanding of kidney function and its disruption in disease. Increased knowledge of metabolism has also been important, particularly the unravelling of the chemistry of the substances involved. This has transformed the character of urine findings: observable signs, some of which were known in antiquity, have become parameters, i. e. variables in a chemical or physical system which are understood in terms of cause and effect. The techniques of urine examination gradually changed in the 20th century. Physical measurement supplanted chemical methods. Mechanisation and automation came to the aid of, or replaced, human labour. Labour-saving technologies are particularly important for urine testing, which is one of the most basic and widely practised medical investigations. The test strip took urinalysis out of the laboratory and made it available everywhere. The long road from matula to test strip has produced reliable and informative tests which can be deployed for patients' benefit under the most rudimentary conditions. Urinalysis was the first area of laboratory medicine to achieve this sort of success.

Erika and Gerd Novotny

Windows onto the building blocks of tissue

The history of histology

Europe witnessed many pioneering discoveries in the first half of the second millennium AD, including the invention of printing and the opening of sea routes to India and America. It was also during this dramatic epoch – around 1590 – that the first microscopes were built, an advance that opened up new horizons for naturalists, physicians and ultimately all mankind. Their introduction offered a window onto a hugely diverse and fascinating microworld and revolutionised ideas about the fine structure of living things. Whereas fibres had previously been considered the smallest structural units of tissues, since nothing smaller was visible to the naked eye during tissue dissection, researchers now focused – literally – on even smaller building blocks of life, namely cells.

Reading stones and spectacles

The use of microscope precursors – magnifying glasses and spectacles – was presumably rare in antiquity. Extant contemporary sources contain no evidence of such devices having been known,[1] although polished hemispheres of quartz or glass have been discovered at the ruins of Nineveh and Pompeii. Initially these plano-convex lenses are more likely to have been used to focus the sun's rays and to light fires, and they may have been worn as jewellery. But at some point it was recognised that placing them on an object or page of writing magnified what was underneath. Seneca (1 BC–AD 65) was the first to record this in writing. Carvers of the time may have used such lenses for their more detailed work.[2] It was long thought that the emperor Nero (AD 36–68) was the first to use an emerald to correct short-sightedness, the better to watch gladiatorial games, but more probably, as depicted by Gotthold

Replica of rivet spectacles from the 14th century.

Ephraim Lessing (1729–1781), he only used it as a shield against the sun.[3]

Ibn al-Haytham, or Alhazen (965–1038), was the first to refer in writing to the use of polished optical lenses as visual aids. For example, he described the magnifying effect of segments from glass spheres. These forerunners of modern spectacles were known as reading stones. They consisted of quartz, rock crystal or the green gemstone beryl (whose Middle High German name, *berille,* is the source of *Brille,*

Laws of optics

As far as we know, the *Optics* of the Greek mathematician Ptolemy (AD 100–178) was the first work to describe the laws of light refraction. The next optics publication, by Alhazen, was not to appear until much later, in the 11th century. Alhazen too described the laws of light refraction and their importance for changes in brightness and size. However, it was Johannes Kepler (1571–1630) who in 1604 described the exact relationships between light rays and the visual image. In 1611 he produced the first mathematical analysis of the path of light passing through a compound optical instrument, thus establishing the foundations still recognised today for explaining the phenomena of physiological optics. Christian Huygens (1629–1695) offered a theoretical analysis of the problem of light propagation, double refraction and reflection, publishing his wave theory in 1690, while Sir Isaac Newton (1643–1727), physicist, mathematician and astronomer, demonstrated by experiment that white light was composed of the colours of the spectrum.

the German word for spectacles). In the 13th century monks were the main users of reading stones, or plano-convex lenses, which were placed directly over a text to magnify the letters. They were familiar to the English Franciscan monk Roger Bacon (1214–1292), who advanced a theory of vision in his *Opus majus,* giving the dimensions of such lenses and instructions for their use. Bacon is also reported to have polished a glass which showed things so strange that its effect was generally attributed to the power of the devil.[4] Commercial lens grinding originated in Italy, where a glass industry emerged in the years between 1284 and 1330. In Venice the glassworkers were known as *cristalleri,* and their work included the polishing of spectacle lenses. The island of Murano, near Venice, produced the first rivet spectacles, consisting of two lenses each screwed into a ring on a stalk, with the ends of the stalks riveted together. Their inventor is unfortunately unknown.[5]

Early microscopy

The construction of the first microscope is attributed to the spectacle makers Hans Janssen and his son Zacharias Janssen (dates of both unknown) from Middelburg in Holland, or alternatively to another Dutchman, Cornelis Drebbel (1572–1633).[6] By that time spectacle grinders had learned to manufacture small lenses from clear glass and to grind them very finely. Instead of contenting themselves with simply looking through a single lens, the Janssens had the idea of mounting two convex lenses one on top of the other in a tube. Galileo (1564–1642) reportedly heard rumours of this invention and built a similar instrument, using it to study the eyes of insects, among other things. In 1611 Galileo constructed a telescope. In contrast to his observations through the microscope, those which he made of the planets through the telescope met with incredulity, despite confirming the cosmic scheme of Nicolaus Copernicus (1473–1543), who had made his observations without optical aids.[7]

The term 'microscope' is thought to have been coined by the Greek scholar Demiskianos. It was also used by a group of naturalists in Rome who in 1603 founded the Academy of Linceans, named after the sharp-eyed lynx and Lyncaeus, the keen-sighted pilot of the Argonauts. Galileo was a Lincean.[8]

Plants and animals under the microscope

Among physicians the prevailing initial response to microscopes was scepticism. Naturalists, by contrast, were enthusiastic. The Janssens themselves performed no studies with their dual-lens microscope. Antonie van Leeuwenhoek (1632–1723), on the other hand, became widely known for the discoveries he made using his simple, one-lens microscopes. A cloth merchant from Delft (Holland) who became fascinated by lens grinding, van Leeuwenhoek manufactured his own lenses from glass and semi-precious stones, achieving up to 270-fold magnification. The principle of his microscopes, which he initially used to examine samples of cloth, was the same as that behind today's dissecting microscope. They comprised a single polished lens fixed between two metal plates, each with a hole in the middle, and an adjustable needle for securing the object of interest – van Leeuwenhoek's solution to the problem of controlling the position of a specimen relative to the lens at high magnification. He was a self-taught researcher, performing a great deal of microscopy and sketching what he saw. He made a different microscope for each object of study – these instruments were found in huge numbers among his personal effects. He was the first to describe the unicellular organisms, e. g. slipper animalcules or paramecia, that arise from sporocysts in hay infusions, and he also described red blood cells, the 'beasties' in his dental plaque, spermatozoa and striated muscle fibres. He even identified the branching of heart muscle cells, which he had the foresight to stain with alcoholic saffron solution. His simple microscope dominated the scene for a century, while the compound microscope, which was in principal superior, remained virtually unused by researchers because of

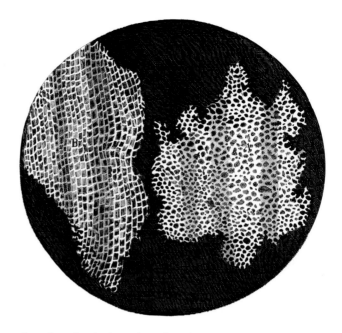

A section of cork, drawn from the microscope by Robert Hooke.

Marcello Malpighi *(1628–1694), physician and professor in Pisa, Messina and Bologna, is today considered the founder of histological microscopy. In 1661 he described capillary blood flow in the lung and mesentery of the live frog, thereby completing the blood circulation doctrine of William Harvey (1578–1657), who had been unable to see capillaries. Malpighi's treatise on the skin,* De externo tactus organo, *was published in 1665. His research ran counter to centuries-old tradition. Some of Malpighi's colleagues went so far as to interrupt his lectures to voice their dissent, and on one occasion even exhorted his students to leave the lecture hall. After a group of masked professors called at Malpighi's country house, assaulted him and smashed his personal effects, he left Bologna. Pope Innocent XII subsequently appointed him as his personal physician.*

Mite, drawn from the microscope by Robert Hooke.

the problems of spherical and chromatic aberration, serving only for the amusement of laymen.

The Londoner Robert Hooke (1635–1703), a naturalist and architect who had studied physics at Oxford, was the first to undertake studies with the compound microscope. He described a method for making short-focus lenses by grinding beads drawn from the finest filaments of molten Venetian glass. To examine objects he prepared 'exceeding thin' slices – sections – using a sharp knife. He recommended introducing liquids between two small plates of clear glass and embedding organic material in water or clear oil. These were the forerunners of slides, coverslips, and coverslip media.[9] Hooke studied plants and insects. In his celebrated studies of thin cork sections he coined the term 'cell', although he accorded it no great prominence, preferring the term 'pores'.[10] He could never have developed the modern concept of the cell as the building block of all living things since the methods of preparation at his disposal made the visualisation of fine detail impossible. In 1665, as secretary of the Royal Society, Hooke reported the results of his micro-

scopy research in the meticulous drawings of his *Micrographia,* which was dedicated to the King of England.

At Bologna University Marcello Malpighi (1628–1694) studied plant and animal morphology. He was the first physician to enthusiastically embrace microscopy, analysing the structure of lung, spleen, kidney (Malpighian corpuscles), liver and skin. He described the sensory papillae and taste buds. In 1686 he published his results in *Opera Omnia,* a two-volume work printed in London.

Microscopes become more accurate

After the emergence of the first microscopes, an artisan-based optics industry developed in the 17th century, mainly in Holland, England, Italy, Germany and France. This resulted in a steady flow of new ideas and improvements, but it was not until the first third of the 19th century that microscope design achieved high magnification using lens combinations. In the early 1820s achromatic objectives[11] were being made with resolutions down to 1 μm (1/1000 mm).

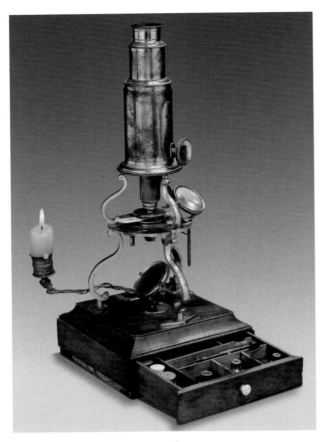

Huntley microscope (London, 1740).

In 1849 the Italian Giovanni Battista Amici (1784–1863) designed a hugely improved multilens microscope. Its innovations soon became standard. To increase resolution, he pioneered the use of immersion objective lenses, which allowed him to fill the gap between the objective lens and the object of interest with a fluid such as water or aniseed oil. By increasing the aperture ratio of the objective lens to values exceeding 1, this significantly enhanced resolution. In 1829 Amici's calculations had incidentally already incorporated coverslip thickness as an important influence on light scatter.[12] Unfortunately, lens makers were still unable to achieve anything approaching consistent lens quality. The multiple lenses required for corrected objectives had to be laboriously selected to minimise chromatic and spherical aberration. In his Jena workshop Carl Zeiss (1816–1888) was keenly aware of this problem. His instruments were highly praised by contemporary experts, and the microscope he presented at the Weimar trade fair won the gold medal. The botany lecturer Jakob Matthias Schleiden (1804–1881) insisted on Zeiss microscopes for Jena University. For Zeiss the trial and error involved in achieving the correct combination of lenses developed

into a nightmare. Initially, however, he had no alternative but to persist with these methods because prevailing opinion held that lenses were so small that theoretical calculation of image errors, and hence their correction, was pointless. In 1867 he asked the physicist and university lecturer Ernst Abbe (1840–1905) whether the laws of optics could be applied to microscope and lens design, and the optics calculated in advance.[13] Their encounter led to a successful collaboration, with Abbe joining the company in 1867. He solved the problem and in 1873 published his theoretical findings on the calculation of objectives. Microscope performance could be reliably determined from the objective lens aperture and light wavelength. Later, with the help of the glass chemist Otto Schott (1851–1935), Zeiss and Abbe managed to extend objective correction from two to three colours of the visible spectrum. The new so-called apochromatic objective lenses became available in 1886, by which time they had virtually achieved the theoretical maximal resolving power of the light microscope: 0.2 μm. Abbe also developed the condenser as a new illumination device for transmitted-light and dark-field illumination, to high praise from Robert Koch (1843–1910). In October 1900 Abbe took on August Köhler (1866–1948) as a scientific officer. Köhler concentrated on microphotography and developed a method – the Köhler illumination principle – which uniformly illuminated the field of view and hence the preparation.

Teased, crushed and cut

Until the mid-19th century microscopy was conducted almost exclusively on unstained objects. This had considerable limitations since contrast is extremely low in unstained tissue. For this reason research concentrated primarily on plants, with their thick, easily identifiable cell walls, and on unicellular and other minute organisms which could also be readily studied without contrast enhancement. While thin sections of plants were at first made free-hand, it was later realised that clamping leaves in elder pith, for example, made them easier to cut. Material thus prepared was then sliced into thin sections with sharp scalpels or cut-throat razors, as described long before by Hooke.

Crush preparations were prepared from fresh tissue by crushing a small tissue fragment or very small insect between two glass slides. Teased preparations were obtained by placing a tissue specimen, for example muscle, in a drop of water and teasing it carefully apart with a pair of needles until cells or fibres could be isolated for microscopy. The preparations

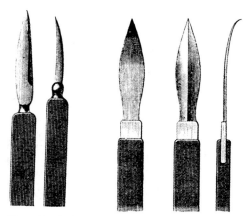

Pieter Harting's preparation instruments (c. 1848).

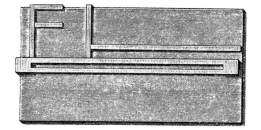

Glass-cutting device built by Harting.

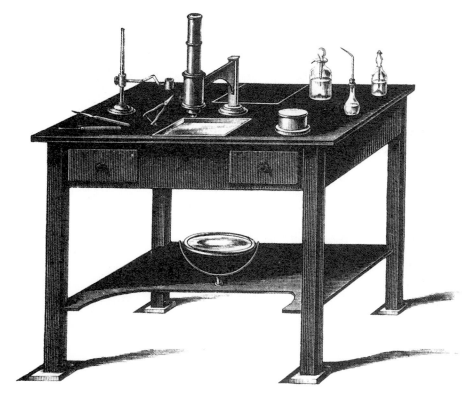

Preparation table (Harting, c. 1848).

were covered with a mica disc to protect the objective lens. Sections were also prepared of dried membranes and fibres.[14] But since they were often too transparent and difficult to identify by microscopy, they were treated with tincture of iodine. This stained the membranes and improved their visibility. We have Jan Swammerdam (1637–1680), famous for his seminal studies on the fine structure of insects, to thank for the technique of injecting vessels with a setting mixture of pigmented fixative. Injection techniques of this type were among the earliest methods of fixing and preserving specimens and were employed, for example, by Malpighi and by Johann Nathanael Lieberkühn (1711–1756), who used a similar mixture to demonstrate the vessels of the small intestinal villi.

Another important step forward was the use of alcohol or acid to harden soft tissue, as this made it possible to prepare sections from animal tissue as well as from plants. At the turn of the 18th century early techniques of chemical analysis became increasingly important for microscopists. The primary aim was to obtain information on the composition of tissue. A by-product was the emergence of the first procedures for enhancing structure visibility. A shared desire to improve these early techniques stimulated successful cooperation between scientists and technicians. Textbooks describing proper micro-

scopy technique and detailing useful methods of specimen preparation soon appeared, for as microscopes became more and more sophisticated, so did the skills and know-how required to take full advantage of their potential. Features which became standard at the time, and which we still find in today's microscopes, included a fixed stand, a mount for the eye tube, an objective lens holder, a stage and a condenser to collect reflected light from the mirror. Good preparation technique was absolutely essential for obtaining information using these microscopes.[15]

Slides and coverslips

Pieter Harting (1812–1885), a professor in Utrecht (Holland), was the first to offer directions on specimen preparation and microscopy technique. An assiduous microscopist, he built his instruments himself. The multi-volume work which he published on the microscope, optics and histological technique provided detailed instructions on specimen preparation and described a specimen preparation bench and various preparation instruments.

Harting also devised a method for producing thin coverslips by fuse-sealing a glass tube at one end and blowing it out from the other end into a large thin bubble. He then broke the bubble into small pieces approximately 0.1 mm thick which he laid over his microscopy preparations. He also investigated the

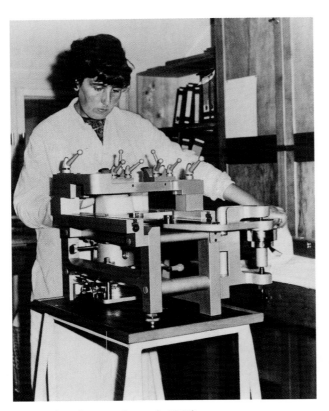

A tetrander microtome in use (c. 1960).

use of protein coagulants to harden tissue. He still preferred to prepare his sections by hand as this yielded him better sections than the as yet primitive sectioning instruments (microtomes) which were becoming available at that time.

The glass support on which specimens were placed for microscopy was an additional problem. Many were still home-made by the scientists themselves as they assembled their collections. Harting developed a purpose-built glass-cutting device. In 1839 the London Microscopical Society agreed a uniform slide size of 1×3 inches (24×72 mm) which has remained standard to this day. Thin coverslips came onto the market a year later. Close inspection reveals that Harting's microscopy 'bible' contained in embryonic form every prerequisite for modern specimen preparation. Paul Mayer (1848–1923) subsequently elaborated important guidelines covering preparation, sectioning and fixation, as well as the staining of both animal and human tissue. With Arthur Bolles Lee (1849–1927), he co-authored a textbook on microscopy technique (*Grundzüge der mikroskopischen Technik für Zoologen und Anatomen*) in 1898, which went to four editions and formed the basis for all subsequent histology manuals.[16, 17]

The emergence of sectioning instruments

Manual specimen preparation required such skill that it was not long before dedicated sectioning instruments were designed. In 1770 John Hill (1707–1775) in England constructed a plane-like device for preparing very thin slices of wood. This was perhaps the first microtome. The term 'microtome', for devices producing ultrathin sections for microscopy, was coined in 1838 by Alphonse Chevallier (1793–1879).

Louis Antoine Ranvier (1835–1922) introduced a hand microtome constructed by Ross in 1855. It became a widely used aid.[18] It consisted of a thick brass cylinder containing a plug, also in brass, which could be moved up and down using a micrometer screw. The object to be sectioned was fixed to the plug and could be advanced by turning the micrometer screw to protrude above the cylinder. A thin section could then be lifted off by drawing a razor over the cylinder top. Specimen advance was thus entirely manual. Many ideas were tested. For example, in 1848 De Capanema developed an inclined-plane specimen guide. Based on these and other pioneering ideas, G. Rivet in 1868 designed a microtome whose working principle was to determine all subsequent models. The object to be sectioned was held in a clamp mounted on a positioning cylinder meshed to a finely threaded adjusting screw. To advance the object to the blade, the screw was adjusted manually or mechanically by a preset amount, thereby raising the stage supporting the object by a defined micrometre value. A feature common to these early microtomes was that either the blade or the positioning cylinder holding the object was advanced towards the other along a slide bar, hence the term 'sledge microtome'. Georg Wilhelm Julius Behrens (1854–1903) offered the following comment on this development in 1884 in the first volume of his journal, the *Zeitschrift für wissenschaftliche Mikroskopie und mikroskopische Technik*:

> In scientific terms, the automatic advancing device is sheer gadgetry... But ours is an age of steam, and in the next everything will run on electricity – so shouldn't it be possible one day to connect the microtome to an electrodynamic machine? The scientist could then sit back with cigar and folded arms behind his mechanical device and observe the automatic brush lifting off the sections and transferring them into a glass dish filled with shimmering aniline mixture. All that then awaits him is the trifling job of examining the slices under the microscope.[19]

Paul Mayer and two colleagues developed the tetrander, a highly stable microtome equipped with their so-called Neapolitan clip, which firmly clamped tissue embedded in paraffin or celloidin and advanced it to the desired position for cutting.

In addition to designing a variety of sledge microtomes, Charles Sedgwick Minot (1852–1914) developed a rotary microtome in which the positioning cylinder was cranked vertically to the perpendicular knife. Given its space-saving design, it was only a matter of time before this device was placed in a refrigerated chamber, similar to a cryostat cabinet. Minot built up an instructive collection of over 1900 serially sectioned mammalian embryos. For this huge task he developed a microtome which not only bears his name to this day but remains faithful to his original design. His first model produced 30 µm sections. Current models can produce 1 µm sections from plastic-embedded tissue. Yet more sophisticated models of the same type of microtome produce ultrathin sections for electron microscopy.

Cryostats and the emergence of peroperative diagnostics

Serendipity presided over the development of the freezing microtome. One night in January 1842, Benedict Stilling (1810–1879) left a tissue sample out on the window ledge; in the morning he found it frozen. The hard tissue enabled him to cut thin sections with a razor, which he then crushed for microscopy. He had unwittingly invented the freezing method for hardening tissue.[20] The English physiologist William Rutherford (1810–1879) reported the first freezing microtome in 1873. Liquid carbon dioxide began to be used as a freezing agent in 1897.

The freezing method eventually led to the development of the cryostat, an invaluable instrument for producing rapid sections for tissue diagnosis during surgery. The first apparatus, introduced in 1938 by the Danish workers Kaj Linderstrom-Lang (1896–1959) and Mogensen, consisted of a rotary microtome built into a coldroom.

Tissue fixation and preservation

Ferdinand Blum (1865–1959) introduced tissue preservation using formaldehyde solution into microscopy technique in 1890. Formaldehyde provided protection against putrefaction and at the same time served to harden or 'fix' tissue, making it easier to section. Originally researchers had boiled their specimens as the simplest method of fixation. This gave way to acetic acid, alcohol and a number of salts of varying toxicity. Johann Evangelista Purkinje (1787–1869) and Martin Heidenhain (1864–1949) are known to have used mercuric chloride solution for fixation. Camillo Bartolomeo

Theodor Schwann *(1810–1882) began working with a microscope while a medical student. In 1835, a year after his finals, he began an internship with the famous anatomist and pathologist Johannes Müller (1801–1858) on a monthly stipend of 15 talers, publishing his most important scientific work,* Mikroskopische Untersuchungen über die Übereinstimmung in der Struktur und im Wachstum der Thiere und Pflanzen, *a mere four years later. This led to his appointment as professor of anatomy at the University of Louvain in Belgium. In 1848 he accepted the chair of physiology and anatomy in Liège, declining offers from German universities on account of the mixed response by German professors to his cell theory. Schwann studied cells from a wide range of tissues and established that all in principle possessed the same structure, with cell membrane, nucleus and nucleolus. Following his studies of the vagus nerve in the calf, he was the first to describe the structure of peripheral nerves, discovering the myelin sheath and the cells, now named after him, which were responsible for its formation. Although happiest studying the microworld, Schwann did not lose sight of the demands and problems of the macroworld. He invented a self-contained oxygen breathing apparatus for mine workers and rescue teams.*

Emilio Golgi (1843–1926) used potassium dichromate and osmium tetroxide. Some of these agents were used to perfuse whole organs or animals by injecting them into an artery. To enable sections to be cut from larger blocks comprising tissues of variable consistency, the blocks had to be not only surrounded by a solid medium but also impregnated with it, i.e. 'embedded', if the various component tissues of an organ were to hold together during sectioning. For this purpose Edwin Klebs (1834–1913) developed paraffin wax embedding, which he reported in 1869.[21] Ten years later Mathias Duval (1844–1907) described celloidin embedding, which was substantially improved in 1882 by Paul Schiefferdecker (1849–1931). Gelatin embedding was another variant, in particular for frozen sections.

Histology: the study of tissue

The evolution of cell and tissue concepts was a slow process, beset by mistakes, in particular because it

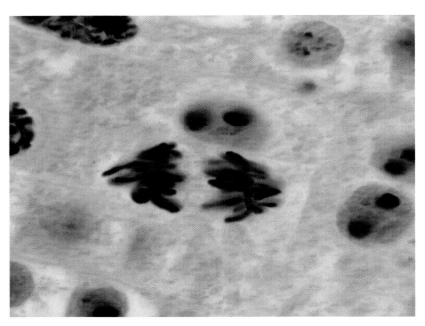

Section through an onion root showing mitoses stained with Heidenhain's iron hematoxylin.

General anatomy deals with the basic forms into which organs can be separated by continued expert division and with the construction of the various organs from these basic forms, which are presumed to include the leaflet, fibre, sphere etc. This approach, which might satisfy the naked eye, is corrected by the microscopy of animal tissue in that the apparently fibrous and cellular forms consist of an infinite quantity of small globules of identical diameter (namely 1/500th of a millimetre)…[24]

Since Brown had seen nuclei in cells, Schleiden in 1838 deduced that a plant develops from a cell. He assumed that new cells arise from the cell nucleus in the intercellular 'cytoblastema'. Another scientist who was interested in cells, and particularly in cell nuclei, was the German anatomist and physiologist Paul Friedrich Theodor Schwann (1810–1882). Influenced by earlier plant cell studies, he began investigating the structure of animal tissues under the microscope, resulting in the fundamental insight that cells are also the building blocks of animal organisms. In his 1839 monograph, *Mikroskopische Untersuchungen über die Übereinstimmung in der Struktur und dem Wachstum der Tiere und Pflanzen*, Schwann set out to demonstrate that plants and animals shared the same structural building block:

As a result of each individual cell entering into the service of the whole, there arises the cell state that we find realised in all higher organisms… The production of cells is the true principle underlying the development of all organic structures.

This marks the turning point when the prevailing view of fibres as the ultimate building blocks of tissue was abandoned in favour of cell theory. Schwann not only described the cell structures he observed through the microscope, he also made many observations about vital processes within cells. Inspired by the atomist theory of antiquity, he discussed them as atomic and molecular processes.[25] Schwann and Schleiden demonstrated that all animals and plants were composed of cells. However, they failed to discover that cells originate through cell division, even though Hugo von Mohl (1805–1872) had already observed plant cells dividing by infolding of the cell membrane to create two new cells in 1835. The essential features of animal cell division were not elucidated until the studies of Walther Flemming (1843–1905) on mitosis in 1882 and Theodor Boveri (1862–1915) on chromosomes in 1904–1909. The cornerstone of the newly emergent field of cytology was the insight described by the Bonn anatomist and histologist Max Schultze (1825–1875) in 1861 when he wrote, in *Über Muskelkörperchen und was man eine Zelle zu nennen hat*: 'A cell is a small lump of

involved learning to see with the microscopist's eye. One common cause of misinterpretation was the inability to distinguish fact from artefact.

Marie-François Xavier Bichat (1771–1802) shunned the use of the microscope, which he did not trust, and instead prepared and described, entirely from the macroscopic viewpoint, multiple categories of 'tissue', a term derived from the French word for 'woven'. Using the Greek *histos* for 'loom', he coined the term 'histology' for the science of tissue structure.[22] The Bonn anatomist August Franz Joseph Karl Mayer (1787–1865) then applied the term histology to tissue microscopy in a book published in 1819.

From fibres to cells

Botanists in the first decades of the 19th century were assiduous microscopists. They defined the plant cell as 'a space enclosed by a vegetable membrane'.[23] The first major observations were made in the second half of the 19th century. Robert Brown (1773–1858) had already identified the nucleus within plant cells in 1831. His observation inspired Schleiden to begin his fundamental studies in plant microscopy, although these fell on stony ground among his fellow botanists. Lorenz Oken (1779–1851) also described vesicular microscopic structures as components of plants and animals. Thus in *Physiologie für Thierärzte* by Eduard von Hering (1799–1881), published in 1832, we read:

protoplasm in which there is a nucleus.'[26] This statement put an end to the still unclear ideas resulting from Schwann's extrapolation of the cell concept from plants to animal tissue in 1839. Even so, cell theory was long questioned. In his 1907 textbook, *Die Funktionen des Zentralen Nervensystems,* the neuropathologist Max Lewandowsky (1876–1918) was still railing against the supposed importance of cell theory, writing in the chapter 'Overestimating the cell principle':

> The body forms cells, not cells the body.

Finally, Robert Remak (1815–1865) demonstrated that spontaneous cell generation from intercellular 'blastema', as postulated by Schleiden and Schwann, does not occur.

Around the same time, Purkinje introduced the protoplasm concept and described ciliary movements of cells. He also prepared sections of bone tissue and teeth. He is incidentally reported to have stained tissue sections with coffee extracts. Gametes were also studied at this time. Purkinje discovered the germinal vesicle in avian eggs, and Karl Ernst von Baer (1792–1876) an ovum in the canine ovary, thereby laying the foundation stone of the science of embryology. This was in 1827, i. e. a full 12 years before the enunciation of cell theory.[27]

The pathologist and the cell

Pathologists naturally also recognised the potential of the microscope and began to deploy this new instrument to sharpen their diagnoses. Rudolf Virchow (1821–1902) concentrated mainly on diseased tissues, although he also studied non-pathological material such as cartilage, bone and connective tissue. His work led to the fundamental insight, expressed in the maxim *Omnis cellula a cellula* (every cell from a cell), that an existing cell had to have come from another cell. He thus confirmed Schwann's position and finally laid to rest the ongoing controversy over cell theory. He viewed the diseases and tumours of an organism quite naturally as cellular diseases too. He coined the term 'leukemia', and described the abnormal increase in leukocyte count characteristic of the disease.[28]

A scientific centre on the Mediterranean

Much important and successful work was undertaken in the marine biology research station founded by Otto Dohrn (1840–1909) in Naples. Dohrn's scientific ambition was to elucidate the prehistory of arthropods and vertebrates. His life's work continues to occupy an important place in zoology. He and

Paul Mayer (1848–1923), who worked at the research station from 1875 to 1913, were nothing if not passionate microscopists. Many young scientists came on training visits, drawn in particular by the station's first-rate technical facilities. They included the brothers Richard Hertwig (1850–1937) and Oskar Hertwig (1849–1922), and it was there that they made the first observation of fusion between pronuclei in the live sea urchin egg and correctly interpreted it as fertilisation. Their experiment was demonstrated in an embryology course for medical students every summer semester from 1956 to 1964. Oskar Hertwig provided a comprehensive account of the well-known but still inadequately characterised process of fertilisation and thereby elucidated the phenomenon of meiosis. His postdoctoral thesis can be summarised in the statement: 'Fertilisation involves the fusion of sexually differentiated cell nuclei'. Boveri also worked for a brief period in Naples, attempting to elucidate the roles of cell nucleus and cytoplasm in heredity using the sea urchin and roundworm parasite *Ascaris* as experimental models. While observing mitoses, he discovered the centrosome, now known to contain the centrioles. Stephan von Apathy (1863–1922) also worked with Dohrn for a while. Primarily interested in the study of nerve tissue, von Apathy succeeded in demonstrating ultrafine fibres running in either parallel or interlaced fashion in the protoplasm of nerve cells, sensory cells and their processes. He visualised these neurofibrils, which are important in modern neuropathology, using gold salt impregnation, a technique calling for the utmost care. Von Apathy, an outstanding microtechnician, authored the two-volume *Die Mikrotechnik der tierischen Morphologie.* He developed instruments and equipment for practising histologists, expounding every step in the method of proper specimen preparation down to the minutest detail. He raised microtechnique to a science.

Anatomy as an aid to physiology

As science's understanding of the fine structure of living things became more detailed, it aided the identification of organ and tissue function. Thus Albert von Kölliker (1807–1905), who in 1850 published the first two-volume work on microscopic anatomy, concentrated on the structure and function of the spleen. He suspected that the spleen broke down erythrocytes and converted their hemoglobin into bile pigment and in the course of his investigations discovered the phenomenon of erythrocyte phagocytosis by spleen macrophages.

Camillo Bartolomeo Emilio Golgi *(1843–1926) was the third son of a country doctor in Coteno, a small mountain town between two Alpine valleys in Northern Italy. Deciding to follow in his father's professional footsteps, he began his studies when barely 16 years of age at the faculty of medicine and surgery in Pavia. After qualifying, he practised in a psychiatric hospital, where he became interested in brain pathology and in 1865 wrote his doctorate on mental illness. He did research on cell pathology while working as a rotating physician in various departments of San Matteo Hospital in Pavia. In 1872 he moved to Abbiategrasso as a consultant. It was there, under the most difficult conditions, that he began his studies on the neural structure of the brain, developing his silver salt technique for visualising nerve cells and describing the extensive branching of nerve cell processes. On the strength of his many publications, he was appointed extraordinary professor of histology at the University of Pavia in 1875. After holding chairs in Siena and Turin, he returned to Pavia as a full professor of pathology and histology in 1881. He remained in Pavia to the end of his life, training many students and making further important discoveries. For his countless contributions to research into the nervous system, he shared the Nobel Prize for Medicine and Physiology with Ramón y Cajal in 1906.*[44]

Santiago Ramón y Cajal *(1852–1934) was born in Petilla, a mountain village in the Spanish province of Saragossa. His father, who held a distinguished degree in medicine and surgery, was also a country practitioner. The long hours that Ramón y Cajal spent outdoors in the mountains as a boy inspired in him the desire to become a painter. Considered an unruly child by his father, he was sent off to the monastery school at Jaca, where he was punished for drawing some all-too-telling sketches of the teachers. Another escapade landed him in prison for three days, after which his father decided that it was time to apprentice him, first to a cobbler and later to a barber. A subsequent period of schooling awakened his interest in anatomy. In 1870 his father became professor of anatomy in Saragossa and took his son with him. Together they worked there for three years in the pathological anatomy department of an old hospital. Ramón y Cajal began to study medicine, qualifying in 1873. He was then conscripted into the armed forces, but received a discharge after contracting malaria and dysentery. This allowed him to return in 1875 to the institute in Saragossa, where he began his morphological research. He became director of the Saragossa anatomy museum in 1879 and professor of anatomy in Valencia in 1885. This was followed by professorships of histology and histopathology in Barcelona and Madrid in 1887 and 1892. In the course of his long career he received multiple honours at home and abroad, culminating in the 1906 Nobel Prize.*

Window onto the brain

The brain has been a prime target of study from time immemorial. It is thus not surprising that two histologists, Golgi in Italy and Santiago Ramón y Cajal (1852–1934) in Spain, should also have devoted their microscopy work to the structure of the brain, its multiple cell types and their processes. Both men developed metal salt staining methods. Golgi was interested in the organisation of the central nervous system. As for so many others in the history of science and medicine, a mishap proved a blessing in disguise for Golgi, leading him to an important discovery. Having fixed some nervous tissue in a mixture of osmium tetroxide and Müller's fluid, he then immersed it by mistake in silver nitrate solution.

This resulted in shimmering, yellowy-red, needle-like crystals. Microscopy of the dehydrated cleared sections prepared from this tissue revealed cells of the most varied shapes with black processes. Golgi was amazed by the diverse shapes of the nerve cells and processes which had suddenly become visible. He discovered the cells in the granular layer of the cerebellum since known as Golgi cells, and the processes of glial cells that terminate on blood vessels. The ultimate fruit of his staining method was the demonstration of the Golgi apparatus in the cytoplasm, not only in nerve cells but also in other cells. However, this discovery could only be interpreted after the invention of the electron microscope. These results would exert a decisive influence

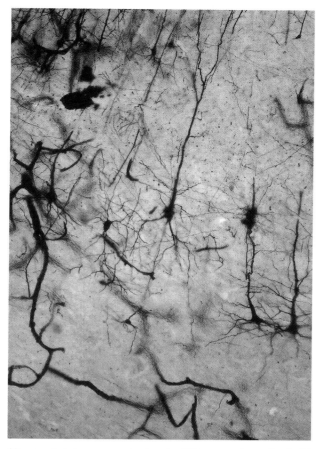

Nerve cells in human cerebral cortex (50 µm section stained with Bubenaite's modification of Golgi's block silver impregnation).

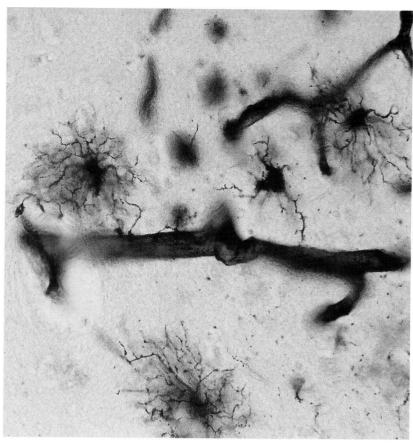

Glial cells with end-feet abutting a blood vessel (50 µm section of human cerebral cortex stained with Bubenaite's modification of Golgi's block silver impregnation).

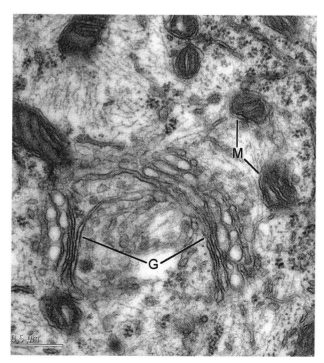

Electron micrograph of the Golgi apparatus (**G**) and mitochondria (**M**) in a spinal ganglion cell.

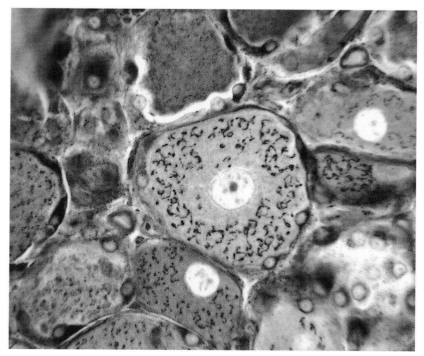

Golgi apparatus in a spinal ganglion (8 µm section stained with osmium tetroxide and silver impregnation).

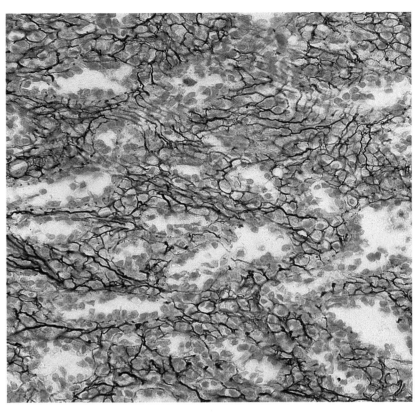

Reticular connective tissue fibres (Gommert-Novotny silver impregnation).

on the future of brain research. Above all they formed the basis for Ramón y Cajal's most important work.[29] Golgi's silver stain triggered the development of various related staining techniques. Ramón y Cajal treated silver nitrate with reducing agents such as hydroquinone and pyrogallol, thereby inventing the so-called reduced silver methods. Since these reactions were performed with tissue blocks, they are also known as block silver stains. The results which Ramón y Cajal obtained by studying tissue prepared in this manner eventually led him to formulate his neuron theory. Ramón y Cajal studied neuron development and proved the connection between the cell processes and cell body. After systematically investigating different segments of the nervous system, he devoted himself from 1899/1900 onwards to cerebral cortex research in man and animals. With his silver method he demonstrated the neurofibrils that von Apathy had already described in gold impregnated preparations. Ramón y Cajal's legacy covered the entire field of neuroanatomy.[30] After the methods and results of Golgi and Ramón y Cajal became known, many other researchers worked with silver impregnation techniques. Max Bielschowsky (1869–1940), for example, demonstrated neurofibrils in frozen sections with a silver method in which diamine silver oxide

was reduced with formaldehyde. Since all these methods were considered unreliable, they spawned a multiplicity of modifications. A further refinement of Bielschowsky's silver method eventually led in 1905 to the demonstration of reticulin fibres in connective tissue. Constantin Levaditi (1874–1953) demonstrated *Treponema pallidum* using block silver staining, while in 1955, to identify fungal mycelia, R. G. Grocott devised a modification of the methenamine silver stain for carbohydrate introduced in 1946 by George Gomori (1904–1957).

Dyes elicit fresh information

With few exceptions, early descriptions in cell microscopy came from studies with unstained tissue samples. Scientists became familiar with cells filled with cytoplasm, containing a nucleus and nucleolus, and surrounded by a cell boundary. They even discovered various epithelial cells – some with cilia – along with muscle fibres and red blood corpuscles. They could also differentiate between the cells of skeletal muscle, heart muscle and smooth muscle. But they felt an increasing need to distinguish more clearly between the various tissue structures. They were bolstered in this desire by advances in the burgeoning field of chemical research and the development of cheap artificial dyes for the textile industry. Fabrics had been dyed since antiquity. It was thus not surprising that scientists should also have coloured cells and tissues with familiar natural dyes, beginning with vegetable pigments such as indigo, madder root, saffron, orcein and chlorophyll. Hematoxylin, extracted from the logwood tree indigenous to Central America, was particularly important. It is not a dye in its own right, but becomes one after conversion to its oxidation product, hematein, either in air or after treatment with oxidants. Widely different tissue fractions can be demonstrated by adding various chemicals to hematein, which has a strong affinity for nucleic acids when combined with a metallic mordant. Many scientists developed their own personal formulations, which were then generally named after them, a notable example being Heidenhain's iron hematoxylin stain. In 1891 Paul Mayer devised a hematoxylin solution which selectively stained the cell nucleus. However, this was not the first nuclear-specific stain This had been found by Joseph von Gerlach (1820–1896), an anatomist in Erlangen, Germany, in 1858. He observed that the nuclei of tissue steeped in ammoniated carminic acid took up the red stain cochineal (obtained from the dried bodies of insects that live on the nopal cactus) more rapidly than did protoplasm or intercellular ground substance. It was von Gerlach who wrote, 'Histology rests on the art of staining',[31] and he believed that

> With few exceptions, human histology has been so thoroughly investigated that without significant improvement in our optical 'aids', there is little prospect of further advance in this field of research.[32]

The latter statement proved grossly off the mark, given the potential of the artificial dyes that were soon available to histologists. From 1854 onwards aniline, a distillate of coal tar, was the springboard for the synthesis of new artificial dyes. Aniline dyes were considerably cheaper than their natural counterparts, although their histological applications could likewise only be determined by a process of trial and error. Paul Ehrlich (1854–1915) was among those who were to play an outstanding role in this regard. Even as a student he had worked on staining techniques in the laboratory of his cousin Carl Weigert (1845–1904). Having established that cells and tissues stained differently when several dyes were used, whether simultaneously or consecutively, and that this could be put to advantage to enhance contrast and differentiation between various tissue types, he embarked on a systematic study of the aniline dyes, dividing them into two major categories, basic and acidic. In his dye theory, published in 1877 (*Beiträge zur Kenntnis der Anilinfarben und ihrer Verwendung in der mikroskopischen Technik*), he was the first to demonstrate that it was not only the molecular structure of the dye that was critical in tissue staining but also and above all the chemical composition of the target tissue fractions. Thus acid substrates, e.g. nucleic acids, stain with basic dyes such as methylene blue, toluidine blue and cresyl violet, while acid dyes such as eosin, erythrosin and many others bind to basic substrates, e. g. in cytoplasm. In 1876 Ehrlich discovered mast cells using basic dyes. While working with methylene blue, he noted the phenomenon of metachromasia (the property of certain dyes to stain particular tissue structures with a colour different from that of the staining solution).

Pathogen stains

Leeuwenhoek was the first to visualise bacteria under the microscope, describing them as tiny worms. Infectious diseases such as typhoid fever, diphtheria and tuberculosis alarmed Western Europeans in Ehrlich's day even more than they do today. In March 1882 he learned of the discovery of the tubercle bacterium at a lecture by Koch in Berlin. He was so impressed that he made it a new focus of study, becoming ever more interested in the potential of stains to identify the causative organisms of infectious diseases. The result was that he was able to establish the acid-fast nature of the tubercle bacillus (i. e. their ability to retain dyes despite an acid wash) and devise an acid fuchsin staining technique which confirmed Koch's discovery.[33]

In 1878 Carl Weigert became the first to stain bacteria in tissue, using an aniline dye. He was also the first to use 'sharp nuclear staining agents', as he called hematoxylin solutions, in histopathology.

New intracellular ultrastructures

Weigert's extensive studies resulted in the demonstration of fibrin in 1884 and of the elastic fibres in connective tissue using resorcin fuchsin in 1886. On becoming head of the Senckenberg Pathology Institute in Frankfurt in 1885, he also turned to neuropathology. He developed important staining techniques used to this day for demonstrating the myelin sheaths of nerve fibres and their degenerative changes. This provided Oskar Vogt (1870–1959) and his wife Cecilie with the tools for their pioneering work on the myeloarchitecture of the brain in the early 20th century. Using the basic dyes cresyl violet and methylene blue to stain nerve cells, the histopathologist Franz Nissl (1857–1919) discovered the bodies named after him, now known to represent rough endoplasmic reticulum, the site of protein synthesis in cells. As with the Golgi apparatus, more detailed characterisation had to await the introduction of electron microscopy.

In 1924 Ludwig Aschoff (1866–1942) and his pupil Max Landau (1886–1915) observed that reticular tissue and some reticular tissue endothelia (reticuloendothelium) stored foreign bodies before all other tissues and that this system, which includes histiocytes and monocytes, was involved in the

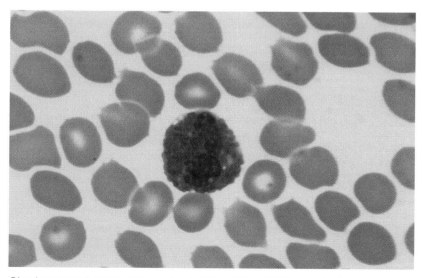

Blood smear with eosinophil granulocyte (May-Grünwald-Giemsa stain).

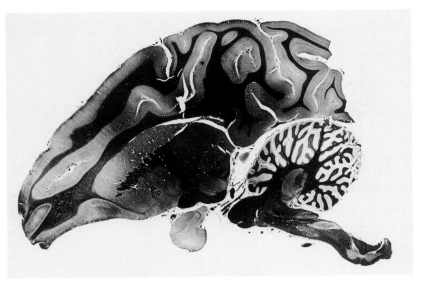

Sagittal section through monkey brain detailing the myelin sheaths around the nerve fibres (modified Weigert stain).

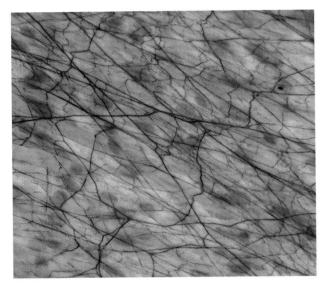

Frog mesentery elastic connective tissue fibres (Weigert's resorcin fuchsin and Goldner's counterstain).

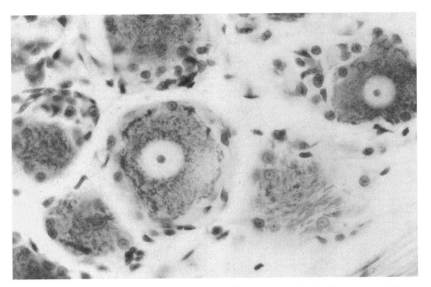

Nissl bodies in spinal ganglion cells (6 µm paraffin section stained with cresyl violet).

immune response.[34] Using vital stains such as pyrrole blue and carmine to explore cell storage and phagocytosis, Aschoff and Landau developed the concept of the reticuloendothelial system.

Heidenhain also contributed greatly to the elucidation of the fine structure of cells and their cytoplasm. His iron hematoxylin stain demonstrated organelles such as the centrosome, the cell division apparatus, lysosomes, zymogen granules in glandular cells, tonofibrils, and many others. 'Über Kern und Protoplasma', Heidenhain's contribution to an 1892 festschrift honouring Kölliker on the 50th anniversary of his doctorate, contains the interesting sentence:

In my view it is certain beyond all doubt that there are microscopic features which even the practised eye misses if it spends only a few minutes on studying a preparation: the retina's ability to discriminate increases over several hours during microscopy up to a certain maximum, after which fatigue sets in.[35]

There is not enough space here to enumerate all of Heidenhain's discoveries. Mention should, however, be made of the azocarmine-aniline blue (azan) stain which he developed. It was extensively used in the 20th century because of its ability to stain nucleus, cytoplasm and connective tissue components in different colours. Heidenhain eventually delegated his technical work to an assistant,[36] whose preparations were of a quality never achieved since.[37] Any histologist who now possesses one such preparation can consider himself fortunate. Heidenhain's work resolved the remaining open questions regarding cell structure as far as was possible using the light microscope, even if the results could only be interpreted with the subsequent arrival of electron microscopy.

Since the work of Ehrlich, Weigert and Heidenhain on differential staining of cells, cell contents and various tissues, an ever-increasing number of new stains and stain combinations have come into use, making it possible to discriminate nucleus, cytoplasm and connective tissue fibres for microscopy and diagnosis, all in a single staining procedure. The hematoxylin-eosin double stain serves as a general-purpose stain. Hematoxylin, a basic stain, demonstrates the nucleus, while acid eosin colours the cytoplasm and connective tissue fibres. Heiden-

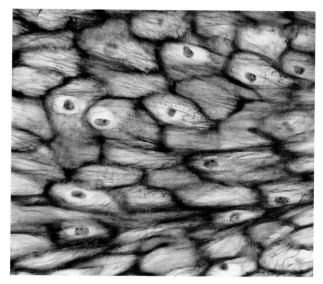

Squamous epithelium (skin), showing tonofibrils (Heidenhain's iron hematoxylin).

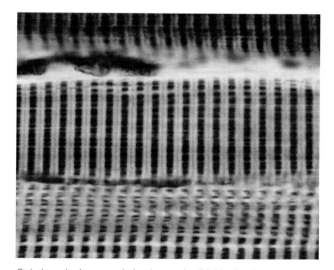

Striations in human skeletal muscle (Heidenhain's iron hematoxylin).

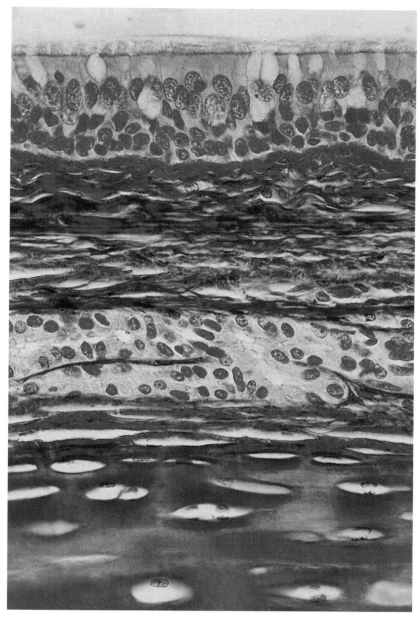

Six–eight micrometre paraffin section of human trachea stained with Heidenhain's azan – azocarmine and aniline blue. This stain was extensively used in the 20th century.

hain's azan stain or one of the many trichrome (3-in-1) stains can be used to impart different colours to the cytoplasm and connective tissue fibres.

Cytology

In the early 1950s cytology parted company with general histopathology to become an independent specialty with a growing capital of new techniques. Cytological analysis was initially performed on stained smears. George Nicolas Papanicolaou (1883–1962) developed a staining method now used on a massive scale in cervical cancer screening. The timely diagnosis of precancerous changes permits prophylactic surgery and saves lives.

Cell chemistry

Advances in biochemistry spawned a new field within histology: histochemistry. Friedrich Miescher (1844–1895), considered one of the first histochemists, founded the 'chemistry of morphological subunits' and 'cell chemistry'. His focus was the cell nucleus and its structure. In 1869 he demonstrated an acid specific to the cell nucleus which he named 'nuclein' or 'nucleic acid' and which subsequently proved to be predominantly **ri**bo**n**ucleic **a**cid (RNA) in the nucleolus and **d**eoxyribo**n**ucleic **a**cid (DNA) in the rest of the nucleus.

Botanists had earlier demonstrated carbohydrate, e.g. starch in plant cells, in 1825 using the iodine

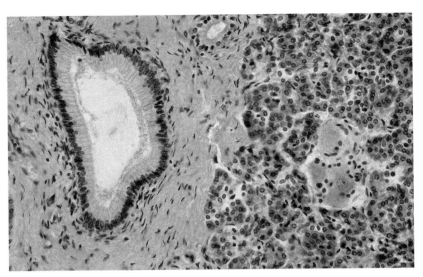

Paraffin section of human pancreas stained with one of the most widely used stains, hematoxylin-eosin.

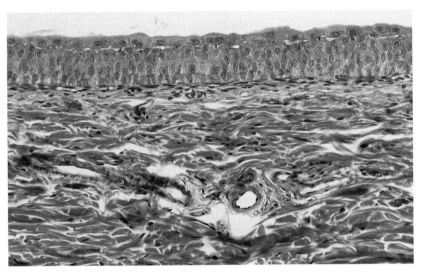

Monkey bladder (Masson-Goldner trichrome stain).

reaction. In 1854 Claude Bernard (1813–1878) demonstrated glycogen in liver cells. Hans Bauer's chromic acid leukofuchsin method of identifying polysaccharide can be termed a true histochemical reaction.[38] Max Schultze described the blackening of lipids with osmium tetroxide in 1864. Up to the end of the 19th century fat droplets were demonstrated in tissue sections by light refraction or solubility in lipid solvents. In 1896 L. Daddi devised a general method for demonstrating lipids which has remained standard to this day using a purely physical reaction with the diazo dye Sudan III.

The most important methods of enzyme detection were only developed in the 20th century, although the earliest reported methods of this kind date from before 1900.[39]

Histochemistry includes the detection of pigments and inorganic compounds. Max Perls (1843–1881) demonstrated ionised iron in 1876. Staining techniques have since been developed for detecting other metals in tissue.

Advances in the 20th century

The rise of laboratory automation in the 20th century made the histologist's work a good deal easier. Tissue fixing and embedding devices were developed. Improvements were made to the paraffin oven – a very early fixture of the histology laboratory which is used to impregnate tissue with paraffin wax. Today there are embedding stations for casting paraffin-impregnated tissue specimens into moulds. Microtomes have been motorised and may have a section ribbon guide. The only tasks still performed by hand are slicing embedded tissue, producing good sections and mounting sections onto slides. Behrens's flight of fancy, in which he imagined the scientist of the future sitting at his automatic sectioning device with his arms folded and smoking a cigar[40] has yet to become reality.

Still, the number of labour-saving devices developed by industry for routine laboratory tasks is considerable. They extend from tissue fixing and embedding systems (mentioned as early as 1905, but not commercially available until the 1950s) to staining machines and coverslippers, which cover stained sections with mountant and a coverslip.

Cryostats have greatly facilitated and enhanced the preparation of frozen sections through fine temperature control and separate cooling of the tissue block.

Microscope design also progressed through the 20th century. The physicist Frits Zernike (1888–1966) developed phase contrast microscopy to observe living cells and examine unstained sections. He demonstrated his new design in 1932 at the Zeiss factory, initially meeting with no response. His idea was then further refined nine years later at Zeiss by August Köhler and W. Loos, with Zernike receiving the 1953 Nobel Prize for Physics for his original idea.

Fluorescence microscopy is now used to study fluorescing tissue inclusions. More radically, once it had become clear that the wavelength of light restricted the theoretical resolution of the microscope, physicists investigated the potential of shorter-wave electromagnetic radiation. In 1931 Ernst Ruska (1906–1988) and Max Knoll (1897–1969) achieved the first picture of an object using electron rays, leading to the construction of the first electron microscope at Siemens in 1937, followed by production in 1939. Magnifications of a previously unimaginable order became possible, with modern instruments achieving resolutions of approximately 0.4 nm (0.4 millionth of a millimetre).

The electron microscope revealed for the first time the details of the cellular subunits which had in fact been seen with the light microscope only to be frequently dismissed as artefacts, e.g. the Golgi apparatus, mitochondria,[41] Nissl granules and endoplasmic reticulum.[42] Although proving a precious research tool in cell biology, electron microscopy has had few applications in medical diagnostics. Sample preparation is expensive and labour-intensive, and the examination field narrow in the extreme (1–2 mm, depending on the microscope), so that only portions of individual cells are visible at the requisite magnification. These characteristics have conspired against the routine use of electron microscopy except in virology, where it has proved indispensable. Ruska received the Nobel Prize for his work in 1986 shortly before his death.

Histological technique has also progressed. Mixing polymers with pure stearine, beeswax or paraffin for tissue embedding has enhanced block sectionability. Artificial embedding agents with epoxy resins have been adopted from the preparation methodology of electron microscopy, enabling sections to be cut down to 0.5 µm. Electron microscopy also revealed the importance of optimal tissue fixing. Organ perfusion with fixing solutions has become the norm for research purposes.

The improvements in microscope optics made possible by number-crunching computer power required new mountants with refractive indices approximating that of glass even more closely than was the case with the first artificial substitutes for Canada balsam. Differential staining techniques have also improved. Whereas early staining guidelines were fairly hazy, leaving much room for the microscopist's personal ingenuity, increasingly precise instructions have been developed over the years, in particular by Benno Romeis (1888–1971), with close compliance guaranteeing a standardised result.

Drawing on the work done by immunologists on antigen-antibody complex formation, Albert Hewett Coons (1912–1978) was using fluorescence-labelled antibodies to demonstrate specific tissue antigens by 1941. In the early 1970s this resulted in a technique – immunofluorescence – without which tumour tissue diagnostics (and much fundamental research) would now simply be unthinkable.

There has even been technical progress in light microscopy. Light scattering in the object is a funda-

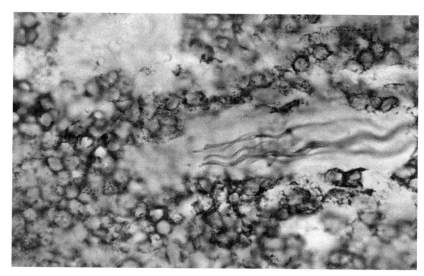

T-lymphocytes in human tonsil labelled by immunocytochemistry, and nerves demonstrated by silver impregnation.

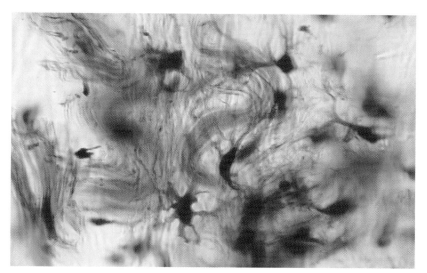

Stereo image of fibrocytes in the human lip.

mental restriction on image quality. By narrowing the illumination beam to the smallest possible point while simultaneously restricting the image field in the objective lens – as is the case with confocal laser scanning microscopy – this problem has been minimised. This breakthrough required the development of practical laser systems, which has resulted in significant labour-savings while yielding substantially better pictures into the bargain.

Digital photography and powerful computers now make it possible with a normal transmitted light microscope to sum a focus series through a thicker than normal section, thereby effectively abolishing the previous limitation on depth of field. In fact with the right computer program 3D images can now be obtained of entire cells.[43]

Robert Tattersall and Rainer Proetzsch

Pisse prophets, polarimetry and patient self-monitoring

The history of diabetes testing

Up to the end of the 18th century, images of physicians typically showed them performing uroscopy.

too much urine'. It is unclear, however, whether the condition referred to is diabetes insipidus (a form of polyuria in which the body may excrete up to five litres of urine per day as a result of inadequate water reabsorption in the kidneys) or diabetes mellitus, the 'sugar disease'.[2] The first clearly recognisable, and marvellously vivid, description of the symptoms of diabetes was given by Arataeus of Cappadocia (AD 81–138), who also gave the disease its name, which derived from the Greek word for 'siphon', 'because the fluid does not remain in the body, but uses the man's body as a ladder whereby to leave it'. He wrote:

> Diabetes is a wonderful affection, not very frequent among men, being a melting down of the flesh and limbs into urine. Its cause is of a cold and humid nature as in dropsy. The course is the common one, namely, the kidneys and the bladder; for the patients never stop making water, but the flow is incessant, as if from the opening of aqueducts. The nature of the disease, then, is chronic, and it takes a long period to form; but the patient is short lived, if the constitution of the disease be completely established; for the melting is rapid, the death speedy. Moreover, life is disgusting and painful; thirst unquenchable; excessive drinking, which, however, is disproportionate to the large quantity of urine, for more urine is passed; and one cannot stop them either from drinking or making water. Or if for a time they abstain from drinking, their mouth becomes parched and their body dry; the viscera seem as if scorched up; they are affected with nausea, restlessness and a burning thirst; …they stand out for a certain time, though not very long, for they pass urine with pain and the emaciation is dreadful; nor does any great portion of the drink get into the system, and many parts of the flesh pass out along with the urine.

The Hindu physicians Charak and Sushrut (5th century AD) were probably the first to recognise the

The earliest known description of diabetes occurs in an Egyptian papyrus discovered by Georg Ebers in a tomb near Thebes in 1862.[1] One of the prescriptions listed in the papyrus, which dates from about 1550 BC, is for a medicine 'to drive away the passing of

Thomas Willis *(1621–1675), physician to King Charles 1 of England, is remembered for his description of the arterial circle at the base of the brain, which is named after him. In his discourse on* Diabetes or the Pissing Evil, *published posthumously, he suggested that, 'diabetes was a disease so rare among the ancients that many famous physicians made no mention of it … but in our age given to good fellowship and guzzling down of unallayed wine, we meet with examples and instances enough, I may say daily, of this disease.' In his own words, 'such as are troubled with this distemper, piss much more than they drink or take of liquid nutriment; and likewise they have a continual thirst.' He described (several times) the urine as being 'wonderfully sweet like sugar or honey', but why this was so was not 'easy to untie'.*

THE
PISSE-PROPHET
OR
CERTAINE PISSE POT
LECTURES.

Wherein are newly difcovered the old fallacies, deceit, and jugling of the Piffe-pot Science, ufed by all thofe (whether Quacks and Empiricks, or other methodicall Phyficians) who pretend knowledge of Difeafes, by the Urine, in giving judgement of the fame.

By THO. BRIAN, M. P. lately in the Citie of *London*, and now in *Colchefter* in ESSEX.

Never heretofore publifhed by any man in the *Englifh* Tongue.

Si populus vult decipi, decipiatur.

LONDON,
Printed by *E. P.* for *R. Thrale*, and are to be fold at his fhop at the figne of the Croffe Keyes, at *Pauls* gate
1637

Frontispiece of Thomas Brian's polemic The Pisse Prophet or Certaine Pisse Pot Lectures, *published in London in 1637.*

sweetness of diabetic urine ('honey urine') and made a diagnosis by tasting it. Ants are attracted to anything sweet, and the Hindu physicians pointed out that, if ants were attracted to a person's urine, this meant that he or she had diabetes. These methods of diagnosis persisted into the 20th century. As late as 1967 a professor of medicine in Accra, Ghana, wrote that about 20 % of diabetic patients reporting for the first time had already confirmed their suspicion of diabetes by tasting their urine.[3] Following this, a correspondent wrote to the *British Medical Journal* that people in Sierra Leone knew they had diabetes when they found ants in the chamber pot the next morning.

Pisse prophets and the pissing evil

Using urine to make diagnoses is probably the oldest medical test and was described by Hippocrates (460–377 BC). Up to the end of the 18th century, paintings of physicians almost invariably showed them inspecting a urine glass, or matula.[4] Charlatans also got into the act with a technique called uromancy,

by which they pretended to divine age, sex, state of health and the duration of disease merely by looking at the urine. In 1637 Thomas Brian published a polemic against these 'pisse prophets' and suggested to his readers that

> it were farre better for the Physician to see his Patient once than to view the Urine twenty times.[5]

That diabetic urine tasted sweet was emphasised by Arabic medical texts from the 9th to the 11th centuries AD but seems to have been forgotten in Europe. Attention was drawn to it again by Thomas Willis (1621–1675). The prevailing view was that diabetes was a disease of the kidneys, but Willis believed that

> the temper or mixture of the blood is so loosened, and in a manner dissolved, that the watery particles cannot be kept in by the thicker ones.

It did not occur to him, however, that the sweetness might be due to sugar, and this connection was not made until the work of Matthew Dobson (1735–1784), physician to the Liverpool Royal Infirmary.[6]

Eugène Chevreul *(1786–1889) was a remarkable man who gave his last communication to the Academy of Sciences in 1888 when he was 102 years old. Apart from being the founder of organic chemistry and the discoverer of the fatty acids, he was also a medical historian and made an intensive study of the principles of colour contrasts which greatly influenced the leaders of the Neo-Impressionist movement, Georges Surat and Paul Signac.*

William Prout *(1785–1850), depicted in a painting from the 1830s. Besides being a practicing physician, Prout held public lectures on 'animal chemistry' and performed extensive experimental studies in his private laboratory. His book* Chemistry, Meteorology and the Function of Digestion Considered with Reference to Natural Theology *was first published in 1834 as one of the* Bridgewater Treatises, *a series intended, in the words of the man who endowed it, to illuminate the 'Power, Wisdom and Goodness of God as manifested in the Creation'. Prout's book went through four editions. After 1830, increasing deafness restricted his contact with other scientists.*[64]

Polarimeter designed and built by Eilhard Mitscherlich. The instrument was used in Johann L. Schönlein's department at Berlin's Charité Hospital around 1843. Now in the collection of the Institute for the History of Medicine, University of Vienna.

In 1772 Dobson admitted a 33 year old man, Peter Dickonson, who had had diabetes for eight months and was passing 28 pints (15 litres) of urine a day. When he came to the hospital he was 'emaciated, weak and dejected; his thirst was unquenchable'. His urine was very sweet to the taste and was usually 'perfectly transparent, and almost colourless'.

Eight ounces of blood were taken from the patient's arm, and Dobson noted that 'the serum was opaque, and much resembled common cheese whey; it was sweetish, but I thought not so sweet as the urine'. He evaporated two quarts of urine and was left with a '[white] cake [which] was granulated, and broke easily between the fingers; it smelled sweet like brown sugar, neither could it by the taste be distinguished from sugar'. Dobson thought diabetes was a disease due to 'imperfect digestion and assimilation' and that the cure was to strengthen the digestive powers and the system in general.

In the 18th century the Edinburgh physician William Cullen (1710–1790) distinguished two forms of polyuria: that in which the urine was sweet he called diabetes mellitus, and when the urine was tasteless he spoke of diabetes insipidus.

Fermentation tests and polarimetry

In 1780 Francis Home (1719–1813), a professor in Edinburgh, showed that diabetic urine could be fermented.[7] He mixed half a pint of yeast with 24 pints of the urine of one of his diabetic patients and

> it soon began to ferment, and exit a vapour, like fermenting liquors. Next day it fermented strongly. On the third, the fermentation seemed over, it had lost all sweetness and tasted like small beer. Murray's [another patient's urine] treated in the same way, fermented into a tolerable small beer.

In 1815 the French chemist Eugène Chevreul (1786–1889) proved that the sugar in diabetic urine was glucose, or grape sugar.[8]

Six years later, in his *An enquiry into the Nature and Treatment of Diabetes, Calculus, and the Affections of the Urinary Organs*, the English physician William Prout (1785–1850), one of the founders of medical chemistry, listed the simple apparatus needed to test the urine; litmus for acidity, boiling for protein, and the slide test for distinguishing between mucus and pus. At this stage sugar was still recognised by taste and by observing white sticky patches where urine had spotted the clothes or shoes.

In the middle of the 19th century tasting the urine was superseded by physical and chemical tests for sugar. One physical method that continued to be used until well into the 20th century was polarimetry. Polarimetry makes use of the ability of glucose molecules to rotate the plane of polarised light. The first device used for 'sugar polarimetry' in Germany was constructed by the Berlin chemist Eilhard Mitscherlich (1794–1863). To determine the sugar concentration in a urine sample, the sample was transferred to a horizontal tube in the device, and the eyepiece was rotated until the brightness was the same in both halves of the visual field. The sugar concentration was then estimated from the angle of rotation of the eyepiece.

Another technique was based on the fact that adding yeast to urine causes it to ferment and produce carbon dioxide. In 1862 William Roberts (1830–1899), physician to the Manchester Royal Infirmary, described the following quantitative method.[9] Two samples of diabetic urine were put in flasks and 'a piece of German yeast about the size of a cobnut or small walnut' added to one. Both were placed on a warm mantelpiece for 24 hours, during which the glucose in the flask with the yeast fermented to carbon dioxide, which was able to escape from the flask. After 24 hours, the specific gravities of the samples were measured, and the amount of glucose was equal to the difference of the specific gravity before and after fermentation multiplied by 0.23. The accuracy of this method was proved in 1907 by the Bostonian Henry Asbury Christian (1876–1951), who argued that it was ideal for the practitioner who wanted to treat his cases of

Claude Bernard *(1813–1878) originally wanted to be a dramatist, but decided to pursue a career in medicine on the advice of a medical professor. It was a fortunate choice, for it is to Bernard that we owe the discovery that the liver is capable of synthesising sugar – a discovery that changed medicine's views about the nature of diabetes. A few years later Bernard discovered a substance in the liver that can be converted to glucose when needed. Bernard interpreted the presence of glycosuria in diabetes as a consequence of abnormally elevated blood sugar levels, which he suspected were caused by reduced glucose metabolism. Though Bernard's hypothesis of the cause of glycosuria was correct, it was not widely adopted by clinicians until the late 19th century.[65] A second discovery of Bernard's (in 1849), and one which made a great impression in an era in which the idea of nervous control of bodily functions was scientifically fashionable, was that a lesion in the floor of the fourth ventricle of the brain produced diabetes, though only temporarily (piqûre diabetes).*

diabetes 'scientifically'. Its advantage was that everything necessary, except the urinometer, could be found in an ordinary domestic kitchen.[10, 11]

Chemical tests for glucose

In 1841 Carl August Trommer (1806–1879) described a method in which urine was heated with cupric sulphate and sodium hydroxide; in the presence of a reducing substance (such as glucose), red cuprous oxide was formed.[12] Because the red colour could be obscured by black copper oxide, the method was not very reliable. Though not widely used, it stimulated further research into the principle of reduction of metallic oxides by glucose. In 1848 Herman von Fehling (1812–1885) added Rochelle salt (sodium potassium tartrate) to the reagent to hold cupric ions in solution, thus greatly increasing the sensitivity of the test.[13] The main disadvantage was that the solution was unstable and had to be remade frequently. Fehling's test was ideal for qualitative purposes but, in the hands of ordinary physicians, too complicated for quantitative analysis. In 1907 the American Biochemist Stanley Benedict (1884–1936) described the first version of his test, which became the most widely used method of de-

Saccharometer designed by Max Einhorn (1885). A urine sample was mixed with yeast and transferred without bubbles to the tube on the right. Left to stand in a warm place, the mixture would form carbon dioxide if the urine contained glucose.

tecting glycosuria (abnormally high levels of glucose in urine) for the next 40 years.[14] Benedict's test was ten times more sensitive than Fehling's.

A problem with all copper-based tests was possible interference by other reducing substances in the urine. In 1923, in his Lettsomian lectures on glycosuria, the London physician Archibald Garrod (1857–1936), discoverer of the concept of inborn errors of metabolism, wrote:

> there is no urinary anomaly of which we should know more than of glycosuria, for thousands of specimens of urine are being tested for sugar every day, in the course of routine examination of hospital and private patients, and of candidates for insurance … [yet] … many observations are vitiated by the absence of conclusive proof that the abnormal substance excreted in the urine is really glucose.[15]

An inscrutable disease

During the first half of the 19th century doctors investigated the etiology of disease by comparing the clinical picture with autopsy findings. Diabetes, however, remained a mystery since, in most cases, nothing abnormal was found at autopsy. It was thought by some to be a disease of the kidneys, while others considered it a disease of the stomach. In 1839, in his *Principles and Practice of Medicine,* the prominent London physician John Elliotson (1791–1868) cited the usual suspects at the time for any kind of ill health: 'grief', 'chills' and 'an excess of venery'. William Prout named 'anxiety and distress' as the most important causes.

The first clue to the pathophysiology of diabetes came from the work of Claude Bernard (1813–1878) in France.[16] When he began his work in 1843, the prevailing theory was that sugar could be synthesised only by plants, and that animal metabolism consisted in breaking down substances originally made in plants. It was also thought that the blood of animals contained sugar only after meals or in pathological states such as diabetes. Between 1846 and 1848 Bernard reported that sugar was also present in the blood of normal animals, even when starved or fed a diet consisting exclusively of meat, a finding which he at first found so astonishing that he doubted his analytical method. He also found that a starch-like substance which, although not a true sugar, could be readily converted into it, was present in 'enormous quantities' in the liver but not in any other organ. He called this substance glycogen (i. e. sugar-forming) and regarded it as analogous to starch in plants. His hypothesis, the glycogenic theory, was that sugar absorbed from the intestine was converted in the liver into glycogen and then constantly released into the blood during fasting.

Testing for glucose in blood

Measuring blood sugar in the 19th century was highly problematic, calling for large volumes of blood, plenty of time and meticulous technique. Most methods in use at the time required 30–50 mL of blood. The first stage was to deproteinise it, then the reducing substances were estimated by means of fermentation, polarimetric analysis or copper reagents. In the 1890s the two methods in common use were those of Friedrich Schenck (1862–1916) and Edward Waymouth Reid (1862–1948). At the beginning of the 20th century blood tests for glucose were still not a normal part of clinical practice. An English textbook published in 1908 states that

> [Blood sugar tests] are never necessary in clinical work but they may be resorted to in suspected frauds connected with life insurance.[17]

Even in hospitals diabetes was diagnosed and monitored with urine tests. Diabetes was defined as a condition in which sugar was constantly present in the urine. Many physicians thought there were two or more types of the disease. In 1880 the French physician Etienne Lancereaux (1829–1910) divided cases by body weight into thin and fat (*diabète maigre* and *diabète gras*). This distinction was only important for prognosis – lean patients died in a year or two, while fat ones survived for ten or more years and eventually developed retinitis, neuritis or kidney failure. The only treatment for either form was a restricted diet. The basis of treatment was to determine the amount of sugar passed in the urine over 24 hours and then reduce the intake of carbohydrates (which are converted by the body into sugar) to the point where no urine sugar could be detected. In this way the patient's 'tolerance' could be determined and checked from time to time. A breakthrough came in 1913 when Ivar Christian Bang (1869–1918), a Norwegian-born chemist then working at the University of Lund in Sweden, devised a micromethod which only needed two or three drops of blood.[18] Unfortunately, the method was anything but easy for anyone except a skilled chemist.

Glucose tolerance tests

During the latter part of the 19th century clinicians such as Rudolf Külz (1845–1895) of Marburg used a variety of test diets to determine their patients' 'tolerance', that is, the amount of carbohydrate which they could eat without developing glycosuria. With the advent of micromethods for measuring blood sugar, repeated measurements could be taken without 'bleeding the patient to death', paving the way for more sophisticated tests of carbohydrate tolerance. One of the first such studies was done in 1913 using Bang's micromethod. After normal subjects drank 100 g of glucose in 250 mL of solution, there was an appreciable rise in blood sugar within five minutes; blood sugar levels usually peaked in about 30 minutes and returned to normal in an hour and three quarters.[19] How to interpret the results of such tests remained contentious for the next 50 years. The upper limit of normal for fasting blood sugar was generally agreed to be 120 mg/dL (6.7 mmol/L). For all other values, there was widespread disagreement, although it was thought that in health blood sugar returned to the fasting level within two hours. In 1975 the epidemiologist Kelly West (1925–1980) asked 20 prominent diabetologists (11 Americans and nine from other countries) what two-hour level in the glucose tolerance test they would consider abnormal. Both the Americans and the others quoted a wide range for the lowest two-hour plasma glucose levels in a glucose tolerance test which were 'clearly abnormal' (130–200 mg/dL) and the highest values considered clearly normal (110–180 mg/dL).[20] These differences of opinion were not merely academic, for, as West pointed out, in one series of glucose tolerance tests in elderly Americans, one of the respondents would have classified 2% as clearly abnormal while another would have so classified 62%.

In 1998 new diagnostic criteria – now standard in most countries except the United States – for interpreting the results of oral glucose tolerance tests were published by a WHO consultation group.[21] Because pure glucose solutions can cause nausea in susceptible persons (e.g. pregnant women), Boehringer Mannheim began marketing a well-tolerated and pleasant-tasting oligosaccharide-based solution for oral glucose challenge (Dextro OGT) in Germany in 1976.

Some clinicians plugged the need for blood sugar tests, especially if, like Hugh Maclean of London, they marketed a kit for doing them. However, in general, blood tests were too expensive and inconvenient for outpatients, and most clinicians managed their patients without them. The famous Boston diabetes specialist Elliott Joslin (1869–1962) wrote in 1923:

> Blood sugar tests are very desirable, but I doubt whether one in ten of my patients has such a test once a month in his own home. The cost of one such test would probably supply them with insulin for a week and they prefer the insulin. Instead of blood sugar

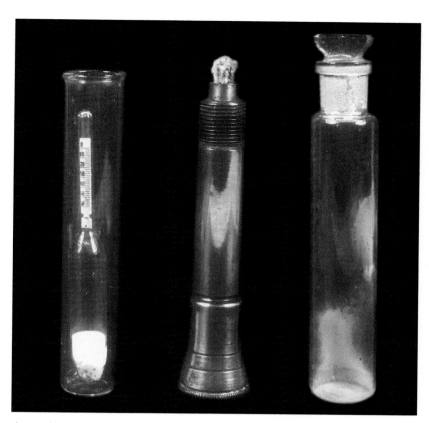

A portable urine test kit for patients (c. 1930). The bottle on the right contained Benedict's solution. The bottom section of the petroleum lamp was unscrewed and used as a cover. On the left: a test tube and a hydrometer, for measuring specific gravity.

tests, they depend on frequent Benedict's tests of each single specimen of urine, of which the cost of one test is one cent.

This reliance on urine tests, in hospital and at home, continued until well after World War Two. Patients who were judged to be capable of monitoring their own condition outside hospital (by no means the majority) were given Benedict's test. The technique was spelt out by Robin Lawrence (1892–1968) of King's College Hospital, himself one of the first people treated with insulin in England, as follows:

> Put 8 drops of urine in a clean test-tube. Add 1 inch (1 teaspoonful) of blue solution. Shake test-tube. Stand the test-tube in a small pan of boiling water and boil for five minutes; or boil in spirit or gas flame for two minutes. Then take out the test-tube. If the fluid remains clear and blue, no sugar is present; if the fluid turns slightly green and a greyish sediment appears at the bottom of the tube, there is still no sugar present. If the solution goes green and there is a yellow deposit after standing for ten minutes, a little sugar is present. If the solution goes yellow, a considerable amount of sugar is present. If the solution goes brown or red, very heavy amounts of sugar are present. There is also very heavy sugar present if a brown or red test turns to a dirty green (olive) colour, which some patients mistake for the light green trace of sugar.[26]

The discovery of life-saving insulin

Despite the progress that had been made in diagnosing diabetes, at the turn of the 20th century medicine was still a long way from having an effective treatment to offer. As so often in human history – and particularly in the history of science – it was chance as much as anything else that eventually put two observant researchers on the right track. In 1889 the Strasbourg physicians Oskar Minkowski (1858–1931) and Josef Freiherr von Mering (1848–1908) were performing digestion experiments which involved removing the pancreas of a dog. Although the dog was housebroken, following pancreatectomy it kept urinating on the laboratory floor. Could it be suffering from diabetes? Acting on an inspired hunch, Minkowski collected a few drops of the dog's urine and tested them for sugar. He found a glucose level of over 10%. In 1892 Minkowski and Charles Édouard Emmanuel Hédon (1863–1933) demonstrated that experimental diabetes induced by pancreatectomy in dogs could be partially relieved with grafts of pancreatic tissue. Minkowski's initial attempts at treating diabetic dogs with extracts of pancreas were a failure, however. In 1908 the Berlin physician Georg Ludwig Zülzer (1870–1949) succeeded in lowering the blood sugar of diabetes patients with alcohol extracts of calf pancreas, but the patients complained of chills, sweats and fever, and the experiments had to be stopped. Today we know that these symptoms were probably due primarily to hypoglycemia. A few years earlier, in 1902, the Russian physician Leonid Vassilievitch Sobolev (1876–1919) had reported his observations following experimental ligation of the pancreatic duct in dogs. While the tissue that secretes digestive enzymes degenerated, the hormone-secreting islet cells of the pancreas survived intact. Sobolev's dogs suffered from digestive disturbances, but did not develop diabetes as Minkowski's dogs had following total pancreatectomy.[22] This pioneering work went largely unnoticed, and it was not until 1920 that Sobolev's experiments were repeated by the American Moses Barron (1883–1974). An article by Barron on his experiments caught the attention of Frederick Grant Banting (1891–1941), a young orthopedic surgeon in Toronto. In 1921 Banting approached the local professor of physiology, John James Rickard MacLeod (1867–1935) and proposed repeating the duct ligations performed by Sobolev and Barron. Banting hoped that making the exocrine tissue degenerate would enable him to obtain an extract of pancreatic islet tissue which would be pure enough to lower blood glucose without side effects. Eventually MacLeod agreed to give Banting a lab and assigned Charles Herbert Best (1899–1978), a medical student who had mastered the techniques of measuring blood sugar, to serve as Banting's assistant. Six months later Banting and Best successfully treated a diabetic dog with an aqueous extract of a degenerated pancreas that had shrivelled to the size of a plum: the dog's blood sugar returned to normal and almost no sugar was found in the urine. To the researchers' delight, the listless animal sprang back to life – but only for a day. The next morning the dog lay dead in its cage. The implications were not lost on Banting and Best: to be effective, treatment with the hormone in their pancreatic extract

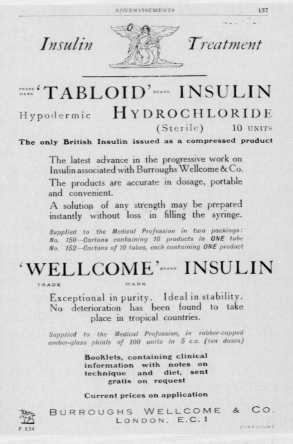

Advertisement for insulin from Burroughs Wellcome (1925).

would have to be given frequently and continued for life. Banting and Best performed numerous animal experiments over the course 1921. Because it contains a high proportion of islet cells, fetal calf pancreas, collected from local slaughterhouses, was used to obtain an extract.[23]

In December 1921 MacLeod hired the biochemist James Bertram Collip (1892–1965), who succeeded in refining the purification technique so that it yielded a pancreatic extract free of toxic impurities.

On 11 January 1922, at Toronto General Hospital, Leonard Thompson, a 14-year-old diabetic who had been on an Allen starvation diet since 1919 and weighed only 65 pounds, received an injection of a purified extract of ox pancreas in each buttock. The patient's blood sugar fell, and further injections on subsequent days rescued the boy from an untimely death. By the end of 1923 standardised extracts of bovine pancreas were available for clinical use in America and most of Europe, and the name 'insulin' had been adopted for the hormone secreted by the islet cells. In 1955 Frederick Sanger (b. 1918) determined the amino acid sequence of insulin, an achievement which had a catalytic effect on modern protein chemistry.[24] Among other things, it paved the way for the elucidation of the three-dimensional structure of insulin in 1969 by Dorothy Crowfoot Hodgkin (1910–1994).[25] For a long time

THE TREATMENT OF DIABETES MELLITUS WITH INSULIN *

RALPH H. MAJOR, M.D.
KANSAS CITY, KAN.

The recent isolation by Banting and his co-workers of an active glycolytic, nontoxic, pancreatic extract opens up a new era in the treatment of diabetes mellitus. Ever since the classical experiment of Mering and Minkowsky proved the existence of pancreatic diabetes, frequent attempts at specific pancreatic therapy have been made. These attempts in the past have been uniformly unsuccessful and now possess little but historical interest.

The isolation of insulin, which is described as the active hormone of the islands of Langerhans, has excited unusual interest among both physiologists and clinicians. Allen [1] has written an excellent summary of all articles published on this subject up to August, 1922, and enables one to trace step by step the various phases in the development of this important discovery.

Fig. 1.—Boy with severe juvenile diabetes, Dec. 7, 1922.

A more recent article by Banting, Campbell and Fletcher [2] describes the results obtained from the use of this preparation, in patients suffering from diabetes. They state that glycosuria is abolished, that ketones

* From the Department of Internal Medicine, University of Kansas School of Medicine.
1. Allen, F. M.: Summary of Publications on Insulin to Date, J. Metabol. Res. **2**: 125, 1922.
2. Banting, F. G.; Campbell, W. R., and Fletcher, A. A.: Further Clinical Experience with Insulin, Brit. M. J. **1**: 8 (Jan. 6) 1923.

disappear from the blood and urine, and that the blood sugar is lowered and maintained at a normal level. They found also that the alkali reserve returns to normal and that the cardinal symptoms are relieved. Perhaps the most interesting statement that they make is that insulin is a specific in the treatment of diabetic coma.

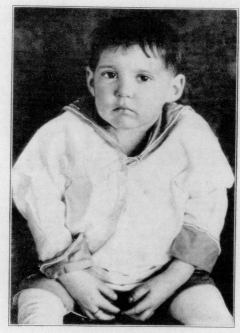

Fig. 2.—Appearance of patient, Feb. 26, 1923.

The preparation of insulin (insulin-Lilly) which is made in the United States has been used extensively in this country during the last few months. We thought it might prove of interest to record the results obtained in this clinic with the use of this preparation. We have used it in the treatment of thirty cases, and the results obtained have confirmed the therapeutic value described by Banting, Campbell and Fletcher. This group consisted mainly of moderately severe cases, but also included four cases of severe juvenile diabetes, four patients on the verge of coma who could be aroused only with great difficulty, and three patients in complete coma. Since a detailed description of the cases is not attempted in this report, a few typical results are shown in the accompanying illustrations and charts.

The boy shown in Figure 1 is an example of severe juvenile diabetes. At the time the picture was taken, Dec. 7, 1922, he had had diabetes for two years, and it had been impossible to render him aglycosuric except on a diet of 5 per cent. vegetables, with days of complete starvation. His weight at this time was 15 pounds (6.8 kg.). Treatment was begun at the St. Louis Children's Hospital under the direction of Dr. W. McKim Marriott, to whom I am indebted for this picture and

*If his family had had its way, **Frederick Grant Banting** (1891–1941) would have become a Methodist minister, but the lingering death of a childhood friend from diabetes led him to study medicine. In late October 1920 Banting, at the time a 29-year-old demonstrator in the physiology department at the University of Toronto, pleaded with the department head, J. J. R. MacLeod, to let him have ten laboratory dogs and one suitable assistant. Two years later Banting and MacLeod were awarded the Nobel Prize for Medicine for the discovery of insulin. Banting shared his half of the prize money with his assistant C. Best, and MacLeod shared his half with J. B. Collip, a biochemist who contributed to the discovery by developing a method for purifying insulin.* [66]

A contribution published in 1923 in the Journal of the American Medical Association *included moving photographs of a diabetes patient before and after treatment with insulin.*

bovine insulin products were used for routine therapy, and porcine insulin was used in patients with insulin resistance or insulin allergies. For various reasons – not least because of the dramatic rise in the global incidence of diabetes – alternative methods of obtaining insulin were urgently needed. The advent of genetic engineering made it possible to manufacture substances occurring naturally in the human body, and human insulin was one of the first to be synthesised using this new technology. Recombinant human insulin was first manufactured in the United States in 1979, using *E. coli* bacteria into which the human insulin gene had been inserted.

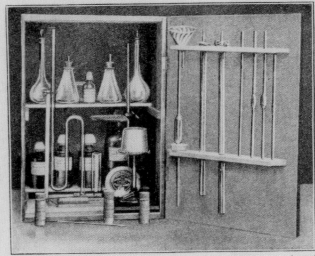
Advertisement for H. Maclean's blood sugar test kit (1924). Maclean hoped that general practitioners would buy and use his 'chemical test'.

Lest the reader think this was rather complicated, Lawrence added that, 'When you have been shown a few tests you will find urine testing quite simple.'

For all Lawrence's reassurances, boiling the urine over an alcohol flame with the accompanying 'bumping' and spurting was not to everyone's taste, especially when away from home. A tablet version of Benedict's test had been devised in 1927 by Sheftel but depended on an external heat source.[27] The big advance for patients came in 1944 when the Ames company introduced Clinitest, which did away with the need for a spirit lamp and thereby made the test much more portable.[28] In 1956 two glucose oxidase-based tests, Clinistix from Ames

and Tes Tape from Eli Lilly, appeared almost simultaneously. In Germany Tes Tape was marketed as Glukotest by Boehringer Mannheim. Clinistix was essentially qualitative and Tes Tape semi-quantitative. Both were more sensitive than Benedict's test or Clinitest, and they were specific for glucose.

What to test, blood or urine?

In an ideal world, urine glucose would provide an accurate estimate of blood glucose at the time of sampling. However, it has repeatedly been shown that it does not. As early as 1919 two researchers found no constant blood glucose level for the appearance of glucose in the urine,[29] and in 1929 Robin Lawrence concluded that there was no such thing as a normal renal threshold. The renal threshold is the blood glucose level above which the kidneys are unable to retain glucose and excrete it in the urine. Unfortunately, the renal threshold can vary between individuals and in different situations (e. g. it can change during pregnancy). Urine testing might therefore be a seriously misleading way of assessing diabetic control.[30] Nor is the variability of the renal threshold for glucose the only reason for blood and urine sugar to be poorly correlated. Another is the time lag between urine formation and the excretion of urine from the body. The shortcomings of urine tests were frequently ignored. The single blood sugar measurement at a clinic visit was an established routine in the 1920s and would remain such for a while to come. In hindsight, its usefulness appears doubtful, since many patients learned that they could 'launder' the result simply by omitting the meal before their clinic visit.

Self blood glucose monitoring

At a meeting in 1956 Priscilla White (1900–1989), a physician at Boston's Joslin Clinic and an acknowledged expert on diabetes in pregnancy and childhood, asked, 'Do you think patients should learn to do their own blood sugars?' This was greeted with laughter from the audience, who clearly regarded it as an outrageous idea.[31] It would be another six years before the first studies on measuring blood sugar under real-life conditions were begun at Guy's Hospital, London.[32] Patients pricked their fingers and put a drop of blood on blotting paper, which was then posted to the hospital. The 'blot method' consistently gave results 30 mg/dL higher than the direct method, but it was suggested it might be used to measure 'blood sugar levels in patients with brittle diabetes at various times of the day and might be of value in improving control of the diabetes'.

The chemist **Hans Wielinger** (b. 1939) was one of the inventors of 'wipe technology'.

It was in this building that a laboratory mishap led to the development of film technology for reagent test strips.

Blood glucose test strips

Dextrostix, a rapid method of measuring blood sugar, was introduced by the Ames company in 1964, and, although it tended to overestimate at low concentrations and underestimate at high ones, there was good agreement between observers in most studies.[33] In 1970 the stick was made machine readable by the Ames Reflectance Meter, a cumbersome device which needed a long warm-up period and careful standardisation. In 1968 Boehringer Mannheim launched its Haemo Glucotest strips, the first semi-quantitative glucose strips employing 'wipe technology'. Hans Wielinger (b. 1939), one of the inventors of the technology, once offered the following account of how it was discovered:

> The year was 1966, the place a Boehringer Mannheim laboratory in Mannheim. A laboratory technician was purifying a chemical developed for use as a colour indicator in a blood glucose test. The purification process involved dissolving the chemical in boiling solvent. On cooling, pure crystals formed in the solution. Luckily, there was a little mishap. Some of the hot solution splattered onto a wall coated with a latex paint and left a light spot that remained visible even after cleaning. A few days later two chemists, both dyed-in-the-wool scientists, had an idea. They sprayed a solution of the enzymes used in glucose testing onto the spot on the wall, wiped it off and let it dry, leaving only the enzymes which had been absorbed by the paint. When the spot was sprayed again, this time with a glucose solution, it turned violet. The enzymes and the glucose had reacted with the light chemical spot to form a violet colour.
>
> This observation showed us that polymer films could be used for test reactions which had so far always been performed using a paper substrate. We embedded all the chemicals needed to test for glucose in a polymer dispersion and then made the material into films. The idea behind the film technology still used to make reagent test strips was born.

The possibility that test strips and reflectance meters might be used by patients themselves was hardly considered until 1975, when Clara Lowy at St Thomas's Hospital, London, suggested that a 26-week pregnant patient with a low renal threshold and repeated episodes of hypoglycemia should be admitted for regular monitoring of her blood sugars. The woman insisted that, if given the equipment, she would be able to do the tests at home, and did so three times a day for the rest of her pregnancy.[34] Most of Lowy's colleagues considered this irresponsible and dangerous. Three years later four groups reported their experience in teaching insulin-treated patients to measure their own blood glucose concentrations with test strips and a reflectance meter.[35, 36] Evidently, patients had little difficulty obtaining blood samples by pricking their fingers, and their results were sufficiently accurate for ordinary clinical purposes. Moreover, home testing led to increased motivation and better control in many patients.

The introduction of a new generation of visually read test strips by Boehringer Mannheim in 1979 was an important advance in that it provided a

WE
MIGHT
HAVE
STOPPED
HERE...

Advertisement for the Clinitest kit, which was launched in 1944.

convenient and reliable test which could be done anywhere without the need for what at the time were expensive and bulky meters. In 1985 there were ten meters on the market, all of which were relatively small and battery operated. By the early 1990s machines had been miniaturised even more, reaction times were down to 20 seconds or less, and most meters had memories and were self calibrating. The latest meters use so little blood that samples can be taken virtually anywhere on the skin surface, not just from very vascular areas such as the finger pulp and ear lobe.

'The spy in the cab'

For nearly 60 years after the discovery of insulin, the great unsolved question was, 'Will good blood glucose control reduce the risk of diabetic complica-tions?' Retrospective studies suggested that it proba-bly did, but the main problem was the difficulty of assessing control in the long term. Often, all physi-cians had to go on was three or four random blood sugars taken in the clinic each year (usually at the same time of day) and, possibly, the results of home urine tests. Some way of objectively assessing glucose control was needed. As so often happens, this came from an unlikely source, proving once again the role of chance in scientific discovery. In 1968 Samuel Rahbar (b. 1929), who was working on hemoglobin-opathies (disorders caused by abnormalities in the oxygen-carrying pigment hemoglobin) in Teheran, published a short report drawing attention to a 'new' hemoglobin in the blood of two patients with diabetes.[37] Initially it was thought this might be a genetic marker of type 1 diabetes. During a one-year sabbatical at the Albert Einstein College of Medicine in New York, Rahbar learned, however, that this glycosylated ('sugared') hemoglobin variant had been identified ten years earlier in the human fetus as HbA_{1c}.[38] A study published in 1971 had reported a two-fold increase in HbA_{1c} as a percentage of total hemoglobin in diabetic patients. And what was even more interesting, this increase did not appear to be related to duration of diabetes, the age of the patient, therapy or complications.[39] In 1975 studies of iden-tical twins discordant for diabetes found that levels of HbA_{1c} were high in the diabetic twin and similar to that for controls in the non-diabetic twin. The authors concluded that the elevation of HbA_{1c} was 'dependent on the disordered carbohydrate metab-olism, and is not an independent component or genetic marker of the diabetic syndrome.' Some of the diabetic patients studied were on diet alone and had normal levels of HbA_{1c}, and it was suggested that this might reflect better control of carbohydrate metabolism.[40] This was subsequently confirmed by a study which found that, when patients on insulin were brought under control in hospital, their HbA_{1c} concentrations returned to normal in four to six weeks.[41] HbA_{1c} was thus the long-sought-after marker of glycemic control rather than a genetic marker for diabetes, and this discovery paved the way for the Diabetes Control and Complications Trial, which in 1993 reported that keeping blood sugars as nearly normal as possible prevented and/or delayed the progression of microvascular complica-tions.[42] It also gave clinicians a way of checking the glycemic control of their patients in the same way that the tachometer allowed truck operators to find out what their drivers were doing – hence the 'spy in the cab' analogy.

Two distinct diseases

In his 1939 Goulstonian Lectures Harold Himsworth (1905–1993) explained that diabetes mellitus was 'a disease in which the essential lesion is a diminished ability of the tissues to utilise glucose ... it is referable either to deficiency of insulin or insensitivity to insulin, although it is possible that both factors may operate simultaneously'. This was an extremely astute observation for the times. Three years earlier Himsworth had suggested that there was an insulin-dependent and a non-insulin-dependent type of diabetes mellitus, and that the former was presumably caused by insulin deficiency. Today we know that the insulin-dependent form – type 1 – is an autoimmune disease in which the insulin-producing cells in the pancreas are destroyed. Eventually, a deficiency of the hormone develops, and the patient has to be put on insulin replacement therapy to maintain an adequate cellular uptake of the glucose cells require as fuel.

Type 2 diabetes is primarily a metabolic disorder in which insulin progressively loses its ability to regulate glucose metabolism. As in type 1, too little glucose enters target cells, and elevated blood glucose leads to debilitating complications. It should be noted that present-day physicians no longer distinguish between just two types of diabetes. And the various subtypes that are still collectively referred to as 'type 2 diabetes' will probably one day be recognised as distinct clinical entities based on the metabolic pathway affected.[43]

Molecular mimicry with disastrous consequences

In 1969 Robert Gamble and Keith Taylor of London rediscovered the seasonal incidence of type 1 diabetes (originally noted in 1926) and suggested a link with coxsackievirus infection.[44] Outbreaks of coxsackie infection are most common in the summer and autumn and cause a variety of illnesses, including flu-like syndromes and respiratory disease. The viral protein P2C in coxsackievirus B4 contains regions similar to regions of glutamic acid decarboxylase (GAD), an enzyme present in the islets of Langerhans in the pancreas.[45,46] Molecular mimicry between GAD and the P2C protein of coxsackie B4 has disastrous consequences. The self-tolerance that normally prevents immune cells such as T lymphocytes from attacking the body's own tissues is disrupted. As a result, insulin-producing beta cells in the pancreatic islets of Langerhans are destroyed. Autoantibodies to GAD can be detected even years before the onset of type 1 dia-

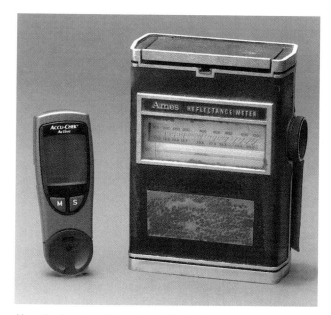

How they've shrunk! A today's blood glucose meter next to one from the early 1970s (right).

betes and have been found in 70%–80% of type 1 diabetics.[47]

How antibodies help diagnose diabetes

Islet cell antibodies (ICAs) were first discovered in diabetics in 1974. They were measured semi-quantitatively by means of indirect immunofluorescence staining under the microscope. The method was difficult and was hardly ever used clinically since it was usually easier to identify type 1 diabetes by its presenting features. Where the test was useful was in predicting who might develop diabetes in the future.

Apart from clinical examination, tests for auto-antibodies directed against components of the pancreas are now the primary tool for establishing which form of diabetes a patient has: type 1, type 2, latent autoimmune diabetes in the adult (LADA) or gestational diabetes. Up to 10% of patients who develop diabetes in middle age, especially those who are not particularly overweight, have anti-GAD antibodies. Within a few months or years these patients fail on oral antidiabetics and, if not treated with insulin, develop progressive ill health.[48] This type of diabetes is now called latent autoimmune diabetes in the adult. Most cases of diabetes that develop during pregnancy resolve after delivery. It has been known for a long time, however, that some women who develop gestational diabetes have latent type 1 diabetes. They can now be identified, and an accurate prognosis made, by testing all women with gestational diabetes for anti-GAD antibodies. In the early 1990s Boehringer Mannheim became one of the first companies to develop antibody tests based on the **e**nzyme-**l**inked **i**mmuno**s**orbent **a**ssay (ELISA) method. The tests were designed to be performed manually or on an automated system in ordinary clinical laboratory settings.

Genetic markers

Research into the immunogenetic basis of type 1 diabetes began with the observations of Jørn Nerup (b. 1938) in Copenhagen and Andrew Cudworth (1939–1982) in Liverpool, showing that type 1 diabetes was associated with certain **h**uman **l**eukocyte **a**ntigens (HLAs).[49] HLAs are genetic markers present on the surface of a variety of cells, particularly leukocytes and other immune cells. In families with several affected members, 95% of diabetic siblings were found to have the same HLA type and, among Caucasians, 90%–95% of patients with type 1 diabetes were positive for either HLA type DR3 or DR4. The role of HLA should not be overemphasised, however, since DR3 and DR4 are found in 60% of the normal population. While these markers indicate a genetic predisposition to autoimmune diabetes, not all carriers develop the disease. For example, only one-third of identical twins are concordant for it.[50] What other factors may play a role? Toxins and early exposure to cow's milk have been considered as possible environmental triggers of type 1 diabetes.[51] One of the aims of diabetes research today is to find markers that can be targeted to detect and halt the autoimmune process that destroys insulin-producing beta cells in the pancreas at an early stage. Considerable effort is also being directed at developing continuous blood glucose monitoring systems that minimise the discomfort of blood testing and are designed for use under real-life conditions. There is no question that close monitoring of blood glucose levels is important for good glycemic control.

Continuous monitoring

If you have diabetes, monitoring your blood glucose is essential, but it is also a chore. Most patients draw the line at around four tests a day. It is especially inconvenient to have to do tests at night to check for hypoglycemia. Ever since the introduction of self glucose monitoring, the dream of diabetic patients (and physicians) has been a non-invasive continuous glucose monitor which would warn of high or low blood sugars without any effort on the part of the patient. Continuous blood glucose monitoring would also provide a clearer indication than HbA$_{1c}$ of how high a patient's blood glucose rises. '[F]or

everyone involved in diabetes care, it would be major step forward, comparable to the introduction of the first spot tests for patient use.'[52]

Measurement in tissue rather than blood

Coagulation makes blood an unsuitable material in which to measure glucose levels continuously over a prolonged period.[53] Alternative techniques are therefore used, such as sensors in the tissue under the skin (subcutaneous tissue) or optical measurement through the skin. The result is the tissue glucose concentration or, more specifically, the subcutaneous interstitial glucose concentration, as the sample in which the measurement is made consists of interstitial fluid, i. e. the fluid bathing the cells and tissues under the skin. In normal weight people with normal blood glucose fluctuations, tissue and blood glucose concentrations are closely matched. However, in the severely obese, who have decreased capillary density in their subcutaneous fat, equalisation between tissue and blood glucose concentrations may be delayed. Fairly marked differences between tissue and blood glucose concentrations can also occur with abnormally large changes in blood glucose, e. g. in patients receiving glucose infusions or intravenous insulin injections. In any event, glucose levels determined in tissue fluid in as stable a glycemic state as possible must correlate with those measured simultaneously in capillary blood if the results are to be expressed as blood glucose levels.

Optical glucose measurement

The ideal solution would be non-invasive optical glucose measurement through the skin. However, only light from the near-infrared region of 600–1300 nm can penetrate intact skin to the deeper skin layers perfused by blood.[54] Below and above this wavelength region, light is absorbed by water, tissue components, skin pigments and blood.

At present infrared spectroscopy can only measure glucose concentrations with sufficient accuracy in solutions, using laboratory spectrometers. Accurate glucose measurement through human skin is thwarted by the fact that the specific near-infrared absorption spectrum of glucose does not differ sufficiently from that of other tissue components. The concentrations of glucose in tissue are also very low compared with those of other light-absorbing substances, especially water. The relatively small changes in glucose concentration that would need to be detected could only be calculated using complicated mathematical techniques.[55] Intensive technological research allied to state-of-the-art data analysis has yet to succeed in filtering out the glucose component of the input signal and converting it to an accurate glucose concentration.

Another optical non-invasive approach, and one which has raised higher hopes than absorption measurement, is to measure the change in the glucose scatter coefficient in the skin. Light scatter depends on the ratio between the refractive indices of the tissue particles and the surrounding medium. Glucose has a direct effect on this ratio. The intensity of diffusely reflected light is measured at distances of, for example, 0.8–10 mm from the point at which the light is directed into the skin. A light scatter intensity profile is obtained from which the scatter coefficient can be calculated. As yet, however, no measurement device incorporating this technique is available for patient use. A Roche research team is working to refine and test the technique.

Measuring glucose with biosensors

In 2001 Cygnus, Inc. (USA), introduced a glucose monitor called GlucoWatch Biographer, which is worn like a wrist watch and measures tissue glucose more or less non-invasively with enzyme electrodes on the underside of the device. The meter works by applying an electrical microcurrent to the skin for several minutes. This draws sodium and other ions through the intact skin, and water follows the sodium and pulls uncharged particles like glucose with it. Sodium ions and glucose move towards the cathode and are absorbed by a hydrogel pad. This process is known as reverse iontophoresis, in contrast to normal iontophoresis, a technique that uses an electrical current to administer medicines transdermally. At the end of the iontophoresis period, a biosensor is activated and the glucose in the hydrogel pad is converted by the enzyme glucose oxidase (GOD) to gluconic acid and hydrogen peroxide. The current generated by the hydrogen peroxide is measured.[56,57] While it has the advantage of being non-invasive, the device also has various drawbacks, including a long warm-up time, frequent skipped readings, local skin irritation and the risk that it may shut off prematurely if the wearer is perspiring heavily. According to the manufacturer, the device should be used in addition to, not as a substitute for, a blood glucose meter.

'Prickly' sensors

The Continuous Glucose Monitoring System (CGMS) from Medtronic MiniMed (USA) uses a needle-type sensor to monitor blood glucose. The system was approved by the US Food and Drug

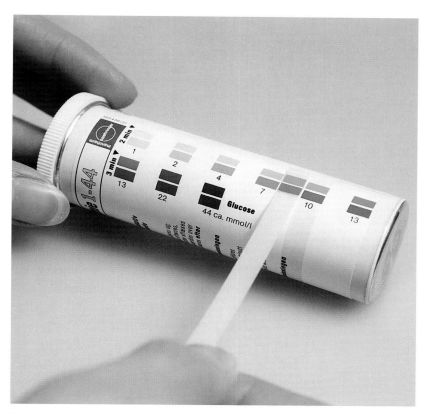

Developed in 1969 and improved in 1979, Haemo-Glukotest is still the gold standard for precise visual blood glucose testing.

Administration (FDA) in 1999. The CGMS measures glucose in subcutaneous tissue, normally in the abdomen, by means of an electrochemical sensor the size of a needle, which remains *in situ* for up to 72 hours.[58] The readings are stored by the system and at the end of each monitoring period are downloaded to a computer for analysis by the physician. Although many patients have expressed a desire to be able to view their own readings, the present system does not include a display.

While needle-type sensors are known for their long-term stability in aqueous solutions, using them to take measurements in the body has long been known to have a major drawback. In living tissue the sensitivity of a sensor steadily decreases, a phenomenon known in technical parlance as 'sensor fouling'. Whether sensor fouling is a result of the sensor being encapsulated by fibrous tissue or is caused by a physical reaction to the enzyme GOD or to the hydrogen peroxide that forms when glucose is broken down is unclear. Another subject of discussion at present is whether the relatively frequent readings indicating a nocturnal hypoglycemic episode might not be system artifacts. According to the manufacturer, sensors of this type should be calibrated at least three to four times per day against capillary blood glucose readings from a conventional glucometer. Interestingly,

Ernst Friedrich Pfeiffer *(1922–1997) developed Biostator, the first artificial pancreas, in collaboration with the Ames division of Miles Laboratories (USA). He was one of the first to call attention to the fact that diabetics frequently experience episodes of nocturnal hypoglycemia (sometimes lasting for hours) without noticing them. The need to monitor glucose continuously at least some of the time in certain patient populations led to the 'Ulm glucose watch' project, undertaken by the Institute for Diabetes Technology at the University of Ulm in Germany.*

studies have shown that needle-type sensors implanted in tissue regain their original sensitivity if they are removed and placed in an aqueous solution. As early as 1990 a working group led by Ernst Friedrich Pfeiffer (1922–1997) concluded from biocompatibility studies of various sensor materials that immune reactions might make it impossible for any sensor to provide stable measurement signals over a period of several days.

> In all species [rats and sheep], foreign-body reactions of the acute type, characterized by hyperemia, exudation and granulocyte accumulation were seen in the first days of implantation, regardless of the material implanted...[59]

Polyvinyl and some polyurethanes were the only sensor coatings found to produce negligible foreign-body reactions in rats. Unfortunately, sensors that worked well for up to four days in rats never worked much beyond 24 hours in man. These findings have been more or less confirmed by research groups from around the world.

Microdialysis

Because of these difficulties, and because of the signal stability and analytical precision offered by microdialysis, Roche's development unit decided at the time to pursue microdialysis, a technology developed by Urban Ungerstedt for sampling interstitial fluid.[60] The aim was to develop a continuous glucose monitoring system combining a microdialysis device with a glucose meter worn outside the body. Microdialysis had been in use since the early 1980s for intermittent sampling of extracellular fluids, for example from the brain.[61] Pfeiffer, the father of the 'Ulm glucose watch' presented a prototype for the project to a group of employees of what was then Boehringer Mannheim. It used an Ungerstedt microdialysis catheter, a delicate, flexible white tube with a second tube inside for introducing

physiological solutions into the body. Together with Ungerstedt and Adelbert Schoonen of Groningen University in the Netherlands, work began to develop a blood glucose monitoring system.

The ultra-fine double-lumen (tube-in-a-tube) microdialysis catheter is implanted in the subcutaneous adipose tissue of the abdomen, and Ringer's solution is pumped through it continuously and circulates back to a sensor. The outer wall of the catheter is a microdialysis membrane permeable to dissolved glucose. Once the local inflammatory reaction to placement of the catheter has resolved (no more than 24 hours after insertion), a data manager unit prompts the user to calibrate the system. A test strip meter built into the data manager measures the glucose in a capillary blood sample and automatically pairs the result with the corresponding sensor reading after a time lag of about 30 minutes, which is the time it takes for glucose in the dialysate to reach the sensor and be measured.[62] Glucose levels are measured and recorded every five minutes for four days, and the system only needs to be calibrated once daily. That means 288 readings per day instead of the usual five to eight measurements with conventional blood glucose testing. This device has a longer continuous monitoring capability than any system now available. A number of trials are currently under way to investigate the system's safety and performance. Another question that is being studied in greater detail is how glucose levels in various body fluid compartments, such as the blood and interstitial fluid, are related. Trials with the system have also shown that it can help shed greater light on the factors that affect metabolism in individual diabetics. Among the questions that continuous glucose readings can help resolve are: What is the right interval between meals and insulin doses? What insulin doses are best in different situations? How should doses of basal and bolus insulin be distributed over the day? When is it most important for optimal therapy to perform conventional blood glucose tests? How long do doses of insulin act? Patients will get to know their metabolic profiles as never before. Moreover, continuous glucose monitoring can help achieve faster, more effective glycemic control with medication, so that metabolic status is kept as close to normal as possible. Further progress should also be possible in managing diabetes during pregnancy and in improving the prognosis in heart attack and stroke patients. The comfort and convenience of using such systems is also likely to increase as further advances are made in miniaturising components, shortening the time be-

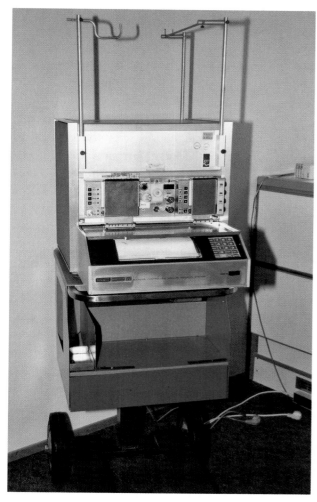

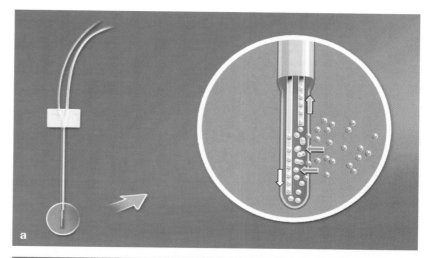

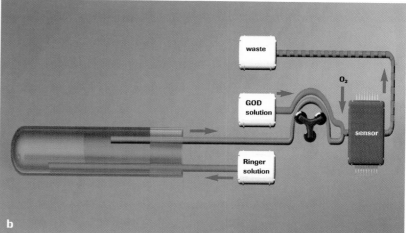

The Biostator artificial pancreas, launched in 1984, was a system designed to automatically control insulin and glucose infusions in hospital settings, the aim being to keep blood glucose levels close to a preselected set-point even during physical exercise (e. g. during a bicycle stress test) and after meals and doses of medication. The system was used during surgery, in intensive care units and especially in research studies. Because intravenous access had to be maintained during use, and because of the relatively large amounts of blood sampled (20–70 mL daily), patients and subjects could not be kept on the Biostator for more than three days at a time. Based on blood glucose readings taken by the system, a control unit calculated the amounts of insulin, glucose and (possibly) electrolytes needed to reach and maintain a specific glucose concentration, and these amounts were then infused by a pump. Biostator was used in studying a variety of metabolic processes and contributed to a number of important findings in diabetology. It was instrumental, for example, in recognising the roles played by numerous hormones and other substances in glucose metabolism and in the discovery that insulin sensitivity follows a circadian rhythm in diabetics and in healthy subjects.

How microdialysis works. A double-lumen catheter roughly 4 cm long which is permeable to water and low molecular weight solutes like glucose (red) but not to proteins is inserted into tissue. A dialysis solution containing sodium ions (white) is continuously pumped through the catheter (**a**). Using a single peristaltic pump to push dialysis solution into interstitial tissue and pull dialysate to the sensor ensures that no more fluid flows into the sensor than is pumped into the catheter. Glucose diffuses across a concentration gradient into the catheter, so that the glucose concentration in the dialysate equilibrates with the interstitial concentration without appreciably depleting it. The enzyme **g**lucose **o**xi**d**ase (GOD) is added to the dialysate outside the body just before the dialysate reaches an electrochemical sensor. GOD reacts with glucose and oxygen (O_2) to form hydrogen peroxide, which is measured by an electrode. The time lag between the uptake of glucose in the dialysate and the sensor response is about 30 minutes (**b**).

tween sampling and measurement and simplifying catheter use.

On the horizon: the automatic pancreas

Management of type 1 diabetes still requires lifelong insulin therapy. A device which administered insulin over long periods, automatically and as needed, without patients having to decide how much to inject in a particular situation, would represent a quantum improvement in the quality of diabetic life.

If we look back two decades, we might think this dream should have long since become a reality.[63]

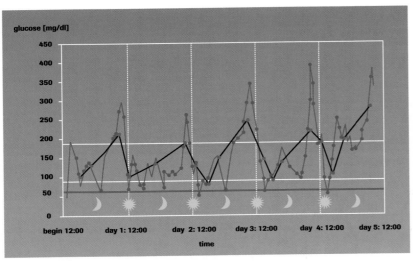

Comparison of findings obtained by intermittent blood glucose measurements (black line) and by continuous microdialysis sampling of interstitial fluid glucose (blue line) in a 47-year-old type 1 diabetic. The two plots clearly illustrate the risk of missing potentially dangerous periods of hyperglycemia and hypoglycemia if blood sugar is monitored intermittently.

Back in 1983 the feasibility of administering insulin with a wearable artificial pancreas configured as a closed loop system was tested in man. The system consisted of an insulin pump operating in a closed feedback loop with components for measuring glucose and calculating insulin doses. Needle-type sensors were inserted into the subcutaneous tissue of the forearm or abdomen in healthy volunteers and diabetics, and the values compared using a hospital artificial pancreas. The subcutaneous levels closely matched those in blood. No time lag was observed between the levels. Perfect regulation of blood glucose fluctuations was achieved by intravenous or subcutaneous insulin administration based on the sensor measurements.

The authors concluded from their results that long-term glucose regulation with the system appeared feasible. Yet despite further improvements and successful studies by many groups in many patients, no such device yet exists for ambulatory patient use, possibly because of long-term sensor instability and insufficiently sophisticated algorithms.

An artificial pancreas will only be reliable once working harmony is achieved between its components: a temperature-independent, continuous and accurate sensor; a central processing unit programmed with insulin dosing algorithms incorporating the measured blood glucose, the change in glucose per unit time, the activity profile of the insulin used, the anticipated food (glucose) intake and other key determinants; and an insulin pump for minutely dosed delivery. Such a device could optimise metabolic control and eliminate the risk of hypoglycemia to a degree indistinguishable from that in healthy subjects. Numerous research groups are committed to ensuring that such an artificial pancreas becomes a reality in the not too distant future.

Burkhard Ziebolz

Arsenic – detection of a folk poison

The beginnings of toxicology

Would everything have turned out differently had George Bodle been easier to live with? Would he have died the tranquil death of a friendly fellow who had lived a long and fulfilled life? It's impossible to say for sure, but there are reasons to think so. James Marsh (1794–1846) might then never have felt compelled to devise a fail-safe test for arsenic, and the history of toxicology would have followed a different course.

George Bodle, a well-to-do farmer from Plumstead near Woolwich in England, died in 1832. The extremely unusual circumstances aroused the suspicion of the authorities. Bodle's demise was attended by some unpleasant symptoms – abdominal cramps, diarrhea, vomiting and weakness of the limbs. The first symptoms had appeared shortly after he had drunk his morning coffee. Bodle's wife, daughter and granddaughter and a maidservant had likewise been seized with violent stomach pains after drinking the coffee. But they recovered. The constellation of coincidence alerted the local forces of law and order: Justice of the Peace Slace and Police Constable Morris became suspicious, particularly as they were acquainted with the situation at the Bodle farm. They knew the 80-year-old Bodle had been a domestic tyrant who treated his children like servants. His son John – 'Middle John' to the locals – was known to be impatient for the old man's death so that he could start life anew with the inheritance. Nor was 'Young John' – Middle John's son and the dead man's grandson – likely to have been unduly upset over the sudden death, as he whiled away his time as a perpetually cadging layabout. However, this in itself was unremarkable, until evidence of foul play emerged from the statement given by Sophia Taylor, the maidservant at the Bodle farm. 'On the morning the old man fell ill, Young John came into

The English chemist **James Marsh** *(1794–1846) developed the arsenic test that still bears his name. For many years he worked at the Royal Arsenal in Woolwich, England, and it was there that he met Michael Faraday (1791–1867). Faraday, who is remembered for his important experimental work in electrochemistry, magnetism and electricity, was Professor of Chemistry at the Royal Military Academy in Woolwich from 1830 to 1851.*

the farmhouse,' Mrs Taylor reported. 'He offered to fill the kettle for the coffee with water from the well – Your Worship, he'd never done that before!' Justice Slace's suspicions grew steadily, fed by new facts. First there was a conversation in the Bodle household some time before the death, when Young John had longingly remarked to his mother: 'I wish the old man dead, then we'd have a few thousand pounds a year.' The second clue was even less ambiguous and was provided by Mr Evans, the local apothecary. Young John had bought arsenic[1] from him twice the previous week, allegedly to be used against the rats on the farm.

Slace found sufficient cause to start an investigation. He immediately had the coffee pot impounded and ordered an autopsy on the body – an unusual, indeed remarkable action for a justice of the peace at that time. This is where James Marsh enters the picture, for it was to him that Slace entrusted the coffee and old Bodle's entrails for further investigation.

Marsh, aged 42 at the time, was a chemist at the Royal Arsenal in Woolwich near London, a capacity in which he was called upon to perform all sorts of duties in His Majesty's service. At the time of the Bodle case he was busy developing a recoil brake for naval cannons, but as he was the only chemist of standing whom Justice Slace could reach in a hurry, the ships' guns had to wait. Methodical scientist that he was, Marsh acquainted himself with the standard contemporary methods of arsenic detection, all of which had been developed in Germany; and he then applied them successfully. In the coffee and stomach contents he found a yellow precipitate that was soluble in ammonia – a sure sign of arsenic. In the subsequent committal proceedings this evidence was enough to convince the jury that they were dealing with a case of poisoning. Young John was duly charged with murder.

The trial in Maidstone in December 1832 proved a fiasco. To understand what happened, we need to realise that the British public at the time harboured certain fundamental, irrational aversions to the police, their inquiries and 'scientific evidence'. When these pet hates were combined, as in the Bodle case, their effect was magnified, with curious consequences for the outcome of the trial.

Yellow precipitate equals witchcraft

'Yellow precipitate', 'hydrogen sulphide', 'ammonia' – what was clear evidence to Marsh was mumbo-jumbo to the jury. Are you telling us that old man Bodle was poisoned with arsenic? Then be so kind as to show us the poison, or else you won't get your conviction. So it was that the accused was acquitted – to his own undoubted surprise and delight, and to the spectators' inexpert jubilation. For the ne'er-do-well Bodle, however, this proved merely a reprieve. He was arrested again ten years later – this time for fraud and blackmail – and sentenced to seven years in prison and transportation to the colonies, an opportunity which he took to set the record straight and confess to his grandfather's murder.

Unfortunately, or perhaps fortunately, James Marsh had no way of foreseeing this odd twist of fate at the time of the murder trial. He saw only the situation as it was, and his failure to ensure that justice had prevailed. Deeply wounded in his professional honour as a chemist, in December 1833 he set about finding a fail-safe method of making arsenic visible. The test would have to be so clear and so irrefutable that it would be understood by even the least educated juror. This was far from an easy task.

Arsenic – the inheritance powder

In order to appreciate the importance of having a reliable test for arsenic – both to society and as a contribution to toxicology – we need to step back in time. References to arsenic sulphide (orpiment) can be found in sources as venerable as the Greek polymath Aristotle (384–322 BC) and the Greek physician and pharmacist Dioscorides (1st century AD). At the time it was considered a kind of sulphur, and was used as a depilatory, as a yellow pigment in painting, and for imparting a golden colour to silver. Alchemists regarded arsenic as a 'bastard metal' (reguline arsenic). Because of its ability to whiten copper they believed they could use it to make a silver-like metal. In reality they were producing an arsenic-copper alloy.

Around 1250 Albertus Magnus (c. 1200–1280) became the first to describe a method of producing arsenic. He heated the mineral orpiment together with soap to obtain metallic arsenic by reduction. The term 'arsenic' is commonly applied to both the metallic element – also known as grey arsenic – and its oxides or sulphides. Jöns Jacob Berzelius (1779–1848) proposed the chemical symbol 'As' in 1814.

The origin of the name 'arsenic' is unclear. It may derive from the Greek term *arsenikon,* first used by Dioscorides for the arsenic mineral orpiment (As_2S_3). The name probably refers to arsenic's volatility and ability to precipitate in metallic form, or to the therapeutic effect of the arsenicals already known to Dioscorides. Another possible source of the name is the Greek *arsenikos,* for 'male'.[2]

Marsh's test

In the Middle Ages it almost seemed as if large sections of the population had come to terms with arsenic poisoning as one of life's natural risks. Ninety to ninety-five percent of poisonings at the time were committed with arsenic. A reliable detection test was thus sorely needed.

Tentative steps had, of course, already been taken in this direction prior to Marsh. Some 30 years before Marsh set to work, it was still assumed that various poisons gave off a characteristic odour when vaporised. Hence proposals that suspect substances be placed on glowing coals and identified by smell. Postmortem examination of the viscera was also

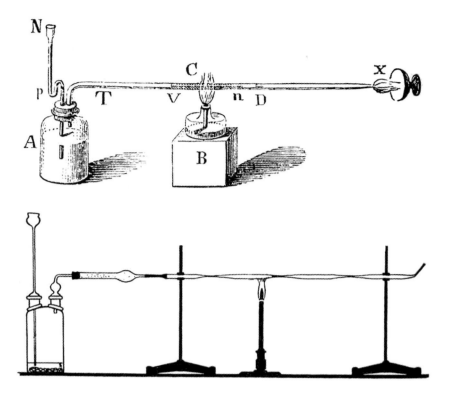

Marsh's apparatus for detecting arsenic.

tried as means of tackling the problem systematically. Except in a few cases (e. g. if there was evidence of tissue destruction by acid), this approach proved useless in practice. Other techniques, when viewed with modern eyes, stand out more for their eccentricity than for their relationship to reality. Georg Adolph Welper, City Medical Officer of Berlin, believed that the bodies of people who had died of arsenic poisoning did not decompose. An estimate of the number of arsenic murders based on this insight would undoubtedly have been much too low. Estimates based on other beliefs, by contrast, would have been much too high: Johann Daniel Metzger (1739–1805), for example, Professor of Medicine and Medical Jurisprudence in Königsberg in the second half of the 18th century, regarded postmortem lividity of the skin – a natural phenomenon – as a typical feature of arsenic poisoning.

For centuries science groped about in the dark. Patients were considered poisoned if they smelled bad or their bodies showed blue-black discoloration. Superstition flourished, as in the theory that the hearts of poison victims could not be destroyed by fire. Evidence based on this belief no doubt often led to unexpected acquittals.

Some approaches, however, were more scientific. As early as 1787, the same Metzger who had been so

The 'art' of poisoning

Other poisons have of course been known since antiquity – henbane, for example, or the hemlock taken by Socrates (470/469-399 BC). However, after white arsenic powder (As_2O_3) was first produced from metallic arsenic in Arabia in the 8th century,[3] it became a much-used instrument of death, gaining great popularity over the centuries as a way of getting rid of one's more troublesome contemporaries. It was odourless, tasteless and easy to administer in food; the symptoms of poisoning were also hard to differentiate from those of cholera, a very common disease at that time. Most important of all, however, was that without an eye witness or a confession by the culprit, there was no way of proving that arsenic was the cause of death.

Just how many arsenic murders have been committed over the centuries will never be known, given the absence or inadequacy of criminal investigations through much of history, but the global toll must be enormous. Such was the popularity of the lethal powder that it was commonly referred to as 'inheritance powder' *(poudre de succession)*.

Cases of murder with arsenic are attested as far back as ancient Rome. Arsenic was the poison with which Agrippina (AD 15-59) had Claudius (10 BC–AD 54) killed to make Nero (AD 37-68) ruler of Rome. Nero, in turn, used the same tried and tested means to eliminate Claudius' son, and any future claim he might have to assume the Roman throne.

The art of poisoning and the use of arsenic reached an undisputed zenith in the years preceding the Renaissance and during the Renaissance itself. The poisoner became an integral part of public life, less as an individual than as a political tool; indeed he served almost as an agent of the state. The city archives of Florence, for example, contain names of victims, prices, contracts and payment records. Most of the entries in these death ledgers end with the note *factum*, indicating that the transaction had been brought to a successful conclusion by the demise of the intended victim.

Rather less organised, but no less pragmatic, was the art of poisoning as practised by the common people. A shadowy figure from this period was Teofania di Adamo (?–1633), also known simply as 'Tofana'. In the 17th century she not only used her Aqua Tofana (a solution of white arsenic)[4] for her own murders, but also conducted a brisk trade in the deadly product. A similarly sinister character was one Marie Madeleine Marquise de Brinvilliers (1630–1676). She too was both a poisoner in her own right and a peddler of *eau admirable*.

Well-attested too are the many murders at the French royal and princely courts of the Middle Ages, and under the princes and popes of the Italian Renaissance. Poisoners such as Pope Alexander VI Borgia (c. 1431–1503) and his son Cesare Borgia (1475–1507) have entered the annals of criminology. Although the Borgias deservedly occupy an exalted place in the poisoner pile, their industry in this regard has often been exaggerated. We now know that a considerable proportion of the victims credited to them died quite naturally of malaria and other infectious diseases.

far off the mark with postmortem lividity heated substances suspected of containing arsenic on charcoal and held a copper plate over the resultant fumes. If arsenic was present, the plate was coated with a whitish layer of arsenic trioxide. When he added white arsenic and charcoal to a glass tube and heated the charcoal in the tube to glowing, the arsenic trioxide fumes reverted to arsenic on contact with the charcoal to form so-called 'mirrors'. In other words, the arsenic precipitated as black-brown metallic spots on the cooler parts of the tube.

In 1806 Valentin Rose, Assessor at the College of Physicians in Berlin, attempted the detection of arsenic in human organs. He was particularly interested in determining whether the poison could still be detected in the viscera and stomach walls after it had left the stomach or been absorbed into the body. Rose's approach was to cut up the stomach of a poison victim and boil the pieces in distilled water. He obtained a mash, which he filtered several times and then treated with saltpetre to destroy the 'organic material of the stomach' and leave, in principle, only the poison of interest. Using carbonate of potash and lime water (in modern terms: potassium carbonate and aqueous calcium hydroxide), Rose obtained a precipitate, which he dried. Like Metzger, he added the precipitate with charcoal to a glass tube and, on slow heating, observed the formation of a metallic arsenic mirror.

This was the state of the art in arsenic testing when Marsh set to work. What does a chemist do when embarking on a new project, then as now? He reads up on the methods and work of others. Marsh's Woolwich Arsenal library stocked several very promising sources. The breakthrough occurred when Marsh came across some papers published around 1775 by Carl Wilhelm Scheele (1742–1786) on the generation of arsine (arsenic trihydride) gas. Scheele, an apothecary in the Swedish town of Köping, discovered the following: if an arsenical liquid was mixed with a little sulphuric or hydro-chloric acid and zinc was added, the zinc reacted with the acid to produce hydrogen. The hydrogen combined with the arsenic to form arsine, a highly toxic gas with the smell of garlic. What is more, this worked with all arsenic compounds. If the gas was then passed through a tube and heated, it decomposed again to hydrogen and arsenic.

Marsh built on Scheele's ideas and took them to what proved a clear and simple conclusion, in the tradition of great discoveries. It had to be possible, he reasoned, to trap and collect the metallic arsenic. He had a U-shaped glass tube constructed for this purpose. One end of the tube was open, while the other was drawn out into a fine nozzle. He then suspended a piece of zinc into the nozzle part of the tube. The apparatus was now ready. Marsh filled the open end of the U-tube with the test solution, which he had previously acidified. When the liquid reached the zinc, it generated arsine – even if it contained only the merest trace of arsenic. The arsine escaped through the nozzle, was ignited, and then deposited in blackish spots as metallic arsenic on a cold porcelain dish held against the flame. The reaction continued until all the arsenic from the sample gradually accumulated on the porcelain dish and became – critically, for jury purposes – truly tangible. Anyone who did not believe it was arsenic could take a lick.

Marsh's discovery was to change toxicology and enter the annals as the standard arsenic test. As would later emerge, the method was so sensitive that it could detect as little as one thousandth of a milligram of arsenic trioxide in the sample fluid. Marsh first published his discovery in 1836 in the *Edinburgh Philosophical Journal,* provoking keen interest within the research community of the day. For one man in particular, Mathieu Joseph Bonaventure Orfila (1787–1853), the new method was little short of inspirational.

Orfila is often called the 'Father of Modern Toxicology'. In 1813 the then 26-year-old published the first part of his two-volume opus *Traité des poisons* or *Toxicologie générale,* the first work of international importance to review contemporary knowledge of poisons. Responding to the demands of the time, Orfila had devoted a large part of his studies to arsenic. Though primarily a collector and systematiser of existing knowledge, he was also very active as a researcher. For example, he established in animal experiments that arsenic migrated from the stomach and intestine to other organs. Thus if the stomach tested negative, the poison might still be detectable in the liver, spleen, kidneys or even the

Mathieu Joseph Bonaventure Orfila *(1787–1853), born on the island of Minorca, studied chemistry and medicine, first in Valencia and then in Barcelona, where they were still teaching that the world was composed of four basic elements: fire, earth, air and water. Orfila, who nourished his mind outside the university on the latest publications, was quickly bored and realised that he had little more to learn there. So he travelled on to Paris, where he became a Doctor of Medicine in 1811. In his apartment in the Rue Croix des Petits Champs he installed a laboratory and devoted himself to the intensive study of poisons. From 1801 onwards he gave private courses on the chemistry of poisons, demonstrating their effects in animal experiments. Orfila established himself as a poisons expert. The second volume of his seminal work appeared in 1815, followed by further books on the subject. In 1819 he became Professor of Medicinal Chemistry at the University of Paris.*

nerves. Orfila also improved on Valentin Rose's method for the 'destruction of fleshy matter', in which the tissue of interest was exposed to saltpetre until it was completely carbonised. Total destruction of the tissue containing the poison made the arsenic easier to detect; the same applied to analysis of the gastric and intestinal contents, where the protein and fat components often made arsenic detection impossible. However, for all his achievements, Orfila repeatedly found himself being hampered by the limitations of his knowledge and his test methods. Why, for example, had he sometimes been unable to find arsenic in dogs that had been given the poison? Surely it could only be that his methods weren't sensitive enough. Marsh's test was exactly what he needed.

Chemistry and circumstance

Orfila and many other scientists worked on applying and improving Marsh's discovery and were delight-

When bodies were exhumed, soil samples were also taken to check their arsenic content.

yards, in particular, contained very high concentrations. Was it possible that the poison detected in corpses had migrated from the soil? This would invalidate analyses performed after exhumation.

The sensitivity of Marsh's apparatus, which had met initially with universal acclaim, now brought a cascade of confusion. New problems emerged in rapid succession, all with the same cause: the immensely wide distribution of arsenic throughout nature.

Orfila worked with all his might on the solution. He obtained bones from the Paris mortuaries and found, as Courbe had claimed, that they regularly contained arsenic. He began to wonder about the causes. Grain was sometimes impregnated with arsenic, particularly in the Département de la Somme. Perhaps the deceased had eaten bread made with such flour. Or perhaps they had received arsenic as a remedy for cancer or venereal disease. Maybe it was an environmental effect: if arsenic was common in nature, perhaps people were constantly taking in small amounts and storing them briefly in the bones without suffering acute poisoning.

Spadework

Bones from the Département de la Somme were thus Orfila's next research objects, together with soil samples from this region and from graveyards. In the soil samples he indeed found arsenic, but only in the form of calcium arsenate, which is insoluble in water. Orfila thus considered it extremely unlikely, although not impossible, that arsenic could permeate into corpses via the moisture in soil.

The first lesson Orfila drew from his experiments was not to rely exclusively on chemical analysis, but also to pay attention to circumstances. Given the frequent presence of arsenic, the circumstances under which a sample was found always had to be considered. These circumstances were just as important as the analytical method itself.

Through the efforts of Orfila and others, all obstacles and sources of error relating to the Marsh test were eliminated over the years, ultimately leaving an extremely reliable method for use in diagnostics and criminology. Thanks to the violent death of one human being and the initiative of a resourceful chemist, arsenic lost its pre-eminence as a folk poison.

Even today, 150 years after its discovery, the Marsh test is still applicable and is learnt by chemistry students in their freshman year.

On the other hand, like other fields, toxicology has not been standing still. Modern technology de-

ed by its accuracy. Then in 1838 came a temporary setback. For in many cases testing with Marsh's apparatus produced the tell-tale mirror even if the sample could not possibly have contained any arsenic. The commotion was great. Could it be that the method was flawed?

Fortunately, the problem was soon resolved. The Marsh test used zinc and sulphuric acid, and Orfila and his colleague Raspal discovered traces of arsenic in both reagents. But this solution raised a fresh problem: How did the arsenic get there? And then there was a further cause for commotion. The chemist Courbe found arsenic in the bones of individuals who had demonstrably not died of arsenic poisoning. Was it a natural component of the human body? This would have posed an enormous analytical problem. Was it generated postmortem by processes as yet unknown? With no clear answers to these questions, reliable analysis was impossible.

Further sources of error were identified. Soil samples were tested from many sites and found to contain arsenic. Samples from some Paris grave-

Gas chromatography is one of the methods used today to diagnose poisonings.

tects poisons in the human body in the **p**arts-**p**er-**m**illion (ppm) range and below. Organic poisons are detected by gas chromatography, mass spectrometry and high-performance liquid chromatography. Heavy metals such as arsenic are detected today by atomic absorption spectroscopy, emission spectroscopy or **i**nductively **c**oupled **p**lasma **m**ass spectrometry (ICP-MS).

Elmer W. Koneman

Old scourges and new

Microbe hunters explore a hidden world

Long before our species existed, the earth belonged to microorganisms – bacteria and their cousins the ·*Archaebacteria,* some of whose descendants, the extremophiles, continue to live in the harshest environments imaginable: in the cores of ancient rock and the intense heat of submarine volcanoes (home to the hyperthermobacteria); in Arctic glaciers and acid and alkaline lakes; and under conditions of severe oxygen deprivation. The arrival of man provided a new niche for a huge and resourceful microbial population which, although already ancient, was – and remains – under continued renewal, forever adapting its genome to environmental demand and ever ready to incorporate foreign genetic material to offset innate deficiencies that might impair its metabolic activity and threaten its survival.

Plague as a shaper of history

Plagues have been a constant in human history, stretching from Moses:

> An immense flight of quail fell by the camp. And the people stood up all that day, and all that night, and all the next day they gathered the quails, and while the flesh was yet between their teeth, ere it was chewed, the wrath of the Lord was kindled against the people, and the Lord smote the people with a very great plague.[1]

to the epicentre of our industrial civilisation, threatened by crows and the West Nile virus. We have the written account of a plague in 1141 BC when the Philistines seized the ark of the Lord and took it to the city of Ashdod, where 'the hand of the Lord was heavy' and He smote the citizens with 'emerods' in their 'secret parts'. Some interpret the 'emerods' as hemorrhoids resulting from bacillary dysentery. Others view them as the buboes of plague. The

Greeks spoke of 'pestilential groins', and the Romans of *pestis inguinaria.* Interestingly, popular belief at the time already associated these afflictions with mice.[2]

Thucydides (c. 471–400 BC), in his *History of the Peloponnesian War,* described the afflictions suffered during the Great Plague of Athens in 431 BC, now believed by many scientists to have been measles.[3] Hippocrates of Cos (460–375 BC) described plagues lasting for three years causing high fever, nosebleeds, dysentery and burning of the eyes. He also reported another epidemic targeting children and young adults, with fever and swelling behind the ears, almost certainly mumps. At the end of the Parthian War (AD 161–166), smallpox is thought to have decimated the Roman army. The returning survivors spread the disease throughout the Roman Empire. Almost 100 years later, a second epidemic under the emperor-philosopher Marcus Aurelius (AD 121–180) left so many dead that Rome and the surrounding cities were largely defenceless. This was probably bubonic plague, which has been seen as the beginning of the decline of the Roman Empire.

Throughout history dysentery has accompanied all armies as a kind of fifth column and has been the uncrowned victor in many battles. Epidemics continued to ravage society in the 16th and 17th centuries: measles, scarlet fever, smallpox, dysentery, malaria, typhus, typhoid fever, influenza and of course the '*morbus gallicus*', or syphilis. The Black Death returned in repeated waves to most European countries. In 1665 the city of London 'looked like a desert' after almost 20% of its population had succumbed to plague. The King, Queen, High Councils and Court of Justice, and most of the rich moved

'The Triumph of Death' by Pieter Bruegel the Elder (1520–1569). The great epidemics of the Middle Ages inspired many artists to produce macabre depictions of human mortality.

west, with the failure of industry only increasing the misery of the poor souls left behind.[4]

The hunt for a cause

It took a long time to realise that microbes could be the cause. For centuries the principles laid down by Aristotle (384–322 BC) in his *Historia animalium* persisted in the public mind. Thus animals were thought to grow spontaneously and not from 'kindred stock'. They came from dew falling on leaves, from decaying mud, dung or timber. New life developed in animal fur or in voided excrement. Flies came from putrefying carcasses; fleas, bugs and lice from moisture and filth; and some fish from mud, sand, or decayed matter.

These were common tenets even in 1675, when Antoni van Leeuwenhoek (1632–1723), observing a drop of rainwater with his primitive microscope, fell upon the hidden world of bacteria. At about the same time, Francesco Redi (1626–1697), an Italian physician and poet of Florence, put the theory of spontaneous generation to the test of experimentation. In addition, one of his students, Giovan Cosimo Bonomo (1663–1696) was finally able to show, using a primitive microscope, that a microbe might be the cause of an infectious disease:

> I dug out from a patient with scabies a minute living creature – resembling a tortoise in shape, of whitish colour, a little dark upon the back, with some thin and long hairs, of nimble motion, with six feet, a sharp head and two little horns at the end of the snout. I was drawing a picture of one of them by a microscope, from behind a part, I saw a drop, a very small and scarcely visible white egg, almost transparent and oblong, like the seed of a pineapple.[5]

Bonomo also demonstrated that scabies was 'produced by the continual biting of these animalcules in the skin' and, of great importance, that 'this distemper can be very catching since these creatures by simple contact can easily pass from one body to

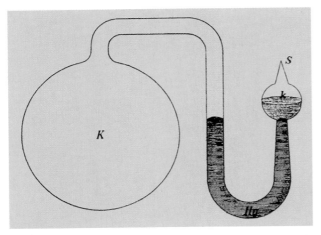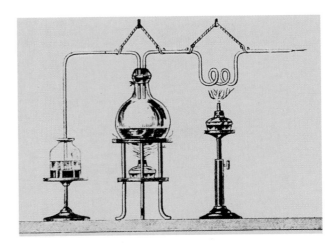

Apparatuses used by Schwann in his experiments to refute the theory of spontaneous generation.

another'. This account is the first hint in writing of contagion and disease transmission via a vector. It was a turning point in the history of medicine. The realisation that microorganisms were directly linked to certain diseases began to be accepted. A subsequent relevant discovery, by the Italian Agostino Bassi (1773–1856) in 1835, revealed that a fungus was the cause of a fatal disease in silkworms, known by the French as *muscardine* and by the Italians as *calcino* or *cannellino*. Bassi found that the affected worms became covered after death with a peculiar hard, lime-like material, which we now know to be colonies of the fungus *Botrytis bassiana*. More particularly, he showed that this material was infectious. After removing a portion of the epidermis, he passed the worm through a flame, and sampled the underlying tissue with a sterilised pin. With a scratch of the pin he could transmit the disease to a healthy silkworm.

The first confirmation that a generalised disease of man could be caused by a microparasite came from the study of trichinosis. James Paget (1814–1899), a 21-year-old medical student working in the dissecting room of St. Bartholomew's Hospital, London, in 1835, first observed the *Trichinella* parasites in a muscle preparation.[6]

Another disease of man soon shown to be associated with a microparasite was ringworm. In 1839 Johann Schönlein (1793–1864) described a fungus in the pustules of a patient with ringworm.[7] In 1840 Jacob Henle (1809–1885) established in his *Pathologische Untersuchungen* that microbes cause disease and that infectious agents multiply in the human body. He was the first to postulate the ability to reproduce disease in a second host using an inoculum from an infected individual. Henle's postulate was

the forerunner of Koch's postulates published 40 years later.

Spontaneous generation refuted

Still, spontaneous generation remained major unresolved issue in the mid-19th century. In particular, scientists sought to determine its relationship to exposure to air and the influence of air on fermentation. Several devised heat-sterilisation experiments, the most significant being those by Theodor Schwann (1810–1882), who is considered by some to be the founder of the germ theory, based on his experiments with of putrefaction and fermentation. His main goal was to prove that putrefaction and bacterial contamination resulted from exposure to air.

In an early experiment Schwann used a large glass globe, bending its neck first horizontally, then into a 'U', and finally blowing a small bulb at the open end. In the bend of the 'U' he placed metallic mercury and into the small bulb an organic infusion. He then sealed the small bulb and heated the whole apparatus. After cooling, he inverted the apparatus to permit the infusion to enter the large flask. Even after several days, no infusoria – the minute organisms found in stagnant infusions of animal or vegetable material – developed within the infusion broth. In a later experiment he demonstrated that it was not the air, but a heat-labile substance in the air that caused contamination and putrefaction of organic infusions.

The controversy over the results of heat experiments continued as subsequent workers failed to duplicate Schwann's results. In particular, Félix-Archimède Pouchet (1800–1872), director of the Natural History Museum in Rouen, presented papers to the Academy of Sciences of Paris in 1858 which, to his mind, proved the existence of spontaneous generation.

Heat-stable or heat-labile?

The controversy over whether or not bacteria could grow after heat treatment was finally resolved by John Tyndall (1820–1893), a British physicist who, in a paper read before the Royal Society of London in 1877, presented his observations that bacteria exist in two forms or phases – one which was relatively heat-labile and the other which was incredibly heat-resistant. In testing the actual heat limitation of germs that had been contaminating infusions in many experiments, he discovered that even after boiling for $5^1/_2$ hours, some microorganisms could still be grown in secondary cultures. Using intermittent heat, he found that the heat-labile (vegetative) forms were killed after the first period of boiling. However, a second or even third period of boiling was needed to kill a second growth of vegetative forms, that had survived the first heating, presumably arising from heat-resistant forms.

At about the same time the resistant spores of anthrax were demonstrated microscopically – first by Ferdinand Cohn (1828–1898), a German-Jewish botanist and microbiologist in Breslau, then by Robert Koch (1843–1910). This proved unequivocally that Tyndall's heat-resistant forms were spores.[8] The science of diagnostic microbiology could now move forward, unfettered by ancient credos and mantras, and based instead on the results of deductive reasoning and careful experimentation.

The fermentation studies of Louis Pasteur (1822–1895) were also instrumental in disproving spontaneous generation. In a number of experiments lasting many months he showed that sugars did not ferment in sterile infusions, i.e. in the absence of bacteria. He reproduced the experiments of Schwann, again demonstrating that air passed through a heated tube into an infusion did not result in the appearance of contaminating organisms. Pasteur's fermentation studies attracted public attention less for their scientific merit than for their impact on the French wine industry. His first fermentation work was done on the production of vinegar. He showed that wine was soured by the contamination of the wine yeast by acid-producing organisms, and that tasteless sparkling or oily wines resulted from secondary fermentation by other bacteria.

With the theory of spontaneous generation disproved and the bacterial origin of infectious disease

The Frenchman **Félix-Archimède Pouchet** *(1800–1872) believed he had experimental proof of the spontaneous generation theory. He heated hay at 100 °C for 20 minutes in an air-bath, then plunged it into a flask of boiling water, closed the flask and sealed it under mercury. Some days later he found that it contained living creatures: moulds, amoebae, monads and vibrios. In further experiments Pouchet demonstrated that the main factors in spontaneous generation were organic matter in solid or dissolved form, water, access to air and suitable temperature. He was convinced that life could appear even though anything previously alive had been destroyed in all elements – putrescible material, air and water. He therefore concluded that life could arise spontaneously. We now know that Pouchet's heat treatments killed only the vegetative forms, but not the heat-resistant spores. Life cannot arise from inanimate matter.*

firmly established by the French school under Pasteur and the German school under Koch, diagnostic microbiology opened up to a myriad of new discoveries. Although each was unique and often historically important, only a few can be discussed in this chapter.

Diagnostic microbiology

In 1876 Robert Koch was among the first to comprehend that bacteria had be captured in the nonmotile state if they were to be adequately studied. He was the first to prepare dried films of bacterial suspensions and stain them with methylene blue. Later, inspired by Paul Ehrlich's (1854–1915) groundbreaking development of stains to visualise intracytoplasmic granules in white blood cells, Koch stained his air-dried smears with aniline dyes, applying a coverslip for protection. These preparations were of superior quality for the time, but their observation became even better after the physicist Ernst Abbe (1840–1905) introduced the practical application of oil immersion lenses and his light-focusing condenser in 1878. Koch was well aware that the growth of bacterial cultures was temperature-

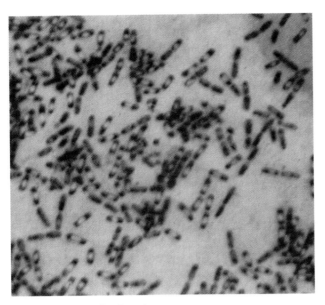
Anthrax spores under the microscope.

dependent. Although many bacteria grow slowly at room temperature, some strains have to be close to body temperature (37.5 °C) for optimum growth. The first incubators were surrounded by a double-walled chamber, often made of copper and insulated on the outside with asbestos. The space between the jackets was filled with water, a relatively poor conductor of heat, enabling a fixed temperature to be maintained. In the pre-electricity era, the temperature was kept constant by heating the jacket water with a gas flame, the height of the flame being the only means – crude and potentially dangerous – of regulating the incubator temperature.

Successful identification of a microorganism depends on understanding its properties. Scientists sought to explain why some microbes were harmful while others were not – a process, incidentally, that will never end, since evolution is constantly renewing the microorganism population. Microbes can harm humans in many ways. For example, the immune response to invading bacteria can be so violent as to be life-threatening in itself, or the bacteria can produce a poison, or toxin, as in the following example.

Diphtheria

Friedrich Loeffler (1852–1915), a professor of hygiene also working in Koch's laboratory, was trying to unravel some of the mysteries surrounding diphtheria and its putative causative organism. The problem was that 'diphtheria' could not be transmitted to animals, making Koch's postulates difficult to apply. Guinea pigs injected intramuscularly with bacterial

colonies developed hemorrhagic inflammation, or keratitis when the material was injected into the cornea. Neither reaction was thought due to the organisms. Loeffler then examined material from 27 patients with diphtheria, including an infant who died several days after becoming hoarse and dyspneic. He recovered chain-forming micrococci from cultures of the throat and pharynx. At autopsy the epiglottis, trachea and bronchi were covered by an inflammatory membrane. In material taken from beneath the denuded membrane, Loeffler observed bacterial rods rather than chains of cocci under the microscope. They were slightly bent and enlarged at the poles. However, they failed to grow on the meat infusion-peptone-gelatin culture medium used at the time.

Loeffler cultured the material on coagulated blood serum at body temperature. Incubation for three days produced the small yellowish colonies of micrococcus; however, among them were occasional larger colonies of the rods seen in the pseudomembrane preparations. In later experiments Loeffler found that these bacteria were highly pathogenic in guinea pigs; yet although the dead animals displayed edema and hemorrhagic areas of dense inflammation in the lungs, the only bacteria he could recover were from the injection sites in the skin. After much reflection and experimentation, he concluded that:

> brownish red areas of consolidation in the lungs, where bacilli could not be demonstrated, were conclusive indications that a toxin generated at the site of injection and transmitted through the blood stream, induced severe damage to the vessel walls. The toxin generated by the bacilli in the guinea pig is undoubtedly similar to the toxin of human diphtheria![9]

It took many more experiments before Loeffler convinced the scientific community that only the pseudomembranous pharyngitis was directly caused by the diphtheria bacteria. The extraoral syndrome was due to the production by the injected bacteria of a lethal toxin with effects manifested far from the injection site.

Loeffler was most puzzled that he could not differentiate between certain nonvirulent strains of the diphtheria bacteria cultured from healthy persons and those producing full-blown disease. Not until later was it discovered that the only virulent strains of *Corynebacterium diphtheriae* were those carrying the *tox* (toxin) gene. This led to the development of procedures to detect the toxin before the diagnosis of diphtheria could be confirmed, and more recently, to nucleic acid assays designed to detect the *tox* gene itself.

Cholera

Microbes make it hard for researchers to track them down, as illustrated by the discovery of the 'comma bacterium', the causative agent of cholera. Two teams, one French, the other German, were commissioned in 1883 to discover the cause of a cholera epidemic that had broken out in Egypt. The German team, under Koch, won out in the end, albeit not in Egypt but in India. Within days of arriving in India, they had a pure culture of the comma-shaped cholera bacterium which they had already observed in autopsy material in Egypt but had failed to culture. The difference in India was the combination of access to fresh material and the use of a culture medium with an elevated pH that was more selective for the growth of the cholera bacterium, separating it from the myriads of other organisms that inhabit the lower intestinal tract.

Sceptics immediately came forward to discredit Koch's announcement that he had found the agent of cholera. An East Indian doctor declared: 'Koch's comma bacillus is not the cause'. This was in spite of the fact that the German Commission had unequivocally related 17 deaths from cholera to the ingestion of water from the large concrete tanks used throughout India not only for storing drinking water, but also for bathing and washing clothes (including those from cholera victims).

The Commission's findings were also discounted by several German notables, including the then 74-year-old Max von Pettenkofer (1818–1901), an eminent Munich hygienist to whom Koch paid a courtesy call on his otherwise triumphal return. To support his scepticism, Pettenkofer ingested a small quantity of a broth culture, developing only mild symptoms. It was later learned that Koch's colleague Georg Gaffky (1850–1918) had sent a partially attenuated strain. Subsequently, an assistant, Rudolf Emmerich (1852–1914), repeated the experiment on himself with another strain and fell severely ill. He recovered, and von Pettenkofer voiced no further doubt. Cholera transmission through the ingestion of contaminated water became fact, and public water supply systems in the developed world have comprised bacterial filters ever since.

Typhoid fever

At about the same time that Loeffler was discovering the bacterial cause of diphtheria, Gaffky cultured *Salmonella typhi* from stool samples of patients with diarrhea. In 1902 a major outbreak of typhoid fever occurred in Trier, a German city on the Mosel River. Koch led an investigation commission. Shortly be-

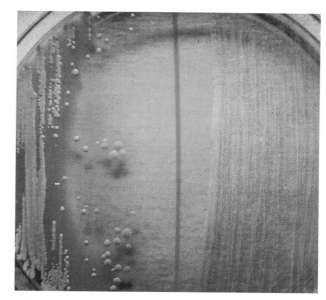

Differential culture medium showing lactose-fermenting coliform bacteria as pink (left), and non lactose-fermenting bacteria, including Salmonella typhi, *as colourless (right).*

fore, a selective culture medium had been developed to separate *S. typhi* from the multiple other stool bacteria. It showed the colonies of lactose-fermenting coliform bacteria as pink, and the colonies of non lactose-fermenting bacteria, including *S. typhi*, as colourless.

Investigations soon eliminated the primary suspect, namely – given Koch's experience with cholera – the public water supply. The team concluded that direct person-to-person transmission was responsible, i.e. transmission from asymptomatic people to others who developed symptoms after ingesting the causative organisms. Koch called these healthy transmitters 'carriers', demonstrating for the first time that individuals could be infected with virulent bacteria without themselves becoming sick. They could then act as a source in transmitting infection to susceptible individuals. The carrier hypothesis was one of Koch's last significant contributions, leading directly to the public health safety practices and procedures familiar to us today.

Plague

In AD 541 and for 52 years thereafter, three separate plagues spread through the Byzantine Empire of Justinian (482–565). Procopius of Caesarea (500?–565?) was the first to describe the detailed symptoms of what we now know as pneumonic plague and bubonic plague. From Egypt, the plagues spread rapidly eastwards over Syria, Persia and India, then penetrated to the west along the coast of

Typhoid Mary

The most famous carrier of the typhoid bacillus was Typhoid Mary.[10] Mary Mallon was a 'good plain cook' who one wintry New York afternoon in 1906, found herself bundled into the back of a city ambulance, subdued by the weight of a female doctor sitting on top of her. During the previous summer, there had been an outbreak of typhoid fever in Oyster Bay on Long Island's north shore, with a suspected source of infection in the home of a New York banker named William Henry Warren, where Mary was a cook. Of the four family members and seven servants living in the house, six had come down with typhoid fever.

Warren hired a sanitary engineer, George Soper, to investigate. Soper immediately suspected the servants, particularly the cook, who had been taken on just three weeks before the outbreak. Mary Mallon was not sick; however, Soper was aware of the chronic carrier state associated with the disease and investigated further. But when he appeared in the kitchen to confront her, she saw him off with a rolling pin. It was then that the ambulance came to pick her up. She saw it coming and fled to a neighbour's house, where the police found her only after a three-hour search. In hospital Mary Mallon was found to be shedding the typhoid bacillus, and she was placed under quarantine. The term 'Typhoid Mary' has been applied to any healthy carrier who resists arrest.

Mary Mallon was given a permanent home in a one-room bungalow on a remote island in the East River, on the grounds of the Riverside Hospital for Communicable Diseases. After two years there, she was released when her lawyer argued that she had never been sick, and therefore could not be a menace to society, but with the proviso that she would never cook again. But anyone who knew Mary knew that she would not keep her word. She was later found cooking in the Sloan Maternity Hospital in New York City, where 25 new cases of typhoid fever had recently been reported. Mary was sent back to her bungalow, where she spent the remaining 26 years of her life, until her death in 1938. During her kitchen career, she had spread typhoid fever to 51 people, three of whom had died.

Africa and over the continent of Europe. The Great Black Plague of the 14th Century, initially cradled in Central Asia, likewise spread westwards to the borders of Europe. During the early years of the 14th century, trade routes had been opened up via land and sea. Commercial caravans crowded the overland highways and ships plied between continents, each with a stowaway cargo of rats, rat fleas and plague bacillus.

By the end of 1348, plague had blanketed all of Italy and most of France, crossed the Alps into Switzerland, and finally reached England. Populations were halved in one city after another. Florence was so severely hit that the Black Death was sometimes referred to as the 'Plague of Florence'. The misery and suffering test our imagination. Descriptions of corpses piled high in the fields or plugging the waterways are legion. Avignon in southern France, the capital of the Roman Papacy from 1309, had to be abandoned 50 years later because of the plague. Almost 75% of its population succumbed, and a reported 7000 homes were boarded up and abandoned. In a nearby field, bought by the Pope and consecrated as a cemetery, 11,000 corpses were buried within a six-month period. The pestilence was graphically portrayed by the Italian poet and humanist Giovanni Boccaccio (1313–1375):

> In men and women alike there appeared, at the beginning of the malady, certain swellings, either on the groin or under the armpits, whereof some waxed of the bigness of a common apple, others like unto an egg, some more and some less, and these the vulgar name plague-boils ... not only did few recover thereof, but well nigh all died within the third day from the appearance of the aforesaid signs.[11]

The agent of plague, *Yersinia pestis*, is named after its discoverer, the Swiss-French microbiologist Alexandre Yersin (1863–1943), who trained under Koch in Berlin and at the Pasteur Institute. Yersin began his investigation in Hong Kong in 1894, in a self-built straw hut on the grounds of the main hospital, with permission of the British government. A plague epidemic had broken out, carrying off 600 people before Yersin's arrival. Those affected developed sudden high fever, often accompanied by delirium. A discrete subcutaneous swelling (bubo) appeared on the first day, usually in the groin. It rapidly reached the size of an egg, with death usually ensuing in the next 48 hours. If a patient survived for four or five days, the prognosis was better, although the reported hospital mortality rate was 95%. Yersin examined the blood and disease tissue of infected patients, describing 'short, stubby bacilli in the pulp of the buboes, that were easy to stain with aniline dyes, but not by the method of Gram'.[12] The ends of the bacilli stained more strongly than the centre. When Yersin seeded the bubo pulp onto agar, he observed transparent white colonies with iridescent margins under reflected light. Growth was enhanced by adding glycerol to the medium. Experimental rats and guinea pigs died soon after being inoculated with bubo pulp; necropsy showed characteristic hemorrhagic lesions, and numerous bacilli in the lymph nodes, spleen and blood. Yersin concluded that plague was a contagious and transmissible disease, and rats the likely vector. Many dead rats were found in the streets and houses of the infected boroughs in Hong Kong; they also harboured large quantities of bacilli in their internal organs; some even developed buboes. Rats and, critically, their fleas, played a major role in plague epidemics.

Tetanus

Although the overall incidence of tetanus in the late 19th century is unknown, the rapidly fatal progression and grotesque facial grimacing, known as *risus sardonicus,* in patients infected with *Clostridium tetani* must have conferred particular urgency on the hunt for the causative agent. After the face, the painful spasms assailed all the muscles of the body. When they affected the muscles of the chest and diaphragm, they made breathing impossible, even as the patient remained fully conscious. Asphyxiation ensued.

In 1889 Shibasaburo Kitasato (1852–1931) grew a pure culture of club-shaped bacilli bearing terminal spores from pus taken from the wound of a soldier garrisoned in Berlin who had died of tetanus.[13] The bacilli had already been described in 1884 by Arthur Nicolaier (1862–1942), who is today credited with the discovery of the tetanus bacillus. These organisms, however, were only found in wounds, but at no other sites in the body. It was therefore assumed that the clinical manifestations were caused by a toxin, as in diphtheria.

Nicolaier had found that the organism would grow on coagulated serum, but only in the presence of other organisms. The reason was unknown at the time. It was later discovered that anaerobes such as the tetanus agent often grow in the company of aerobic bacteria that extract oxygen from the immediate environment. Kitasato, however, devised a culture method involving preincubation at 36–38 °C in coagulated serum containing oxygen-reducing proteins. He observed growth of the typical bacilli and spores within 24 hours. He then placed the culture in a water bath at 80 °C for one hour, after which only spores remained. Mice injected with these spores promptly died of tetanus.

During his tenure at the Koch Institute, Kitasato also worked with Emil von Behring (1854–1917) and

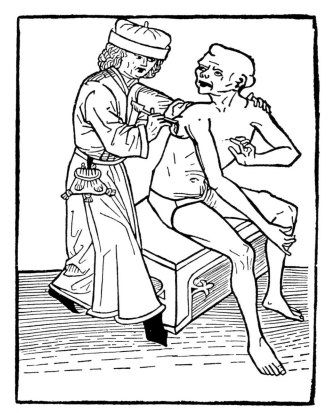

Physician incising buboes (1482 woodcut).

Ehrlich on the toxins of the diphtheria and the tetanus bacteria. Much basic groundwork was laid; however, it was ultimately Ehrlich who developed an effective antitoxin that could be used treat tetanus patients. Behring received the Nobel Prize in 1901 for the discovery of diphtheria antitoxin; Ehrlich was the Nobel Laureate in 1908 for major contributions in immunology and chemotherapy. Unfortunately, between these years, the two scientists parted company; after having worked famously together, they died bitter enemies.

Bacillary dysentery

In 1898, an assistant of Kitasato, Kiyoshi Shiga (1870–1957), became acutely aware of the high prevalence of dysentery in all provinces of Japan. Between June and December of that year the reported cases reached 89,400, 24 % of which were fatal. The hunt for the causative agent was stumbling over the inadequacy of contemporary bacterial culture methods. Animal studies were of little use, since experimental animals did not develop a dysentery syndrome similar to that in humans. Shiga then announced that he had found a specific organism causing the Japanese variety of dysentery that satisfied all of Koch's postulates. He even added a postulate of his own: 'if the serum from an actively sick or convalescent patient afflicted with the disease in

The Swiss-Frenchman **Alexandre Yersin** *(1863–1943) worked for a short time as an assistant in Koch's laboratory in Berlin, where he helped Friedrich Loeffler (1852–1915) with his diphtheria toxin experiments. He then moved to Paris to work with Émile Roux (1853–1933), a personal friend and admirer, at the Pasteur Institute. In one account, Yersin was described as the vector transporting Koch's methods into the Pasteur Institute. Yersin had an irresistible desire for adventure. One day he simply left the Pasteur Institute, leaving behind a long letter of explanation for Roux, boarded a ship of the Messageries Maritimes, spent time in Saigon and Manila, and ultimately ended up in Indochina. He joined a small expedition to explore the mountainous region between China and Laos. During the trip he was shot in the leg, developed malaria, suffered a bout of severe dysentery, and on one foray was attacked by a tiger. He was under constant threat from hostile tribes. Exhausted by the misery and privation, Yersin returned to civilisation and accepted an assignment in Hong Kong to help investigate the causes of an outbreak of bubonic plague. There he met up with Shibasaburo Kitasato (1852–1931), who had also been an assistant in Koch's laboratory. Yersin and Kitasato, together with a small team, rapidly identified the bacterial cause of plague, a discovery which Yersin soon followed by a long paper[34] describing his work in Hong Kong. As a final privation one of his local workers absconded with his money.*

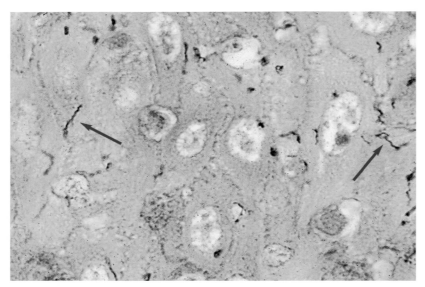

Tissue section showing the ultraslender, tightly coiled spirochetes of Treponema pallidum *(arrows), the causative agent of syphilis (Warthin-Starry silver stain).*

question agglutinates a specific organism, the organism has an intimate association with that disease'; he described his pathogen – now known as *Shigella* – as 'a short rod with rounded ends, similar in appearance to the typhoid bacillus and most types of enteric coli'.[14] The nonflagellated Gram-negative bacteria did not produce spores. Growth was optimal at 37 °C and in an alkaline environment. He also found that the bacillus was difficult to recover from

the stools early in the disease but then multiplied to yield almost pure cultures at the height of infection. Although subcutaneous injection of pure cultures into mice, guinea pigs, rabbits and cats proved fatal in each instance, it did not produce the intestinal changes seen in man. Shiga did not shrink from self-experimentation. He inoculated himself with a 'vaccine' he had produced from attenuated cultures. The effects were anything but pleasant:

> I administered ½ of an agar culture subcutaneously in the rump. Several hours later I developed a headache and tenderness at the site of injection. In 8 hours there were chills and fever followed by lassitude and pain in the knee joint and calves. The local tenderness increased and on the next day, the swelling reached the size of a dish, the local axillary glands were swollen and sensitive to pressure … On the 8th day the local swelling increased and the lesion was incised. The more superficial layers were hard and thickened; the deeper layers were pussy and infiltrated. The pus was sterile. The changes therefore were due to toxemia. The symptoms abated on the 9th day. Blood serum taken on the 10th day agglutinated dysentery bacilli at a 1:10 dilution.[15]

Four species of *Shigella* have since been characterised, of which *Shigella dysenteriae* is the most virulent.

Syphilis

In number and volume published accounts of syphilis probably exceed those on any other infectious disease. In the pre-modern era diagnosis was difficult because symptoms were often vague. The spirochetes that cause syphilis are very slender and take up most stains poorly, making them difficult to recognise. Because of its relationship with sexual activity, syphilis has often been shrouded in secrecy and treated more as moral failing than communicable disease.

Disagreement persists among archeologists and paleontologists as to the evidence of syphilis in the bones of mummies. It has been claimed that syphilis was native to America and that it was spread across Europe in the 16th century by sailors returning from the New World. The Italians called syphilis the Spanish or French disease. The French called it the Italian disease. The English called it the French disease. Whatever its origin, syphilis has been a major scourge of mankind.

The name 'syphilis' was coined by Girolamo Fracastoro (1478–1553), physician, astronomer, geographer, poet, humanist and chief physician to the Council of Trent, who in 1530 published a didactic poem entitled *Syphilis sive Morbus Gallicus,* in tribute to a Shepard boy named Syphilus, who was afflicted with a strange infection. However, the watershed year in diagnosis would not come until 1905. The causative agent, which Fritz Schaudinn (1871–1906) first named *Spirochaeta pallida* and later *Treponema pallidum,* was apprehended through the efforts of several researchers.[16] Only a year later August Paul von Wassermann (1866–1925) developed the complement fixation diagnostic test described in detail in the 'Blood lines' chapter. Several additional tests have since been developed, including the Venereal Disease Research Laboratories (VDRL) test in the United States for post-treatment serological follow-up, and the **r**apid **p**lasma **r**eagin (RPR) test, used as a rough screening procedure in situations demanding high specimen throughput in a short time.

Even with our sophisticated battery of diagnostic procedures, certain bacteria continue to elude us, several of which are described in the following sections.

Swimming pool granuloma

In the mid-1950s a striking increase in the number of patients with subcutaneous abscesses and granulomas was observed in various clinical and pathology practices in the Denver (Colorado) metropolitan area. Granulomas are nodular changes caused by collections of activated immune cells under the skin. Clinically these skin lesions were consistent with a chronic bacterial infection, as might be observed in brucellosis, syphilis or one of the subcutaneous mycoses. Acid-fast bacilli were observed in tissue sections; however, the organism could never be recovered in culture.

Gardner Middlebrook (1915?–1986) of the National Jewish Hospital in Denver was assigned to the problem. He and his colleagues had considerable expertise in the diagnosis and treatment of tuberculosis and in the laboratory detection of *Mycobacterium tuberculosis* and **m**ycobacteria **o**ther **t**han **t**uberculosis (MOTT). After much trial and error in the use of a variety of culture media, and several animal experiments, Middlebrook finally discovered the right medium and culture conditions to recover the elusive agent. Middlebrook agar is an enriched non-selective agar-based medium for mycobacteria. Not only was the correct formulation of this medium essential for culturing the Denver strain, but, more importantly, Middlebrook discovered that the strain grew only at incubation temperatures below 32 °C.[17]

Epidemiological studies by the Colorado Department of Health revealed that most patients pre-

Depiction of syphilis by Albrecht Dürer (1471–1528).

The American **Gardner Middlebrook** (1915?–1986) studied medicine at Harvard Medical School, where he contracted pulmonary tuberculosis, later described as the spur to his scientific work. After qualifying, he became a bacteriologist and pathologist at the Rockefeller Institute for Medical Research. In the early 1950s he was appointed research director at the National Jewish Hospital in Denver, Colorado. This photograph is from that period. From 1962 to 1964 he was a professor of microbiology in Buenos Aires. In the mid-1960s he returned to the United States, where he was a professor of pathology at the University of Maryland until 1980. He introduced the use of two antibacterial agents in the treatment of bacterial disease to combat the development of resistant organisms. He developed a number of microbial culture media that still bear his name. He received several national and international awards, including the Pasteur Medal in 1954. He was not only an outstanding microbe hunter, but also a multi-talented craftsman, building for example a home-made organ which he donated to the Hallmark Church of the Nazarene in Baltimore. He published works of fiction and articles on music and philosophy in addition to his papers on microbiology.

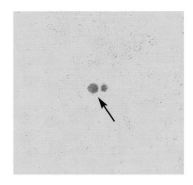

Chlamydia *inclusion bodies (iodine stain).*

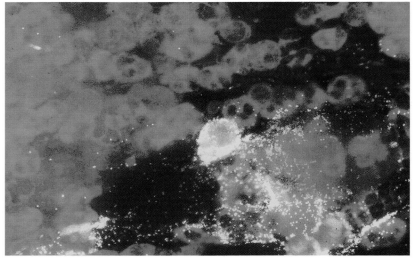

Elemental bodies of Chlamydia trachomatis *(fluorescent label).*

senting with these subcutaneous granulomas had frequented a well-known hot-water mountain spa resort in Glenwood Springs, west of Denver. The same organism recovered on Middlebrook agar from infected patients was also present in the natural thermal water of the pool, which was teeming with bacteria. This organism, *Mycobacterium marinum*, produces an infection called 'swimming pool granuloma', or more recently 'fish tank granuloma', as most current infections are related to the care of heated contaminated fish tanks.

Chlamydia

Trachoma, a contagious disease of the conjunctiva and cornea that can lead to blindness, was known several thousand years ago in China, where it affects millions to this day. It was familiar to the Romans, an alleged sufferer being Marcus Tullius Cicero (106–43 BC). The Egyptians and Chinese discovered empirically that copper salt paste applied around the eyes inhibited the conjunctivitis, while also serving as a mascara-like cosmetic.

The legitimacy of describing trachoma as an emerging infectious disease is based on the fact that for a long time the causative agent could not be recovered in culture. *Chlamydia trachomatis* was not grown until 1957, when it was inoculated into embryonated hen's egg.[18] Two years later, it was recovered for the first time from both the eyes of a child with conjunctivitis and its mother's cervix.[19] From then on, *C. trachomatis* was found repeatedly in women and men with nongonococcal genital infections, sometimes with complications such as salpingitis, urethritis or epididymitis. Chlamydia are nonmotile, Gram-negative, obligate intracellular bacteria. They replicate within the cytoplasm of host cells, where they form characteristic inclusion bodies that can be seen under the light microscope after staining with iodine. They have restricted metabolic activity and are totally dependent on the host cells for their energy needs. They are susceptible to many broad-spectrum antibiotics.

Chlamydia infection of the conjunctiva, urethra or uterine cervix can be diagnosed by identifying inclusion bodies within infected host cells using light microscopy, iodine or immunofluorescence staining.[20] The use of fluorescein-conjugated monoclonal antibodies for cytological staining and visualisation of infectious elementary bodies was developed in the 1980s. Elementary bodies are the infectious forms seen in acute disease. They measure only 0.25–0.35 µm in diameter and have sharp, well-defined margins. In the hands of an experienced microscopist, fluorescence staining techniques are highly sensitive and specific.

The introduction of nucleic acid amplification methods in many clinical laboratories has increased the sensitivity of positive results and decreased the turn-around time. The COBAS Amplicor test for chlamydiae is based on amplifying **d**eoxyribo**n**ucleic **a**cid (DNA) specific for *C. trachomatis* using the **p**olymerase **c**hain **r**eaction (PCR). The fully automated procedure is highly sensitive in detecting chlamydial DNA in urethral and endocervical swab specimens. This is particularly useful for subclinical infection screening in asymptomatic individuals. At the same time, the extremely high specificity – 99.9% – means that a negative test rules out chlamydial infection, thus preventing misdirected therapy.

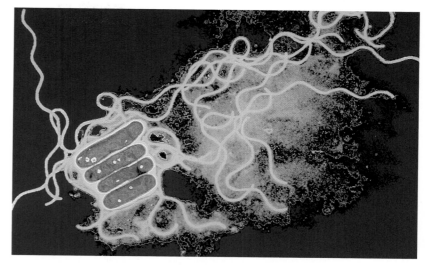

The bacterial pathogen of Legionnaires' disease, L. pneumophila.

Legionnaires' disease

On the Bicentennial of the United States Declaration of Independence in 1976, celebrations were scheduled throughout the summer. Philadelphia, the cradle of this historic event, was to be the centre of the festive activities. However, the occasion was dampened by community anxiety. Earlier in the year the newspapers had reported that the strain of influenza virus that had caused the devastating influenza pandemic of 1918 was very likely to return during the summer. Hence the panic when 182 members of the Pennsylvania American Legion who were attending a convention developed an acute respiratory illness and 29 of them died shortly after returning home.

Epidemiological and environmental data on the outbreak were minimal at the start of the investigation. Viral and various toxic causes were sought, the former because the clinical presentations closely resembled the pneumonia seen in severe influenza. A bacterial etiology was near the bottom of the list, except in the minds of a few astute infectious disease clinicians. The study of stained tissue sections of lung biopsies also pointed away from an acute bacterial agent, as the airways of most patients showed a preponderance of the immune cells known as macrophages. Although attention was soon directed at transmission via the drinking water and/or air-conditioning cooling towers, months went by, even with all the resources available to the Centers for Disease Control (CDC), before the causative agent was identified and remedial measures taken. Eventually, thanks to the persistence of Joseph McDade (b. 1940), the CDC was able to culture a previously unknown bacterium, given the name *Legionella pneumophila* in 1977,[21] from a single post-mortem biopsy specimen.

Initial attempts to recover the organism on embryonated eggs had failed, probably because the protocol required the inclusion of penicillin and streptomycin to suppress the growth of other microorganisms. McDade became interested in these inhibitory antibiotics and prepared cultures without them. After much trial and error, and the testing of a wide variety of culture media and new formulations, he and his colleagues developed buffered charcoal-yeast extract agar as the selective medium of choice for recovering *Legionella* species from clinical specimens.

In retrospect, several background factors could be related to the outbreak. For example, the water required to fill the air conditioning cooling towers was taken from nearby rivers and, when heated in the towers, was optimal for the growth of legionellae. Also, the outlets of the duct systems delivering cool air to the hotel rooms were often located above the head of the beds, creating a direct highway for the airborne pathogens to the unsuspecting sleepers.

Toxic shock syndrome

The bacteria known as Gram-positive cocci were discovered in 1880 by Alexander Ogston (1844–1929), a surgeon at the Aberdeen Royal Infirmary in Scotland, in an extended study of wound abscesses. He found that the inflammation and suppuration were caused by micrococci, which he observed in wound exudates.[22] He recognised two types of cocci: one, arranged in clusters, he named *Staphylococcus,* based on the Greek *staphylo* meaning a bunch of grapes; the other, arranged in chains, he named *Streptococcus.* He further observed that the first type surrounded itself with a fibrous capsule, like a castle

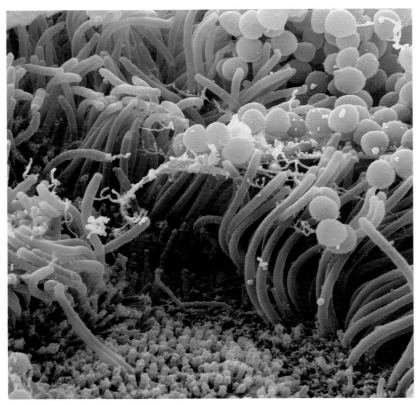

Staphylococci on nasal mucosa.

within a moat, producing lesions such as boils and carbuncles. The typical streptococcal infection was an acute suppurative inflammation which he called phlegmon. If the pus-producing organisms escaped from the inflammatory foci to circulate and multiply in the bloodstream, the result was septicemia.

The most recent staphylococcal syndrome is **t**oxic **s**hock **s**yndrome (TSS), first described in 1978.[23] An illness characterised by high fever, headache, confusion, conjunctival injection, a scarlatiniform rash, reduced urine output and low blood pressure was observed in seven children aged 8 to 17 years over a period of several months. They also showed varying degrees of sore throat, vomiting, watery diarrhea and shock, in all cases with fine desquamation of the affected skin, particularly on the palms and soles. Toxin-producing strains of *Staphylococcus aureus,* phage group 1, were isolated from various body sites in five cases.

Early in 1980 an additional 52 cases were reported to the CDC.[24] Females aged 13–52 years were almost exclusively affected. Striking associations were uncovered with the menstrual cycle – 38 of 40 women (95%) developed TSS within five days of starting a period.

We now know that the hemolytic bacterium *S. aureus* – normally a harmless resident of the human upper respiratory tract and skin – can also colonise blood and mucus in the vagina. A tampon concentrates this material, providing ideal conditions for the growth of staphylococci.[25] The symptoms of TSS are caused by the bacterial toxin known as **t**oxic **s**hock **s**yndrome **t**oxin 1 (TSST-1). An intriguing new concept was that the toxin functioned as a superantigen, bypassing the usual antigen-processing steps by mononuclear immune cells and binding directly to monocytes and lymphocytes. The result was a brutal immune reaction with systemic inflammatory effects. Chemical messengers such as lymphokines and monokines were directly released into the systemic circulation, explaining the low blood pressure and various multisystem manifestations of TSS. TSS has since been reported in males as well as females and in association with many other conditions, including staphylococcal abscesses, osteomyelitis,[26] postoperative wound infections, and post-influenza pneumonia.[27]

Gastritis and peptic ulcer

Classic textbooks listed many causes of gastric mucosal inflammation (gastritis) and peptic ulceration: individual predisposition, excess caffeine (coffee, tea) and/or alcohol, certain drugs (salicylates) and a variety of other stimuli to gastric acid production. In specific instances, any one of these may be involved. However, in most cases the cause is a microorganism, *Helicobacter pylori,* unidentified until 1982. Two Australians, gastroenterologist Barry Marshall (b. 1951) and pathologist J. Robin Warren (b. 1937), isolated and cultured spiral bacteria from gastric mucosal specimens of patients with chronic gastritis.[28]

In 1979 Warren, a pathologist at Royal Perth Hospital in Western Australia, noted spiral *Campylobacter*-like bacteria on histological sections from patients with gastritis. Over the next two years he routinely treated all gastric biopsy specimens with the selective Warthin-Starry silver stain until he had established a clear link between the curved bacteria and chronic gastritis. The gastric mucosal changes he found associated with these bacteria were epithelial cell damage, immune cell migration into the tissue, and increased mononuclear cells. However, the bacteria were difficult to culture. Following a report describing the recovery of a spiral bacterium from mouse intestinal mucosa, Marshall and Warren cultured the bacteria on chocolate agar.[29] Success depended on incubation in a jar containing a special oxygen-free gas mixture of 85% nitrogen, 10% hydrogen and 5% CO_2, continued over five days – a period gifted by serendipity: before leaving for the Easter weekend of 1982, the laboratory technicians forgot to destroy some culture vessels at the end of the 2-day culture period. Returning after a total of five days' incubation, Marshall and Warren were greeted by the culture which for months they had been trying to grow in two days.

A key biochemical characteristic that they also discovered was the profuse production of the enzyme urease, which splits urea into ammonium ions and carbon dioxide. The ammonium ions provide an alkaline buffer for the growing bacteria that protects them from the strong gastric acid.

Did these bacteria colonise the stomach in the wake of inflammation or did they cause the inflammation? To answer this question, Marshall and his New Zealand colleague Arthur Morris experimented heroically on themselves by swallowing first an acid inhibitor and then the bacterial cultures – with the result that Marshall developed acute, readily treatable, gastritis and Morris chronic gastritis which it took years to eradicate.[30]

Bacterial identification

Microbiology laboratories devised various schemes to improve identification of the ever increasing number of bacterial species. The best-known and most widely used identification grids were the King charts published by the CDC, based on the exhaustive work of Elizabeth O. King (1912–1966).

Although flow diagrams and grid systems are still widely used in clinical laboratories, several commercial identification systems have also been available since the 1960s. Microbiologists with long experience of conventional culture media and biochemical tests initially treated these kits as a curiosity. However, acceptance levels grew steadily. Common rapidly growing, biochemically active species, such as Enterobacteriaceae, could be identified much more easily and accurately with the commercial systems. Enterobacteria infect wounds and the urinary and respiratory tracts. Once the pathogen had been isolated on a selective medium, the strain can be identified using a commercial multitest system, such as Enterotube or API 20E.

Enterotube, introduced in 1971, was a pencil-shaped, self-contained, sterile, compartmented plastic tube containing eight different conventional media capable of performing eleven standard biochemical tests. Threaded through the centre of the tube was a needle that sequentially inoculated each compartment with a sample from an isolated colony of the test organism. Compartmental colour

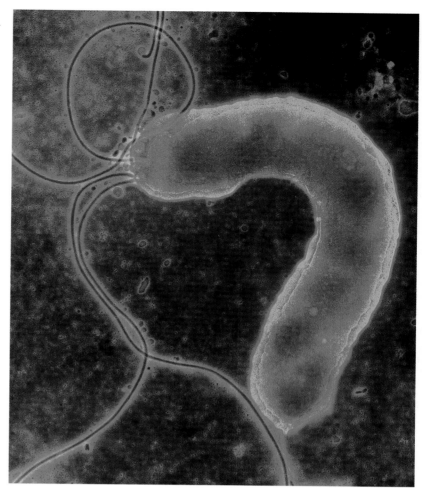

Helicobacter pylori, *the 'stomach bug'.*

reactions after 24-hour incubation were readily visible and were either read off the manufacturer's pattern recognition grid or given by a 4-digit biocode number derived by adding the numbers opposite the various compartments.

The first-generation Enterotube, for Enterobacteriaceae, was extended some two years later into the Oxi-Ferm system, targeting the more common non-fermentative and oxidase-positive Gram-negative bacilli. Its eight chambers included formulations of selective nutrient media designed to promote bacterial growth and detect various metabolic products. However, the Oxi-Ferm never enjoyed the widespread use or popularity of the Enterotube, as the reactions were often weak, producing fuzzy endpoints. Studies at the time managed to assign only two-thirds to three-quarters of isolates to genus and species.

The API 20E identification system, introduced shortly after the Enterotube, marked a major advance. It consisted of a plastic strip with 20 miniaturised cupules containing dehydrated substrates rather than the wet media of the Enterotube. De-

Barry Marshall *(b. 1951) (left) and* **Robin Warren** *(b. 1937) of the Royal Perth Hospital, Western Australia. The photograph was taken in 1984, shortly after they discovered the pathological significance of the stomach bacterium* Helicobacter pylori.

Elizabeth O. King *(1912–1966) joined a CDC diphtheria laboratory in 1948. Three years later she developed a strong interest in the Gram-negative bacteria associated with disease, particularly those not belonging to the family Enterobacteriaceae. Many of these species were poorly classified and their identification presented a particular challenge to clinical laboratories, a situation which she made up her mind to resolve. Her efforts resulted in the exhaustive King charts, which provide clinical microbiologists with valuable guidelines to the identification of the more elusive bacterial isolates.*

hydration was a breakthrough in miniaturised technology and significantly extended test shelf-life. All reactions were colour-coded and were either read off from the manufacturer's grid matrix identification table or given by a seven-digit biocode number.

Several additional miniaturised systems came onto the market. Although as a group these packaged, self-contained identification systems represented an important advance over the cumbersome and poorly standardised conventional plate and tube media systems, many laboratories have come to use them less and less, given the availability of larger automated systems.

Automated identification

The United States space programme was a shot in the arm for diagnostic microbiology. The National Aeronautics and Space Administration (NASA) was concerned that the astronauts might bring a deadly 'Andromeda strain' back from the moon. To forestall such an eventuality, it was essential to intercept the pathogen before the spaceship re-entered the earth's atmosphere. NASA therefore commissioned the aerospace manufacturer, McDonnell Douglas, to develop a compact microbiological test system for the automated on-board detection, identification and susceptibility testing of potential pathogens picked up on the moon walk.

The response was a piece of plastic barely larger than a credit card with several rows of tiny compartments having a total capacity of 30 tests. Each compartment contained reagent reacting with a specific bacterial metabolite, accessed via a pore-sized opening for the injection of a couple of microlitres of fluid inoculum, usually urine. On reaching each compartment, the fluid dissolved the reagent, initiating the process of metabolite detection. The card was then inserted into a reader which identified the organism by integrating all the reactions into a computer program.

The card became the core of the **AntiMicrobic System** (AMS) marketed by McDonnell Douglas after expiry of the NASA contract. As the first automated bacterial identification and antimicrobial susceptibility test system, it was the forerunner of the current Vitek System and a major breakthrough in its day, accelerating turnaround times and the delivery of informed and effective antimicrobial therapy.

Antimicrobial susceptibility testing

The inspiration for antimicrobial susceptibility testing is generally credited to Sir Alexander Fleming (1881–1955) and his famous observation in 1929 that the growth of *Staphylococcus* colonies was inhibited in the vicinity of a colony of *Penicillium notatum*. The following decade saw the development of the disk diffusion test in which filter paper disks impregnated with a concentration of antibiotic were laid over a culture plate. The disks surrounded by a zone of inhibited growth were those containing an antibiotic to which the test organism was 'sensitive'; no zone meant that the organism was resistant. After several modifications, Professors William M. M. Kirby (1914–1997), Alfred W. Bauer (1923–1998) and associates at the University of Washington in Seattle standardised a test endorsed by the FDA that serves as the basis for the Kirby-Bauer test still used today.[31]

Macrodilution method

By the 1970's, the near-logarithmic proliferation of new antibiotics and the increased difficulty of treating infections in the growing population of immunosuppressed patients highlighted the need for a more sophisticated and labour-saving susceptibility test system for estimating an antibiotic's minimum inhibitory concentration (MIC), defined as the lowest concentration of antibiotic that inhibits bacterial growth in a test culture. Knowing an antibiotic's MIC value for a susceptible pathogen provides an accurate guide to dose. Macrodilution was the first method used to determine the MIC.

Microdilution method

However, macrodilution proved too cumbersome for the high-volume needs of larger clinical laboratories. It was displaced by microdilution in 96-well polystyrene trays. This method, officially introduced in 1977 by Clyde Thornsberry and coworkers at the CDC in Atlanta, Georgia, defines the MIC as the value in the last well showing visible inhibition of bacterial growth.

The Epsilometer (E-test)

The widely used Epsilometer, or E-test, manufactured by AB Biodisk in Sweden, bridges the gap between disk diffusion and automated dilution for determining the MIC. As in the disk diffusion test, an organism suspension is evenly streaked onto a plate. An 'E-strip' impregnated with antibiotic at increasing concentrations is then laid in the centre of the plate. After incubation for 18 hours the MIC is read

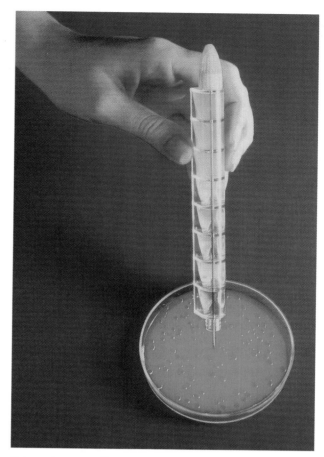

Enterotube, a self-contained bacterial identification system launched by Roche in 1971.

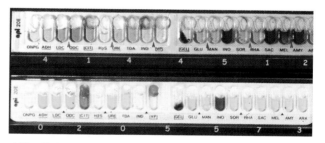

API 20E identification strips from Analytab Products Inc. The miniaturised kit system contains dried pre-reduced substrates for identifying members of the family Enterobacteriaceae. Along the bottom of each strip are the biocode numbers, each derived from octal conversions of the substrate reactions within each triplet between the arrows. The organism was then 'decoded', i.e. identified, using the manufacturer's handbook.

from the point at which the zone of growth inhibition intersects with the strip. Since only one antibiotic can be tested per strip, the E-test is not cost-effective for testing multiple drugs. However, it has proven effective in specific situations requiring an MIC result for a given antibiotic against a given test organism, notably certain anaerobes and species of yeasts.

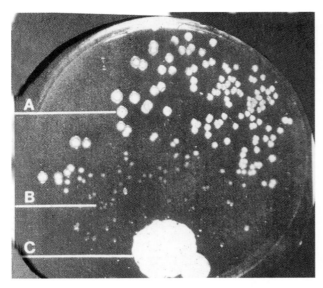

Agar plate on which Sir Alexander Fleming in 1929 observed the inhibitory effect of the contaminant mould Penicillium notatum on the growth of staphylococci. **A**: viable growing staphylococcal colonies; **B**: colony lysis in the zone in which the fungal colonies (**C**) have produced antibiotic substances. Fleming's discovery launched the new technology of antimicrobial susceptibility testing.

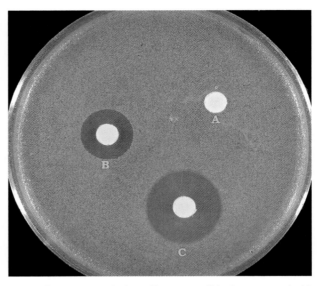

Disk diffusion test with three filter paper disks impregnated with different antibiotics, one showing resistance (no zone of inhibition, **A**), another sensitivity (wide zone of inhibition, **C**) and the third an intermediate reaction (medium zone of inhibition, **B**).

Automated antibiotic susceptibility test systems

The first MicroScan instrument, the TouchScan, was operated manually. Results derived from a pattern of positive and negative reactions visualised by the operator in incubated microtitre trays were keyed in via a dial pad. This was the starting point for several series of AutoScan instruments offering organism identifications within seconds. The panels were incubated off-line, then inserted into the instrument for consistent standardised identifications. The main users were smaller laboratories. The latest generation MicroScan is the WalkAway, which literally automates incubation, reagent addition and data interpretation using standard microdilution trays read photometrically (overnight) or fluorometrically (short incubation), generating substantial labour savings.

The Sensititre Automated Microbiology System offers a full range of user options from manual and semi-automated to fully automated reader output. Like the AutoScan range, it uses standard microdilution trays, a video plate reading system, and a robotic system that positions the incubated trays under the photometer or fluorimeter, depending on the application. The ability to upgrade from manual to automated applications – depending on laboratory need and budget – is a distinct advantage of the modular design.

Nonculture techniques

The diagnostic applications of antigen/antibody reactions grew out of several investigations of immunity in the 1870s and 1880s that focused on the recognition of mysterious properties or substances in the bloodstream and body fluids of animals inoculated with attenuated viruses and live bacteria. In 1891 the zoologist, microbiologist and later Nobel laureate Ilya Ilyich Mechnikov (1845–1916) observed that certain body cells incorporated infective material and destroyed it by a process of intracellular digestion that he called phagocytosis. In 1889 Behring and Kitasato discovered substances active against diphtheria and tetanus toxin. Émile Roux (1853–1933) and Yersin confirmed their observation of these 'antitoxins' the same year, prompting the use of neutralising antitoxins to combat the morbidity and mortality of infection with several bacterial pathogens.

Also in 1889, Albert Charrin (1856–1907) and a colleague found that *Pseudomonas aeruginosa* cultured with serum from animals that had recovered from induced *P. aeruginosa* infection formed clumps that sank to the bottom of the test tube. The diagnostic potential of this finding became apparent later in the year, when Fernand Widal (1862–1929) added a uniform suspension of actively motile typhoid bacteria to a small quantity of serum from an animal previously injected with the same bacteria. Motility was instantly arrested, the suspension forming clumps visible to the naked eye. Widal's reaction – bacterial clumping on exposure to specific immune serum, later called agglutination – was to become a cornerstone in bacterial identification.

In 1894 Richard Pfeiffer (1858–1926), while serving as professor of hygiene in Königsberg, demonstrated that cholera vibrios were destroyed in vitro in the serum of animals immunized against cholera. He further demonstrated that cholera bacilli disappear in the peritoneal fluid of animals previously immunised with this organism, a process known as 'Pfeiffer phenomenon'. Pfeiffer regarded the active agent as a kind of pro-ferment that became converted into a ferment or enzyme in the body of the living animal. This lytic action could also be demonstrated against red blood cells, causing them to hemolyse. Both actions could be eliminated by heating the serum to 55 °C, indicating the presence of a thermolabile substance.

Jules Bordet (1870–1961), a Belgian bacteriologist working in the Pasteur Institute in Paris, characterised the role of this unknown thermo-labile factor, later termed 'complement'. For this pioneering work, he received the 1919 Nobel Prize. Bordet also discovered that complement binds to antigen-antibody complexes (so-called complement fixation) to produce antibody-mediated immunity.

In 1897 Rudolf Kraus (1868–1932), director of the State Serotherapeutic Institute in Vienna, demonstrated an additional property of immune serum. The injection of experimental animals with clear filtrate from liquid cultures of cholera, typhoid or plague bacteria produced specific substances in the animals' serum that in turn precipitated the bacteria when these were mixed in vitro with the inoculatory filtrate. This precipitation reaction formed the basis of the precipitin test. It had thus become clearly established by the end of the 19th century that antigen injection into an animal was followed by the appearance of serum antibodies. Antibodies varied in type but were always specific to the eliciting antigen, defined by reaction-specific components of the bacterial cell wall.

The first agglutination tests used bacterial cells in suspension as the endpoint for determining if a specific antibody was present in the test sample. These direct agglutination tests included the Weil-Felix test for diagnosing rickettsial disease (using a *Proteus* species that has cross-reacting antigens on the cell surface), the Widal test for typhoid fever, and the brucellosis test devised by the Danish veterinarian Bernhard Laurits Frederik Bang (1848–1932).

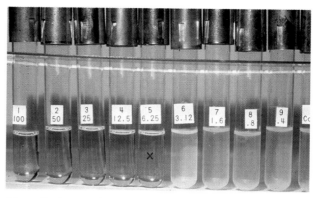

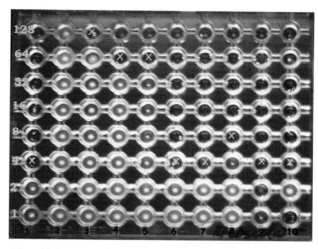

Macrodilution test for determining the lowest concentration of antibiotic producing visible inhibition of bacterial growth (minimum inhibitory concentration, MIC). Here the MIC reads 6.25 µg/ml.

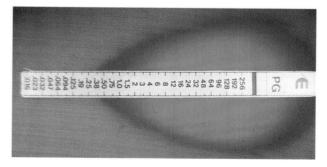

Microdilution assay in a 96-well polystyrene tray. The numbers across the abscissa at the bottom represent different antibiotics; those along the ordinate to the left are the concentrations of the serially antibiotic dilutions in each well. Yellow X: antibiotic MICs.

Epsilometer (E-test) for determining MIC by the gradient diffusion technique. The MIC in this case is 0.38 µg/ml, read at the point at which the lowest part of the ellipse of growth inhibition transects the filter paper strip.

For many years these and subsequent agglutination tests were included in a febrile agglutinin panel for diagnosing febrile illness.

They were soon superseded, however, by direct particle-agglutination tests in which antigens or antibodies were attached to the surfaces of inert

Latex agglutination. Right: particle aggregation typical of a positive test. Left: negative test.

particulate carriers. For example, many antigens adsorbed directly onto the surface of red blood cells. This formed the basis for a variety of hemagglutination tests, many of which are still used today. However, because red cells deteriorated unless specially treated, inert particles appeared more practical candidates as antigen carriers in agglutination tests. Latex particles, for example, were uniformly smooth, unlike the irregular and rough clay particles used in many agglutination tests. The 0.18 µM polystyrene latex particles used for calibration in electron microscopy were found to adsorb **immunoglobulin G** (IgG) onto their surfaces. This observation led to the development of latex agglutination tests for the direct diagnosis of infectious disease by identifying type-specific antigens in the test sample.

Later the use of certain strains of *S. aureus* as the antibody carrier was investigated to avoid certain problems with latex particles. The protein outer coat of *S. aureus* (protein A) readily and directly combines with the receptor-binding Fc region of the IgG molecule. The coat is also less affected by nonspecific reactions from stray proteins in the sample. In what became known as coagglutination tests, serological reagents were subsequently developed using bacterial cells as carriers which adsorbed a variety of ligands[32] onto their surface.

Current technology thus diagnoses many infectious diseases without resorting to culture confirmation. The serological era in microbiological diagnostics dates back to the Wasserman reaction, which inaugurated a long line of agglutinating, precipitating and complement-fixing antigen/antibody tests, many of which are still in use today.

Immunoassays

The development of technologies leading to the modern use of immunoassay has been a particularly important feature of the last several decades, and is hence the subject of a separate chapter of this book.

The technique is based on tagging antibodies with a label that allows antigen detection, either visually or through the use of semi-automated and automated instruments. Variants of the technology are particularly useful for typing bacterial strains.

Bacterial strain typing

Infection control practitioners often need laboratory assistance to complement their investigations. Clinicians may want to know the strain of a certain pathogen they have cultured, to determine if it represents relapse of an old infection or a new episode caused by a different bacterial strain. The term 'strain' has long been used for organisms or homogeneous populations of organisms that can be differentiated within a given species. It reflects the heterogeneity within a given species. Strain typing has recently taken on a new dimension in the recognition and classification of the bacterial agents of bioterrorism.

Nucleic acid typing methods

Strain typing using PCR analysis of nucleic acid is highly accurate and differs from conventional methods in several respects. Conventional methods, for example, invariably require culture of the strains concerned whereas DNA typing is performed directly on the clinical specimen. Also, certain bacterial strains are untypable by conventional methods because they lack or have lost the relevant cell-surface receptors, whereas molecular typing bypasses these phenotypic characteristics by focussing solely on the differences in genomic sequence. Only molecular typing can therefore detect silent mutations involving changes in nucleotide sequence but no phenotypic effect. This is an important advantage as a silent mutation can inactivate the recognition site of a restriction enzyme, in turn affecting any additional tests that depend on this enzyme for cutting nucleic acids. Another merit of molecular typing is that it identifies conserved or species-specific genomic sequences that may then be used in the design of targets for other DNA-based methods. Nucleic acid-based typing methods have increased almost exponentially in number and diversity over the past decade.

Prions

Hidden in this skein of technology old and new is a new challenge with an as yet relatively low profile, the 'prion'. We can sympathise with the frustration microbiologists and chemists must have felt in the late 19th century when they became aware that bac-

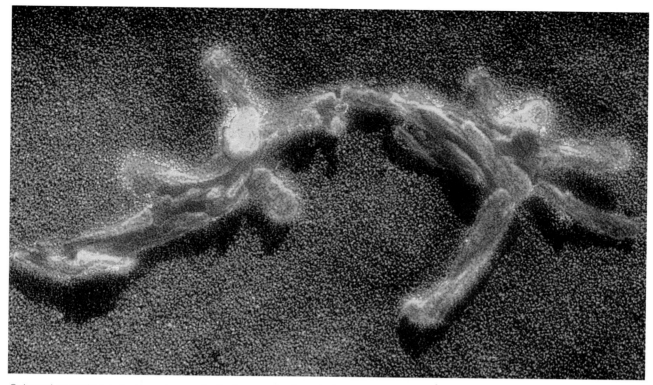

Coloured transmission electron micrograph of prion proteins from the brain of a TSE-infected hamster.

teria, fungi and unicellular parasites were not the smallest agents of infectious disease. Despite careful filtration of contaminated fluid, disease could still be transferred to a new host via an unknown filterable agent, the virus. Today we are in a similar situation. A type of self-replicating protein, called a prion, has been discovered which is relatively resistant to protein-degrading enzymes (proteases), and which accumulates in the brains of people with a degenerative brain disease known as transmissible spongiform encephalopathy (TSE).

Heating to 90 °C inactivates viruses, but does not affect prions. Similarly, radiation damages viral genomes, but does not harm prions. Certain enzyme treatments destroy DNA and RNA, but not prions. However, agents such as phenol that denature proteins also destroy prions, prompting the hypothesis that we are dealing with a self-replicating protein that contains neither DNA nor RNA. The American Nobel laureate Stanley B. Prusiner (b. 1942) coined the term 'prion' from the phrase 'proteinaceous infectious particle' as an easier to pronounce variant of the more obvious abbreviation 'proin'.[33]

How can there be transmissible self-replicating information that is not coded in the primary amino acid sequence? Prions apparently represent a life form differing from anything with which we are so far familiar. Intensive research is underway to unlock the mysteries of this newly discovered entity.

Prions are proteins that are part of the normal plasma membrane of mammalian brain cells and other cell types. Research indicates that this usually harmless protein has been incorrectly folded, possibly from mutation, resulting in a **pr**ion **p**rotein (PrP). These PrPs on a cell stick together, forming fibres that cannot be incorporated into the plasma membrane. Loss of normal membrane function then leads to cell death. Transmission from human to human, animal to human, or animal to animal may occur through the ingestion of infected tissue. In past times, eating the brains of deceased relatives was a ritual widely practised in Papua New Guinea. Recent 'mad cow' disease in parts of Britain and elsewhere is most likely related to the ingestion of prion protein in feeds supplemented with rendered prion-infected sheep and cattle. Formal diagnosis of TSE in humans is currently only possible in post-mortem brain tissue.

Predicting the future?

The scientist is barely more qualified than the philosopher or poet when it comes to predicting the evolution of diagnostic microbiology. There is no way we can foresee where the infinite separation and sequencing of DNA and RNA codes will eventually lead us. Even less can we predict the strategies which microorganisms may yet evolve to ensure their survival and further development.

Elmer W. Koneman

The fungus among us

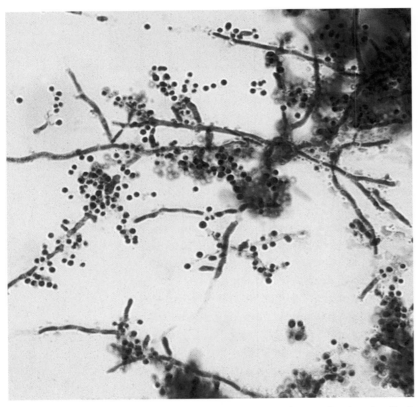

Photomicrograph of a mount of Trichophyton mentagrophytes, *showing the 'finely interlaced narrow septate mycelia, within which characteristic swellings appear', as first described by Gruby from his microscopic observations.*

Fungal plant diseases were known in early times, and mushrooms were used for food – at times to the dismay of the poor souls who suffered from life-threatening poisoning. There is evidence that an etymologist long ago derived the word 'fungus' from the Latin *funus*, meaning 'funeral'. However, more exacting taxonomists have traced the origin to the Greek word *sphongis*, meaning 'sponge', evidently from the appearance of certain mushrooms, or perhaps of certain plant diseases caused by fungi. Knowledge of fungal disease dates back to ancient Greece and Rome. The infection of the scalp that we call favus (or honeycomb ringworm) was known to Aulus Cornelius Celsus (c. 30 BC – AD 38), perhaps the greatest of the Roman medical writers, who, in his classic treatise *De medicina*, first described this condition.

The roots of diagnostic mycology go back to 1834. Agostino Bassi (1773–1856), after several years of work and many failed experiments, finally convinced the professors at the University of Pavia that a fungus was the cause of the dread disease of silkworms known as *calcino* (or *muscardine*), which threatened to close down the silk industries in Italy and France. He called the fungus *Botrytis bassiana*, although it is now known as *Beauveria bassiana*. But in an era when the doctrine of spontaneous generation was still prevalent, convincing the professors of this relationship was no easy task. Silkworm disease was attributed by all but a few critical thinkers to circumstantial factors, such as the changing state of the atmosphere, the poor quality of food being used, or unfavourable methods of silkworm breeding.

But only a few years later, in 1837, Robert Remak (1815–1865), a medical practitioner in Berlin, first recognised mould filaments in the skin crusts of a

Agostino Bassi *(1773–1856), the Italian bacteriologist who identified the fungal cause of muscardine disease in silkworms. He is also widely considered to be the founder of the parasitic theory of infection.*

David Gruby *(1810–1898), who identified the underlying fungal nature of several diseases, such as favus infection of the skin, caused by* Trichophyton mentagrophytes, *and thrush in infants, caused by the fungus he named* Oidium albicans.

patient with favus. He observed spherical bodies and branched threads in microscopic preparations but did not immediately appreciate their causal role. Two years later Johann Schönlein (1793–1864) first identified favus as a fungal disease, a finding subsequently proved by Remak himself. Having injected some material from one of his patient's lesions into his own skin, Remak observed the progression of a typical favus infection. In honour of his colleague, Remak named this fungus *Achorion schoenleinii* (it is now called *Trichophyton schoenleinii).*

In 1842 the fungal nature of favus was also described by David Gruby (1810–1898), who at that time was working in Paris. More importantly, however, he elucidated the etiology of ringworm of the beard. The causative agent was described by Gruby as follows:

> In order to recognize the true tinea (favus), microscopic examination is adequate. A small amount of crust is collected and smashed in a drop of pure water. The preparation is placed between two glass slides and observed at 300-fold magnification. One will see a large number of round to oblong corpuscles $1/300$ to $1/100$ of a millimeter long and $1/300$ to $1/150$ of a millimeter wide. They are transparent with a smooth surface, are either without color or slightly yellowish and contain only one substance. One also notes articulated filaments of a diameter of $1/1000$ to $1/250$ of a millimeter, transparent and colorless. The general shape of these filaments is cylindrical or branched depending on the part of the crust with which they are associated.[1]

In 1843 Gruby further linked the contagious human scalp infection tinea capitis to a fungus he named *Microsporum audouinii,* in honour of Victor Audouin, the director of the Natural History Museum in Paris. Gruby studied infected hairs from

patients with *M. audouinii* and found that they were covered on the outside with spores. He also observed that, at the point where it emerges from the skin, the hair shaft becomes greyish and breaks off within eight days. As more hairs are so affected, the patient is left with a patch of alopecia. Another important contribution by Gruby was to establish the fungal nature of *muguet* or thrush in infants. This condition is caused by the fungus he named *Oidium albicans* (now called *Candida albicans),* one of the more common fungal isolates recovered from clinical specimens. Gruby's work was challenged by many scientists, some of whom believed that ringworm infections were caused by animal parasites. Ultimately, Gruby's observations – that various dermatophytic fungi, rather than animal parasites, were the underlying cause of these skin infections – were confirmed by Raymond J. A. Sabouraud (1864–1938), the eminent Parisian dermatologist. Sabouraud was a multitalented Renaissance man who may have been more famous as a sculptor and for his book on Montaigne than for his scientific achievements. At the Third International Congress of Dermatology, held in London in August 1896, he lectured for a whole afternoon on *Trichophyton* ringworm infections. Whether there was any connection between his status as a world expert on scalp diseases and the baldness of his own pate is open to conjecture. On this occasion Sabouraud exhibited over 300 cultures from various patients with ringworm infections. This was the man who introduced peptone dextrose agar for the cultivation of fungi, a growth medium that still bears his name and a modification of which is widely used in diagnostic microbiology laboratories today.

Emergence of diagnostic mycology

The modern era of diagnostic mycology began in 1936 with the work of Chester Emmons, a mycologist serving with the United States Department of Health. He established a sound taxonomic classification for the three dermatophyte species, *Microsporum, Trichophyton,* and *Epidermophyton,* as well as other fungal species. Although the two fungal diseases, coccidioidomycosis and histoplasmosis, were discovered near the turn of the 20th century, the dimorphic nature of the fungus was not appreciated until 1940; that is, the appearance of a mould form when cultivated at room temperature and a yeast form at incubator or body temperature. This observation provided an important initial clue for future identification of the dimorphic fungi, which cause the majority of disseminated fungal infections in humans.

Interest in clinical mycology increased greatly following the Second World War. Norman F. Conant (b. 1908), a mycologist at Duke University School of Medicine, North Carolina, developed an ongoing summer course in medical mycology that inspired researchers throughout the world. In 1944 he published the *Manual of Clinical Mycology,* a universally used text that not only raised the standard of medical mycology to new heights but established the foundations of laboratory practices that are still employed today.

Modern mycology laboratory practices

The preliminary identification of fungi is based on observation of the morphology of colonies grown on culture media. This is generally sufficient to distinguish yeasts from filamentous moulds. Yeast colonies are smooth, pasty in consistency and usually white to buff-yellow in colour. The identification of mould colonies is based on their rate of growth, surface morphology, the appearance of the reverse of the colony, and on whether or not pigment is seen. Surface morphology is described using terms such as 'cottony', 'fluffy', 'woolly', 'sugary' or 'granular', with the appearance depending on the degree of sporulation. Pigments range from white to yellow, buff, brown, green, green-blue, lavender, orange, red and black. Colonies that are black both on the surface and on the reverse side are immediately included in the dark, or dematiaceous, group. Colonies may have irregular or radial folds, known as rugae.

Microscopic preparations for direct examination may be made by teasing a small portion of the colony into a drop of saline on a glass slide. Lactophenol aniline blue stain is often used to improve visibility of the colourless filamentous hyphae and the fruiting bodies. Many laboratories prepare a transparent ('Scotch') tape mount, in which the sticky side is gently pressed to the surface of the colony, and the tape then stretched over a drop of lactophenol aniline blue on a glass slide.

Presumptive or definitive genus/species identifications are made by observing one or more of the above-described preparations under the microscope. The nature of the hyphae is first examined. Submerged hyphae are called vegetative; those that extend upwards from the surface of the agar are called aerial. Hyphae may be divided by cross-walls, or septa, in which case they are termed septate, in contrast to aseptate species. The hyphae of the dematiaceous moulds display varying degrees of yellow-brown pigmentation.

Fruiting bodies: an aid to identification

More precise identifications are based on the nature of the fruiting bodies. Many fungi form spores within confined structures such as sporangia. Other fungi produce asexual spores, called conidia (from a Greek word meaning 'dust'), which are shed from specialised cells known as phialides on the surface of the fruiting body. Conidia may be borne in chains, in clusters or singly, each of which is an important observation in making a presumptive identification. Spores and conidia vary in shape, size, arrangement and pigmentation. Macroconidia are often multicelled and are formed from the hyphae in clearly recognisable patterns.

Detection of antigens

In cases where microscopic identification is not possible because the typical spore-forming fruiting bodies cannot be observed, an exoantigen test is performed. Fungal hyphae produce cell-free antigens, known as exoantigens, which can be extracted by overlaying the surface of the primary culture with a 1:5000 solution of thimerosal, followed by overnight incubation. The surface fluid is then aspirated, concentrated and placed in microimmunodiffusion wells opposite reference antigens and antibodies representative of the fungal species being tested. After incubation for 24 hours the preparation is observed for the presence of telltale lines between the sample well and its complementary antibody well.

Biochemical tests

Few biochemical tests are helpful in identifying fungi. *Aspergillus fumigatus,* for example, cannot be

A case study

Let us suppose that you have recently consulted a doctor because of intermittent sharp pain in the upper right of your chest, particularly aggravated on taking a deep breath. You have had a mild cough for some time but did not become concerned until one morning when you spat up some blood. In contrast to the usual patient, who only sees the doctor but not what happens to a specimen after it is collected, we will take you on a behind-the-scenes tour of your local diagnostic mycology laboratory. Although in some cases the diagnosis of a fungal lung infection can be made by obtaining a culture of sputum, in your case the chest X-ray reveals a solid mass in the right upper lobe of the lung, appearing to be within a cavity. The French call this type of appearance *grelot*, referring to the bell-like image with a 'clapper' inside. Your doctor explains that you have a 'fungus ball', which means that a fungal colony is growing within a pre-existing cavity. You confirm that many years ago you had a bout of tuberculosis, which you thought was healed. The doctor goes on to explain that you have inhaled some fungal spores, probably from contaminated dust, with a few spores finding their way into your old tubercular cavity via an open air passage.

In order to identify the fungal species, an aspiration biopsy of the fungus ball is performed. The aspirate is sent both to the pathology laboratory for histological examination and to the mycology laboratory for culture. In the mycology laboratory the specimen is inoculated onto the surface of a Sabouraud's dextrose agar plate. The inoculated plate is then placed in an incubator set at 30 °C. As most fungi take several hours to grow, the plate will not be examined until 48 hours have passed.

In the meantime the pathologist has had the opportunity to analyse the stained histological sections, observing a club-shaped expansion of a hyphal strand, a structure known as a vesicle. On the top half of the vesicle is a row of short cells that are producing spores. These spore-bearing cells are called phialides. The structure bears a distinct resemblance to the device used in churches to sprinkle holy water, known as an aspergillum (from the Latin *aspergere*, meaning 'to sprinkle'). The pathologist identifies a species of *Aspergillus*. Two days later the green, granular colonies of this fungus have grown in culture. Under the microscope the aspergillum structures are now readily recognisable. A diagnosis is made of *Aspergillus fumigatus* – one of the fungi more commonly recovered from fungus ball infections of the lung. A treatment plan is drawn up.

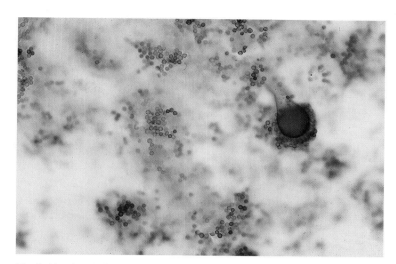

The fruiting head of Aspergillus fumigatus, *with its club-shaped vesicle and a row of spore-bearing phialides, resembling the device used for sprinkling holy water (aspergillum).*

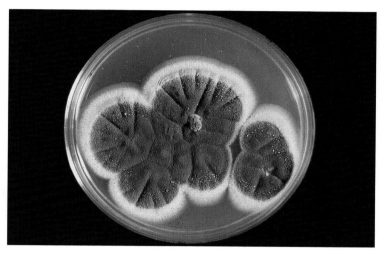

Colony of Aspergillus fumigatus *after incubation for 72–96 hours at 30 °C on Sabouraud's dextrose agar.*

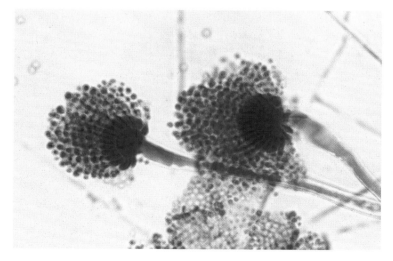

A fruiting body of Aspergillus fumigatus *viewed under the microscope in a lactophenol blue mount prepared from the surface of a colony.*

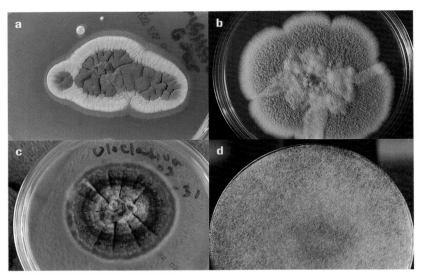

Colonies of various filamentous moulds. **a**) A fluffy colony producing a wine-red water-soluble pigment that is diffusing into the surrounding agar. **b**) A granular colony similar to that seen with the Aspergillus fumigatus *recovered in the case study.* **c**) A dark brown to black woolly colony suggestive of one of the dark or dematiaceous moulds. The reverse side is typically jet black. **d**) A rapidly growing woolly colony of a zygomycete, typically growing from border to border in the culture dish. Observation of these colony types is helpful in making a provisional genus/species identification.

A typical yeast colony growing on the surface of an agar plate. The colonies are smooth, yellow to pink in colour and typically have a pasty to mucoid consistency.

identified by tests of this kind. Most commonly, biochemical tests are used to identify yeasts. The selective fermentation and assimilation of carbohydrates are particularly useful for distinguishing different yeast species within a given genus. In the past, studies of this type were performed in conventional tubes containing the various carbohydrates to be measured. Currently several self-contained kits are available, including the Uni-Yeast Tek plate.

Both the exoantigen extraction test and biochemical assays provide rapid identification of young cultures, i. e. prior to the onset of sporulation, as observed microscopically using conventional culture techniques. Often a definitive diagnosis can be made from the results of biochemical tests many days before the telltale spores are produced, permitting the initiation of a definitive course of therapy based on knowledge of the genus and species of the causative agent.

Serological diagnosis

Lastly, fungal infection can be diagnosed by demonstrating circulating antibodies in blood specimens. This technique is only successful in cases where antibodies are actually produced as a result of a fungal infection. However, particularly for infections caused by dimorphic species, it can be very helpful in establishing a diagnosis when conventional culture methods fail. The serological procedures most commonly used for the detection of serum antibodies are complement fixation, immunodiffusion and ELISA (**e**nzyme-**l**inked **i**mmuno**s**orbent **a**ssay).

In order to determine whether a fungus infection is active, it is most helpful to demonstrate at least a fourfold increase in antibody titre over a baseline value. This can be done by comparing the titres determined for blood samples drawn approximately three weeks apart.

Antifungal susceptibility testing

In cases where therapy proves ineffective, an antifungal susceptibility test may be performed. Ideally an in vitro antifungal susceptibility test should provide a reliable measure of the relative activity of the drug being tested, correlate with in vivo response and predict the likely outcome of therapy. It should also serve to monitor for emerging resistance. Much progress in antifungal susceptibility testing was made in the 1990s through the efforts of the National Committee for Clinical Laboratory Standards (NCCLS). First of all a standard procedure was established for testing yeasts, particularly *Candida* species, against fluconazole and itraconazole. Interpretive breakpoints for *Candida* species were also defined. This was an important step forward, making it possible to achieve some degree of consistency in results from different laboratories.[2]

Unfortunately, in the case of the *Aspergillus* mould, developing standardised procedures for antifungal susceptibility testing has been more difficult. The chief problem is how to produce a standard inoculum of conidia and sporangiospore suspensions without significant interference from hyphal fragments that may enter into the suspension. The degree of sporulation varies between species and strains, making it difficult to obtain a standard suspension.

On the horizon are methods serving to shorten the time between the onset of symptoms and the administration of directed therapy. By identifying fungal nucleic acid sequences after **p**olymerase **c**hain **r**eaction (PCR) amplification a definitive diagnosis can be made without the need for culture.

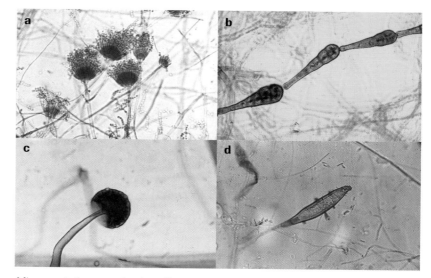

*Microscopic features of various filamentous moulds. **a**) Fruiting heads of an* Aspergillus *species. **b**) Large, multicelled spores described as muriform because of their resemblance to the façade of a stonemason's wall (Latin* murus*); characteristic of* Alternaria *species. **c**) Spores enclosed in a bag-like structure called a sporangium; characteristic of one of the Zygomyces species. **d**) Large, multicelled conidia known as macroconidia. The macroconidium shown here is characteristic of* Microsporum canis. *The sizes, shapes, internal structures and arrangements of spores are observed by mycologists in order to establish a genus/species identification.*

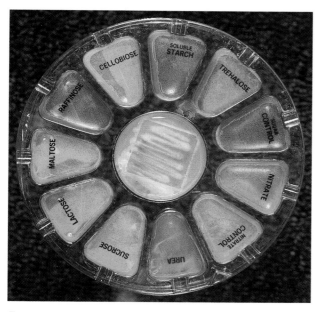

The Uni-Yeast Tek 'wheel' (Remel Laboratories, Lenexa, Kansas, USA), one of the commercial systems available for the identification of yeasts. The peripheral compartments contain various culture media substrates; the central well contains cornmeal agar, which can be inoculated for microscopic observation of growth patterns. Each of the peripheral compartments is inoculated through a small pore with the yeast suspension to be examined. After incubation, the colour reactions observed in these compartments provide a biochemical profile from which yeast genus/species identifications can be made.

Elmer W. Koneman

Living worms in living flesh

The diagnosis of parasitic diseases

FRANCESCO   REDI
ARETINO   CELEBERRIMO
FILOSOFO,   E POETA.
nato a 18.Febb.ͤ MDCXXVI.   m.ͭ in PISA p.ͤ Mar.ᵒ MDCXCVII
Dedicato al merito sing:ͤ dell' Ill.ᵐᵒ Sig.ͬ Cav.ͬ Ignazio Redi
dell'Ord.ͤ di S. Stefano Patrizio Aretino Pronipote del suͤ:
Preso da un Quadro esistente nell' Imperial Galleria di Firenze.

*The Italian scientist and poet **Francesco Redi** (1626–1697) was personal physician to the Grand Duke of Tuscany. In 1668 he demonstrated experimentally that maggots do not develop on putrefying meat that has been carefully protected from flies, thereby disproving the theory of spontaneous generation. In flasks containing meat and fish which were covered with very fine Neapolitan muslin and placed inside a wooden frame also covered with muslin, Redi showed that no maggots appeared despite the large numbers of flies on the frame. Maggots were however observed to develop from eggs laid by the flies on the cloth. Redi thus convincingly refuted the notion that maggots arise spontaneously in meat.*

Francesco Redi (1626–1697) has been called the father of parasitology, an honour he earned in 1671 by publishing the first book exclusively devoted to the subject: *Osservazioni intorno agli animali viventi che si trovano negli animali viventi*. Having collected a wide variety of impressions and unfounded theories concerning the nature of parasites, he produced an illustrated scientific work that was far ahead of its time. Redi had an advanced knowledge of ectoparasites and studied in particular the effects of lice on animals and humans. He discovered many new parasite species by dissecting diseased animals and was among the first to recognise that ascaris worms are hermaphrodites. He was also among the first to illustrate the scolex (holdfast) of a tapeworm. As court physician to the Grand Duke of Tuscany, Redi undoubtedly had access to a library containing many earlier writings. His attention may have been drawn to an account of people living along the shores of the Red Sea in ancient times who suffered from stinging sensations under the skin of the arms and legs. He may also have read the views of Galen (129 – c. 216), who had recognised a link with Guinea worm infestation but attributed the malady to a 'nervous concretion'. His scientific mind may have been bemused by the Old Testament account of how 'the Lord sent fiery serpents among the people, and they bit the people, and much people of Israel died.' He undoubtedly could visualise clearly in his mind the bladder worm cysts (found on the tongue in pigs) that were likened to hailstones by Aristotle (384–322 BC). He may have been puzzled by accounts of toothaches being caused by 'toothworms' and sudden death by 'heart worms', and entertained by the Chinese maxim that one should harbour at least three worms to remain in good health.

The science of parasitology was further advanced by Nicolas Andry (1658–1742), who presented an early, primitive classification of parasites in his important text *De la génération des vers dans le corps de l'homme.*[1] As a physician, he also dealt with the signs and symptoms of worm infestations, which were divided into two types – intestinal and extraintestinal. The book includes advice on how to avoid infections with worms: breathe good air and eat good food, avoiding certain items such as melons, sugary food and especially vinegar, which is frequently 'full of worms and their seeds'. It also includes the pithy observation that 'one cannot hope to avoid worms after death but can hope to do so during life.' Andry distinguished three types of intestinal worms: long, short and flat. The first, which reside in the duodenum, he called strongyloides (a name deriving from the Greek *strongylos* 'round'). The second group, found in the rectum, he called ascaris (from a Greek root meaning 'agitation', as these 'little worms' are always in active motion). In fact, these are more likely to have been what we now call pinworms (*Enterobius vermicularis*). The third group consisted of the flatworms known as *Taenia*. Here, Andry recognised two distinct types and carefully illustrated the differences in his text, which contains the first description of the differences between pork and beef tapeworms (*Taenia solium* and *Taenia saginata*).

In the late 18th and early 19th century several parasitologists and other interested individuals, building on Andry's achievements, began to develop a more systematic classification of parasites.[2] Johann August Ephraim Goeze (1731–1793), a German pastor, described various species of parasites in great detail and was the first to identify two additional types of tapeworm in humans besides the broad tapeworm. Goeze grouped parasites according to their hosts: humans, other mammals, birds, fishes and amphibians. He was hailed as an 'indefatigable helminthologist' by his colleagues.

Incidentally, the beef tapeworm reportedly affected 100% of Abyssinians at the turn of the 19th century. This startling figure, if true, would make the headlines today. But perhaps it is less surprising in the light of the fact that the Abyssinians were quoted as saying they preferred to eat their beef 'fresh and raw' and, if possible, 'still warm and quivering'. As the connection between infestations and parasitic diseases became better defined, parasitologists began to appreciate more fully the prevalence of such diseases around the world. As knowledge of epidemiology grew and people became more aware of the origins and modes of transmission of parasitic diseases,

The botanist, zoologist, anatomist and physiologist **Karl Asmund Rudolphi** *(1771–1832) was professor of medicine at Greifswald University before being appointed to the first Chair in Anatomy and Physiology at the newly established University of Berlin (now Humboldt University) in 1810. He subsequently also served as rector of Berlin University, in 1813/14 and 1824/25. Rudolphi investigated the anatomy of nerves, studied plant growth and was an early champion of the view that the cell is the basic structural unit of plants. He was the first to describe in detail the life cycle of parasitic worms and is regarded as one of the founding fathers of parasitology. Under his direction, the holdings at Berlin's Anatomical Institute were expanded to form one of the most important collections in Europe. He constantly stressed the importance of chemistry and the role of the exact sciences in medicine and biology.*

attention was increasingly focused on sanitation and dietary practices.

The taxonomy of parasites took on new dimensions as a result of the work of Karl Asmund Rudolphi (1771–1832), the founder of Berlin's Zoological Museum. Thanks to a number of monumental works published by Rudolphi in the early 19th century, the number of known species of parasites trebled. He provided systematic descriptions of their general anatomy and physiology, genus and species characteristics and normal habitats, together with references to older scientific writings. Texts by other authors concerned with prophylactic measures, clinical manifestations and the treatment of parasitic diseases subsequently appeared. In 1816 J. S. Olombel, a medical officer in the army of Napoleon, published his *Remarques sur les maladies vermineuses,* and in 1819 J. G. Bremser, a curator at the Natural History Museum in Vienna, published his book *Über lebende Würmer in lebenden Menschen,* which included high-quality colour plates of many of the parasites known at that time.[3]

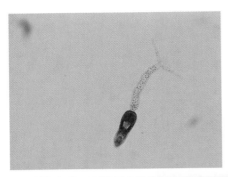

Photomicrograph of a cercaria, the infective larval stage in the life cycle of trematodes (parasitic flatworms).

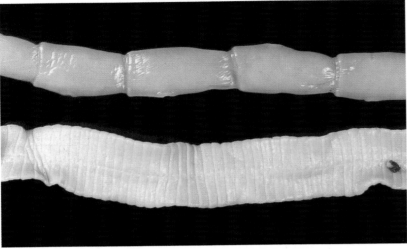

Reproductive, egg-containing segments, known as proglottids, from a Taenia *species of tapeworm (top) and from the broad tapeworm,* Diphyllobothrium latum *(bottom)*

Complex life cycles

Picture yourself on the banks of a small pond where, among the usual freshwater molluscs, myriads of animalcules known as cercariae are swimming. On closer inspection, they can be seen to have a long tail and to be actively motile. Would you wonder what they were? Certainly these fascinating creatures aroused the curiosity of Johannes Japetus Steenstrup (1813–1897), a Danish naturalist who systematically studied the life cycles of various parasites. Steenstrup observed that cercariae would become encysted, sometimes on snails, and sometimes on other objects. Then, after several months, they would develop into the adult form of the parasite known as *Distoma* (liver fluke), found beneath the skin and in the liver of some species of freshwater fish. Where did the cercariae come from? They were released from what L. Bojanus had called the king's yellow worm, an encapsulated structure in the viscera of snails. Observing these yellow worms under the microscope, Steenstrup found that they were filled with small cercariae. From further studies, he finally elucidated the complex life cycle of the liver fluke, which involves two intermediate hosts. He later concluded that 'all trematode animals are developed in this way, that all are obliged to undergo such alterations.' From this beginning, and as the science of parasitology developed, it soon became obvious that not all parasites have the simple life cycle of direct transmission from animal to animal, animal to human, or human to human.

Felix Dujardin (1801–1860), professor of zoology at Rennes, first recognised that cestodes (tapeworms) also spend part of their lives in an intermediate host, and that bladder worms are part of their life cycle. He established that shrews acquired *Distoma* parasites when they ate slugs infested with the intermediate forms. This was an important first step in understanding the transfer of parasitic forms through intermediate hosts. Dujardin also introduced the term 'proglottis' to describe the body segments of tapeworms.

Most microbiologists will remember the French bacteriologist Casimir Davaine (1812–1882) for his contributions to the discovery of the anthrax bacillus by Robert Koch (1843–1910). However, Davaine was also a parasitologist, and was among the first to recognise the importance of microscopic examination of feces in establishing the diagnosis of helminthic disease. He first observed the intestinal flagellate *Pentatrichomonas hominis* and showed that ascaris eggs remain infective for long periods in damp environments. He also published a major text in which the classification of parasites was updated, including full accounts of their natural history, geographical distribution and role in clinical disease.[4]

The second half of the 19th century saw an explosion of knowledge in the field of parasitology. The scientific discoveries made during this period concerning life cycles, habitats, modes of infection and pathogenicity for the various genera and species of parasites could fill several volumes. For reasons of space, only a few key developments will be discussed.

Life cycle of *Fasciola hepatica*

In 1880, following failed experiments by his mentor, George Rolleston (1829–1882), Algernon P. Thomas, a 25-year-old graduate of Balliol College, Oxford, began to investigate the life cycle of *Fasciola*. He scoured flooded hillsides day and night, and brought back various species of molluscs in his search for larval trematodes. In one specimen of *Lymnaea truncatula* he found peculiar cercariae that had a strong tendency to encyst on any object, with forms resembling very closely the young forms of *Fasciola* he had seen in sheep. Thomas next gathered a great multitude of *L. truncatula,* placed them in water teeming with miracidia (the first larval stage) and observed how the snails soon became infected. In further studies he was able to follow the whole process: the entry of the miracidia into the snail, the formation of sporocysts and the development of rediae (reproductive structures). The rediae, in turn, released cercariae, which showed the same encystment on water plants, fish and other aquatic organisms. The various stages of the life cycle in the environment had thus been worked out.

In 1892, a Brazilian named Adolpho Lutz – a pupil of the great parasitologist Rudolph Leuckart (1822–1898) – successfully demonstrated in Hawaii that herbivorous animals became infected by eating cercariae encysted on plant life. However, it was not until about 20 years later, in 1914, that the Russian parasitologist Dimitry F. Sinitsin demonstrated the path taken by the larval flukes after ingestion. He charted how the parasites penetrated the gut wall and migrated across the peritoneal cavity before finally infesting the liver.

Schistosoma haematobium

During the Second World War British troops stationed in Egypt became familiar with a urinary tract condition they called 'Bill Harris disease' – a corruption of the name 'Bilharz'. In 1852 the parasite responsible for this disease had been discovered by Theodor Maximilian Bilharz (1825–1862), a German pathologist working as a tropical medicine physician in Cairo. Bilharz later found this parasite within and adjacent to the urinary tract in 30–40% of the autopsies he performed while working in Egypt. The parasite was thus initially called *Bilharzia haematobium.*

Thomas Spencer Cobbold *(1828–1886) worked in the Department of Anatomy at Edinburgh University, but became intensely interested in parasitology after encountering numerous parasitic creatures in the course of his animal dissections. On one occasion, while dissecting a giraffe, he found that the bile ducts were teeming with a hitherto unknown species of liver fluke, which he named* Fasciola gigantica *(after the size of the parasite, not the host). Cobbold later moved to London, where he became professor of botany and helminthology at the Royal Veterinary College. With permission to dissect animals from the Zoological Society's Gardens, together with animals acquired from farms or markets, or donated by friends, he was able to compile a wide-ranging treatise on parasites and parasitic diseases entitled* Entozoa, an Introduction to the Study of Helminthology *(1864).*

T. S. Cobbold, a distinguished British parasitologist, described a similar worm in the body of an ape dying at the London Zoological Garden. He recognised that this parasite was anatomically not a *Distomum* and thus required an alternate name. He originally suggested the genus name *Bilharzia,* in honor of the discoverer. But, as fate would have it, David Weinland, known for his discovery of the cercaria of the liver fluke *Fasciola hepatica,* had three months previously suggested the genus name *Schistosoma* for this new worm, after the split-body appearance of the adult male (*schistos* = cleft; *soma* = body). Following the rules of zoological nomenclature, the name *Schistosoma* took precedence. Nonetheless, *Bilharzia* is still used to denote the disease characterised by the passage of schistosome eggs in bloody urine. It is estimated that approximately 250–300 million people are now affected by these parasites worldwide, with around 600 million at risk of infection.[5]

The life cycle of the schistosomes was elucidated between 1908 and 1910, when Kan Fujinami and

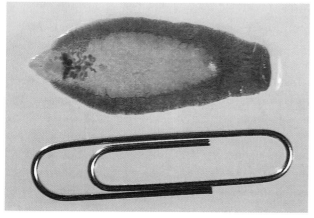

The adult liver fluke, Fasciola hepatica.

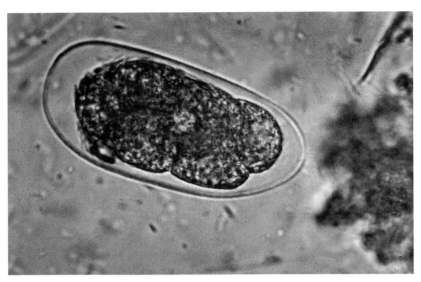

Photomicrograph of hookworm eggs. The average diameter of these eggs is approx. 60 μm.

Hachitaro Nakamura at the University of Kyoto, in Japan, successfully infected mice with cercariae of *Schistosoma japonicum*.[6] In 1915 Robert T. Leiper was sent to Egypt by the British War Office to investigate the life cycle of the parasite that had ravaged so many British troops during the Boer War. Leiper infected monkeys, mice, rats and guinea pigs by submerging them in cercaria-infested waters. He showed that cercariae shed their tails when they enter the skin in mice, and he used tissue sections to demonstrate how they penetrate into the host. Thus, the life cycle of one of the most important human parasites was explained some 65 years after the initial identification of the adult worm.

Trichinella spiralis

Were the Mosaic and Mohammedan prohibitions on the eating of pork based on observations of outbreaks of trichinosis? Quite likely. Heavy infestations can cause sudden severe illness, and people may well have made the association with the ingestion of pork. In 1822 the pathologist Friedrich Tiedemann (1781–1861) found white, stony concretions at autopsy in most of the muscles of a man who had died with gout.[7] However, these nodules were not composed of urates, but of phosphate, carbonate of lime and animal matter resembling fibrin. Tiedemann had no idea what these 'little bodies' were. In 1835 Sir James Paget (1814–1899), at that time a 21-year-old medical student at St Bartholomew's Hospital in London, noticed little specks in the muscles of a cadaver he was dissecting. He microscopically detected a 'worm' in one of the specks, opening the door to the discovery of *Trichinella spiralis*. The life cycle of the trichina worm was subsequently unravelled by several researchers. Finally, in 1851, Carl Friedrich Reinhold Herbst (1824–1868) of Göttingen demonstrated the transmission of trichinellae from one animal to another in a series of feeding experiments. While dissecting a pet badger that had been in the habit of feeding on scraps from the dissecting room table, Herbst found worms encysted in all of the animal's voluntary muscles. He then fed some of the contaminated badger flesh to three young puppies, two of which he killed two months later. Dissecting these in turn, he found vast numbers of trichinellae throughout their voluntary muscles.

A general practitioner, a one Dr Konigsdorfer of Plauen in eastern Germany demonstrated encysted trichinellae in a small piece of biceps muscle excised from a patient suffering from marked prostration and limb pains. Muscle biopsy thus became an important technique for establishing the diagnosis of trichinosis.

From an 1863 newspaper we learn of a dramatic outbreak of trichinosis in the German town of Heltstadt following a celebration of the fiftieth anniversary of the Battle of Leipzig. As part of the festivities, as a token of appreciation for the good work being done by the local miners and smelters, a picnic dinner was provided, including large quantities of pork. This turned out to be a dubious reward, as 158 of the guests contracted trichinosis, with 28 ultimately dying as a result. One of the fatal cases involved an old teacher from a neighbouring village, who had himself fought in the Battle of Leipzig. A cruel irony, indeed, to have survived the immediate dangers of the battle only to succumb to the commemoration 50 years later!

Hookworm

If you had lived in ancient China, you might have heard of 'able-to-eat-but-too-lazy-to-work, yellow disease'. Severe anemia and intestinal disturbances are also described in the Egyptian Papyrus Ebers, dating from around 1550 BC. We now know that these debilitating diseases reported throughout history were due to intestinal hookworm infestation, involving relentless tapping of the host's blood supply. Hookworm has been called 'mankind's worst helminthic pathogen'; it has caused more human disease than any other parasite, with the exception of ascaris. As early as 1940, when the total world population was 2,166 million, an estimated 457 million cases existed worldwide (i.e. an infection rate of approximately one in five).

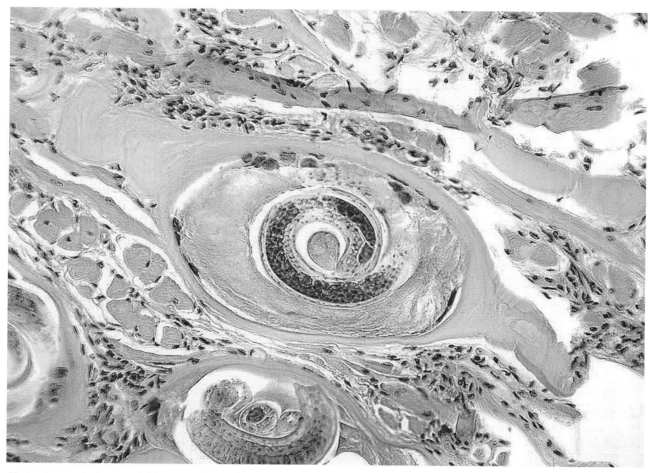

Photomicrograph of a muscle biopsy specimen infested with the larval form of Trichinella spiralis.

The hookworm parasite was discovered in 1843 by Angelo Dubini (1813–1902), a physician of Milan. He first observed the worm in the gut of a peasant who had died at the local hospital. Having recognised the parasite and its association with anemia, he later found worms of the same type in the intestines of approximately 20% of subjects examined at autopsy. He named the worm *Ancylostoma* ('hooked mouth') *duodenale* (referring to the site where most of the worms were found).

Anemia from blood-letting

It was Theodor Bilharz and Wilhelm Griesinger (1817–1868), one of his associates at the Cairo Medical School, who first attributed the severe anemia seen in patients with hookworm infection to the voracious blood-letting of myriads of worms firmly anchored to the intestinal mucosa by their teeth and cutting plates. In 1866 the causal link was also confirmed by Otto Wucherer (1820–1873) at the General Infirmary of Bahia, in Brazil, when he found *Ancylostoma* hookworms in the duodenum of a black slave who had died from severe anemia.

In 1878 Giovanni Battista Grassi (1854–1925) first demonstrated that the diagnosis of hookworm infection could be made by microscopically observing the typical thin-shelled embryonated eggs in stool specimens. An interesting related story concerns a severe outbreak of anemia among Italian miners employed to construct the St Gotthard tunnel between Italy and Switzerland. The anemia was found to be secondary to *Ancylostoma* infection. Upon completion of the tunnelling work, the miners dispersed all over Europe, after which ancylostomiasis became a much more widespread disease.

The final chapter

What still remained to be determined was how humans became infected with hookworms. It had been assumed that infections occurred simply from ingestion of the embryonated eggs. In 1898 the mode of infection was accidentally discovered by the German parasitologist Arthur Looss (1861–1923), who had moved to Egypt to take advantage of the opportunities afforded by that country for research. As part of an experiment, he was dropping a culture of *Ancylostoma* larvae into the mouths of guinea pigs, and some of the fluid fell onto his hand. He subsequently experienced an itching sensation and erythema at the site of contamination. When he examined samples of his own feces at intervals thereafter, he found in due course that he was also excreting hookworm eggs. He later applied drops of *Ancylostoma* larvae culture to the skin on an Egyptian boy's leg an hour before a planned amputation. In microscopic studies, he observed that the larval hookworms had penetrated the skin, thus confirming this part of the life cycle.

Subsequent attempts by other researchers to confirm Looss's findings failed. Finally, in 1902, C. A. Bently, a medical officer working at an Assam tea plantation, published a paper proposing that so-called ground itch was related to the presence of *Ancylostoma duodenale* larvae in the soil. In the clinching experiment one batch of soil was mixed with feces contaminated with *Ancylostoma* larvae and another batch was mixed with normal feces. The two samples were applied to each of his own wrists, one on the left, the other on the right, and held in place with a bandage for eight hours. Typical ground itch developed only where the sample containing the living larvae had been applied. This knowledge of the life cycle of hookworms led to the development of regulations in many parts of the world concerning the hygienic disposal of human feces.

Filariasis

In 1866 the German physician Otto Wucherer (1820–1873), who had been born in Portugal and was working in Brazil, noticed 'filarial worms' in a specimen from a patient whose urine also contained chyle (milky fluid). In fact, he had been looking for schistosomal parasites. Over the next two years he found additional cases of filarial chyluria and published his findings in the *Bahia Medical Gazette*, a journal of very limited circulation. Microfilariae were also observed in chylous urine by researchers elsewhere, including Timothy Richard Lewis (1841–1886). Born in England, Lewis spent most of his medical career in Calcutta, serving in the 1870s as an army attaché to the Sanitary Commission of India. Investigating a patient presumed to have cholera, he wrote:

> The colour [of urine] so closely resembled many rice water stools that I examined it and was repaid in a way not anticipated … [T]here were embryos of a round worm.[8]

His findings, however, were never disseminated beyond the annual report to the Sanitary Commissioner. He later observed the same embryos in the blood of an Indian patient with diarrhea.

Next to appear on the scene was the Scotsman Sir Patrick Manson (1844–1922). In the 1860s he served as a medical officer with the Chinese Imperial Maritime Customs Office at the port of Takao. Among the commonest and most disabling conditions he had to treat was elephantiasis. Turning to surgery, he impressed the local population by removing vast scrotal tumours from many patients. In a paper he expressed the desire to demonstrate that the condition known as lymph scrotum was caused by the 'filaria of Lewis'. On one occasion he made a bargain with the wife of a dying man that, for the sum of $ 200, he would be allowed to perform an autopsy. He and his brother duly began the procedure in a very hot, ill-lit room. Before they could complete their task, a mob had gathered, wanting to know what these 'foreign devils' were up to. Manson and his brother had to run for their lives. Manson later carried out an autopsy on another Chinese victim of elephantiasis at the dead of night in a local cemetery, working by the light of a dimly burning lantern. On this occasion he was able to detect adult filarial worms in the lymphatic channels of the upper leg.

At about the same time, in 1887, adult filarial worms were independently identified by Joseph Bancroft (1836–1894), working in Brisbane, Australia. However, what happened to the circulating embryos remained a mystery, and how humans became infected was still a matter of pure conjecture. Knowing that microfilariae could be found in the circulation of infected humans, Manson reasoned that the disease might be transmitted by an animal that fed on blood. To test his theory, he allowed mosquitoes to obtain a blood meal from a patient with elephantiasis. He then made slide preparations each day from expressed drops of mosquito stomach fluid and finally observed that the ingested microfilariae underwent a series of highly interesting metamorphoses in the mosquito gut, leading to the infective form. The complete life cycle was confirmed when it was demonstrated in follow-up experiments that humans became infected through the bite of the mosquito.

Manson made an additional important discovery: microfilariae could not be found in the circulation of infected humans at all times of the day. When the blood of a patient with elephantiasis was examined over a 24-hour period, microfilariae were identified far more frequently by the night-time observer than during the day. The microfilariae re-

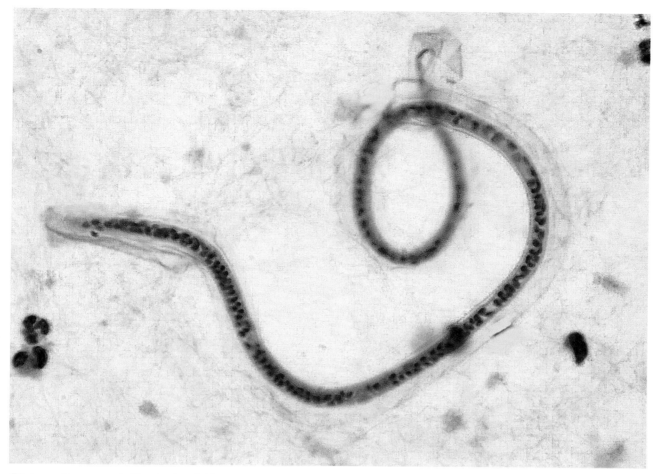

Filariae, as they appear in blood or lymph. These worms are approximately 150 µm in length.

appeared in the blood around sunset, and their numbers increased until around midnight, coinciding with the time when mosquitoes took their blood meals. When this finding was presented at a medical meeting, one heckler inquired 'Do the filariae carry watches?' Nonetheless, the nocturnal periodicity of microfilariae had been established. At this meeting it was proposed that the parasite should be named after Lewis, Manson and Bancroft collectively; however, the name *Wuchereria* was adopted in recognition of the initial publication in the *Bahia Medical Gazette.*

The above examples illustrate how the science of parasitology progressed in the latter half of the 19th century, and also how advances were often made by far-flung individuals at a time when communication was a slow and arduous process. Through a combination of intuition, luck and persistent experimentation, the morphology of parasites became well defined, one life cycle after another was elucidated, and clinical parasitologists recognised the links between organisms and the associated diseases.

Protozoology

Advances in man's understanding of protozoan (single-celled) parasites were facilitated by improvements in the compound microscope. The first observation of protozoa is of course attributed to Antoni van Leeuwenhoek (1632–1723), who noted 'motile animalcules' in the gut of a horsefly and, shortly thereafter, in his own feces. He is now believed to have been looking at *Giardia lamblia.*

After these observations, however, more than a century passed before any further progress was made in the study of protozoans. In 1841, with the aid of a microscope, Gabriel Gustav Valentin (1810–1883), an anatomist and professor of physiology at the University of Berne, Switzerland, observed dark, motile, bullet-shaped objects lying between the red blood cells of a trout he was dissecting. This was the first time that trypanosomes had been observed. The first adequate description of these organisms was provided in 1843 by David Gruby (1810–1898), when he presented a short paper to the Academy of Sciences in Paris. He called the parasite *Trypanosoma*

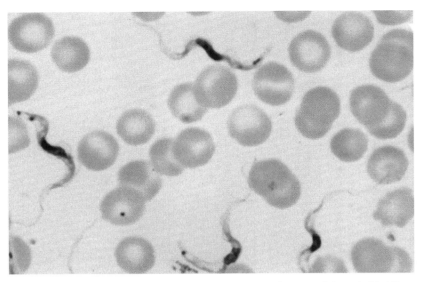

Trypanosomes, as observed in the peripheral blood smear of a person infected with African trypanosomiasis.

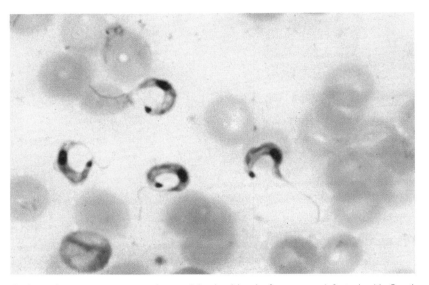

C-shaped trypanosomes, as observed in the blood of a person infected with South American trypanosomiasis (Chagas' disease). These trypanosomes range from 50 to 100 µm in length.

sanguinis, the name being derived from the Greek trupanon ('borer') on account of the organism's auger-like motion.

Sleeping sickness

Sir David Bruce (1855–1931), a surgeon-major with the British Army in South Africa, searched in vain for a bacterial cause of the endemic cattle disease known as nagana (from a Zulu word meaning 'in low or depressed spirits', referring to the unfortunate animals' appearance). With the aid of stains developed by Paul Ehrlich (1854–1915) for the study of peripheral blood smears, Bruce soon found organisms in his preparations. He thought they were filariae, but the morphology did not fit. These 'infusorial' parasites were found to be present in the blood in every case of nagana.

It was John Kirk who, in 1865, first linked this disease of cattle with the bite of the tsetse-fly – which was later found to be a vector for the transmission of human disease as well. With the assistance of Robert Koch, who happened to be in German East Africa working on the cause of rinderpest at the time, Kirk suggested that the trypanosomes undergo cyclic changes in the tsetse-fly. Once the life cycle of the parasite had been clarified and the roles of both the trypanosomes and the tsetse-fly had been defined, commissions were soon established to study sleeping sickness in Africa. This work laid the foundations for much of our current knowledge of trypanosomiasis.

Kissing bugs

In the meantime Carlos Chagas (1879–1934) had discovered yet another variant of trypanosomiasis, which was prevalent in certain remote parts of Brazil. The peripheral blood manifestations of South American trypanosomiasis differed from those of the African form in that the circulating trypanosomes had a distinctive 'C' shape. In addition, instead of the classical symptoms of sleeping sickness, patients suffered heart failure as a result of tissue invasion by leishmanial parasites, and the outcome was often fatal. Chagas first linked the disease with a species of reduviid bugs that infested many people's houses. These nocturnal marauders obtained blood meals particularly by attacking the faces of the sleeping inhabitants, hence the name 'kissing bugs'.

Although Chagas was convinced that infections were caused by the bite of the reduviid, he was puzzled by his discovery of numerous flagellate parasites in the hind gut of the bug. The reduviid was then found to have a peculiar trait – it defecates at the same time as it takes a bite. The infective parasites are thus inoculated into the bite wound when the agitated victim rubs the area to relieve the intense pain.

Dysentery

As has often been pointed out, in the American Civil War dysentery was more destructive to the troops on both sides than powder and shot. Although in most cases the disease was probably due to the much more readily communicable bacterial enteric pathogen *Shigella dysenteriae*, the protozoan parasite *Entamoeba histolytica* is also known to have taken its toll. As clinical experience accumulated, it became possible to distinguish the syndromes caused by these two agents, even before the agents themselves were known.

Entamoeba histolytica, discovered in 1873 by Fedor Aleksandrevitch Lösch (1840–1903) in the stools of a young Russian peasant in St Petersburg, proved to be the more feared agent, as the resultant disease was frequently complicated by extraintestinal sites of infection in the form of amebic abscesses, primarily in the liver but also in other organs. Lösch left detailed accounts of the clinical features, post-mortem findings and parasitology of the agent. The characteristic intestinal amebic ulcers had also been observed by Robert Koch in the course of autopsies he performed on patients presumed to have died of cholera in Egypt. Although liver abscesses were also observed in two such cases, Koch disregarded these findings, as they had little to do with cholera.

Malaria

Many months of persistent efforts were required to define the life cycle of *Plasmodium,* the causative agent of malaria. A major contribution was made by Charles Louis Alphonse Laveran (1845–1922), the French physician, pathologist and parasitologist who in 1907 received the Nobel Prize in Physiology or Medicine for his work on the identification of *Plasmodium* and his discovery of the pathogenic role of protozoa. Laveran identified four different morphological forms of the malarial parasite and described the appearance of characteristic elements in the blood: crescent-shaped forms (gametocytes), transparent pigmented spherical bodies with actively moving flagella, and small ring forms (trophozoites) within red blood cells.

The discovery that malaria is transmitted from human to human by the *Anopheles* mosquito was made by Sir Ronald Ross (1857–1932), a surgeon-major and the 1902 Nobel Laureate in Physiology or Medicine. Ross's untiring, repeated dissections of mosquitoes also revealed how the sexual stage of the parasite develops in the gut and proboscis, resulting in the formation of mature infective sporozoites. Credit must also be given to Patrick Manson for his part in these discoveries, as Ross was in almost constant contact with his mentor during his prolonged struggle. After finally observing the sexual union of the micro- and macrogametes in the mosquito gut, Ross wrote to Manson:

> I feel most justified in saying that I have completed the life-cycle of proteosoma, or rather one life-cycle of proteosoma, and therefore in all probability of the malaria parasite.

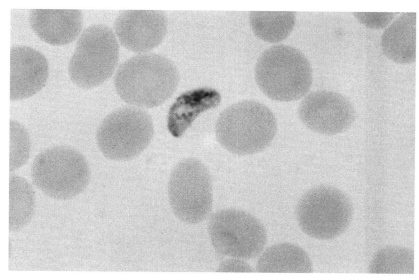

A banana-shaped gametocyte of Plasomodium falciparum, *as observed in the peripheral blood of a patient with malignant tertian malaria.*

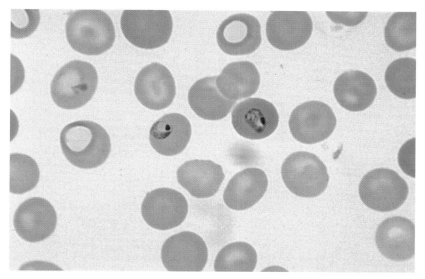

Early trophozoites of a Plasmodium *species, as observed in a peripheral blood smear of the type used to diagnose malaria.*

Humankind has benefited from these dedicated efforts. In many parts of the world malaria has been eradicated through mosquito control measures, and prophylactic and curative treatments have been developed to reduce morbidity and mortality.

Laboratory techniques in parasitology

The observation of distinctive parasitic forms in direct wet-mount, iodine-treated or stained fecal smear preparations remains the cornerstone of the diagnosis of parasitic diseases. Most intestinal parasitic conditions are diagnosed by the identification of characteristic trophozoites, cysts or eggs in stool samples. Their relative size and shape and the presence of distinctive internal structures provide the

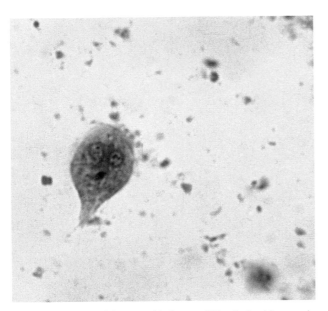

Photomicrograph of the parasitic forms of Giardia lamblia, *as observed in stool specimens from patients with giardiasis. Note the 'monkey face' of the motile trophozoite form, with two prominent 'eyes', a central axostyle ('nose') and a 'moustache'.*

experienced microscopist with the morphological evidence necessary to make an identification. On occasion larvae or key parts of adult forms may also be observed.

Stool specimens are usually stored in a container with a preservative. Some laboratories use formalin, in concentrations between 3% and 10%, usually buffered with sodium phosphate. More recently additions to formalin have been made to improve preservation and yield sharper microscopic images of various parasitic forms. For example, Merthiolate and iodine have been added to produce a mixture known as MIF (**M**erthiolate **i**odine **f**ormalin solution). MIF helps to prevent the deterioration of almost all parasitic forms and also adds colour to any forms that may be present, making it unnecessary to prepare a stained smear. Another advantage with MIF is that protozoa, eggs and larvae can be identified in temporary direct wet mounts without the need for further staining. The fixative used most commonly is **p**olyvinyl **a**lcohol (PVA), which employs a resin incorporated into Schaudinn's fluid. Cysts, trophozoites and other parasitic forms are well preserved in PVA and can thus withstand long-distance transport or prolonged storage.

At the laboratory a saline suspension of the stool sample is first prepared. This is then centrifuged to enable any parasitic forms to be concentrated in the sediment. Alternatively, a flotation technique may be used, employing a liquid of high specific gravity, commonly zinc sulphate solution (specific gravity 1.18). With this method, protozoan cysts, coccidian oocysts and certain helminth eggs are concentrated in the surface film. The advantage, compared with the centrifugation procedure, is that most of the background debris settles to the bottom of the tube, leaving a clear liquid that can be examined directly or used to prepare smears. One disadvantage is that operculated eggs and unfertilised ascaris eggs will not be recovered.

In the case of parasitic forms that do not concentrate well, such as *Giardia* trophozoites and cysts, smears need to be prepared and stained. A technique commonly used in most clinical laboratories is Wheatley's trichrome staining, based on a method previously introduced by Gomori. The procedure is rapid and simple to perform and provides for even staining. Protozoan trophozoites and cysts in particular are readily seen; helminth eggs and larvae may be more difficult to identify, as a result of excess stain retention. Fecal smears have to be well preserved to obtain the best staining results. One option is the time-honoured iron hematoxylin stain[9], which makes morphological detail clearly visible in most parasites. *Cryptosporidium* or *Cyclospora* infection can be detected with the aid of an acid-fast stain; the oocysts of these parasites will appear red when examined under the microscope.

Additional techniques have been used for detecting the larval stages of certain nematodes in cases of light infection. In the Harada-Mori filter paper method, for example, small portions of a fecal suspension are inoculated onto the surface of a filter paper strip, which is continuously soaked, by capillary action, with fluid from a tube in which the end of the strip is immersed. As the larvae migrate through the fibres of the filter paper into the fluid in the tube, they are concentrated and can be observed microscopically.

If no parasites are detected in stool specimens, other tests may need to be considered, e.g. the examination of duodenal secretions. To obtain a sample, the 'string' test can be carried out: the patient has to swallow a small weighted capsule attached to a long string, which is allowed to enter the duodenum before being pulled back out several minutes later. The string is then stripped of its mucin, which is affixed to the surface of a glass slide and examined under a microscope.

Stained tissue sections or bone marrow aspirates are required to identify the leishmanial forms of visceral (kala-azar) or cutaneous leishmaniasis and the

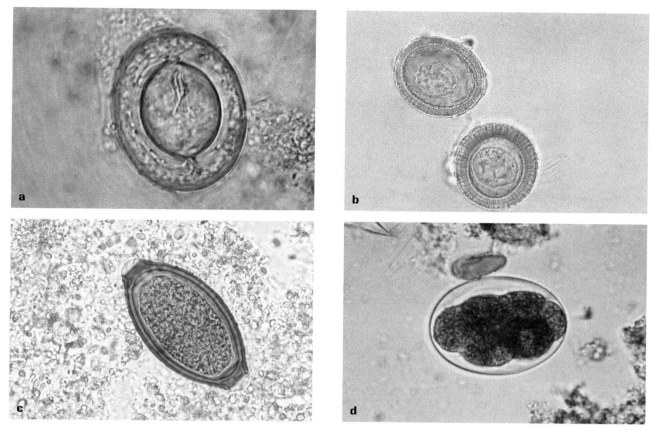

Various eggs that may be microscopically observed in stool specimens at a clinical parasitology laboratory, permitting genus/species identification of parasitic worms. These eggs range from 40 to 60 μm in greatest dimension. **a**) Spherical egg of the dwarf tapeworm, Hymenolepis nana: *inside the outer shell a hexacanth embryo is visible within an inner membrane.* **b**) *Eggs produced by a* Taenia *tapeworm, with characteristic thick, striated shells.* **c**) *Barrel-shaped egg of the whipworm,* Trichuris trichiura, *with a characteristic smooth, thick shell and two hyaline polar plugs.* **d**) *Thin-shelled hookworm egg undergoing internal cleavage and retraction; at this stage, a clear space appears beneath the inner membrane.*

intracellular leishmanial forms seen in Chagas' disease. The intracytoplasmic cyst forms of *Trichinella spiralis* and of *Sarcocystis* disease are characteristic. Tissue sections obtained from intestinal ulcers may also be helpful in establishing the diagnosis of invasive amebiasis and balantidiasis. To identify the brood capsules of hydatid disease, tissue sections may also be needed, although aspirates of bladder worm fluid may reveal the presence of characteristic scolices and/or hooklets (hydatid sand).

Newer diagnostic methods

In the early 1980s immunological assays were developed for the detection of *Giardia* antigen in stool specimens to establish the diagnosis of giardiasis. During the course of infection *Giardia* antigen was detected more commonly than cysts in stool specimens, particularly during periods of latency in individuals known to be infected. The antigen was also found more commonly than cysts during therapy,

the release of antigen most likely being the result of the destructive effects of antiparasitic drugs on trophozoites.

The *Giardia* specific antigen against which monoclonal antibodies were produced is called GSA-65. In the prototype ELISA tests, the anti-GSA-65 antibody was attached to a solid-phase material. In performing such tests, an extract of the stool specimen is added to the reagent, and the mixture is incubated to allow any available antigen to adsorb to the antibody. After any extraneous material has been washed away, an enzyme-labelled antiglobulin reagent is added. The presence of GSA-65 was indicated by a blue colour reaction. By 1996 at least nine immunoassay kits were commercially available, all showing a high degree of sensitivity and specificity. It is therefore now common practice in most clinical laboratories to test for the presence of *Giardia* antigen in stool specimens instead of searching for trophozoites or cysts.

Diarrheal outbreaks

Cryptosporidiosis and cyclosporiasis, diarrheal diseases caused by protozoa that were briefly mentioned above, have recently aroused a great deal of medical interest.

Early in the spring of 1993 the city of Milwaukee, Wisconsin, suffered a major outbreak of acute watery diarrhea. By the time the epidemic subsided in the following summer, approximately 400,000 people (25% of the total population) had been affected. The outbreak was caused by *Cryptosporidium parvum,* as was confirmed by positive fecal specimens in one-third of the people affected. How could this happen in such a modern city? An investigation at one of the municipal water treatment plants in April 1993 revealed a two- to fourfold increase in the turbidity of water that had passed through conventional bacterial filters. As many as 13 *Cryptosporidium* oocysts were found per 100 L of water. Oocyst counts were particularly high in water that had been melted from ice blocks. The source was later traced to nearby cattle-holding pens, where manure run-off was sufficiently contaminated to overwhelm the water filtration system. *Cryptosporidia* are well known to inhabit the intestine of calves and cows, causing explosive diarrhea.

In October 1993 the principal of an elementary school in rural, central Maine notified the public health authorities that a large number of his pupils were absent because of an outbreak of acute diarrheal disease.[10] The source of this outbreak was traced to a one-day agricultural fair attended by the students eight days previously, which had featured a farm animal petting zoo, a hayride, a cider-pressing demonstration and light refreshments. Over the next few days approximately 26% of those attending the fair were affected, including several high-school students who had helped out at the fair or served as chaperones; in a third of all cases *Cryptosporidium* oocysts were detected in stool specimens. Those who had drunk apple cider were found to be at highest risk. *Cryptosporidium* oocysts were detected in the cider, on the cider press and in a stool specimen from one of the calves on the farm that had provided the apples.

Outbreaks of cyclosporiasis also occurred in North America in the 1990s. From May 1995 to July 1997, 150 clusters of *Cyclospora* infections, involving a total of almost 3000 people, were reported in Florida, the Washington, DC, area and Canada, primarily in the province of Ontario.[11] The majority of these cases were related to the consumption of raspberries imported from Guatemala. After conventional washing procedures contaminated soil or dust was still harboured in the deep fissures within the fruit. Other isolated outbreaks reported in the US during this period were most often due to ingestion of fruit salads, berry desserts and fresh basil. Time and again we are reminded of the many avenues that microbes may discover to enter the water supply or food chain, provoking fresh outbreaks of infection in humans.

Parasites versus humans

Outdoor people who camp under the stars or in abandoned cabins continue to be susceptible to arthropod-borne parasitic diseases, a prime example being infections with *Babesia* parasites from the bites of *Ixodes* and other tick species. In North America babesiosis is caused primarily by *Babesia microti,* whereas in Europe infections are more commonly due to *Babesia divergens.* Babesiosis is less frequently reported in Europe but is more often lethal. Immunosuppressed individuals, particularly those with AIDS, are particularly vulnerable to parasitic infections. In such cases symptoms are commonly more severe and prolonged, and reactivation of latent conditions such as toxoplasmosis continues to pose a problem. The individuals concerned should therefore take special precautions, avoiding certain activities and minimising potential contacts with animals or other people that involve a high risk of contracting parasitic diseases.

Parasitology is a science that provides challenging and exciting work for all those involved – clinical parasitologists endeavouring to diagnose and aid in the treatment of parasitic diseases, and pure scientists attempting to understand in more detail the life cycles of parasites in widely varying environments. Each day, new discoveries are being made in a field comprising many hundreds of parasitic forms. It is safe to predict that in the years ahead diagnostic and epidemiological capabilities in parasitology will be expanded by the application of newer technologies, such as multiplex PCR and other signal and target amplification systems, to a number of clinically relevant pathogens.

The emergence of routine diagnostic laboratories (from 1840 on)

From hobby horse to
applied science

Johannes Büttner

These subjects of study are immense, and it is to implement them that it would be so important for hospitals to establish a ward flanked by a laboratory for the sole purpose of pursuing them with all the care and in all the detail which they warrant.[1]

Antoine François [de] Fourcroy, 1755–1809

From hobby to practical science

Physicians discover the diagnostic utility of chemistry

From the 17th century on, many medical faculties possessed a *laboratorium chymicum* as well as a botanical garden and an anatomy theatre. The existence of these laboratories, which were mainly places for preparing drugs, can be viewed as a response to the teachings of Theophrastus Bombastus von Hohenheim (1493/4–1541), better known as Paracelsus, and his disciple iatrochemists (physician-chemists), who advocated a medicine based on chemical principles. The present chapter, however, is devoted to another kind of chemistry laboratory, which emerged only in the 19th century and whose main purpose was the diagnosis of disease. These 'clinical' or 'medical' laboratories were the nucleus for the rise of laboratory medicine as a new medical speciality in the 20th century.

A new means of investigating the nature of disease

If the French Revolution was the signal event of late 18th century European politics, it was paralleled in chemistry by a scientific revolution associated with the name of Antoine Laurent Lavoisier (1743–1794). In addition to his momentous achievements in general chemistry, Lavoisier pioneered new ways of explaining human bodily processes such as respiration in chemical terms. For example, he described the generation of 'animal heat' (i.e. the body heat of animals and humans) as a combustion process involving the oxygen in inspired air. In celebrated experiments in human subjects he measured oxygen consumption and carbonic acid production and related them to body temperature and muscle activity. Lavoisier broke new ground in physiology and medicine, and gave his contemporaries fresh hope of finding characteristic chemical changes that could

aid the diagnosis and understanding of disease. His untimely and violent death amid the turmoil of Revolutionary France prevented him from completing his work.

We first encounter the idea of establishing special laboratories in hospitals in the writings of the French physician and chemist Antoine François [de] Fourcroy (1755–1809), who in 1791 published a plan for a hospital laboratory, describing it 'as a new means of investigating the nature of disease'. His proposal:

> At such a distance from a ward with twenty or thirty beds would be built a chemistry laboratory equipped with all materials and all implements necessary for animal analysis.[2]

Fourcroy[3] himself was unable to establish such a laboratory in a hospital, but his department of medical chemistry at the École de Santé in Paris boasted a large, well-equipped laboratory where medical students were taught chemistry and which afforded every research tool possible. In some hospitals chemistry was the province of the hospital pharmacist, and to this day clinical chemistry remains a branch of pharmacy in France.

The next clinical laboratory was established in 1808 at the University of Halle, where Johann Christian Reil (1759–1813) was professor of therapeutics at the Schola Clinica, or university hospital. Reil was keenly interested in applying chemistry to medicine and, in a proposal to the rector in 1803, suggested that clinical instruction would be best served by establishing a 20- to 30-bed ward and engaging a pharmacist

> to investigate … everything pathological that can be investigated chemically. More observation and less conjecture, more truth and less hypothesis, would enter medicine as a result …[4]

Antoine Laurent Lavoisier *(1743–1794) with his wife and co-worker* **Marie-Anne Pierrette**. *A talented artist who studied drawing with Jacques Louis David (1748–1825), Madame Lavoisier recorded her husband's experiments in pictures. Lavoisier, who came from a family of lawyers, earned his licentiate in law at the Sorbonne in 1764, but then devoted himself entirely to the natural sciences. In 1768 he was accepted into the Royal Academy of Sciences as an associate chemist, and in the same year he joined the Ferme Générale, a private company of tax farmers who collected import duties and other taxes for the crown. In 1775 he became director of the Régie des Poudres et Salpêtres, the state gunpowder administration at the Royal Arsenal, where he set up a very well-equipped laboratory. In 1784 he was appointed director of the Academy. During the Revolution, the National Convention dissolved the Ferme Générale in 1791, and its members were all sentenced to death by the Revolutionary Tribunal on 8 May 1794. The condemned were executed by guillotine the same day. The president of the Tribunal was a former physician, Pierre André Coffinhal (1762–1794), who had become public prosecutor at the Châtelet prison. He is reported to have said: 'The Republic has no need of scientists. Let justice take its course.' Oil painting by Jacques Louis David, 1788.*

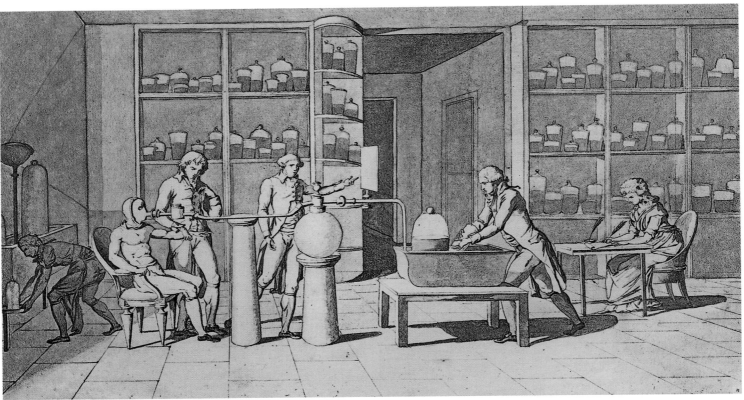

Lavoisier performing an experiment on human respiration in his laboratory (from a drawing by Madame Lavoisier). The experimental subject holding a breathing mask to his face and breathing oxygen from the large glass container is Lavoisier's assistant, Armand Seguin (1767–1835). Lavoisier is shown standing at the pneumatic trough used to collect the exhaled air for analysis. Madame Lavoisier is recording the experiment at the table on the right.

During Napoleon's Prussian campaign, Halle was the first city to fall to the French in October 1806. Napoleon, who took up residence in the house of the anatomist Johann Friedrich Meckel the Younger (1781–1833), was angered by the anti-French sentiments of the students and general populace and summarily closed the university. Two years later – with Halle now part of the Kingdom of Westphalia – the university was reopened. The medical faculty was allocated a building with space for a ward and an adjacent laboratory. Following Reil's appointment to the newly founded University of Berlin, he opened a laboratory there too. However, he died of typhoid fever in the war year of 1813, and the laboratory was closed. As a result of his essay 'Über die Lebenskraft', Reil had become known far beyond the frontiers of medicine. *Lebenskraft,* or 'vital force', was a vague expression invoked at the time to describe the inexplicable phenomena of life. Reil gave the expression a new meaning grounded in the natural sciences, thereby helping to pave the way for the use of chemical methods in medicine.

Organic chemistry in physiology and pathology

Several decades passed before any further laboratories appeared in hospitals. To be sure, there were a few physicians who, out of personal interest, set up laboratories of their own. There – inspired by the teachings of Fourcroy, Reil and others – they studied the chemistry of clinical materials from patients. But the further development of clinical chemistry, or chemical pathology, required other stimuli.

The first requirement was to develop simple methods for analysing biological materials. In 1784 Lavoisier had discovered that organic compounds, i. e. substances formed by plants and animals, were composed of just a few elements. Lavoisier identified three: carbon, oxygen and hydrogen, with nitrogen being added to the list a short time later. He also developed a method of quantifying the elements present in organic matter, namely by burning samples in oxygen gas and analysing the resulting gas mixture. This method was not suitable for general use, however. Explosions were frequent. Many great chemists[5] of the first half of the 19th century strove to make Lavoisier's 'elemental analysis' reliable and safe. But it was only in 1831 that Justus [von] Liebig[6] (1803–1873) introduced a method simple enough for non-specialists. Though scientists were now able to identify pure organic compounds by analysing their constituent elements, it would be a while longer before they learned to understand their structure, i. e. how elements were linked to one another within a compound. Also, elemental analysis required careful purification of the substance of interest. This proved a particularly tricky problem with many substances found in the excreta and constituents of the diseased body, notably complicating the analysis of the compounds first described as proteins by Gerrit Jan Mulder (1802–1880).

The availability of a method that even non-specialists could use was only one prerequisite for promoting the application of chemistry in medicine. The other, more important, requirement was to convince physicians of the value of chemistry. In the first decades of the 19th century medical students at most universities in German-speaking countries received little theoretical and absolutely no practical instruction in chemistry. The task was to show the medical profession that bodily processes in health and disease could be largely explained in terms of chemical reactions. To a great extent this was the achievement of Liebig in two books, published in 1840 and 1842, describing in broad and convincing brushstrokes the chemical changes in the living organism. His second book, in particular, *Organische Chemie in ihrer Anwendung auf Physiologie und Pathologie* – often referred to simply as *Animal Chemistry* in English – had a profound influence on the medical fraternity. His description of animal life, and especially of the chemical transformations for which the term 'metabolism' came to be used, convinced many readers that chemical tests could be useful for studying processes in the living organism.

'Medicine wishes to be a natural science'

Medical men were also among those advocating a greater role for the natural sciences in medicine. The clinician Johann Lucas Schönlein (1793–1864), for example, encouraged his students in Würzburg, Zurich and Berlin to study disease in greater detail using the tools of the natural scientist, and his students responded enthusiastically. Physicians, in Schönlein's view, needed to familiarise themselves with 'chemistry, and chiefly analytical chemistry and the theory of reagents',[7] if they wished to describe and recognise disease. Schönlein's teachings, which

Johann Christian Reil *(1759–1813), in the uniform of a member of the State Mining Board (after 1802), was appointed professor of therapeutics at the University of Halle in 1787, and later became the city's* Stadtphysikus *or medical officer. Under his direction the Schola Clinica became a leading centre of medical training. Johann Wolfgang von Goethe (1749–1832) valued Reil very highly as a physician. In 1810 Reil was appointed to the newly established University of Berlin, and in 1813, during the Napoleonic Wars, he was responsible for the military hospitals west of the Elbe. In a report to Baron Heinrich Friedrich Karl vom und zum Stein (1757–1831), he described the wretched plight of the 20,000 sick and wounded soldiers requiring medical attention after the Battle of the Nations, which raged in Leipzig from 14 to 19 October 1813. Reil himself died soon after, on 22 November 1813, in Halle. Goethe commemorated him in a prologue written for the reopening of the theatre in Halle that Reil had founded years before.*

Johann Lucas Schönlein *(1793–1864) had a somewhat unsettled career. He became an associate professor of special pathology and therapeutics at the young age of 27 and just four years later was already a full professor and medical director at the Juliusspital in Würzburg. In 1827 the city even made him an honorary freeman. Because of his liberal politics, he was dismissed from his post in 1830 after the July Revolution. He went to Switzerland, taking a position at the newly established University of Zurich. Würzburg demanded the return of his certificate of honorary freedom. Schönlein sent it immediately, inscribing the envelope with the words 'Worthless papers'. In 1839 the University of Berlin appointed him head of the Department of Medicine at Charité Hospital. Schönlein retired to his native city of Bamberg in 1859, dying there five years later on 22 January.*

became known as the natural history school of medicine, found adherents but also opponents.

The pupils of the great Berlin physiologist Johannes Müller (1801–1858) went even further. They not only sought to use the natural sciences as a tool, but called for making 'the scientific method' the basis of medical practice. The 23-year-old Rudolf Virchow (1821–1902), then a student at Berlin's Pépinière, a military medical school officially known as the Friedrich Wilhelm Institute, proclaimed in a special lecture: 'Medicine wishes to be a natural science.'[8] He reported this speech to his father as if it had contained a 'formal medical profession of faith'. General Eck of the Army Medical Corps recalled: 'he often sounded like a member of the French Academy'.[9]

Rudolf Virchow *(1821–1902). Like Schönlein, Virchow spent a number of years in the university medical departments in Würzburg and Berlin. After studying medicine at Berlin's Pépinière military medical school, he became assistant to the prosector Robert Froriep (1804–1861). In 1848 he was dismissed for being involved in the disturbances of the March Revolution in Berlin. The following year he was appointed professor of pathology in Würzburg. In 1856 he accepted the chair in pathology at Berlin University, a position he would hold for the next 46 years. In 1848/49 Virchow campaigned for 'medical reform', i. e. for a reorganisation of the health system. After his return to Berlin he was politically active as a city councillor, and later as a member of the Prussian and German parliaments. He died on 5 September 1902 after falling from a tram and breaking his femur. His large body of scientific work, and particularly his work in cellular pathology (1855–1858), made Virchow one of the founders of modern pathology.* Virchows Archiv, *which he established in 1847 with Benno Ernst Heinrich Reinhardt (1819–1852), was the journal of record in the field. In his early years he had himself attempted to clarify some problems in pathology using chemical methods. In Berlin he left this work to the scientists in the chemistry department of his new institute. In later life he took an intense interest in anthropology and the origins of man.*

Handbuch

der

angewandten

medizinischen Chemie

nach dem neuesten Standpunkte der Wissenschaft
und nach zahlreichen eigenen Untersuchungen

bearbeitet

von

Dr. J. Franz Simon,

der physikalisch - medizinischen Societät zu Erlangen, des Vereins badenscher Medizinalbeamte, des naturwissenschaftlichen Vereins zu Hamburg und anderer gelehrten Gesellschaften korrespondirendem und Ehrenmitgliede.

I. Theil.

Medizinisch-analytische Chemie.

Johann Franz Simon *(1807–1843). Perhaps because of his untimely death at age 36, there are no known portraits of Simon. In place of a portrait, the title page of the first volume of his major work is reproduced here. A contemporary described him as 'small in stature, thin, brown-haired, of sanguine temperament'. After apprenticing as a pharmacist, he studied pharmacy in Berlin, graduating in 1832. In 1835 he switched to the study of chemistry, obtaining his PhD in 1838 with a thesis on the chemistry and physiology of breast milk. When Schönlein was called to Berlin in 1840, Simon obtained a position as assistant in the department of medicine. Two years later he qualified as a university lecturer in chemistry. The professors pronounced the candidate 'not of sterling general education, but very competent in his subject'. Alexander von Humboldt (1769–1859), by contrast, was full of praise for Simon and urged the ministry to make him an associate professor. Simon's initial interest had been toxicology. His two-volume* Handbuch der angewandten medizinischen Chemie, *which is based on a wealth of observations and analyses, was the first comprehensive account of clinical chemistry. Simon was the first to attempt a systematic presentation of the diagnostically important pathological changes in blood. He was also responsible for establishing the first journal and the first scientific association for the new discipline. On his way to the Congress of Naturalists in Graz, he died – 'mentally deranged', possibly from cerebral tuberculosis – in Vienna on 23 October 1843, before the chemistry laboratory he had striven to establish at the Charité could become a reality.*

'This science requires a man's undivided attention'

It was Schönlein who took the first concrete step towards the regular use of chemical tests in clinical diagnosis after his appointment to Berlin's Charité Hospital. When he began to lecture there at Easter 1840, he hired the chemist Johann Franz Simon (1807–1843) to demonstrate the chemical and microscopic examination of urine, blood and other materials from the patients he presented. Simon had set up a laboratory in his private quarters close to the Charité, where he performed more complicated quantitative analyses and also held private courses for the students. 1840 saw the publication of the first volume of his manual of applied clinical chemistry, in which he described his analytical methods and detailed the results of his investigations in patients. The second volume appeared two years later.

Meanwhile Schönlein strove hard to establish a laboratory for Simon at the Charité. But negotiations dragged because the medical corps generals at the Pépinière – to which the Charité belonged – did not want to set up a laboratory in Schönlein's department, but in the *prosectorium*, i.e. the morbid anatomy department where autopsies were performed. They had selected the young Virchow for this task, advising him to learn chemical methodology. Simon died before a decision was reached. Schönlein then entrusted two of his assistants with continuing Simon's work. Wilhelm Heintz (1817–1880) took over the chemistry, and Robert Remak (1815–1865) the microscopy. However, no actual laboratory was yet available. Moreover, until 1856 the Berliners had to do without Virchow, whose political activities during the 1848 Revolution had led to his dismissal.

In the interim Virchow was appointed professor of pathology at the University of Würzburg, where he secured a new building for the pathology institute, which included a large chemistry laboratory. The clinical professors at Würzburg were very progressive for the times. Impressed by Liebig's writings, they had acquired a small collection of chemical apparatus. In an application to the university authorities they wrote, with reference to Liebig, that a new discipline was emerging in their institution 'that requires a man's undivided attention'. In Johann Joseph [von] Scherer (1814–1869), they found their man. Scherer had studied medicine and chemistry and, after working with Liebig for a year and a half, was eminently well trained for work as a 'chemical pathologist'. His laboratory worked closely with Würzburg's Juliusspital. Analytical results were 'always publicly announced in the hospital and used by the attending physicians for diagnosis, etc',[10] giving us our first glimpse of the role of a modern hospital laboratory. A short time later another clinical laboratory opened at the General Hospital of Vienna University. Its director was the Moravian chemist Johann Florian Heller (1813–1871), who had to contend with a much greater local credibility problem than Scherer faced with his clinicians in Würzburg.[11]

These early clinical laboratories were headed by chemists or chemically trained physicians. Their further evolution through the second half of the 19th century and into the 20th century saw physicians increasingly taking charge of the laboratory work.

Johann Joseph [von] Scherer *(1814–1869) obtained his MD in Würzburg in 1836 with a thesis on the effects of poisons in various classes of animal. He took an early interest in chemistry and, while working as a spa physician at Wipfeld in Franconia, accepted an invitation from the naturalist Ernst von Bibra (1806–1878) to undertake chemical work in the latter's private laboratory at Schloss Schwebheim near Schweinfurt. Under the influence of von Bibra, Scherer decided to study chemistry in Munich. The Bavarian government gave him a travelling scholarship in 1840 that took him to Giessen for a year and a half as an assistant to Liebig. Afterwards he returned to Würzburg, where he initially found employment as a chemistry teacher at a technical school. In 1842 he was appointed to the university as an associate professor. Five years later he became a full professor. Scherer's scientific papers during his early Würzburg years dealt with chemical pathology. In an 1843 monograph he published his chemical and clinical findings in 71 patients. His many pupils included the famous Max [von] Pettenkofer (1818–1901). After Scherer's death on 17th February 1869, his chair and the large new institute built for him in 1865 were taken over by the Philosophical Faculty.*

An accurate balance: the most important instrument

Let us take a look at a clinical laboratory of the time. According to Simon, every analysis had to start with a specific question raised by a specific clinical case. In other words, no analysis without a reason. What was analysed? Primarily urine and blood, but also pathological formations such as kidney and bladder stones. The 'total analysis' developed by Scherer – the leading method of blood analysis between 1843 and 1850 – was typical of the times. The most important instrument was an accurate balance. However, techniques like Scherer's were undoubtedly too demanding for the ordinary medical practitioner. Adapting laboratory methods to physicians' resources and abilities was a particular ambition of Heller in Vienna.

Unfortunately, there are no surviving photographs of early clinical laboratories. However, archival records do convey an idea of their equipment and general appearance. For example, we have a sketch and a list of the requisite apparatus for the laboratory planned by Heintz for Schönlein's

Scherer's total blood analysis

Systematic chemical analysis of the blood, encompassing as many components as possible, was a particular challenge. Test material was available in abundance, for bloodletting was still a common therapeutic practice at the time. However, blood coagulates shortly after being drawn, with the solid red blood clot separating from the liquid yellowish serum, and hence a special analytical technique was necessary. Clean separation of clot from serum was difficult as the centrifuge had yet to be invented. Protein, the main component of serum, was coagulated with boiling water, separated and weighed. The 'extractives' remaining in the serum water posed a formidable analytical problem. Scherer spoke of the Herculean task of cleaning the 'Augean stables of extractives'. Isolation of individual components was attempted after evaporating the water. The blood clot was analysed by squeezing a second sample of clotted blood through a linen cloth, which retained the 'fibrous material' known today as fibrin. The fluid that passed through the cloth contained dissolved substances which could be determined after evaporating the water. All in all, it was a complicated and hugely time-consuming method. Eugen Franz von Gorup-Besanez (1817–1878), professor of chemistry in Erlangen, included Scherer's method in his *Lehrbuch der Zoochemischen Analyse,* recommending it

> for its neatness of execution, which presents no significant difficulties to those with some practice in chemical work, and for the fact that all components are found by weighing.[12]

Zusammenstellung der Resultate.

Die auf 1000 berechneten Zahlen stellt man in folgender Weise zusammen :
In unserem gewählten Beispiele :

In 1000 Serum sind enthalten :		In 1000 Blut sind enthalten :	
Wasser	910,45	Wasser	783,18
Feste Stoffe	89,55	Feste Stoffe	216,82
Eiweiss	74,15	Faserstoff	2,30
Extractivstoffe	5,96	Blutkörperchen	139,25
Lösliche Salze	8,74	Eiweiss	63,78
	88,85	Extractivstoffe	5,13
Differenz	0,70	Lösl. Salze	8,86
			219,32
		Differenz	2,50

Die Gesammtmenge der anorganischen Salze des Serums betrug: 10,49 in 1000 Th.

Die Gesammtmenge der anorganischen Salze des Blutes betrug: 10,71 in 1000. In 1000 Th. defibrinirten Blutes waren ferner 2,68 Fett enthalten.

Laboratory report of a blood analysis performed using Scherer's method (c. 1843).

department. The laboratory was to include an instrument room equipped with analytical balances, microscopes and other sensitive devices, and a chemist's room furnished with fireplaces, distillation apparatus, sand and water baths and a place for storing coal. A large room with workbench space for about 25 students was to be devoted to practical instruction. The range of equipment in the clinical laboratories headed by chemists was already astonishingly large. Particularly noteworthy were the instruments available for quantitative analyses. In addition to the balance, the mid-1840s saw the arrival of the polarimeter in laboratories, a notable advance particularly because it afforded a simple means of measuring the 'sugar' concentration in urine.[13] Laboratories like Scherer's and Heller's also possessed an apparatus for Liebig's method of combustion analysis. Nor was there any lack of powerful microscopes. First used to detect and identify crystals obtained in chemical separations, they later served mainly for the study of cells and other biological structures.[14] Until the invention of the Bunsen burner in 1857, heating was usually done with spirit lamps or the Berzelius lamp, which provided a readily adjustable flame.

The French model

In France and Great Britain the clinical laboratory developed along largely different lines. In France, where clinical medicine had played an important role since the late 18th century, scientific methods were applied early on in medicine, though for the most part the methods employed were physical, such as percussion of the chest and auscultation of chest sounds through the stethoscope. French clinicians developed these techniques into a fine art. Chemical investigations took a back seat by comparison. Their main purpose, if performed at all, was to support the diagnosis of diseases thought to originate in body fluids, i. e. in the 'humours', rather than in organs. This was a revival of the humoral pathology of antiquity, which interpreted disease as an imbalance of humours. Gabriel Andral (1797–1876) and other clinicians conducted systematic blood tests in an effort to advance understanding of disorders of the blood. In contrast to Scherer's detailed blood analyses, however, Andral contented himself with determining the proportions of fibrin, red blood cells, serum solids and water.

Despite Fourcroy's efforts, few clinical laboratories were set up in French hospitals. In 1839 the German clinician Carl Reinhold August Wunderlich (1815–1877), like many German physicians of the day, visited the Paris hospitals and described them in detail, noting little interest in chemistry among his French colleagues. In most cases samples were presumably sent for analysis to private commercial laboratories, which were generally run by pharmacists. Considering the great contributions made by French physicians to the development of morbid anatomy in the first half of the 19th century, their lack of interest in the use of the microscope for examining tissue is striking. It was above all three German-speaking physicians, Hermann Lebert (1813–1878), Louis Mandl (1812–1881) and David Gruby (1810–1898), whose courses introduced microscopy to the Parisian medical fraternity.

If the hospital chemistry laboratory got off to an inauspicious start in France, the medical research laboratory flourished there as nowhere else. The Parisian physiologist François Magendie (1783–1855) began studying physiological processes by opening the bodies of live animals, an experimental approach termed 'vivisection', which provoked widespread protests in England, Italy and the German-speaking countries. Magendie was a prosector at the Paris Faculty of Medicine before being appointed professor of physiology and general pathology at the Collège de France in 1836.

'The laboratory is the inner sanctum of medicine'

Magendie's pupil and successor Claude Bernard (1813–1878) used vivisection to investigate the chemical processes of digestion and the function of the liver. This enabled him to replace Liebig's hypotheses on metabolism with exact descriptions of the processes that actually occurred. His studies on the role of the liver in glucose metabolism, including the discovery of the glucose storage substance glycogen, are just one example of his work.[15]

In his famous theoretical work *Introduction à l'étude de la medicine expérimentale,* often described as the bible of scientific medicine, Bernard spoke of the laboratory as the inner sanctum of medicine.[16] And in his book on diabetes he proclaimed that:

> rich in facts gathered in hospital, [medicine] can now leave the hospital for the laboratory.[17]

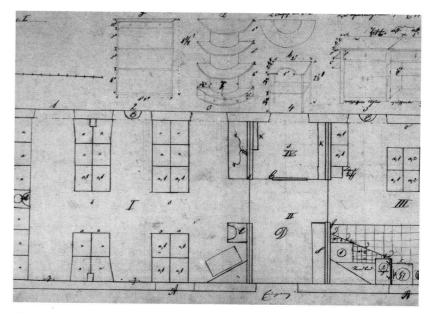

Plan for a chemical pathology laboratory at Berlin's Charité Hospital. Autograph sketch from a handwritten application by Heintz, 1847. I: Teaching laboratory with workbenches for the students; II: anteroom; III: chemist's workroom; IV: instrument room.

Work at Bernard's laboratory was primarily physiological rather than clinical, at the service of science. Yet its huge influence extended to clinical laboratories worldwide. Incidentally, Bernard rejected the emergent application of statistical methods in experimental medicine, as the following passage from his *Introduction* vividly illustrates:

> Imagine a physiologist collecting urine from the lavatory of a train station frequented by travellers from all nations, and believing that this provided him with an analysis of the average European urine.[18]

Bernard's scepticism notwithstanding, statistical data were needed to ascertain reference values for the composition of 'normal urine'.[19]

The British model

As a legacy of the Enlightenment, and thanks particularly to the work of the Royal Society in London, the experimental method was widely accepted in British medical circles at the start of the 19th century, which was not the case in Germany. In 1808 the Animal Chemistry Club was formed within the Royal Society, primarily as a forum for the new discipline of organic chemistry. An institution that was to have an even more profound influence on the future of medicine was the Medico-Chirurgical Society of London, founded by Alexander Marcet (1770–1822) and a group of physicians who shared his interest in the natural sciences. Originally from Geneva, Marcet emigrated to Britain during the Napoleonic Wars and became a physician at Guy's

Hospital in London. In addition to his clinical duties, he taught an experimental chemistry course at the medical school attached to Guy's.

Chemistry is to the physician as anatomy is to the surgeon

William Prout (1785–1850), the pre-eminent clinical and physiological chemist of his day in Britain,[20] likewise had close ties to Guy's Hospital, although he held no post there. He carried out his research as a private physician. In 1814 he began to hold lectures on animal chemistry in his apartment. Today Prout's name is primarily associated with his hypothesis that the atomic weights of elements are whole-number multiples of the weight of hydrogen. As far as the history of clinical chemistry is concerned, however, his main claim to fame rests in his extensive work on the chemistry of digestion and his division of 'alimentary substances' into three broad classes, namely 'saccharine' (carbohydrate), 'oily' (lipid) and 'albuminous' (protein), which are still current today. Another achievement that received considerable attention was his discovery of hydrochloric acid in gastric juice in 1824. In his Goulstonian Lecture at the Royal College of Physicians of London in 1831, Prout predicted with astonishing far-sightedness:

> What the knowledge of anatomy at present is to the surgeon, so will chemistry be to the physician, in directing him generally, what to do, and what to shun.[21]

In the mid-19th century Guy's Hospital was the leading centre for the application of chemistry to medicine. Two of the hospital's lecturers, Golding Bird (1814–1854) and George Owen Rees (1813–1889), published widely read books describing the analytical methods they developed at Guy's and their uses. From 1864 onwards, Ludwig Johann Wilhelm Thudichum (1829–1901) embarked on an extensive research project funded by the Privy Council 'to improve the chemical identification of diseases', partly at the laboratory of St Thomas' Hospital, which he headed, and partly in his superbly equipped private laboratory. Using new analytical methods, he discovered and characterised a number of previously unknown substances in the body fluids of the healthy and sick.

Two groundbreaking projects are cited here as indicative of the high standard of research in mid-19th century England. In 1843 Richard Bright (1789–1858) established two wards with a laboratory at Guy's Hospital for the study of kidney disease. Extensive chemical and microscopic studies there led to the description of Bright's disease[22] – an early

Ludwig Johann Wilhelm Thudichum *(1829–1901) at age 33. Thudichum studied medicine at Giessen University and also attended Liebig's chemistry lectures, but did not work in the latter's laboratory. Unable to obtain a university post in Giessen (probably because of his political activities after 1848), he emigrated in 1853 to England, where he worked as a physician at several London hospitals and taught chemistry at various London medical schools. In his well-equipped private chemistry laboratory he devoted himself extensively to research. His equipment included a combustion apparatus, presented to him by Liebig, which Thudichum once described as his 'most precious possession' In 1866 he was appointed lecturer in pathological chemistry and head of the newly established pathological chemistry laboratory at St Thomas' Hospital. Thudichum is mainly remembered today for his pioneering studies on the chemical constitution of the brain, in which he laid the foundations of cerebral biochemistry. In addition to his many journal publications, Thudichum wrote important books on subjects ranging from gallstones and the analysis of urine in disease to basic chemical anatomy and clinical chemistry. His writings also include* A Manual of Chemical Physiology including its Points of Contact with Pathology, *monographs on public health and (according to the foreword) a rigorously scientific book on the chemistry of wine. Although Thudichum never worked in Liebig's laboratory, he regarded Liebig as the teacher who had most influenced him. He helped promote Liebig's meat extract by publicly endorsing it when it was introduced in Britain. After Liebig's death Thudichum published a detailed article on Liebig's discoveries and philosophy.*

example of disease research at a university hospital. And at University College, also in London, the physician Alfred Baring Garrod (1819–1907) demonstrated that uric acid was consistently present in the blood of gout sufferers. To detect this characteristic 'disease matter', he devised a 'thread test' in which uric acid crystallised as the sodium salt on a thread immersed in the sample. This enabled Garrod to distinguish gout from rheumatic diseases with similar

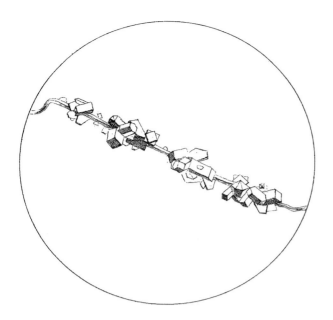

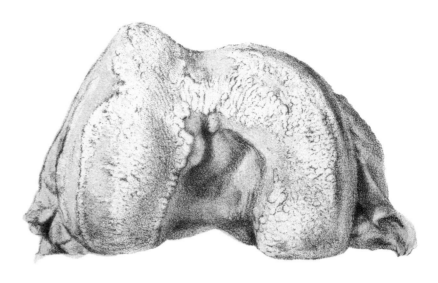

Garrod's thread test to detect uric acid in blood.

Deposits of sodium urate (sodium salt of uric acid) on the articular surface of the knee joint in a patient with gout.

symptoms, since patients with the latter showed no marked increase in uric acid.

These achievements contrast sharply with the general lack of interest in chemistry's potential clinical applications among Bright's and Garrod's British contemporaries. Lecturing to students in 1848, the famous Dublin clinician Robert Graves (1796–1853), expressed the prevailing sentiments of the period well when he remarked:

> I have seen students led astray by false notions, wasting half the time which should be spent in hospital and by the sickbed, in wandering through the fields on botanical excursions, or working in the laboratory, engaged in the solution of some unimportant problem.[23]

It is from Robert Graves, incidentally, that the form of hyperthyroidism known in the English-speaking world as Graves' disease takes its name (in Continental Europe the name 'Basedow's disease' [from Carl Adolph von Basedow, 1799–1854] is preferred).

One reason why British clinicians were so hesitant to acknowledge the value of chemistry in medicine was the still widely held belief that chemistry contributed nothing to clarifying the 'mysteries of life', and hence could contribute nothing to understanding disease.

Wanted: more than just 'diagnostic signs'

There were also setbacks on the path to progress, for various reasons. The Leipzig chemist Carl Gotthelf Lehmann (1812–1863) lamented:

> It is hard to understand how one could hope to recognise the abnormal when one is still unfamiliar with the normal.[24]

This complaint was particularly pertinent to protein chemistry. Three types of protein had been distinguished, and chemical formulae postulated. But there was no agreement. Liebig and the Dutch chemist Mulder became embroiled in a fierce argument over the chemical structure of proteins. The knowledge and methods of the day were incapable of differentiating between normal and abnormal proteins. As an understanding of proteins was critical for understanding sickness and health, progress faltered.

To gain its clinical credentials, chemical pathology had to provide more than confirmatory evidence for the diagnostic signs long familiar to physicians. Another cause for scepticism was the inadequacy of contemporary knowledge of physiology, particularly among chemists. In his 1831 Goulstonian Lecture Prout had stressed that physicians would have to acquire a knowledge of chemistry for this very reason. In Germany, in particular, there was the added difficulty that the physiology taught at the universities in the first decades of the 19th century was heavily influenced by natural philosophy, which pushed the discoveries and methods of natural science into the background.

A final factor was the growing shortage of qualified staff as advances in the chemical synthesis of organic compounds opened up new and attractive careers for chemists in the second half of the 19th

The Virchow solution: a department of chemistry at Charité's Institute of Pathology

After moving to a professorship in Berlin in 1856, Virchow won approval for a new building, including a large chemistry laboratory, for the Institute of Pathology at Charité Hospital. Even as a student, Virchow had been fascinated by chemical pathology and had done some experimental work of his own, for example on the role of proteins in disease. In a report on a study trip for the Ministry of Education and Culture in 1846, he had written:

> Lastly, it should be mentioned that the morbid anatomist, if he wishes to be a physiologist, must also be a chemist. But he cannot also be expected to perform all the chemical work himself. He would not have the time for this. However, he should be familiar with the methods.[28]

The laboratory set up at the new institute in Berlin operated as an independent department of chemistry. It became the pre-eminent training site for chemical physiology and pathology and the incubator for many of the institute's subsequent directors. The medical historian Erwin Ackerknecht has described Virchow as the 'grandfather of biochemistry' for this reason.

The Frerichs solution: The laboratory in Charité's 1st Department of Medicine

In 1859 the Breslau clinician Friedrich Theodor [von] Frerichs (1819–1885) succeeded Schönlein as head of the 1st Department of Medicine at Berlin's Charité Hospital.[29] As a pupil of the Göttingen chemist Friedrich Wöhler (1800–1882), he was greatly interested in the clinical application of chemistry. In Berlin he established a hospital chemistry laboratory at the Charité, run at his request by a junior physician employed as a chemical assistant. Thanks to the obliging anatomist Karl Bogislaus Reichert (1811–1883), Frerichs managed to obtain several large rooms at Berlin University's newly built Institute of Anatomy for his research in chemical physiology and pathology.

century. They migrated into organic chemistry laboratories and the fledgling chemical industry, where prospects were more salubrious than the 'messy work' of handling biological samples.

Disease as dysfunction

Fortunately, the situation changed as a result of a shift in thinking about the nature of disease.[25] Since antiquity disease had been viewed as a phenomenon that befell man, producing signs and symptoms.

It was a view that assumed a fundamental divide between health and disease. The French physician François Joseph Victor Broussais (1771–1839) was the first to advance the contrary position that disease was subject to the same laws as health and that the differences between physiological and pathological states were quantitative, not differences in kind. Thus Broussais wrote:

> Diseases are derangements to which the functions are subject and which distance them from the normal or physiological state.[26]

Disease thus became a process. This new school of medicine was known as 'physiological medicine'. Incidentally, readers familiar with the novels of Honoré de Balzac (1799–1850) will have encountered Broussais immortalised as Dr Brisset, one of the three medical committee doctors in *La Peau de Chagrin* (variously translated as *The Wild Ass's Skin* and *The Magic Skin*).

From about 1840 onwards younger clinicians began adopting Broussais's doctrine of physiological medicine because of the scope it afforded for applying scientific methods in clinical medicine. Competing groups chose different names for this new direction in medicine and launched journals to champion their ideas. The *Archiv für Physiologische Heilkunde*, published by Wilhelm Roser (1817–1888) and Carl Reinhold August Wunderlich (1815–1877), the *Zeitschrift für rationelle Medizin*, founded by Jacob Henle (1809–1885) and Karl von Pfeufer (1806–1869), and Virchow's *Archiv für pathologische Anatomie und Physiologie und für klinische Medizin* all date from this period. All the groups were allied in their opposition to 'ontology', a term Virchow borrowed from philosophy to denote a belief in the existence of independent disease entities, and in their insistence on seeking rational, evidence-based explanations for observed phenomena. Even the infectious pathogens discovered in subsequent decades were – as Virchow stressed – not the disease, but the cause of physiological changes in the affected body.[27]

Bernard made a major contribution to the new view of disease as a deviation from normal bodily function with his concept of the *milieu intérieur*, or internal environment, defined as the circulating fluid (plasma, lymph) that bathes the body's cells. The constancy of this environment is a necessary condition for normal function, and characterising it would be one of the major tasks of 20th century clinical chemistry. The myriad parameters that can now be measured in the laboratory make possible to detect and correct abnormal increases and decreases in the constituents of the internal environment before they become a serious problem.

Between hospital and pathology laboratory

The new doctrine of physiological medicine encouraged physicians to start applying chemistry on their own to resolve clinical questions. This meant establishing chemistry laboratories which, unlike their predecessors, were directed by physicians and employed physicians trained in chemistry. Two models were tried at Berlin's Friedrich Wilhelm University (today Humboldt University; see box). Both were very successful and were widely imitated at other institutions in Germany, and later in other countries.

The Virchow solution, linking a chemistry laboratory with a pathology institute, aroused great interest, particularly among American physicians. The model was adopted at many American universities. It also explains the common American usage of 'clinical pathology' to denote a speciality that includes clinical chemistry. German-speaking countries preferred Frerichs' 'clinical solution'. The first head of Virchow's laboratory was the physician Ernst Felix Immanuel Hoppe-Seyler (1825–1895), who was subsequently the first appointee to the chair of chemical physiology at Tübingen University, inaugurating a branch of science that became biochemistry.

Ward and hospital laboratories

In the last decades of the 19th century many hospitals had facilities for performing simple chemistry and microscopy on the wards or in ward laboratories. At their most rudimentary these consisted of a table in the doctors' room with a microscope and a few simple pieces of apparatus. University hospitals usually had a separate small room close to the patients. The investigations were performed by a student or young physician, known in German universities as a *famulus* (Latin: servant) or *amanuensis* (Latin: a slave secretary), who thus received on-the-job training in the methods employed. The American educationalist Abraham Flexner (1866–1959), who studied medical training in Europe before the First World War with a foreigner's critical eye on behalf of the Carnegie Foundation for the Advancement of Teaching, reported on the Prussian regime in these ward laboratories:

> The immaculate appearance of these little laboratories is ascribable not to lack of work – an immense amount of material is daily handled in them – but to a system of fines for offenses against good housekeeping; a

Ernst Felix Immanuel Hoppe-Seyler *(1825–1895) had Friedrich Ludwig Jahn (1778–1852), the "father of gymnastics", as a godfather, and retained a lifelong interest in sporting activity as a result. Felix Hoppe lost his parents as a child and grew up in the home of his brother-in-law, the physician Dr Seyler. Many years later, when Hoppe became professor in Tübingen, his brother-in-law adopted him. From then on he called himself Hoppe-Seyler. The young Felix studied medicine in Halle, Leipzig and Berlin, developing a particular interest in chemistry. In 1854 he obtained a post as prosector in anatomy at the University of Greifswald. Two years later Virchow offered him the post of prosector and head of the Chemistry Department at the Charité Hospital's new Institute of Pathology, in which he proved highly successful. In 1861 he was appointed Associate Professor in Applied Chemistry at the University of Tübingen. Finally, he took on the newly created chair of Physiological Chemistry at Strasbourg University, where a large institute was built for him. In his scientific work Hoppe-Seyler began by concentrating exclusively on developing and improving analytical methods for the new physiological chemistry, which he described in a small "guide", which appeared in 1858. Over the course of the years this grew into an extensive "Handbook of Physiological and Pathological Chemical Analysis", which remained the standard work on analytical methods in physiological chemistry until the mid-20th century. Another important factor in he development of the discipline of physiological chemistry was the journal – "Zeitschrift für Physiologische Chemie" [Journal for Physiological Chemistry] – that he launched in 1877. From his extensive body of scientific work, all we mention here are his blood pigment studies which led to accurate methods for measuring hemoglobin and its derivatives.*

penalty of two cents is imposed if a gas-jet is left burning, one of ten cents if a lens is left lying about.[30]

During the *Gründerjahre*, the boom years following the Franco-Prussian War of 1870–71, superbly equipped laboratories were set up in Germany, particularly at the universities. One example was the 'Clinical Institute', conceived by the clinician Hugo von Ziemssen (1829–1902), which opened in Munich in 1878. Built next to the university hospital, the institute was richly endowed with instruments and clinical teaching materials, and had a dedicated clinical chemistry laboratory for research. The William Pepper Laboratory of Clinical Medicine at the University of Pennsylvania, which opened in Philadelphia in 1894, was similarly well appointed. Explicit reference was made to the Virchow and Ziemssen institutes at the dedication ceremony.

Several German universities created spacious new buildings for their teaching hospitals around this time. When the Tübingen Medical Hospital opened in 1879, only the doctors' room was available for simple chemistry and microscopy. By 1890, new

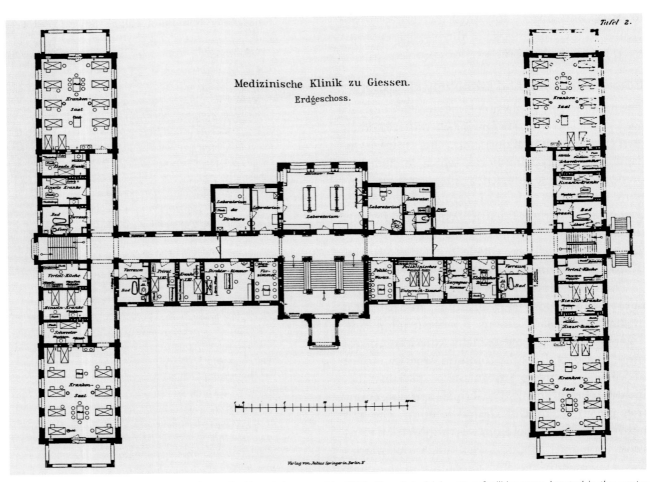

Medizinische Klinik zu Giessen.

Erdgeschoss.

Verlag von Julius Springer in Berlin N

Ground floor plan of Giessen University's medical hospital, opened in 1892. The clinical laboratory facilities were located in the centre section of the building, opposite the main entrance. The wards occupied several floors in the wings.

departments and hospitals were being built with extensive laboratories devoted to patient care, teaching and research. For example, the new medical hospital at the University of Giessen, which commenced operations in 1890, was designed with a large laboratory at its centre, giving concrete expression to Bernard's description of the laboratory as the inner sanctum of medicine.

Clinical chemistry analysis became a regular part of the medical curriculum in the last decades of the 19th century, creating a demand for textbooks. In his memoirs, Friedrich [von] Müller (1858–1941), a Munich clinician, related that students asked him to run a revision course on the subject. This grew into the *Taschenbuch der Medicinisch-klinischen Diagnostik,* produced in collaboration with Otto Seifert (1853–1933). First published 1886, the book was still a best-seller when the 73rd edition appeared in 2000.

At the start of the 20th century, smaller hospitals and sanatoria also incorporated small diagnostic laboratories.

Colour as a guide to diagnosis

Spurred by the medical community's growing interest in chemical analysis and improvements in analytical methods and instrumentation, the second half of the 19th century saw spectacular advances in techniques based on the detection or measurement of colours. Even the very earliest practitioners, in examining their patients, had looked for telltale colour changes, notably of the skin or urine.[31] Similarly, careful attention to the colour changes that occur during chemical reactions had long been standard practice in chemical laboratories. What was new was the advent of optical, i.e. physical, methods of colour measurement for chemistry and clinical chemistry.

In 1860 the chemist Robert Wilhelm Bunsen (1811–1899) and the physicist Gustav Robert Kirchhoff (1824–1887) invented spectral analysis, initiating a methodological revolution in analytical chemistry.[32] In the 17th century, Isaac Newton (1642–1727) had made a detailed study of the dis-

Small clinical laboratory at the sanatorium of Maximilian Oskar Bircher-Benner (1867–1939) in Zurich (c.1910). Bircher-Benner is still remembered for his contributions to nutritional therapy (Bircher muesli). His laboratory possessed equipment that was state-of-the-art at the time. Items on the benches include (from left to right) a centrifuge, pipettes, a water bath, a sugar polarimeter and a microscope.

persion of sunlight into separate bands of colour as it passes through a glass prism. The English term 'spectrum' (which originally meant 'an apparition or ghost') entered common use for describing the phenomenon of separated light. Bunsen and Kirchhoff studied the changes in the colour of a flame caused by introducing the salts of various elements.[33] Flame coloration by minerals had long been known, and had found practical application in the manufacture of fireworks. But Bunsen's and Kirchhoff's purpose was to use it to identify chemical elements. On separating the coloured light with a glass prism, they observed characteristic 'coloured lines'. They constructed a spectroscope, which enabled Bunsen, only a short time later, to discover two new elements, which he called 'rubidium' and 'caesium'.

The spectroscope – which soon became commercially available – began to interest the medical profession in 1862, when Hoppe-Seyler made an exciting discovery. He observed that an aqueous blood solution held in a glass bath in front of the spectro-

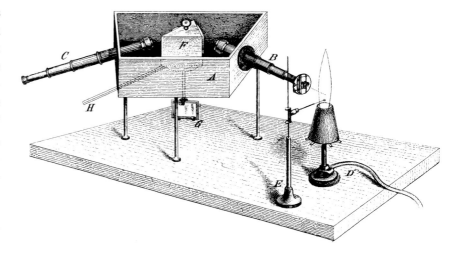

Sketch of the first Bunsen-Kirchhoff spectroscope, consisting of a box (**A**) blackened on the inside, telescopes (**B**, **C**), a Bunsen burner (**D**), an arm holding a platinum wire (**E**), a hollow prism filled with carbon disulphide (**F**) and a handle (**H**) for rotating the prism and mirror (**G**).

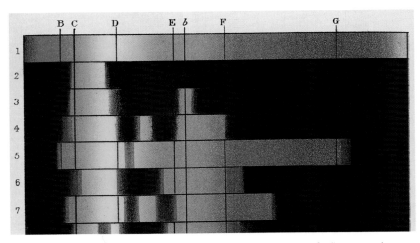

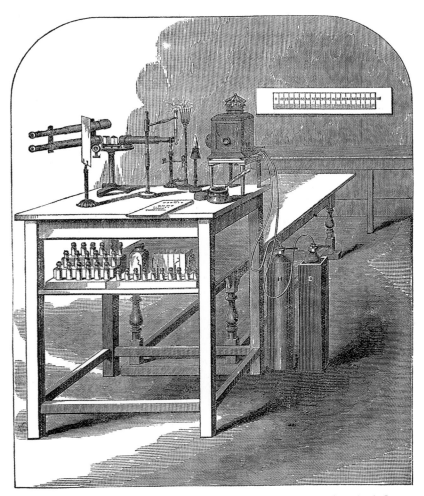

Solar spectrum and blood spectra. 1: Solar spectrum with Fraunhofer lines; 4 and 5: oxy-hemoglobin; 6: reduced hemoglobin; 7: carboxyhemoglobin.

Thudichum's well-equipped spectroscopic observatory in London (1867). A Bunsen spectroscope is shown on the left of the bench. On the right is a Drummond light, which produced an intense limelight using oxygen and hydrogen from the bottles to the right of the bench. An additional telescope was mounted on the spectroscope for accurate spectra measurement using a scale projected onto the wall.

scope no longer showed the complete solar spectrum, but displayed extinctions ('bands') in various regions of the spectrum. Two years later the Irish physicist George Gabriel Stokes (1819–1903) showed that what Hoppe-Seyler had seen was the spectrum of oxygenated arterial blood: deoxygenated venous blood exhibited quite different bands. This provided a method of confirming the presence of blood, and of distinguishing arterial from venous blood. Soon after, the spectroscope was successfully used to detect carbon monoxide-laden blood in victims of coal fume poisoning, which was common at the time due to poorly ventilated stoves.

The discovery of blood spectra alerted physicians and biologists to the potential of this new physical method in studying the hitherto chemically obscure pigments from the animal and vegetable kingdoms. Many clinical laboratories also acquired a spectroscope or its handier version, the 'direct-vision spectroscope'.

First test for anemia

The increasing focus on pigments in medical laboratories prompted the idea of measuring colour intensity to gauge the strength of a pigment solution. A particularly important task was to determine the concentration of the red blood pigment, hemoglobin, and thus provide more accurate estimates of anemia severity. Industry had already devised simple comparative methods for determining the concentration of a dye solution against reference solutions of known strength. For example, there were already devices for testing the purity of vegetable dyes, such as indigo. These devices for visually comparing two dye solutions were known as colorimeters. Hoppe-Seyler had designed a similar apparatus for blood even before the discovery of the blood spectra, but the real breakthrough was achieved by the Parisian instrument maker Jules Duboscq (1817–1886), whose instruments remained in use, with minor modifications, for over 100 years. These colorimeters were highly accurate. Constructed of brass and glass and mounted on polished wood, they were the jewels of the laboratory. Many methods of quantitative clinical chemistry analysis were subsequently developed for Duboscq colorimeters. The American biochemist Otto Folin[34] (1867–1934) created one of the most complete analytical programmes for blood and urine in the early 20th century. His methods used colorimetry to perform virtually all the clinically important laboratory investigations. However, the techniques were still too time-consuming for clinical practice. The preparation of reference solutions was also too complicated. For important parameters such as hemoglobin estimation, the simple instruments designed by the Englishman William Richard Gowers (1845–1915) and the Swiss Hermann Sahli (1856–1933) entered common use. These hemometers compared the colour of blood dilutions with a sealed tube containing a suitable stable pigment at a precisely adjusted concentration.

Spectrophotometry

Simple colorimetry, however, was not enough for medical research. New developments led to the technique of spectrophotometry. In 1873 the Tübingen physiologist Karl Vierordt (1818–1884) modified the Bunsen-Kirchhoff spectroscope to allow comparison between a pigment solution of unknown strength and a standard in a precisely defined region of the spectrum. His spectrophotometer quantified the concentration of pigment in a solution in a specific narrow wavelength region. The Vierordt method inaugurated a glittering period of progress in instrumentation, led first by skilled institute technicians, but soon dominated by the emergent optical instrument companies. The mechanisation and automation that began in the mid-20th century are in many cases still based today on photometric methods.

Duboscq colorimeter.

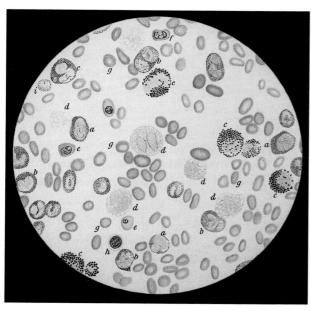

*Blood smear demonstrating the elevated white cell count characteristic of myeloid leukemia. Ehrlich's triacid stain clearly differentiates the granulations in the white blood cells, identifying neutrophils (**b**) and eosinophils (**c**). This stain does not show the basophilic granulation in mast cells (**d**).*

Differentiation of blood cells

Researchers in the 19th century had already begun to stain their biological preparations to facilitate visual identification. In addition to natural pigments, synthetic dyes were available for this purpose from mid-century on. As aniline was used in the synthesis of many of these dyes, they were collectively known as aniline dyes. The young medical student Paul Ehrlich (1854–1915) – encouraged by his cousin, the pathologist Carl Weigert (1845–1904), and his anatomy professor, Wilhelm von Waldeyer-Hartz (1836–1921) – became interested in the use of aniline dyes to stain cells and tissues. He developed novel methods of staining microscopy preparations which made it possible to demonstrate chemically distinct cell structures.[35] Ehrlich applied his staining techniques with great success to blood,

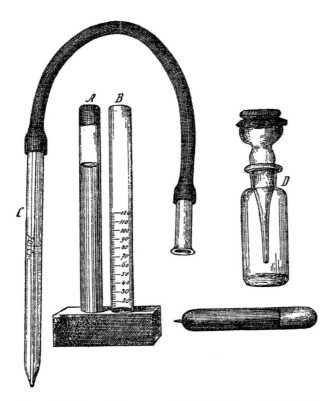

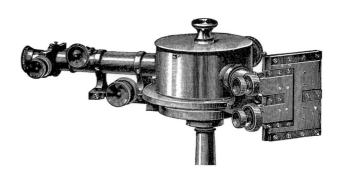

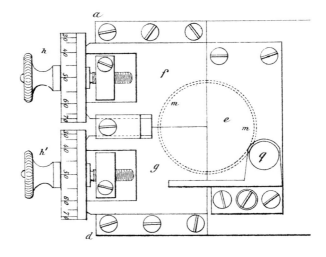

Gowers' instrument for measuring blood pigment (1879). The sealed tube (**A**) contained a stable solution of the red dye picro-carmine as the reference standard. Twenty microlitres of blood were transferred to the other tube (**B**) with the pipette (**C**), and distilled water was added with the dropper (**D**) until the colour in B matched that in A. The hemoglobin content was read from the scale on B as a percentage of normal.

Vierordt spectrophotometer. Above: View of the instrument with double slit. Below: Double slit for sample and reference beams.

differentiating between various types of white blood cells (leukocytes). He discovered mast cells, which contain granules staining with basic dyes (e. g. methylene blue), eosinophils, which show granules on staining with acid dyes (e. g. eosin), and neutrophils. For direct microscopy, he also developed the smear method still in use today, in which a drop of blood is smeared onto a slide and air-dried. Ehrlich was the founder of modern blood morphology. His method of differentiating leukocytes removed the cloud of uncertainty that had previously hovered over this family of cells.

The staining techniques still used for blood counts date back to a method originally developed by Dimitri Leonidovich Romanowsky (1861–1921) for identifying the malaria pathogens (plasmodia) found in the red blood cells of malaria patients.[36] The Romanowsky stain as modified by Gustav Giemsa (1867–1948) was widely used. The new blood staining techniques differentiated between the various forms of leukemia for the first time, yielding more accurate diagnoses of the disease

first described by the young Virchow as 'white blood'. In large part thanks to Ehrlich, blood microscopy rapidly became one of the most important fields of laboratory medicine.

Near-patient research

These methods of chemical and microscopic investigation brought near-patient research into the clinical laboratory for the first time. The clinician Bernhard Naunyn (1839–1925), who worked as a young assistant in Frerichs' department, wrote in his memoirs:

Experimental work virtually forces itself on the physician; the ward is the most fertile source for topics of normal and pathological physiology.[37]

It was also Naunyn who made the much-quoted pronouncement:

Medicine will be a science or it will be nothing.[38]

And, speaking at the Congress of Internal Medicine in Vienna in 1908, Friedrich [von] Müller could confidently declare:

The times are past when superficial dilettantism dominated chemistry studies and hypotheses. In medical department laboratories, good and useful chemical work is now being done that is acknowledged not only by chemical physiologists, but also by professional chemists. We have created a solid foundation for teaching the pathology of nutrition and metabolism.[39]

A new specialty is born

From about 1840 onwards there were definite signs pointing to the birth of a new scientific discipline. Special laboratories were set up, textbooks written, professorships created, research proposals drafted, and journals and societies founded to promote the exchange of ideas.

Laboratories now became a fixture of university and non-university hospitals, but had little freedom to pursue research agendas of their own choosing. Their focus was restricted to clinical diagnosis and disease research. Still, the years that clinical chemistry laboratories spent in the bosom of the hospital were critical to the scientific development of the specialty.

One by-product of this 'chequered history' was that there was no single universally accepted name for the new field. The designations 'medical chemistry', 'chemical pathology' and 'clinical chemistry' were used more or less interchangeably. The preferred terms in English-speaking countries were 'chemical pathology' and 'pathological chemistry', and in French *chimie médicale*, and later *'biochimie clinique'*.

The last decades of the 19th century witnessed the emergence of a variety of additional specialities, including bacteriology, serology and immunology, which likewise strove to establish themselves as sciences in their own right. Internists, in particular, resisted granting independence to clinical chemistry and the other new fields. At the first Congress of Internal Medicine in 1882, Frerichs expressed this in the following words:

> We welcome with pleasure the achievements of morbid anatomy, chemistry, and experimental pathology, which have provided us with valuable, in some cases invaluable, fundamental facts and considerably furthered the development of our science. But we remain masters in our own house, requiring no tutelage ...[40]

One of the most eminent British biochemists of the early 20th century, Frederick Gowland Hopkins (1861–1947), took the contrary view when he predicted independence in a lecture in 1908:

> But I believe it is not going too far to say that the rise of chemical pathology to its full importance will call almost for a new profession.[41]

Paul Ehrlich *(1854–1915) was still a schoolboy when he developed an interest in the natural sciences. Assigned to write an essay on Calderón's play* Life is a Dream *as part of his school-leaving examination, he got into trouble for proposing that brain activity was an oxidative process, and dreaming a 'phosphorescence of the brain'. Ehrlich began his medical studies in Breslau but transferred the following year to Strasbourg University, where he attended the lectures of chemist Adolf von Baeyer (1835–1917) and experimented with microscopic stains under the anatomist Wilhelm [von] Waldeyer-Hartz (1836–1921). At the age of 24 Ehrlich obtained his MD with a groundbreaking thesis on the theory and practice of histological staining. He became a consultant physician in the department of medicine at Charité Hospital under Frerichs, who left him a free hand to pursue his research. Ehrlich sought to explain the binding between stains and tissues in terms of the relationships between their chemical constituents. He developed far-reaching ideas on how and where chemical reactions take place in the cell, using stains as indicators of underlying chemical processes. He set out his theoretical ideas in a monograph on the oxygen requirements of the body, which he submitted as a* Habilitationsschrift, *the postdoctoral thesis required for qualification as a university lecturer, even though he had already been granted the title of professor. After Frerichs' death Ehrlich left the department and began to collaborate with Robert Koch (1843–1910) on immunisation in infectious diseases. In 1896 he was asked to head a new institute for serum research and serum testing in Berlin, which was moved three years later to Frankfurt am Main and grew into the large research institute which today bears Ehrlich's name. In Frankfurt he devoted himself increasingly to the chemotherapy of infectious diseases. This work culminated in the discovery of salvarsan for the treatment of syphilis. For his work on immunity, Ehrlich shared the 1908 Nobel Prize for Physiology or Medicine with Ilya Ilyich Mechnikov (1845–1916).*

Donald Dexter Van Slyke *(1883–1971) studied chemistry at the University of Michigan, where he obtained his doctorate in organic chemistry under Moses Gomberg (1866–1947), the discoverer of free radicals. He trained as a biochemist under Phoebus P. Levene (1869–1940) at New York's Rockefeller Institute for Medical Research, which was founded in 1901. In 1911 Van Slyke travelled to Berlin for a year to work with Emil Fischer (1852–1919). Before starting work as a chemist at Rockefeller Hospital, which had opened just a few years before, he was sent back to Europe to observe arrangements for cooperation between clinicians and biochemists at medical institutions in London, Paris, Berlin, Strasbourg, Freiburg and Munich. Van Slyke remained at Rockefeller Hospital until his retirement in 1948, and his laboratory there became the 'Mecca of clinical chemistry'. The year after his retirement he joined the newly founded Brookhaven National Laboratories in Upton, New York, where he remained active in research until his death on 4 May 1971.*

The term 'laboratory medicine' appeared only in the mid-20th century. While the term neatly captures an important common feature of a group of disciplines – namely, that they are all at home in the laboratory – it is a bit odd for a branch of science to be named for its setting rather than its subject matter. Or is the name a homage to Bernard's description of the laboratory as the inner sanctum of medicine?

The United States led the way in the 20th century. The very close collaboration that continued there for decades between the rapidly expanding fields of biochemistry and clinical chemistry was a decisive advantage. The science historian Robert E. Kohler has spoken of the 'American school of clinical biochemistry'. This success story began with Folin, and Donald Dexter Van Slyke (1883-1971), the 'father of modern clinical chemistry', played a particularly important role. His two-volume textbook *Quantitative Clinical Chemistry*, co-authored by the clinician

John Punnet Peters (1887–1955) and published in 1931 and 1932, was largely responsible for establishing the name 'clinical chemistry' worldwide.[42]

Medicine or science?

A heavy sigh echoes down to us from an early pioneer of laboratory medicine. In a letter to Virchow, written in 1869, Thudichum remarked:

> I am nothing if not both chemist and physician, but this union constitutes the difficulty of my existence.[43]

This one sentence nicely sums up the competing imperatives of medicine and natural science which shaped the development of laboratory medicine and have remained a fact of its existence to this day. Unlike most scientific disciplines, laboratory medicine did not originate as an offshoot of a parent discipline, that is, through specialisation, but through the fusion of several scientific fields. This accounts for many of its distinctive features. On closer examination, the fundamental divide between clinical or bedside medicine and the natural sciences could not be more apparent. It is the divide between the art of medicine, which involves the exercise of practical judgement and skill, and the imperatives of scientific research. Even the ancient Greeks distinguished between art, which they understood to include practical medicine as well as the crafts and fine arts, from scientific knowledge, which they termed *theoria*. The Yale epidemiologist Alvan R. Feinstein once spoke of two cultures, and others, such as Wolfgang Wieland have distinguished more recently between practical and theoretical science. The bedside physician deals with individual patients and has to make decisions that will help them. The research physician uses the methods of science to discover general truths.

Both approaches have an essential place in the medical or clinical laboratory. The methods of investigation are scientific, but they are used to obtain results that apply to one specific patient at a time. In a very real sense, the specialties that make up laboratory medicine can thus be seen as a kind of bridge between science and medical practice.

Ralf Bröer

Motes, protective ferments and hormones

Pregnancy testing from antiquity to the present day

Women always want to find out whether they are pregnant or not, and whether they are expecting a young gentleman or a little lady. If the doctor cannot give them a proper answer, they have scant regard for his skill.[1]

This quotation from the *Heilsame Dreck-Apotheke*, a book from 1696 by the Eisenach town physician Christian Franz Paullini (1643–1712), could readily be supplemented by hundreds of similar warnings in the medical literature from antiquity to the present day. Confirmation of pregnancy was always of the utmost importance for women (and men). Correct diagnosis at the earliest possible moment qualified or disqualified a physician in the eyes of his patients. It is therefore unsurprising that methods of pregnancy detection should have preoccupied every generation of medical practitioner for thousands of years. What may be surprising, though, is the overwhelming importance that all have attached to a pregnant woman's urine, from the early advanced civilisations to the monoclonal antibody era, regardless of the medical knowledge of the times.

Fumigation and urination

The oldest information on pregnancy detection methods is found in ancient Egyptian papyri, although we cannot always be certain whether the techniques described were actually pregnancy tests or sterility tests. Two prescriptions from Berlin Papyrus 3038 were probably intended as pregnancy tests. The first, Prescription No. 195, reads:

Other investigation in a woman who does not give birth…, she shall be fumigated with hippopotamus dung. If she passes urine and feces, she will give birth, but if not, she will not give birth, for she is in the normal state.[2]

It remains unclear whether this refers to fumigation of the vagina, nose or body in general. The use of dung should cause no surprise, given that the medicinal use of excrement formed an integral part of ancient medical practice.

Berlin Papyrus 3038, found in Saqqara and now housed in the Egyptian Museum in Berlin, was written around 1250 BC. However, its 204 prescriptions are much older, dating from the Middle Kingdom (2040–1781 BC), if not from the Old Kingdom (2670–2195 BC).[3] Prescription No. 199 reads:

Another procedure to determine whether a woman will or will not give birth: barley *[Hordeum vulgare]* and emmer *[Triticum dioccum]*. The woman must moisten it with urine every day like [she does the] dates and the sand, after it has been placed in two bags. If

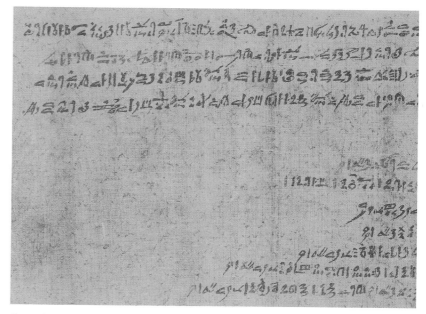

Page from Berlin Papyrus 3038 with Prescription No. 199 for diagnosing pregnancy from urine.

Christian Franz Paullini *(1643–1712) was personal physician to the Bishop of Münster and the Duke of Wolfenbüttel. He spent his twilight years as city medical officer in his home town of Eisenach. In place of a portrait, this is the copperplate engraving that graced the title page of the fourth edition of his* Heilsame Dreck-Apotheke *from 1734, last reprinted in 1847. It began with the words: 'Never be idle, listen and look: God's wonders are to be found even in the smallest speck of dirt. Each creature is a pledge of His goodness and tinder of His love, in excrement and urine lie God and Nature.'*
Apart from Heilsame Dreck-Apotheke, *Paullini also wrote* Flagellum salutis *and* Das hoch- und wohlgelehrte teutsche Frauenzimmer, *in praise, respectively, of the therapeutic value of the whip and the highly educated German woman. He also wrote works on the nutmeg, earthworm, toad and donkey.*

both grow, she will give birth. If the barley grows, it means a male child. If the emmer grows, it means a female child. If neither grows, she will not give birth.[4]

The reference to sand and dates relates to a similar test described in the Carlsberg Papyrus Collection. It required the woman to moisten two bags of silt and dates with her urine. If they grew worms, she would not give birth; if no worms grew, she would bear a healthy child. It goes without saying that the ancient Egyptians knew nothing of pregnancy hormones in the urine, but they had probably noticed that pregnant urine had a positive effect on the germinability of cereals. As for gender prediction, this is clearly based on magical thinking by analogy: in ancient Egyptian the word for barley was masculine and the word for emmer (wheat) feminine.[5]

Does the wheat germinate or not?

The Egyptian germinability test using pregnant urine for gender prediction turns up again several hundred years later in *De remediis parabilibus*, written by Galen of Pergamum (129 – c. 216), personal physician to the Roman emperor Marcus Aurelius:

> Take the urine of a pregnant woman and dig two little pits. In one throw barley, in the other wheat. Pour in the urine and cover with earth. If the wheat sprouts first, she will bear a boy, but if the barley, a girl.[6,7]

The sexes were reversed compared to the Egyptian original, but matched the genders of the words for the two cereals in Greek. In the Middle Ages the germinability test became part of European folk medicine. Paullini described it as late as the 18th century in his popular *Heilsame Dreck-Apotheke*:

> Dig two pits in the earth, throw barley in one and wheat in the other, but pour the urine of the pregnant woman into both and cover with earth. If the wheat shoots up before the barley, it will be a son, but if the barley comes up first, you must expect a daughter.[8]

In German as in Greek, 'barley' is feminine and 'wheat' masculine.

The 20th century saw several attempts to prove that the old germinability test was based not only on magic, but also on empirical knowledge. Ancient Egyptian urine testing first captured the attention of Selmar Aschheim (1878–1965), a Berlin gynecologist with an interest in history. In 1927, together with Bernhard Zondek (1891–1966), Aschheim presented to the public the first functional pregnancy test based on the hormonal effects of pregnant urine. In the same year the *Archiv für Gynäkologie* published a paper on 'Midwifery among the ancient Egyptians', in which the author mentioned the famous Prescription No. 199 from the Berlin Papyrus.[9] Aschheim was evidently referring to this essay when in 1928 he introduced an 'historical note' into the description of his method, remarking with surprise that 'the ancient Egyptians were already using urine for pregnancy testing 3000–4000 years ago.'[10] Together with Zondek he investigated the effect of pregnant urine on plant growth. However, it was Walter Schoeller (1880–1965) and Hans Göbel from the Berlin laboratory of Schering AG who in 1931 first reported accelerated flowering in hyacinths, onions and maize in response to the addition of estrone from pregnant urine.[11]

Julius Manger from the Institute of Pharmacology, University of Würzburg, recognised the parallels between the ancient Egyptian prescription and the Berlin researchers' studies of plant physiology. In 1932 he re-ran the folk medicine germinability test,[12] moistening with urine grains of wheat and barley that had been left to swell in tapwater for 20 hours in open Petri dishes. The result was that urine inhibited growth, whether it came from a pregnant woman or not. Astonishingly, however, he seemed to confirm the possibility of gender prediction:

> We observed the rule that more rapid growth by barley compared to wheat signified a girl, while unaccelerated or delayed growth by barley signified a boy. On this basis urine tests from 100 pregnant women yielded 80% correct diagnoses and 20% wrong diagnoses.[13]

Two doctoral studies at the University of Heidelberg in the 1930s examined Manger's controversial results. In 1934 Walther Hoffmann concluded that it was possible in principle to diagnose pregnancy from germination tests in cereals. Pregnant urine clearly accelerated the growth rate of the seedlings. Hoffmann made no attempt at gender diagnosis.[14] In 1938 Margarete Schwind found 'that compared to tap-water any urine inhibits the germination of wheat and barley grains.'[15] However, pregnant urine had a consistently greater growth effect than urine from non-pregnant women or men. Fetal gender played no role. Interest in pregnancy testing based on cereal germinability or plant growth waned after the Second World War when animal models became the new focus of attention. But as late as 1947, almost 4000 years after ancient Egyptian Prescription No. 199, the germinability test was investigated using flowers of the *Gladiolus* genus.[16]

The eyes have it

Elements of Egyptian pregnancy and sterility testing were incorporated into the Greek Hippocratic Corpus (400 BC – AD 100). They shared a common basis in the assumption that a pregnant woman's body differs fundamentally from that of a non-pregnant woman. Although the Hippocratic texts do not mention the cereal growth test with pregnant urine, there is a parallel in Prescription No. 198 from Berlin Papyrus 3038 which reads:

> Another test for telling whether or not a woman will give birth. Get her to stand in an open doorway. If her eyes appear of different colours, one like an Asian, the

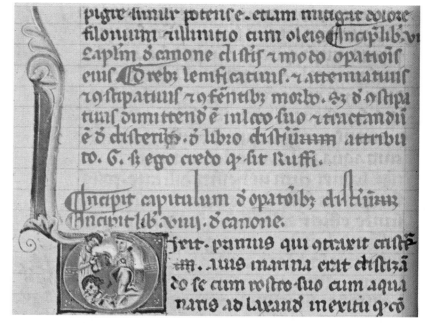

The Arab physician-philosopher **Rhazes** (865–925), who first described 'little clouds' in pregnant urine, was born in Ray near Tehran in Iran. As a young scholar he was interested in, among other things, alchemy, literature and music. At the age of 30 he devoted himself to medicine after his eyes had been injured by chemical fumes. Around 900 he was appointed head of the famous Baghdad hospital founded by Harun al-Rashid. Later he visited many royal courts as a consultant, but died blind and impoverished in his home town in 925. Rhazes opposed religious and scientific dogmatism. Although he valued the writings of antiquity, especially those of Galen, he was critical of many ideas propounded by the 'ancients'. He wrote the first work on smallpox and measles. As a zither player and singer Rhazes also used music therapy and recommended calming pregnant women with song. In place of a portrait, a page is shown from a Latin manuscript of his Liber continens, *which contains an early description of urinary pregnancy testing.*

other like a Southerner, then she will not give birth. If you find the eyes of one skin [colour], she will give birth.[17]

The Hippocratic text *De sterilibus (Concerning infertile women)* reads as follows with regard to eye testing:

> If by no other way, one can recognise pregnancy in a woman by the following feature: the eyes are contorted and lower-set; the whites do not have their natural whiteness, but appear paler.[18, 19]

Prescription No. 193 in the Berlin Papyrus likewise entered Greek medicine:

> To tell between a woman who will give birth and one who will not. Crush watermelons, steep in the milk of a woman who has given birth to a boy, and fashion into a food. If she vomits, she will give birth, but if she only has flatulence, she will not give birth.

De sterilibus offers a markedly similar version:

> If you want to know if a woman is pregnant, make her drink, on an empty stomach, butter and milk from a woman who is nursing a boy. If she vomits, she will give birth, otherwise not.[20]

Title page of 1674 edition of the forensic medicine book De relationibus medicorum *(first edition 1602) by Fortunatus Fidelis.*

Cravings and motes

Apart from incorporating the magical empiricism of the ancient Egyptian urine tests, Greco-Roman medicine of antiquity accorded no great importance to urine assessment for detecting pregnancy. Authors were more concerned with women's feelings after intercourse, symptoms in the cervix, vagina, vulva, breasts, eyes and skin, the cessation of menstruation, nausea, and the pregnant woman's abnormal cravings. The *Gynecology* of Soranus of Ephesus (c. 100 AD) is typical in this regard:

> Yet in our opinion, one must work out the evidence for conception from the many signs lumped together and by their differentiation. For instance from the facts: that at the end of intercourse the woman has been conscious of a shivering sensation, that the orifice of the uterus is closed but soft to the touch and lacking in resistance (for in coldness and inflammation it closes too, but there is roughness and hardness), that the vagina is not kept moist by the seed or only slightly, the whole of the moisture (or) its greater part having been directed upward. Later on also from the facts: that the monthly catharsis is held back or appears only slightly, that the loins feel rather heavy, that imperceptibly the breasts swell, which is accompanied by a certain painful feeling, that the stomach is upset, that the vessels on the breast appear prominent and livid and the region below the eyes greenish, that sometimes darkish splotches spread over the region above the eyes and so-called freckles develop. And still later, from the appearance of pica and from the swelling of the abdomen in proportion to the passage of time; and then from the fact that the gravida perceives the movement of the fetus.[21]

Soranus belonged to the 'Methodist' school of physicians, which attributed disease states to the mechanical tension between organs consisting of atoms. The properties of bodily fluids such as urine therefore played no role for Soranus in connection with the early diagnosis of pregnancy. However, it was not the atomism of Soranus that informed further development in the Middle Ages and Early Modern period, but Galen's humoral theory with its emphasis on examination of the pulse and urine. Uroscopy, in particular, took on ever greater importance, shown by the fact that physicians were depicted for centuries with a urinal, or matula, as their professional symbol. *Liber continens,* by the Arab physician Rhazes (865–925), contains the first description of pregnancy diagnosis by uroscopy. Pregnant urine was described as essentially clear, but with surface turbidity and multiple ascending and descending granules or motes (dust particles).[22] Half a millennium later we encounter a very similar urine diagnosis in the midwifery book *Ein schön lustig Trostbüchle von den Empfengknussen und Geburten der Menschen,* by the Zurich lithotomist and herniotomist Jacob Rueff (c. 1500–1558) from 1554:

> The urine or water, is white, a little cloud floating or swimming aloft, and many motes are seen in it, as in the beames of the Sun: but first of all, in the first moneth, when many such like things do sinck to the bottome, they are drawn out in length like unto wooll, the Urinall being moved in which they are in.[23]

Pregnancy before the law

Insights into the implications of early pregnancy diagnosis can be gleaned from the forensic medical literature of the Early Modern period (1500–1800). Thus to spare her innocent child a pregnant woman could not be tortured or killed. A diagnosis of pregnancy was also important in matters of inheritance and legitimacy. For example, if a deceased man was intestate, his widow could claim pregnancy to prevent the inheritance passing to relatives. Many women simulated pregnancy to avoid the conjugal duty of sexual intercourse. Unmarried pregnant women, on the other hand, tried to conceal their condition for the purposes of abortion, infanticide or subsequent misrepresentation of the child's parentage.[24] In his *De relationibus medicorum* of 1602, the Sicilian physician Fortunatus Fidelis (c. 1550–1630) – like Rhazes and Rueff – considered pale urine with turbidity a sign of pregnancy. Fidelis also described the genital fumigation practised in antiquity, but considered it dangerous to mother and child. If the smoke re-emerged from the mouth and nose, pregnancy was discounted according to the persistent concept of intercommunicating channels in the woman's body. Fidelis also described the symptoms of early pregnancy known to Soranus. At conception the woman feels a shudder, followed by teeth chattering and cramps, then relaxation. The man notices how his member is pulled inwards by the womb's avidity for his seed. After intercourse involving conception, seminal fluid does not drain outwards; instead, the neck of the womb closes tightly. But others remarked that without the woman's cooperation, it was often impossible to diagnose pregnancy with confidence.[25] In 1621 the famous Roman forensic physician Paolo Zacchia (1584–1659) even asserted that it was no more possible to tell from a woman's urine that she was pregnant than to divine her innermost thoughts.[26]

In 1688 Nicolas Venette (1633–1698), professor of medicine in the French city of La Rochelle, published under a pseudonym, a manual of sexual advice, *De la génération de l'homme, ou tableau de l'amour conjugal,* which went through many reprints and was also translated into German under the title *Abhandlung von Erzeugung der Menschen.*[27] In the section on pregnancy signs he reported a number of 'ancestral' urine tests:

> Others leave the urine throughout the night in a copper basin containing a thin knitting needle, and if they find a few red drops on the needle in the morning, they no longer doubt that the woman is pregnant. Some others take urine and wine, of one as much as of the other, and afterwards decant the urine; if it now looks like beans that have been brought to the boil, they maintain that the woman is pregnant. Still others leave a woman's urine to stand in the shade for three days in a tightly closed glass vessel before straining it through clear taffeta; if the taffeta shows no animalcules or worms, they confidently claim pregnancy.

Frontispiece of treatise On performance of the conjugal duty *(1733) by Johannes Jodocus Beck: matrimonial court with a disproportionate number of men.*

For Venette, however, 'nausea, vomiting and other accidents' were more reliable signs 'than all the tricks the ancients ostentatiously performed to recognise a pregnant woman'.[28]

Doubts about urine testing

The long article on pregnancy signs in *Zedlers Universallexikon* from 1743 highlights the controversial status that had come to surround pregnancy urine diagnostics by the mid-18th century.[29] Even so, it continued to be practised by many physicians. The author of the encyclopedia entry, as befitted the Enlightenment, made no attempt to disguise his contempt:

> Indeed, even today, physicians can be found who presume to pass judgement on pregnancy from female urines brought to them. They say that where the urine contains small particles that go up and down in a little cloud on gentle shaking of the jar and then settle when the jar is set down to rest, this signifies impregnation in otherwise healthy women. Moreover, the urine of a pregnant woman is said to be almost golden yellow and very cloudy from the first month to the sixth, with

Jean-Alexandre Le Jumeau Vicomte de Kergaradec
(1788–1877), the discoverer of fetal heart sound auscultation.

small particles like motes floating on its surface; when these cluster together, they form a cloud, or eneorema, in the middle of the urine like closely coiled wool.[30]

The frequent contradictions between the descriptions of pregnant urine were proof in themselves, as far as the author was concerned, that 'nothing certain could ever be determined by inspecting jars'. He even went so far as to denounce the uroscopists as charlatans:

> If now and then we come across physicians boasting that they can recognise pregnancy from the urine, we can rest assured that their secret is pure trickery: such 'urine physicians' are practised in recognising pregnancy not so much from the water as from the other circumstances which they have learnt and discovered by skilled inquiry.[31]

In reality there were no infallible signs of pregnancy: the conscientious physician had rather to 'gather together each and every sign'. The author of the encyclopedia article proceeded to list a multiplicity of pregnancy signs – 20 very common, 24 less common and 10 rare – in which uroscopy was conspicuous by its absence.

As the male discipline of obstetrics began to supplant female midwifery in the 18th century, so efforts to 'shed enlightenment' on the mystery of pregnancy intensified. The manifest aim was to establish complete male control over female reproductive function. Thus the 'definite' signs recorded by the obstetrician during his examination were contrasted with the 'uncertain' signs perceived by the woman, the most important role in this regard devolving to external and internal palpation of the female genital tract. Urine status continued to be documented even though it had become profoundly questionable. Yet despite their best efforts, male researchers, general practitioners and forensic physicians were unable, until into the 19th century, to produce incontrovertible empirical evidence against the word of 'respectable' women. Until shortly before confinement, a woman could persist in maintaining, even in the face of midwives and physicians, that she was not pregnant. In 1794 the General Prussian Legal Code permitted failure to recognise pregnancy until the 30th week![32]

Compressibility and kyestein

A first important advance was auscultation of the fetal heart sounds, described in 1822 by the French physician Jean-Alexandre Le Jumeau Vicomte de Kergaradec (1788–1877). This sign was unsuited, however, to the early diagnosis of pregnancy.[33] By contrast, Alfred Hegar (1830–1914), professor of gynecology in Freiburg, claimed in 1884 to have found a reliable early diagnostic sign.[34] As early as the second month of pregnancy, striking 'compressibility' of the lower uterine segment is apparent on bimanual palpation: 'At times one feels one has only a playing-card-thick layer of tissue between the fingers; another time this seems 4–5 mm thick.'[35] Hegar presented a second sign, the formation of a fold from the uterine wall, in 1895. He was able

> to form an artificial fold by pressing the finger located in the vaginal vault against the finger of the other hand which is directed down from the abdominal wall with pressure on the uterus. One thus forms a fold from the uterine wall as one forms a fold from intestinal wall if one wishes to demonstrate the bowel loop in a hernia.[36]

It soon emerged, however, that Hegar's pregnancy signs by no means eliminated the essential uncertainty of early pregnancy diagnosis.

This also applied in 1900 to urine testing, which meanwhile had gained a new and unexpected lease of life in 1831 when the Paris physician Jacques-Louis Nauche (1776–1843) believed he had discovered a specific substance in pregnant urine.[37] He considered the formation of so-called kyestein, an iridescent pellicle or film on the surface of the urine, as a definite sign:

> If one leaves the urine of a pregnant woman or nursing mother to stand for some time, in about thirty to forty hours a precipitate of white, loose, dusty, grumous material develops, consisting of the caseous or actual components of the milk that forms in the breasts during pregnancy.[38]

Nauche appeared unaware that this description slotted him into the long tradition of pregnant urine diagnostics dating back to Rhazes. His sign was soon roundly criticised but it prompted others to investigate pregnant urine more closely with the chemical and physical methods that had become available. The university lecturer Mark Aurel Hoefle (1818–1855), a pioneer of clinical chemistry in Germany, conducted extensive comparative experiments at the Heidelberg Birthing Institute[39] which showed that Nauche's pellicle was as likely to form on male as on female urine.[40] Alternative urine constituents had their day over the following decades: sugars, cell derivatives, blood corpuscles, protein and phosphates.[41] In 1881, for example, Gaspard Adolphe Delattre believed, mistakenly, that he had discovered a new pregnancy sign in an absence of urinary phosphates.[42] None of these discoveries had any impact on clinical practice.

Lysines and protective ferments

The blood of pregnant women had also been investigated for specific properties in the 19th century. But the results in terms of water content and red and white cell counts were contradictory.[43] The beginnings of immunology in the final years of the century then encouraged Wilhelm Liepmann (1878–1939), a junior physician at the University Department of Obstetrics and Gynecology in Halle, to attempt the first serological diagnosis of pregnancy. This came against the background of the first report of placental material in the blood of eclamptic pregnant women by the Leipzig pathologist Christian Georg Schmorl (1861–1932) in the 1890s. The new century saw studies by the Leiden professor of gynecology Johann Veit (1852–1917) on the 'deportation' of entire chorionic villi into maternal blood, even in normal pregnancies. Veit also tried to account for eclampsia, a kidney disease that occurs after the 28th week of pregnancy and whose cause has remained a mystery to this day. It is characterised by edema, proteinuria (abnormal excretion of protein in the urine), hypertension, nausea, dizziness and visual disturbances. Convulsions and coma can occur without warning, and are so life-threatening to mother and child that intensive care monitoring and emergency delivery are almost always necessary. Building on the side-chain theory of Paul Ehrlich (1854–1915), Veit postulated that lysines formed in maternal blood due to the interaction of maternal erythrocytes with fetal syncytial cells.[44, 45]

On this basis, in late 1902, Liepmann attempted to obtain a pregnancy-specific serum by injecting

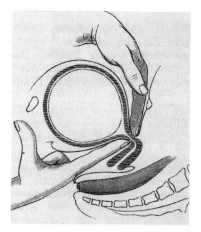

Hegar's first pregnancy sign: increased compressibility of the lower uterine segment.

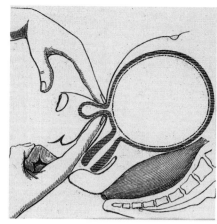

Hegar's second pregnancy sign: formation of a fold in the uterine wall.

human chorionic villi into the abdominal cavity of rabbits. His aim was to use the resulting serum to detect placental tissue in the maternal circulation, tantamount to 'a serum diagnosis of pregnancy'.[46] In early 1903 Liepmann announced that he had indeed succeeded in identifying placental material in precipitates of pregnant serum.[47] Erich Opitz (1871–1926), a lecturer in the Department of Obstetrics and Gynecology at Berlin University, checked Liepmann's results the same year and failed to confirm them. No placental tissue was present in pregnant serum, nor any antibodies against fetal cells. A diagnosis of pregnancy based on Liepmann's method therefore seemed completely impossible.[48] Liepmann and Opitz continued to debate the issue in public for a while, but conducted no further studies on the possibility of a serum diagnosis of pregnancy.

While Liepmann turned to other topics, eventually becoming the founder of social gynecology in Germany, his Halle colleague Richard Freund (1878–1943) continued in the following years to pursue the villus deportation theory advanced by Veit, who also worked in Halle from 1904. Freund's goal was not to diagnose pregnancy, however, but to treat eclampsia. First he confirmed Liepmann's results in 1904, but met fierce resistance to his findings at the German Congress of Gynecologists in 1905. He remained undeterred and in the following years demonstrated that the liquid released on compression of the placenta – a placental pressure extract – had a toxic effect that was neutralised by the addition of serum. This result encouraged him to treat his first eclamptic patients with a therapeutic serum in 1909.[49] In the same year Freund moved to the Department of Obstetrics and Gynecology at Ber-

Emil Abderhalden *(1877–1950) in the laboratory. Abderhalden was born in Oberuzwil in the Swiss canton of St Gallen. After medical studies he worked under Nobel Prize winner Emil Fischer at Berlin University's Institute of Chemistry. Abderhalden studied the digestion of dietary proteins and demonstrated the need for 'essential amino acids'. At the tender age of 31 he was appointed professor of physiology at the Berlin Veterinary College. In 1909 he postulated specific 'defensive ferments' against parenterally administered exogenous protein, and went on to develop a serological pregnancy test on this basis. Although the test proved non-reproducible, Abderhalden – professor at Halle from 1911 onwards – remained dogged in its defence. In 1931 he became president of the Leopoldina German Academy of Natural Scientists in Halle. Ordered to leave Halle by the US army at the end of the Second World War, Abderhalden returned to Switzerland, where he died in 1950.*

lin's Charité Hospital and in summer paid a visit to Emil Abderhalden (1877–1950), professor of physiology at the Berlin Veterinary College. Accounts differ on what actually transpired between the two. All that is certain is that they agreed on joint experiments to investigate eclampsia and develop a serum diagnosis of pregnancy. The aim was to use Abderhalden's 'optical method'[50] to identify the products of placental protein degradation by the proteolytic protective ferments, which Abderhalden postulated in the serum of pregnant women. After initial difficulties the experiments were crowned with success, and were jointly published in 1910.[51] They diagnosed pregnancy without error in a total of 50 cases, albeit only in the first trimester. After Abderhalden moved to Halle in 1911 he continued the experiments, introducing a second so-called dialysation procedure which in 1912 he reported as providing a reliable diagnosis of pregnancy in every month.[52] He published a detailed monograph on protective fer-

ments the same year.[53] In the *Münchener Medizinische Wochenschrift* of 11th June 1912 Abderhalden proudly observed:

> We have thus succeeded in diagnosing pregnancy by means of the optical method and the dialysation procedure. Our methods detect the reaction of the maternal organism to penetration by chorionic cells. The reaction releases ferments which comprehensively degrade the nonself material, thus stripping it of its singularity.[54]

Reactions in the scientific community were euphoric. Over the next two years well over 400 publications appeared on the topic worldwide. In a 1914 survey 15 German university obstetrics and gynecology departments reported consistently positive results with the new pregnancy test. By 1914 Abderhalden's monograph on the proteases – which were termed 'defensive ferments' – was already into its fourth edition. There were proposals to extend the technique to the investigation of infectious diseases, cancers and even schizophrenia. Abderhalden, a pupil of the Nobel Prize winner Emil Fischer (1852–1919), had become professor of physiology at the tender age of 31 and was being touted for the post of director of the Kaiser Wilhelm Institute of Physiology. As well as a plethora of articles, he published influential manuals and textbooks, and edited dictionaries as well as series of books on specialist topics. He was awarded the Helmholtz Medal by the Prussian Academy of Sciences in 1913 and the Cothenius Medal by the venerable Leopoldina German Academy of Natural Scientists in 1914.[55] Yet all this glory was based on scientific self-deception, perhaps even on deliberate fraud, for the 'defensive ferments' that Abderhalden described as 'conclusively demonstrated' did not exist at all.[56]

The first intimations of the inadequacy of the new pregnancy test, and hence of the dubiousness of the underlying theory, emerged shortly after Abderhalden's first optimistic publications. In February 1913 Paul Lindig (1886–1924), an assistant in the Department of Obstetrics and Gynecology at Jena University, published studies on the enzymatic ('fermentative') reaction which stripped it of any specificity.[57] Even at this early stage Abderhalden reacted with pique and irritation, arguing that Lindig's preparations had simply been insufficiently boiled.[58] Abderhalden's defence strategy in the face of negative findings proved extremely successful, both with Lindig and in all subsequent cases. It was based on three key arguments. First: the fermentative reaction required considerable practice; if Abderhalden's instructions were not followed to the letter, errors would inevitably occur. Second: the fermentative reaction was still being perfected; Abderhalden modified and tightened his own procedures at frequent intervals. Third: the large number of confirmatory studies by eminent researchers disqualified any negative finding as erroneous. Thus Abderhalden criticised Lindig for poor experimental technique while conceding the need for stricter purity testing of the placental material, and referred to over 50 researchers who had successfully conducted the test at his institute.

No substantive response was forthcoming by Abderhalden to the sceptical reports from his former comrade-in-arms Richard Freund and the Erlangen consultant physician Ernst Engelhorn in spring 1913. Both Engelhorn and Freund had raised doubts about whether pregnant and non-pregnant subjects could be reliably distinguished by serodiagnosis.[59,60] Abderhalden vehemently contested Freund's claim that he had inspired Abderhalden with the idea for a serological pregnancy test during his visit in 1909.[61] The hardest blow to Abderhalden came in 1914 from the eminent biochemist and head of the bacteriology laboratory at the Berlin Am Urban city hospital, Leonor Michaelis (1875–1949), who shortly before had revolutionised biochemistry by developing a technique that for the first time enabled scientists to calculate mathematically the kinetics of enzyme-catalysed reactions (Michaelis-Menten equation). Michaelis could thus be considered the greatest authority of his day on enzymatic reactions. His verdict on Abderhalden's reaction was thus all the more devastating:

> We cannot confirm that the serum of pregnant women yields the specific reaction described by Abderhalden with the aid of the dialysation method in a manner suitable for practical use. Neither have our investigations persuaded us that a methodological difficulty is responsible for the fact that Abderhalden's reaction has so far been of no practical use in individual cases. They have instead entirely failed to convince us that the serum of pregnant women contains a specific enzyme for placenta with the properties described by Abderhalden that is always absent in the serum of nonpregnant women or of men.[62]

Michaelis and his co-investigator von Lagermarck had adhered 'pedantically and in all details' to Abderhalden's instructions and conferred with him. Von Lagermarck had even worked for a week with Abderhalden in Halle in order to master the method. Yet no reproducible differences between sera from pregnant and non-pregnant subjects could be found using the dialysation method. It was not even pos-

Selmar Aschheim *(1878–1965) was born in Berlin, the son of a Jewish businessman. After his medical training he worked as a gynecologist in Berlin-Charlottenburg and from 1908 onwards also held a research post in the laboratory of the Charité Hospital's Obstetrics and Gynecology Department. Because of his long military service in the First World War and lack of recognition by his head of department, he was never able to qualify as a university lecturer. From the early 1920s he investigated the function of ovarian hormones together with the young Bernhard Zondek. Aschheim was the first to discover a gonadotropin (a hormone acting on the sexual organs) – namely **h**uman **c**horionic **g**onadotropin (HCG) – in pregnant urine, and used this as the basis for developing a reliable pregnancy test. He reported this sensational discovery in the summer of 1927. In 1936 Aschheim was driven into exile. He went to Paris, acquired French citizenship and survived the Occupation by going underground. He died in Paris in 1965 at the age of 87.*

sible to compile statistics on positive and negative reactions, as the distinction between the two 'often appeared all too arbitrary'. Yet Michaelis' criticism was to prove more harmful to himself than to Abderhalden. As an unsalaried associate professor and deprived of further career prospects, Michaelis left Germany after the First World War to work for a few years in Japan, before moving in 1926 to the United States. In a letter from 1920, he expressed the justified suspicion that Abderhalden had blocked his advancement in Germany.[63] Officially he remained on the academic staff of Berlin University until 1933, when his licence was revoked because of his Jewish origins.

The fermentative reaction was already obsolete in America by the early 1920s, but Abderhalden held to it for the rest of his life, even though he cannot have failed to be aware of its worthlessness. In Germany no criticism was voiced of the defensive ferments until well into the Nazi era, by which time Abderhalden had risen to the presidency of the Leopoldina. Indeed, Josef Mengele (1911–1979), camp physician at Auschwitz, dispatched blood samples to be investigated for racial differences by Abderhalden's reaction. In 1939 Abderhalden himself had already referred to the possibility of using his technique to 'diagnose' racial differences. In the 1950s, the method enjoyed a renaissance thanks to the obscure fresh cell therapy advocated by Paul Niehans (1882–1971).[64] Abderhalden's attempts to

Bernhard Zondek *(1891–1966) came from Wronke in the province of Posen (Poznań) in Poland. After medical school and military service he joined the Charité Hospital's Obstetrics and Gynecology Department and was soon collaborating closely with Selmar Aschheim. In 1923 he qualified as a university lecturer with a paper on the inefficacy of ovarian extracts. Through implantation experiments with anterior pituitary fragments he became the first to demonstrate the existence of a hormone acting on sexual organ function which he described as the 'motor of sexual function'. He presented his discovery to the world in early 1926. Further joint experiments with Aschheim led just a few years later to the development of the first hormonal pregnancy test. As a Jew he was forced out of Germany in 1933. He continued his research at the Hebrew University of Jerusalem, dying in New York in 1966 during a study trip.*

make a name for himself by taking an outspoken stance on various social and ethical issues are also psychologically revealing – and were perfectly in tune with his blatant disregard for acceptable standards of scientific ethics and his insistence after 1945 that he had known nothing about the exclusion of Jewish Leopoldina members. In the First World War he belonged to the national-conservative 'camp' and in the 1920s he edited the journal *Ethik*. Eugenics and racial hygiene so moulded his views that he held 'eugenics to be the highest expression of ethics'.[65]

Hormones in urine

Given Abderhalden's eminence, it is scarcely surprising that Aschheim, the developer of the first hormonal pregnancy test, was still voicing only very mild criticism of Abderhalden's 'brilliant protective ferment hypothesis' in the second edition of his monograph *Schwangerschaftsdiagnose aus dem Harne*, which appeared in 1933. He acknowledged Michaelis' doubts and insisted that the results of any method should be reproducible, which was not the case with Abderhalden's reaction.[66] Aschheim

was undoubtedly well informed about the controversy, having worked with Freund in the Obstetrics and Gynecology Department of Berlin's Charité Hospital since 1908. Aschheim soon headed the departmental laboratory where he studied the changes in endometrial histology during the menstrual cycle. He never qualified as a university lecturer because the head of department favoured other colleagues and he had to do several years of military service. Back in Berlin, he embarked in 1919 on a close collaboration with Zondek, who was 13 years his junior and had just obtained his doctorate. Zondek investigated the effect on the guinea pig uterus of the ovarian extracts in vogue at the time and, in 1922, came to the damning conclusion that all preparations on the market were endocrinologically inactive and hence clinically worthless.[67,68] Yet shortly thereafter the pioneering publications from St Louis, Missouri by Edgar Allen (1892–1943) and Edward A. Doisy (1893–1986) triggered a fresh wave of research into the ovarian hormone. Allen and Doisy injected spayed rats and mice with ovarian follicular fluid from pigs and cattle. Two days later the rodents were sexually aroused and ready to mate. In the vaginal mucosa the extracts stimulated the development of the cornified cells (anuclear squames) found only in estrous animals. These cells were readily detectable in vaginal smears, a response that formed the basis for the first highly sensitive biological estrogen test, which soon gained worldwide acceptance as the Allen-Doisy test.[69]

Zondek and Aschheim too made use of the new detection method in their series of experiments begun in 1924, and fully confirmed the Americans' results. By injecting ovarian material from humans, mice and cattle into the thigh muscles of spayed white mice, they induced the vaginal cytological changes characteristic of estrus after 72–96 hours. More detailed studies led them to the hypothesis that the ovarian hormone was produced in the theca cells of the follicles. They also found 'folliculin' in the ovary and placenta during pregnancy.[70] When Aschheim and Zondek presented their results at the German Congress of Gynecologists in Vienna in early June 1925, their contention that there was only one ovarian hormone provoked fierce criticism. The Kiel professor Robert Schröder (1884–1959) maintained that there had be a second hormone acting as a stimulant to uterine growth. To refute this objection, Zondek and Aschheim, like Allen and Doisy before them, conducted experiments with folliculin extract in infantile, sexually immature mice and achieved marked growth of the uterus

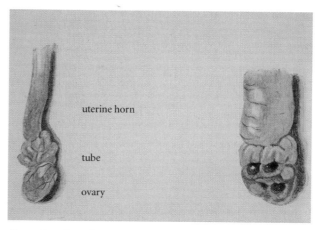

Genitals of an immature mouse 100 hours after injection of pregnant urine. From Aschheim and Zondek's 1928 article in the Klinische Wochenschrift on pregnancy diagnosis from urine.

Illustrations from Aschheim's monograph Schwangerschaftsdiagnose aus dem Harne. Left: ovary of a normal immature mouse; right: ovary of a mouse injected with pregnant urine. Hemorrhagic spots and corpora lutea are the signs of a positive pregnancy reaction.

and vagina. Surprisingly, however, the ovaries of these immature mice showed virtually no changes.[71] Zondek and Aschheim next wondered whether there were substances that could induce ovarian maturation. They unsuccessfully implanted a vast array of tissues, extracts and glands in their mice. Only when Zondek implanted fragments of cow and human anterior pituitary gland into the mouse thigh for the first time on 8 July 1925 did the characteristic anuclear squames appear in the vagina 100 hours later. Precipitate ovarian maturation brought the animal into premature sexual maturity *(pubertas praecox)*. The ovaries showed the three characteristic findings of follicular growth, blood-filled follicles (hemorrhagic spots) and corpora lutea, the latter each with an included ovum *(corpora lutea atretica)*. Aschheim was also able to demonstrate a similar response to extracts of *decidua gravitatis* and placenta, as well as to blood from pregnant women. This was the first proof of the probable existence of an anterior pituitary hormone that controlled the ovary, of a 'hormonotrophin' as the 'motor of sexual function', as Zondek put it. Zondek and Aschheim first reported these sensational experiments at a meeting of the Berlin Society of Obstetrics and Gynecology on 22 January 1926. By 1928 they had substantiated their hypothesis, despite abysmal laboratory conditions, by experiments in over 5000 immature mice.[72,73,74] The gonadotropin that Aschheim and Zondek described as an anterior pituitary hormone would only later prove to be the structurally and functionally similar placental hormone **h**uman **c**horionic **g**onadotropin (HCG).

In the course of his studies Aschheim discovered that the gonadotropic hormone became undetectable in the serum from three days after delivery. What had happened to it? There were several possibilities. It could have been destroyed in the body, secreted into the milk or excreted. Aschheim first investigated urinary excretion and found exceptionally large amounts of gonadotropin and folliculin. The concentration was so high that he was able to dispense with extraction and inject the urine directly into the experimental animals. Aschheim then tested pregnant urine and by the subcutaneous injection of 1–2 ml detected gonadotropin just a few days after a missed period. By contrast, he could only find definite evidence of the follicular hormone from the fourth month of pregnancy onwards. Aschheim first presented these results in public at the XXth German Congress of Gynecologists in Bonn in June 1927, and even then referred to the possibility of a new pregnancy test:

> Anterior pituitary hormone appears in the urine as early as the second month of pregnancy. We found it only 35 days after the last menses. The control urines we have examined to date from women at various menstrual phases, menopausal women, cancer patients, and men, etc, have yielded negative results. Large longitudinal studies are underway, especially of controls. If the present results are further confirmed, it should prove possible to diagnose pregnancy by detecting the anterior pituitary hormone in urine.[75]

On 27 April 1928 Aschheim and Zondek reported the results of these studies to the Berlin Society of Obstetrics and Gynecology. In 511 urine samples the two researchers, using a blinded design and some 2500 mice, had succeeded in diagnosing pregnancy with an accuracy of 98%. The diagnosis was based on identifying hemorrhagic spots (pituitary reaction II) and *corpora lutea atretica* (pituitary reaction III) in the ovaries of mice killed and dissected four days after injection of the test urine. A highly reliable diagnosis of early pregnancy in the laboratory had thus become possible for the first time in the history of medicine.[76,77]

Researchers throughout the world swiftly confirmed the reliability of the Aschheim-Zondek test. Zondek himself related the following anecdote: on testing some urine samples given to him by the director of the Berlin Zoo, he found a positive result in a female orangutan. The Zoo director was adamant that pregnancy was out of the question, since the only possible male was much too old to produce any offspring. After the baby orangutan was born, Zondek warned the director 'in future not to underestimate the abilities of aging gentlemen.'[78] A survey of German obstetrics and gynecology departments organised at the end of 1929 by the *Deutsche Medizinische Wochenschrift* found a failure rate of less than 2% in 892 urine tests.[79] Unlike Abderhalden's reaction, these results were not based on autosuggestion and were repeatedly confirmed over the following decades.

Their international renown failed to save Aschheim and Zondek, as Jews in Germany, from being stripped of their posts and forced into exile. The first casualty was Zondek, who lost his position as head of department at Berlin-Spandau City Hospital at the start of 1933, immediately after Adolf Hitler assumed power. In September 1933 his teaching licence was revoked, and in the same year he left his homeland for ever, emigrating via Sweden to Palestine. As head of the Hormone Research Laboratory at Hadassah Medical School in Jerusalem, he continued his research until his retirement in 1961. Aschheim was at first left alone as a war veteran. At the end of 1935, however, his teaching licence too was revoked. He emigrated to France in 1936 and became director at the Centre National de la Recherche Scientifique in Paris.[80]

Tests in rabbits and toads

Although the Aschheim-Zondek test was a highly sensitive test for diagnosing early pregnancy, it had considerable drawbacks preventing its wide-scale routine use. For example, five immature mice had to be killed for a single test. Also, the fact that it took four days made the test unsuitable for rapid diag-

Lancelot Hogben *(1895–1975), the inventor of the first practical frog test, was a brilliant biologist, but also a famous writer and committed socialist. After university Hogben taught in various posts around the world, first in London, then in Edinburgh and Montreal, and from 1927 in Cape Town, South Africa, where he found superb conditions for a zoologist. There were many lakes with masses of clawed frogs* (Xenopus laevis), *which were ideally suited to laboratory use. Hogben concentrated on the melanophore-stimulating hormone of the pituitary intermediate lobe. As a by-product of his experiments he discovered that female frogs laid eggs after being injected with anterior pituitary extracts. This observation led to the first pregnancy test with amphibians. Hogben left Cape Town in 1930 because of his distaste for Apartheid and returned to England. His book* Mathematics for the Million *became a world best-seller that is still in print today. Hogben turned to eugenic problems and spent the remainder of his academic career as professor of medical statistics at the University of Birmingham.*

nosis. However, a possible solution was not long in coming. In 1929, Maurice H. Friedman (1903–1991), of the University of Pennsylvania in Philadelphia, presented the rabbit test that would later bear his name. Since female rabbits ovulate spontaneously on contact with bucks, and even on rubbing against other females, they first had to be kept in isolation for four weeks. Ten millilitres of pregnant urine was then injected into the ear vein of a sexually mature doe, providing a result in just 24 hours. The abdominal cavity was opened, without necessarily killing the animal, and the hormonal effect of the urine was assessed. Blood-filled follicles in the ovaries were diagnostic of pregnancy. However, the method proved impractical due to high costs and the animal husbandry effort involved.[81,82]

The early 1930s brought mounting evidence, thanks to the work of Ernst Philipp (1893–1961), that the Aschheim-Zondek test did not detect an anterior pituitary hormone, but a gonadotropin produced in the placenta (HCG). The pituitary gland produced the related luteinising hormone (LH), as well as follicle-stimulating hormone (FSH).

However, a simple and rapid pregnancy test remained elusive. In this situation the British biologist Lancelot Hogben (1895–1975), professor of zoology at the University of Cape Town from 1927 to 1930, had the idea of experimenting with the South African clawed frog (Xenopus laevis) as a new test animal.[83,84] Hogben dreamed of making *Xenopus* for endocrinology what *Drosophila* had already become for genetics. He injected pregnant urine into the dorsal lymph sac of female clawed frogs and within 18 hours recorded the laying of a large number of eggs, which was extremely easy to observe. After the first publications in 1933/34 the test was successfully repeated many times and practised throughout the world, especially in Great Britain. Its advantages were the short test time, the simplicity of the result and the fact that the animals did not have to be killed. For decades the greatest impediment to its use in Europe was the sensitivity of these exotic animals to ambient temperature, diet and handling.[85] As for the significance of the clawed frog as an experimental animal for biology, however, Hogben would eventually be proved right. In 1975 *Xenopus* became the first vertebrate to be cloned and remains to this day an inextricable feature of the modern laboratory. In 1930 the pugnacious socialist Hogben moved to London University as professor of social biology, joined the reform wing of eugenics research and militated for the incorporation of mathematical principles into genetic research.

After the Second World War amphibians returned to the fore as experimental models in the development of new biological pregnancy tests. However, attention now focused on the males. One centre for research since the 1920s had been the

Argentine capital Buenos Aires. Bernardo Alberto Houssay (1887–1971), winner of the Nobel Prize in 1947, had taken an early interest in the effect of the pituitary gland on the sexual function of toads, and particularly of the Argentine toad (Bufo arenarum). With his co-worker J. M. Lascano González, he demonstrated at the Buenos Aires University Institute of Physiology in 1929 that implantation of anterior pituitary tissue in adult male toads triggered the release of spermatozoa into the seminal ducts.[86] However, almost 20 more years were to pass before this observation was translated into a usable pregnancy test, thanks to Houssay's Buenos Aires colleague Carlos Galli Mainini (1914–1961), who published his results in 1947.[87] Galli Mainini injected pregnant urine into the dorsal lymph sacs of male toads at brief intervals, releasing spermatozoa into their urine after 2–5 hours. Accuracy was similar to that of the Aschheim-Zondek test. Galli Mainini's 'male toad test' was taken up and adapted to local circumstances surprisingly quickly. In Central Europe both the edible frog (Rana esculenta) and common toad (Bufo bufo) were established as suitable test animals by 1950. The 'Galli-Mainini test' with toads and frogs gained rapid acceptance and was being performed at many hospitals with suitable laboratories into the 1960s. The animals were in some cases caught in the wild, then sexed, weighed and kept in slanting glass jars. They could be 'recycled' several times. A positive result was sometimes obtained within half an hour, and after no more than 8 hours. The earliest at which a definite diagnosis could be made was 10 to 14 days after a missed period. Using graduated tests with concentrated urine the method could also be adapted to the tentative diagnosis of abnormal pregnancy, malformations of the placental chorionic villi (hydatidiform mole), malignant tumours of the chorionic epithelium (choriocarcinoma), and of pregnancies taking root outside the uterus (ectopic pregnancy).[88]

Antigens and antibodies

The immunological detection of **h**uman **c**horionic **g**onadotropin (HCG) further simplified pregnancy testing. However, its development required considerable groundwork. Back in 1947 at the Pasteur Institute Alain Bussard (b. 1917) and Pierre Grabar (1898–1986) had shown that HCG stimulates the production of specific antibodies. A few years later Grabar, together with Curtis A. Williams (b. 1927), also developed the important method of immunoelectrophoresis, which brought the identification of particular antigens to new heights of specificity

The clawed frog (Xenopus laevis)*, so called because of the short black claws on its three inner toes, was the model used in the first hormonal pregnancy test with amphibians.*

Leif Wide *(b. 1934) developed the first immunological pregnancy test. During his medical training in Stockholm Wide was already interested in laboratory medicine and assisted Carl Axel Gemzell (b. 1910) in his growth hormone work. Gemzell eventually took Wide on as a research student, assigning him to the development of an immunoassay for growth hormone. When this project was unsuccessful, Wide switched to human chorionic gonadotropin (HCG) and developed the first immunological pregnancy test. In 1960 he followed Gemzell to the University of Uppsala, where he still works. Together with his wife he presented the first immunological pregnancy test for mares in 1963. In 1965 he moved to the Department of Clinical Chemistry. His RAST test for detecting IgE antibodies in allergies became a worldwide success for the Pharmacia company. At the end of the 1960s Wide returned to reproductive medicine. Many publications on the hypothalamic-pituitary-ovarian axis followed. His most recent achievement was the development of a drug screening test for exogenous erythropoietin in athletes.*

and sensitivity.[89] In 1959 René Got in Paris used this technique to separate HCG from antigenic impurities.[90,91] A further prerequisite was created by Stephen Vickers Boyden (b. 1925) in 1951 with the method of passive hemagglutination. By treating erythrocytes with tannic acid, Boyden altered their surface properties to enable them to bind proteins and hence be used as antigen carriers.[92] In 1959 the Swedish reproductive endocrinologist Carl Axel Gemzell (b. 1910) asked a young medical student Leif Wide (b. 1934) to determine human growth hormone (HGH) in serum by hemagglutination inhibition, or what was now known as Boyden's test. These experiments would lead to the first immunological pregnancy test.[93]

At the Karolinska Institute in Stockholm Gemzell had already been working for some years on the extraction from human anterior pituitary lobes of hormones that promoted the growth of male and female gonads and controlled endocrine function. His aim in administering anterior pituitary hormones was to induce ovulation in sterile women with ovarian insufficiency. Success was not long in coming. 1958 saw the first report of successful clinical trials by Gemzell, together with Egon Diczfalusy (b. 1920) and Karl-Gunnar Tillinger. Two years later he announced the first twin pregnancy after hormonal induction of ovulation. For his

treatments with follicle-stimulating hormone (FSH), followed by luteinising hormone (LH) or HCG, Gemzell collected human pituitary glands from autopsies throughout Sweden.[94,95] The material was also needed for clinical studies with HGH. In 1958 Maurice S. Raben treated a child with short stature with HGH for the first time. Hemagglutination inhibition as a detection method for growth hormone had just been described in the literature when Gemzell entrusted Wide with the task of developing a corresponding immunological test for serum HGH. Wide had been studying medicine in Stockholm since 1954 and had first met Gemzell on the gynecology course. A year later Gemzell took on Wide as a research student in his laboratory. Although Wide developed a new method for stabilising the sensitive erythrocytes that acted as antigen carriers, the HGH hemagglutination test worked only with pituitary extracts, not blood serum. Surprisingly, however, the new method performed very well in urine. When Wide failed to find growth hormone in urine, he looked for HCG:

> The problem was that I could not find any hGH in normal urine. I wanted to utilize my discovery with the assay method and decided to try it on a hormone that was known to be excreted in large amounts in urine, human chorionic gonadotrophin (hCG). Rabbits were immunized with hCG and the first antiserum that I obtained functioned excellently in the hemagglutination inhibition reaction. Urine specimens were obtained from Carl Gemzell's ward. Only pregnant women gave a positive reaction in the test. The first immunological pregnancy test with a high accuracy had been developed (1960).[96]

Wide had first spent weeks sensitising rabbits with HCG isolated by immunoelectrophoresis. In the first stage the resulting anti-HCG rabbit serum was mixed with pregnant urine containing HCG, leading to the formation of antigen-antibody complexes. In the second stage Wide checked whether this reaction had really occurred by adding HCG bound to stabilised sheep erythrocytes. If the urine contained HCG, the sheep red cells did not agglutinate (clump) because the previously added anti-HCG serum had been 'used up' by the pregnant woman's HCG. The unagglutinated sheep erythrocytes settled as a reddish-brown ring on the bottom of the test tube. The pregnancy test was positive.[97]

Wide subsequently developed test ampoules containing lyophilised (freeze-dried) reagents and achieved good results. Together with Gemzell he approached the Dutch firm of Organon, which in 1962 launched the first commercial immunological pregnancy test under the name of 'Pregnosticon'. When Gemzell was appointed professor at the University of Uppsala in 1960, Wide followed him and wrote his 1962 doctoral thesis on the new method, which was 10–50 times more sensitive than the bioassays from day 35–38 after the last menstrual period. A further advantage was the speed of the test, which produced a result within 1–2 hours.[98] In 1967 Wide had another great success with his development of the **r**adio**a**llergo**s**orbent **t**est (RAST) for determining allergen-specific IgE antibodies. He continued to teach at Uppsala and last caused a stir in the 1990s when he succeeded in differentiating injected recombinant **e**rythro**po**ietin (EPO) from its endogenous counterpart, thereby making it possible to detect athletes taking banned EPO.

Additional pregnancy tests based on the Wide-Gemzell reaction were developed in rapid succession. First, in 1961 sheep erythrocytes were successfully replaced with latex particles. Just two years later the first rapid slide test entered the market as the 'Gravindex' test. A drop of urine and a drop of anti-HCG serum were mixed for 1 minute on a black slide. If HCG was present in the urine, it absorbed the anti-HCG serum. On addition of a solution of latex coated with HCG antigen, the resulting mixture did not clump because there was no more free anti-HCG serum. The solution became homogeneously milky and the test was positive. A negative test was shown by a granular white precipitate. The result could be read within 2–3 minutes. The accuracy of the test was 95%. Sensitivity was half that of the Wide-Gemzell reaction.[99]

The early 1970s saw a further leap in the development of immunological pregnancy tests, based on the discovery of the α- and β-chains of HCG and LH. It soon emerged that the α-chains were identical, but the β-chains showed small differences. By immunising rabbits with HCG β-chains it became possible for the first time to produce specific anti-HCG antisera that did not cross-react with LH. Based on this discovery, the American Judith L. Vaitukaitis (b. 1940) in 1972 developed the first **r**adio**i**mmuno**a**ssay (RIA) differentiating between serum HCG and LH.[100] It was the culmination of a decade of RIA studies into the measurement of the two hormones. The assay was so sensitive that pregnancy could for the first time be diagnosed before the first missed period, namely on the eighth or ninth day after ovulation.[101]

The paper published in August 1975 by Georges Köhler (1946–1995) and César Milstein (1927–2002) on their successful production of monoclonal antibodies also heralded a new, and so far the last, important phase in the history of immunological pregnancy testing. At the same time the technique of diagnostic ultrasound, developed in the 1960s, entered routine clinical use.[102] The first pregnancy tests using monoclonal antibodies came onto the market in the 1980s, following the critical identification in 1977 of a carboxy-terminal domain of 30 amino acids specific to the HCG β-chain.[103] To distinguish the complete HCG molecule reliably from free α- and β-chains and from LH, an antibody was developed against an antigenic determinant of HCG that occurs only in the complete molecule. Today serum tests can diagnose pregnancy just a few days after ovulation. Using tests freely available in the shops women can now exclude or confirm pregnancy the day after a missed period.

Erika Keller

Blood lines

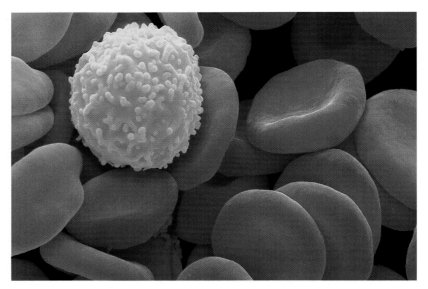

One litre of blood contains 5–10 billion white blood cells and about 5 trillion red blood cells. Red cells have a mean diameter of 7.7 micrometres. Lymphocytes can have a diameter of 6–16 micrometres.[17]

The notion that blood has healing or rejuvenating powers is an ancient one. Drinking the blood of youths or young animals, preferably lambs, was recommended for a variety of mental and physical illnesses. Introduction of small amounts of the blood of a healthy, vigorous donor into a debilitated recipient by scoring the skin has been practised since antiquity in many different cultures. However, only with the discovery of the circulation of the blood by William Harvey (1578–1657) did scientific research into direct blood transfusion become possible. From about 1615 Harvey studied the action of the heart in humans and animals. In its role as the 'fount of the arterial system', as it had been referred to around AD 1000 by the Persian physician and philosopher Abū Ali al-Husayn Ibn Abd Allah Ibn

Sina, also known as Avicenna (980–1037), the heart formed the basis of Harvey's studies and of his calculations of the body's blood volume. His findings, published in 1628 in the treatise *Exercitatio anatomica de motu cordis et sanguinis in animalibus,* revolutionised medical science. In this work he described the arteries, the veins, the heart valves, the movement of blood in both the greater (systemic) and the lesser (pulmonary) circulation and the heart actions that are responsible for the pulse. He also provided mathematical proof that the circulating blood could not originate in the liver.[1] Harvey's work met with virulent criticism, both justified and unjustified, since the nature of the connection between the systemic and the pulmonary circulation was still unclear. Harvey himself had proved that the interventricular septum contained no pores through which blood could pass between the two sides of the heart, thus contradicting a commonly held assumption. However, it was only after 1661, when the Italian anatomist Marcello Malpighi (1628–1694) showed that the arteries and veins are connected to each other via the capillary system, that Harvey's description

> The left ventricle expels the blood into the aorta, the right into the lungs. The blood flows from the right ventricle through the lungs and thence into the left ventricle (lesser circulation).

came to appear plausible. Thenceforth more and more scientists attempted to demonstrate the correctness of Harvey's theses by experiment. Experiments of this kind involving animal-to-animal transfusions were conducted for the first time in 1665 in England, while experiments involving animal-to-human transfusions were conducted for the first time in 1667 in France. The use of human-to-human transfusions to treat massive blood loss was a controversial issue since, as statistical studies by Leonard Landois (1837–1902) confirmed, its outcome was not predictable.[2] Though most transfusions failed, the number of transfusions of human blood that had a favourable outcome was surprising considering the physical conditions under which they were given: advocates of transfusion performed the procedure in front of large audiences in the lecture theatres of medical schools while their opponents protested against the practice, sometimes raising a considerable uproar. Blood donors were celebrated by all as heroes – and with good reason, since direct blood transfusion involved their arteries or veins being opened with a scalpel and either sutured directly to the similarly opened veins of the recipient or else connected end-to-end to the veins of the recipient via a tubular connecting piece. Items used as connecting pieces included preserved calf arteries, glass or silver tubes and rubber hoses with glass attachments dipped in liquid paraffin to prevent coagulation of the blood. The operation on the blood vessels was performed without anesthesia, in unsterile conditions and with no way of estimating the amount of blood lost by the donor. The risk of clotting was a serious problem for the recipients. Though in 1771 William Hewson (1739–1774) had reported the possibility of preventing fresh blood from clotting by agitating it, the available time generally did not permit agitation of the blood for long enough to cause complete precipitation of its fibrin component. Transfusion was always used only as a last resort, mostly in women bleeding to death as a result of childbirth – a fact sometimes lost in the furore surrounding the practice. Despite the unpropitious circumstances in which they were performed, only slightly more than half of all human-to-human transfusions were unsuccessful, a fact that might be explained by the normal distribution of the ABO blood groups within the population.

The discovery of the ABO blood group system

It had long been known that people who recovered from infectious diseases such as smallpox were protected for life against further infection, i. e. they were immune. Early in the 20th century researchers set themselves the task of elucidating the nature of this protection. They found that immunity was due partly to the formation of antibodies whose presence could be demonstrated in the individual's blood and serum. This led to the development of a new scientific discipline, serology, which deals with the laws governing the formation and action of antibodies in response to the presence of antigens. It was discovered, for example, that the serum of patients with typhoid fever causes typhoid bacilli to clump together (agglutinate). This observation led to further studies on the agglutination of antigen-bearing cells, bacteria and even red blood cells that occurs when these are brought into contact with patient serum or antibody-containing animal serum. At that time antibody formation was regarded exclusively as an immune response to infection with a pathogen. Karl Landsteiner (1868–1943) then had the brilliant idea of investigating the agglutination of blood cells in the serum of healthy individuals. In 1901 he reported his experiments in the journal *Wiener klinische Wochenschrift:* He used 0.6% saline solution to prepare an approximately 5% suspension of the red blood cells (erythrocytes) of each of 12 different blood samples and then mixed each of these suspensions in approximately equal parts with the serum of the other blood samples, either in a test tube or in a 'hanging drop' on a cover glass.[3] On the basis of the results obtained in this way he postulated a rule to the effect that the serum of individuals of group A contains naturally occurring antibodies against antigens of blood group B. He referred to these 'isoantibodies' (antibodies produced in the same species), also known as isoagglutinins, as anti-B antibodies. Similarly, the serum of individuals of group B was found to contain anti-A isoantibodies, while the serum of individuals of group C was found to contain both anti-A and anti-B antibodies. The group to which an individual belongs is determined by which antigen (e. g. A) is present on the surface of their red cells. The antibody that reacts with that antigen and thereby agglutinates the red cells bears the same name but has the prefix 'anti' (e. g. anti-A). The occurrence of a reaction between A and anti-A results in agglutination or lysis of the red cells and

Number of blood transfusions from 1666 to 1874

Human blood	347	Animal blood	129
Favourable outcome	150	Favourable outcome	42
Unfavourable outcome	180	Temporary improvement and doubtful success	25
Doubtful outcome	12		
Success not to be expected	3	No improvement and death	62
Death as a result of operation	2		

First page of Landsteiner's pioneering article on human blood groups.

thus in death. The naturally occurring isoantibodies (i. e. those present in accordance with Landsteiner's rule) are therefore always those of the other blood group. Landsteiner's blood group C was later referred to as zero because of the absence of A and B antigens. Thus began a dispute about the naming of blood group antigens that still rages today. Some serologists advocate the use of letters, others numbers, while yet others use the name of the discoverer of an antigen or of the individual in whom a particular antigen was first found. Though a 'standing committee for standardisation' was formed as long ago as 1928, even the nomenclature of the ABO letter) or AB0 (number) blood group system has yet to be standardised.[4]

Even today, an individual's ABO blood group is determined essentially in accordance with Landsteiner's method: Antibody-containing sera obtained from healthy blood donors whose blood group is known are mixed with the subject's red cells to form a suspension as specified by Landsteiner. The resulting serological reaction identifies the red cell antigens that determine the subject's blood group. The result is always checked by adding the subject's serum to red cells of donors whose blood group is known and observing the cells for agglutination. Only if the blood group determination performed using the subject's red cells and that performed using the subject's serum yield results that conform to Landsteiner's rule is the subject's ABO blood group considered to have been correctly determined. Though most known blood group characteristics can now be demonstrated using industrially manufactured monoclonal antibodies and the reactions can be performed not just in test tubes but also in other reaction vessels such as microtitre plates and gel-containing capillaries, the method described by Landsteiner is still used in serology laboratories because it is economical and simple to perform. The presence of cold agglutinins is likewise still demonstrated using Landsteiner's method. Cold agglutinins are proteins that can cause lysis of red blood cells at low temperatures.[5]

From his observation of the three isoagglutinins anti-A, anti-B and anti-AB, Landsteiner concluded that

these provide an explanation of the variable results of therapeutic transfusion of human blood.[6]

The fourth blood group of the ABO system, namely that in which no agglutinins at all are present (AB), was discovered in 1902 by Landsteiner's colleague Adriano Sturli (1873–1964).

It was ten years before Landsteiner's findings were incorporated into medical practice and determination of the blood group of both donor and recipient came to be regarded as an essential precondition for blood transfusion. Awareness of the ABO blood group system alone reduced the number of unsuccessful transfusions to such an extent that blood transfusion became the most important form of treatment for massive blood loss. This led inevitably to an increased demand for healthy blood donors.

The establishment of blood banks

In America the possibility of transfusing blood from one human to another became a topic of public discussion after publication of a treatise by the surgeon George Washington Crile (1864–1943).[7] Agencies were set up to refer blood donors to hospitals, and the hospital or prospective recipient of the blood had to pay the donor a fee of up to 50 dollars, from which the agency deducted a commission of 20–30%. Professional donors developed criminal methods of extorting money from rich patients, while the poor simply could not obtain blood. The necessary reaction to this unsatisfactory situation originated at Washington University, St. Louis, where students took the initiative of donating their blood to poor patients at no charge. Of course, they were not able to provide blood for all those in need of it. Unpaid blood donors therefore had to be recruited. As an incentive, potential blood donors were promised a free blood transfusion whenever they might need it, i.e. they 'deposited' blood in order to be able to 'withdraw' it if necessary later. Thus arose the concept of 'blood banking', a term which, though strictly speaking out of date, remains in use today. The blood bank principle proved unable to cope with the increasing demand for blood on the battlefields of the First World War, and the shortcomings of the blood donation system became clear once more.

One only has to picture a direct blood transfusion – like the scene in the lecture theatre described above, but with direct suturing of the donor's artery to the recipient's vein as recommended by Crile – being performed on a battlefield to realise that an army surgeon would greatly prefer to have preserved blood for indirect transfusion.

The search for a stabiliser

A search thus began in the First World War for a stabiliser that could preserve blood in a container while preventing it from coagulating. A first breakthrough was achieved in 1914 with the use of

After completing his studies in clinical chemistry, **Karl Landsteiner** (1868–1943) worked firstly as an assistant at the Institute of Pathological Anatomy of the University of Vienna. Following the revolutionary discoveries made by the great bacteriologists of the late 19th century, research at this institute was directed mostly towards the production and use of immune sera. Landsteiner set out to investigate the antigenic properties of the blood of healthy people and in so doing discovered the human blood groups, publishing his groundbreaking findings in 1901. In 1923 he accepted a post at the Rockefeller Institute for Medical Research, as his scientific achievements had still not received their due recognition in Vienna and as, moreover, working and living conditions in post-war Vienna were wretched. It was for this reason that Landsteiner had moved firstly to The Hague, where, despite unsatisfactory working conditions and financial hardship, he continued to publish important scientific findings, e.g. on the subject of allergy and anaphylaxis and substances that trigger such reactions, on haptens (molecules that act as antigens only after being conjugated to a protein) and on the composition of hemoglobin, the red pigment of blood. He also proved that the pathogen of poliomyelitis is a virus, not a bacterium, and showed that this virus could be grown in a culture medium made from the kidney tissue of monkeys.[16] In 1930 he was awarded the Nobel prize for Medicine for his discovery of the major human blood groups.

sodium citrate to prevent coagulation, and a second in 1916 with the use of the sugar dextrose to prolong red cell survival. Even today sodium citrate and dextrose form the basis of all stabilisers. By the closing stages of the First World War the Americans had learned how to collect whole blood in bottles to which a precisely measured amount of sodium citrate and dextrose had been added. Blood preserved in this way and kept on ice could be taken to the combat zone and transfused into a wounded soldier after puncturing an arm vein, in some cases saving the life of soldiers who otherwise would not have survived transport to the nearest field hospital.

After 1918 a number of newly established privately owned American laboratories developed improved stabilisers by use of additional substances. These laboratories later evolved to become pharmaceutical companies that still supply blood transfusion systems, stabilisers and blood group tests.

Another way – other than by transfusion of preserved whole blood – of making it possible to transport wounded soldiers to hospital was first described in 1918 in an article published in the *British Medical Journal*. This involved the use of blood plasma.

The cells of blood can be separated from the fluid, or plasma, by centrifugation. Plasma is still used today to replace lost fluid in patients with massive bleeding, shock or burns. It was soon found that plasma could be evaporated to produce a coarse-grained powder that can be stored for long periods. Dried plasma was first used successfully on a large scale in a devastating fire in Boston in 1920.

Early guidelines for blood donation

Early in the Second World War, before becoming involved in hostilities itself, the USA launched a major operation to provide dried plasma for British troops. In a patriotically oriented propaganda campaign entitled 'Blood over water', thousands of unpaid blood donors were recruited at 33 centres on the East coast of the USA. This triumph of organisation was made possible by preliminary work undertaken by the Blood Transfusion Betterment Association, founded in 1929 in New York under the chairmanship of Landsteiner, who since 1923 had worked in New York at the Rockefeller Institute for Medical Research while hoping – in vain, as it turned out – to be offered a post at Vienna University. Landsteiner buried himself in administrative work for the Betterment Association in order to ease his homesickness. He merged this association

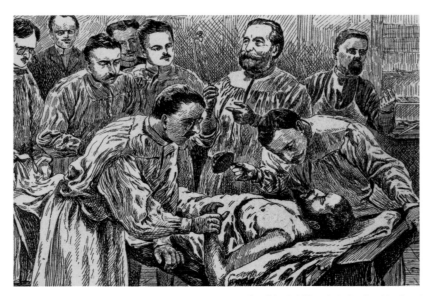

Ernst von Bergmann performing an operation in the Charité Hospital, Berlin. Idealised anonymous drawing from 1899.

with the Rockefeller Foundation, not for any financial reason, but in order to obtain a pool of thoroughly investigated, healthy blood donors and to promote basic research in transfusion medicine. In 1930 the Association issued a set of guidelines for blood transfusion services, including rules for the selection and remuneration of blood donors. The USA thus played a trailblazing role in the normative aspects of transfusion medicine.

As in the USA, the experience of the Russian medical corps on the battlefields of the First World War led to an intensification of research in the field of transfusion medicine in Russia. The years 1926/27 saw the establishment in Moscow and Leningrad of central institutes that played a role similar to that of the Blood Transfusion Betterment Association in the USA. Based on the American model, the role of the two central institutes and the subsequently established regional blood donation centres was defined and selection criteria for blood donors – all of whom were paid – were established. By the 1930s blood transfusion research in the USSR had achieved international standing. As well as investigating many aspects of the composition of blood, Soviet scientists looked into the possibility of transfusing cadaveric blood, which, because of the fibrinolysis that occurs after death, does not coagulate and consequently requires no stabiliser. In Western Europe, by contrast, use of cadaveric blood was firmly rejected, firstly for psychological reasons – despite the fact that transplantation of other cadaveric organs (blood, too, is an organ) is accepted – and secondly for organisational reasons, namely that in order to be suitable for this purpose blood would need to be transfused within four hours of the death of the donor. Within this time the presence of any transmissible disease in the donor would need to be excluded, however this is possible in 30 % of cases at most. With the start of the Second World War blood research in the USSR was subordinated to the necessities of war and conducted under conditions of strict secrecy, no further scientific work being published.

In the period between the two world wars many countries, e. g. France, Poland, Italy and the Netherlands, followed the USA and the USSR in setting up central institutes to regulate blood transfusion.

Blood transfusion: the 'latest fashion'

The German medical fraternity of that time took a highly sceptical view of what it regarded as merely the 'latest fashion' in treatment. This may have been due in part to the lasting influence of the great

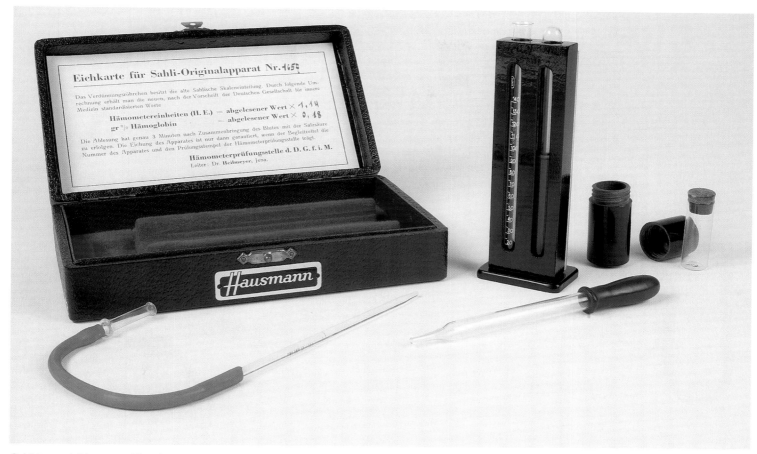

Sahli hemoglobinometer: The closed tube (right) contained a pigment that served as a reference standard. The open tube (left) served as a mixing tube. This was filled up to the graduation mark with hydrochloric acid. A measured quantity of blood obtained using a graduated pipette from a drop of blood on the subject's fingertip or earlobe was then added. Distilled water was then added drop by drop until the colour matched that of the reference tube. The hemoglobin level (Hb) was read from a scale. Nowadays every blood donation is preceded by determination of the donor's hemoglobin level. To this end a small cuvette is filled with capillary blood from the donor's fingertip and the hemoglobin level is measured by photometry.

surgeon Ernst von Bergmann (1836–1907), who in 1883, on the occasion of a foundation day of the Military College in Berlin, had condemned blood transfusion in such scathing terms that his speech came to be regarded as a 'funeral oration for transfusion'. The few transfusions given in Germany were of fresh blood transfused directly from donor to recipient. This required no central institute for blood donation and transfusion. Instead, individual hospitals had so-called blood donor registers with index cards detailing the name, date of birth, address, place of employment and ABO blood group of individuals who had indicated their willingness to give blood. If and when the need arose the potential donor was fetched by messenger, or if possible by telephone, from their home or workplace and taken directly – often still in street clothes – to the operating theatre, where they were placed alongside the recipient and a connection established between the blood vessels of donor and recipient.

In return for this the donor demanded to be paid, with the result that as in the USA, blood donation in Germany came to be characterised by attempts at extortion, especially during the years of famine that followed the First World War and the Great Inflation.

The surgeon Ernst Unger (1875–1937), a student of Ernst von Bergmann, recognised the need for an officially regulated, national blood donation institute in Germany. In 1932 the mayor of Berlin responded to Unger's insistent demands by ordering the founding of the Berlin blood donation service at the Rudolf Virchow Hospital. On 14th December 1932 Unger reported to the Berlin Medical Association on the new body, of which he had been appointed head, stating that thenceforth blood donors were to be paid a standard rate of 10 Reichsmark for 350 mL, 15 Reichsmark for 500 mL, and 20 Reichsmark for 1000 mL, of donated blood. The initial examination, at which the would-be blood donor's general health and nutritional state were

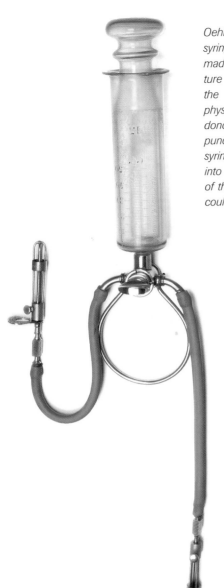

Oehlecker's apparatus consisted of a glass syringe, a connecting piece with a two-way tap made of nickel or nickel silver, and two puncture needles. Before a transfusion was started the whole system had to be irrigated with physiological saline solution. After both the donor vein and the recipient vein had been punctured, donor blood was drawn up into the syringe and immediately injected unchanged into the recipient vein by changing the position of the two-way tap. Up to 1000 mL of blood could be transfused in 20 minutes in this way.

The Lampert beaker was made of an amber material which, because of its poor wettability, delayed coagulation. After being filled with fresh blood from a donor, the beaker was taken immediately to the patient's room. There the blood was drawn out of the beaker into Oehlecker's apparatus and injected into the patient.

assessed, was undertaken by a clinically trained physician. The would-be donor's ABO blood group was then determined in a laboratory using Landsteiner's method and the hemoglobin (Hb) level of his or her blood was measured. The level of this oxygen-transporting pigment of red blood cells rises and falls with the red cell count and is used as an indicator of whether the blood contains a sufficient number of red cells. If the value is found to be below a certain level (e. g. in people with iron deficiency), the would-be donor is rejected for his or her own protection. In those days hemoglobin determination was performed using the hemoglobinometer described by Hermann Sahli (1856–1933). The results of the examination were recorded in the donor's index card. Individuals accepted as regular donors were provided with a photo identity card and required to make a written undertaking to

present themselves for re-examination at quarterly intervals without being summoned, to report any illness immediately and not to donate blood at any other hospital without first obtaining permission from the blood donation service.

Risk of infection of donors

The risk of donors becoming infected by the recipients of their blood became strikingly clear on an occasion when diphtheria patients in the infectious diseases unit of the Rudolf Virchow Hospital required blood transfusions. In this situation the need for physical separation of donor and recipient was imperative, however at that time in Germany direct transfusion of fresh blood was still regarded as the only method of transfusion that offered any hope of success. Unger was well aware that as long ago as 1914 Albert Hustin (1882–1967) had successfully transfused blood rendered incoagulable by addition of sodium citrate and that red blood cells could be kept viable for 30 days by addition of sodium citrate and dextrose. He also knew that in other countries transfusions were performed using citrated blood stored in a refrigerator for up to 14 days. Nevertheless, he considered the use of unaltered blood to be preferable. He therefore needed a container via which uncoagulated fresh blood could be transferred to a recipient. To this end he combined the transfusion apparatus devised by Franz Oehlecker (1874–1958) that he had used up till then with the amber beaker devised by Lampert.[8] Unger's wide-ranging research activities both on questions of immunology and on the subject of coagulation confronted him again and again with the same problems that arose in transfusion medicine. With the benefit of his research results German transfusion medicine could have risen to the highest international standard, however in April 1933 Unger became one of the first Jewish chief physicians to be forced out of his hospital.

Blood for the war

Ideological distinctions and exclusions also resulted in experience on the use of blood transfusion gained in the Spanish Civil War failing to make its way to Germany and therefore not being incorporated into the early preparations for war. Thanks to the advanced state of Soviet transfusion medicine as outlined above, the USSR was largely able to meet the requirements of the 'antifascist fighters' in Spain for blood, with the result that the lives of many wounded combatants were saved. While fighting in the Polish campaign, Wilhelm Heim (1906–1997), who since 1938 had been investigating the possibility of indirect blood transfusion using heparin (then known by the proprietary name Vetren) as a stabiliser, learned from a soldier who had previously fought in Spain of the transfusions performed on the enemy side.[9] Spurred on by these reports, Heim made it an urgent priority to save the lives of wounded soldiers by means of blood transfusions. At the very least, he considered, transfusions could make it possible to get wounded soldiers to the nearest field hospital alive. In December 1939 Heim took advantage of his home leave to present this idea to the responsible army departments. He met with an enthusiastic reception and a research unit was set up for him in what was then the Robert Koch Hospital in Berlin-Moabit. In 1941 Heim gained his qualification as a university lecturer with a thesis on 'clinical and experimental studies on the problem

of blood preservation'. Via Heim, the Minister for the Army informed the Minister for the Interior of Germany's need for a uniformly regulated blood donation system. In March 1940 the Ministry for the Interior issued guidelines for the establishment of a blood donation authority in the German Reich. Though Unger's name was totally suppressed, his ideas and demands bore fruit in these guidelines. The Robert Koch Institute in Berlin was made responsible for all matters relating to transfusion. It controlled the production of test sera and blood products until 1993 and is still responsible for gathering epidemiological data on diseases that can be transmitted by blood.

Risk of infection of recipients

The most important risk of this type was that of contracting syphilis, a disease which in 1940 was still an unsolved problem. Though the causative pathogen, *Treponema pallidum,* had been discovered in 1905 and the presence of antibodies against this organism could be demonstrated, the recently discovered antibiotic penicillin, which was the only curative treatment for syphilis, was still in very short supply. From 1942, when Hartmann and Schone discovered that even blood donors with latent (inapparent) syphilis could transmit the disease, examination of donor blood for syphilitic infection was regarded as essential. In addition to a physical examination for evidence of the disease, every blood donor had to undergo a Wassermann test, the original serological test for syphilis which had first been published in 1906.

Discovery of the Rh blood group system

In 1936/37 Peter Dahr (1906–1984), a serologist working at the Hygiene Institute of the University of Cologne, was investigating monkey blood groups. The results he published led to a lively exchange of ideas between himself and Landsteiner. In August 1941 Landsteiner sent his still unpublished instructions on how to obtain anti-Rh serum from guinea pigs to Dahr.[10] This put Dahr

> in the fortunate position of being able to produce anti-Rh sera myself and perform Rh tests at the Cologne Hygiene Institute.[11]

In 1940/41 Landsteiner and Alexander S. Wiener had injected blood from rhesus monkeys into rabbits and guinea pigs. In the serum of animals immunised in this way they found antibodies that agglutinated not just the erythrocytes of rhesus monkeys but also those of about 85 % of the white human population. They therefore referred to the serum as anti-rhesus

Detection of syphilis

The Wassermann test for syphilis combines two test systems: a **c**omplement **f**ixation **r**eaction (CFR) and a hemolytic system as an indicator. In this test hemolysis, i.e. lysis of red blood cells by destruction of their cell membrane, leads to release of hemoglobin and red coloration of the reaction mixture of the indicator system. The CFR is based on the ability, first observed in 1898 by Jules Bordet (1870–1961), of fresh serum to lyse red blood cells in the presence of specific antibodies. Bordet used the term 'complement' to refer to the heat-sensitive, high-molecular-weight proteins that are responsible for this activity.

August von Wassermann (1866–1925) observed that the serum of syphilitic patients contains antibodies that combine with antigen and in so doing consume complement. He used a lipoid extract of mammalian organs as an antigen. As a means of rendering consumption of complement visible, Wassermann used sheep red cells that are hemolysed by antibodies in rabbit serum in the presence of complement. Basically, the Wassermann test is as follows: To the patient serum suspected of containing antibodies to *Treponema pallidum* are added the antigen (lipoid extract) and complement in the form of fresh serum, e.g. from a guinea pig. If antibodies are present in the patient's serum, they bind to the antigen and thereby consume complement. In the second step of the test, sheep red cells and rabbit serum are added. If the complement has been consumed by the primary antigen-antibody reaction, the sheep red cells are not hemolysed and the supernatant in the reaction vessel remains clear. In this case the Wassermann test is positive and it is concluded that the patient has syphilis. If, on the other hand, the primary reaction does not result in consumption of complement, the sheep red cells are hemolysed and hemoglobin is released, causing the reaction mixture to take on a characteristic translucent red colour. In this case the Wassermann test is negative and it is concluded that the patient does not have treponemal infection. From 1906 until the late 1960s the test described by Wassermann was the only available method of demonstrating the presence of syphilis. Nowadays the ***T****reponema* ***p****allidum* **h**emagglutination **a**ssay (TPHA) is used as a screening test for syphilis. This test uses avian red blood cells sensitised (coated) with *Treponema pallidum*. If the patient serum contains antibodies against the pathogen of syphilis, these bind to the *Treponema pallidum* on the avian red cells. This antigen-antibody reaction causes the sensitised red cells to undergo agglutination which is visible to the naked eye after centrifugation. If no antibodies are present, centrifugation causes the red cells to sediment to form a 'button' on the floor of the reaction vessel. A positive TPHA is confirmed by the fluorescent treponemal antibody test, in which the pathogen is observed directly under a fluorescence microscope. In other words, the transfusion blood firstly undergoes a highly sensitive screening test for infectious diseases that is more likely to yield false-positive than false-negative results. A positive result is confirmed by means of a highly specific test. This approach, i.e. performing a sensitive screening test followed by a specific confirmatory test, is now standard practice.

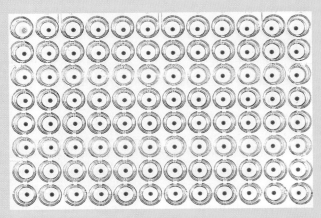

The Treponema pallidum *hemagglutination assay. Above left is the positive control; all the other test results are negative.*

serum and to those individuals whose erythrocytes reacted with it as Rh-positive, the remainder of the population being Rh-negative.

Rh incompatibility between mother and child

In 1939 Philip Levine and R. Stetson had reported the occurrence of a hemolytic transfusion reaction in a woman who had been given a transfusion of her husband's blood after a stillbirth.[12] They found not only that the woman's serum contained antibodies against her husband's erythrocytes, but also that it agglutinated the erythrocytes of 80 out of 104 ABO-compatible blood donors whose blood they tested. Levine and Stetson conjectured that the mother had been immunised by an antigen present on the erythrocytes of her unborn child. The child must have inherited this antigen from its father.

At the same time, Wiener and his coworkers were examining the sera of patients who developed intolerance reactions after ABO-compatible transfusions. They found that these sera showed the same specificity as that described by Levine and Stetson and as that present in Landsteiner's anti-Rh sera. They attributed this specificity to the presence of Rh-antibodies and learned two things: firstly, that the tolerability of transfused blood depends not just on the ABO blood group system but also on the Rh blood group; and secondly, that Rh incompatibility between mother and child can result in severe fetal damage and even stillbirth.

In contrast to the ABO system, the antigens of which are present on all human somatic cells and also in certain bacteria and plants, the Rh blood group is determined by factors that are present only on the surface of red blood cells. Rh antibodies arise only as a result of 'genuine' immunisation after Rh-incompatible transfusions, pregnancies or organ transplants. Antibodies that arise in this way are said to be 'irregular' in that their occurrence does not follow Landsteiner's rule. Regular anti-A and anti-B antibodies arise as a result of 'natural' immunisation by antigens present in the environment.

It was soon found that a person's Rh blood group is determined not by a single antigen, but by a system composed of a number of factors. By 1943 four more rhesus antigens had been identified. The first Rh antigen to be discovered was named D, the others C, c, E and e. About 40 antigens of the rhesus blood group system have now been identified and named on the basis of a variety of criteria. Wiener's nomenclature, in which factor D is referred to as Rh, C as rh', E as rh", c as hr' and e as hr", is still employed to some extent in the English-speaking world. In the Rosenfield nomenclature all Rh antigens are numbered in the order of their discovery. In addition, many antigens are named after the scientist who first described them or the individual in whom they were first identified. Only after discovery of the manner in which they are inherited did the letter-based CcD.Ee nomenclature introduced by Fischer and Race in the late 1940s achieve widespread use on the basis that it best represents the genetic relationships of these five most important Rh antigens.

Rh antigens are proteins that span the erythrocyte membrane and thereby help to stabilise it. The D gene either produces the D antigen or is 'silent', i. e. produces no antigen. People with a silent D gene are said to be rhesus-negative. When the immune system of a Rh-negative individual is exposed to Rh-positive erythrocytes as a result of transfusion, organ transplantation or pregnancy, there is an 80% probability that it will form an antibody, anti-D, against factor D. No other antigen is known to induce the formation of antibodies in such a high proportion of cases. If repeat exposure to factor D occurs in an individual in whom anti-D antibodies have already been formed, antigen-antibody binding can cause a potentially fatal transfusion reaction, organ rejection or fetal damage of variable severity. Passage of

large amounts of maternal rhesus antibodies into the fetus during pregnancy can result in intrauterine death or stillbirth. Even after the birth of an affected child a risk remains, as the hemoglobin released as a result of destruction of the erythrocyte membrane is converted into a toxic yellow pigment, bilirubin. This substance can damage the newborn infant's brainstem centres and thereby cause severe mental and physical impairments. For a long time the only way of saving the life of such infants was by exchange transfusion. This involved repetitive withdrawal of small amounts of the patient's blood and simultaneous replacement of it with Rh-negative donor blood.

For 20 years exchange transfusion was the only hope for 'rhesus babies'. Then, in 1964, Rh prophylaxis was made an obligatory part of antenatal care in Germany. In this technique Rh-negative women are injected with small, harmless doses of anti-D hyperimmune serum during their first pregnancy and immediately after delivery. Rh-positive fetal erythrocytes that find their way into the maternal circulation are destroyed by the injected anti-D antibodies, with the result that no anti-D antibodies are formed in the mother and the next pregnancy is not endangered.

Antibodies directed against the Rh antigens Cc and Ee can have the same effects as anti-D antibodies, but the probability that they will be formed is much lower, namely less than 8%. Other Rh factors will not be discussed here, as they are of little clinical relevance.

Routine testing of blood donor and recipient for the presence of Rh factor D was introduced in the late 1940s. In this test anti-D-containing serum from donors immunised with Rh-positive blood is incubated at 37°C in a test tube with the subject's erythrocytes. Serum containing Coombs' anti-human globulin is then added and the presence or absence of agglutination is noted.

This method is still used today, also for the Rh factors Cc and Ee, though use of monoclonal Rh antibodies is now generally preferred.

Discovery of the Kell blood group system

The Kell blood group system is similar to the rhesus system in that anti-Kell antibodies can damage a fetus with the corresponding antigens in the same way as can anti-D antibodies.

In contrast to the Rh system, however, only 5–10% of Kell-negative recipients form anti-Kell antibodies after transfusion of Kell-positive blood. The lower immunogenicity of the Kell system as compared with the frequency of anti-D formation in the Rh system is presumably due to the fact that the *K* and *k* alleles of the Kell system really exist. The peculiarity of the Kell system is the statistical distribution of its alleles: 92% of populations of Western European descent carry the kk allele combination and are referred to as Kell-negative; 7.98% of the population carry the *Kk* antigen combination and are referred to as Kell-positive, as are the 0.02% who bear the homozygous *KK* allele combination. This distribution explains why the Kell system only took on practical importance in the late 1970s, when the number of blood transfusions rose sharply. Since 92% of donors and recipients possess the same Kell antigen combination (kk), antibodies are not formed when blood is transfused between them and the Kell blood group system is therefore of no relevance in such cases. Recipients with the Kk antigen combination form neither anti-K nor anti-k antibodies, since neither of these antigens is foreign to them; therefore, the Kell system does not make itself manifest here either. Only two out of every 1000 blood transfusion recipients bear the KK antigen combination and are therefore potential antibody formers who could react to a subsequent transfusion. Once a KK patient has formed anti-k antibodies, any subsequent transfusion of Kell-negative erythrocytes must be expected to result in a potentially fatal transfusion reaction. Such patients must be given only KK blood, however an adequate supply of this can be very difficult to maintain. Blood from Kell-positive donors can of course stimulate the formation of anti-K antibodies in Kell-negative recipients. Though it is easy enough to ensure that any subsequent transfusions given to such patients are of Kell-negative blood, it is better to avoid antibody formation in the first place. Blood pack labels must therefore specify not only the blood's ABO and Rh group characteristics but also its Kell group characteristics. There is no obligation to state the characteristics of the blood in terms of any of the other blood group systems (Duffy, Kidd, Lutheran etc.) that can cause transfusion reactions once antibodies have been formed. These systems are taken into account only in blood recipients who have already developed antibodies. Prior to any transfusion, the recipient's serum must be screened for the presence of such antibodies.

Antibody screening

In the antibody screening test the patient's serum is incubated with a panel of donor red cells whose blood group antigens are known. Any antibody present in the serum will agglutinate donor red cells bearing the corresponding antigen. This antigen defines the antibody present in the patient. In order to identify blood that will be suitable for transfusion into the patient, preserved blood is then tested for absence of the corresponding antigen using the defined antibody. Sometimes a large number of preserved blood specimens have to be tested before a compatible one is found. In order to spare the patient's blood, antibody-containing serum from appropriately immunised donors is used. Since their development in 1975 by César Milstein (1927–2002) and Georges Köhler (1946–1995), monoclonal antibodies have increasingly been used for antigen testing, since they can be produced in almost unlimited quantity at constant quality.

Compatibility testing

In order to ensure that the right blood has been chosen for the patient, one more test is performed. Now that packed red cells, rather than whole blood, are used for transfusion, this is referred to as compatibility testing rather than crossmatching, since – like the antibody screening test – it tests only for the presence in the recipient's serum of antibodies directed against the donor's red cells. Correctly performed compatibility testing following correct donor and recipient blood group determination and a correctly performed antibody screening test, with antibody differentiation if necessary, has a high probability of preventing the occurrence of any transfusion reaction due to blood group incompatibilities of the red blood cells.

White blood cell antigens

Like the blood groups of the red blood cells, the histocompatibility antigens, or transplantation antigens, of the white blood cells (leukocytes) are determined using antibody-containing sera. Such sera used to be obtained mostly from women who had become immunised via a number of pregnancies. **H**uman leukocyte **a**ntigen (HLA) characterisation, or typing, is performed by placing antiserum – e.g. that of a pregnant woman – containing a known antibody into the tiny wells of a test plate and then adding to this a cell suspension of specially prepared white blood cells, e.g. those of a potential blood or organ donor whose HLA characteristics are unknown. If antigen-antibody binding occurs, the cell membrane of the white blood cells breaks down in the presence of complement. Addition of a vital dye renders the antigen-antibody reaction visible under the microscope, since only cells whose membrane has been destroyed take up the dye, whereas intact cells do not. HLA typing is now being largely replaced by DNA determination using molecular biological methods.

Only in special cases are blood products specifically tested and selected in order to avoid the immunologically determined side effects of transfusion resulting from antigens present on the surface of white blood cells. In most cases removal of the white cells by filtration is sufficient for this purpose. In certain situations it can be necessary to irradiate cell-containing blood products (generally with x-rays) in order to eliminate immunogenic action of the lymphocytes.

Transmission of pathogens

Pathogens can be transmitted via blood transfusions if the blood was contaminated while being obtained or prepared or if the donor was infected. Contamination can and must be avoided by good manufacturing practice. Nevertheless, it can be difficult to prove that a donor is free of transmissible pathogens. This is especially true of pathogens that remain in the blood over long periods without causing symptoms but which can infect a blood transfusion recipient. Such pathogens must be detected by detailed questioning of the donor about any possible risk of infection and by the performance of suitable laboratory tests.

After penicillin largely eliminated the spectre of syphilis, transmission of hepatitis became the most feared infectious complication of blood transfusion. The hepatitis A virus was known to persist for only a short time in the blood and to be transmitted mostly by direct person-to-person contact. Transmission via blood products can occur only during the brief viremic phase, however during this phase the affected person feels too ill to donate blood. Hepatitis A therefore plays no significant role as a cause of post-transfusion hepatitis. The **h**epatitis **B** **v**irus (HBV), by contrast, has a long incubation period of up to 240 days. Desperate efforts were therefore made to develop a means of detecting HBV.

Hepatitis B

In 1963 Baruch Samuel Blumberg (b. 1925) discovered in the blood of Australian Aborigines a protein that induces formation of a specific antibody when injected into another human being.[13] In 1970 Dane and coworkers described the same antigen as a viral coat protein and identified it as the coat protein of HBV.[14] 'Dane particles' were then given the name

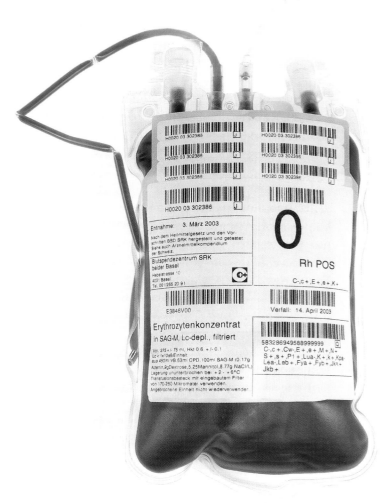

Packed red cell preparations must contain information on the Landsteiner blood group and the Rh and Kell characteristics.

HBsAg (**h**epatitis **B** **s**urface **a**nti**g**en). Within the viral coat is the core particle HBcAg (**h**epatitis **B** **c**ore **a**nti**g**en). These antigens, together with their corresponding antibodies anti-HBs and anti-HBc, can be detected via an ELISA (**e**nzyme-**l**inked **i**mmuno**s**orbent **a**ssay) method developed by Blumberg himself. In this ingenious method nonspecific antibodies bound to a solid support such as the floor of a test tube bind antigens (e.g. HBsAg) present in an added solution. If the patient or donor serum to be tested is then added, the now bound antigens attach via their free binding site to the corresponding antibodies, in this case anti-HBs. In order to render this reaction visible, an anti-antibody, e.g. anti-human globulin, labelled with an enzyme is added to the mixture in the test tube together with the enzyme's substrate. The enzyme, e. g. peroxidase, alters its substrate and in so doing brings about a measurable colour change.

By employing different reagents, the ELISA technique can be used to measure other antigens, e. g. HBsAg, or other antibodies, e. g. anti-hepatitis C virus (HCV) antibodies.

Although ELISA is a sensitive and highly specific method, its introduction failed to reduce the rate of post-transfusion hepatitis to any significant extent. Therefore, even after obligatory HBsAg testing of blood donors was introduced in 1970, routine measurement of the level of the hepatic enzyme SGPT (**s**erum **g**lutamic-**p**yruvic **t**ransaminase, now known as ALAT) in donor serum was continued. It has been known since the mid-1960s that an elevated level of this enzyme in donor serum (released by destroyed liver cells) correlates with transfusion-associated hepatitis in the recipient.

Hepatitis C

Even after exclusion of all would-be blood donors with a history of infectious hepatitis, an elevated SGPT level or a positive HBsAg test result, the rate of transfusion-associated hepatitis fell by only about 5 %. It was therefore conjectured that one or more other types of hepatitis virus might exist, and in 1975 the term non-A, non-B hepatitis was introduced to refer to these. Fifteen more years passed before the main pathogen of non-A, non-B hepatitis, namely **h**epatitis **C** **v**irus (HCV), was identified and an ELISA method of detecting the corresponding antibody (anti-HCV) became available. Hepatitis C virus could not be grown in cell culture, however in 1988 scientists identified regions of the viral genome from which they were able to engineer viral proteins for use as an antigen in an ELISA test. An anti-HCV test based on this novel viral construct was introduced early in 1990. This breakthrough in the battle against hepatitis C received relatively little public attention, however, since over the ensuing decade all eyes were focused on a new disease that can also be transmitted by blood: **a**cquired **i**mmuno-**d**eficiency **s**yndrome (AIDS).

AIDS

In 1981 five cases of an unusual form of pneumonia and a number of cases of a rare skin cancer (Kaposi's sarcoma) were reported in the USA, all in young homosexual men. A sexually transmitted organism that weakened the immune system was postulated as the cause. When a similar illness was observed in a group of known drug addicts, it was conjectured that in this case the pathogen had been spread by shared use of injecting equipment and therefore that it could also be transmitted via blood. In November 1982 the first two cases of what appeared to be this new disease – now known as AIDS – were reported in Germany. In December 1982 the case of a one-and-a-half-year-old child who developed a series of severe and in some cases rare infections after receiving multiple blood transfusions was reported. It was not until January 1984, however, when a report was published in the USA on the cases of 18 AIDS patients who had previously received blood transfusions, that the connection between the blood transfusions and the child's immunodeficiency was recognised.

In 1983 Luc Montagnier (b. 1932), of the Pasteur Institute in Paris, and a short time later Robert Gallo (b. 1937), of the US National Cancer Institute, discovered a new virus. In 1986 this virus was given the name 'human immunodeficiency virus', or HIV. A scientifically unhelpful dispute as to which of these two researchers had discovered the virus raged for almost ten years, finally ending with an admission by Gallo that he had conducted his research using the virus isolated by Montagnier.

In 1984 the AIDS pathogen was isolated for the first time from both a blood donor and the recipient of that donor's blood. This proved that AIDS could be transmitted via blood. For some time, however, this finding was overshadowed by the almost medieval view that marginal groups such as homosexuals and drug addicts 'deserved' to be struck down by AIDS as a punishment for their immoral lifestyle. The gutter press mounted a veritable hate campaign against AIDS patients, who consequently became afraid to admit to their condition. This placed an additional burden on patients who had been infected via blood products. The biggest group infected in this way was that of hemophiliacs, in particular people with hemophilia A or B, who have a genetically determined deficiency of coagulation factor VIII or IX, respectively. These coagulation factors, which can be obtained from the plasma of donated blood, have to be administered to these patients at regular intervals. Plasma for this purpose is obtained and prepared either in plasmapheresis units or in blood donation centres. Coagulation factors are obtained by 'pooling' many litres of plasma from many donors, separating this plasma into individual fractions and packaging these fractions as batches. The plasma of a single infected donor can thus contaminate many batches. Methods of killing viruses in plasma by application of heat had been available since 1983 – having been developed for use on hepatitis viruses – but they were expensive and not always sufficiently effective. For reasons of cost, therefore, patients were treated not only with virus-inactivated, but also with untreated, pooled plasma. In 1984, when the catastrophic situation of hemophiliac patients and the possibility of transmission of AIDS via blood transfusion had permeated into the public consciousness, a frantic search began in blood donation services for methods of reducing this risk. It also became clear that the worldwide, scarcely controllable trade in plasma products could promote the spread of new or previously highly localised infectious diseases. National self-sufficiency in blood products was therefore made a priority goal in the European Union (EU).

Not uncommonly, a justifiable fear of acquiring transmissible infections led potential blood recipients to refuse urgent transfusions. Only from mid-1986, when an ELISA test for anti-HIV antibodies finally became available, did patients' confidence in treatment with blood products begin to recover.

The first generation of anti-HIV ELISA tests were able to detect antibodies only from about day 45 after infection, at which stage the affected person was already infectious. This period has been progressively reduced in subsequent test generations, though even now a certain risk of nondetection remains, even with tests based on direct demonstration of HIV in the blood.

A positive result in an ELISA-based HIV antibody test requires confirmation using a different test method. As described above for syphilis, the first step in diagnosis is to perform a highly sensitive screening test, in this case an anti-HIV ELISA, that may give a false-positive result but will almost certainly not give a false-negative result, i. e. will not fail to detect antibodies that are present. A positive antibody screening test is confirmed by means of a Western blot analysis. In this technique concentrated, purified HIV components are separated by gel electrophoresis on the basis of their molecular weight and then transferred onto a cellulose matrix, where they specifically bind any HIV antibodies present in a sample of patient or donor serum. Enzyme-labelled anti-antibodies are then used to render the reaction visible as bands on the cellulose strip. If no bands appear, the sample is HIV-negative. A strip is deemed to be positive if it contains at least two bands that can be unequivocally assigned to an HIV component. Strips with only one band typical of the virus are classified as indeterminates. In December 2002 the US Food and Drug Administration (FDA) approved the use of PCR-based

The cellular components of blood, namely the red blood cells, or erythrocytes (42.8%), the white blood cells, or leukocytes (0.07%), and the platelets (2.14%), can be separated by centrifugation from the blood plasma, which contains proteins (4.4%), sugar, fats, salt (1.09%) and water (49.5%). The figure shows centrifuged blood. The blood and plasma are additionally separated from each other by an added translucent separating gel.

hepatitis C and HIV tests that can be performed simply and rapidly using the Cobas AmpliScreen system.

The BSE scare

Creutzfeldt-Jakob disease, which leads to neurological deficits and eventually to unconsciousness and death, was previously thought to result from a genetic predisposition. Research into bovine spongiform encephalopathy, or BSE, a new disease of cattle, led to the discovery of an infectious protein, referred to as a prion, which by causing other protein molecules to assume its three-dimensional conformation can destroy the normal brain structure. A cut section of affected brain has the appearance of a sponge. The encephalopathy of humans that can be transmitted by prions was given the name 'new-variant Creutzfeldt-Jakob disease' (nvCJD). This differs from the classical form of CJD both in that affected individuals become ill at an early age and in that the causative agent is found especially in the patient's white blood cells. During the BSE crisis there was a great deal of public discussion about the theoretical, though as yet unproven, possibility that prions might be transmitted via blood transfusions. Severe restrictions on blood donation, e. g. for anyone who had visited the United Kingdom, were called for. In September 2001 removal of white blood cells from transfusion blood by filtration was made obligatory in the EU.

Blood component manufacture

From the mid 1960s the white blood cells were removed from blood for transfusion in order to reduce the likelihood of immune reactions in patients who had received multiple blood transfusions. The whole blood was firstly centrifuged in the collection bottle in order to separate it into a supernatant of plasma and a layer of packed red cells. The white blood cells lying on top of the red cell layer were then aspirated off using a long cannula. The only way of eliminating the risk of bacterial contamination associated with this process was by performing it inside a closed system. A compound plastic bag was developed for this purpose. The donor blood is firstly collected in the primary bag, to which a stabiliser has been added, and then centrifuged. The plasma, the packed red cells and in some cases the platelets are then squeezed into satellite bags. The white blood cells are collected in an integrated filter. This process yields storable blood components which in Germany have been classified since 1978 as proprietary medicinal products that have to be manufactured in accordance with the German Drug Act.[15] In Germany the production of blood products is also subject to the Pharmaceutical Manufacturing Act, the guidelines and directives of the German Medical Council, the recommendations of the Council of Europe and the requirements of the WHO Technical Report. Since 1998 the care and selection of blood donors and quality assurance with regard to the administration of blood products to recipients have been regulated in Germany by a special transfusion law.

Laboratory testing procedures, legally regulated good manufacturing practice and quality-assured use pursue a single objective: to provide effective and safe blood components for the patients who need them.

Sabine Päuser

Cancer signs

Hippocrates *(c. 460 – c. 375 BC) was born on the island of Cos and was the sixth of possibly seven members of a family of Asclepiads to bear that name. He trained as a physician in Athens and acquired further knowledge in the practice of medicine on his travels through Thessaly, Asia Minor and Egypt. Even during his lifetime he was considered an eminent physician, and his medical advice was much sought after by members of the ruling classes. Of the 58 writings comprising the* Hippocratic Corpus, *a collection of treatises summarising the knowledge of various medical schools, none can be confidently attributed to Hippocrates – not even the* Hippocratic Oath, *certainly the most famous work in the collection. However, this in no way diminishes the significance of Hippocrates, who was the 'first to free medicine from the bonds of mysticism and speculation and base it on the observation of nature and on experience'.[71] Hippocrates was an adherent of the humoral theory, attributing disease to a lack or overabundance of the four humours: blood, phlegm and black and yellow bile. He was also familiar with cancers of the internal organs, a knowledge that was later lost and does not resurface even in the works of celebrated Galen. According to Galen, cancer was caused by inspissated black bile, a conclusion he drew from his observation that melancholy women were particularly prone to cancer. While Hippocrates and Galen stressed the need to detect cancer at the start of the disease, they were able to diagnose it, if at all, only by its course.[72]*

That cancers were known to Egyptian medicine is documented in several surviving papyri. The Edwin Smith Papyrus, for example, which dates from about 1600 BC, describes tumours of the breast.[1] And the Ebers Papyrus, from approximately 1550 BC, contains detailed teaching texts on tumours, which even recommend a number of remedies for them. The Hippocratic writings frequently mention cancer, a term which the Ancient Greeks may have used to describe any type of benign or malignant tumour, including hemorrhoids. Hippocrates of Cos (c. 460 – c. 375 BC) was the first to use the term *karkinoma* (carcinoma) for malignant non-healing cancers, in addition to the term *karkinos* (crab/cancer) for any non-healing ulcer.[2] These terms are thought to derive from *karkinousthe* – roughly translatable as 'attacked by the crab' – and to have been inspired by the 'crab claw-like' network of blood vessels glimpsed under the skin in certain superficial, outwardly visible tumours. The words 'cancer' and 'carcinoma' were already in common use among the Ancient Romans. However, for the Roman physician Aulus Cornelius Celsus (30 BC – AD 38), 'carcinoma' was an umbrella term for all tumours. Cancer was indirectly diagnosable from the fact that all treatment was ineffective. The celebrated Galen (AD 129 – c. 216) emphasised the need to diagnose cancer in its earliest stages. However, even he could only make presumptive diagnoses, obtaining confirmation of cancer only from the disease course. Leonides of Alexandria (fl. c. AD 180) gave one of the first descriptions of a cancer sign, and one which we still consider a particular cause for alarm: nipple retraction as an indication of breast cancer.[3]

Henry Bence Jones *(1813–1873), who was born in Yoxford, Suffolk, in England, originally intended to take holy orders. He studied theology at Trinity College, Cambridge, but, shortly before being ordained, paid a visit to a relative in Liverpool which was to steer his life in another direction. After working in a hospital dispensary for six months, he not only wanted to become a doctor, but had also developed an interest in medical chemistry. On completing his medical training at Cambridge and St George's Hospital in London, he therefore went to the laboratory of Thomas Graham (1805–1869), at University College, London, and, in 1841, to the world-famous laboratory of Justus [von] Liebig (1803–1873) in Germany, to extend his knowledge of chemistry. In 1842 he set up in practice in London and equipped himself with a small laboratory in which he analysed urinary stones from the museum at St George's Hospital.[73] In the same year he published his first book on urinary stones and gout, which he dedicated, as a 'friend and pupil', to Liebig. While it was customary in his day to describe diseases with a whole catalogue of symptoms, Bence Jones endeavoured to apply pathological and physiological chemistry in diagnosis and treatment, and to promote these disciplines in England through lectures and publications. He developed the concept of a 'chemical circulation in the body that is based above all on diffusion processes between blood, tissues and excretory organs'. He published numerous studies on the chemical analysis of urine, including one in 1847 on a patient with mollities ossium.[74] He is said to have started work in the laboratory every day at the crack of dawn, visiting his hospital patients in the afternoons and evenings.*

A serious heart condition, the result of rheumatic fever in his youth, put an end to this double life as a practising hospital physician and basic researcher in 1862. From then on Bence Jones devoted himself entirely to scientific research. He was a contemporary and friend of Charles Darwin (1809–1882) and Michael Faraday (1791-1867). His last book was a two-volume biography of Faraday, published in 1870. He prescribed such a strict diet for his patient Darwin that the renowned naturalist wrote (despite the 'therapeutic' success) that Bence Jones had 'half-starved me to death'.

Hair diagnostics, uroscopy and boiling tests

Cancers that failed to externalise in visible tumours or hemorrhages were very difficult to diagnose correctly until the 20th century. There often remained only the sad and very vague criterion of complete treatment failure. As understanding of the different presentations of cancer increased, so did efforts to identify trustworthy cancer signs. These efforts were also stimulated by the advances made in cell pathology by Rudolf Virchow (1821–1902)[4] and by an expanding array of therapeutic and, particularly,

surgical options.[5] Many of these early diagnostic criteria strike us today as ranging from the desperate to the bizarre. According to Hermann Schridde, a German pathologist born in 1875 and the discoverer of Schridde's hair abnormality, jet-black, strikingly thick hair at 'sites on the head especially exposed to light, at the anterior hair margin, in the temporal and nuchal regions' indicated an increased risk of cancer. Writing about his findings in a 1922 issue of the *Münchener Medizinische Wochenschrift*, Schridde confidently asserted:

> Whereas I was able to observe black pigmentation of the hair and pigmentation of the skin, as mentioned, in cancers of all organs – only red-haired subjects appear an exception – I have not seen this change in sarcomas … My experiences thus leave no room for doubt that whether a cancer of the internal organs is present can be concluded from the changes described in the head hair. In many cases I have made the diagnosis simply on the basis of examination of the hair, without knowledge of the clinical diagnosis and before starting the autopsy, and I have never been mistaken.[6]

Schridde's 'cancer hair' was still being investigated in 1936. In that year a study involving 300 patients reached the following conclusion:

> The increased incidence of the hair abnormality that we have shown in certain families supports the view that Schridde's cancer hair is only the expression of an abnormality of the constitution, which is combined with, among other things, a predisposition to malignant tumours. Whether this connection between the two constitutional abnormalities, which is certainly hereditary, presupposes particular humoral or neuronal pathways cannot as yet be decided. We can summarise our findings by saying that the absence of the Schridde hair abnormality appears a sure sign that carcinoma or a carcinomatous disposition is absent. On the other hand, the demonstration of cancer hair is not proof that cancer is present; it can, however, be said that individuals with cancer hair have a greater probability of cancer than those without.[7]

Kaminer's inoculation reaction is likely to strike the modern reader as similarly misguided. Its proponents had no compunctions about injecting serum from patients probably suffering from cancer under the skin of healthy subjects and basing a diagnosis on the resulting eruption.[8]

Attention naturally also focused on the examination of body fluids, such as blood and urine, which were relatively simple to obtain. The general practitioner Reinhold Köhler wrote in 1853 in his book *Die Krebs- und Scheinkrebs-Krankheiten des Menschen*, in a section on the 'Influence of cancer on the characteristics of blood and secretions':

Cancer develops in all possible constitutions and temperaments. If in cancer there is a primary change in the blood components, then this probably concerns neither the fibrous material, nor the blood corpuscles, nor the protein, but the little-known extractives.[9]

History was to prove him hugely mistaken.

Uroscopy in a host of variants was integral to these endeavours. In the so-called Davis reaction, for example, urine was heated with hydrochloric acid and extracted with ether. The residue remaining after evaporation of the organic solvent was then examined. A pink-violet colour was thought to signify cancer, while yellow-brown coloration was interpreted as a negative result.[10]

Efforts to wrest clues about cancer from serum and urine by heating them and subjecting them to all sorts of other processes continued into the 20th century – but with dubious success.

First tumour marker in urine

Yet not all of these efforts can be dismissed as completely useless. The fact is, the first tumour marker was discovered by 'boiling urine', even if the physicians who made the discovery in 1845 were not yet aware of what they had found. 'What is it?' With these words the London physician Thomas Watson (1792–1882) ended a letter which he dispatched on 1 November 1845, together with a urine sample containing an unusual precipitate, to the 'chemical pathologist' Henry Bence Jones (1813–1873) at St George's Hospital. On the previous day Watson had asked a colleague, William MacIntyre (1792–1857), to examine his 45-year old patient Thomas Alexander McBean. MacIntyre had duly examined not only the patient but also his urine with great care and had made an astonishing discovery. He heated the urine, which was by no means an unusual thing to do: as far back as 1694 Fredericus Dekkers (1648–1720) had reported heating a urine sample acidified with acetic acid as a test for protein.[11] However, the reaction which MacIntyre observed was odd indeed. As he heated the urine, a milky cloudiness formed, followed by the formation of a gel-like precipitate which disappeared on further heating to 160–170 °F (71–77 °C).[12] Bence Jones repeated the experiments with urine samples from his own patients, observing that acidification of the urine with nitric acid produced precipitates which dissolved on boiling and reprecipitated on cooling.[13] In 1847 he published his observations on the precipitates, which later became known – a little unjustly, given the contributions by Watson and MacIntyre – as Bence Jones proteins.[14, 15]

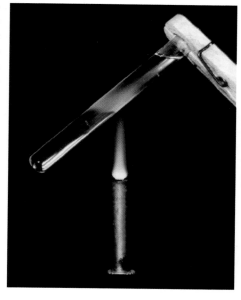

The presence, after moderate heating (50–60 °C), of slightly whitish opalescence in the middle of a test tube filled with acidified patient urine, which then disappears after further heating, was used to test for Bence Jones proteins in urine until the mid-20th century.

Patient McBean died on 1 January 1846. 'Atrophy from albuminuria' (albumin excretion in the urine) was given as the cause of death.[16] The diagnosis was not actually mistaken, as the term 'albuminuria' was used non-specifically at the time for increased protein excretion in the urine. However, Watson, MacIntyre and Bence Jones suspected that their patient had actually died from something else, possibly a cancer. The post-mortem then revealed that there was something wrong with the deceased's bones. The ribs, sternum and thoracic and lumbar vertebrae were soft and fragile. The 'interior' of these bones was red, sodden and 'gelatiniform'.[17] They therefore changed their diagnosis to '*mollities et fragilitas ossium*'.[18] MacIntyre described the case of 'Mr M.' in 1850 as a 'case of mollities and fragilitas ossium, accompanied with urine strongly charged with animal matter.'[19, 20] That the cause was a cancer of the bone marrow did not become clear until 1873, when Ossip J. von Rustizky (1839–?), a professor in Kiev, published a report in the *Deutsche Zeitschrift für Chirurgie* on a patient with a pulsatile, fist-sized mass on the temple who was found at autopsy to have some soft bones and eight tumours. Von Rustizky examined the tumours and wrote:

> Overall, the tumour cells were identical in structure to the cells taken from the adjacent bone marrow, so that one would have mistaken one for the other had not the distinctive presence of larger fat droplets alerted the observer to the genuine bone marrow cells.[21]

Using the Latin prefix *multi* and the Greek adjective *myelogen* (concerning bone marrow), von

Rustizky gave the disease the name by which it is still known today, 'multiple myeloma'.

In 1889 the *Prager Medizinische Wochenschrift* published a paper 'On the symptomatology of multiple myeloma. Observation of albumosuria' by Otto Kahler (1849–1893), a professor of medicine in Prague. This paper provided the first complete clinical description of multiple myeloma,[22] and as a result the condition also became known as Kahler's disease. The same issue of the journal also included a detailed report on the properties of the urine in Kahler's patient, which was found to contain the same strange precipitates described by Bence Jones after heating. One year later Santiago Ramón y Cajal (1852–1934) produced the first accurate microscopic description of plasma cells, which were first identified in the blood of multiple myeloma patients in 1905/1906 by Hermann Schridde, the pathologist mentioned earlier. The hypothesis that malignant plasma cells in the bone marrow were responsible for myelomatous bone disease was first proposed in 1909.[23]

Although no one knew exactly what Bence Jones proteins were, the boiling test to detect them entered the battery of laboratory investigations in the late 19th century. Starting with Kahler, there was an awareness of the diagnostic importance of Bence Jones proteins as a sign of malignant bone marrow disease, though surely no one was describing them yet as a tumour marker, a concept which was not developed until the 1970s. Yet by 1898 seven cases had been described in which these proteins occurred in the urine in Kahler's disease. Barely ten years later over 100 cases had been documented in the medical literature.[24]

Experts differed widely in their views on what caused the production of these proteins. However, a look at the 11th edition of the textbook *Analyse des Harns. Zum Gebrauch für Mediziner, Chemiker und Pharmazeuten* (1913) indicates that by the early 20th century a consensus was emerging:

> that Bence Jones protein should not be considered as something foreign to the human body. It thus in no way represents immediately re-excreted dietary protein, but protein which has been transformed into body protein.[25]

The same textbook went on to caution that the Bence Jones test was far from straightforward. Above all, it could yield false-positive and false-negative results. Many different factors, including the salt and acid content of the urine, could affect this 'strange coagulation phenomenon'.

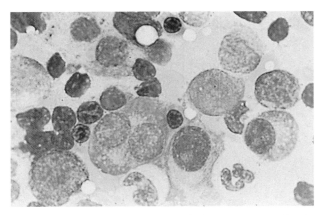

Mono- and binucleate cells as seen in bone marrow under the microscope in multiple myeloma.

Thus the temperature limits at which precipitation occurs vary with the acidity and salt content of the urine. Other urine constituents, such as the urea content, also affect the behaviour of this protein.[26]

In 1934 the celebrated hematologist Edwin Eugene Osgood (1899–1969) and a colleague reported on the infiltration of liver, spleen, bone marrow and lymph nodes by malignant plasma cells in multiple myeloma.[27] But the nature of Bence Jones proteins remained unexplained, posing a continuing obstacle to the routine diagnosis of multiple myeloma, despite the discovery, in 1903, that the bone lesions in this disease were visible on x-ray. Diagnosis would remain an uncertain undertaking until bone marrow biopsy became more frequent in the 1930s and urine electrophoresis was developed.[28]

Thomas Watson's original question thus continued to preoccupy researchers and would remain a puzzle until scientists began to unravel the structure of antibodies. The man who finally found the answer was the American biochemist Gerald Maurice Edelman (b. 1929), who shared the 1972 Noble prize for medicine or physiology with the British biochemist and immunologist Rodney Porter (1917–1985) for their discovery of the chemical structure of antibodies. How was the answer found? In a sense by chance. Edelman's aim was to elucidate the structure of antibodies, a daunting challenge given the huge diversity of antibodies. He therefore went in search of 'simpler molecules'. Bence Jones proteins were relatively simple to isolate. They were also relatively homogeneous, had a relatively low molecular weight and were known to show antigenic properties similar to the immunoglobulins.[29]

Edelman's hypothesis was that

> Bence Jones proteins may be polypeptide chains that have not been incorporated into the myeloma globulins because of a failure in the linkage process.[30,31]

One afternoon at the Rockefeller Institute in New York he and a colleague performed a simple but exciting experiment. They 'heated solutions of [antibody] light chains isolated from immunoglobulins from our own serum using the classic boiling test to detect Bence Jones proteins'[32] and made the same observations in their samples as Watson, McIntyre and Bence Jones had done almost 120 years previously. What must researchers think and feel at such a moment? In 1962 they published a study not only itemising the amino acid composition of Bence Jones proteins, but also showing – and confirming by several methods – that the light chains of IgG immunoglobulin from the blood of a patient with Bence Jones proteins were identical to those in urine.[33] In the discussion of their results they proudly concluded:

> A urine sample containing reversibly coagulable protein was sent to Dr. Jones in 1845 by a practitioner, Dr. Watson, who also sent a note describing its behaviour. The description terminated with the question 'What is it?' Dr. Jones concluded that it was the 'hydrated deutoxide of albumin.' The above studies would supply the question with another qualified answer: Bence-Jones proteins appear to be polypeptide chains of the L type that have not been incorporated into myeloma proteins.[34]

It was not long before the last major question marks surrounding Bence Jones proteins disappeared. In August 1967 their amino acid sequence was published[35] and in 1974 Robert Huber (b. 1937) and his group published their three-dimensional structure, obtained by X-ray structural analysis.[36]

We now know that multiple myeloma is characterised by the uncontrolled proliferation of malignant undifferentiated antibody-producing plasma cells (B cells) of a single cell type, which establish themselves in the bone marrow, where they suppress the growth of normal blood cells.

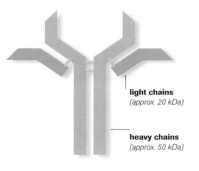

light chains
(approx. 20 kDa)

heavy chains
(approx. 50 kDa)

Schematic drawing of an IgG immunoglobulin, consisting of two light and two heavy chains. Each of the chains has a constant and a variable domain.

Extract from the textbook Analyse des Harns. Zum Gebrauch für Mediziner, Chemiker und Pharmazeuten *(1913).*

The presence or absence of Bence Jones proteins in urine is neither the sole diagnostic criterion for multiple myeloma nor an adequate exclusion criterion. On the one hand, only approximately half of all patients with multiple myeloma excrete the proteins, while on the other, Bence Jones proteins are also found in the urine of patients with other so-called proliferative B-cell diseases, such as certain leukemias[37] and lymphomas,[38] and also Waldenström's macroglobulinemia.[39] The test for Bence Jones proteins is thus still in use in the diagnosis of such diseases, even if immunofixation has long since replaced the laborious 'boiling test' for detecting the free monoclonal immunoglobulin light chains.[40,41]

The first tumour marker to be described thus consists of incomplete, identical (monoclonal), low-molecular antibody chains produced by malignant plasma cells that are incompetent to mount an effective immune response.[42] These immunoglobulin light chains have a lower molecular weight than the complete antibody molecules. They can therefore be excreted by the kidneys and detected in urine.

It took decades for this first tumour marker in urine to be identified as such, and over a century for its nature to be elucidated. Only recently a report was published on the value of testing serum

Robert Huber *(b. 1937) elucidated the three-dimensional structure of Bence Jones proteins in the early 1970s, together with colleagues at the Max Planck Institute of Biochemistry in Martinsried, the Institute of Physical Chemistry at Munich Technical University and the Institute of Medical Biochemistry at the University of Graz. Huber was born in Munich, where he studied chemistry, obtained his PhD and qualified as a university lecturer at the Technical University. Since 1972 he has been a scientific member of the Max Planck Society and* director of the Max Planck Institute of Biochemistry in Martinsried. In 1976 he became an adjunct professor at Munich Technical University. He is editor of the Journal of Molecular Biology *and a member of many international scientific societies. He has received numerous awards, including the Nobel prize for chemistry in 1988, which he shared with his German colleagues Johann Deisenhofer (b. 1943) and Hartmut Michel (b. 1948) for the crystallisation and x-ray structural analysis of the photosynthetic reaction centre from the bacterium* Rhodopseudomonas viridis. *His main areas of research interest are in elucidating the structure and function of biological macromolecules, especially large, complex aggregates, and developing and improving various physicochemical methods for this purpose. Huber is shown here with a model of the protein-cleaving enzyme trypsin.*

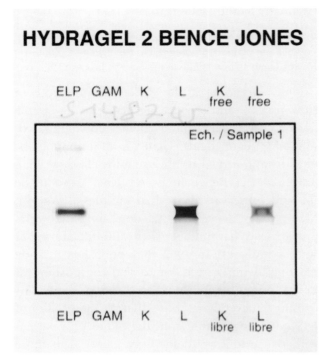

Today Bence Jones proteins are detected by immunofixation electrophoresis on agarose gels. The proteins in a sample are first separated by electrophoresis on an agarose gel and then incubated with antisera of differing specificity. The antisera diffuse into the gel and the corresponding antigens are precipitated and fixed with a fixing solution. Unbound proteins are removed in a washing step. The precipitated antigen-antibody complexes are stained and visually assessed.[75]

for Bence Jones proteins in monitoring chemotherapy for multiple myeloma. The study used an immunoassay specific for immunoglobulin light chains.[43]

During the 20th century, scientists learned to use the metabolic products, enzymes and hormones[44] produced by tumour cells or certain antigenic structures on the surface of malignant cells (tumour antigens) as tumour markers. However, since these are often compounds that can also be found at low concentrations in the body fluids of healthy subjects, most tumour markers are unsuitable by themselves for making an initial diagnosis, but are used instead for monitoring treatment response.

Cervical smear for cancer screening

Something of an exception is the cytological analysis of the cervical smear to detect cervical cancer. Is this a case of a sign which is reliably diagnostic in itself? If the staining technique developed in the first half of the 20th century by George Nicholas Papanicolaou (1883–1962) reveals cancer cells in the cervical smear (Pap smear), the answer is 'Yes': the case is clear-cut and action is necessary.

Papanicolaou was by no means the first to look at tumour cells under the microscope. In 1838 Johannes Müller (1801–1858), an anatomist, pathologist and physiologist at Berlin University, had described the microscopic appearance of tumours in his monograph *Über den feineren Bau und die Formen der krankhaften Geschwülste*. It was also in Müller's laboratory that the young Rudolf Virchow became acquainted with the cell theory. Later Virchow would inject fresh impetus into the study and diagnosis of cancers with his work on tumours and his irritation theory of oncogenesis.[45]

Although Emil Küss (1815–1871) had recommended the use of tissue specimens for the histological diagnosis of cancer as far back as 1847,[46] it was probably the gynecologist Carl A. Ruge (1846–1926) who first performed tissue biopsies – i. e. the removal and examination of tissue from living patients –

for tumour diagnosis, in 1878.[47] Carl Friedländer (1847–1887), in his *Mikroskopische Technik*, published in 1883, stated:

> In uterine carcinoma one finds cellular elements and even tissue particles in the discharge that originate in the carcinomatous ulceration and aid diagnosis by virtue of their morphological structure.[48]

And yet it would be another 60 years before cytological analysis – thanks to Papanicolaou – became practicable and accepted in cancer screening. Actually the Greek cytologist, who emigrated to the United States with his wife in 1913, had at first only been interested in the sexual cycle of humans and animals (guinea pigs). To study the estrous cycle, he embarked in 1920 on the first systematic examination of vaginal smears. The first report on his findings, published in 1925, attracted little attention. This all changed in 1933, when Papanicolaou published a 118-page monograph that laid the foundations of vaginal cytology and cytopathology. The findings were based on over 1000 smears from 13 healthy women, including his own wife. Papanicolaou had made two very important modifications to the methodology then prevailing. First, he fixed his vaginal smears with isopropyl alcohol before they dried, having discovered that drying altered the appearance of the cells to such an extent that characteristic cell changes became unrecognisable.[49] Secondly, to Harris's hematoxylin nuclear stain he added a second stain with orange G or a mixture of dyes (orange G, light green, Bismarck brown and eosin). This provided better definition of the various stages of the cytoplasm.[50] The cell nuclei are then stained blue-violet, and the nucleoli red. The cytoplasm may be blue, blue-green or red, depending on hormone status. It is impossible for us now to determine with any certainty exactly when, in his extensive studies, Papanicolaou identified cancer cells for the first time. He reported his findings on cervical cancer cells at a conference in 1928,[51] but at first failed to convince his colleagues of their importance. As Papanicolaou himself later remarked, this was probably due to his short report in the conference proceedings. The report, which appeared in the *Proceedings of the Third Race Betterment Conference* under the promising title 'New Cancer Diagnosis', was inadequately documented and 'contained many stenographic errors that changed the meaning of the text'. These deficiencies, as well as the proceedings status of the publication, may have been largely responsible for the work being ignored by pathologists and physicians.[52] From 1939 onwards Papanicolaou worked intensively in cancer cytology,[53]

George Nicholas Papanicolaou *(1883–1962) was the son of a successful general practitioner in Greece. After obtaining his MD in Athens in 1904, however, he felt no desire to follow in his father's footsteps and went to Vienna to study philosophy. Shortly thereafter, he moved on to the Institute of Zoology in Munich, at that time the largest zoological research centre in the world.[76] There, in 1910, he earned a PhD in zoology with a thesis 'On sex determination and differentiation of the sexes in daphnids'.[77] In the same year he married, once again choosing not to heed his father. Instead of marrying the daughter of a rich wholesaler, as his father wished, he proposed to a friend of his sister's, Andromache (later called Mary) Mavroyeni, who, as a military officer's daughter, received only a small dowry from the government. Papanicolaou never regretted his decision. As he later remarked, his wife became his loyal and tireless companion and assistant.[78] In a letter to his parents he wrote on 4 October 1910:*

> *It is not my ideal to be wealthy or to live happily, but to work to create – to do something worthy of a strong moral man.[79]*

On their honeymoon the couple visited the Oceanographic Museum in Monaco, one of the best marine research stations in the world at that time. In a corridor of the museum Papanicolaou ran into a friend from Germany who was just packing to leave and who suggested that Papanicolaou could apply for his job as a physiologist. Papanicolaou was hired and accompanied Albert I, Prince of Monaco, grandfather of today's Prince Rainier of Monaco, on his yacht L'Hirondelle II *on an ecological expedition in 1911. After the outbreak of the Balkan War he fought in the Greek army against the Turks from 1912 to 1913 and got to know some Greek-American volunteers, who painted an enticing picture of the opportunities in America. These reports awoke in him the desire to work in biomedical research in the United States. As soon as the war was over he set about turning this dream into reality, and on 19 October 1913 he arrived in New York with his wife. His first post, which paid $60 per month, was as a part-time pathology assistant at New York Hospital; his wife worked as a shop assistant. A few months later Papanicolaou obtained a new post as a research biologist in the Department of Anatomy at Cornell University Medical College in New York. This job was not only more interesting, but better paid. Two months later Mrs Papanicolaou joined him as his assistant. This was the start of a research partnership which over the next half-century contributed a string of groundbreaking results in several specialties.[80] Papanicolaou remained in the department for 48 years, until shortly before his death, occupying in turn the posts of assistant, lecturer, assistant professor, associate professor and finally professor of anatomy. In late 1961, aged 78, he left his laboratory and comfortable home in New York to head a research and training institute for exfoliative cytology in Miami. He had just a short time left to live.*

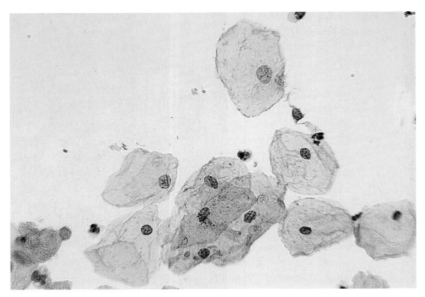

Photomicrograph of a Pap-stained cervical smear with a normal cell pattern at 400x magnification. The specimen shows normal squamous cells of the uterine cervix. The nuclei are relatively small compared with the surrounding cytoplasm and exhibit a fine nuclear reticulum.[81]

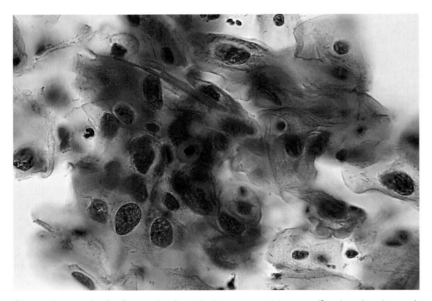

Photomicrograph of a Pap-stained cervical smear at 400x magnification showing early precancerous cell changes (mild dysplasia) caused by human papillomavirus. The nuclei are larger and darker, but the cell bodies are still intact. The nuclei are surrounded by a clear halo. HPV-infected squamous cells of this type are known as koilocytes.[82]

and in 1943, together with the gynecologist Herbert Frederick Traut (1894–1963), published the famous monograph *Diagnosis of Uterine Cancer by the Vaginal Smear*.[54] The profession took note at last. The monograph reported cytological smear examinations in 3014 women with a diagnostic accuracy of 98.4% in cervical cancer and 90.7% in endometrial cancer (cancer of the body of the womb). From then on many of Papanicolaou's colleagues devoted themselves to advancing the cytological diagnosis of cancer. He himself led the way in extending his method to the detection of cancers of the airways and urinary and gastrointestinal tracts, publishing over 50 papers on cytology in cancer detection between 1943 and 1961. In 1948 the American Cancer Society recommended the creation of additional cytology laboratories for genital cancer screening. And by the start of the 1960s cytology had established itself as a sensitive screening method for cancers of many organs not only in the United States, but also in numerous other countries.[55] Yet these cancer signs are not 100% reliable either. In the case of cervical cancer, up to 30–50% of serious precancerous lesions may be missed, depending on the patients screened and the quality of the cytological specimens.[56] Since we now know that cervical cancer is caused by certain high-risk types of **h**uman **p**apillomavirus (HPV), there has been no lack of effort to develop suitable tests for these HPV types. One approach introduced in the late 20th century involves the use of genetically engineered monoclonal antibodies to the coat proteins of the particularly aggressive viruses responsible for cervical cancer. These antibodies can detect and type HPV even in Pap-stained histological and cytological specimens. Researchers at Roche are currently developing a test based on the **p**olymerase **c**hain **r**eaction (PCR) for screening cervical cells for the genetic material of high-risk HPV.[57]

First serum tumour markers

In 1938 Alexander B. Gutman and Ethel Benedict Gutman of Columbia University and New York-Presbyterian Hospital published their discovery of the increased presence of **ac**id **p**hosphatase (ACP) in the serum of patients with metastatic prostate cancer.[58] The prostate gland, found only in men, was known to contain particularly high concentrations of this enzyme. If metastatic prostate cancer cells entered the lymphatics and bloodstream, the Gutmans reasoned, then increased levels of ACP should be detectable in the blood. Experiment proved their hypothesis correct. The first serum tumour marker had been found. This enzyme is still used to monitor the course of prostate disease. However, various isoforms of ACP occur in the secretory cells of many organs and tissues. As its name suggests, ACP catalyses the cleavage of phosphomonoesters in an acid environment. For this reason, all tests for the enzyme have long depended on the colour change it causes by removing a phosphate residue from organic dyes, which is detectable by photometric methods. An isoform of the enzyme known as **p**ro-static **a**cid **p**hosphatase (PAP) is specific for prostate cancer. It is distinguished from other phosphatases by the fact that its activity is inhibited by the addition of tartrate. This isoform can now be identified by immunoassay, although this test is only of secondary importance today. Screening and monitoring in prostate cancer are now based on the detection of **p**rostate-**s**pecific **a**ntigen (PSA).

Tumour antigens as tumour markers

The era of tumour antigens as tumour markers began in 1964 with the identification of **c**arcino-**e**mbryonic **a**ntigen (CEA) in colorectal cancers by Phil Gold (b. 1936) and Samuel Orkin Freedman (b. 1928).[59] Their discovery was the result of a search for tumour-specific antigens. One of the methods employed at the time was to treat animals with human tumour extracts and then look for antibodies in their blood. Gold and Freedman immunised rabbits by injecting them intramuscularly with tissue extracts from human colon cancer, normal bowel tissue or human plasma. In the rabbits treated with the tumour tissue extracts, they detected circulating antibodies directed against a glycoprotein with a 50% carbohydrate content and a molecular weight of about 180 kDa which occurs in primary colorectal carcinoma and its liver metastases at concentrations up to 500 times those in normal bowel mucosa or other epithelial tissues. Increased levels are also found in other cancers, but are not as high as in colon cancer. CEA is now detected by immunoassay. In 1973 Roche became the first company in the world to market an immunodiagnostic ELISA test for CEA.[60] ELISA (**e**nzyme-**l**inked **i**mmuno**s**orbent **a**ssay) techniques exploit the lock-and-key principle of antigen-antibody reactions. As a separate chapter is devoted to this topic, it will not be discussed further here.

From treatment monitoring to treatment decision

Immunohistochemistry – a body of qualitative or semiquantitative techniques for characterising sur-

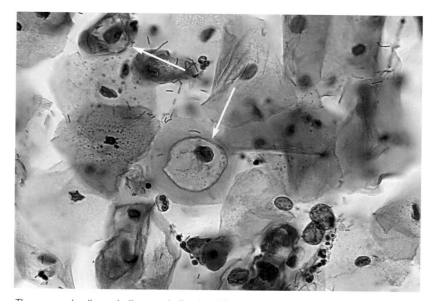

The arrowed cells are koilocytes, indicating infection with human papillomavirus. The cell in the centre of the picture provides a particularly striking example of the perinuclear halo. The blue rods are lactic acid bacteria (Lactobacillus adidophilus), *which are normal inhabitants of the vagina.*[83]

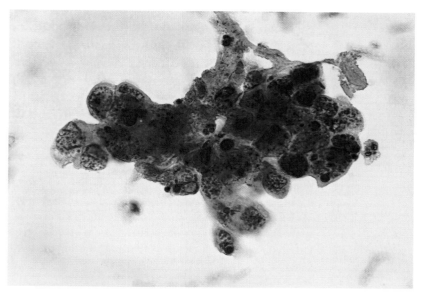

Typical cancerous cervical squamous cells. The cells are so closely adherent that they form a multinucleate mass of cytoplasm, resulting from the fusion of mononucleate cells. This is a characteristic of squamous cell carcinomas. The malignant cells have much larger nuclei than normal squamous cells. The nuclear reticulum shows clumping. The nucleoli are particularly prominent.[84]

Today cytological preparations are normally stained and coverslipped by machine. On the left: A medical laboratory technician places fixed preparations in an autostainer. The illustration on the right shows the stained smears after they have left the automated coverslipper.

gically removed tumour tissue or biopsy material – has been used in tumour diagnosis since the mid-20th century. While the question 'Malignant or benign?' can be answered by preparing a histological section, staining it appropriately and having it read by an experienced pathologist, immunohistochemistry can provide useful information about the presence or absence of growth factors, hormone receptors, enzymes and other substances in tumours. Surface structures on metastatic cancer cells, for example, may indicate where to look for the primary tumour, since metastatic cells carry the same structures on their membranes as cells at the primary cancer site. And such structures can also help to predict treatment outcome. Treatment with the genetically engineered (recombinant) humanised monoclonal antibody trastuzumab (Herceptin), which blocks the HER2 human epidermal growth factor receptor on the surface of breast cancer cells, can be successful only if these receptors are actually present in increased numbers. A test for HER2 overexpression is therefore obligatory before starting treatment, and a positive immunohistochemical test result is currently still required for eligibility to receive the drug. Dye-labelled antibodies are used to ascertain the HER2 receptor protein density in tissue samples, which are graded under the microscope into four staining levels. Only if the biopsy specimens show grade 3+ is treatment worthwhile. Other HER2 tests are also available. In the 25–30 % of patients with an increased HER2 receptor protein density, Herceptin therapy improves life expectancy by up to 50 %.

Visualising genes

Where immunohistochemical analysis is equivocal, the more expensive **f**luorescence **in situ h**ybridisation (FISH) technique is used. An increased number of cell surface receptors for a given growth factor may be due to the presence of multiple copies of the gene coding for the receptor. This is where the molecular cytogenetic FISH technique comes into its own. Fluorescent probes applied to tumour tissue samples can detect repeated **d**eoxyribo**n**ucleic **a**cid (DNA) segments – DNA repeats – coding for HER2. The HER2 gene, which is located on chromosome 17, is identified using gene probes labelled with a

What are tumour antigens?

Tumour antigens are substances on the surface of tumour cells that can provoke an immune response. They are therefore 'targets' for the diagnosis and treatment of cancer. Some occur only on the surface of tumour cells, while others occur in normal tissues but are present at their highest concentrations in tumours. The following types are distinguished on the basis of function, origin or location.

- Cancer-testis antigens. These antigens are produced in various tumours and in the testis, but not in other tissues. Their function is unknown.
- Melanocyte differentiation antigens, which are produced only in normal melanocytes and in melanoma cells.
- Specific tumour antigens, which result from point mutations in normal genes.
- Viral antigens found on the surface of tumours in which a proven relationship exists between viral infection and tumour occurrence, e.g. in cervical cancer due to **h**uman **p**apilloma**v**irus (HPV).
- Antigens that occur in normal tissues but are produced in greater amounts and presented on the cell surface at higher densities in malignant tissues. Such 'over-expressed self-antigens' include HER2 proteins on the surface of breast cancer cells.[61]

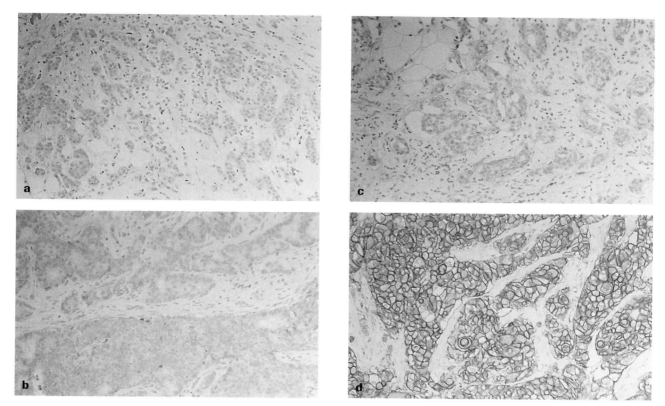

Immunohistochemical testing for increased expression of the HER2 receptor protein on the surface of breast cancer cells helps to identify patients who will benefit from treatment with Herceptin. Breast tumour biopsy specimens are immunostained using the HercepTest kit (DAKO), and then assessed for staining intensity under the microscope. Four levels of staining intensity are distinguished and provide semiquantitative measures of HER overexpression: *a*) Grade 0: no staining of membranes observable, no detectable presence of tumour protein on tumour cell surfaces; *b*) Grade 1+: weak, barely perceptible staining of cell membranes in over 10% of tumour cells; *c*) Grade 2+: weak to moderate staining of membranes in over 10% of tumour cells; and *d*) Grade 3+: strong complete staining of membranes in over 10% of tumour cells.

fluorescent dye. This clarifies whether the cell nucleus contains the usual one copy of the gene on each chromosome or multiple copies. Under the fluorescence microscope the HER2 genes are recognisable as light signals. In addition, tests using quantitative PCR have been developed to detect the increased presence of HER2 DNA or HER2 **m**essenger **r**ibo**n**ucleic **a**cid (mRNA) in tumour tissue. In tumour cells isolated from tissue samples by microdissection,[62] PCR-based techniques produce results in 100% agreement with those obtained by FISH.[63] The LightCycler, a PCR instrument offering real-time fluorescence detection, can identify up to ten copies of a DNA fragment specific to the HER2 oncogene and composed of 112 nucleotide base pairs within 70 minutes. At present, however, this HER2 DNA test is supplied only to research laboratories and is not available for routine diagnostic use.

Tumour marker studies: indications

Tumour markers are substances encountered in increased concentrations in malignant tissues or in the body fluids of people with malignancies. They are produced either by the tumour itself or by the body in response to a tumour. These conventional tumour markers have been used primarily for cancer treatment follow-up, assessment of treatment efficacy, prognosis and detection of cancer recurrence – and often still are. If treatment is successful, the concentration of a tumour marker should fall from its pretreatment baseline value. A renewed rise in concentration after treatment indicates the recurrence of cancer foci. Because of their inadequate specificity and sensitivity, tumour markers should not be used as screening tests unless there is a reasonable suspicion of disease, not least because elevated tumour marker serum levels can also occur in benign diseases. The prognosis of a malignant disease cannot be deduced from a single measurement of a tumour marker, but only by serial determination at defined intervals.[64] The hunt for new highly specific tumour markers continues. Moreover, it is hoped that the analysis of new oncological biomarkers will permit targeted therapeutic decisions in the future.

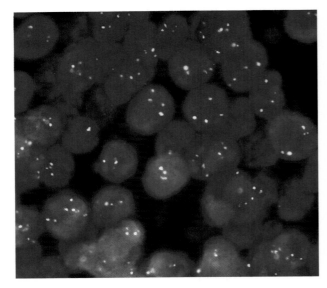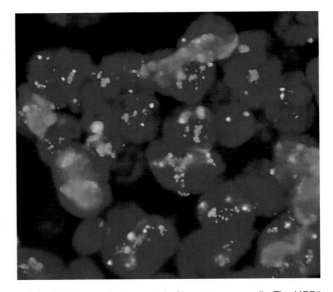

Result of a fluorescence in situ hybridisation (FISH) test for extra copies of the HER2 gene in the nuclei of breast cancer cells. The HER2 gene, which is located on chromosome 17, is identified using gene probes labelled with a fluorescent dye. This shows whether the cell nucleus contains the usual two copies of the gene (left figure) or many copies (right figure). After hybridisation, every copy of the HER2 gene is recognisable under the fluorescence microscope as a fluorescent signal. The red signals mark the HER2 gene sequences. The green signals show the centromere of chromosome 17 as a reference sample.[85, 86]

Oncological biomarkers

Biomarkers are defined as characteristic, objectively measurable parameters that can serve as indicators of normal biological processes, disease processes or pharmacological responses to therapeutic intervention.[65] Oncological biomarkers are expected to help predict how patients will react to specific anti-cancer agents, thereby avoiding the trial-and-error use of medication. The presence or absence of certain metabolic enzymes in tumour tissue, for example, could indicate whether a particular treatment is worthwhile in a particular patient. Thus, if a patient's tumour contains insufficient amounts of enzymes needed to convert a drug into its active cytotoxic form, the patient could be spared treatment with that drug. Xeloda, a fluoropyrimidine developed by Roche for oral use in chemotherapy, is first absorbed via the digestive tract and then enzymatically modified in the liver. Conversion to the actual cytotoxic agent, **5-f**luor**o**uracil (5-FU), requires the enzyme **t**hymidine **p**hosphorylase (TP), which is more abundant in certain tumours than in healthy tissue. On the other hand, such tumours also contain another enzyme, **d**ihydro**p**yrimidine **d**ehydrogenase (DPD), which degrades 5-FU.

5-FU exerts its cytotoxic effect by inhibiting the enzyme **t**hymidylate **s**ynthase (TS), thereby decreasing tumour cell division. Its efficacy naturally depends on the ratio between the enzymes involved in its synthesis and breakdown, i.e. on the TP/DPD ratio. However, this varies from patient to patient and from one tumour type to another. For this reason researchers have focused on devising tests that measure the production of these enzymes. Moreover, researchers have also trained their sights on molecules that help to determine the efficacy of 5-FU in the tumour. There is, for example, a membrane transport protein, known as hCNT1, that carries a metabolic intermediate of 5-FU into tumour cells but not into the surrounding stroma. This molecule too is a potential marker for predicting tumour responses to 5-FU treatment and identifying treatment-resistant patients with a degree of high accuracy. Roche scientists have already developed various test platforms for detecting these biomarkers in clinical research, including enzyme-linked immuno-assays (ELISA), antibodies for immunohistochemical assays and PCR methods for quantifying mRNA from fresh tumour tissue or from tumour tissue that has been fixed in formalin and embedded in paraffin for histology. The ability of these tests to predict therapeutic responses to Xeloda is currently under clinical trial, with a view to setting cutoff values that identify the patients in whom treatment is likely to be most effective.[66]

The search continues

We know today that cancers are genetic diseases. Tumours develop when the genome of somatic cells suffers an accumulation of mutations in genes that control and regulate processes of cell division and growth.[67] The gene alterations present in a particular case play a role in determining the aggressiveness of tumour growth and metastasis. Thus profiling the 'genetic properties' of tumours can enhance prognostic accuracy and enable physicians to prescribe individualised drug treatments.

High hopes have been placed in so-called microarray technologies, which measure the expression level, i.e. degree of activation, of many thousands of genes. The test sample in this case is messenger RNA obtained from tumour cell tissue. The messenger RNA is detected by binding to specific single-stranded complementary DNA anchored to a biochip. This identifies which gene changes characteristic of a particular tumour are present and manifested via messenger RNA.

It is also hoped that information on the nature and aggressiveness of tumours can be obtained by analysing the DNA methylation pattern of tissue samples. Methylation is a naturally occurring phenomenon in which a methyl group, $-CH_3$, attaches to cytosine, one of the four bases in a DNA molecule. DNA methylation is one of the most important biological mechanisms controlling gene expression or activity. Regulatory regions are methylated in the DNA of many tumour cells. Recent studies have shown, for example, that over 90% of the promoter region of the GSTP1 gene is methylated in prostate cancers.[68] The promoter region is the DNA sequence at which synthesis of the RNA gene copy begins. If a gene's promoter region is highly methylated, transcription is prevented. This in turn can lead to cancer if the gene product helps to suppress tumour formation or growth, as is the case with **g**lutathione-**S**-transferase **pi** (GSTpi) – the enzyme coded for by the GSTP1 gene – which plays a role in detoxifying carcinogens.[69]

But why look for a new prostate cancer marker when we can already detect prostate tumours at a very early stage with PSA? PSA is an organ-specific

The LightCycler Instrument quantifies messenger RNA – for example, for the Xeloda biomarkers TP, DPD and TS from patient tumour tissue – using PCR (see page 170 for explanations of abbreviations).

tumour marker, but it is not tumour-specific. It cannot be used to diagnose prostate cancer, but merely to decide if prostate biopsy is indicated to establish whether an enlarged prostate is malignant or benign. About four out of five biopsies do not show malignant tumours. The hope is therefore that a new test for methylation of the GSTP1 promoter sequence will lead to fewer biopsies with higher positive hit rates.[70] Since a methyl group is either present or not, DNA methylation patterns can be digitised and easily interpreted.

Nor is the search for new and reliable cancer signs confined to analysing the genetic material of tumour cells. Using the tools of proteomics, to which a separate chapter of this book is devoted, researchers are also looking for proteins that can indicate tumour growth at a very early stage.

Rolf Steinmüller

The medium matters

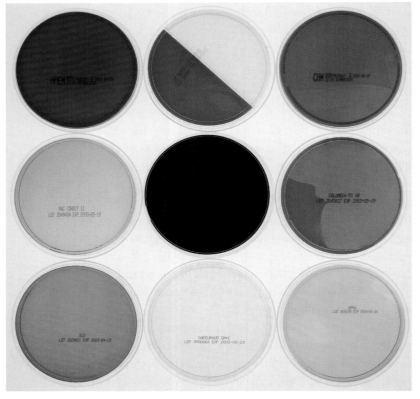

Petri dishes containing various culture media.[39]

Studies on the physiology, biochemistry and genetics of microorganisms usually cannot be performed on individual cells. Populations consisting of many millions of individuals are required. To obtain such populations, microorganisms are propagated by culturing them on an appropriate substrate or culture medium under favourable conditions. The substances an organism requires for growth in a laboratory setting must be contained in sufficient concentrations in the culture medium used. Micro-

organisms are extremely diverse, and their nutrient requirements differ greatly. Some microbes are fairly undemanding and need only a few inorganic substances to grow. Others are more fastidious, requiring complex organic compounds. The amounts and combination of nutrients contained in culture media thus need to be finely tuned to the needs and capabilities of each organism of interest. The number of recipes for preparing microbial culture media is therefore vast.

Most of the techniques that have been devised for cultivating microbes on culture media date from the second half of the 1800s, and some of the methods developed over a century ago are still in use today.

The quest for pure cultures

In nature microbes virtually never occur as pure cultures. It is therefore not surprising that the first investigations of microbes were performed with mixed cultures. The French scientist Louis Pasteur (1822–1895) developed a method of isolating pure cultures relatively early on. However, in practice it proved to be too time-consuming, difficult and unreliable for routine use. His method was to allow microbes to grow in a clear liquid culture medium and to repeat this procedure several times by subculturing. In this way the mixture of different bacteria is successively diluted until finally only bacteria of a single species are left. Following on from experiments to disprove the theory of spontaneous generation, for which he and others had used the famous swan-necked flask, Pasteur was the first to introduce a semi-synthetic, transparent liquid medium. This medium, known as 'Pasteur's fluid', consisted of water, cane sugar, ammonium tartrate and ash of yeast.[1] Pasteur recognised that the differences between fermentation processes were attributable to the presence of different types of microorganisms. However, because he worked only with liquid culture media, his efforts to isolate specific organisms failed. While these simple transparent liquid media of known chemical composition were adequate for selective cultivation of fermentative microorganisms, successful isolation of microorganisms, and particularly of microbial pathogens, required media of a different kind. Innumerable attempts were undertaken to obtain pure cultures by modifying Pasteur's fluid,[2,3,4] but with varying degrees of success. For example, in 1873 Edwin Theodor Klebs (1834–1913) used the so-called fractional method for cultivating pathogenic bacteria. He believed that with frequent subculturing of small amounts of the liquid to be tested the microorganism present in the greatest numbers in the original culture would finally prevail. For this purpose Klebs used fine glass capillaries, which he dipped into the original fungus-containing culture. The capillary with fluid from the culture was then sealed by melting the ends, disinfected with alcohol and

Along with Robert Koch (1843–1910), the Frenchman **Louis Pasteur** (1822–1895), the son of a tanner, was the first important scientist to investigate infectious diseases and ways of combating them. But Pasteur was not only a brilliant microbiologist, he was also a gifted chemist. In 1848 his work with the salts of tartaric acid led him to the discovery of optical isomerism. In 1865 he recognised that living yeast cells and other microorganisms were the cause of fermentation and putrefaction, disproving the theory of spontaneous generation in rotting substances. He found out that alcoholic fermentation could be suppressed by molecular oxygen (Pasteur effect) and that unwanted fermentation and decomposition of food could be prevented by moderate heating (pasteurisation). His discovery of the immunising action of attenuated pathogens provided the basis for vaccination against anthrax, chicken cholera, swine erysipelas and rabies. In 1867 he moved to Paris. There, in 1887, he founded the Institute of Microbiology and Hygiene that bears his name, a non-profit-making institution devoted to the prevention and treatment of disease. Today the Institut Pasteur is a world-renowned centre for basic research in biology.

broken open again in a fungus-free vegetation fluid contained in a stoppered flask under a layer of oil. After vegetation was complete … the procedure was repeated. This makes it possible to remove any contamination which may have been present in the original fluid and to obtain the predominant organism in pure form. The method can be described as fractional culture.[5]

However, Klebs probably never obtained a pure culture in this way.[6]

Joseph Lister (1827–1912) also developed a method for obtaining pure cultures in liquid media.[7] He used a graduated syringe with a plunger which was advanced by a screw thread, thus allowing him to work with very small volumes of fluid. With the aid of a microscope he determined the shape and number of the bacteria. In his crucial experiment on the significance of asepsis (absence of microorganisms), Lister identified two different types of microorganisms and calculated their concentrations. This enabled him to determine the dilution statistically required to dispense a single organism into culture vessels with his syringe. The greatest problem for all these scientists was that they worked with liquid media (nutrient broths).[8]

From 'blood spots' to solid media

In 1872 Joseph Schroeter (1837–1894) published a paper on chromogenic bacteria,[18] i. e. bacteria which produce pigments. He had observed that isolated

bacterial growth occurred in the form of coloured spots, or colonies, on solid substrates such as potatoes, starch paste, bread and egg white. These colonies differed from each other, but within each colony the bacteria were all of a uniform type. Herrmann Hoffmann (1819–1891) also experimented with cut potato surfaces. However, potatoes have certain disadvantages. For example, the cut potato is moist, which enables motile bacteria to spread over the entire surface, and because the surface is not transparent the colonies are difficult to see. But the main drawback is that potatoes are a poor nutrient medium for many bacteria.

Further important work on the subject of culture media was performed by the pioneering mycologist Oscar Brefeld (1839–1925) of the Botanical Institute at the University of Münster in Germany. In 1875 Brefeld published his principles for obtaining moulds in pure culture. These stated: first, that the medium should be inoculated with only a single spore; secondly, that the medium should be clear and transparent and provide optimum conditions for microbial growth; and thirdly, that the culture should be carefully protected from contamination. Brefeld also introduced the cultivation of fungi on solid media, adding gelatin to his culture fluids for this purpose. His methods for obtaining pure cul-

Serratia marcescens and the miracle of the bleeding bread

Discoloration of food can be caused by the growth of bacteria. If the organism present produces a red colour, the colonies can easily be mistaken for drops of blood. *Serratia marcescens* stands out amongst the microorganisms producing a red pigment. Its former name, *Bacterium prodigiosum,* the 'miracle microbe', is a reference to its colourful history. Not every blood-like discoloration is caused by *S. marcescens,* but this bacterium was probably the agent most frequently responsible for the so-called blood miracle, and its bloodstained path can be traced throughout history, from its first mention by Pythagoras of Samos[9] (6th century BC) through the military campaigns of Alexander the Great and into the 19th century. In 322 BC soldiers in the Macedonian army of Alexander the Great noticed blood-like spots on their bread during the siege of the city of Tyre in Phoenicia (modern-day Lebanon). The Macedonian soothsayer Aristander interpreted the miracle as a sign that blood would flow in Tyre and Alexander would be victorious. The observation that 'blood' had flowed from inside the bread was thus taken to indicate the fate awaiting the besieged city. These events were reported by the Greek historian Diodorus Siculus[10] and by the Roman historian Quintus Curtius Rufus[11] (both 1st century BC).

It was not until 1819 that the first attempts to find a scientific explanation for the phenomenon were made. Again it was 'bloodstained' food that provoked agitation and unrest. At the beginning of July 1819 a child in the house of a small Italian farmer fell ill. At the same time red flecks began appearing daily in the family's polenta, a cornmeal mush that is a staple food in Italy. The family linked the child's illness to the discoloration of the food and thought it was witchcraft. Some accusingly insisted that the polenta had been made from meal which had been hoarded during the famine of 1817 and withheld from the starving people, and that this was now a punishment from heaven. The authorities instructed the district physician of Piove di Sacco, Dr Vincento Sette, to investigate the phenomenon. Independently, the young pharmacist Bartolomeo Bizio also began to investigate. Bizio – like Sette[12] – showed that the red colour was a pigment produced by a microbe. However, they wrongly believed the causative organism to be a fungus. Bizio published his results first and thus could claim priority of discovery and the right to name the organism.[13] He chose the genus name *Serratia* in honour of the Italian physicist Serafino Serrati, whom Bizio mistakenly believed had invented the steamship. (Though Serrati did not invent the steamship, he was the first to travel up Italy's Arno River on one.) As a species name, Bizio added *marcescens,* from the Latin *marcesco* meaning 'spoil' or 'go bad', as the pigment rapidly decomposes and fades on exposure to light.

Culture of the 'miracle microbe' Serratia marcescens.

In 1872 Ferdinand Cohn (1828–1898) – the famous Breslau botanist who promoted the career of the young, as yet unknown Robert Koch (1843–1910) – wrote:

> It has been related since antiquity that from time to time a drop of blood could suddenly form on food, particularly on bread. Once it had appeared, the blood spread, dripped and covered wide areas; when this was observed in ancient times it was considered a portent that showed the anger of the gods, revealed hidden crimes and called for bloody atonement. Up to recent times history contains numerous reports of people succumbing to a dark superstition whenever blood miraculously appeared on food and particularly when it became visible on the sacramental wafer. In the Century of Enlightenment the blood miracle gradually ceased, but only in recent decades has it been realised that the reports of the miracle have a basis in scientific fact.[14]

Once all the myth and mystery had been dispelled, the bacterium, which was considered harmless, was used as an indicator organism to demonstrate the spread of microbes, for example by hand-shaking. In 1906 Mervyn Henry Gordon (1872–1939) demonstrated in the British House of Commons, by gargling with a culture of *S. marcescens* and reciting passages from Shakespeare, that microbes were spread over long distances through the air by speaking, sneezing and coughing. In this experiment the bright red colour on the open dishes of nutrient agar distributed throughout the chamber showed that the bacteria had travelled into its furthest corners. In the late 1970s *S. marcescens* again hit the headlines when the US army had to admit having released the bacterium as a marker in tests to simulate germ warfare attacks.[15]

S. marcescens causes a variety of infections in humans, particularly in drug addicts and hospitalised patients. These include airway infections in ventilator patients, nosocomial urinary tract infections, wound infections, peritonitis and catheter infections, and it is also a cause of endocarditis and osteomyelitis (infection of bone and bone marrow), especially in heroin addicts. In addition localised conditions, passage of the bacterium into the bloodstream can precipitate generalised sepsis and polyarticular septic arthritis. So the bacterium of the 'bleeding bread' is by no means harmless and certainly not miraculous. Another person who should be mentioned in connection with historical observations about *Serratia marcescens* is Christian Gottfried Ehrenberg (1795–1876), one of the leading naturalists of his time. In September 1848 he was brought a piece of boiled potato which had blood-like spots on it. Inoculation to other boiled potatoes, and later to white bread and Swiss cheese, led to the growth of red colonies. Even though Ehrenberg's description is less detailed than those of Bizio and Sette, his results became more widely known than those of the Italian authors.[16, 17]

tures worked well with fungi but were unsuitable for the considerably smaller bacteria.[19]

In 1883 Klebs had also developed a solid culture medium, isinglass, which only became liquid at 50 °C.[20] Isinglass is derived from the lining of the air bladder of the beluga and other types of sturgeon. This is composed of very hygroscopic, high-molecular-weight proteins which, after heating and subsequent cooling, solidify to a clear jelly. Because of its good adsorptive properties, isinglass has been used as a clarifier, particularly for the fining of wine, as a dressing or finishing agent (a term applied to various fillers and starches which are added mainly to cotton fabrics to improve their appearance, handle and weight) and as a glue.

Solid culture media catch on

Robert Koch (1843–1910) thus had predecessors in cultivating microorganisms on solid culture media: Klebs with isinglass and Hoffmann and Schroeter with potatoes, starch paste, solidified egg white, etc.[21] Koch himself acknowledges this, but, in the eyes of the medical historian, it is still Koch who must be credited with introducing the transparent solid culture medium into bacteriology.[22]

Even during his lifetime Koch was considered an institution. Together with his French rival Pasteur, who was about 20 years his senior, Koch was one of the most important pioneers in microbiology and medicine. A gifted scientist, he developed important bacteriological techniques for growing microorganisms in pure culture and rendering them visible under the microscope. By working with pure cultures, Koch was able to develop rules for establishing whether a microorganism causes a particular disease. He was 32 years old when he published the manuscript of his first bacteriological study, on anthrax, in 1876. He had performed the experimental investigations for this study in the consulting room of his medical practice, where he had set up a laboratory. After several fruitless attempts he succeeded in cultivating the anthrax microbe by using a complex nutrient fluid as a substrate:

> Fresh anthrax blood from guinea pigs was diluted with aqueous humour from the eye of a calf and incubated in several preparations, with and without a hollow-ground slide, for 10–12 hours at temperatures of approx. 35 °C.[23]

However, Koch soon realised that further groundbreaking discoveries would only be possible if simpler procedures for obtaining pure cultures could be developed. If a bacterial culture were streaked onto a solid medium, the organisms would

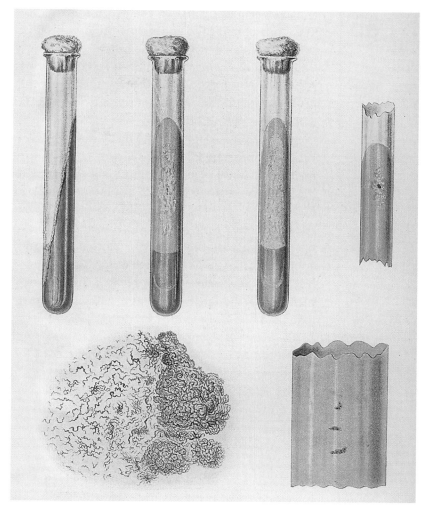

Probably the best-known achievement of Robert Koch is his discovery of the tuberculosis bacillus. The mycobacteria were cultivated on solidified blood serum in test tubes. On this type of nutrient medium the bacteria produce characteristic colonies with a clumped, wrinkled structure.

continuously divide and thus form many new cells which would be immobilised. Although the original culture might have been composed of many different types of bacteria, the colony formed at a particular site would consist of a single species. He soon came to the conclusion that a universally applicable solid culture medium could not exist. They all had certain shortcomings. He therefore focused his attention on the search for a transparent gelling agent which would make it possible to solidify a better known and widely accepted liquid medium. Many of the pathogenic microorganisms he wanted to experiment with thrived beautifully in beef broth.

Gelling agents from the kitchen

To solidify his culture media, Koch initially borrowed a leaf from cookery books. Drawing on knowledge about certain fungi that grow on a gelatin-based medium, he began by using gelatin. The Italian mycologist Carlo Vittadini (1800–1865) had already been using this substance for 30 years.[24] On a transparent solid culture medium of this type, the colonies that develop are much more clearly visible. At the same time the individual nutrient requirements of the various bacteria could be more readily taken into account by modifying the medium while it was still liquid.

In early August 1881, at the instigation of Lister, Koch demonstrated his transparent, solid culture medium at the Seventh International Congress of Medicine, held at the Institute of Physiology, King's College, London. The European colleagues present considered his innovative culture methods one of the highlights of the congress. Pasteur, who also attended, and who at that time was at the height of his fame, was also very impressed by the new methods. Although Pasteur, as a patriotic Frenchman, had not forgotten the Franco-Prussian War of 1870–71, he rushed up to Koch to congratulate him. His words, as reported by Lister, who witnessed the encounter, were: 'C'est un grand progrès, Monsieur.'[25] In the same year, Koch published a spectacular paper on the investigation of pathogenic organisms, in which he described, amongst other things, the use of culture media which were both transparent and solid.[26]

However, gelatin does have some disadvantages. It is a glue-like protein substance which is highly susceptible to microbial digestion and liquefaction. Also, it changes from a solid to a liquid state as soon as the temperature rises above 28 °C. This means that gelatin melts at body temperature, the preferred incubation temperature for pathogenic microorganisms. Nor was it very suitable at the height of summer, as electric refrigerators had yet to be invented. In 1882 a new gelling agent, agar-agar (a complex polysaccharide), was introduced on the basis of domestic lore.

Agar-agar

The discovery of the gelling agent agar-agar is usually attributed to Koch. He first mentioned the use of agar-agar as a gelling agent for culture media on 24 March 1881 in his lecture to the Berlin Physiological Society on the etiology of tuberculosis.[27, 28] One year later, in his famous paper on the isolation of *Mycobacterium tuberculosis,* the use of agar-agar was mentioned for the first time in a publication, although only in passing.

> The tubercle bacilli can also be cultured on other nutrient substrates if the latter have similar properties to congealed blood serum.[29]

The special culture medium Koch initially used for the cultivation of the tubercle bacillus was sterile, coagulated cattle or sheep serum. Further details on the preparation of cultures followed, including the reference to agar-agar:

> For example they grow on a jelly prepared with agar-agar which remains solid at incubating temperature and which contains a meat broth and peptone as additives.[30]

These achievements, however, were not made without the help of Koch's colleagues – even though their contribution is not mentioned in the publication cited.

Agar-agar was introduced at the suggestion of Fanny Angelina Hesse (1850–1934), née Eilshemius, the American wife of Walther Hesse (1846–1911), a colleague of Koch's. In 1877 Hesse, who had been born in Bischofswerda (Saxony), became district medical officer of Schwarzenberg (Erzgebirge), where for ten years he treated the men working in the uranium mines, who often suffered from a disease called mountain sickness (Schneeberg lung cancer). To expand his knowledge of environmental hygiene, Hesse studied at the University of Munich from 1878 to 1879 under Max von Pettenkofer

Agar-agar – the rise of a seaweed extract

The Malay word 'agar' or 'agar-agar' was originally used to refer to various edible East Asian seaweeds (*Euchema, Gelidium, Gracilaria,* etc.). Agar-agar is a complex-structured, gelatinous natural product (mucilage) which is obtained from marine red algae by extraction with hot water. Chemically, agar is a mixture of at least two polysaccharides, the gelling agarose (approx. 70%) and the non-gelling agaropectin (approx. 30%). It has some excellent properties which make it the ideal solidifying agent for microbiology. Unlike gelatin, agar is not quickly broken down (liquefied) by microorganisms occurring on dry land. Its melting and solidifying properties in an aqueous milieu deserve particular mention. A 1.5% aqueous suspension of agar melts at 80–90 °C. On cooling, it solidifies again to a clear, stable jelly at 38–32 °C. Agar-agar is available commercially in various forms and grades.

(1818–1901). There he devoted himself primarily to investigating carbon dioxide and dust pollution in the air. The results of this work led him to spend a few months (1881–82) working at Koch's Imperial Health Office in Berlin, where he also investigated airborne bacterial contaminants.[31] After returning home, he continued the research he had begun in Berlin on measuring airborne microbial levels – working under primitive conditions and using his kitchen as a laboratory – and in 1884 published his results in a paper 'On the quantitative determination of microorganisms in the air', which appeared in the second volume of the *Reports* of the Imperial Health Office. It was in his kitchen in Schwarzenberg that Hesse first used agar-agar in his scientific work.[32] For his investigations Hesse used an apparatus which initially consisted of tubes lined with gelatin through which air was passed.[33] This allowed him to determine the number and types of microbes in the air. Because it was summer, he was having a great deal of trouble keeping his culture media solid. Many of his experiments were ruined because the culture media melted. In his search for an alternative gelling agent he was helped by a stroke of good fortune. His wife, who came from a Dutch merchant family living in New York, frequently helped out as a laboratory assistant – not an uncommon thing for a bacteriologist's wife to do in those days. One of her duties was to boil her husband's nutrient broths, and as a result she was very familiar with the difficulties associated with the use of gelatin as a gelling agent. To prevent any more experiments from being spoiled, she suggested using agar-agar instead. She herself had been introduced to the substance in New Jersey by a Dutch neighbour who had previously lived in Java. Fanny had been using agar-agar in the kitchen for years to make jellies and puddings.[34] Agar-agar had been used in Asian households for centuries as a thickener for soups.[35] Fairly soon thereafter, probably at the end of 1881, Hesse wrote to Koch, informing him of the new discovery.

Koch and Fanny Hesse therefore jointly deserve the credit for the discovery of this simple method. It took quite some time for agar-agar to become widely used, as the substance was in short supply in those days. However, the situation changed dramatically once agar-agar became generally available. In a contribution to the *Handbuch der pathogenen Mikroorganismen* (1929), Gildemeister wrote:

> Agar culture media have practically superseded gelatin culture media, so that the latter are now reserved almost exclusively for special purposes.[36]

Petri dishes dating from the early 20th century (*Medizinhistorisches Museum, University of Zurich*).

Petri dishes: a perfect fit

Originally Koch applied his culture media to slides, later to flat glass plates. Preparation of these gelatin or agar-agar plates required a pouring apparatus. The finished plates were then stacked on top of each other in large glass bell jars using glass-stacking supports – a very lengthy and arduous procedure which required not only manual dexterity but also various aids. Then in 1886 one of his assistants, the Berlin physician Julius Richard Petri (1852–1921), had the idea of using shallow covered dishes instead.

> For more than a year I have been using for this purpose shallow two-piece dishes having a diameter of 10–11 cm and a depth of 1–1.5 cm. The top half serves as a lid and has a slightly larger diameter … Shallow dishes of this nature can be recommended particularly for agar-agar plates which, as we know, do not adhere well to simple glass plates without additional fixing.[37]

The dishes later named after Petri are shallow, round glass containers with an overlapping lid, which protects the contents against contamination from the air. They also have the advantage that the

Streaked culture plate after inoculation (left) and after incubation at 37 °C (right).

culture media do not dry up as quickly as on a glass plate and can therefore be stored or incubated for longer periods.

Petri dishes are still used for culturing microorganisms on and in solid media, and today's versions are almost identical to the originals. The dishes most commonly used have a base diameter of about 90 mm and a depth of about 16 mm (standard Petri dishes). Originally Petri dishes were made of glass. However, glass dishes have now been largely supplanted by disposable Petri dishes made of polystyrene. These are transparent, light and easy to stack

From meat extract to culture medium

The roots of the Oxoid company go back to the 19th century. The company's history began with the German chemist Justus von Liebig (1803–1873), who suggested a procedure for the extraction and concentration of meat. An English company (Frey Bentos), which owned large cattle farms in Uruguay, took up these suggestions and used them for the production of meat extract. The Liebig Extract of Meat Company (Lemco) began production in 1865 under the direction of George Giebert. The meat was freed of fat, tendons and bone and heated to about 70 °C, and the aromatic, mineral-rich extract was drawn off. What was left was extracted meat with a high protein content, which was dried and ground and then sold throughout the world as Liebig's Extract. A simple and cheap way had thus been found to transport meat from America to Europe. In 1899 the product name of the meat extract was changed to Oxo. In 1910 Oxo was first sold in the cube form which is still famous today. Even today the Oxo cube is still such a success that it is used by more than half the households in the United Kingdom (more than 2 million cubes per day). One in six cooked meals in Britain contain an Oxo cube. The name Oxoid was introduced in 1924 for granulated extracts and other products for hospital and laboratory use. In 1965 the Medical Division of Oxo was set up as a separate company, Oxoid Limited.

but cannot be heat-sterilised. As they are produced under near-sterile conditions and any microorganisms present are usually destroyed by the high temperatures during production, the dishes are suitable for many microbiological purposes even without additional sterilisation. For particularly critical culture media or investigations and for longer incubation times the more expensive gamma-irradiated Petri dishes should be used.

Koch initially used agar in liquid form so that he could resuspend bacteria in it. This 'pour plate method' is still sometimes used today as a reliable means of estimating bacterial counts. In the classic procedure, 0.1–1 mL of sample suspension is mixed with 10–20 mL of an agar medium kept liquid at 45 °C and then allowed to set on a Petri dish. The advantage of this procedure is that although interference through overgrowth of the culture medium with motile organisms is not completely ruled out, it is at least less likely since the microorganisms are suspended in the culture medium. The effort involved and the large number of Petri dishes that have to be filled are, however, definite disadvantages. It is also essential that the liquid culture medium should be kept at the right temperature. If the temperature is too low, there is a danger that the medium will solidify during pouring, whereas if the temperature is too high, the microbes might be damaged.

It was eventually discovered to be far more convenient to cultivate bacteria on the surface of agar plates rather than in a culture medium – particularly if the medium was filled into shallow dishes (Petri dishes). This spread-plate method has not changed significantly since its introduction. A sterile inoculation loop is used to spread a small amount of the cell suspension over an agar plate in several series of parallel streaks. Each successive streak leads to increasing dilution of the organism to be identified (inoculum) on the plate. Ideally, by the time the last streaks are applied, only single cells, widely spaced, will be inoculated onto the surface of the agar and grow into isolated colonies on incubation.

Commercial culture media

The era of industrially produced culture media was rung in at the close of the 19th century, soon after the discovery of agar-agar. Many of the large companies that sell dehydrated and ready-to-use culture media today have been in business for a long time. Quite a few of them were founded around the turn of the century.

Shortly after he began working with agar, Hesse developed a tuberculosis nutrient agar together with a company called Heyden in Radebeul. This solid agar medium made it possible to evaluate cultures just two or three days after inoculation of the plate.[38]

Merck, one of the leading and oldest manufacturers of culture media, began producing peptones for scientific use as far back as 1892. Peptones are a mixture of soluble peptides of different chain lengths which are formed from proteins by incomplete acid hydrolysis or enzymatic hydrolysis. They are an intermediate product of protein digestion (using endopeptidases). Peptones obtained from casein and muscle protein are used to produce culture media for use in microbiology. The groundbreaking discovery of peptones goes back to the chemist Carl Grosschopf from Güstrow. He developed manufacturing processes for peptones and a number of other preparations, including pepsin, in 1873 and for rennet powder in 1877, enabling Friedrich Witte (1829–1893) to make these products on an industrial scale in his Rostock factory. Witte's peptone became world-renowned as a result of Koch's bacteriological research.

Dehydrated culture media are industrially prepared dry mixtures of the components of a culture medium, which are reconstituted by adding the appropriate amount of water and sterilised shortly before use. The important features of these dehydrated culture media are that they are quick and convenient to use, leave far less room for error during preparation and have a largely constant, standardised composition.

A number of products for routine use, particularly in the medical sector, are also available in the form of ready-to-use culture media. These are sterile culture media, usually agar plates in disposable Petri dishes in packs of 20 or 100, or tubes of nutrient solution. Ready-to-use culture media can be useful if there are no facilities for the preparation and sterilisation of culture media or if only a few plates or tubes of a culture medium are needed.

New generations of culture media

Modified forms of the ready-to-use culture media are also available, which are suitable for microbial hygiene monitoring, for example. Contact slides (agar-coated slides in closed transport containers) or RODAC plates (**R**eplicate **O**rganism **D**etection **and**

A medical laboratory technician inoculating a culture medium on a Petri dish in the Bacteriology Laboratory at Basel's Cantonal Hospital.

Counting), for example, are ready-to-use products for the detection of microbial contamination of surfaces or liquids. The culture media slides or plates are coated or filled in such a way that the agar forms a convex surface. The plates are placed on the surface to be sampled and are pressed down so that the entire area of the culture medium comes into contact with the surface.

The detection of characteristic bacterial enzymes with the aid of chromogenic substrates allows rapid identification of bacteria. The bacteria can be identified directly on the culture medium on the basis of the characteristic colour of the colonies. The composition of the culture medium selectively promotes the growth of the target organisms and at the same time enhances the activity of characteristic enzymes.

Even today microbial culture is the most important and informative means of detecting, characterising and identifying microorganisms. Modern molecular biological techniques, such as the **p**olymerase **c**hain **r**eaction (PCR), can of course also be used to identify microbes. However, in the case of many of these techniques, cultures are still indispensable, since they are the only way to produce enough cells of the species of interest (biomass) to permit testing.

Christoph Gradmann

Fighting the White Death

Robert Koch, tuberculosis and tuberculin

At the end of the 19th century medical bacteriology was considered the quintessence of modern, scientifically based medicine. Though not the first medical discipline to follow the *Zeitgeist* and rely entirely on observation, measurement and experiment, it differed from other branches of medical science in one important respect. With its promise that discoveries in the laboratory could be put to practical use in everyday life, it raised euphoric hopes unmatched by any other discipline. Bacteriology put a new face on contagious diseases by showing that they were the work of invisible microbes, and at the same time promised to rid the world of these diseases. The role of bacteria in infectious disease was recognised, and bacteriologists were the men best equipped to meet this peril. Their prestige was closely bound up with the object of their research. The isolation of dangerous pathogens and the prospect of being able to control them transformed scientists into warriors against epidemic disease.

There is no disease to which the above applies more than to tuberculosis, and no scientist to whom it applies more than to the German bacteriologist Robert Koch (1843–1910). The careers of the 'Bacillus Father' and the White Death were intimately linked. In 19th century Europe the disease generally called 'consumption' was probably the number-one cause of mortality and responsible for around 15% of all deaths. This was also a time when ideas about the disease were undergoing dramatic change. At the beginning of the 19th century there was a lung disease known as 'pulmonary consumption' (or more technically as 'phthisis') because of its typical wasting course and which was believed to be related to a collection of other diseases. By the end of the

Robert Koch *(1843–1910) at the Imperial Health Office in 1884.*

century lupus, scrofula and the other diseases in the collection – their names now familiar only to the specialist – were recognised as clinical forms of a single infectious disease: tuberculosis.

There is no question that Robert Koch deserves much of the credit for this altered state of affairs. When he identified the pathogen known today as *Mycobacterium tuberculosis*, it was his greatest triumph yet, and, although this discovery came earlier in his career as a medical bacteriologist, it is still considered his most important scientific achievement. In the eyes of his friend and colleague Friedrich Loeffler (1852–1915), Koch became 'overnight the greatest, most successful and most laudable scientist of all times'.[1] On 24 March 1882 Paul Ehrlich (1854–1915) attended the celebrated Berlin lecture in which Koch first presented his discovery of the tubercle bacillus, and the impression it made on him is recorded in his obituary for Koch. '[T]hat evening', he wrote, 'is engraved in my memory as the most majestic scientific event I have ever participated in.'[2] Koch's work was immediately hailed as a breakthrough. In his *Geschichte der Tuberkulose*, published in 1883, Albert Johne (1839–1910) wrote that 'as a result of Koch's latest work the pathogenetic aspect of the tubercle question can be regarded as essentially settled'.[3] For Koch personally, the overwhelming response led to an appointment as Privy Councillor in June 1882. Together with his cholera expedition of 1883–84, which gained him general acclaim, the identification of the tuberculosis bacillus was the scientific sensation that launched him to fame in the early 1880s. In presenting his results, Koch declared:

> In the future our battle against this terrible scourge of the human race will no longer be a battle against an undefined something but against a tangible parasite.[4]

Indeed, the day on which Koch presented his work in Berlin stands out like no other as a milestone in the rise a specialty from relative obscurity to scientific glory. Yet there is another reason why Koch's work on tuberculosis must be regarded as epoch-making: it combined the most important laboratory methods and technologies developed by medical bacteriology up to that time. At the beginning of the 1880s a stage of development had been reached which appeared to open the way for a wider exploration of infectious diseases. A short time later Koch's colleague Loeffler would coin the expression 'Koch's postulates' to refer to the criteria derived from these methods for identifying pathogenic organisms.

But how did this success come about? What were its methodological and technological foundations? What previous work by other scientists did Koch build on? What impact did his work have on the contemporary understanding of tuberculosis? And finally, how do 'Koch's postulates' fit into the story?

Tuberculosis in the 19th century

Koch presented his discovery of the tuberculosis bacterium in two stages in 1882–84. First, there was his celebrated lecture to the Physiological Society of

Friedrich Loeffler (1852–1915) and Robert Koch. Loeffler studied medicine in Würzburg and Berlin where, after his doctorate (1874) and a few years' service as an army doctor, he was finally ordered to the Imperial Health Office in 1879. There, together with Georg Gaffky (1850–1918), he became Koch's right-hand man and was responsible for a significant part of the work on tuberculosis. In 1888 Loeffler became professor of hygiene at the University of Greifswald. He introduced numerous technical innovations into bacteriology. Today he is remembered primarily for discovering the first submicroscopic pathogen, the virus which causes foot-and-mouth disease. In addition to hygiene, he also taught the history of medicine and became the first historian of bacteriology.

Berlin in 1882. This was followed by a few short papers and then finally, in 1884, by his monumental paper 'Die Aetiologie der Tuberkulose', in which he described and reflected on his methods in minute detail.[5]

Koch had started his career as a bacteriologist with work on anthrax – an animal disease which very rarely affects humans. He later studied wound infections, i. e. disease processes whose infectious origins appeared obvious. In turning his attention to tuberculosis, Koch was tackling a research topic which was as significant as it was controversial. The characteristic features of the disease were that it occurred regularly in the population and its course in the individual patient was usually chronic. In the early 19th century the name 'tuberculosis' was

The room in which Robert Koch held his lecture on the etiology of tuberculosis on 24 March 1882. At the time the room belonged to the Physiology Institute; it is now used by the Institute of Microbiology and Hygiene at Humboldt University, Berlin.

The Imperial Health Office in 1880.

applied not to one but to a variety of diseases, which were distinguished by their clinical course and morbid anatomy. In 1819 the French clinician Théophile Laënnec (1781–1826) had proposed that such seemingly distinct conditions as lupus, phthisis and scrofula were manifestations of one and the same disease process, pointing to the fact that the same characteristic nodules, or tubercles, were always present in the diseased tissue. However this view did not take hold. In the second half of the century, attention was focussed more on the distinguishing clinical features of disease than on searching for a unifying cause. Tuberculous processes accordingly tended to be seen as metamorphoses of other diseases, notably pneumonia.

There were also speculations about the cause of the disease. In addition to transmission by (at that time still hypothetical) germs, factors such as disposition, age, environmental influences, heredity and a putative relationship to malignant diseases

were prime suspects. Of course none of these factors could be regarded as a necessary cause on a par with the role now accorded bacteria in the pathogenesis of bacterial diseases. This may sound surprising, but at the time people were more interested in processes of disease transformation than in causes. This led to the criticism that it was

a confusing linguistic usage to employ the expression 'tuberculosis' to refer both to a characteristic form of neoplasm and to a characteristic form of transformation.[6]

Felix Niemeyer (1820–1871), the physician quoted above, was naturally more interested in the latter, for example in the transformation that occurred when cancers became tuberculous. However, there were also researchers who tried to demonstrate the infectious nature of the disease. In 1865 Jean Antoine Villemin (1827–1892) showed that tuberculosis could be induced experimentally in animals by inoculating them with diseased tissue and thus concluded that the disease was infectious. In 1877 Edwin Klebs (1834–1913) suggested that a bacterium should be regarded as the infectious agent. At the University of Breslau there was a whole group of scientists working on the subject. In 1879 Carl Weigert (1845–1904) put forward the idea that the unity of the different forms of tuberculosis derived not from the morbid anatomy of the diseased tissue but from their etiology (cause). Julius Cohnheim (1839–1884) and Carl Salomonsen (1847–1924) confirmed Villemin's experiments and suggested using animal experiments to establish the cause. Koch's exchanges with these scientists at Breslau University in the 1870s were an important stimulus for his work. Choosing tuberculosis as an object of research was thus a bold but also a clever decision. Koch was able to build on existing research and at the same time could reasonably expect that proof of a bacterial etiology would have a dramatic impact on the complex scheme of tuberculous processes, even if the notion of tuberculosis as an infectious disease was not in itself new. It would be the first time a bacterial cause had ever been demonstrated for a human disease and would moreover serve as a model for a new understanding of infectious diseases which gave the bacterial etiologies reconstructed in the laboratory priority over clinical observation.

Identification

Of course medical bacteriology was still a very young science. However, the significance of Koch's discovery – if we listen to Koch – did not lie in the fact that he had tracked down the tubercle bacillus with completely new methods. In his view, the bacillus had been identified largely by modifying and extending existing methods to fit a new question. The speed with which this work was performed was indeed impressive. Only eight months passed between the start of Koch's investigations in August 1881 and his famous lecture in March of the following year. It should be noted, however, that Koch was no longer alone as he had been in his earlier work. Since 1880 he had been at the Imperial Health Office, where he was the leader of a rapidly growing team and where, in the two years prior to March 1882, such fundamental things as pure cultures and the solid culture media indispensable for growing them had been developed.

The first step was to find the causative agent – by no means a simple task. The suspected bacterium proved to be considerably smaller than the pathogens already known and was not readily visible even under the microscope. In his studies on anthrax Koch had originally worked without staining. He later adopted staining techniques, particularly from Weigert, to distinguish between bacteria and host tissue and to prepare specimens for microphotography. While examination of tuberculous tissue under the microscope initially revealed nothing which could have been identified as a bacterium and stained, staining with alkaline methylene blue produced results.

> When coverslip preparations were treated with this staining solution for 24 hours, very fine, rod-like structures appeared for the first time in the tubercle mass…[7]

The next task was to make these 'rod-like structures' more clearly visible so that they would stand out from the surrounding tissue. This was achieved by a further refinement in staining technique. When a second, brown dye (vesuvin) was applied to Koch's blue-stained preparations, only the tissue was decolourised. As a result, the rods now appeared blue, and everything else brown. This also made it possible to distinguish the rods from almost all other bacteria:

> Under the microscope the structures of the animal tissues, such as the nucleus and its breakdown products, are brown, while the tubercle bacteria are a beautiful blue. Indeed, all other types of bacteria except the bacterium of leprosy assume a brown colour.[8]

With Ehrlich's help, Koch's staining procedure was very soon replaced by a much more effective one. This made it possible to find the rods consistently in tuberculous tissue and to describe their characteristic arrangement. The bacteria typically formed 'small groups of cells which are pressed

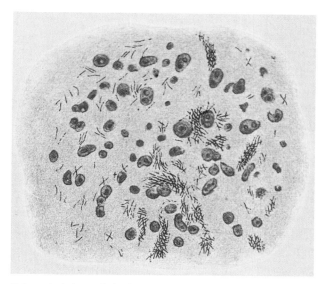

Tuberculosis bacteria in tissue. Drawing of a slide preparation by Robert Koch, 1884. After staining the cell nuclei appear brown, the bacteria blue.

together and arranged in bundles'. Their appearance also reflected the course of the disease:

> In all locations where the tuberculosis process has recently developed and is progressing most rapidly, these bacilli can be found in large numbers … As soon as the peak of the tubercle eruption has passed, the bacilli become rarer…[9]

The fact that Koch was able to render the tubercle bacilli visible by staining not only corroborated his 'firm belief'[10] in the 'parasitic' nature of tuberculosis, but also relieved him of the need to compare his bacteria with those found previously by others. As no one had ever used a similar staining procedure before, and the bacteria (as noted above) were invisible without staining, other investigators must have seen something different:

> Because of the quite regular occurrence of the tubercle bacilli, it must seem surprising that they have never been seen before. This can be explained, however, by the fact that the bacilli are extremely small structures and are generally present in such small numbers, that they would elude the most attentive observer without the use of a special staining reaction.[11]

Thus the double stain was more than just a technical innovation. Far more than any other microorganisms previously studied, the tubercle bacilli were artefacts of the methods used to study them. Incorrect use of the staining technique, for example, could lead to other components of a specimen appearing blue instead of the bacteria.

Despite the intensity with which the staining procedure was discussed, Koch remained surprisingly silent about two serious problems. The Königsberg physician Paul Baumgarten (1848–1928) had not only seen tubercle bacilli at almost the same time as Koch, but had done so without a staining procedure – i. e. he had seen identical shapes under the microscope and described their association with the morbid changes in tuberculous tissues. Not many of the notes made by Koch about his work have survived, but those which have show that in March 1882 his work was still in full progress and that many of the experiments described in his detailed paper of 1884 were not performed until after March 1882. So Koch was in a hurry and had every reason to be. The second problem Koch omitted to mention was that, despite every effort to do so, he, the man who pioneered the use of photomicrography in bacteriology, had not succeeded in photographing his preparations. He attached tremendous significance to photographic illustration and had emphasised only shortly before that photography, as the only 'purely objective view free of any prejudice',[12] was to be distinguished from the subjective form of illustration afforded by drawings. The fact that his preparations could only be published as drawings was something that Koch only mentioned in passing. We know from Koch's colleague Loeffler, who later became the first historian of medical bacteriology, that the double stain was in fact developed while Koch was attempting to photograph the microorganisms rendered visible by methylene blue. The reason why it is so interesting to analyse Koch's staining technique is that in his paper of 1884 he described the presence of spores, i. e. resistant forms

of the tuberculosis bacterium – something which, so far as we know today, does not exist. It is important to realise that in the 1870s the demonstration of such a spore stage was a crucial step towards demonstrating the stability of bacterial species. The concept of spores had been introduced into bacteriology by Koch's teacher Ferdinand Julius Cohn (1828–1898). In Koch's own work on the etiology of anthrax the discovery of *Bacillus anthracis* spores had been pivotal, because it explained the (apparent) temporary disappearance of the bacteria. The spores of the tubercle bacterium had similar properties. Koch described them as a 'resistant form necessary for preservation of the species'[13] and was thus able to account for the fact that dried sputum, for example, remained infectious for extended periods of time. The existence of spores also explained the infectiousness of the caseous (cheese-like) mass at the centre of the tubercles, in which bacteria could often not be demonstrated. According to Koch, spores were unstainable and thus invisible:

> … as there is as yet no means of staining the spores of the tubercle bacilli in any way, their presence after the disappearance of the bacilli is only revealed by the infectious properties of the caseous substance in which they are embedded.[14]

Koch provided a drawing of these spores, which he described as being 'of oval shape' and usually numbering 2–4 distributed along the length of a bacterium.[15] As Koch's statements on this topic are contradictory, all one can do is note the significance of the spores for his argument, namely that they made it possible to postulate the presence of bacteria in places where none could be detected. Koch's ostentatious references to his established methods thus also served to conceal problems. Certainly his spores were a potential pitfall for him. For example, his account of the life cycle of the bacillus was complete only as long as one was prepared to accept their existence.

Culture

By contrast, the difficulties encountered in culturing and inoculating the bacillus could largely be solved by modifying existing methods. Experiments showed that only tissue containing bacteria were capable of transferring tuberculosis to animals in the laboratory. And animal experiments also showed that various tuberculous diseases were forms of one and the same disease and identical to tuberculosis induced experimentally by inoculation, and that human tuberculosis was identical to that in susceptible animals. Essentially Koch was reproducing the

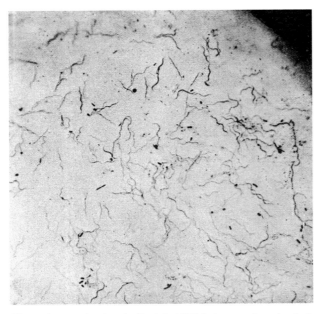

Photomicrograph taken by Koch in 1877. It shows anthrax bacteria which have formed spore filaments while growing in liquid.

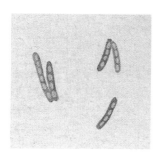

Drawing by Koch of the spore stage of the tubercle bacillus, 1884.

experiments of Villemin and his Breslau colleagues Cohnheim and Weigert. As his work progressed, he discovered that guinea pigs were the ideal experimental animals: they did not acquire tuberculosis naturally outside the laboratory but were extremely susceptible to inoculation tuberculosis. Moreover, the disease had a rapid and typical course in these animals. Amongst Koch's papers there is a record, compiled by Koch himself, listing his experiments and documenting a shift away from the use of diseased tissue to experiments with cultures in the spring of 1882. In order to prove that the disease was caused by bacteria and not by some other, as yet unknown components of tuberculous material, it was crucial to separate the bacteria and grow them in pure culture outside the body. If inoculation of animals with the cultured bacteria resulted in tuberculosis, then the bacteria, and they alone, must be the cause of the disease. In preparing his cultures, Koch was faced with two difficulties. One was the special growth requirements of the bacteria,[16] and the other their extremely slow rate of growth, which meant that there was always a risk of cultures becoming contaminated over overgrown by other microbes. The first problem was solved by using a culture medium made of coagulated blood serum, which remained solid at 30 °C. As for the second problem, the guinea pig – along with scrupulous laboratory hygiene – provided an answer. As human tissue samples were usually contaminated, a passage through the guinea pig was added between the removal of tissue and culture. The rapid progression of the disease in these animals provided a far better starting material for seeding, so that pure cultures could be obtained with a reasonable degree of certainty. Material applied to the culture medium was not supposed to show signs of growth sooner than 10–15 days after seeding. Earlier growth was a sign of contamination as cultures of the tuberculosis bacteria grew very slowly. There were a number of other ways of verifying the identity of the cultures, e. g. by their typical appearance as 'very small spots, dry and scale-like'. Also, the cultures always

Handwritten notes by Robert Koch about his experiments on tuberculosis between 1 November 1881 and 30 January 1882. The experiments were performed with tuberculous material obtained from different forms of the disease, which are noted in the second column. On the right, the number of days to the death of the experimental animals is noted; underlining indicates animals that were killed.

remained on the surface of the transparent culture medium. Penetration into the medium or liquefaction of the medium, which was not uncommon with other bacteria, was a sign of contamination. Finally, an additional means of verification, independent of the culture procedure, was to identify the bacteria by staining.

Infection experiments with pure cultures

Koch's investigations culminated in his infection experiments with pure cultures. For these a large number of different species were inoculated in numerous different ways, or infected in some other manner, to simulate the various routes of natural infection. If the animals were susceptible to tuberculosis, the pure cultures induced the disease. Koch

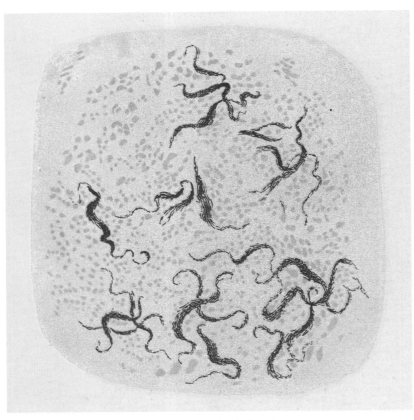
Cultures of the tuberculosis bacillus; drawing by Koch, 1884.

The bacterial origin of tuberculosis

When he presented his work in 1882, Koch placed particular emphasis on the aspect of bacterial etiology, which was received with practically no opposition. Koch's eminently thorough procedure appeared to rule out any doubt about his results in this respect. Even the pathologist Rudolf Virchow (1821–1902), who was decidedly critical towards bacteriology, could not dispute that the tubercle bacterium played a role in causing the disease. However, the immediate positive response to Koch's 1882 paper was due not only to the thoroughness of his work; it was also important that Koch initially avoided voicing any overly harsh opposition to other, non-bacterial factors in the etiology of tuberculosis and expressly acknowledged the significance of disposition, inheritance and social conditions. Koch had thus merely found the causative agent of tuberculosis and not redefined the disease itself. His statement that 'phthisis [was considered] by doctors to be a non-infectious disease based on constitutional abnormalities',[20] but that the means were now available 'to draw the boundaries of the diseases understood as tuberculosis, which we were not hitherto able to do with certainty'[21] is a little exaggerated. What he had in fact done was add the causative agent to an existing concept of the disease. The idea that tuberculosis was an infectious disease had already been developed by others; Koch's work helped this to become the consensus view. Central to this view was a firm rejection of clinical manifestations and an emphasis on bacteriological findings. It was now the latter, not morbid anatomy, which was crucial:

> Now ... as regards the confusion of non-tuberculous nodules with genuine tubercles, nothing is simpler than to rule this out: the true tubercles are infectious and contain tubercle bacilli, the false ones do not.[22]

Moreover, Koch did not present his discovery as the result of his eight months' work on the subject – about which he revealed nothing. In summing up his results, he went all the way back to the anthrax studies that marked the starting point of his career as a bacteriologist:

> With regard to knowledge of its etiology tuberculosis thus follows the pattern of anthrax. The tubercle bacilli bear exactly the same relationship to tuberculosis as do the anthrax bacilli to anthrax.[23]

From clinical presentation to pathogen

Koch's work on tuberculosis is a milestone in the history of how bacteriology transformed medicine. As advances were made in identifying the bacterial

described the pure cultures used for these experiments with obvious pride:

> It is therefore not going too far to say that in most of the experiments absolutely pure masses of bacilli were used.[17]

What Koch wanted to see in these experiments was not just whether signs of tuberculosis occurred – i.e. whether bacteria and pathological tissue changes could be demonstrated – but whether the tuberculosis induced using pure cultures was identical to the tuberculosis previously induced by inoculating fresh tuberculous material. This was the case. In Koch's first four series of experiments in 1882

> the inoculation of cultures of bacilli into the abdomens of the experimental animals produced an inoculation tuberculosis which showed exactly the same course as if fresh tuberculous substances had been inoculated.[18]

With his pure cultures Koch had reproduced the inoculation tuberculosis of Villemin, Cohnheim and others. The pathogen, the missing link in their experiments, had been identified. In 1882 Koch memorably summed up his work as follows:

> All of these facts taken together lead to the conclusion that the bacilli which are present in the tuberculous substances not only accompany the tuberculosis process, but are the cause of it. In the bacillus we, therefore, have the actual tubercle virus.[19]

causes of infectious diseases, definitions of disease based on morbid anatomy were supplanted by new definitions based on necessary causes. In differentiating diseases from each other, the biological classification of causative agents became more important than clinical symptomatology. It became possible to base diagnoses on tests for pathogenic organisms rather than on clinical signs and symptoms.

Internal process or a product of external causes?

The bacteriological concept of infectious disease was also associated with a shift in emphasis from disease as an internal organic process to disease as a phenomenon produced by external causes. The term 'etiology' had initially been used to refer to a whole range of pathogenic factors, from climate to inheritance to disease-causing microorganisms, but as the 19th century drew to a close 'etiology' in the bacterial sense became a central concept in medicine. Koch's work on tuberculosis marks a breakthrough in the understanding of human infectious disease based on bacterial etiology. The sum of his work up to 1884 furnishes the first complete bacteriological model of infectious diseases. In its description of microbial pathogens, this model is modern in that it views them as necessary causes. Koch did not accord pathogenic organisms just any role in disease causation but singled them out, precisely and logically, as necessary causes: without the tubercle bacillus there was no tuberculosis, without *Vibrio cholerae* no cholera. This not only made it possible to classify infectious diseases according to their causative agents, something which we take for granted today, but also provided a logical target for agents – from disinfectants to antibiotics – designed to fight such diseases.

'Koch's postulates'

In view of the high standards Koch applied to his work on tuberculosis, it is not surprising that, in addition to his arguments on the immediate issues of interest, he also systematically discussed the problem of establishing cause-and-effect relationships between bacteria and specific diseases. In his paper of 1884 in particular, he did this in some detail, formulating abstract criteria for demonstrating bacterial pathogenicity which made it possible to use the 'methodological fruits' of his previous work in the investigation of other diseases. In their most basic form these criteria consisted of the three steps of identifying a suspected pathogen in infected tissue, growing pure cultures of the pathogen outside the diseased organism, and then successfully infecting laboratory animals with the cultured pathogens. The essence of Koch's position was that conclusive proof could only be obtained

> by completely separating the parasite from the diseased organism and from all of the products of the disease which could be ascribed a disease-inducing influence, and then introducing the isolated parasite into healthy organisms and inducing the disease anew with all its characteristic symptoms and properties.[24]

A few years later Koch's colleague Loeffler named these criteria 'Koch's postulates'. This name is both appropriate and misleading. It is misleading because it can be shown that Koch had no such blueprint and varied his own methods and standards of evidence substantially from case to case. In 1878, for example, when he was working on wound infections, he had not yet developed his technique for obtaining pure cultures and rejected the use of other culture techniques as an unnecessary luxury. In the case of cholera, he believed he could do without a demonstration of the disease in animal experiments and, in his work on tuberculosis, his animal experiments with infectious material acquired a significance which is not reflected in the postulates. But the expression is nevertheless fitting. It directs our attention to the fact that, in addition to bacteria

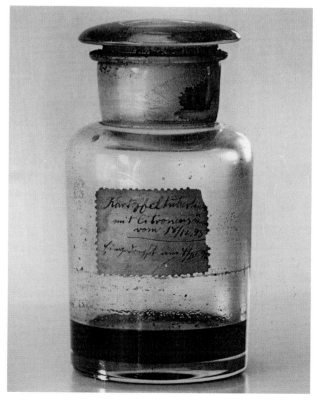

Tuberculin bottle. The label reads: 'Potato tuberculin with citric acid, 18 Dec 93'.

Ein Wohlthäter der Menschheit.

Der neue Ritter St. Georg.

Redakteur: Siegmund Haber in Berlin.   Druck und Verlag von Rudolf Mosse in Berlin.

Two caricatures of Robert Koch: Ein Wohlthäter der Menschheit (A benefactor of mankind), published in Ulk, *a supplement to the* Vossische Zeitung, *14 Nov. 1890, and* Aus der Welt der unendlich Kleinen (Scenes from the world of the infinitesimal), *published in* Kladderadatsch, *23 Nov. 1890.*

and microscopes, medical bacteriology was also rooted in a specific concept of infectious diseases which can be summarised in Koch's postulates. This remains true even if the statement is qualified by adding that the postulates describe a regulative idea rather than reflecting actual research practice and that Koch himself never formulated any postulates in this way.

Tuberculin: the story of a mistake

Even if the expression 'Koch's postulates' can be said to sum up the theoretical consequences of Koch's work on tuberculosis, we should not overlook the fact that this work also had other, much more concrete consequences. By establishing the role of minute bacteria as specific causes of infectious disease, Koch's results gave these diseases a new, more clearly defined identity, but at the same time, and for the same reason, also raised hopes that medical science was half-way to finding a treatment. In 1882 he declared:

> But in the future our battle ... will no longer be against an undefined something but against a tangible parasite[25]

thus giving voice to expectations, already widely held at the time, that the identification of specific pathogenic organisms would soon lead to equally specific remedies. However, these expectations were not fulfilled. On the contrary, for decades the applications which resulted from the discoveries of Koch and other bacteriologists were limited essentially to techniques of preventive hygiene, such as disinfection. From about 1883 onwards Koch himself focused on finding a cure for tuberculosis, a search that would eventually plunge him from the heights of professional fame into a fiasco. The pressure on him to succeed was in no way lessened by the fact that in the 1880s his French rival Louis Pasteur (1822–1895) was successfully developing effective vaccines against infectious diseases such as rabies. Koch's work on a cure continued for years with varying intensity. In time he obviously decided to alter his research strategy. Having first tried to develop an 'internal disinfectant' that would destroy the tubercle bacillus in the body, Koch set off in a new direction with his work on tuberculin, which drew on his understanding of the etiology of tuberculosis. At the time Koch regarded infectious diseases as a kind of bacterial invasion in which entry into the body, infection and disease were essentially simultaneous events. The healthy body, he believed, was normally free of pathogenic microorganisms, but, once an invasion had begun, it was completely at the mercy of the invaders. The disease then proceeded to consume the body like a culture medium, coming to a halt only when the medium was used up. In the case of tuberculosis, Koch believed that the result of this consumptive process was the death (necrosis) of tuberculous tissue and that tissue death was brought about by a (hypothetical) substance excreted by the bacteria. If it were possible to isolate this substance, he reasoned, then necrosis could be induced in the tissue without the spread of bacteria. In the mind of its inventor, tuberculin was thus not designed to attack the bacteria directly but, by destroying tuberculous tissue and robbing it of its nutritional value, was supposed to prevent the further spread of the disease in a kind of bacteriological variant of the scorched earth tactic.

The tuberculin euphoria of 1890

No-one apart from his closest colleagues knew anything about this when, at a large congress in Berlin in August 1890, Koch made his sensational announcement that he had found a cure for tuberculosis. The scientist stated succinctly that he had

> encountered substances which are able to halt the growth of the tubercle bacilli not only in the test tube but also in the animal body.[26]

While admitting that his experiments had not yet been completed, he felt confident enough to say that in the case of guinea pigs

> which are in the advanced stages of general tuberculosis, the disease process can be brought to a complete halt.[27]

He said nothing at all about the composition, method of preparation or mode of action of the cure. Starting in October of the same year Koch published a series of articles in which he disclosed snippets of information about tuberculin over the course of practically a whole year.[28, 29, 30] He initially revealed nothing about its composition, confining himself to providing information about dosage and action and reporting some successful experiments in humans. At first the treatment could only be obtained from a colleague of Koch's, but even this limited availability, starting on 13 November 1890, triggered a general euphoria. Over-hasty use of the treatment precipitated the publication of similarly hasty reports of successful cures, which fuelled even more excitement. In all this 'the world's doctors were thus experimenting with a completely unknown substance, a "secret remedy" to which they gave credence solely on the strength of Robert Koch's scientific reputation.'[31] The degree of ignorance

Tuberculin on draft. Damit es noch mehr fluscht *(A way to improve cash flow), published in* Ulk, *a supplement to the* Vossische Zeitung *16 Jan. 1891.*

about the composition of the remedy is reflected in the factually incorrect but commonly used names 'Koch's lymph' and 'Koch's antiserum', which only gave way to the name 'tuberculin' in the course of the winter.

Tuberculin fails

The euphoria was short-lived. After only a few weeks there were reports of patients deteriorating following use of the substance and even of fatal outcomes. The secrecy surrounding Koch's wonder drug – which at first seemed so fitting given the drug's apparently sensational properties – now began to reflect badly on its originator. There was increasing pressure on Koch to provide information about the ingredients and the method of preparation. In January 1891 he finally issued a general

The Institute of Infectious Diseases in Berlin, opened in summer 1891, forerunner of today's Robert Koch Institute.

description of tuberculin, which turned out to be a glycerine extract of tuberculosis cultures. What were the reasons for Koch's secrecy? Apart from the difficulty of producing tuberculin – which Koch may well have mentioned merely as a handy excuse – there are a number of other plausible explanations. First, such behaviour was quite common at the time. Koch hoped to make a fortune from tuberculin, which would have allowed him to say goodbye to his unloved university career and set up his own institute. In the autumn of 1890 Koch was still planning to establish an institute to study and manufacture tuberculin. He anticipated that annual profits from his cure would amount to the colossal sum of around 4.5 million Marks (about € 50 million today) and, in a letter to the Prussian Ministry of Culture, even did a little simple arithmetic based on the health statistics to show why this was so:

> As regards the prospects of sufficient sales of the amounts produced, allow me respectfully to point out the following. Per million people it can be estimated that there are, on average, 6–8000 people suffering from tuberculosis of the lungs. In a country with a population of 30 million there will thus be at least 180,000 phthisics.[32]

But the secrecy not only concealed Koch's bold business scheme, it also concealed scientific problems with tuberculin: there was far less to hide than met the eye. Koch had little more to show than his method of production, a few animal experiments

and a speculative theory of how the cure worked. He had not been able to isolate any active principles that would account for the alleged effect. In the spring of 1891 it became evident that Koch had been fishing in decidedly muddy waters and that this was the true reason for the secrecy. By early 1891, when critics were finally able to prove that tuberculin injections could even promote the spread of the disease in the body, and Koch had failed to produce any cured guinea pigs, tuberculin as a treatment was scientifically finished. In the summer of 1891 one of his critics summed up the numerous animal experiments that had been done in the meantime with tuberculin as showing

> that large doses make the established inoculation tuberculosis worse, while small and moderate doses are of no help.[33]

From remedy to diagnostic tool

Even in Koch's day the diagnostic use of tuberculin was discussed far more favourably than its therapeutic action. However, the idea behind it was also very strange. Koch attached no particular diagnostic significance to the systemic reaction to tuberculin which was observed in practically all adults. Instead, he used a localised or particularly strong reaction to diagnose acute disease. He explained the absence of a systemic reaction in guinea pigs by postulating that their sensitivity to tuberculin was much lower, estimating it to be 1500 times lower than in humans! To us this interpretation may appear absurd, but at the time it would have hardly been possible for Koch to interpret the systemic reaction to tuberculin (which he had even observed in himself) as an indication of previous infection. Yet it is precisely this reaction, almost completely ignored by Koch, which is the basis of the modern tuberculin test. In contrast to Koch's method, which was used to detect the presence of acute disease, this modern test determines whether a person has been immunised in the past with the BCG vaccine[34] or has been previously infected with tuberculosis. The modern interpretation of the tuberculin reaction thus presupposes a clear conceptual divide between infection and disease which is foreign to Koch's invasion model of infectious diseases.

As far as his career plans were concerned, Koch was also in a tight spot at the beginning of 1891. In October 1890 he had taken a leave of absence from his post as professor of hygiene at the University of Berlin. His new institute was not yet finished and in negotiations between the Prussian government and Koch over possible purchases of tuberculin, the ministerial bureaucracy had played for time. This was a clever ploy. When tuberculin proved to be a 'flop', they had the scientist under their thumb and could set up the sort of institute they wanted. Instead of a tuberculin institute, an institute for infectious diseases with a broad scientific brief established, the forerunner of today's Robert Koch Institute. Although Koch became its first director in the summer of 1891, he had to accept a number of harsh conditions imposed by the Prussian government, which wanted to guard itself against the bacteriologist's possible future forays into business. Koch had to agree to refrain from private practice and to transfer all future inventions to the state without compensation.

The consequences of the tuberculin scandal were complex. For Robert Koch there was not only the damage to his personal reputation, which was intensified by his separation, at almost the same time, from his first wife and his affair with a 17-year-old art student, Hedwig Freiberg, who later became his second wife. When tuberculin failed, his dependence on the Prussian establishment, from which he had hoped to free himself with the help of his tuberculin profits, had if anything increased. In addition, the failure damaged the reputation of bacteriological hygiene as a discipline and was, for example, to prove a handicap in the development of serum therapy, at that time still in its infancy. Further investigation of the action of tuberculin gradually led in the direction of the allergological and immunological questions which it is relevant to today. As a result, Clemens von Pirquet (1874–1929) was able to develop a test procedure in 1907 which allowed the diagnosis of previous infection with tuberculosis. Koch however – like a good many of his contemporaries – never abandoned his on views on tuberculin. He produced an improved version in 1897 and probably remained convinced to the end that he had found a cure for tuberculosis.

Naotaka Hamasaki

The analysis of biocatalysts

The development of clinical enzymology

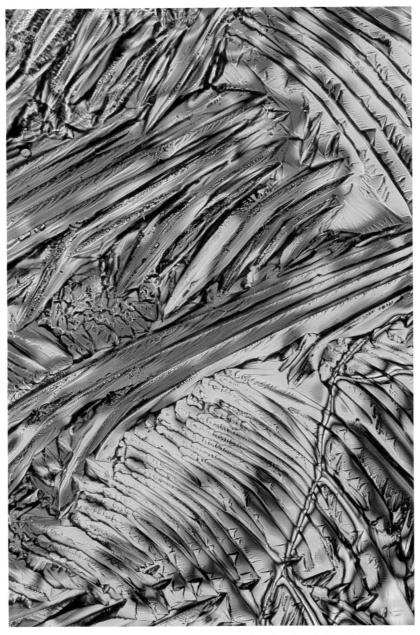

Micrograph of crystals of the digestive enzyme trypsin, taken in polarised light.

Until the nineteenth century it was widely believed that a special life force or *élan vital,* operating only in higher living beings, was required to convert inorganic material into organic compounds. For the 'vitalists' it was simply inconceivable that biological functions might one day be explained by chemistry. By the end of the nineteenth century, however, opposition to vitalism was growing, and with it the tendency to explain the phenomena of life in terms of physicochemical processes.[1] This was also the century that saw the first discovery of an enzyme, although enzymatic phenomena had in fact been observed long before. Some 200 years earlier, for example, it had been noted that meat liquefied in the gastric juice of hawks, which therefore had to contain some protein-dissolving substance. Anselme Payen (1795–1871) and Jean-François Persoz (1805–1868) were probably the first to isolate an enzyme of plant origin. They treated an aqueous extract of malt with ethanol and precipitated a heat-labile substance which promoted the hydrolysis of starch. They called the fraction thus extracted 'diastase', deriving the term from the Greek word for 'separation', as this enzyme separates sugar components from starch. It is now recognised that Payen and Persoz's diastase was in fact an impure preparation of amylase.[2] The next enzyme to be partially purified was of animal origin. Theodor Schwann (1810–1882), the German physician and biochemist to whom we owe ground-breaking descriptions of cell structure and metabolism, isolated a substance from gastric juice that cleaved and dissolved protein. He called it 'pepsin'.

Pepsin was clearly one of those long-sought substances that initiated and accelerated changes in organic compounds. As yet they had no name, and it was only possible to speculate about their effects. In 1836, the same year that Schwann described pepsin, the Swedish naturalist Baron Jöns Jacob Berzelius (1779–1848) wrote:

> We have good reason to suppose that, in living animals and plants, thousands of catalytic processes take place between tissues and fluids and bring forth the multitude of heterogeneous decompositions that we shall in future perhaps discover in the catalytic power of the organic tissue of which the organs of the living body consist.[3]

It was these initial observations of enzymatic activity that paved the way for the notion of 'catalysis'.[4] Between 1849 and 1877 other enzymes were identified, such as pancreatic lipase[5] (discovered by Claude Bernard, 1813–1878) and invertase in yeast[6] (Marcelin Berthelot, 1827–1907).

At the time of these early discoveries it was not yet clear that yeasts were unicellular organisms. That they were alive and responsible for fermentation was demonstrated independently, and almost simultaneously, in 1837 by Charles Cagniard-Latour (1777–1859), Schwann and Friedrich Traugott Kützing (1807–1893). As so often in the history of science, these convergent discoveries were due to improvements in instrumentation – in this case, the development of microscopes with achromatic lenses.[7] Cagniard-Latour noted that the cells of brewer's yeast consisted of a mass of small round units capable of reproduction and were not simply an organic or chemical substance. The idea that fermentation was caused by living organisms was confirmed and pursued further by Louis Pasteur (1822–1895).[8] He also coined the noun 'ferment' for the catalysts involved. While Pasteur considered the processes that occur during fermentation to be essential physiological activities of certain microorganisms, contemporary chemists – notably Justus [von] Liebig (1803–1873) – advocated a purely chemical theory of fermentation. A distinction was drawn between 'organised ferments' (most famously espoused by Pasteur), which were believed to be present in or on the surface of living cells, and 'unorganised ferments' such as diastase and pepsin, the activity of which was clearly not associated with microorganisms (the view championed by Liebig).[9] The dispute between Pasteur and Liebig was not settled until 1897, when two brothers, Hans Ernst August Buchner (1850–1902) and Eduard Buchner (1860–1917), obtained a cell-free yeast extract that converted sugar to alcohol.[10, 11] The term 'enzyme' (from the Greek for 'in yeast') as a name for biocatalysts, or ferments, was introduced by Friedrich Wilhelm Kühne (1837–

The German biochemist **Eduard Buchner** (1860–1917), working with his brother Hans Ernst August Buchner (1850–1902), showed that a cell-free extract of yeast was capable of fermenting sugar to alcohol. After observing that gas formed when a concentrated cane sugar solution was added as a preservative to yeast juice, he realised that a fermentation reaction had occurred which could help to settle the dispute between Pasteur and Liebig. On 11 January 1897, Buchner's six-page paper on 'Alcoholic fermentation without yeast cells' was read at a meeting of the German Chemical Society; the impact of his finding was similar to that of the discovery of X rays by Wilhelm Konrad Röntgen (1845–1923) two years earlier. Buchner showed that substances can have catalytic properties which do not necessarily depend on cellular structures. Ten years later, in 1907, he received the Nobel Prize in Chemistry for validating the concept of enzymes and establishing its general applicability to biochemical catalysts acting inside and outside cells.[36] Although he was 54 when the First World War broke out, he volunteered for active service and died in 1917 from a shrapnel wound suffered in action at the front in Romania.

1900), and led naturally to the idea of a science of enzymes, i.e. enzymology. However, the fact that enzymes are proteins was not recognised until the late 1920s. When James Batcheller Sumner (1887–1955) crystallised urease in 1926,[12] many argued that the enzyme was simply an impurity adsorbed onto or occluded within the protein crystals. But in the early 1930s John H. Northrop (1891–1987) and co-workers crystallised pepsin, trypsin and chymotrypsin, and conclusively demonstrated that the protein crystals were pure enzymes. By 1943 about 25 enzymes had been crystallised, and enzymology was firmly established as a scientific discipline.

Enzymatic analysis and clinical enzymology

In the early 1900s the events involved in enzymatic reactions were studied more closely, and the concept of kinetic analysis was established by Leonor Michaelis (1875–1949) and Maude Leonora Menten (1879–1960) in Berlin and George Edward Briggs (1893–1985) and John Burdon Sanderson Haldane (1892–1964) in Britain. In 1913 Michaelis and Menten rediscovered the equation derived by Victor Henri (1872–1940).[13] The Henri-Michaelis-Menten equation, which is based on simple principles of chemical equilibrium,[14] is a measure of the affinity between enzymes and substrates. In 1925 Briggs and Haldane introduced the concept of steady state into enzyme kinetics.[15] In the 1940s and 1950s hundreds of new enzymes were discovered, many of which were purified to homogeneity and crystallised. Key metabolic pathways were elucidated, and biochemists began to focus on the mechanisms of

Leonor Michaelis *(1875–1949), a biochemist, was in charge of the bacteriological laboratory at Urban Hospital in Berlin. Together with Maude Menten (1879–1960) – a Canadian physician and biochemist, who was a visiting researcher at the University of Berlin in 1912 – he developed the famous Michaelis-Menten equation. This enabled scientists for the first time to describe biochemical reactions mathematically. Michaelis and Menten's findings still serve as a basis for describing the catalytic activity of proteins. Their work also helped pave the way for the development of industrial biotechnology.[37]*

Enzymes and substrates

Enzymes are large proteins which play an essential role as biocatalysts in a multitude of metabolic reactions. Intensive study in the early part of the 20th century revealed them to be highly complex molecules of varying molecular weight, consisting of long chains of 20 amino acid building blocks whose arrangement (sequence) differs for each enzyme. These chains have to be folded into specific three-dimensional shapes for enzymes to function as catalysts.

The substances converted by enzymes into other compounds are referred to in scientific parlance as 'substrates'. Conversion occurs when a substrate binds to a special region of an enzyme, known as its 'active site'. The enzyme itself remains unchanged by this reaction. Each substrate fits the active site of a specific enzyme as neatly as a key fits the lock it was made for – a property known as 'substrate specificity'.

Enzymes are denoted by the names of their substrates, followed by '-ase'. The enzyme that cleaves maltose (malt sugar), for example, is called 'maltase'. The vast number of enzymes which have been discovered to date are divided into six groups according to the reactions they catalyse. Hydrolases, for example, are a group of enzymes that cleave certain chemical bonds, whereas ligases catalyse the formation of new chemical bonds.

enzyme activity and regulation. Reactions catalysed by enzymes were described in the equations of enzyme kinetics. During the same period Otto Heinrich Warburg (1883–1970) developed a method of 'enzymatic analysis' based on the absorption of light by the pyridine coenzymes NADH and NADPH at a wavelength of 340 nanometres.[16] The introduction of the spectrophotometer by Arnold Orville Beckman (b. 1900) and Carl Zeiss (1816–1888), and the commercial production of purified metabolic enzymes by Boehringer Mannheim, established enzymatic analysis in the laboratory.

During this period biochemists were also attempting to standardise a variety of measurement systems, nomenclatures and units for properties such as molecular weight. Amidst this welter of information, Hans Ulrich Bergmeyer (1920–1999) resolved to publish a handbook that would make enzymatic analysis practicable even for non-experts. Recognising the biological significance of enzyme reactions, Bergmeyer was convinced that progress in biology would depend on the availability of reliable methods of enzymatic measurement. His *Methods of Enzymatic Analysis,* published in 1963, was intended not as a theoretical treatise but as an introduction to the fundamentals of measurement. This handbook has introduced generations of clinical chemists to the principles and methods of enzymatic analysis.[17]

Clinical enzymology and laboratory medicine

The foundations of clinical enzymology were laid in the early 1900s, when serum **amy**lase (AMY) was first measured in patients with pancreatic disease.[18] At the end of the 1930s (acid and alkaline) phosphatases and cholinesterase were found to be clinically relevant in prostate cancer and liver disease.[19, 20, 21] They were joined approximately 20 years later, in the mid-1950s, by **al**anine amino**t**ransferase (ALT), **as**partate amino**t**ransferase (AST) and **l**actate **d**e**h**ydrogenase (LDH) – markers of liver disease and myocardial infarction, and mainstays of contemporary clinical enzymology.[22, 23] These were soon followed by the contribution of **cr**eatine **k**inase (CK) and γ-**g**lutamyl**t**ransferase (γ-GT) to the understanding and management of skeletal muscle disorders, myocardial infarction and liver disease. Measurements of enzyme activity in body fluids provided such useful diagnostic information that they became an increasingly important adjunct to routine clinical examination.[24, 25]

The adoption of enzymatic analysis in routine laboratory settings was facilitated by the development of excellent assay methods and by remarkable innovations and improvements in assay equipment. The growth and progress of clinical enzymology may thus be regarded as a product of collaboration between industry and academia.

Apart from its importance in the clinical laboratory, enzymology occupied centre stage in biochemistry and the life sciences until about 1970. By that time most of the body's metabolic pathways and key metabolic enzymes had been investigated in detail. Today the cellular metabolic reactions once viewed as 'vital phenomena' can be reproduced in the test tube (in vitro) and elucidated without invoking any mysterious life force. Moreover, enzyme kineticists are now able to go beyond qualitative 'all-or-nothing' descriptions and characterise biological phenomena in the quantitative language of mathematics and trace metabolic changes to changes in the balance between enzyme systems.[26,27] Quantitative analysis is an important tool for interpreting metabolic phenomena generally, and not only the role played by enzymes. Replace the first word in 'enzyme kinetics' with 'protein', and you have an effective quantitative/kinetic approach for analysing biological processes and events based on protein-protein interactions. Signal transduction events in cells, for example, cannot be precisely elucidated except by means of quantitative/kinetic analysis.[28] Thanks to advances in the quantitative analysis of enzyme reactions, it is now possible to explain 'vital phenomena' on the basis of structures at the amino acid side chain level ('structural biology'). Viewed from this perspective, enzymology is at the origin of today's life sciences.

Since its inception in the early 1900s, the mission of clinical enzymology has been to apply research findings in the diagnosis of disease, essentially by measuring enzyme activity in serum or plasma. In almost every case – the exceptions being blood coagulation factors and enzymes involved in lipid metabolism – the enzymes of interest are released into the circulation from damaged cells or tissues, whose identification thus becomes of critical importance. The main tools used by enzymologists for this purpose have been isoenzymes, or isozymes, and mapping techniques which have assigned these isozymes to tissues, cells and even cell components. Isozymes – the concept dates from 1959[29] – are enzyme variants present in the same organism and catalysing the same reaction, but differing in their molecular protein structure and physicochemical properties. Analysis of the primary structure[30] of released enzymes also sheds light on the etiology

From 1954 until his retirement in 1985, **Hans Ulrich Bergmeyer** (1920–1999) worked as a chemist and manager at Boehringer Mannheim in Tutzing, near Starnberg Lake in Upper Bavaria. His initial task was to determine the activity of the enzyme extracts which the company produced for therapeutic use. For this purpose he developed new methods which he subsequently systematised in what was to become a standard reference work. Bergmeyer's Methods of Enzymatic Analysis, which has gone through more than ten editions since it was first published in 1963, contains hundreds of detailed analytical methods. The translation of his findings into commercial products, including enzymes and substrates for research and enzyme-based diagnostic tests, established him as a pioneer of modern diagnostics.

and pathology of enzyme abnormalities. Such analyses were once confined to specialised facilities, but advances in genetic engineering have made them routine procedures in clinical laboratories. Most of the enzymes currently investigated have been known since the early days of clinical enzymology. The prescience and foresight of the pioneers in this field beggar belief.

While clinical enzymology's mission remains unchanged, the automated analysers introduced over the last few decades have dramatically improved the measurement of circulating enzymes. Not only have measurements of enzyme activity become significantly more accurate, but automation has also reduced the time and sample sizes required for testing. Results are also available faster because today's systems are able to analyse large numbers of samples simultaneously. Moreover, these revolutionary performance characteristics are now packaged in analytical instruments so compact and simple to use that they can provide precise, accurate and rapid enzyme data at the bedside.

Measuring released enzymes

As it circulates through the body, blood not only supplies oxygen to cells and tissues, but also transports waste generated at various sites to the lungs and kidneys for elimination. Thus enzymes released from injured cells or tissues enter the circulation, where – unless they are inactivated – their increased presence indicates damage to their source organ. Enzymes commonly measured for their clinical implications include the transaminases (AST, ALT), LDH, γ-GT, **al**kaline **p**hosphatase (ALP), CK, AMY, **ch**olinesterase (ChE) and lipase. Since they catalyse major metabolic reactions, many of them occur in organs. If an organ containing significant amounts of a given enzyme is damaged, it will release greater amounts of that enzyme into the blood. The elevated enzyme level thus becomes a sensitive marker of organ damage. Typical examples include CK and ALT: an increase in blood CK levels indicates muscle injury, while elevated blood ALT levels are almost certainly a sign of liver damage. By contrast, the distribution of LDH is less organ-specific, making it difficult to identify the injured organ on the basis of increased blood LDH levels. However, analysis of LDH isozymes is effective for this purpose. Similarly, CK isozyme analysis can distinguish myocardial damage from skeletal muscle injury. Enzyme kinetics can also be recruited to identify the site or severity of damage, e. g. by measuring the slope of the increase in levels of an enzyme or the time of the increase. It is generally thought that enzymes are released into the bloodstream through damaged cell membranes, but this has not been experimentally proven. For example, although glucose-6-phosphatase is specific to hepatocytes, its clinical usefulness in diagnosing liver damage has proved to be no greater than that of ALT. The pre-

sumed reason is that glucose-6-phosphatase, which occurs in the membrane of the endoplasmic reticulum, is not released from the cell as readily as ALT or LDH, which are present in the cytoplasm. But, again, experimental evidence to support this hypothesis is lacking.

Isozymes

Since the same enzymes may occur in many organs, an increase in the activity of a particular enzyme in a body fluid does not always identify the damaged organ. This is where isozyme analysis comes to the rescue. LDH and CK are prime examples of enzymes routinely subjected to isozyme analysis. In the case of LDH, five isozymes have been identified: H4, H3M1, H2M2, H1M3 and M4 ('H' denoting a subunit expressed primarily in **h**eart tissue, and 'M' a subunit expressed primarily in skeletal **m**uscle). The gene for the H subunit is located on chromosome 12 (12p12.2-p12.1) and that for the M subunit on chromosome 11 (11p15.1-p14).

The IUPAC-IUB[31] Joint Commission on Biochemical Nomenclature recommends restricting the term 'isozymes' to multiple forms of enzymes arising from genetically determined differences in primary structure (e. g. proteins encoded by different genes) heteropolymers with these proteins as subunits (hybrids) and a group of polymorphic molecules that have clearly resulted from mutations. However, in the clinical laboratory setting, enzymes resulting from post-translational protein modification are also recognised as isoforms. The techniques used for isozyme analysis include electrophoresis, ion exchange column chromatography and immunological methods. Electrophoresis separates isozyme fractions according to their charge characteristics. Immunological methods use specific antibodies to distinguish between isozymes.

Measuring enzyme activity

Virtually every clinical laboratory now uses automated analysers to measure enzyme activities, and as a result there have been significant gains in the precision of such measurements. Also, at the level of individual laboratories, precision has been greatly enhanced by the application of internal quality controls. However, standardisation of test results between laboratories has emerged as a major problem. A satisfactory solution is urgently required, particularly given the move towards electronic patient records and the related prospect of more and more strictly regimented standards of care. Where quantities of a substance can be expressed as concentra-

Enzyme markers in clinical diagnosis

Enzyme	Diagnosis	First reported
Amylase	Acute pancreatitis	1910
Acid phosphatase	Prostate cancer	1938
Cholinesterase	Liver disease	1938
Alkaline phosphatase	Liver disease	1940
Aspartate aminotransferase	Myocardial infarction	1954
Aspartate aminotransferase	Hepatitis	1956
Alanine aminotransferase	Liver disease	1956
Lactate dehydrogenase	Myocardial infarction	1956
Glutamate dehydrogenase	Leukemia, cancer	1956
Lactate dehydrogenase	Cancer	1957
Lactate dehydrogenase	Muscle disease	1957
Creatine kinase	Muscle disease	1959
Creatine kinase	Myocardial infarction	1960
γ-Glutamyltransferase	Liver disease	1960

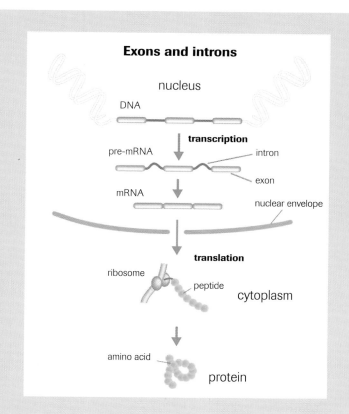

Exons and introns

nucleus

DNA

transcription

pre-mRNA

intron

exon

mRNA

nuclear envelope

translation

ribosome

peptide

cytoplasm

amino acid

protein

Genetic polymorphisms and abnormal proteins

The gene regions that code for proteins are known as exons, and their adjacent non-coding regions as introns. During the editing process that results in a mature **r**ibo**n**ucleic **a**cid molecule (messenger RNA, or mRNA), the introns are removed, leaving behind the sequences that contain instructions for protein synthesis. If a variation associated with substitution of an amino acid in a protein is detected in an exon region, this suggests the presence of a gene polymorphism, which may or may not result in expression of an abnormal protein. To establish whether a variation is a polymorphism, the gene of interest can then be analysed in 50–100 individuals to determine the frequency of the variation. An enzyme molecule can be confirmed as abnormal by introducing the abnormal gene into cell cultures (transfection) and then examining the enzyme's specific activity.

Introns are removed during RNA maturation. The resulting strand of mRNA carries the instructions for constructing a protein from the cell nucleus to the ribosomes in the cytoplasm, where protein biosynthesis takes place.

tions (as with electrolytes and glucose), measurements can be standardised relatively easily with the aid of standard reference materials. However, this is not readily applicable to enzyme measurements. The activities measured for one and the same enzyme preparation vary with the conditions of measurement. In addition, the commercial reagents used in laboratories are prepared for measurements based on different principles and performed under different conditions, which inevitably gives rise to discrepancies in the results obtained by different laboratories. But if that is the case, is inter-laboratory variation something we can reasonably hope to eliminate? Is standardisation a realistic aim in clinical enzymology? The answer is 'Yes', for the following reasons.

Although the term 'true value' surfaces from time to time in discussions about measuring enzyme activity, there is no such beast: all values are 'apparent'. Once this basic principle is grasped, the standardisation problem looks less intractable. Ultimately, it is impossible to evaluate the accuracy of measurements of enzyme activity. However, the values obtained using one assay can be correlated with those obtained using another. A method that unequivocally validates the specific activity of an enzyme with a high degree of precision should be selected as the reference method. Practical standard-

isation of measured enzyme activity values is not difficult provided the method chosen gives a high specific activity and is precise, and there is a reference enzyme preparation. Progress on this front has recently been facilitated by the advent of commercial enzyme reference materials (ERMs).

Lipid metabolism and blood clotting

Research into lipid metabolism has made remarkable progress in recent times, a fact reflected by increased clinical testing for lipoprotein fractions and other components of lipid metabolism. This development has been paralleled by the increasingly frequent measurement of enzyme activities relevant to lipid metabolism, e. g. of **l**ipo**p**rotein **l**ipase (LPL). **C**holesteryl **e**ster **t**ransfer **p**rotein (CETP) is also measured, although it is not an enzyme. Until recently, cholesterol levels in lipoproteins rather than total serum cholesterol were considered an important atherogenic factor, with lower concentrations of **l**ow-**d**ensity **l**ipoprotein (LDL) and higher concentrations of **h**igh-**d**ensity **l**ipoprotein (HDL) cholesterol being thought to lower the risk of atherosclerosis.[32] However, improved understanding of substances such as **h**epatic **t**ri**g**lyceride **l**ipase (HTGL) has sparked a growing controversy over the protection afforded by high HDL levels. Certainly it would be premature to base arguments about the

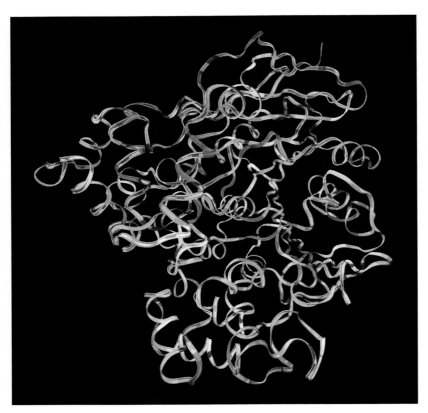

Computer image of lipase, an important enzyme in lipid metabolism.

promotion or prevention of atherosclerosis simply on measurements of HDL cholesterol.

While thrombosis among Japanese was once thought to be less common than among Europeans or Americans, its incidence in Japan is now recognised as relatively high. Thrombosis is a multifactorial disorder caused by a combination of lifestyle and environmental factors. Moreover, low anticoagulation factor activity has been found in many people with an increased tendency to thrombosis.[33] There is growing recognition of the importance of measuring the activity of anticoagulation factors such as protein C, protein S and antitrypsin, and of fibrinolytic factors such as plasminogen and plasmin inhibitor. Although they do not all have enzyme activity, some are proteinases or enzyme activators or inhibitors.

These enzymes and factors involved in lipid metabolism and blood coagulation have physiological functions in the circulation. Changes in their activity reflect direct physiological effects on metabolic systems and carry greater clinical significance than the levels of disease-marker enzymes released into the circulation by damaged tissue. However, no basis has yet been established for their investigation in the clinical laboratory. Whether they eventually become incorporated into routine tests depends on the development of suitable assay methods.

Abnormal enzyme molecules

When a clinical sample shows abnormally low or high levels of enzyme activity that cannot be attributed to the patient's disease, immunoglobulin[34] binding or a molecular abnormality may be the cause. Immunoglobulin-bound enzymes can be detected by a combination of isozyme analysis and immunological staining. The presence of abnormal enzyme molecules is indicated by a discrepancy between the activity and quantity (concentration) of an enzyme. Until a few decades ago, when genetic engineering was still in its infancy, identifying abnormal molecules involved the use of cumbersome techniques of protein chemistry. Today, however, identification is relatively easy. After obtaining the patient's informed consent, a blood sample is taken, and **d**eoxyribo**n**ucleic **a**cid (DNA) is extracted from the white blood cells. This genetic material is then amplified (copied many times) using the **p**olymerase **c**hain **r**eaction (PCR) technique, and the DNA sequence is examined for abnormal sites.

Prospects

Clinical enzymology owes its current standing to a series of tremendous advances that began in the 1950s. Its clinical utility is beyond question, and its techniques are an indispensable part of modern diagnostic practice. Yet at the same time it could be argued that few developments of note have occurred since the 1980s. Be that as it may, the techniques used in clinical enzymology to detect disease in microlitres of blood will continue to play an important role in the future. Enzymes with physiological functions in blood and those released into the circulation by damaged tissue will remain key parameters in laboratory diagnostics. The next leaps forward are likely to occur when pathological changes can be assessed by testing for circulating levels of various proteins involved in intracellular signal transduction as well as for enzymes, tumour markers and cytokines.

Beckoning on the more distant horizon is a new era in measurement technology. Nothing would be more desirable than to be able to perform clinical chemistry tests non-invasively. I have a vision of the future in which hospitals will be equipped with walk-through diagnostic systems capable of doing a laboratory workup of patients as soon as they arrive. For patients this will mean that some of the familiar 'trials' of the examining room will be replaced by a procedure as simple and non-invasive as stepping through a metal detector gate at the airport.[35]

Monika Barthels

The development of coagulation diagnostics: a detective story

A drop of blood issues from a wound and in less than five minutes turns into the gelatinous blob that we call a clot. Another drop falls on a rose petal and barely clots at all. Why not?[1] A boy with the bleeding disease hemophilia injures himself and bleeds nonstop for hours, even days – the wound is forever rebleeding. But if you take blood from one of the same boy's veins, the bleeding, as in a normal person, is minimal, even nonexistent. How can this be, if he's a hemophiliac?[2] Normally blood flows uninterruptedly throughout life in a closed circuit, without clotting. But in one in a thousand individuals thrombosis occurs, i. e. a thrombus (blood clot) forms, causing a sudden and highly undesirable obstruction of a blood vessel and thereby disrupting the circulation to an extent that can occasionally be life-threatening.[3]

Such phenomena have now, at the start of the 21st century, been all but fully elucidated. The feats of scientific investigation responsible for the current state of knowledge have been reminiscent, on occasion, of detective work. They have helped shape our present-day understanding that there are clearly diagnosable congenital and acquired clotting disorders. These are associated with an abnormal bleeding tendency (hemorrhagic diathesis) or with increased coagulability, sometimes even with both together. The final diagnosis, e. g. of hemophilia, can only be made on blood samples in the laboratory.

From antiquity to 1836

Very few descriptions of hemostatic mechanisms have reached us from before the mid-19th century. Renowned physicians of antiquity recognised that blood jellifies on cooling. The great Greek physician Hippocrates of Cos (c. 460 – c. 375 BC) also de-scribed a fibrous material (fibrin) which formed in the process. He noted that cooling the wound has-tened hemostasis – probably the first reference to enzymatic processes in blood coagulation.[4] The first description of a bleeding tendency and its trans-mission through the female line occurs in the Baby-lonian Talmud of the 3rd century AD. The first accounts of abnormal clotting in veins date from the 17th century. The same period saw the first reports of experiments on the response of blood to cooling, which hastened clotting, and to movement, which delayed it.[5] Successful attempts at hemostasis using hypnosis had presumably already been made before the treatment of the last tsarevitch, who was a hemo-philiac.

What happens when body fluids are mixed

In the second half of the 19th century hard work and simple experiment achieved a basic understand-ing of coagulation, hence of coagulation diagnostics. The main approach was to mix blood or plasma with serum or body cell extracts, add various chemicals and then measure the clotting time. The results naturally left many questions unanswered on the characterisation of substances whose presence was often only suspected, leading to heated debate. The existence of the central clotting enzyme, thrombin, was reported in 1836 by the Scottish surgeon Andrew Buchanan (1798–1882), who had observed some five years earlier that certain body fluids clotted quickly after freshly clotted blood or serum was added to them.[6] Alexander Schmidt (1831–1894), a physiologist from Dorpat (now Tartu, Estonia) on the Baltic and one of Virchow's students, created the basic framework for classic coagulation theory between 1860 and 1890. His experiments

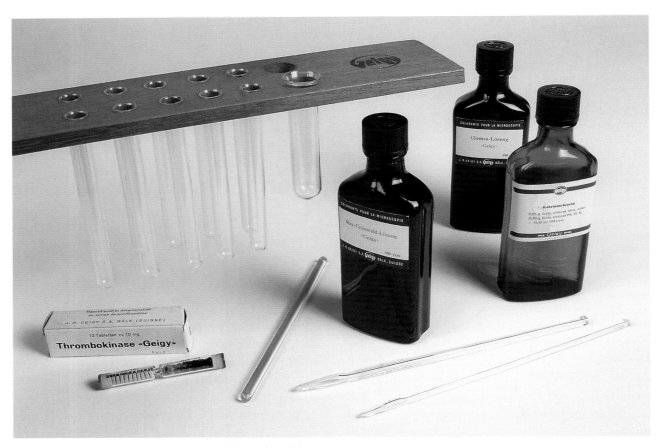

Reagents of an early thrombokinase test manufactured by Geigy.

consumed horse blood by the litre, earning him the nickname of 'bloodsmith' from his colleagues. In his detailed review of Schmidt's life and work, A. H. Sutor wrote:

> When we consider the classic coagulation scheme, as recorded by Morawitz 11 years after Alexander Schmidt's death, we can detect a certain similarity with the final position in a chess game between two grand masters. Little would one suspect from the simplicity of that immaculate, unimprovable configuration that it was the result not of rigorous logic but of flashes of brilliance and dogged positional play, with some moves being freely chosen and others forced by the opponent, whose different approach imposed a lasting change in the situation ... Schmidt was a central participant in this story, playing a crucial role in the discovery and classification of fibrinogen, prothrombin, thrombin and thrombokinase.[7]

The coagulation scheme published in 1905 by the Leipzig clinician Paul Morawitz (1879–1936) was to inform coagulation research and diagnostics over the subsequent 50 years.[8] On the basis of his literature studies Morawitz decided that blood plasma had to contain calcium, prothrombin and fibrinogen, that tissue thrombokinase + calcium + prothrombin led to the formation of thrombin, that

blood or plasma required a wettable surface, that thrombin converted fibrinogen to fibrin and that a substance present in serum inactivated thrombin.[9] It was also Morawitz who named the tissue factor 'thrombokinase'.

The decade from 1910 to 1920 saw a fundamental discovery, that of a substance which prolonged clotting time. As it was obtained from liver, William Henry Howell (1860–1945) called it 'heparin'.[10] Years later, as direct-acting anticoagulants, heparins were to prove remarkable drugs for preventing thrombo-embolism. They remain widely used to this day.

Early clotting tests

The clotting tests performed during this period were global tests, i. e. they encompassed all phases of fibrin formation. A prolonged clotting time was thus a nonspecific and somewhat insensitive indicator of abnormal coagulation. Some tests remained in use for decades. They included the whole-blood clotting time, in effect an early instance of **p**oint-**o**f-**c**are **t**esting (POCT), published by Lee and White in 1913,[11] and also Howell's recalcification time,[12] determined using platelet-rich plasma made uncoagulable with oxalate or citrate salt; ionised calcium was

Present-day knowledge

NB: Clotting (coagulation) is not the same as the arrest of bleeding (hemostasis), which only occurs in the living organism (in vivo) through the interplay of three 'partners': vessel wall, blood platelets and the coagulation of plasma – the classic triad, with minor modifications, described by the great Berlin pathologist Rudolf Virchow (1821–1902). Clotting can also take place in vitro, in the test tube, although the ground rules in vitro are somewhat different from those in vivo.

A cascade is unleashed…

Clotting requires three totally different components: various proteins, ionised calcium and procoagulant lipids. A certain protein, fibrinogen (factor I), is constantly present in the blood in soluble form. During the clotting process fibrinogen is slightly but so effectively modified that it precipitates as a solid net-like (reticular) substance, fibrin, which in vivo then seals the wound. The trigger for this modification is a protein-cleaving (proteolytic) enzyme, thrombin (factor IIa). Understandably, thrombin does not circulate in its active form, but as an inactive precursor, prothrombin (factor II). Activation to thrombin is the result of a chain reaction by other proteolytic clotting enzymes (e.g. factors IXa, VIIa and Xa) – at the time and place of need, i.e. at the site of injury. This is triggered by the release of a protein called 'tissue factor' from injured tissue cells. (Tissue factor and the tissue extract tissue thromboplastin are both used as reagents in Quick's test.) Tissue factor forms a complex with blood factor VII to initiate the clotting process. The enzymatic reactions are accelerated by the presence of high-molecular-weight proteins, clotting factors V and VIII and procoagulant phospholipids which are not present in blood but are a tissue factor component contained in platelets and in many tissue cells. The presence of ionised calcium (factor IV) is essential. Clotting is concluded by 'stabilisation' of fibrin, brought about by the most recently discovered clotting factor, factor XIII, among other influences.

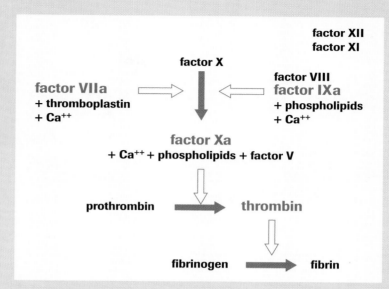

The coagulation cascade.

…then arrested

Many substances play a role in inhibiting clotting, confining it to the time and site at which it is required. The best-known circulating inhibitors are also proteins: antithrombin, protein C and its cofactor, protein S. The clot is ultimately broken down, or rather dissolved, in a process termed fibrinolysis, which again is performed by proteolytic enzymes (in vivo: thrombolysis).

All these processes generate reaction products, e.g. fibrin degradation products (D-dimers), which can be readily measured. Changes in their concentrations often provide useful information on fibrinolysis or disease processes.

 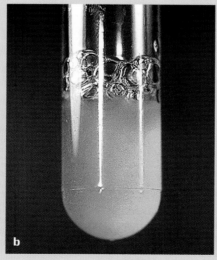 

Fibrin formation in the test tube: **a**) Plasma, the yellow, cell-free fluid portion of unclotted blood. **b**) A dense gel forms after clotting has been initiated by adding calcium ions. **c**) End result of the clotting process: a thick fibrin clot has formed, leaving the fibrinogen-free liquid called serum as a supernatant.

Armand James Quick *(1894–1978) from Wisconsin, who obtained a PhD in chemistry in 1922 and his MD in 1928. From 1944 until his retirement in 1964 he was Professor and Head of the Department of Biochemistry at Marquette University in Milwaukee, Wisconsin. He is known mainly for the test he pioneered in the 1930s, which he called the prothrombin time (PT). The PT is still used today to monitor coumarin therapy. The prothrombin consumption test which Quick described in 1949 was important for understanding the clotting process. In 1966 he published the aspirin tolerance test for identifying latent bleeding disorders.[64]*

The Norwegian **Paul A. Owren** *(1905–1990) studied medicine at Oslo University, where he became Professor of Internal Medicine after initially working as a general practitioner. In 1943 he made the seminal discovery that the pathological PT of a female patient with a severe bleeding disorder was due to a deficiency not of prothrombin but of a previously unknown clotting factor which he isolated and named factor V. Owren subsequently worked on many other aspects of hemostasis, e. g. platelet aggregation.[65]*

The biochemist **Walter H. Seegers** *(1910–1996) was a pioneer of coagulation research, not least because of the biochemical techniques which he introduced. He was still in his twenties when he published his isolation of prothrombin and thrombin in 1937 and 1938. From 1946 to 1980 he chaired the Department of Physiology and Pharmacology at Wayne State University School of Medicine in Detroit, attracting many workers to his institute from both the United States and abroad. He and his group were the first to isolate and characterise many other clotting components, e. g. factor V, factor X, antithrombin and protein C.[66]*

then added at a certain point, after which the time to visible fibrin formation was measured. The advantage of all these tests was, and remains, the fact that fibrin formation is observed with the investigator's naked eye. Older physicians who still performed these tests themselves often say how useful they were for assessing clotting in their patients.

Discovery of the factors

All the clotting factors except fibrinogen, which was already known, and prothrombin were discovered between 1935 and 1959. Roman numbering, in the order of factor discovery, was proposed as early as 1956 so as not to prejudice the often inexactly understood function of the factor concerned.[13] At that time the 'factors' were defined much less by their biochemical properties than by their associated clotting time profiles under defined experimental conditions. They thus tended to remain abstractions, in particular for clinicians without any laboratory experience, thereby presumably contributing to the generally perceived esoteric nature of coagulation diagnostics.

Prothrombin time (PT, 'Quick's test')

The first real, and subsequently standardisable, coagulation test was developed by the American Armand James Quick (1894–1978) and published in 1935.[14] Quick's test, or its synonym, thromboplastin time (both terms have long been widely used in continental Europe), is the (one-stage) **p**rothrombin **t**ime (PT). In a slightly modified version, it is still widely used, in particular for monitoring coumarin therapy. The basis for Quick's idea was the Morawitz clotting scheme. He assumed that the rate of clotting was proportional, and thus the clotting time inversely proportional, to the thrombin concentration. His innovation, in terms of quantitative measurement, was to add all the known factors in excess except for the factor of interest, i. e. only one variable factor remained, which was prothrombin. Under these conditions, he argued, the prothrombin concentration should determine the coagulation time. Quick therefore called his test the 'prothrombin time'. Although the name was soon to prove misleading, his approach created an immutable basis for all quantitative tests of individual clotting factors, in which clotting time is inversely proportional to factor concentration.

The discovery of the 5th clotting factor

In 1947 the Norwegian hematologist Paul Arnor Owren (1905–1990) published in *The Lancet* the case of a female patient with a severe congenital hemorrhagic diathesis.[15] He showed that despite the markedly prolonged PT value of the patient's plasma, the cause had to lie in a deficiency not of prothrombin but of some previously unknown clotting factor. His experiments, performed single-handed without specialist training, were brilliantly simple, worthy of Sherlock Holmes, and characteristic of the deductive reasoning displayed in clotting analyses. They were also blessed by a good measure of luck, in that he achieved valid pioneering results despite what we now recognise as partially flawed arguments. Owren first established that the patient's plasma PT value and recalcification time were so prolonged that they would have to have been equivalent to a prothrombin concentration of about 10%. Yet the patient had neither hypovitaminosis K nor severe liver disease. 'In view of these findings', he wrote, 'it was natural to doubt the correctness of Quick's method of prothrombin determination.' Owren's next step was to assume, based on Quick's approach, that the clotting time must have been influenced by another factor. He began by excluding a deficiency of the basic clotting factor, fibrinogen, together with decreased responsiveness of fibrinogen to thrombin (as, for example, in the dysfibrinogenemias). In this regard he was far ahead of his time. He then isolated prothrombin from normal plasma (i. e. plasma from normally clotting subjects) by adsorption onto aluminium hydroxide and added different amounts of this prothrombin-free plasma to the patient's plasma. He discovered that increasing volumes of this plasma shortened and eventually normalised the patient's plasma PT. Together with other experiments, this led him to conclude that the patient's blood lacked a substance that was present in normal blood and necessary for normal clotting, but not included in the clotting schemes current at the time. He named it factor V. Owren went on to isolate factor V and demonstrate that intravenous injection of the factor shortened the patient's PT. Independently of Owren, and also in 1947, the great biochemist Walter H. Seegers (1910–1996) and his team described the isolation of a protein that accelerated clotting, which later proved identical to Owren's factor V.[16] Owren called his patient's clotting defect 'parahemophilia', 'as the faulty coagulation of para-

In 1944, after completing her medical studies, **Rosemary Biggs** (1912–2001) entered the Department of Pathology in Oxford under R. G. Macfarlane, who encouraged much of her important work. It was she who was responsible for the first description of hemophilia B. She also developed the thromboplastin generation test. In 1967 she became director of the newly founded Oxford Haemophilia Centre, where she soon set up a central database for hemophiliac patients. Biggs was the editor of Thrombosis and Haemostasis for a number of years and received many scientific awards.[67]

haemophilia is not returned to normal by addition of thrombokinase as is the case of haemophilia'.

The history of the discovery of factor V is typical of the discovery of most clotting factors: it begins with an unusual and severe hemorrhagic diathesis in an individual patient. Tests in which that patient's plasma is mixed with plasma from patients with an already defined clotting disorder point to either another case of a known disorder or a new type of clotting defect. In the second stage, more sophisticated methods are used to identify the defect.

Hemophilia A or B?

The discovery of clotting factors VIII and IX, and the realisation that their absence was responsible for hemophilia A and hemophilia B, respectively, is also a story of deductive reasoning. A coagulation-accelerating protein, subsequently designated factor VIII, had been isolated as early as 1937.[17] It shortened the abnormal clotting time of hemophiliac blood. Not until 15 years later did Rosemary Biggs (1912–2001) and her colleagues establish that there were two forms of hemophilia instead of the single entity previously known, although both were identical in terms of hemorrhagic diathesis and sex-linked transmission.[18] The Oxford group had observed, like other scientists before them, that blood from some patients with hemophilia shortened the clotting

The thromboplastin generation test: a two-stage test

In this test three components are first obtained from the patient's blood and the blood of a normal subject. Two normal components and the test component are then added to each other. The components concerned comprise plasma adsorbed onto aluminium hydroxide which is stripped of prothrombin complex factor but still contains factors V, VIII and I (fibrinogen) only, serum also containing no prothrombin but factors VII, IX and X only, and platelets as a source of phospholipids. Although these three components, together with calcium ions, cannot generate thrombin, since prothrombin is absent from the test mixture, they can activate factor X. What Biggs called 'thromboplastin' is the prothrombinase complex generated in stage 1. In stage 2 the generated prothrombinase complex is then added to the patient's plasma, or 'substrate plasma', and the degree of factor X activation is measured from the rate of thrombin generation and, ultimately, from the rate of fibrin formation. The test is abnormal, i.e. gives a prolonged clotting time, with adsorbed patient plasma in hemophilia A and with patient serum in hemophilia B.

time of blood from other hemophiliacs – an obvious anomaly, if all hemophilias were the same. Using the methods then available to them, they first showed that the suspected other factor differed clearly from 'antihemophiliac globulin', i.e. factor VIII, in being detectable in serum, similarly to the factor VII which had been discovered in the meantime, and also in being precipitable with aluminium hydroxide. The two factors could also be differentiated by means of the two-phase test developed by Biggs and Stuart Douglas, the thromboplastin generation test.[19] They christened the new factor – the future factor IX – 'Christmas factor', and the new form of hemophilia 'Christmas disease', after their first patient. Classic hemophilia due to factor VIII deficiency was later named hemophilia A, and hemophilia due to factor IX deficiency hemophilia B.

This screening test proved useful despite being impossible to standardise. In the 1950s and 1960s, together with the PT, it was the only way of differentiating between hemophilia A and B and other clotting disorders. The concept behind this test had a major impact on theories of the coagulation cascade and the development of further tests. For example, it formed the basis of the commercial two-stage test for factor VIII introduced in the 1980s, which is used to standardise factor VIII in clotting factor concentrates.

A further example of a two-stage test was that for prothrombin.[20] Common to all these two-stage tests is that the development of full enzymatic activity can be observed over time, which to some extent protects them from the influence of interfering factors. This principle of rate-based (kinetic) measurement was subsequently revived in the chromogen substrate test.

The discovery of factors 'VI', VII and X

The serum factor initially numbered VI subsequently proved to be activated factor V (factor Va), leaving the number VI unassigned ever since. Owren already had evidence in 1947 that there had to be another factor whose blood concentration, like that of prothrombin, was decreased by coumarin anticoagulant therapy.[21] Around 1950 a Boston research group[22] and Fritz Koller (1906–1999) and his colleagues in Zurich, Switzerland[23] characterised factor VII in greater detail as a heat-stable serum protein. The Boston group were also the first authors to describe a case of factor VII deficiency, detectable from a prolonged PT despite normal factor V and prothrombin levels. In 1955 Koller's group in the person of François-Henri Duckert (1922–1998) described a further factor isolated from plasma which they named factor X in several publications.[24] Factor X deficiency was subsequently demonstrated in 1956 in an English female patient, Audrey Prower, and in 1957 in an American male patient, Rufus Stuart, with the result that factor X was also known as Stuart-Prower factor.[25, 26, 27]

A snake venom leads to factor X

The new factor X was initially almost indistinguishable from factor VII in terms of its biochemistry and performance in laboratory tests, with one exception: factor VII-deficient plasma could correct the clotting defect in factor X-deficient plasma. Bachmann from Koller's group[28] developed a specific test for factor X using Russell's viper venom (RVV) based on work by Cecil Bowie and the Macfarlane-Biggs group in Oxford, who had established that the conversion of prothrombin to thrombin in the presence of RVV required factor X but not factor VII. We now know that RVV contains an enzyme which directly activates factor X, rendering factor VII unnecessary. The curious RVV reagent was not a stroke of luck at the right time in the 1950s, but had already been in occasional use in coagulation diagnostics for 20 years. Snake venom in general had been recognised as having anticoagulant activity since the late 19th century and had already been studied from a variety of viewpoints. Since the 1980s RVV has been used as an important reagent, above all in the diluted RVV (dRVV) test for the antibodies in the blood known as lupus anticoagulants. Although these prolong clotting time in some tests, they do not cause abnormal bleeding; paradoxically, they may cause life-threatening thromboembolism.

Factors XI and XII

1953 also saw the discovery of a further bleeding disorder, initially classified as a hemophilia.[31] However, it was soon realised that the new entity differed from the classic hemophilias in that the bleeding tendency was far milder, despite the same degree of factor deficiency. The cause was identified as the absence of a factor initially designated **p**lasma **t**hromboplastin **a**ntecedent (PTA), later factor XI.

In 1955 a previously unknown clotting defect, due to factor XII deficiency, was discovered in a patient named John Hageman.[32] Factor XII has puzzled the scientific community for many years in that its absence is unassociated with a bleeding disorder, despite a PTT so grossly prolonged that it exceeds that seen in the severest forms of hemophilia. Although John Hageman himself died from thromboembolism, it has yet to be conclusively determined that factor XII deficiency even predisposes to venous thromboembolism. Factor XII is a 'contact factor', i. e. it is activated by adsorption onto negatively charged surfaces, presumably injured cell membranes in vivo. The factor has also aroused interest because it plays a role in other biosystems, notably the complement system, which is involved in inflammatory processes.

Gross prolongation of the aPTT as in factor XII deficiency has also been observed in two other extremely rare factor deficiencies, likewise unassociated with a bleeding tendency: kallikrein deficiency and high-molecular-weight kininogen deficiency. Both are contact factors and closely associated with factor XII.[33]

The final factor: factor XIII

In 1960 Duckert, a member of Koller's group, concluded that a previously unknown cause had to underlie a case of familial bleeding disease, since all the known clotting tests had proved normal.[35] Since those affected also had a wound healing disorder with abnormal scar formation, he suspected a connection with fibrin generation. It had long been recognised that fibrin could vary in quality. It was not just that due to delayed fibrin formation, as in hemophilia, the fibrin clot was of visibly poor

PTT and aPTT

In 1953 a test was reported which was called the **p**artial **t**hromboplastin **t**ime (PTT), since it gave a clotting time which, unlike the thromboplastin time in Quick's test, was abnormal in the plasma of hemophiliac patients: it was prolonged, as was also, for example, the recalcification time.[29] A brain tissue extract, 'cephalin', was used as the partial thromboplastin. Its critical components were the same procoagulant phospholipids as occur in blood platelets, whose use had already been validated as the third component in the thromboplastin generation test. Thereafter the combination of PT + PTT could be used to detect almost all defects of fibrin formation. It was far simpler and faster than the thromboplastin generation test. There was only one snag: the PTT was subject to substantial inter- and intraindividual variation. In addition, prolongation of the clotting time did not always mean a hemorrhagic diathesis. Since a wrong diagnosis can have devastating consequences in bleeding disorders, the test could not be retained in this form. It was improved in 1961 by optimising the activation of coagulation,[30] which had long been recognised to require, at least in vitro, a wettable surface, e. g. glass. In this improved version of the test, termed the **a**ctivated **p**artial **t**hromboplastin **t**ime (aPTT), a suitable phospholipid is first added to the plasma in the presence of an active surface. Only then is coagulation set in motion by adding ionised calcium. Ever since, the aPTT has been the most widely used clotting test after the PT, not least on account of its initially unforeseen applications, namely for monitoring therapy with the anticoagulant heparin and for detecting lupus anticoagulants. The classic single-stage tests for factors VIII, IX, XI and XII, as well as other factors, are based on the principle of the aPTT.

macroscopic quality – scanty, friable and fragmented – but prematurely dissolving fibrin could also be distinguished from a 'stable' fibrin that was resistant in particular to physiological fibrinolysis. This could be demonstrated relatively rapidly, as the unstable fibrin soon dissolved in 5-molar urea in contrast to its stable counterpart. The explanation was that an optimal fibrin clot required a fibrin-stabilising factor, namely factor XIII, and calcium ions. Factor XIII too has to be activated to the enzymatic form, via the action of thrombin and calcium ions. It is the only clotting enzyme which does not cleave proteins but instead acts as a transglutaminase to crosslink long fibrin chains. This peculiarity makes diagnosis considerably more difficult, as the standard clotting tests such as the PT and aPTT do not detect factor XIII deficiency. Even into the 1980s factor XIII activity could only be investigated using time-

Thrombin time

It was only natural to introduce into the diagnostic arsenal yet another, third global test of fibrin formation in which standard concentrations of the enzyme thrombin are added to the test plasma. The subsequent clotting time then depends solely on the interaction between (standard) thrombin and its fibrinogen substrate, with prolonged clotting times being attributable only to disorders within this narrow field. In theory the reaction can be influenced by the concentration and quality of the fibrin, but also by possible inhibitors – indeed, these proved the principal determinants. As a result the thrombin time developed into a clinical test for monitoring the therapy of the anticoagulant heparin, assessing the inhibitory effect of fibrinogen breakdown products in systemic fibrinolytic therapy, and supplementing the PT and aPTT in the diagnostics of fibrin formation. However, because it gives widely ranging results when used to monitor the anticoagulant therapy with heparin, this task was later entrusted to the aPTT. The first thrombin time test was presented as early as 1952,[34] not least because a relatively pure thrombin preparation, the Roche product Topostasin, was by then available both for topical therapy and as a laboratory diagnostic aid.

consuming and approximate 'solubility tests' or elaborate biochemical methods. An elegant photometric method applicable to routine diagnostics was only published in 1991.[36]

Measurements in slow motion

The first clotting tests soon proved very insensitive, in particular for the important diagnosis of mild hemophilia. The simple solution, devised in the 1940s, was to make small changes easier to detect by artificially prolonging the test clotting times, as in the sodium chloride tolerance test and the heparin tolerance test, in which increasing concentrations of sodium chloride or heparin were added to plasma in a series of test tubes and clotting times correspondingly extended.[37] However, these tests proved too time-consuming and also too inaccurate as clotting times lengthened. They are worth mentioning because even today the standard method can still occasionally be modified in a similar manner – in full knowledge of the implications – when an otherwise undetectable clotting disorder is suspected.

Detection of hypercoagulability

Given the procoagulant activity of serum and the occasionally shorter clotting times seen in individual plasmas, it was suspected that blood could become hypercoagulable under certain circumstances. This inspired the physicians' dream of an in vitro hypercoagulability test for the timely detection and appropriate treatment of impending thrombosis. One of the earliest hypercoagulability tests was the 'thrombin generation test' of 1964:[38] thrombin generation and inactivation were monitored in a series of test tubes and accelerated thrombin generation was demonstrated in certain patient groups. The test failed to gain acceptance for methodological reasons. However, the search for a hypercoagulability test continued to be intensively pursued, at times with near-goldrush fervour. The most promising method to date appears to be determination of endogenous thrombin potential as described by H. C. Hemker (b. 1934).[39] However, this test also seems unlikely to fulfil the hope of detecting impending thrombosis.

Thromboelastography

Thromboelastography, a global test based on a new measurement principle that differed radically from the coagulation diagnostics of its time, was first described in 1948.[40] According to its developer Hellmut Hartert (1918–1993), clotting was best evaluated if intervention in the natural course of events was kept to a minimum. For this purpose Hartert designed a device, the thromboelastograph, which measured the viscoelasticity and strength of the forming blood clot and monitored its development and the duration of the various phases, including as appropriate the clot dissolution phase. Clot strength was measured using the shear forces generated by rotating a cuvette of blood. The method gives a rapid overview of the clotting process, including the ability of platelets to bind fibrinogen to their surface. Thromboelastography can also detect the premature clot lysis that may occur in markedly raised circulating fibrinolytic activity or severe factor XIII deficiency.

Coumarin therapy monitoring

Coumarin therapy was already well established at the start of the 1960s. Physicians monitored it on an ambulatory basis, often in dedicated anticoagulant clinics housed in university hospital outpatient departments, mostly with their own coagulation laboratories, then increasingly, from the early 1970s, in physicians' offices and contract laboratories. Eventually patients learned self-monitoring, which by the early 1990s had developed into the best-standardised example of POCT. The PT reagent, thromboplastin, was already widely available in the late 1950s from a variety of manufacturers. Thromboplastins of various origins were used.

Most thromboplastin reagents were of animal origin, obtained from rabbit or bovine brain, but also from human brain and placenta. It was soon realised that thromboplastins of differing origin differed in their sensitivity to the individual factors in the prothrombin complex, in particular factor VII, and that in addition their effect was species-specific, i.e. that thromboplastin from the same species gives the shortest clotting time. This differing specificity means that plasma samples from the same patient will give different PT values with two different reagents, therefore the same PT value could mean that a patient's dose of anticoagulant was too low or too high. Study results were not comparable. From the outset this led to heated debates that at times resembled religious wars.

Methodological variants were another cause of conflicting results. One of the first was the one-stage 'prothrombin test' proposed by Owren in 1959 and still in use today (Thrombotest).[43] The reagent consists of bovine brain thromboplastin, adsorbed bovine plasma as a source of factor V and fibrinogen to enhance specificity, and calcium ions. The test can be performed in plasma, whole blood or capillary blood. Another variant is the HepatoQuick test, which virtually excludes interfering variables such as heparin or factor V deficiency.

Beginning in 1966, after it became clear that PT values could differ by more than 100%, Rosemary Biggs and Kenneth Denson (b. 1922) sought to exclude the influence of thromboplastins by introducing the '**p**rothrombin **t**ime **r**atio' (PTR), defined as the patient's observed PT divided by the laboratory's calculated mean normal PT,[44] each determined using the laboratory's standard reagent. Comparability improved as a result, but remained unsatisfactory for almost 20 years until the World Health Organisation (WHO) solved the problem by introducing the **i**nternational **n**ormalised **r**atio (INR) in 1983.[45]

Patient self-monitoring

Standardisation of the PT was the precondition for patient self-monitoring of coumarin therapy, the impetus for which, fittingly, was provided by a patient. In 1985 a German student, Heike Möller-Jung (b. 1963), underwent heart valve surgery. After the operation she felt understandably dejected at the prospect of life-long coumarin therapy combined with lifelong monitoring by physicians. Deciding to take matters into her own hands, she contacted a laboratory that provided PT results. The idea sud-

Hellmut Hartert (1918–1993) developed the thromboelastograph while at the Heidelberg University Department of Medicine. The device, which he first described in 1948, measured the viscoelasticity and strength of developing blood clots and recorded clot formation and the duration of its various phases, including clot dissolution. As befitted his interest in physics and electrical engineering, he worked primarily in hemorheology, developing the rheosimulator in 1972 and the concept of resonance thromboelastography in 1981. From 1962 until his retirement in 1983 Hartert headed the Department of Medicine in Kaiserslautern. In recognition of his scientific achievements he received the Poisseuille gold medal at the 5th International Congress of Biorheology in 1983.[68]

denly occurred to her: 'What they do in the laboratory, I can do too. I'll monitor myself.' In February 1986 Heike Möller-Jung received her own coagulometer, a KC 1A (Amelung, Lemgo, Germany), and the matching HepatoQuick test from Boehringer Mannheim. Since this test did not need venous blood – it worked with capillary blood – a simple prick in the finger pad was now sufficient. There was no longer any need to go to the doctor or laboratory, the result was immediately available and the patient remained mobile, a huge advantage in terms of quality of life. Möller-Jung's constant companion and instrument of independence was a small case containing a relatively small coagulometer. In May 1986, at a doctor-patient seminar for heart valve patients at Bad Berleburg Hospital, Germany, organised by her cardiologist Carola Halhuber (b. 1936), Möller-Jung put forward her 'crazy' new idea, initially with great trepidation. But instead of the disapproval she feared, her presentation was greeted

Biochemical methods

Biochemical methods have been used in coagulation research since the 1930s, when Seegers and coworkers isolated prothrombin and thrombin.[41] The following decades saw increasing purification and characterisation of clotting factors in terms of their biochemistry and physiology, e. g. molecular weight, half-life in blood. This led to the development of the first factor concentrates – prothrombin complex concentrate[42] and increasingly pure factor VIII and IX concentrates – for the therapy of bleeding disorders.

Heike Sichmann *(formerly Möller-Jung), shown here checking her coagulation status at home, was the inspiration behind patient monitoring of anticoagulant therapy after she underwent heart valve surgery in 1985. Determined to lead a more independent life, she began self-monitoring with a KC 1A in February 1986.*

with enthusiasm by Halhuber and fellow-clinician Angelika Bernardo (b. 1958). They embarked on a pioneering collaborative program to develop the self-monitoring of coumarin therapy. Several centres were soon set up in Germany to train patients in self-monitoring and the use of the KC 1A coagulometer. Initially some physicians and health insurance authorities were deeply opposed to the idea, but in 1989 a patient obtained a judgement awarding him the right to reimbursement for the costs entailed – the basis for the current refund provisions in Germany. The German Anticoagulation Self-Monitoring Study Group (*Arbeitsgemeinschaft Selbstkontrolle der Antikoagulation* [ASA]) was set up as a registered society in 1992.[46]

In the late 1980s industrial R&D became aware of the potential contained in a patient-friendly system for determining the PT. The groundwork was performed in the USA. Biotrack in California was the first to bring a simple system onto the market.

In 1989 Boehringer Mannheim began to develop a system based on patents from Cardiovascular Diagnostics Inc., North Carolina, designed mainly for the self-monitoring of coumarin therapy and use in the physician's office. The result was the CoaguChek system, introduced in 1993. In 1994 Boehringer Mannheim took over the Biotrack system and upgraded it to determine three clotting parameters simultaneously. The current model is the Coagu-Chek Pro.[47] Using a single drop of freshly obtained whole blood, this device can measure the parameters aPTT, PT and activated clotting time.

Individual factor tests

Of the clotting tests from the 1950s, only one, simple test displayed sufficient specificity and standardisation potential for it to remain in use to this day, virtually unchanged: Arnold Clauss's test for coagulable fibrinogen.[48] In the 1950s it was known that clotting times were influenced by minimal changes in the thrombin concentration, but very little by fluctuations in the concentration of the substrate, fibrinogen. Clauss (b. 1927) merely varied the thrombin time by diluting the plasma fibrinogen to concentrations that correlated linearly with clotting times. For diagnostic purposes, hospitals at the time initially also used other, cruder methods of fibrin determination, e. g. precipitation using heat or salting out.

By the late 1950s a few companies, notably the Marburg-based company Behringwerke, as it was then known, were producing test kits with reagents for determining individual clotting factors such as V and VII. But these were not manufactured commercially on a larger scale and under improved conditions until advances in basic biochemistry and the increasing clinical applications of coagulation diagnostics made this possible in the late 1960s. During these years further acquired clotting disorders were discovered and defined, e. g. the complex clotting disorders in liver disease, and later those in liver transplantation. The basic mechanism of disseminated intravascular coagulation (DIC), also known as consumption coagulopathy, was elucidated in the 1960s, together with its clinical implications.[49, 50] The development of intensive care medicine, e. g. cardiac surgery on a heart-lung machine (extracorporeal circulation), increased the requirement for acquired coagulopathy diagnostics. New treatments to prevent bleeding and thrombosis using clotting factor concentrates and fibrinolytic clot-busting drugs demanded dedicated monitoring of clotting potential. The early 1970s also saw the introduction of hemophilia centres where experienced physicians treated (and still treat) patients with very rare but life-threatening congenital bleeding disorders.

Precipitation and agglutination tests

The coagulation diagnostics of intensive care medicine increasingly became emergency diagnostics. Basic research into intermediate and breakdown products of fibrinogen and fibrin in the mid-1960s had shown that like their parent molecule, fibrinogen, many breakdown products could be precipitated with a variety of agents, e.g. alcohol, and thus identified in a naked-eye screening test. Other tests were based on the visible clumping (agglutination) of biological material. Although these methods were vigorously challenged, they frequently yielded valuable diagnostic clues. At the same time the initial results alerted physicians to the fact that the identification and, if possible, accurate quantification of the reaction products of coagulation and fibrinolysis were at least as important diagnostically as fluctuations in factor concentrations.

Immunological tests

Immunological techniques are now an essential part of coagulation diagnostics. By introducing accurate protein identification they put an end to the previous exclusive dependency on speculation as to nonspecific clotting activities. This partly made up for their inability to provide any information on the activity or functionality of the molecules concerned. Indeed, diagnosis was enhanced by combining the measurement of clotting activity with immunologically determined protein concentrations, making it possible to identify inherited dysfunctional molecular mutations or inactive protein inhibitor complexes formed during clotting.

Immunological techniques were introduced in the 1960s with the use of polyclonal antibodies primarily to determine the breakdown products of fibrinogen and fibrin. The initial radial immunodiffusion tests were fairly insensitive. It was the 'rocket' immunoelectrophoresis developed in 1966 which inaugurated the modern era of immunology in coagulation diagnostics.[51] It appeared enticingly elegant, producing on gel plates visible rocket-shaped precipitates whose length corresponded to the protein concentration. Even factor XIII and antithrombin could now be quantified. A further important development in this period was the immunological determination of what was known at the time as 'factor VIII-associated antigen', which subsequently proved to be the independent von

von Willebrand factor

Congenital von Willebrand disease was first observed in 1926 by the Finnish physician Erik Adolph von Willebrand (1870–1949) on the Aaland Islands. Initially it was regarded for many years as a disorder of platelet function due to the prolonged bleeding times in von Willebrand patients. But von Willebrand himself already referred to it as 'pseudohemophilia'. In the 1950s patients' factor VIII levels were found to be decreased. In 1957 Inga Marie Nilsson (1923–1999) and her team in Sweden reported that infusion of a concentrate containing factor VIII/von Willebrand factor in patients with von Willebrand disease not only increased factor VIII activity but also, to their utter surprise, shortened bleeding time, which was known to be a measure of platelet function. This meant that von Willebrand disease was a disorder not of platelet function but of plasma coagulation.[52] Much later, from the 1980s onwards, the investigation of von Willebrand disease was to become the most interesting story in coagulation diagnostics.[53] Von Willebrand factor is an independent factor that binds to factor VIII. If it is absent or severely decreased, factor VIII degradation is accelerated and factor VIII levels in the blood are correspondingly low. It was then discovered that von Willebrand factor agglutinated platelets, including formalin-fixed normal platelets, a property that proved to be of diagnostic value. An observation in the early 1970s that von Willebrand factor bound in vitro to normal platelets and agglutinated them in the presence of a barely used antibiotic, ristocetin, led to the only test currently capable of measuring a function of von Willebrand factor immediately and with almost total specificity. This function is known as ristocetin cofactor activity and the corresponding test as the ristocetin cofactor test.[54]

However, conclusive evaluation of the von Willebrand factor macromolecule, which is made up of multiple polymers (multimers), remains the preserve of specialist laboratories using labour-intensive gel separation techniques to determine whether all the multimers are present and, if not, to identify the defect involved and classify it accordingly.

Recent research has identified giant von Willebrand factor multimers as a cause of small blood vessel microocclusions in isolated patients, resulting in the rare, life-threatening and treatment-refractory syndrome of thrombotic thrombocytopenic purpura.[55]

Willebrand factor. Until well into the 1980s specialist laboratories could make the differential diagnosis between hemophilia A and von Willebrand disease simply by combining the determination of this antigen with an assay for factor VIII activity.

An immunological technique based on an entirely different measurement principle – the cloudiness (turbidity) of a solution – was laser nephelom-

Electron micrograph of early clot formation showing how blood platelets, appearing as spherical particles, are incorporated into a network of fibrin.

etry, introduced in the mid-1970s to determine individual clotting factors including antithrombin.[56] Its advantage over immunoelectrophoresis, which takes several hours, was that it provided an immediate result, which was becoming increasingly important, for example, for antithrombin estimation in the diagnosis of life-threatening consumption coagulopathy. Antithrombin is a normal blood constituent which inhibits most clotting enzymes, slowly inactivating them in such a way as to confine normal coagulation to the site and time of need, namely wound closure. The ability to detect a decrease in antithrombin (i. e. antithrombin consumption) was regarded at the time as a significant advance in the diagnosis of life-threatening consumption coagulopathy. However, it was only when congenital antithrombin deficiency was recognised as a cause of familial predisposition to thrombosis (thrombophilia) that the central role of antithrombin in normal clotting became apparent.[57]

The 1980s saw two huge advances in immunodiagnostics: the development of highly specific monoclonal antibodies, which increased the accuracy of protein identification, and the introduction of the enzyme-linked immunosorbent assay (ELISA). ELISAs have become probably the most widely used immunological test, earning them a separate chapter in this book. They have permitted a whole palette of clotting and fibrinolysis determinations, from individual components, e.g. factor II, protein C, protein S and the plasminogen activator (fibri-

nolysis) inhibitor PAI-1, to the most diverse reaction products, e.g. prothrombin fragment 1 + 2, thrombin-antithrombin complex, fibrin monomers, fibrinopeptide A, platelet factor 4 and fibrin(ogen) degradation products (especially D-dimers).[58]

Chromogen substrate assays

Having known since the mid-1950s that the protein-cleaving enzymes (proteases) that play a role in clotting could also cleave amino acid esters, biochemists synthesised peptides comprising three to four amino acids bound to a *p*-nitroaniline ring which were highly protease-specific. Cleaving of the *p*-nitroaniline ring from the amino acids colours the test fluid yellow, a reaction which can be measured in a photometer. The technique is currently used to measure clotting and fibrinolysis parameters (e. g. plasminogen) and their inhibitors such as antithrombin. In principle, chromogen substrate assays can also serve as global clotting tests. Together with fluorogen substrate assays they have radically changed coagulation diagnostics. Measurement by photometry permits rapid and extensive automation, e. g. on the Cobas Fara analyser, delivering clotting enzyme and inhibitor activities according to standardised clinical chemistry criteria. Not least it was hoped that these synthetic peptide substrates would eventually supplant the natural but ultimately elusive substrate fibrinogen. This has failed to materialise, as the short-chain peptide substrates are also cleaved by other biological molecules. Overall, however, these methods have substantially enhanced the quality and standardisation potential of coagulation diagnostics.[59]

Predisposition to thrombosis (thrombophilia)

The description in 1965 of a case of familial antithrombin deficiency,[60] which confers an increased risk of venous thromboembolism, inaugurated a new era in coagulation diagnostics. The search for congenital and acquired causes of thrombophilia began in earnest in the 1980s. Several new, primarily congenital, risk factors have since been discovered. Such hereditary thrombophilia is due mainly to quantitative or qualitative abnormalities in normal blood-borne coagulation inhibitors, above all antithrombin, protein C, and its cofactor, protein S. Diagnostic efforts to identify thrombophilia have now far outstripped those for congenital bleeding disorders. A further cause of thrombophilia was discovered by chance in the 1990s. First described by Björn Dahlbäck in 1993, it was due to a previously unknown mechanism, resistance to activated protein C (APCR).[61] How exactly does this work? If activated protein C (APC) is added to normal plasma, the aPTT is prolonged, since APC inactivates the thrombin-activated clotting factors Va and VIIIa, which are therefore no longer available to accelerate coagulation. Dahlbäck's laboratory, however, discovered that plasmas from some patients, whose clinical thrombophilia was unassociated with laboratory evidence of thrombophilia in the tests then available, failed to react to the addition of APC by prolongation of the aPTT: their aPTT remained normal, i. e. it was APC-resistant.

One year later it was shown using modern genotyping techniques that 95 % of cases of APCR are caused by a single point mutation in the factor V gene.[62] As a result, APC no longer recognises the cleavage point in activated factor Va, so that factors Va and VIIIa remain active, driving the continuous generation of thrombin in a vicious circle which only accelerates coagulability. The factor V mutation is also known as factor V_{Leiden} after the Dutch city in which it was first described. It is fairly common in northern Europe, where approximately 7 % of the population are heterozygotes with a partial predisposition to thrombosis. However, it is found in 20–30 % of patients suffering a thrombosis before the age of 40. Although large studies have shown that APCR is a weak risk factor, it confers an overall risk of thrombosis which is sevenfold higher than in normal subjects. Another defect favouring thrombophilia is the prothrombin gene mutation, which again is fairly common in that 1–2 % of the normal population are heterozygotes.

Thrombophilia diagnostics is a fast-moving field. Firm conclusions as to the implications of the defects diagnosed, some of which may be paired, cannot yet be drawn in the absence of large-scale epidemiological studies. Meanwhile many other risk factors have been described, including raised clotting factor levels, clotting factor mutations and metabolic disorders.[63]

Summary

Research into normal and abnormal clotting dates back a mere 150 years, due less to lack of interest

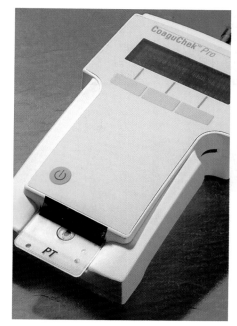
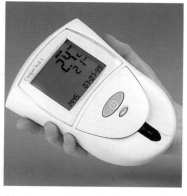

Modern self-monitoring devices: CoaguChek S (left) and CoaguChek Pro (right). The systems are equivalent and work on similar principles. A drop of blood is aspirated into a capillary tube and mixed with reagent to start the clotting cascade. Time to clotting onset is then measured.

than to unavailability of the requisite technology, namely methods of obtaining plasma – the fluid component of blood which retains the clotting factors, in contrast to serum, the fluid that remains after blood has clotted – and of measuring clotting times in the test tube, i. e. the actual clotting tests. In the second half of the 20th century the field was opened up by sophisticated biochemical techniques, e. g. enzymatics and gel separation, and by immunology and molecular biology, nowhere more so than in the broad field of thrombophilia diagnostics, where we are still only at the threshold of understanding. Coagulation diagnostics and the treatments which it has made possible have incontrovertibly saved and/or enhanced the quality of many lives. Hemophiliacs can now lead a normal, pain-free existence. The frequency of thromboembolic disease with its disabling late sequelae has been roughly halved. Patients on coagulation-controlling drugs routinely monitor their treatment using simple devices, and many studies are investigating how these diagnostic systems for self-monitoring can be improved.

Elmer W. Koneman

It's a small world

The history of virological diagnosis

Dmitri Iosifovich Ivanovsky *(1864–1920), studied botany at the University of St Petersburg (Russia). While investigating tobacco plants affected by mosaic disease, he discovered that the sap of diseased plants remained infectious after passage through a bacteria-retaining filter; the filterability of viruses had thus been demonstrated.*

Imagine the jubilation among bacteriologists during the last decade of the 19th century. Louis Pasteur (1822–1895) and Robert Koch (1843–1910) had relegated the theory of spontaneous generation to the dustbin of history. The germ theory prevailed and one infectious disease after another was linked to a newly discovered bacterial species. For a short time it was believed that new bacteria would sooner or later be discovered as the cause of almost all human and animal infections. But this elation soon subsided. Koch's postulates[1] were beginning to break down. The third postulate had to be revised early on, as infections such as cholera, leprosy and typhoid could not be transmitted to experimental animals, and subsequent isolation of the organism was

thus precluded. André Victor Cornil (1837–1908) and Victor Babès (1854–1926), in their popular textbook *Les bactéries* (1885), indicated that the bacterial etiologies of infectious diseases associated with certain skin eruptive fevers, such as smallpox and measles, had not been adequately confirmed by experiment. By this time the methods for isolating and identifying bacteria were highly sophisticated and could not be faulted. Yet it soon became clear that bacteriologists had failed to uncover the cause of many important infectious diseases, the agents of which remained an enigma. In 1894 William Henry Welch (1850–1934) stated:

> [W]e have a large number of infectious diseases which have thus far resisted all efforts to discover their infectious agents – yellow fever, typhus fever, dengue, mumps, rabies, Oriental pest, whooping cough, smallpox and other exanthematous fevers ... these are the most typically contagious diseases, which it might have been supposed would be the first to unlock their secrets ...[2]

The idea began to emerge, particularly among scientists engaged in microbial research, that microbial forms may exist that are too small to be detected by the microscope. The possibility of the existence of submicroscopic germs was supported by John Tyndall (1820–1893), when, in his light-beam experiments, he demonstrated tiny particles in the air 'beyond the reach of the microscope'. As early as 1876 he wrote:

> 'Potential germs' and 'hypothetical germs' have been spoken of with scorn, because the evidence of the microscope as to their existence was not forthcoming. Sagacious writers had drawn from their experiments the perfectly legitimate inference that in many cases the germs exist, though the microscope fails to reveal them ... Directing it [the concentrated beam] upon

media which refuse to give the coarser instrument any information as to what they hold in suspension, these media declare themselves to be crowded with particles – not hypothetical, not potential, but actual and myriad fold in number – showing the microscopist that there is a world beyond even his range.[3]

In 1887 the Scottish physician John Brown Buist described in his book *Vaccinia and variola* – which included photographs – tiny spherical particles with a diameter of about 0.15 μm that were observed in the 'pure lymph' obtained from variolar pustules.[4] He regarded these as 'spores' that develop by artificial cultivation in solid media into the larger bacterial forms. He went on to conclude that the spores represented an immature stage in the life cycle of the bacterium supposedly causing variola (smallpox) and vaccinia (cowpox), and also apparently represented the active principle of the vaccine that he was preparing. In retrospect Buist's spores were probably the elementary viral particles of variola and vaccinia, which on account of their size were barely visible with the improved optics of the microscope used at that time. Thus in 1886 Buist was the first to see and develop a stain for viral particles, the true identity of which he did not, of course, appreciate.

The term 'virus' was probably introduced by Pasteur, who developed an effective vaccine against rabies even without demonstrating the infectious agent, which could not be cultured by traditional bacteriological methods.

The discovery of the filterable infectious agent

Enter on the scene the Russian botanist Dmitri Iosifovich Ivanovsky (1864–1920). While studying the causal agent of a disease of tobacco plants that produces leaf mottling – now known to be the tobacco mosaic virus – Ivanovsky noted that it would pass through a bacterial filter.

A few years earlier Adolf Eduard Mayer,[5] a German chemical technologist, had also studied tobacco mosaic disease. Using Koch's methods of artificial culture, Mayer was unable to isolate the causal microorganism. When these efforts failed, he filtered sap extracted from diseased plants through a single layer of filter paper and determined that the filtrate was still infectious. However, as the filtrate became non-infectious when passed through two layers of paper, Mayer ruled out the possibility of an 'enzyme-like body'. He also discovered that infectivity could likewise be eliminated by heating the sap at 80 °C for several hours.

Martinus Willem Beijerinck *(1851–1931), professor of bacteriology at the Technical School in Delft (the Netherlands). Following his unsuccessful attempts to isolate the agent of tobacco mosaic disease, he concluded that the cause was a living, fluid, infectious agent, for which he coined the term* 'contagium vivum fluidum'. *His discovery that the pathogenic agent reproduced only in cells that were undergoing division marked the beginning of the modern science of virology.*

Familiar with Mayer's work, Ivanovsky repeated the experiment and discovered – contrary to the earlier findings – that the disease could be transmitted even after filtration through two layers of paper. He also found that infectivity was retained after passage of infected sap through Chamberland filter candles, which were used at that time both in research and commercially to produce bacteria-free water. Ivanovsky initially suspected that the disease was caused by a 'poison elaborated by bacteria present in the tobacco plant and dissolved in the filtered sap'.

Independently, the microbiologist Martinus Willem Beijerinck (1851–1931) also attempted unsuccessfully to isolate the agent of tobacco mosaic disease. He came to the conclusion that it 'is an infective disease but is not provoked by microbes'. In a now famous follow-up experiment Beijerinck placed the sap from infected tobacco leaves on the surface of a solidified agar medium, which was incubated for ten days to allow diffusion to occur. He then cleaned the surface of the medium and discarded the top 1 mm of agar. The freshly exposed agar was then removed and injected into tobacco plants, again resulting in disease. Beijerinck concluded:

A virus (infectious agent) composed of small, discrete particles will remain on the surface because it cannot diffuse into the molecular pores of the agar plates. In this situation the deeper layers of agar will not become virulent. Conversely, a water-soluble virus (infectious agent) will be able to penetrate a certain depth into the agar plates.[6]

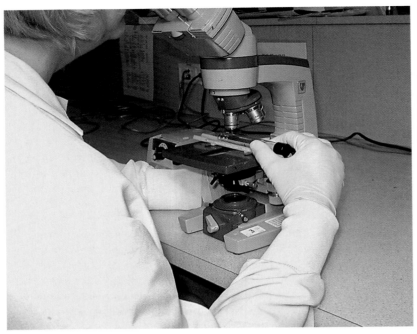

Examination of tissue culture for cytopathic effect in a roller tube, using direct bright-field microscopy. The rack fitting into the specimen holder on the microscope stage serves to prevent the tubes from rolling off.

From this experiment Beijerinck inferred that the disease agent, as it was able to diffuse, had to be 'liquid' or 'dissolved' and therefore non-cellular. He further concluded that the cause of tobacco mosaic disease was a living, fluid, infectious agent, for which he coined the term *contagium vivum fluidum*. This concept drew public criticism, as it was in direct conflict with the dictum of Rudolf Virchow (1821–1902) *'Omnis cellula e cellula'*,[7] i. e. with the widely accepted view that anything which reproduced was alive and cellular in form. In further experiments Beijerinck demonstrated that infections occurred only where plants were actively growing, and he therefore correctly concluded that the pathogenic agent reproduced only in cells that were undergoing division. Thus the 20th century opened with a new understanding of infectious diseases caused by submicroscopic viruses.

Identification of viruses as causative agents

In quick succession the viral etiology of a number of animal infections was established – African horse sickness, fowl plague, sheep pox, cattle plague and fowl pox. By the end of the first decade of the 20th century, the viruses responsible for many human infections had also been discovered – yellow fever, rabies, dengue fever, poliomyelitis and measles. By the end of the 1920s transmission of tumours by means of cell-free infiltrates had been demon-

strated, and techniques were established to propagate viruses in tissue culture. It was also at this time that Frederick William Twort (1877–1950) discovered viruses capable of infecting and breaking up (lysing) bacteria, for which the term 'bacteriophages' (literally 'bacteria eaters') was later coined by Félix d'Hérelle (1873–1949).

The phenomenon of lysogeny was described by Jules Bordet (1870–1961). Via this process viral genetic material, which is incorporated into the genome of the infected bacterium, can be transferred from one bacterium to another and transmitted from one generation to the next. The best example of lysogeny is the incorporation of a lysogenic phage into virulent strains of *Corynebacterium diphtheriae*, leading to toxin production.

Viruses: a cause of tumours

In 1908 it was discovered that cell-free filtrates could also transmit certain tumours.[8] A cell-free emulsion of liver, spleen and bone marrow was prepared from a chicken with leukemia, and following centrifugation and passage through three layers of filter paper, it was injected into normal hens. Of the five hens thus treated, two contracted leukemia. This experiment proved that cell-free filtrates can produce leukemia and, as the transmission of cells was not involved, the disease was most likely caused by a virus. Three years later Francis Peyton Rous (1879–1970), working in the laboratories of the Rockefeller Institute for Medical Research in New York, demonstrated that not only could leukemia be so transmitted, but sarcomas could also be induced in chickens by transfer of sterile, cell-free fluids.[9]

Yet at this time it was still assumed that the 'ultravisible' (submicroscopic) microbes were bacteria, although confusion existed as to why there was such difficulty in isolating them using the culture techniques of the day. A step forward was made as early as 1909 with the observation of cellular inclusions by several investigators. There were indications that these inclusions were somehow related to a virus. But were they the actual pathogens, intracellular stages in the life cycle of a protozoan, or simply material produced by cells in reaction to the virus? In 1909 Stanislaus von Prowazek (1875–1915), a Bohemian microscopist working at the Institute of Tropical Hygiene in Hamburg, dubbed these inclusions 'Chlamydozoa' (mantled animals) and proposed the theory that they were filterable microorganisms which developed intracellularly.

In 1913 the Austrian dermatologist Benjamin Lipschütz (1878–1931) also observed these intracellular round, darkly-staining bodies, which he called 'strongyloplasma' (round bodies). In a classification of diseases associated with these filterable agents, Lipschütz found that inclusions or elementary bodies were microscopically visible in 16 of 41 such conditions.[10] In 1929 the question of the viral nature of elementary bodies was finally resolved, with the discovery that the inclusion bodies of fowl pox did actually contain the virus.[11]

Viruses: a diverse group

Once the concept of virus was accepted, it became apparent through further studies that they are a heterogeneous group, differing in size and in biochemical composition.

In 1935 Wendell Meredith Stanley (1904–1971), while working as a biochemist at the Rockefeller Institute for Medical Research at its Princeton site in New Jersey, announced in a seminal paper that he had crystallised the virus of tobacco mosaic disease.[12] He found that the 'crystalline protein' was highly infectious and considered the tobacco mosaic virus to be an autocatalytic protein that required the presence of living cells for duplication. In 1946 Stanley received the Nobel Prize for Chemistry for this work. In the meantime, Stanley's observations had been amplified by experiments conducted in 1937, which showed that viruses consist mainly of nucleic acid and protein.[13]

It was not until the application of electron microscopy, however, that the structure of viruses and their differences could be elucidated. The first direct observation of a virus in electron micrographs, the tobacco mosaic virus, was published in 1939.[14] Electron microscopy opened up new doors, permitting the measurement of viral size, and ultimately provided more detailed information about virus morphology and function. The detection of empty protein coats attached to bacterial cell walls, for example, suggested that only the nucleic acid component of phagee replicated within the bacterial cell. It was also soon discovered that phage particles are liberated from lysed cells to infect intact cells.

The clinical diagnostic virology laboratory

By the mid-20th century the fundamental structure and function of viruses had become well known, and terms such as 'capsid', 'capsomere', 'envelope', 'matrix proteins', 'naked virus', 'nucleocapsid' and 'virion' were common currency within virology laboratories and the clinical practices they serve. Several laboratory techniques were developed for the isolation and/or observation of effects on tissues and cells,

Influenza epidemics throughout history

If sufficient evidence for the diagnosis of influenza is provided by the sudden appearance of a respiratory disease, persisting for several days or weeks and then as suddenly disappearing, major epidemics can be traced back to ancient times. Such an epidemic was described in 412 BC by Hippocrates (c. 460 – c. 375 BC), and several outbreaks were also recorded in the Middle Ages. More recently a major epidemic occurred in 1889, caused by a virus antigenically similar to the 'Asian' strains which originated in China. This epidemic was severe, but more importantly it marked the start of a wave of new outbreaks that struck in subsequent years. Influenza epidemics and pandemics (affecting several continents) occur as a result of changes in influenza virus coat proteins. Minor variations in surface proteins, which occur constantly, are known as antigenic drift, while major changes are termed antigenic shift (responsible for pandemics), for example, an antigenic shift in the virus caused a repeat outbreak in 1900, which was due to a 'Hong Kong'-like strain.[17] Moreover, in the epidemics of both 1889 and 1900, individuals in the age range 20–40 were more commonly affected than ever before.[18]

The catastrophic 'Spanish influenza' pandemic of 1918 was caused by a swine-like influenza virus. An estimated 20–40 million people worldwide succumbed to this infection, with an estimated 80% of the war deaths in US Army troops resulting not from enemy fire, but from influenza. Major outbreaks of influenza also occurred in 1957, 1968 and 1977.

as were more up-to-date techniques to permit the direct detection of viral antigens.

Initial cultures using embryonated eggs

It has been known for many years that viruses are dependent on living cells for reproduction. As early as 1931 Alice Miles Woodruff and Ernest William Goodpasture (1886–1960), pathologists at Vanderbilt University in Tennessee, demonstrated that the fowl pox virus could be grown on the chorioallantoic membrane of developing chick embryos.[15] Virus-containing lesions could be observed growing on the membrane after inoculation. Thus was introduced a new, inexpensive technique that was readily available for use in virology laboratories and offered the opportunity to isolate different viruses. This technique was quite useful in the decades that followed; the use of embryonated eggs waned, however, as more convenient approaches to viral diagnosis were provided by the evolution of cell cultures and other new procedures.

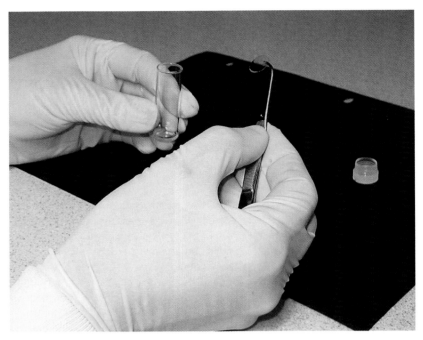

A round coverslip on which cells are grown, ready to be placed into the bottom of the shell vial tube.

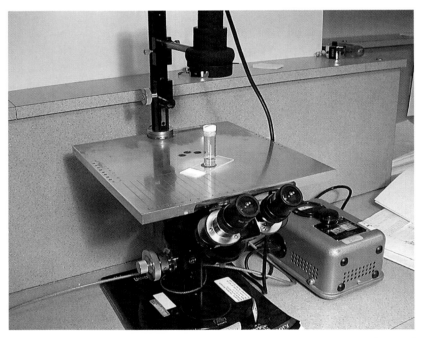

Examination for cytopathic effect: a coverslip is observed through the bottom of the shell vial tube, using inverted microscopy.

Cell cultures

In virology 'cell culture' refers to the in vitro cultivation of viruses in dissociated single cells. Such cultures are of three types: primary, diploid or semicontinuous, and continuous. Primary cell cultures are prepared directly from tissue, usually from an animal or an embryo. Monkey kidney, human amnion or chick embryo cells are most commonly used. The tissue preparations are minced, digested with prote-

olytic enzymes and seeded onto appropriate glass or plastic dishes containing antimicrobial agents.

Diploid or semicontinuous cell cultures can be passaged for more generations than primary cultures. Human embryonic lung fibroblasts are most commonly used. Continuous cell cultures are transformed cell lines that are 'immortalised' and can be passaged indefinitely. The cell lines most frequently used include Hep-2, HeLa and RK-13.

A variety of containers are used to support monolayer cultures, e. g. roller tubes containing the culture media that provide the nutrients, salts, vitamins and buffer which are essential to maintain the viability of the cell lines. After inoculation and incubation for periods that vary according to the type of virus, the tubes are examined for cytopathic effects. For this purpose, they are fixed in a specimen holder that fits on the stage of the microscope, and low-power magnification is used for observation.

The shell vial technique offers an alternative method for the rapid isolation of certain viruses, particularly cytomegalovirus (CMV), which may require as long as 21 days for detection using standard cell culture techniques. In this method, a monolayer is prepared on a round glass coverslip, which is placed in a flat-bottom vial. The inoculum is centrifuged onto the monolayer, which allows more rapid and effective inoculation of any viral particles present into the cells. Viral detection may be carried out directly through a microscope or alternatively the monolayer can be stained with fluorescein-conjugated antiserum or tested with a molecular probe. With the aid of the shell vial technique, most isolates of herpes simplex virus, for example, can be detected within 24 hours and CMV within 48 hours.

Detection of the virus is based on the observation of specific virus-induced damage to the monolayers, i. e. the cytopathic effect (CPE). Experienced microscopists can make a tentative or definitive identification of the causative virus by assessing the shape assumed by the involved cells, the characteristics of the CPE (whether it is focal or diffuse, how rapidly it appears and progresses) and which types of cell culture are affected.

Viral antigen detection

Immunological methods utilising antibodies, commonly type-specific monoclonal antibodies, may be used to detect the presence of complementary antigens. The binding of antibodies and antigen can be detected using techniques such as agglutination, hemagglutination or hemadsorption, direct and indirect fluorescence, nucleic acid probes and other recently developed molecular diagnostic procedures. The use of DNA probes, coupled with **p**olymerase **c**hain **r**eaction (PCR) amplification of specific pieces of DNA in vitro, allows the detection of viral nucleic acids in quantities so small that they may be missed by traditional viral diagnostic techniques.

Viral serology

Diagnosis of viral disease may also be accomplished using standard serological methods. Demonstrating that circulating antibodies are present in serum or plasma, or that there has been a change in antibody levels or titres, can provide valuable information concerning the status of a given viral disease.

A case in point is the appearance of antigens and antibodies after self-limited infection with hepatitis B virus. **H**epatitis **B** **s**urface **a**nti**g**en (HBsAg) appears first in the blood of an infected individual, but is cleared within a few weeks. Antibodies to HBsAg are produced, which can be detected for many weeks after elimination of the surface antigen. However, there is a short window of time even during the clinical course of disease, when the antigen may have been cleared but the antibody is not yet detectable. In cases where serological diagnosis may be necessary, an indication is provided by the detection of core antigen (HBcAg). Antibodies to core antigen (anti-HBcAg) and to surface antigen (anti-HBsAg) return to baseline over a period of several months to years. The absence of these antibodies indicates that the residuals of hepatitis B infection have subsided and that therapy has been successful.

'Unvarying disease caused by a varying virus'[16]

Fortunately certain viral diseases have been virtually eliminated, or their incidence markedly reduced, by mass vaccination programmes. Smallpox, for example, is no longer encountered, the last case having been recorded in Somalia in 1979. Poliomyelitis is now a rare disease, at least in the western world.

The fight against influenza, however, has not been as successful. Outbreaks due to 'new' influenza viruses causing the same disease are a regular occurrence. Influenza viruses are unique among the respiratory tract viruses in that they undergo significant antigenic variation. This not only leads to the periodic emergence of new strains, but makes it necessary to develop new vaccines against these new antigenic variants. This variation, known as antigenic shift, has been responsible for the major outbreaks that have occurred in the past.

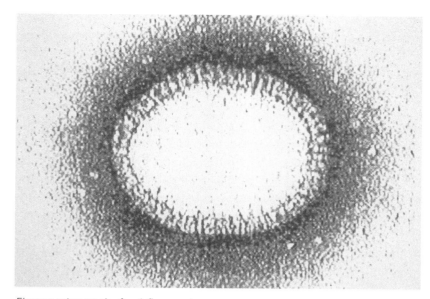

Electron micrograph of an influenza virus.

Influenza A viruses infect swine, horses, seals and a large variety of birds as well as humans. The transmission of influenza A between animal species is quite complex. Humans may contract infections from contact with infected animals, particularly from poultry, such as domestic turkeys, chickens, geese and ducks. A 1979 epidemic of avian influenza passed to pigs was the probable source of an increase in human infections, particularly in Europe. Once one or more humans are infected, the disease spreads rapidly via inhalation of respiratory droplets produced when an infected individual coughs or sneezes; through the exchange of oral secretions, as may occur during kissing; from sharing of contaminated objects, such as eating utensils; or by other routes of transmission, e.g. contaminated dust.

As future influenza pandemics in humans are inevitable, coordinated efforts will be required among scientists throughout the world to establish effective plans for influenza surveillance, vaccine development and production, chemoprophylaxis and continued research on the genetic characterisation of newly evolving pathogenic strains.

Hepatitis viruses

The term 'viral hepatitis' refers to infections of the liver caused by one of five hepatitis viruses. The cardinal clinical sign is jaundice – the orange-yellow discoloration of the skin and sclera – accompanied by increases in plasma bilirubin levels. Several outbreaks of jaundice have been reported in the past, often in military personnel (so-called campaign jaundice).[19] The initial form of hepatitis was a self-limited disease, characterised by jaundice, lassitude and low-grade fever. The incubation period following exposure is approximately two weeks, during which time an infected patient sheds virus in the feces, which is easily transmitted to others via fecal-oral mechanisms. This classic type of infection, known as hepatitis A, is also transmitted by contaminated food and water. Several outbreaks of this disease have been produced by shellfish from contaminated waters, as they are often eaten raw or steamed at temperatures below that necessary to kill the virus.[20] As **h**epatitis **A v**irus (HAV) occurs only in very low concentrations in the blood, transmission through blood exchange is rare. Although HAV can be cultured from infected feces, the diagnosis of disease is more commonly made by detecting specific **i**mmuno**g**lobulin **M** (IgM) anti-HAV antibodies in serum samples, with titres increasing rapidly during the first three to six months of illness.

A second parenterally transmitted[21] form of the disease is called hepatitis B. With a longer incubation period (ranging from 45–120 days), it has a propensity to cause lingering, chronic infections and has been associated with cancer of the liver. The existence of this form of viral hepatitis was first described in 1885[22]: an outbreak of jaundice was reported, affecting 15% of 1289 shipyard workers in Bremen, Germany, two to nine months after they had received smallpox vaccines prepared from 'human lymph'. Several other outbreaks were encountered in association with vaccinations where human serum was used as the vehicle, and also with tattoos and blood transfusions. These clinical entities were grouped together as 'homologous serum jaundice'.[23] The terms 'hepatitis A' and 'hepatitis B' were introduced in 1947 to distinguish the infectious and homologous serum forms of jaundice.[24] Initially the diagnosis of hepatitis B in an individual patient was made primarily by clinical and epidemiological studies. However, the discovery in 1965 of the Australian antigen, later called 'HBsAg',[25] led not only to a convenient method for establishing a diagnosis but to a clearer picture of viral hepatitis in general.

It was soon discovered, however, that not all patients with transfusion-related jaundice had hepatitis B. In a study of 30 distinct bouts of community-acquired hepatitis in 13 patients, only two cases were due to the hepatitis A and 12 to the hepatitis B virus, while 16 were caused by another virus, which was soon called **n**on-**A**, **n**on-**B h**epatitis (NANBH).[26] It was later discovered that NANBH could be a serious disease, possibly leading to chronic liver disease and cirrhosis, whereas the acute illness was often relatively mild compared with post-transfusion hepatitis B.

Because NANBH, subsequently known as hepatitis C, was transmitted primarily through transfusions and intravenous drug use, diagnostic tests were developed particularly for use in blood banks to screen blood donors. These assays are based on the detection of serum antibodies to various **h**epatitis **C v**irus (HCV) antigens which are universally present in patients who are chronically infected with HCV. Unfortunately the results of these tests may be negative in acute infections prior to the appearance of serum antibodies. Current assays utilise advanced technologies such as ELISA (**e**nzyme-**l**inked **im**muno**s**orbent **a**ssay) and its supplemental test RIBA (**r**ecombinant **i**mmuno**b**lot **a**ssay), or the detection of specific nucleic acid determinants with the aid of nucleic acid amplification techniques. Using a specific PCR test, it is possible to determine viral load, which is important in determining the efficacy of antiviral therapy for HCV infection.

Other hepatitis viruses have also been identified, but these will only be mentioned in passing. The **h**epatitis **d**elta **v**irus (HDV) – a defective virus transmitted only in association with HBV, which it needs for replication – has been detected in epidemics throughout the world, but particularly in Italy. When the delta virus is present, the symptoms of HBV infections are considerably more severe. The diagnosis is made by detecting serum IgM antibodies to HDV (IgM anti-HDV), **h**epatitis **d**elta **a**nti**g**en (HDAg), or HDV RNA (by PCR). Another hepatitis agent, the **h**epatitis **E v**irus (HEV), produces a hepatitis A-type infection. Specific tests for detecting serum IgM anti-HEV antibodies are commercially available in Europe, Asia and Canada. The pathology, clinical manifestations, available diagnostic procedures and molecular biology of these hepatitis viruses have recently been described in detail.[27]

Human immunodeficiency virus

In the past two decades since the **h**uman **i**mmuno**d**eficiency **v**irus (HIV) was first discovered to be the cause of **a**cquired **i**mmuno**d**eficiency **s**yndrome (AIDS), an immense volume of literature has accumulated.[28] A brief summary of the discovery of HIV is to be found in the chapter 'Blood lines' in this book.

What was the origin of HIV? Although the initial cases of AIDS were reported from California, evidence suggests that it is an old endemic disease in Africa, previously unrecognised.[29] The lack of adequate diagnostic facilities in many regions of Africa perhaps explains how this disease could have remained hidden for centuries. On the other hand, HIV has not been detected in any stored serum samples obtained from African populations prior to 1980. To cut a long story short, the currently prevailing theory of the origins of today's AIDS pandemic assumes that the agent responsible arose from mutation of the simian immunodeficiency virus (SIV), which crossed the species barrier to infect humans. The virus was subsequently introduced into the western world, where its initial spread was accelerated by the sexual practices of homosexual men. By 1996 a cumulative total of 29.4 million cases of HIV infection had been reported worldwide, of which 60% were in men, 30% in women and 10% in children. To date there is no evidence that the pandemic has abated.

The first-generation test, developed in 1985, was a viral lysate assay in which the antigen was derived from a lysate obtained from chemically digested virus particles. In the ELISA test these antigen lysates were attached to a solid phase, to which was added the sample suspected of containing HIV antibodies. In a second phase of the test antigen-antibody coupling was then detected by adding an enzyme- or fluorescent-tagged antiglobulin. For a detailed account of the principles of ELISA see the chapter entitled 'Immunoassays'. Although this first-generation test was useful for screening individuals in cases where HIV infection was clinically suspected, its specificity was low, resulting in many false-positive reactions.

Second-generation ELISA tests represented a great improvement, with both sensitivity and specificity reaching 99% in some studies.[30] It was now possible for body fluids other than blood, particularly saliva, to be tested. Other technologies, particularly latex agglutination, are less complex and have been widely used as screening tests in developing countries. Presumptive diagnoses have also been facilitated by the separation and detection of several specific proteins, such as inner core proteins, envelope proteins, and virus enzymes, encoded by *gag*, *env* and *pol* genes in the HIV genome. The core protein p24 has proved to be a particularly useful marker.

Over the past few years antigen detection tests have been developed which are particularly useful for screening blood donor samples. HIV nucleic acid assays, including PCR amplification of DNA sequences, have not only improved the sensitivity of detection but have permitted the quantitative deter-

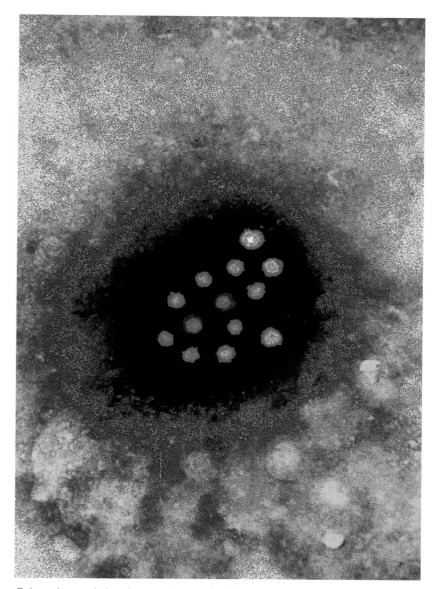

Coloured transmission electron micrograph of hepatitis A particles (red).

mination of viral load – a helpful adjunct in assessing the efficacy of therapy.

Newly emerging viruses

In 1967 African green monkeys were imported from Africa to Europe for experimental purposes. Some of these animals were infected with a filovirus (Marburg virus). Among the workers handling the monkeys or their tissues, 31 cases of hemorrhagic fever occurred, of which seven were fatal.[31] This zoonotic transmission[32] resulted from close contact between the humans and the monkeys, with substandard precautions being implemented in the handling of the animals and/or their tissues. Several filoviral hemorrhagic fever infections and contained hospital outbreaks have been reported in Africa,

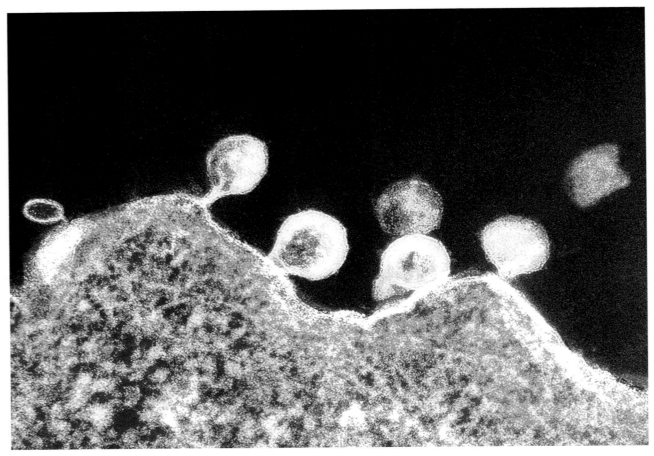

HIV particles emerging from a T cell.

caused by the Zaire and Sudan subtypes of Ebola virus. The disease spread as a result of close contact with infected patients and the use of contaminated needles and syringes. In 1989 an Ebola outbreak was also reported in the United States, affecting workers at the primate import quarantine facility in Reston, Virginia. In these cases the diagnosis was based on the detection of type-specific antibodies in the serum of infected individuals. A full account of emerging filovirus infections has recently been published.[33]

Hantaviruses

From 1951 to 1953, during the United Nations military operation in Korea, troops deployed near the Hantaan River along the disputed border between North and South Korea were subject to a febrile illness that carried a substantial mortality. An estimated 3000 cases of a flu-like illness of varying severity occurred, accompanied by hemorrhagic manifestations and kidney complications in many fatal cases. Although the causative agent was not immediately recovered, later investigations using the convalescent sera of infected patients led to the detection of viral antigens of unknown classi-

fication.[34] The viral agent was later detected in the field mouse *Apodemus agrarius*, which was identified as the natural host.

In the spring of 1993 twelve cases of an acute pulmonary disease, nine of which were fatal, were reported by the Indian Health Service to the New Mexico Department of Health. The typical illness was characterised by abrupt onset of fever, myalgia, headache and cough, followed by progressive pulmonary edema, respiratory failure and hypotension. In the fatal cases death occurred within two to ten days after the onset of symptoms. Most of the patients were healthy young adults, 35% were American Indian, and the sex distribution was even.

With the assistance of the Centers for Disease Control (CDC), a new hantavirus was identified.[35] The rodent reservoir was found to be the deer mouse *Peromyscus maniculatus*. Epidemiological data from central New Mexico indicated that from May 1992 to May 1993 the deer mouse population had increased tenfold as a result of increases in available food and cover, associated with heavy snow and rain during this period. It was found that about 80% of infected patients reported exposure to rodents in their homes.

West Nile virus

In the summer of 1999 flamingos and pheasants were mysteriously found dead at the Bronx Zoo in New York City. A sudden increase in the number of dead crows was also noted around the city. The possibility of an avian virus disease was immediately pursued. Genetic analysis of the probable agent recovered from the dead birds revealed a virus with nucleic acid sequences similar to those of the West Nile virus – a flavivirus first discovered in Africa in 1937. Since then, the virus had also been found in West Asia and the Middle East, primarily in a wide variety of birds, horses and other animals, with only occasional human cases recognised before 1999.

As the summer of 1999 turned into autumn, 83 human cases of West Nile fever had been encountered in New York City alone. Some of those infected had mild, influenza-like symptoms; others suffered from meningitis and meningoencephalitis, varying in severity and clinically resembling Western equine and St Louis encephalitis. In nine cases the infection was fatal. Much as the shadow of a solar eclipse wends its way across a continent, West Nile virus infections spread first in New York and surrounding states and then extended the following year along the eastern seaboard into many of the southeastern states. By 2002 it had reached the midwest, spreading as far west as Nebraska and Colorado. In that year alone over 3000 human cases with laboratory evidence of West Nile virus were reported to the CDC through the various state public health facilities.

How did the West Nile virus gain access to the United States? One suggestion which is perhaps fanciful but not impossible, is that an infected *Culex pipiens* mosquito travelled from an endemic area of the Middle East or Africa to New York City on a transatlantic flight. Having left the aeroplane along with the passengers, and desperate for a blood meal, it may then have found an unsuspecting crow near the airport, or made its way to the Bronx Zoo to infect the animals there. Other mosquitoes joined the fray, and the alarm bells rang when not only dead crows and flamingos were found but humans became infected as well. The West Nile virus is spread via the bite of the *Culex* mosquito, which prefers to obtain blood from birds and horses but does not object to tapping into humans in the absence of other options.

The most recent dilemma posed by the West Nile virus is associated with its isolation from patients who have received organs or blood products from infected donors. Intense research is currently under way to develop donor screening tests. Precautions are also to be taken when people encounter dead birds, which should be carefully retrieved for delivery to the nearest local health department for West Nile virus assays. Animal caretakers and ranchers have been alerted to notify health authorities of any tell-tale signs of stumbling and staggering in horses or other animals. Indeed West Nile virus has become established in the western hemisphere and seems likely to extend throughout North America and into Central and South America as well.

SARS

Capturing the headlines in recent months has been the newly discovered virus that causes the highly infectious disease known as **s**evere **a**cute **r**espiratory **s**yndrome (SARS). The SARS epidemic is the latest example of humankind's recurrent struggles with the constantly changing world of microorganisms. In only a small proportion of cases does the ongoing process of mutation produce a new microbial strain that poses a threat to the health of animals and humans. However, even with a probability of one in a million – as presumably was the case with the SARS virus – a highly infectious strain may emerge, producing turmoil worldwide.

The SARS infections that occurred in endemic areas of China were not initially recognised and reported as such. As a result it was possible for new variants of the coronavirus to spread unchecked locally and soon spill over into neighbouring regions and countries. As a result of intercontinental air travel, the causative agent spread to more than 30 countries.[36] On 29 May 2003, the WHO reported a cumulative total of 4994 SARS cases worldwide, with 750 deaths. Overall the case fatality rate is estimated to be 15%.[37]

To date the highest numbers of deaths have been recorded in China (327), Hong Kong (273), Taiwan (81) and Singapore (31). The occurrence of 141 cases (with 22 deaths) in Canada, mainly in Toronto, illustrates how new diseases can rapidly spread to distant countries. The threat of a global spread precipitates major public health and economic crises, casting a shadow not only over the cities and regions affected, but over the entire global economy. Both tourism and international trade have been severely hit by widespread hysteria and restrictions on travel.

The new agent was identified by microbiologists as belonging to the **co**ronavirus (CoV) group, so called because of the projections which give the virus a crown-like (Latin *corona*) appearance under

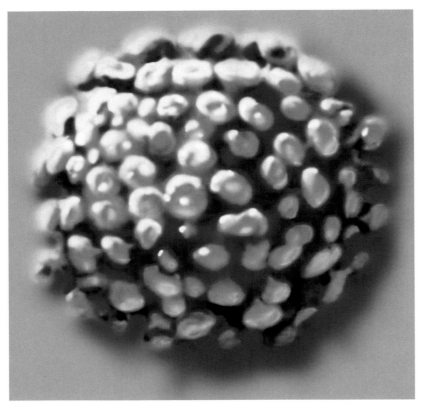

Coronaviruses, which include the causative agent of SARS, are so named because of the surface projections that give them a crown-like appearance (corona, *Latin for 'crown'*) under the microscope.

the microscope. The RNA of the SARS virus consists of 29,727 nucleotides, and the genome has already been decoded; this represents a major achievement, coming as it does only a few months after the diagnosis of the first case of SARS. The genome organisation is similar to that of other coronaviruses, e. g. influenza viruses. The sequencing studies were carried out jointly by the National Microbiology Laboratory in Winnipeg (Manitoba/Canada), the University of California at San Francisco (US), Erasmus University in Rotterdam (the Netherlands) and the Bernhard Nocht Institute in Hamburg (Germany). The sequences produced by the Canadian and US researchers are available online.

As a result of collaboration between the WHO, the CDC and numerous other bodies, scientific knowledge of SARS was acquired and disseminated in record time. The data required for disease management was efficiently collated by think-tanks established around the world: laboratory, radiological and clinical findings from SARS cases worldwide were compared, and diagnoses and treatment recommendations were collected.

Researchers and clinicians from Germany, Switzerland, various other European and Asian countries and the US, for example, formed internet-based networks for the research, diagnosis and treatment of SARS. In addition, various online databases were established to facilitate the collection and rapid analysis of new information from all over the world and to promote the universal adoption of new guidelines.

At present, laboratory diagnosis of SARS is mainly carried out at national health facilities and selected leading laboratories. SARS-CoV antibodies can currently be detected in blood with the aid of ELISA and immunofluorescence assay (IFA). Positive findings are reported if a negative antibody test on acute serum is followed by a positive antibody test on convalescent serum, or if a four-fold or greater rise in antibody titre is detected between acute and convalescent-phase sera tested in parallel. The SARS virus can also be isolated directly in cell cultures from various specimens.

In cases where SARS is clinically suspected, rapid diagnosis can be achieved with the aid of PCR testing. In this procedure RNA viruses extracted from specimens are investigated. For the confirmation of positive results strict criteria need to be adopted, especially in low-prevalence areas, where the positive predictive value may be lower. The diagnosis of a SARS infection can be confirmed in various ways: by positive findings obtained with two different clinical specimens (e. g. nasopharyngeal and stool); by tests involving the same type of specimen collected on two or more days; or with the aid of two different assays or repeat PCR testing using the original clinical sample. If appropriately-timed PCR tests are performed, the results are highly reliable; with positive findings, therefore, treatment can be initiated directly. As with other newly discovered viral infections, the number of new SARS cases recorded will doubtless decline over time.

As soon as containment measures begin to take effect and vaccines become available for at-risk population groups, the current SARS epidemic will presumably be relegated from the limelight into the medical history books. In the meantime SARS serves as a reminder that microorganisms are subject to constant change, and that outbreaks of new infectious diseases – with serious short- and long-term consequences – are to be expected at any time.

Equally, the SARS epidemic has demonstrated how a new pathogen can be identified and classified in record time through open communication among scientists in the health sector worldwide. Work on laboratory diagnostic tests is continuing, and accelerated vaccine development should soon make it possible for the disease to be effectively contained.

Factors promoting the spread of viral pathogens

Several characteristics contribute to the 'success' of particular viral pathogens, possibly leading to outbreaks of infectious disease in humans.[38]

Chief among these is the capacity of the virus to grow rapidly, which is contingent on its ability to complete its life cycle very quickly in reservoir hosts, particularly in vectors such as mosquitoes that may only be active for short periods. Together with the ability to grow rapidly, a high replication rate in tissues is necessary if the virus is to be transmitted via vectors that obtain a blood meal from the infected host. However, even viruses that do not grow quickly may still be infective if they can be readily shed. Another factor that may promote the spread of viruses is the capacity to replicate in certain key tissues that favour transmission: examples include the spread of the pox virus through infected exfoliated skin, the rabies virus through the shedding of salivary gland epithelium, and HIV through genital secretions and blood; likewise, the Ebola virus has been transmitted to humans via contact with green monkey tissues.

Extensive spreading is also facilitated if a virus can be shed even in the face of increased host immunity: this involves the capacity to evade host defenses and establish permanent infection. Models include the recrudescent shedding of herpesviruses from ganglionic neurons and the long-term survival and shedding of hepatitis B and C viruses from carriers.

Viruses transmitted by the fecal-oral route are by their nature environmentally 'tough'. These include the poliovirus, parvoviruses (e.g. causing fifth disease in children) and reoviruses, notably the rotavirus.

Viruses are metabolically inert, infectious, but not necessarily pathological. They are smaller than cells but larger than most macromolecules. They reproduce exclusively within viable cells and consist of an outer protein coat and a nucleic acid core – either DNA or RNA, but not both. Over the years, a comprehensive classification of viruses associated with human infections has evolved.

It is often important that a definitive viral diagnosis should be made. Although the diagnosis of many viral infections may be established on clinical grounds alone, less characteristic infections in immunosuppressed patients may require laboratory confirmation. Since the 1950s numerous diagnostic techniques have been developed, involving, for example, the cultivation and isolation of viruses and the observation of cytopathic effects in cell cultures. More elaborate procedures have been developed for the detection of antigen or antibodies in body fluids, as well as nucleic acid assays for direct detection of viral antigen in biological fluids. In addition, through the extensive application of immunisation programmes, many viral infections have been virtually eradicated or are rarely seen; if and when they recur, they may not be recognised, as physicians may no longer be familiar with the presenting symptoms.

A definitive diagnosis may also be important for infection control or epidemiological studies. For example, if a hospitalised patient or staff member is found to have chickenpox, measles or rubella, the hospital staff and patients in the immediate vicinity must be checked for immunity. Infection control studies of viral infections such as influenza can also be relevant not only for the local community but as part of worldwide surveillance for the emergence of possible epidemics and pandemics.

The laboratory revolution

Heinz Fiedler

Immunoassays open up new possibilities in diagnostic testing

The immune system is an adaptable and highly sophisticated set of mechanisms that serve to defend the body against microorganisms and foreign, harmful or toxic substances, as well as against malignant tissue and debris from disintegrated cells. A smoothly functioning immune system is vital to the integrity of higher organisms. The human immune system is dependent on the complex interplay of protective substances (antibodies) dissolved in the blood serum and cellular defence mechanisms interlinked in a network. Apart from the phylogenetically older non-specific defence mechanisms, scientific interest over the past century has focussed largely on specific immune reactions, in which antibody molecules are produced and specific lymphocytes (B lymphocytes, plasma cells) mature in response to stimulation by antigens (peptides or complex proteins recognised as foreign). Each B lymphocyte recognises a specific antigen and, as a plasma cell, produces a matching antibody. Once stimulated, a B lymphocyte proliferates rapidly to form a large population (clone) of identical cells. Regions on the surface of an antigen known as epitopes fit into the two binding sites (paratopes) located at the ends of a specific antibody like a key into a lock. This biochemical lock-and-key analogy is, of course, also applicable in other areas of crucial biological significance: the enzymatic catalysis of metabolic reactions, for example, in which a substance to be converted (substrate) binds to the active site of an enzyme, or signal transduction processes, in which a chemical messenger binds to a receptor molecule that receives and relays chemical signals.

The first practical application of immunological processes dates back to 1796, when Edward Jenner (1749–1823) injected fluid from a cowpox sore into

Emil Adolf [von] Behring *(1854–1917), the 'children's saviour', was himself the fifth of 12 children. He studied medicine at the Friedrich Wilhelm Institute of Military Medicine in Berlin, known as the Pépinière. This carried the obligation to remain in military service for nine years. While in the army Behring became interested in infectious diseases and the burgeoning field of bacteriology. In 1889 Robert Koch (1843–1910) appointed him to a post at the Hygienic Institute of the University of Berlin. Together with Shibasuro Kitasato (1852–1931) and his friend Erich Wernicke (1859–1928) he produced the first antisera against diphtheria and tetanus, and together with Paul Ehrlich (1854–1915) he developed the methods of analysis and measurement required for their large-scale production. Hoechst Dye Works enabled him to set up private research facilities, which he transformed in 1904 into Behring-Werk OHG (AG from 1920), using the proceeds of his Nobel Prize. Overwork and the hostility he encountered caused his health to fail, but this was followed by a period of astonishing productivity. In 1937 the toxin-antitoxin vaccine against diphtheria was widely introduced in Germany. Behring was raised to the nobility in 1901. His marriage to Else Spinola, whose mother was Jewish, produced six sons, whom Adolf Hitler declared in 1934 to be 'honorary Aryans'. The magazine* Der Stürmer *wrote at the time that Behring had 'contaminated' his own blood. The National Socialist state commemorated the 50th anniversary of the discovery of serum therapy with a spectacular celebration.*

Rosalyn S. Yalow *(b. 1921) received the Nobel Prize for Physiology or Medicine in 1977 for the development of radioimmunoassays (RIA) for peptide hormones, together with the Frenchman Roger Charles Guillemin (b. 1924) and the Pole Andrew Victor Schally (b. 1925), who had discovered the production of peptide hormones in the brain. The significance of the highly sensitive immunoassay for peptide hormone research can be gauged from the fact that Guillemin and Schally had had to collect 5 million sheep and pig hypothalami in the course of their efforts to isolate just 1 mg of pure TRH (**t**hyrotropin **r**eleasing **h**ormone), a low-molecular-weight peptide that stimulates the pituitary and ultimately the thyroid. Yalow's former teacher and co-worker, Berson, with whom she developed the RIA in the 1950s, had died in 1972. Until his early death the two scientists investigated hormonal regulation in the gastrointestinal tract and differentiated the various molecular forms of gastrin produced in the stomach. She expanded the analytical armamentarium by using a physiological binding protein (intrinsic factor) instead of an antibody in an immunoassay for vitamin B$_{12}$, a substance essential for hemoglobin synthesis. From 1970 she served as Chief of the Nuclear Medicine Service at the Bronx Veterans Administration Hospital in New York and from 1972 to 1992 as Director of the Solomon A. Berson Research Laboratory. She also taught at Mount Sinai School of Medicine and at Albert Einstein College of Medicine (Yeshiva University) in New York. Politically she actively supported the responsible use of radioisotopes in nuclear medicine. She has been particularly concerned with promoting public understanding of science, lecturing to students, for example, at Nobel laureate meetings held in Lindau, Germany.*

a healthy child. Jenner proved the success of the vaccination six weeks later by inoculating the boy with lymph obtained from a smallpox patient. His paper 'An Inquiry into the Causes and Effects of the Variolae Vaccinae' was rejected by the Royal Society, which advised Jenner not to risk the scientific reputation he had earned as an investigator of the nesting habits of the cuckoo. Despite resistance from various quarters – including many doctors, for whom smallpox patients had been a lucrative source

of income – the practice of smallpox vaccination spread swiftly. In 1805 Napoleon ordered mandatory vaccination of all soldiers. In 1881 Louis Pasteur (1822–1895) succeeded in conferring protection against anthrax and in 1885 against rabies by means of vaccination with attenuated pathogens.

About 100 years after Jenner, Emil Adolf von Behring (1854–1917), who in 1901 was awarded the first Nobel Prize for Physiology or Medicine, developed antidotes to non-fatal doses of diph-

Susumu Tonegawa (b. 1939) discovered that, in accordance with combinatorial principles, approximately 1000 combinable gene segments can give rise to about a trillion different antibodies, so that ultimately a specific antibody can always be produced to match an invading antigen. 'This diverse combination of various segments, inaccuracies in recombination (rearrangement), and the shifting permutations of different, randomly selected light and heavy chains produces an endless repertoire of different antibody arms.'[19] He thus solved the enigma of how humans, who have a limited number of genes, are able to produce such an immense diversity of antibodies. In 1959 Tonegawa began to study chemistry at the University of Kyoto, where he was introduced to the emerging discipline of molecular biology and also delved into virology. In 1969 he received a PhD from the Biology Department of the University of California at San Diego. From 1971 he spent several years at the Basel Institute for Immunology, where he began investigating antibodies. In 1981 he returned to the US to become Professor of Biology at the Center for Cancer Research, Massachusetts Institute of Technology. In addition to the Nobel Prize he has received numerous other national and international awards.

theria toxin. From animals that had survived the disease he isolated serum containing antitoxins (antibodies), which he successfully used during a diphtheria epidemic in 1892. Working with Behring, Paul Ehrlich (1854–1915), whom we have encountered on several occasions in earlier chapters, developed methods of analysis and measurement for standardising the production of antisera. In recognition of this work, he was appointed head of the Institute for Sera Testing and Serum Research.

From an erroneous hypothesis to a new approach

Many key discoveries in the field of immunology were made between 1900 and around 1960. During this period the development of immunodiagnostic tests was significantly influenced by metabolic research.

After the Second World War Oak Ridge National Laboratories, a nuclear research facility in Tennessee, began to produce radioisotopes such as ^{131}I, ^{3}H (tritium) and ^{13}C for non-military applications. At the Radioisotope Service of the Bronx Veterans Administration Hospital in New York Solomon A. Berson (1918–1972) and Rosalyn S. Yalow (b. 1921) took advantage of this opportunity to track the metabolism, distribution and excretion of radiolabelled endogenous substances in vivo. Berson and Yalow

first turned their attention to iodine in the thyroid gland, the metabolism of various proteins and the lifespan of red blood cells. In this context they tested a hypothesis proposed by I. Arthur Mirsky (1907–1974), which postulated that adult-onset diabetes is not due to reduced insulin secretion but rather to abnormally rapid breakdown of insulin by a hepatic enzyme. However, Berson and Yalow found that intravenously administered radiolabelled insulin disappeared from blood plasma more slowly in diabetic patients previously treated with exogenous insulin than in those who had never been treated with insulin.[1] Evidently, in the patients who had previously received treatment, the ^{131}I-labelled insulin bound to antibodies that had formed as an immunological reaction to exposure to animal insulin. As early as 1928 Franz Depisch (1894–1963) had identified an insulin-weakening factor in the serum of diabetic animals treated with insulin. However, using the classical methods of immunology available at the time, e. g. agglutination and precipitation, it was not possible to detect the extremely low concentrations of antigen (insulin)-antibody complexes present. The results of the experiments performed by Solomon and Yalow were at odds with the prevailing view that only high-molecular-weight proteins or cell components are able to induce the production of antibodies. The manuscript was therefore initially rejected by *Science* and *The Journal of Clinical Investigation* with a request that the term 'insulin antibodies' be expunged from the title.[2,3] But it was evident that relatively small molecules in foreign organisms are also able to stimulate the production of antibodies. Perhaps even more relevant for the development of a new generation of diagnostic tools was the fact that the high level of antigen-antibody binding strength made it possible to identify and measure minute quantities of antigen – less than a trillionth of a gram. Thus the testing of Mirsky's false hypothesis led to the development of a novel analytical approach: the competitive radioimmunoassay (RIA). In 1959, after years of experimentation, Berson and Yalow first described a competitive RIA method that could be used in practice for assaying insulin in human plasma.[4]

A new tool: radioimmunoassay

How does competitive RIA work? First radiolabelled and unlabelled antigen are mixed together with polyclonal antibodies, which at that time were obtained from immunised foreign organisms. The radiolabelled and unlabelled antigen compete for the limited amounts of antibody present. The proportion of radiolabelled antigen that binds to a given quantity of antibody decreases as the concentration of unlabelled antigen in the sample increases. The antigen-antibody complexes are then separated from any unbound antigen and the radioactivity is measured. Concentrations of unlabelled antigen are determined under identical experimental conditions by comparison with standard solutions containing a known amount of the target antigen. While it is essential that the immunological behaviour of the antigen in the unknown sample and in the standard solution should be identical, the behaviour of the labelled and unlabelled antigen may differ.

Though largely ignored initially, by the late 1960s RIA had become a standard method in the field of endocrinology. The Karolinska Institute's citation at the Nobel Prize ceremony for Rosalyn Yalow in Stockholm in 1977 referred to the development of radioimmunoassays for peptide hormones as a 'revolution in biological and medical research'.

RIA is an extremely sensitive and specific method, requiring less than 1 mL (usually 5–20 µL) of blood plasma. It therefore permits functional tests to be performed on blood samples withdrawn at short intervals. RIA created a new basis for investigating hormonally regulated processes in the body.

For the first time it was demonstrated that many hormones are released in brief bursts, a process known as pulsatile secretion. Disturbances in this mechanism can, for example, cause infertility in women. Successful treatment depends on the ability to simulate the pulsatile process. Once it became possible to produce antibodies to thyroid and steroid hormones by coupling these non-protein hormones to immunogenic proteins, the scope of RIA applications grew rapidly.

Use in the diagnosis of thyroid disorders

The thyroid is one of the most extensively studied hormone-producing glands in the human body. In 1909 the surgeon Emil Theodor Kocher (1841–1917) was awarded the Nobel Prize for 'his work on the physiology, pathology and surgery [thyroidectomy for goiter] of the thyroid'. Three years later the biochemist and Nobel laureate Edward Calvin Kendall (1886–1972) discovered that the thyroid gland has a high content of iodine and in 1915 he isolated the hormone thyroxine (T_4). The diagnosis of thyroid disorders was initially based solely on clinical observations and on unreliable measurements of basal metabolism. In 1951 the chemical determination of protein-bound iodine represented a breakthrough, but this method was also error-prone. The introduction of a rapid and specific immunoassay placed diagnostics on a firmer footing. The high specificity of the antibodies used made it possible to assay substances that differ only slightly from each other, such as the T_4 molecule, which contains four iodine atoms, and triiodothyronine (T_3), which contains three. The further development of highly sensitive and specific assays even made it possible to distinguish free (biologically active) thyroxine (FT_4), which makes up less than 0.03 % of the total thyroxine in the body, from thyroxine bound to carrier protein (99.97 %). Immunoassays also shed light on the regulatory mechanisms involved in the hypothalamic-pituitary-thyroid axis. It was discovered that increased concentrations of thyroid hormones counteract the stimulatory effects of hormones secreted by the hypothalamus and pituitary through a negative feedback mechanism. With the development of highly sensitive immunoassays for thyroid-stimulating hormone (TSH), it became possible to establish a diagnostic strategy based on testing the hypothalamic-pituitary-thyroid regulatory system. Only when TSH levels were found to be abnormal were FT_4 and FT_3 determinations subsequently performed. Without immunoassays, it would be impossible to diagnose and monitor the course of thyroid disorders.

Use in steroid hormone analysis

Similar progress was made in elucidating the chemistry and mechanism of action of steroid hormones. Four Nobel laureates were involved in the isolation and synthesis of sex hormones and adrenocortical hormones.[5] Before the advent of the immunoassay these hormones and their metabolites were determined mainly in the urine using chemical methods. It was not usually possible for hormones to be assayed individually but only as groups (e. g. all estrogens).

Variants of RIA

Competitive RIAs were soon followed by non-competitive assays, known as immunoradiometric assays (IRMAs), using an excess of antibodies coupled to a solid phase. The generally higher sensitivity of IRMAs depends essentially on the specific activity of the radiolabelled antibody, with the long-lived radioisotope ^{125}I now generally being used as the tracer. To facilitate use in practice, the reagents and tools required were introduced in kit form. As the method was refined, antibodies were replaced by other ligands.[6] For example, specific binding proteins were used in protein binding assays in place of antibodies. Binding proteins had long been known and were used, for example, in assays for vitamin B_{12}, vitamin D and cortisol. Receptors (docking sites) for peptide hormones proved difficult to isolate and purify. Although the use of receptors in immunoassays yields better results than use of antibodies (in terms of characterising the biological activity of hormones), such tests remain the preserve of research laboratories due to their prohibitive costs.

A quantum leap: monoclonal antibodies

The production of monoclonal antibodies is one of the most significant achievements in the field of immunology. At the Basel Institute for Immunology Niels Kai Jerne (1911–1994), an outstanding theoretician and director of the Institute from 1969 to 1980, encouraged Georges Jean Franz Köhler (1946–1995) to analyse the diversity of antibodies to an enzyme from the bacterium *Escherichia coli*. To pursue his investigations, Köhler collaborated from 1974 to 1976 at the Medical Research Council in Cambridge with César Milstein (1927–2002), who was cultivating cancer cells in tissue cultures and studying how genetic information is converted (translated) into antibody structure. He was able to build upon earlier work by Jerne, who had described an experimental method (plaque assay) for identifying and isolating individual immune cells. Köhler had the bold idea of fusing an 'immortal' antibody-secreting cancer cell (myeloma cell) from mice with a genetically equivalent cell producing a specific antibody. The resultant hybridoma combines the ability to divide indefinitely with the ability to produce a specific antibody. When these cells divide, the daughter cells (clones) are genetically identical to the parent cell, i. e. they are monoclonal.[7] From 1000 or 10,000 hybridoma clones produced, the most suitable one is chosen by careful testing and selection of the antibodies (by sensitivity, specificity, antigen recognition). This clone is then further cultivated in mass cultures or in ascites (fluid that accumulates in the abdominal cavity) obtained from laboratory animals. By contrast, the polyclonal antibodies formerly produced by a costly and time-consuming method in animals still had to be purified and selected, if this was at all possible, by means of chromatography or absorption, e. g. with cross-reactive antigens.

The press release on the decision to award the 1984 Nobel Prize to Jerne, Köhler and Milstein stated:

Comparison of polyclonal and monoclonal antibodies

Antibody	Antigen requirements	Properties of the antibody	
		Binding sites	Cross-reactivity
Polyclonal	Highly purified	Heterogeneous	Reduced by absorption
Monoclonal	Purity not necessarily required	Homogeneous	Eliminated by selection

Monoclonal antibodies have opened up completely new fields for theoretical and applied biomedical research and allow precise diagnosis and also treatment of disease.

Thanks to their outstanding specificity, stability and reproducibility, and the avoidance of the need for cumbersome purification steps, monoclonal antibodies have supplanted polyclonal antibodies in many immunoassays.[8]

Since monoclonal antibodies can be selected for reactions with specific parts of antigen molecules (epitopes), it became possible to develop tests for proteins and hormones that are structurally similar. Monoclonal antibodies are even used therapeutically, e. g. in the treatment of cancer.

Enzyme immunoassays

It is still not possible for radioactive isotopes to be used in all laboratories or countries. Radiological protection regulations, costly equipment and disposal procedures, and short isotope decay times must all be considered. For this reason researchers began looking for other markers (tracers) that can be easily attached to antibodies without altering their immunogenic structure.

In 1971 Eva Engvall and Peter Perlmann from Sweden and Bauke Klaas van Weemen and Antonius H. W. M. Schuurs from the Netherlands independently reported a new test principle based, like RIA, on immunological reactions between antigens and antibodies, but in which an enzyme is used instead of a radioisotope to label the antibody.[9, 10] The assay method of this type now most widely employed is ELISA (enzyme-linked immunosorbent assay), in which antigen binds to antibodies fixed to a solid phase (test tube, microtitre plate). Horseradish peroxidase, alkaline phosphatase or glucose-6-phosphate dehydrogenase are commonly used as marker enzymes. A substrate (hydrogen peroxide or phosphoric acid esters) is then added, and the amount of bound conjugate is determined by measuring enzyme activity with the aid of photometry, fluo-

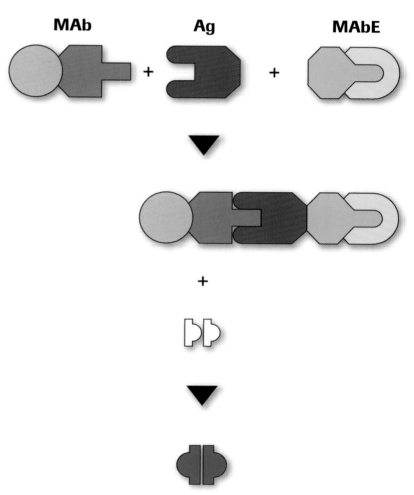

*How a sandwich enzyme immunoassay with monoclonal antibodies works: The first step is an immunological reaction. The **anti**gen (Ag) in the serum or plasma sample binds to a **m**onoclonal **antib**ody (MAb) attached to a plastic surface. A mobile **m**onoclonal **antib**ody coupled to an **e**nzyme (MAbE) binds to a different site on the antigen, forming an MAb-Ag-MAbE sandwich complex. In a second (enzymatic) reaction, the complexed enzyme reacts with a dye added to the solution. The change in colour intensity, measured photometrically, is proportional to the amount of antigen present.*

César Milstein *(1927–2002), who was born into a Russian immigrant family in Argentina, worked at the Medical Research Council Laboratory of Molecular Biology in Cambridge (UK). His interest in immunology was aroused by his friend and mentor Frederick Sanger (b. 1918), who in 1958 was awarded a Nobel Prize for elucidating the amino acid sequence of insulin. When Jean Franz Köhler (1946–1995) arrived in Cambridge in 1974, Milstein was investigating whether mixed antibodies form when two antibody-producing cancer cells (myeloma cells) are fused. Köhler was looking for cancer cells that produced antibodies with an affinity for a predetermined antigen – a search for a needle in a haystack, given the immense variety of antibodies. One night Köhler had the idea of fusing an antibody-producing myeloma cell with a normal antibody-producing cell, a lymphocyte that produced antibodies to a predetermined antigen This flew in the face of conventional wisdom, which held that antibody production would be suppressed or lost if two different cell lines were fused.[20] Nevertheless, it worked, and the problem of how to produce monoclonal antibodies had been solved.*

rometry or electrochemical sensors. One advantage of enzyme immunoassays is that existing equipment and technologies for measuring enzyme activity can be directly used and, in particular, readily integrated into laboratory automation systems.

Fluorescence and luminescence immunoassays

Substances that fluoresce or luminesce when excited can also be used as tracers, often with greater sensitivity. When ions of rare earth elements, such as europium or samarium, are incorporated into complexes, their longer decay times mean that fluorescence can be measured after the confounding influences of fluorescent organic molecules (e. g. proteins) have subsided. So-called time-resolved fluorescence immunoassays and other sophisticated test protocols have further increased sensitivity and lowered detection limits, making it possible to assay extremely low concentrations, e. g. of hormones in saliva or cytokines and growth factors in serum.

Cell-bound antigens

Researchers have also learned how to detect antigens in living cells using monoclonal antibodies labelled with fluorescent dyes. In the case of fixed cells it is also possible to label antibodies with enzymes or streptavidin-biotin. Using monoclonal antibodies, more than 140 different antigens and adhesion molecules have so far been identified on the surfaces of white blood cells (leukocytes), platelets and, in particular, lymphocytes. Each of these has been assigned a **c**luster of **d**ifferentiation (CD) antigen number. Precise analysis and differentiation of molecules on the surface of B lymphocytes, T helper cells, T suppressor cells and natural killer cells with the aid of fluorescence-labelled antibodies and flow cytometry is used for the diagnosis of numerous diseases, including AIDS, ankylosing spondylitis, septicemia, lymphomas and platelet disorders.

In microbiological and virological diagnostics many indirect antigen-antibody tests, such as the latex and hemagglutination test or the complement binding reaction, have been supplanted or supplemented by direct and indirect immunofluorescence tests, immunoassays and immunoblot tests.

Immunoassays without tracers

At the end of the 1960s methods were developed for the direct measurement of antigen-antibody complexes in solution. In immunoturbidimetry, for example, changes in the turbidity, or cloudiness, of a solution are determined photometrically as a function of time (kinetic measurement) or after a defined period.[11] In nephelometry laser light is used, the scattered light being analysed by a photodetector.[12] Both methods are suitable for rapid and reproducible determination of clotting factors, apolipoproteins and drugs, as well as proteins in serum and urine.

Heterogeneous immunoassays

With the immunoassays so far described, the antigen-antibody complexes had to be separated from unbound antigens or antibodies. In the early years established physicochemical methods were used for this purpose: precipitation with organic or inorganic agents or addition of 'anti-antibodies', electrophoresis, chromatography, absorption of free antigen and many other elaborate manual techniques. A simpler approach was provided by two-site (sandwich) assays: for large molecules with at least two different epitopes, two different antibodies can be used to 'sandwich' the antigen.[13]

There is another analytical reason for this approach. The aim in developing immunoassays is to detect a single defined molecule without the results being distorted by other members of the same protein family or by metabolites. This kind of distortion can be avoided by using two monoclonal antibodies or one monoclonal and one polyclonal antibody (labelled and unlabelled) directed against different characteristic epitopes of the molecule of interest. For example, **l**uteinising **h**ormone (LH) and **f**ollicle-**s**timulating **h**ormone (FSH) (pituitary hormones that act on the ovaries), **t**hyroid-**s**timulating **h**ormone (TSH) (also produced by the pituitary) and **h**uman **c**horionic **g**onadotropin (hCG; a hormone produced by the placenta during pregnancy) all share an identical alpha peptide chain. They differ only in a section making up a quarter of their second (beta) chain. At least one monoclonal antibody must therefore bind to this section of each hormone if the hormones are to be distinguished from each other. The same applies if one wishes to distinguish the hormones being measured from precursors, i. e. prohormones and their cleavage products, or from the products of proteolysis in the liver, kidneys or plasma. Since breakdown products often accumulate more abundantly in the blood than do the intact molecules, cross-reactivity (i. e. reaction between an antibody and an antigen other than that which elicited production of the antibody) has to be virtually eliminated. The lower the cross-reactivity, the greater the analytical specificity of the assay.

Niels Kai Jerne (1911–1994) (left) and **Georges Jean Franz Köhler** (1946–1995) (right). Jerne found his vocation relatively late in life: he began his medical studies at the age of 28. At 40 he published his dissertation on antigen-antibody reactions, taking the diphtheria toxin as an example. This was to become a standard work in the field of immunology. During his research work at the California Institute of Technology in Pasadena (1954–1955) he developed a natural-selection theory of antibody formation. From 1956 to 1962 he was a Section Head at the WHO while also teaching biophysics at Geneva University. In the Department of Microbiology at the University of Pittsburgh (1962–1966) he developed together with Albert Nordin a simple quantitative test for individual cells that produce antibodies to a specific antigen. The Jerne plaque assay became a cornerstone of cellular immunology. Jerne then served for three years as Director of the Paul Ehrlich Institute and Professor of Experimental Therapy in Frankfurt. From 1969 to 1980 he helped to develop the Basel Institute for Immunology, which was funded by Roche, into an international centre of immunological research. During this period he put forward many new hypotheses, including his network theory, according to which the immune system is held in balance by an antibody cascade, in which the various generations are able to stimulate or suppress the production of one another.[21] Köhler joined the Basel Institute in 1971 and completed his doctoral thesis there. In 1974 he moved to Cambridge, where he met Milstein. On 7 August 1975 the epoch-making hybridoma study was published, in which Köhler and Milstein described how monoclonal antibodies could be produced. Köhler is said to have repeatedly pointed out the dangers of allocating funds for basic research purely on the grounds that the findings were expected to have immediate practical applications. He is reported to have stated: 'I'm not inclined to keep refining a method until it's usable. I'm interested in the fact that the method essentially works. Then I turn to other things.'[22] From 1985 until his early death he was Director of the Max Planck Institute of Immunobiology in Freiburg.

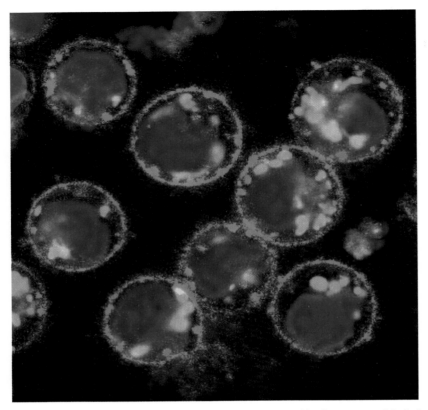

Images of live human T lymphocytes were highlighted in red by fluorescence-labelled antibodies. Mitochondria were stained green with a vital marker and cell nuclei were stained blue with a specific DNA marker.

Detection limits for immunoassays

Tracer	Minimum amount [mol/L]
^{125}I (RIA)	10^{-18}
Enzyme (photometry)	10^{-15} to 10^{-16}
Fluorescent dye	10^{-15} to 10^{-17}
Rare earth complexes and	
Time-resolved fluorescence	10^{-18} to 10^{-20}
Luminescence	10^{-18} to 10^{-20}

10^{-15}: femtomole	1 mole contains 6.0235×10^{23} molecules
10^{-18}: attomole	
10^{-21}: zeptomole	

In solid phase immunoassays an antibody is attached to a solid plastic surface (test tube, microtitre plate) by chemical or physical forces. In other respects the same test format can be used as in a sandwich assay. One universally applicable and highly stable coupling element is a system consisting of biotin (a vitamin) and avidin or streptavidin ('antivitamins'). The two elements can be bound to the antibody, the solid phase or the marker enzyme, thus permitting a large number of combinations.

Homogeneous enzyme immunoassays

The step of separating bound from unbound tracer can only be dispensed with if the signal from the tracer is altered when it binds to antibody.[14] In the EMIT method (enzyme-multiplied immunoassay technique) the activity of the enzyme bound to the antigen is reduced as a result of steric hindrance by the antibody. Addition to the sample of the antigen being measured partly neutralises the antibody and reactivates the enzyme in a proportional manner.[15] However, the detection limit is only about 10^{-9} mol/L.

Detection of pharmaceuticals and drugs of abuse

The principle underlying CEDIA (cloned enzyme donor immunoassay) is the formation of an active enzyme, beta-galactosidase, from two genetically engineered fragments – an enzyme donor, bound to the antigen, and a (larger) enzyme acceptor. In the assay the antibody, which is added in excess, first reacts with the antigen in the sample. The remaining free fraction of the antibody reacts with the antigen-bound enzyme donor. Only the part of the enzyme donor that remains free now associates with the enzyme acceptor to form a complete enzyme, whose activity is directly proportional to the concentration of antigen in the sample. CEDIA is the most sensitive type of homogeneous enzyme immunoassay (detection limit 10^{-11} mol/L), with linear 2-point calibration, and it is eminently suitable for assaying pharmaceuticals and drugs of abuse.[16]

The competitive fluorescence polarisation immunoassay is widely used for the same applications. In this method emissions of polarised fluorescence are measured after the formation of antigen-antibody complexes in a solution.[17]

Immunoassays allow near patient testing

Emergency physicians, various other specialists and also an increasing number of informed patient groups are calling for point-of-care tests that permit rapid detection of metabolic products, toxic substances and drugs of abuse. As long ago as 1986 a commercially available pregnancy test was developed in which a monoclonal antibody on a nylon membrane was used to capture hCG, a hormone produced in the placenta.[18]

In currently available tests antigen-containing sample and enzyme-labelled antigen compete for limited quantities of antibody immobilised on cellulose acetate. The unbound portion of the enzyme-labelled antigen diffuses out of the reaction zone to react with the enzyme substrate. A different strategy is adopted, for example, in an assay for cardiac troponin, used in the diagnosis of myocardial infarction. Two monoclonal antibodies are dissolved in a blood sample – a signal antibody labelled with colloidal gold and a capture antibody labelled with biotin (biotinylated). After the cellular components have been separated out, the two antibodies form sandwich complexes with any troponin T present and are visualised in a reading area as a red (gold) line. Excess antibodies are bound at a second line, which serves as a control, indicating that the test has been correctly performed.

Other point-of-care tests are designed to determine increased albumin excretion in the urine (e. g. for early detection of diabetic nephropathy), myoglobin (diagnosis of myocardial infarction) and D-dimer (detection of thrombosis and fibrinolysis). Still others are used to test for antibodies to viruses, drugs and narcotics.

The development of specific immunoassays is expected to progress rapidly, thus helping to improve the care of patients with acute and chronic heart disease, pulmonary embolism, clotting disorders and poisoning, both in emergency settings and in doctors' offices.

Dieter J. Vonderschmitt, Rita Roth,
Leo Schwerzmann and Thomas Caratsch

The rise of automation

The importance of laboratory medicine, and especially clinical chemistry, for diagnosing disease and assessing treatment grew enormously after the Second World War. The period from 1950 to 1970 witnessed an exponential expansion in the number and scope of tests. Only after 1970 did some degree of consolidation creep into view, thanks on the one hand to the enormous strides made in the understanding of metabolism, and on the other to the nascent automation which largely fulfilled clinicians' wishes for faster, cheaper and better analytics. However, automation does not merely rationalise tasks in the clinical laboratory. It also outperforms manual methods in every way that matters: primarily as regards precision and accuracy, but also as regards error rates.

Mechanisation, automation, robotics

Even today there is nothing straightforward about quantifying a chemical compound in blood. An untreated blood sample cannot as a rule be analysed directly. It contains components that have to be removed to give plasma or serum. Neither of these viscous liquids can be equated with a simple aqueous solution, however, and as a result even sampling them already poses specific challenges. For this reason, early quantitative analyses were characterised by relatively large volumes of sample material, in the millilitre range, and by laborious sample preparation, precipitation reactions, weighings and titrations. Simplification only came with the introduction of the first photometers and colour reactions.

A typical photometric analysis comprised the following sequence of steps: centrifuging the sample tube, decanting the plasma or serum, pipetting an exact sample volume, adding an exactly measured volume of precipitant to remove the protein (deproteinisation), centrifugation, re-pipetting an exact volume, adding an accurate volume of reagent, mixing and incubating, decanting into a measuring cuvette, reading the absorbance from the (analogue) display, and calculating or plotting the concentration. Naturally the method had to be calibrated using an appropriate standard solution.

For those confronted with the task of measuring a dozen or more samples in this way – and at this stage we are only talking about measuring a single parameter per sample – mechanisation could only be a godsend. By mechanisation[1,2] we mean the implementation of some or all of these analytical steps by means of motor-driven mechanical modules. Early mechanisation could only manage a few steps, from pipetting the deproteinised sample to the analogue recording of the results, and even then only for a single parameter per instrument. Early 1960 laboratories were therefore replete with pipetting aids and dedicated analysers, e.g. for blood glucose, protein or creatinine.

The key difference between mere mechanisation and automation is the ability to recognise and act upon events requiring an appropriate response from the mechanical system, such as 'No sample present' – 'Stop sample pipetting and activate acoustic alert'. This presupposes the use of sensors, control elements and actuators.

Robots are freely programmable automated instruments.[3] A typical pipetting robot, for example, can be programmed for any kind of primary vessel and can pipette reagent and sample into any kind of secondary vessel, e.g. microtitre plates. Other robots are programmed to load centrifuges or prepare samples.[4] There are seamless borders between mechanisation, automation and robotics.

Functional air bubbles

Leonard Tucker Skeggs (1918–2002) described the first usable 'automaton' in a paper published in 1957.[5] The resulting 'AutoAnalyzers' from Technicon enjoyed great success and remained the most widely used analysers into the 1980s. Skeggs' stroke of genius was to make no attempt to mimic the modus operandi of a laboratory technician in a mechanical system. Instead, all analytical steps took place in a stream of liquid in which sample, dilution buffer and reagents were mixed, each component being propelled through tubing by a peristaltic proportioning pump before entering a mixing coil. However, this system only worked if the nonlaminar stream of liquid was segmented by air bubbles to restrict sample dispersion over a relatively long distance. Varying diameters of Tygon tubing determined the volumes of the various components. The number of possible reagents and type of different operations were practically unlimited. Auto-Analyzers owed their worldwide success not least to the resourcefulness of a whole army of creative people who found hundreds of new applications and processes that could be handled by these simple instruments. Deproteinisation, for example, could be readily accomplished in the flow system by continuous dialysis. The applications eventually ranged from extractions and back-extractions to enzyme-coated coils which readily coped with enzymatic substrate assays.[6] As for the air bubbles, these were removed just before they reached the photometric flow-through cell.

A new kind of analytics

Skeggs broke completely new ground and conventional analysts vented their scepticism. How could peristaltic pumps confer accuracy and precision? Critical and sarcastic comments soured the literature.[7] But closer dispassionate examination revealed that while a peristaltic pump could not convey an exactly metered volume per unit time, the amount conveyed remained remarkably constant, thus ensuring precision. The system did not deliver absolute measurements, and results were based on the concentrations of a standard solution. This was nothing new in analytics. Other instruments had to be calibrated with standard solutions too. Discussion revolved mainly around the measurement of enzyme activities, which in the AutoAnalyzer depended on the use of standard enzyme solutions for calibration. Purists insisted that a measurement based on the known molar absorbance of substrates or cosubstrates had to be possible.[8] What finally made the AutoAnalyzer the most popular instrument of its day was the sheer range of its advantages over other instruments.[9,10] The first was that it had only two mechanical moving parts, the sampler and the peristaltic pump. The mechanics of each were as simple as they were sound. All other movement was impressively accomplished by flow and the dynamics of the air-segmented solutions. The second advantage was that the solution moved only in one direction. All modern systems, without exception, use pipettors to aspirate the sample and then dispense it into the reaction vessel. If a clot covers the pipette opening during the aspiration process, the resulting obstruction prevents the correct volume from reaching the reaction vessel. Modern analysers

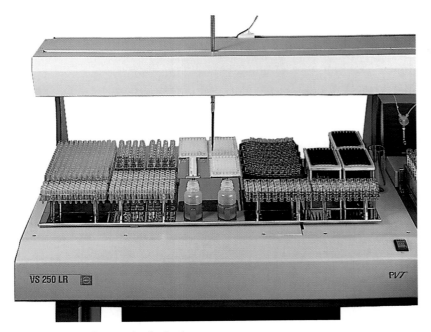

Pipetting system for sample distribution.

have been carefully designed to detect such clots and are thus considerably more reliable, although errors can still occur. In a flow system, by contrast, partial or total obstruction is clearly identifiable from the signals received, enabling the error to be corrected.

The main disadvantage of the AutoAnalyzer was its high reagent consumption. Even with the miniaturisation incorporated into the newer AutoAnalyzer systems, reagent consumption remained higher than with so-called discrete systems.

Profiles

Analyses of the type just described initially involved measuring a single parameter. However the system proved readily expandable. The stream of segmented and buffer-diluted sample could be easily divided. It then became possible to analyse four, six or even more parameters in the divided sample stream. In the early days this required a multichannel recorder to plot the resulting curves. Only the advent of the first simple and affordable processors in the 1970s enabled the signals to be digitised and evaluated accordingly. Co-determination of four or six parameters made perfect sense. In suspected liver disease, for example, clinicians always requested the same test battery: bilirubin, alkaline phosphatase and the two transaminases. This resulted in the various profiles, or multitest panels, which are still offered by most laboratories today.

SMAC

The last model to use air segmentation technology for higher throughputs was the **s**equential **m**ultiple **a**nalyser with **c**omputer, or SMAC, which could measure 20 parameters simultaneously in a single half-millilitre sample. Its two sample per minute throughput, delivering over 2000 results per hour, was revolutionary for its time. It was the first instrument to replace flame photometry, the traditional method of measuring sodium and potassium, with ion-selective electrodes, which were ideally suited to a flow system. Nevertheless, this type of analytics provoked heated debate[11] and eventually had to be abandoned. The problem was that 20 results were obtained from each sample, i.e. for each patient, whether they were wanted or not. Even if the clinician only needed the glucose, he still received 20 results. And if one of the 19 unrequested results was abnormal, this could lead to unnecessary investigations. For example, a low serum iron does not in itself signify iron deficiency, since there are various conditions in which it does not require medical intervention. One solution would have been – and was – to convey the requested result and simply suppress the rest. However, this was open to the ethical objection that the patient was paying – directly or indirectly – for all the tests and therefore had a right to the results, particularly if they were grossly abnormal and could have revealed unsuspected disease. On the other hand, there was also a potential for abuse if only the abnormal results were supplied in addition to those requested, since physicians would then only have had to order the cheapest test to be sure of receiving all the abnormal results. Moreover, laboratories would always have been obliged to perform all tests, including, for example, in cases where one analysis channel was not working but all the others were delivering valid results. The fact that SMACs continued to consume huge volumes of reagent solution, combined with the appearance of the first functional selective analysers, forced the demise of air-segmented AutoAnalyzer systems in the early 1980s.

Profile, batch and selective analysers

Although certain profiles continue to make medical sense today, it is important to realise that those just described were the result of a specific technology, particularly if they included a large number of parameters. One approach to eliminating these drawbacks was the batch analyser, introduced back in the 1960s,[12] which determined a single parameter in a batch of samples virtually simultaneously, as in manual analysis. Before performing a test it was therefore necessary to collect a batch of samples requiring the test in question. The approach is sometimes described as test-oriented analytics. In contrast, selective analysers process one sample after another – the way samples are usually received in the hospital setting – regardless of how many parameters are to be determined.[13] Selective analysers are sample-oriented, as too are profile analysers. Laboratories now use selective analysers almost exclusively, unless special conditions prevail, such as the requirement for enzymatic and serological determinations at blood donation centres.

Batch analysers

There was an economic case for batch analysis only if batches occurred normally, i. e. if enough samples accumulated that required a particular test. In practice this meant selecting from the sample pool those which, for example, needed to be tested for glucose. An aliquot[14] then had to be pipetted from each of these samples and delivered to the analyser. After processing the batch, the instrument could then generally proceed to a different test on a new batch. Before the advent of laboratory informatics, the results had to be collected at the end and matched with the samples. The handling of samples, aliquots and results required great discipline; it was not easy, and mix-ups were frequent.

The first centrifugal analysers

In 1969 the first centrifugal analyser was presented in a scientific publication.[15] It consisted of a rotor with three concentric rings of wells to hold the sample and reagents. Once the rotor was inserted in a centrifuge and spun, centrifugal force drove the reagents outwards from the wells, flushing the sample into the cuvette at the outer edge, where a light beam parallel to the rotor axis measured the absorbance (the light absorbed by the sample) during rotation. Various commercial platforms applying this principle were developed. They could only analyse one parameter per run, with the great disadvantage that if, for example, glucose was required from a sample that arrived just after the start of the run, it had to wait until the next run.

Batch-selective centrifugal analysers

The Cobas series of centrifugal analysers developed by Tegimenta AG – now Roche Instrument Center – were selective instruments, but still suffered from the drawback that no further samples could be added during the run. They nevertheless incorporated

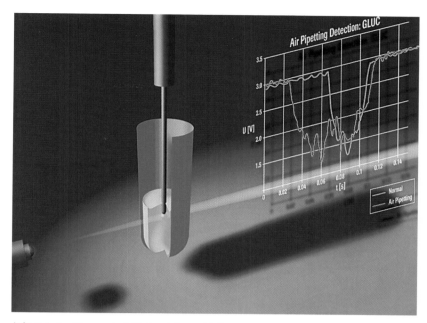

Infrared pipetting control (Cobas Integra 800).

significant advances over first-generation centrifugal analysers.[16] For example, the light beam was no longer transmitted in parallel to the rotor axis, but radially, so that it traversed the measuring cell longitudinally.[17] This offset inaccuracies in reagent dosing and made precision dependent solely on exact sample dosing and a constant cuvette cross section. Although the high-quality plastic rotors in the Cobas Fara were designed for single use, they were washed and reused by some laboratories. The analyser's versatility was unsurpassed for its time. Not only could it measure absorbance, but it also offered fluorometry, fluorescence polarisation, nephelometry and turbidimetry, opening the door to a wide range of immunoassays. In addition to these optical measurements, the system included a module for determining sodium and potassium by means of ion-selective electrodes. Centrifugal analysers were particularly valuable for measuring enzyme kinetics, since the start of the reaction was clearly defined by the start of centrifugation and the kinetic profile could be monitored at high resolution thanks to the very short time intervals from measurement to measurement. The number of applications was exceptionally large,[18] and to this day there are many users who regret that the instrument is no longer in production. Further advantages were its very low reagent consumption per measurement, less than half a millilitre (500 microlitres), and small sample volume, 5–50 microlitres. On the other hand, why it should be necessary to spin reaction mixtures in order to analyse them remained a legitimate question.

Centrifugation remains a batch process

In clinical chemistry there are only a few tests which do not require blood cell removal. Ion activity measurements in whole blood using ion-selective electrodes are feasible for a few electrolytes, but unsuitable for large series and automation. As a rule all blood samples must therefore be centrifuged. This means loading the centrifuge by hand or with a robot, centrifuging (which generally takes about 10 minutes), then unloading the centrifuge, manually or by robot. Since the entire process takes about 15–20 minutes, it is sensible to wait until a minimum number of samples have accumulated before loading the centrifuge. Once the centrifuge has started, further samples must wait until the process is completed. Centrifugation is thus an unavoidable batch process. As such, it prevents the samples that are continuously arriving at a clinical laboratory from being continuously processed. This impediment to continuous fully automated analytics represents one of the last unsolved problems in total laboratory automation (TLA).

Selective analysers

Selective analysers are sample-oriented. They are called selective because on each sample, unlike with profiles, they perform only those tests that the hospital or physician has requested. Except for emergency or 'stat' analyses, samples are processed according to the FIFO principle (**f**irst **i**n, **f**irst **o**ut), meaning that the first results come from the first sample to be processed. The methodology of the selective continuous analysers had far-reaching repercussions on laboratory organisation, as will be clear if we take a brief look back at the traditional clinical laboratory. After being received by pneumatic tube, messenger, post, or other transport system, the samples were registered and the requested tests keyed in, assuming they were not already available electronically. The samples were then arranged by order of arrival and centrifuged before proceeding to the sorting and aliquoting station, where the serum or plasma was pipetted for each test, profile or analyser into daughter tubes that also had to be labelled. This work was complex and demanded great concentration. For a long time it was the major laboratory bottleneck and a dangerous source of error. However, because the modern selective analyser provides such a wide range of tests, in 90 % of cases it can meet every request directly from the pri-

mary tube. Modern analysers are therefore not only analysers, but have also largely taken over the function of sorting station. As a result the laboratory bottleneck has now shifted away from the sorting station to centrifugation.

There is no doubt that modern selective analysers have largely displaced the other methods. But they also have some definite disadvantages. The systems have become highly complex, contain a plethora of electronic components and limit user freedom. Any laboratory technician with a little talent for DIY was able to repair an AutoAnalyzer. With today's systems, repairs and troubleshooting remain the province of contract service engineers who provide continuous 'intensive care' facilitated by online communication via modem and telephone line. The contractor has to keep hundreds of spare parts and printed circuits in stock to guarantee a rapid response when needed. Laboratory technicians must undergo lengthy and demanding training if they are to master the instrument and keep it properly maintained. It is not at all a matter of inserting a sample and pressing a few buttons.

Clockwork precision

One of the first large selective analysers was produced in a watch factory in close collaboration with a university institute. The **G**reiner **S**elective **A**nalyzer (GSA) was largely inspired and designed by Roland Richterich (1927–1973), professor of clinical chemistry at the University of Berne.[19] The instrument was the epitome of Swiss precision, containing dozens of synchronous motorised pipettors. The reaction vessels travelled on a long chain through a temperature-controlled water bath and were vibrated, while pipetting stations along the chain added various reagents. In its mode of operation the analyser was to a large extent the robotic reincarnation of a laboratory technician, matching each manual step. The GSA was the prototype of an 'open' analyser[20] in that it gave users a free choice of reagents and the ability to adapt and develop assays which they could then transfer to the analyser. Its main drawbacks were its size and multiplicity of mechanical parts.

Creation of the measuring cell during the analysis

In contrast to the GSA, DuPont's **A**utomatic **C**linical **A**nalyzer (ACA) was an absolutely 'closed' system. It used a disposable plastic packet for each test. For each sample submitted for analysis, the instrument was loaded with a sample cassette and one test cas-

Blood cells have to be removed by centrifugation for virtually all clinical chemistry tests.

sette per requested test. The remainder of the analysis up to and including the result was fully automatic, without further operator intervention. Inside the analyser, the sample was applied to the individual test cassettes and mixed with the reagents in the cassette's plastic packet. An interesting detail was the chromatographic pretreatment incorporated in some of the tests: these test packets were fitted with small chromatography columns that removed substances interfering with the test. When the reaction or incubation was complete, the plastic packet was compression-moulded into a photometric cuvette. The manufacturer offered an extensive range of analytical parameters, including chemistry, enzymes, immunology, electrolytes, drugs, hormones, toxicology, coagulation, and special tests such as ammonia and lactate.

The early 1980s saw the appearance of other closed systems. In 1978 Kodak introduced its Ektachem system[21] at the International Congress of Clinical Chemistry in Mexico City. Clinical chemists swarmed into the auditorium eager to find out about the new system. Dire predictions about the impending demise of clinical chemistry

as a speciality followed but went unheeded. The system could perform about 40 different tests with a throughput of 540 analyses per hour. It used a dry chemistry technique[22,23] in which the various reagents were incorporated into thin films where they reacted with the sample components to form coloured products. The test packs, which resembled Kodak photographic slides, included sodium and potassium measuring kits that used miniaturised ion-selective disposable electrodes.

In the late 1980s the Abbott Vision analyser represented an attempt to work with unprocessed whole blood.[24] The plastic cassettes were fixed to a rotor and rotated during centrifugation to decant off a defined amount of plasma and mix it with the reagents.

The closed systems were remarkably easy to use and often achieved great precision and accuracy. However, their advantages were offset by the user's total dependence on the manufacturer. Only the methods provided by the manufacturer could ever be used because the systems brooked no alternatives. This could be a hindrance, especially when new developments occurred. If a new test appeared in

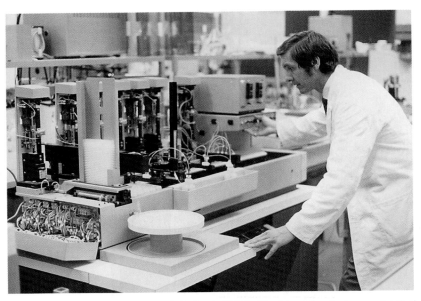

An analyser driven by compressed air (early 1970s). The idea of replacing mechanical drive systems with pneumatic ones was intriguing, but failed to stand the test of time.

the literature or on the market, the user had to rely on the company to implement it in their system.

Pneumatics challenges mechanics

The first analyser which Hitachi exported to Europe puffed in the laboratory almost like an old-fashioned steam engine. The reason for its distinctive behaviour was that it used compressed air to drive its components, especially the pipettors. However, although an interesting innovation, the method failed to displace conventional parts and motors: the very next generation was again exclusively mechanically driven. The Japanese analysers did not differ greatly in design from the prototypical selective analyser, the GSA. They used one or more multi-way valves in place of the multiple synchronous motors to direct the many reagents from their containers to the sample tubes. The long chain of reaction vessels was replaced by a large reaction plate, and the reagent vessels doubled as cuvettes. Mixing was performed by small stirrers. Pipetting needles, stirrers and cuvettes were washed and dried in an instrument cycle. All this was again strongly reminiscent of the steps in manual analytics. Hitachi scaled up their analysers to modular systems which could be assembled into an entire analysis line.[25]

The Mira miracle

The Cobas Mira developed by Tegimenta was likewise based on the technology just described. Outwardly there was nothing to suggest that the instrument was particularly sophisticated, a view which

the manufacturers evidently shared, given the somewhat modest production run they originally scheduled. However, the Cobas Mira soon became the best-selling clinical chemistry analyser. Its design was simple and straightforward, and its test range met the needs of most small and medium-sized laboratories.

Miniaturisation

Meanwhile there was enormous progress in miniaturisation, virtually paralleling that in electronics. Obviously, all analysers were quick to incorporate printed circuits and microprocessors. But the sample and reagent processing hardware was seriously miniaturised too. New analysers work with sample volumes of 1–10 microlitres, creating their own specific requirements for sampling. If the pipetting needle dips too far into the sample, there is a risk that more sample will cling to the outside of the needle than is aspirated into the bore. For this reason the needles in all modern analysers only just pierce the sample surface. The risk here is that the concentration of the aspirated sample may be increased due to surface evaporation and poor mixing of the surface material with the remainder of the highly viscous sample. The sample needle or sampling device must also be equipped with a sensitive surface detection sensor. The danger then is that insufficient or no sample is aspirated, for example if the needle touches the inner wall of small sample tubes that are not fully vertical.

Working with small sample volumes has obvious patient benefits, especially in pediatrics. It naturally also has the advantage of correspondingly low reagent consumption; in addition, every process – whether mixing, heating, thermostating, or equilibrating a heterogeneous reaction – goes faster than with large volumes. This dramatically shortens analyser cycle times, which in turn increases sample throughput and shrinks the time from sampling to result. Most analysers deliver results in 5–10 minutes, except for immunoassays which often take considerably longer because an equilibrium has to be reached. However, this can be countered by reaction rate analysis, which also has the advantage of detecting excess antibody or antigen (hook effect). Thus the Dade Stratus, a solid-phase analyser incorporating radial chromatography, delivers immunoassay results within one minute.

The automation of immunology

There has been a colossal expansion in immunodiagnostic tests in the last 20 years, paralleled by

Today's laboratory staff cope with a range of complex tasks that go far beyond just inserting samples and pressing buttons.

the number of instruments designed to run them.[26] The primary divide is between heterogeneous and homogeneous systems, the latter having proved far more amenable to automation.[27] Indeed these could be automated in practically the same way as ordinary chemical reactions, or could be run directly on standard analysers.

A patronised physicist

Walter Dandliker was a somewhat singular physicist in the biochemistry department of Scripps Clinic and Research Foundation in La Jolla, California, an object of indulgence for the immunologists drawn to this 1960s Mecca, where they concentrated on more important matters such as unravelling the complement system. In a darkroom in his laboratory, standing on a heavy steel plate that rested on four tennis balls, was a home-made spectrofluorometer which Dandliker used to lay the foundations of a new analytical system for haptens, low-molecular-weight antigens, e.g. drugs or hormones, which only initiate an antibody response if complexed to a carrier.

Fluorescence polarisation: a methodological breakthrough

It was not until many years after Dandliker published his method that Abbott incorporated it in one of the first automated analysers suitable for routine use. The principle is fascinating. If surface-adsorbed fluorescent molecules are excited with polarised light, the light which they emit is similarly polarised.[28, 29] However, small fluorescent molecules moving freely in solution can take up any position during the lifetime of the excited state, and the light which they emit is no longer polarised. This also applies to haptens complexed to a fluorescent molecule. However, as soon as such haptens react with a large antibody, the inertia of the large molecule limits their movement, and fluorescence polarisation is partially preserved. Thus by measuring fluorescence polarisation the original concentration of haptens in homogeneous solution can be determined.

A large number of instruments went on the market, making it difficult in the early 1980s to decide on the right automated or semi-automated analyser.

The Cobas Mira, launched in 1984, was one of the best-selling analysers on the market. Its test menu was tailored to the needs of the small and medium-sized laboratory.

Selective electrodes

Selective electrodes were nothing new, the pH electrode – in ubiquitous use throughout the natural sciences – being probably the best-known example. The selective glass membrane develops a potential with respect to the test solution which depends on the solution's proton activity. The opposite side of the membrane develops a potential that remains constant and depends on the pH of the buffer solution inside the electrode. The small potential difference between the inner and outer surfaces can be measured and is a linear function of pH. Other membrane electrodes[30] work on the same principle.

Concentrations and activities

Ion-selective electrodes are used to measure ion activities. These differ from the ion concentrations, but are the critical variables in biosystems.[31, 32] Ions and uncharged molecules and proteins interact; oppositely charged ions attract each other and form short-lived ion pairs, whereas ions of like charge repel each other. These effects only disappear in very dilute solutions but are marked in blood plasma. Cell membranes – like the membranes of ion-selective electrodes – only respond to activities, in other words, to the bioactive ionised fraction, which is always smaller than the concentration. It is, however, possible to calculate or estimate the concentration from the activity. The alkali ions Na^+ and K^+ are the ions with the highest concentration and activity in plasma. There is in practice no chemical reaction that could be used for simple and reliable quantification of these ions. The use of selective electrodes is therefore a very important advance in clinical chemistry analysis. The electrodes are also ideally suited to measurement in flow-through systems.

Measurement in whole blood

Ion-selective electrodes can also be used to measure ion activities directly in whole blood. As no chemical reactions are involved, but solely physical measurements, the red blood cells are not harmed, nor do they interfere with the measurement process. All that matters is to prevent the blood from clotting (e.g. with lithium heparin). The measurements are relatively simple, and the aspiration and subsequent washing process can be automated, so that the tests can be performed beside or near the patient. As potassium determination is often a 'stat' analysis, such instruments are particularly useful during surgery or in intensive care units.

Nevertheless, ion-selective electrodes also have their problems. Surface equilibria are reached relatively slowly, and the first electrodes were correspondingly sluggish in their response. Sensors that come into contact with the sample suffer from numerous interactions that do not occur on exposure to photons in the photometer beam. Proteins and other substances such as drugs may deposit on the membrane surface, affecting the potential, and in particular the time to equilibration. It took relatively long before instrument developers learnt to overcome these difficulties and produce usable electrodes.

A special case among ion-selective electrodes is the calcium electrode, used to determine calcium activity or 'free' calcium. Calcium is about 50% bound to proteins and chelators. Binding is strongly dependent on pH. When the sample tube is opened, carbon dioxide escapes because its pressure in venous blood is higher than in ambient air. The blood pH increases, and calcium protein binding with it, resulting in falsely low measurements of alcium activity. 'Free' calcium therefore has to be measured immediately after opening the sample tube, which in practice precludes automation. On the other hand, 'free' calcium is a crucial parameter, more important than total calcium, and can only be determined with ion-selective electrodes.[33]

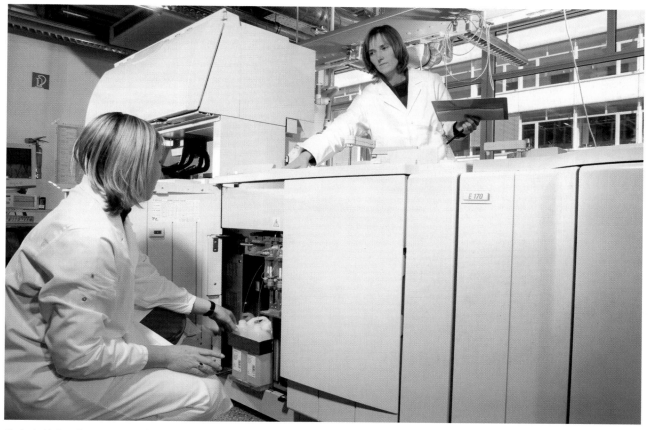

Today's high-volume systems from Hitachi are supplied as modules that can be configured into a variety of complete laboratory solutions.

The multipurpose analyser

Aliquoting – the preparation of identical daughter tubes from a centrifuged primary – is problematic. If done by hand, it requires intense concentration. If automated, then high-use equipment is required which is often not online, i. e. the aliquots have to be introduced into the analysers by hand. It is thus an advantage if one and the same analyser can process as many parameters as possible. However, such an analyser would require a maximum of methods on board. The Cobas Integra was one of the first analysers to combine chemical, immunological and ion selective methods. It has proved extremely robust and efficient. The systems of the Cobas Integra family now offer a menu of over 150 tests. Their resulting complexity makes them closed analysers in practice, meaning that users have very little freedom to adapt their own methods to them, and can only do so in collaboration with the manufacturer. However, this is not impossible. Also, the Cobas Integra systems are not alone in this regard: automated immunology almost always implies a closed system on quality assurance grounds.

The optimisation challenge

Three factors inform the planning and automating of laboratory work: reliability, speed and cost-effectiveness, i. e. the same factors that apply to industrial production generally. Since the most reliable method is usually not the fastest, the fastest not the most cost-effective, and the most cost-effective not the most reliable, optimisation is a constant challenge.[34] The medical laboratory is a service facility with almost all the features of a regular production unit. For this reason the goal in routine analytics is to achieve the highest possible level of automation.

Enter the robots

The early 1990s saw increasing calls – mainly from the United States – for consolidation, meaning the concentration, ideally, of all analytical tasks in a single instrument system. In fact, the target has become even more ambitious. Sample tubes should arrive in the laboratory pre-barcoded; scanning the barcode then downloads the electronic test request to the laboratory information system that also controls the analyser array. Ideally, after arrival and

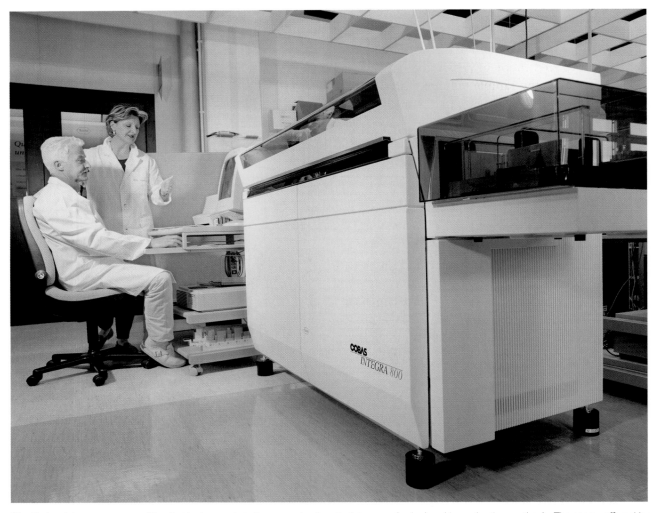

The Cobas Integra was one of the first instruments to incorporate chemical, immunological and ion selective methods. The menu offered by systems of the Cobas Integra family now exceeds 150 tests.

inspection, the samples are arranged in racks: their barcodes are read, they are loaded into centrifuges, decapped, and loaded into the analyser(s) – all by robot. The robot prioritises 'stat' samples, sorts out the samples that do not require centrifugation, and takes aliquots from those requiring tests outside the analyser's competence. Once inside the analyser, the samples are dispatched directly to the correct module.

Heavy artillery

The first such systems were heavy, inflexible and expensive. They were really only feasible where laboratories were built around the system, i.e. in new buildings, mainly in Asia: Japan, Taiwan, South Korea and Hong Kong. But they were soon followed by neater second-generation systems currently offered by at least four companies. The new systems are modular in design and can generally be assembled in any desired combination, depending on the range of analyses, sample throughput and available space (despite being more compact, and more flexible to assemble, today's systems still need space).

A new era thus dawned in analytics, although we can already foresee its limitations. The flexibility of these systems in design and combination is offset by their inflexibility as to quality control. For product liability reasons, quality control is integrated into the systems, leaving users little freedom to make their own decisions and exercise individual responsibility.

Dry chemistry

In classic analytics, exactly measured volumes of reagent solutions are added to a certain amount of sample. This dilutes the particles to be determined in the sample, as well as the products deriving from the analyte. After measurement, back-calculation is needed to derive the original concentration. This does not apply with support-bound reagents. Since these are in solid form, their volume is negligible compared to the sample volume.[35,36] The solid reagents are after all dissolved in the sample. So because the concentration of analytes in the sample does not change, the sample volume is irrelevant. All that matters is that the reagents dissolved in the sample volume are still present in excess. In practice, however, it has been found that despite this theoretical independence of volume, more accurate results are obtained if the sample volume is exactly measured.

Near-patient testing (point-of-care testing)

Centralised laboratory testing is reliable and economical, but often suffers from being too slow, meaning that too much time elapses between blood collection and receipt of the result. Since much of this time is spent in transport to the laboratory, rather than in the laboratory itself, near-patient or **point-of-care t**esting (POCT) – i. e. at the bedside – has great advantages under certain circumstances,[37] in particular where vital and rapidly changing parameters are concerned. There is of course a danger that the number of such instruments will increase, leading to the re-emergence of small peripheral laboratories that are less reliable and economical than their central counterpart. This can now be avoided by reducing the transport time to, and analysis times in, the central laboratory. Comparison shows that the longer turnaround time in central laboratories is chiefly due to centrifugation. POCT is a whole-blood technique, making centrifugation unnecessary.

Summary

Space does not allow us to do justice to the full complexity and scope of automation in laboratory medicine. The examples described represent a small fraction of the instruments that have marked its evolution. We have not even mentioned, for example, the hematology analysers offering automated differential blood cell counts.

The time from the development of a method to its automation has shrunk. Fears have often been voiced that large-scale automation would make medical laboratory technicians redundant. The years have failed to bear this out. New methods will initially always be manual, and the profession of medical laboratory technician has become considerably more challenging. The view was once

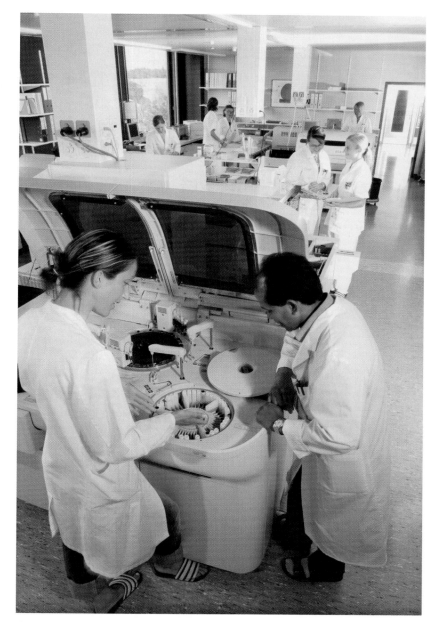

Operating today's complex analytical systems is a demanding job requiring considerable skill.

widely held that operating analysers involved no more than pressing or turning buttons. This has long been discredited. The complexity of modern analysers makes their operation a challenging task. Besides, irrespective of all the automation, robotics and computerisation, the mission of clinical chemistry has never changed: it remains the prevention, diagnosis, treatment and prognosis of disease in our fellow man. Automation has simply ensured that this mission is increasingly better served.

Peter Stiefelhagen and Sabine Päuser

Matters of the heart

The laboratory contribution to cardiodiagnostics

From antiquity the heart was considered the seat of the soul, indeed as the embodiment of the life force. The beating sensation in the chest was viewed as proof of life, since it was recognised that when the beating ceased, life ceased with it. At the same time the heart came to symbolise passion and love. For the Greeks, the heart was a glowing furnace which

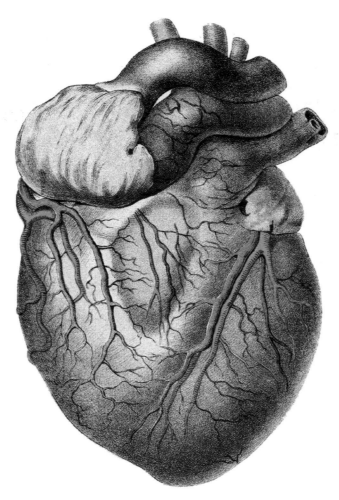

A 19th century depiction of a healthy heart and its blood vessels.

burnt the impurities in blood. However, rather than a furnace it is a tireless pump that each day performs a phenomenal amount of work. In a person at rest it pumps 4.9 litres of blood per minute or roughly 290 litres per hour round the body.[1] The heart of a 70-year-old will have beaten some three thousand million times, the blood feeding the 100 million million cells with oxygen and nutrients and removing metabolic waste. Cardiodiagnostics as we know it today developed from a discipline long based on physical techniques. Circulating biochemical markers by means of which life-threatening heart disease such as myocardial infarction (heart attack) and heart failure could be identified in the clinical chemistry laboratory were not discovered until the second half of the 20th century.

Beginnings: physical techniques

In 1761 the Viennese physician Leopold Auenbrugger (1722–1809) published *A New Discovery that Enables the Physician from the Percussion of the Human Thorax to Detect the Diseases Hidden Within the Chest* (commonly abbreviated to *Inventum novum*).[2] The purpose of percussion was to determine whether a patient's lung was filled with water or air. Auenbrugger had tested his invention over seven years in patients with lung and heart disease and in experiments in which he investigated the change in sound caused by injecting fluid into the thorax of cadavers.[3] Some years later, in 1819, Théophile-René-Hyacinthe Laënnec (1781–1826) published his discovery of auscultation of the heart. The development of his method of listening to heart sounds with an instrument which later became the stethoscope marks the true beginning of cardiodiagnostics. Auscultation has retained a

*In 1819 the Breton physician **Théophile-René-Hyacinthe Laënnec** (1781–1826) described his method of listening to heart sounds – auscultation – using the first stethoscope.[25] This marked the beginning of cardiodiagnostics. In addition, Laënnec was the first to describe bronchiectasis (dilatation of the bronchi), emphysema (distension of the lungs) and pulmonary infarction. He was also the first to recognise tuberculosis as an independent disease entity and provide an accurate description of the tubercles. He himself died of pulmonary tuberculosis.[26]*

clinical role into the modern imaging era. Even before the inauguration of this era in 1895 with the discovery of X-rays by Wilhelm Conrad Röntgen (1845–1923), other instrumental techniques had already become available to physicians: mechanocardiography – the recording of the mechanical pulsation of the heart from the thorax – in 1865 and phonocardiography – the amplification of heart sounds and murmurs – in 1894. But without doubt the greatest advance in cardiodiagnostics was the development in 1903 of electrocardiography, in which the electrical events occurring during cardiac activity are recorded in the electrocardiogram (ECG). Cardiac catheterisation followed in 1941, echocardiography (ultrasound imaging) in 1954, and coronary angiography, which visualises the coronary arteries using contrast media, in 1962. These techniques continue to play an essential role in routine clinical practice.

On the trail of myocardial infarction

Cardiodiagnostics developed in parallel with research into the most important heart diseases, for example coronary artery disease. In 1761 Giovanni Battista Morgagni (1682–1771), the founder of organ pathology, reported lesions of the coronary arteries and myocardium, the muscle that forms the middle layer of the heart wall. In 1768 William Heberden (1710–1801) provided a masterly description of angina pectoris (tightness in the chest) based on his clinical observations of the condition. In angina, attacks of pain in the heart region are associated with a characteristic feeling of constriction. They are triggered by an inadequate cardiac oxygen supply following occlusion or spasm in one or more coronary arteries. Angina is usually the harbinger of myocardial infarction. The great Rudolf Virchow (1821–1902), physician, ethnologist, archaeologist, anthropologist and politician rolled into one, also made a lifelong study of the characteristics of coronary arteries and blood clots. His era saw the publication of the first scientific studies on the topic of risk factors in cardiovascular disease, notably on the pathogenic role of smoking. Although particularly severe, and fatal, forms of angina pectoris were reported as early as 1850, myocardial infarction was not described as a separate disease entity until early in the 20th century, and for many years thereafter could only be diagnosed at autopsy. Thus the term 'infarct' was initially synonymous with a fatal anatomical disease. A breakthrough came in 1912, when James Bryan Herrick (1861–1954) provided the first clinical description, incriminating a coronary artery clot (coronary thrombosis) as the actual cause.[4] The typical features of myocardial infarction were identified as severe chest pain and a fall in blood pressure. Four clinical forms were distinguished: sudden death, early death after several minutes of intense chest pain and shock, late cardiac death after an initial period of more or less severe pain, and finally non-fatal forms with milder but more protracted angina.

Enzyme markers of myocardial infarction

For many years the only diagnostic signs of dead myocardial tissue in blood were elevations of the white blood cell count and erythrocyte sedimentation rate. Not until 1954 was decisive progress made by showing that the blood level of **g**lutamate **o**xaloacetate

A Frerichs stethoscope from the 19th century.

The Italian physician and naturalist **Giovanni Battista Morgagni** *(1682–1771) founded organ pathology in his work* De sedibus et causis morborum per anatomen indagatis libri quinque, *published in 1761,[27] in which he attributed diseases to morphological changes in individual organs. Morgagni began his medical studies at the age of 16 and became professor of medicine at 29, first in Bologna, then four years later in Padua. His practice of 'the art of anatomy' led him to discover numerous anatomical features of the human body. He had a special interest in congenital heart disease.*

The London physician **William Heberden** *(1710–1801) coined the term 'angina pectoris' in a lecture to the Royal College of Physicians in London on 21 July 1768: 'But there is a disorder of the breast marked with strong and peculiar symptoms, considerable for the kind of danger belonging to it, and not extremely rare… The seat of it, and sense of strangling, and anxiety with which it is attended, may make it not improperly be called angina pectoris.' Heberden observed some 100 patients with the disease and reported the typical calcifications of the aorta at autopsy.[28] He distinguished angina pectoris from other chest conditions, but mistakenly ascribed the cause to cramp or an abscess.*

transaminase (GOT), now known as **as**partate amino**t**ransferase (AST), is raised in acute myocardial infarction.[5] This marked the beginning of laboratory diagnosis in this field. AST was initially measured by paper chromatography, a laborious procedure with an 18-hour incubation time. It was replaced by a spectrophotometric assay based on a kinetic test of enzyme activity in which the level of enzyme activity correlated with the reaction rate. NADH, the reduced form of the pyridine moiety in the coenzyme **n**icotinamide **a**denine **d**inucleotide, acted as indicator, i. e. as the marker of the measurement result. The change in light absorption by this indicator per unit time provided a measure of the rate of reaction and hence of the enzyme activity present. Two years later, in 1956, another enzyme, **l**actate **deh**ydrogenase (LDH), was reported as a diagnostic biochemical marker of myocardial infarction.[6] In contrast to AST, it could be detected in infarct patients for up to 11 days after infarction. Thus for the first time a laboratory parameter was available which could also detect less recent myocardial infarctions.

Another enzyme of cardiodiagnostic importance, **c**reatine **k**inase (CK), was first described in 1959 in patients with progressive muscular dystrophy.[7] It was soon also found to be released in increased amounts in myocardial infarction. Circulating CK

activity increases markedly a few hours after myocardial infarction, often peaking after 24 hours.[8] It was even believed that the enzyme could be a prognostic indicator in that patients with elevated CK values on post-infarct day 3 had a markedly poorer prognosis. The explanation for the relationship was simple: the larger the infarct, the greater and more sustained the increase in CK.

Since CK is released not only from myocardium but also from skeletal muscle, total CK activity is a nonspecific, even if highly sensitive, parameter. In the search for more specific cardiac markers, the initial candidates were the CK isoenzymes. Isoenzymes are variants of an enzyme having the same substrate specificity but different primary structures, for example by consisting, like CK, of different subunits. CK molecules are dimers, consisting of two subunits. Three monomeric subunits of CK are known: M (**m**uscle), B (**b**rain) and Mi (**mi**tochondrial). The CK of cardiodiagnostic interest consists of one CK-M and one CK-B subunit. However, since CK-MB is released not only from myocardium but also, in certain diseases or in extreme physical exertion, from skeletal muscle, isolated determination of CK-MB barely enhanced diagnostic specificity. Nor was the diagnostic time window increased, since the profile of CK-MB activity is similar to that of total CK. However, by calculating the CK-

MB/CK index it was possible to enhance diagnostic specificity, notably for differentiating a myocardial lesion from skeletal muscle disease.

CK isoenzymes were initially analysed by electrical gradient separation (electrophoresis) and quantified by densitometry. Not until 1974 was the analysis markedly simplified and standardised by the development of anion exchange column chromatography. CK-MB is now measured by immunoassay: the non-cardiospecific isoenzymes are selectively neutralised by specific antibodies so that only CK-MB activity is ultimately determined. A notable advantage of the method is that it gives a result within 15 minutes.

Though the foundations for rapid and reliable laboratory diagnosis of myocardial infarction were in place in the early 1960s,[9] it was not until 1979 that the World Health Organization recommended enzyme diagnostics as the third pillar of infarct diagnosis alongside clinical signs and ECG changes.[10] Other enzyme detection methods followed before protein assays entered laboratory diagnostics. The information provided by protein markers was not only diagnostic, but also prognostic.

From enzyme activity to protein concentration

Until the mid-1980s acute myocardial damage could be detected only by the elevated activity of enzymes such as AST, LDH and CK and its isoenzymes. But none of these tests was either particularly sensitive or cardiospecific. This led to diagnostic problems, notably for small myocardial infarcts that failed to show up on the ECG, unstable angina, myocarditis (heart muscle inflammation), multiorgan disease, and patients who had undergone cardiopulmonary resuscitation, who usually have additional skeletal muscle lesions. It was also clinically important, in an era in which new treatment modalities were available for recanalising an infarct artery using drugs or a balloon catheter, to be able to detect myocardial damage as early as possible. New biochemical cardiac markers were needed not only for making the initial diagnosis but also for monitoring treatment and assessing prognosis, with due allowance for additional criteria such as rapidity, practicability, specificity and cost. The first important step was the introduction of a CK-MB mass assay using the enzyme-linked immunosorbent assay (ELISA) technique in the mid-1980s.[11] It marked a decisive switch in laboratory cardiodiagnostics from assaying an enzyme's activity to measuring its concentration (or mass) as a protein. The result was enhanced diag-

The German cardiologist **Hugo Albert Katus** (b. 1951) introduced the use of troponins for the detection of myocardial infarction. He studied medicine in Heidelberg from 1970 to 1976 and obtained his MD with a thesis on cardiac anaphylaxis: changes of membrane parameters and contractility. In 1988 he qualified as a university lecturer in internal medicine with a paper on the Diagnosis and volume determination of acute myocardial infarction using antibody dependent measurement methods. His awards include the 1995 German Industry Prize for Innovation for the development of the troponin T assay and the 1998 German Cardiology Society Arthur Weber Prize for his seminal contribution to myocardial infarction diagnostics.

nostic sensitivity, in particular in the early phase of acute myocardial infarction and in smaller, electrocardiographically silent, myocardial necroses. Furthermore the new marker could be used to monitor the response to clot-busting (thrombolytic) drug therapy. A fourfold increase in CK-MB mass within 90 minutes reflects successful recanalisation of an infarct artery. It also serves as a prognostic parameter in unstable angina: elevation of the CK-MB mass indicates an increased risk of myocardial infarction and mortality.

Early diagnosis with myoglobin

In the late 1970s myoglobin was reported as a screening parameter for myocardial infarction in the emergency setting. This oxygen-binding protein is produced in striated muscle, including the myocardium, whereas it is absent from smooth muscle. Myoglobin is more avid than hemoglobin for molecular oxygen and is therefore important for oxygen transport and storage in striated muscle. Because of its low molecular weight it is released with relative ease and rapidity by damaged myocardium, while returning to the normal range markedly earlier than the standard cardiac enzymes.

Myoglobin is non-cardiospecific and is also elevated in renal disease. However, its early sensitivity is high, meaning that an acute myocardial infarct can

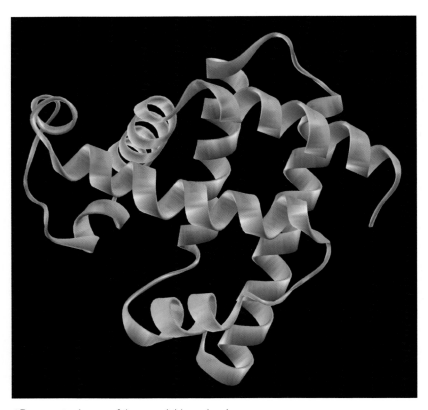

3D computer image of the myoglobin molecule.

be very rapidly and reliably excluded. Whereas CK and CK-MB activities do not begin to rise until at least four to six hours after the onset of pain, myoglobin elevation occurs within two hours. A normal myoglobin six to ten hours after the acute pain episode excludes acute myocardial infarction with a high degree of certainty. Thus in the early diagnosis of myocardial infarction only the CK-MB mass assay displays comparable diagnostic sensitivity.

Myoglobin is also used to assess response to thrombolysis. Rapid sharp elevation exceeding four times the normal level within 90 minutes of initiating thrombolytic therapy is evidence of successful revascularisation.

Absolute cardiospecificity

The early 1990s witnessed the introduction of the cardiac troponins – troponin I (cTnI) and troponin T (cTnT) – into laboratory cardiodiagnostics. In partnership with Boehringer Mannheim, the German cardiologist Hugo Albert Katus (b. 1951) developed a new diagnostic test for myocardial infarction based on the detection of cTnT.[12] Troponin T is found in adults only in the myocardium. Troponins are myofibrillary proteins in heart muscle which are released by myocardial cells in response to the slightest injury. With troponins I and C, cTnT

forms a troponin complex. This is involved in the regulation of myocardial contraction. Circulating troponin levels rise in infarct patients within three hours of pain onset and remain raised for over two weeks. It soon became apparent that the troponins were highly sensitive parameters for detecting minimal heart lesions such as small or micro infarcts, which often herald more extensive myocardial infarction.

A positive troponin result in unstable angina reflects a markedly poorer prognosis and is an indication for initiating maximal drug therapy, including an antiplatelet agent.

cTnT is useful in diagnosing myocardial infarction and in monitoring recovery and response to treatment. If a coronary thrombus is dissolved pharmacologically using a thrombolytic, the circulating cTnT level will show whether the infarct vessel has been adequately recanalised. It can also detect the occurrence of even tiny myocardial necroses in invasive cardiac procedures.

The qualitative whole-blood rapid test has proved valuable in routine practice. If the first result is negative in a patient with unstable angina, it should be repeated two hours later. If it is still negative eight hours after pain onset, a myocardial lesion can be excluded with extremely high probability. Quantitative determination by ELISA is required for assessing infarct size and response to thrombolysis.

Troponin estimation meets clinical criteria for an ideal cardiac laboratory marker in patients with unelucidated chest pain: simplicity, rapidity, absolute accuracy and unlimited availability. The late 1990s saw the development of the first rapid point-of-care tests for the emergency bedside diagnosis of myocardial infarction. Thus the Roche Cardiac

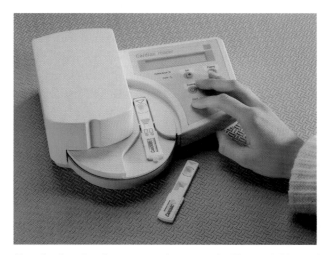

The Cardiac Reader can monitor troponin T, myoglobin and D-dimer both in the laboratory and at the bedside.

Reader measures a combination of two complementary parameters: myoglobin as an early nonspecific marker, and troponin T as a specific marker that can be demonstrated for up to two weeks after the acute myocardial syndrome and that detects even small myocardial lesions. The same device can also measure D-dimers – fibrin degradation products elevated in venous thromboembolism due to coagulation activation and increased fibrinolysis – to exclude a diagnosis of deep leg vein thrombosis or pulmonary embolism. In 2002 the Swiss company Vitest introduced the rapid Myokard Status test in Switzerland and Germany, offering simultaneous determination of three myocardial proteins: myoglobin, cTnI and CK-MB. In November of the same year, at Medica, the world's largest specialist medical trade fair, the Berlin biotechnology company rennesens introduced CardioDetect, a monoclonal antibody test which can identify myocardial infarction from the increased blood level of **h**eart-type **f**atty **a**cid-**b**inding **p**rotein (h-FABP) released from infarcted myocardial cells.

Laboratory markers of heart failure

In addition to laboratory parameters that detect structural changes in the heart, there was a need for a parameter of heart function. The clinical diagnosis of heart failure is not always simple, in that the cardinal symptom, breathlessness, is relatively nonspecific: patients with lung disease or obesity also suffer shortness of breath. As a result the correct diagnosis is often made relatively late, thereby needlessly delaying the initiation of the requisite therapy. Since early 2002 a reliable biochemical laboratory parameter has been available in Europe that helps to eliminate this uncertainty: NT-proBNP, the **N**-terminal fragment of **b**rain **n**atriuretic **p**eptide (BNP) **pro**hormone. Natriuretic peptides help to control electrolyte balance and blood pressure. BNP increases the urinary elimination of sodium ions and water. ProBNP is released by myocardial cells in response to volume and pressure overload. The NT-proBNP marker is the climax to a gripping, near 50-year research story at the outset of which no one imagined that it might one day result in the development of a longed-for laboratory indicator of heart failure.

Discovery of the natriuretic peptides

In 1953/54, in the USA, the German physiologist Otto Heinrich Gauer (1909–1979) conducted the following experiment: he introduced a balloon catheter into the right atrium of dogs, inflated it,

*The German physiologist **Otto Heinrich Gauer** (1909–1979) was a pioneer of circulation research and of space physiology. He described how the circulation is controlled by blood volume in addition to osmoregulation, and associated this control with renal function, showing that an elevation of blood volume increases urine output – an association now indexed in textbooks as the 'Gauer-Henry reflex'. Gauer studied medicine from 1928 to 1935 in Heidelberg and gained his doctorate in 1937 with a thesis on a topic from cardiovascular research for which he was awarded a prize from Heidelberg University. His scientific work on gravitation physiology before and during the Second World War at the Air Ministry's Aeromedical Research Institute in Berlin brought him to the attention of the occupying Americans, who transferred him in 1947 to the Aviation (later Aerospace) Medical Laboratory at the Wright Air Development Center, Wright-Patterson Air Force Base, in Dayton, Ohio. In 1953 he became Associate Professor at Duke University, in Durham, North Carolina. On returning to Germany in 1956 he worked for five years at the Kerkhof Institute in Bad Nauheim while holding a full professorship at Giessen University. In 1963 he was appointed to the chair of physiology at the Free University in West Berlin, where he successfully continued his studies on circulatory and gravitational physiology. Gauer was a dedicated scientist with a gift for the practical, reflected in considerable artisanal skills. Thus in 1957 he designed a catheter-tip manometer for his studies in animals, notably giraffes, and built it himself in the Institute workshop. He introduced the terms 'high-pressure system' and 'low-pressure system' into circulation physiology in Germany. The main focus of his scientific work was the regulation of blood volume and of its distribution along the body axis. According to Karl Kirsch (b. 1938), his pupil and successor at the Institute for Physiology of the Free University, Gauer also had an unerring eye for quality in research and distinguished himself by his farsightedness and optimism, confronting research difficulties with the attitude: 'You get nowhere without trying'. He was extremely alert to the potential of space physiology and viewed it as holding the key to further developments in physiology as a whole. This attitude rubbed off on his colleagues and pupils to the extent that in 2000 the Institute for Space Medicine and External Environments was founded at the Free University, complete with endowed chair.*

then observed an increase in urine output (diuresis) and in urinary excretion of sodium ions (natriuresis).[13] In the early 1980s Adolfo J. de Bold explained these findings as follows: distension of the atrial wall causes small granules contained therein to release **a**trial **n**atriuretic **p**eptide (ANP), a hormone that directly increases water excretion by the kidneys. To demonstrate this, de Bold and his coworkers performed an experiment typical of physiological research: using a tissue extract, they attempted to restore a physiological function – in this case water excretion – which had been suppressed or markedly impaired in experimental animals. They injected anuric rats intravenously with the supernatant from homogenised atrial or ventricular tissue. The atrial

Biochemistry and modes of action of the natriuretic peptides

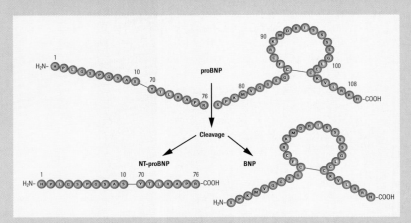

To permit molecular activity on the organs of salt and water excretion, proBNP is split into BNP and an N-terminal proBNP fragment (NT-proBNP) which is detectable in blood for longer than bioactive BNP and is thus a more stable target for clinical chemistry analysis. The letters in the circles stand for the following amino acids: A = alanine, C = cysteine, D = aspartic acid, F = phenylalanine, G = glycine, I = isoleucine, L = leucine, M = methionine, N = asparagine, Q = glutamine, R = arginine, S = serine, Y = tyrosine.

Like most peptide hormones, ANP (**a**trial **n**atriuretic **p**eptide) and BNP (**b**rain **n**atriuretic **p**eptide) are produced as larger precursor molecules (precursor peptides or preprohormones). The preprohormones are split in the myocardium into a signal peptide and the corresponding prohormone. Each prohormone is then split into one bioactive and one bioinactive fragment and released from the heart into the blood. The bioactive forms of the natriuretic peptides possess a 17-amino-acid ring structure essential for their physiological activity. The 108-amino-acid BNP prohormone is released in response to stretch stimulation of the myocardial cells, most typically by an increase in blood volume, and split by a protease into a bioactive 32-amino-acid C-terminal fragment[21] (BNP 77-108) and a bioinactive N-terminal fragment[22] (NT-proBNP 1-76). ANP and BNP are similar in physiological activity in terms of vasodilatation, natriuresis, diuresis (increased glomerular filtration rate) and inhibition of the renin-angiotensin-aldosterone system, thus contributing to blood pressure control. Both peptides are valuable noninvasive indicators of hemodynamic status and ventricular function. They are normally found only at low circulating levels.

extract increased sodium chloride excretion 30-fold and water excretion tenfold, whereas the ventricular extract had no such effect. The mystery natriuretic factor was thus to be sought in atrial tissue. Atrial muscle cells were found to contain a large amount of rough endoplasmic reticulum and numerous membrane-bound storage granules or vesicles. Morphologically and histologically these granules were reminiscent of those of polypeptide-producing cells. De Bold and his coworkers concluded that the atrium produced a polypeptide which influenced the volume of water excreted by the kidneys.[14] In 1985, in *Science,* de Bold published the results of his systematic investigations into atrial muscle cells.[15] He had discovered ANP, a polypeptide hormone with diuretic and natriuretic activity. According to de Bold the hormone also inhibited the secretion of renin[16] and aldosterone[17] and was thus probably involved in the short- and long-term control of water and electrolyte balance and blood pressure.

In the late 1980s the Norwegian physician Christian Hall (b. 1950) undertook a PhD on ANP release in cardiogenic shock and found that ANP values were elevated in heart failure. However, ANP did not fully match cardiologists' fond hopes for a simple biochemical laboratory test to aid the diag-

nosis of heart failure, since it proved a very unstable parameter for clinical chemistry analysis. Hall's Norwegian colleague, the clinical chemist Johan Sundsfjord (b. 1934), inspired him to study an inactive N-terminal residue cleaved from the ANP prohormone: NT-proANP. This proved to be not only more stable in the laboratory but also a more reliable prognostic indicator. Subsequently, in 1988, Japanese researchers published in *Nature* their discovery of B-type natriuretic peptide in porcine brain.[18] Since many neuropeptides are found not only in brain but also in other organs, ventricular myocardial tissue was fairly soon identified as the main source of circulating BNP.[19] Higher natriuretic peptide levels were found in the blood of heart failure patients due to the increased fluid volume and pressure in the heart. As its name indicates, ANP is secreted predominantly by the atrium. BNP, on the other hand, is a more faithful marker of left and right ventricular function, as has been shown in most comparable studies. It thus soon came to be considered a more sensitive and specific parameter for left ventricular failure, which is far commoner than right-sided heart failure. Two further natriuretic peptides have since been identified: urodilatin in 1986, which is produced in the kidney, excreted in the urine and involved in the control of sodium

The Norwegian physician **Christian Hall** *(b. 1950) has worked in various fields of experimental medical research, as seen from his many publications. His main interest has been in various aspects of the pathophysiology of heart failure. Among other topics, he has studied the regulation of blood volume and endocrine mechanisms in heart failure. He developed a new approach to the diagnosis of heart failure based on the measurement of cardiac natriuretic peptides, for which he received the Medinnova Prize in 1990. He has headed the Cardiovascular Endocrinology Research Group in the Clinical Chemistry Department at Oslo University since the early 1990s and became chairman of the university's Research Institute for Internal Medicine in January 2000.*

and water reabsorption in the renal collecting ducts; and **C**-type **n**atriuretic **p**eptide (CNP) in 1990, which is produced mainly in vascular tissue and has vasodilator properties.[20] But it quickly became clear that the best markers of heart failure would be BNP and NT-proBNP.

Bioinactive molecules are easier to measure

Whereas the cleaved bioinactive fragment NT-proBNP has a circulating half-life of 60–120 minutes, the half-life of the bioactive BNP hormone is only some 20 minutes. Not least for this reason, the blood concentration of NT-proBNP is about one order of magnitude higher than that of BNP. Since circulating NT-proBNP values are less subject to intraindividual fluctuation and the molecule is more stable in vitro than BNP, attempts were made, beginning in 1996, to raise antibodies for an NT-proBNP immunoassay. Clinical trials began a mere three years later. The test has proved almost 100% reliable at excluding chronic heart failure. The NT-proBNP parameter is thus highly sensitive. It is also specific,

in that it is elevated exclusively in patients with heart failure. Moreover, it is raised in early heart failure – which is otherwise difficult to diagnose – and regardless of which ventricle is involved. Elevation is thus unambiguous evidence of heart failure. It excludes other causes of breathlessness, in particular lung disease, with a high degree of certainty. Since in addition the NT-proBNP blood level correlates with the severity of the heart failure, it also has prognostic significance.[23] An elevated NT-proBNP is an indication for further investigation by ultrasound and other techniques. Conversely, a normal value renders such investigations unnecessary. A dream long cherished by cardiologists – the ability to detect heart failure immediately using a simple laboratory parameter – has finally come true. The European Society of Cardiology has now incorporated natriuretic peptide analysis into its diagnostic guidelines for heart failure. Further research is being conducted to develop a rapid test for these parameters that can be performed outside the laboratory, directly at the bedside.[24]

Nucleic acid amplification and chip technologies expand the frontiers of diagnosis (advances since 1983)

The human genome and the road ahead

Hans-Joachim Burkardt and Sabine Päuser

The dawning of a new era

PCR revolutionises diagnostics

What is PCR? The three letters are short for 'polymerase chain reaction'. But, of course, knowing what the abbreviation stands for doesn't explain what PCR is all about. To really understand what PCR is and why many believe it to be **the** revolutionary diagnostic method of the 20th century, we have to start our story at the beginning. In a nutshell, PCR is a technology that enables scientists to copy minute amounts of the genetic material **d**eoxyri**b**o**n**ucleic **a**cid (DNA) an unlimited number of times. As a result, genetic material extracted from organisms, both living and dead, can now be investigated in ways that were previously impossible. New methods of microbiological analysis based on the detection of trace amounts of genetic material from infectious microorganisms allow the identification of pathogens that are difficult to grow in culture.

What is more, these methods reduce the time required for analysis from days or even weeks to hours. PCR has also given rise to exciting new techniques for diagnosing diseases associated with genetic changes, including classic hereditary diseases and cancers, which are now also known to have a genetic component. And PCR marked the advent of molecular biology in forensic medicine. But how was this ingenious method which has revolutionised so many branches of medical diagnostics discovered and developed?

Inspirational night-time musings

What does a scientist do during a night-time drive while his girlfriend is asleep in the passenger seat? He lets his thoughts stray. We can forgive Kary Banks Mullis (b. 1944) for allowing his thoughts to turn, not on the woman asleep at his side, but to the experiments he was planning for the coming week. In the early 1980s Mullis was employed as a researcher at Cetus, one of the many small and innovative biotechnology companies that were shooting up like mushrooms at the time. In 1983, the year in which PCR was conceived, Mullis was working on oligonucleotides, short segments of single-stranded DNA. But let's let Mullis describe his drive north from San Francisco in his own words:

> The polymerase chain reaction wasn't the result of a long development process or a lot of work. It was accidentally invented late one evening in May 1983 by the driver of a grey Honda Civic during a drive along Highway 128 through the mountains between Cloverdale and Anderson Valley in California. It happened at a very specific moment, and I count myself among the luckiest of people that at that moment a series of unrelated thought processes – some correct, some misguided, but all quite common – converged in

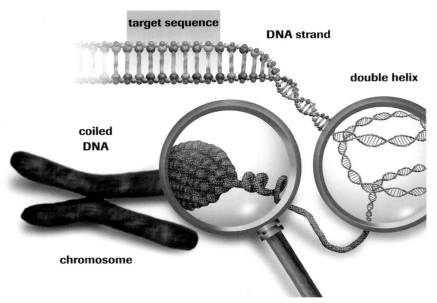

target sequence

DNA strand

double helix

coiled DNA

chromosome

PCR is a method of multiplying specific target sequences of DNA.

my mind in such a way that I suddenly recognized the process which I later called the polymerase chain reaction. Everything else that was going through my mind that evening came to a sudden standstill, as did the Honda, which came to a halt at the edge of the road around 45 miles from the coast. The Californian buckeye trees were in full bloom, and a gentle tropical fragrance filled the air.[1]

What had happened? Mullis was pondering how the technique being used at the time to analyse the sequence of nucleotides, the building blocks of nucleic acids, could be made more effective. One problem in particular niggled him: In addition to the radioactively labelled nucleic acid probes he was using, his samples inevitably also contained unlabelled nucleic acid building blocks from the environment that could distort his results. What, he thought, if all those unlabelled, 'dirty' molecules could be broken down in a chain reaction before the actual probes were added? They would then no longer interfere with his detection reaction. Suddenly Mullis realised that a chain reaction would also produce millions of copies of the nucleic acids of interest. Was it really possible that no one had ever happened on this ingeniously simple idea before? In fact, no one ever had.[2]

Mullis's nocturnal musings won him the 1993 Nobel Prize for Chemistry. It should be noted, however, that a number of other researchers at Cetus were involved in developing the method. Their role in the research and development work that led to PCR becoming an established technology is vividly described in Paul Rabinow's book *Making PCR*.[3]

How does it work?

PCR is frequently explained in non-technical parlance as method of finding a needle in a haystack by multiplying (amplifying) it into a stack of needles. The needle in this analogy is a nucleic acid or, more precisely, a nucleic acid fragment, e. g. from a pathogen such as a virus or bacterium. Tests that detect pathogens by targeting their genetic material make good sense, as all known pathogens, except perhaps the causative agent of BSE, have nucleic acids that uniquely identify them. Pathogens and their nucleic acids are usually present in very low concentrations in a clinical sample (a blood sample from a patient, say) and can therefore easily be obscured by the large amounts of nucleic acid and other biological material present from the host – i. e. the sick person or animal the sample was taken from. This host material corresponds to the haystack in our analogy.

The chemist **Kary Banks Mullis** *(b. 1944; shown on the right) is a multifaceted personality. He has described himself as a 'generalist with a chemical prejudice'.[8] Not only is he the inventor of the polymerase chain reaction (PCR) but he has also devised a plastic that changes colour rapidly when exposed to ultraviolet light. While still a graduate student he published a paper in* Nature *entitled 'The cosmological significance of time reversal'. After earning a PhD in biochemistry from the University of California at Berkeley in 1972, he held several postdoctoral fellowships before joining Cetus Corporation in Emeryville, California, as a nucleic acid chemist in 1979. He remained with Cetus for seven years, during which time he discovered PCR. In 1986 he was appointed Director of Molecular Biology at Xytronyx, Inc., in San Diego, where he concentrated on DNA technology and photochemistry. In recognition of the importance of PCR technology, the Royal Swedish Academy of Sciences awarded Mullis the 1993 Nobel Prize for Chemistry for his contributions to the development of methods in DNA-based chemistry. (The prize was shared by Professor Michael Smith [1932–2000] of the University of British Columbia in Vancouver, Canada, who was honoured for his fundamental contribution to the establishment of oligonucleotide-based site-directed mutagenesis and its development for protein studies.)[9] Mullis has been the recipient of numerous other distinctions, including the 1993 Japan Prize. The photo shows him together with Henry Erlich (left), with whom he shared the 1990 Biochemical Analysis Prize, awarded by the German Society for Clinical Chemistry and Boehringer Mannheim, for devising the polymerase chain reaction and for major contributions to developing the method for practical use. In 1994 he received an honorary doctorate from the University of South Carolina. His numerous publications range from scientific papers and popular science articles to his 1998 autobiography entitled* Dancing Naked in the Mind Field. *He is currently Vice President and Director of Molecular Biology at Burstein Technologies in Irvine, California.[10]*

Henry Anthony Erlich *(b. 1943) is a molecular biologist, geneticist and immunologist. He received a PhD in genetics in 1972 from the University of Washington in Seattle, after which he held postdoctoral fellowships in the Department of Biology at Princeton University and in the Department of Medicine at Stanford University. He joined Cetus Corporation the same year as Mullis and as head of a large team was actively involved in the early 1980s in developing PCR and investigating its potential applications in basic research, medical diagnostics, anthropology and forensics. He is interested in the genetic causes of complex multifactorial diseases. His major research interests include the analysis of polymorphisms in HLA genes and the development of HLA tests for tissue typing, determining disease susceptibility and establishing individual identity. He has authored more than 250 articles and has received numerous scientific distinctions. Since 1991 he has been Director of the Department of Human Genetics at Roche Molecular Systems, Inc., in Pleasanton, California.*

Scientists at Cetus Corporation obtained thermostable Taq *polymerase for PCR from* Thermus aquaticus *bacteria isolated from Mushroom Spring in Yellowstone National Park (Wyoming, USA).*

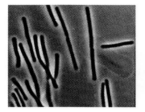

The bacterium Thermus aquaticus *as seen under a light microscope (left) and under an electron scanning microscope (right).*

PCR has been such a success because it is able to identify these numerically underrepresented microbial nucleic acids with the help of so-called primers. Expanding on our analogy slightly, the primers are like powerful magnets that pull the needle out of the haystack. And, secondly, because it can be used to produce billions of identical copies of DNA (our 'stack of needles') in the test tube, which can then be readily identified.

To obtain a sufficient number of copies, multiple (20–30) amplification steps are required. In each step, or cycle, the sample is heated to about 90 °C or higher. At this temperature the polymerase from *Escherichia coli* that was used originally (i. e. prior to Mullis's invention) for the test-tube synthesis of DNA is destroyed. As a result, fresh enzyme had to be added for each cycle. This was not only time-consuming and expensive but also affected the efficiency of amplification. A solution to this problem was therefore imperative.

It had been known for some time that certain ancient and exotic bacteria had managed to survive from the planet's dim past by colonising extreme habitats. For example, bacteria that feel just fine at temperatures approaching the boiling point of water had been isolated from hot springs in Yellowstone National Park in the United States. But if a bacterium can tolerate such unusually high temperatures for a living organism, it must possess enzymes that are also able to withstand such heat, including heat-resistant DNA polymerase.

It occurred to Mullis that, by employing a thermostable polymerase – a polymerase that wouldn't be phased in the least by the temperatures needed to separate the strands of double-stranded DNA – he would be able to copy genetic material over and over again in a chain reaction. The first thermostable DNA polymerase used was derived from *Thermus aquaticus,* a thermophilic eubacterium isolated by Thomas Brock from hot springs in Yellowstone National Park.[4] Cetus scientists Susanne Stoffel (b. 1950) and David H. Gelfand (b. 1944) isolated DNA polymerase from this bacterium and gave some to Mullis, Henry Erlich (b. 1943) and Randall Saiki (b. 1955) for use in PCR. Cetus patented this enzyme in 1989 and marketed it as 'Taq polymerase' (deriving the name from *Thermus aquaticus*).[5] This proved to be a decisive breakthrough. Fresh enzyme no longer had to be added at the start of each cycle; instead, *Taq* polymerase was added just once, at the beginning of the amplification process. New DNA strands produced in each cycle served as templates for the polymerisation of additional strands in subsequent cycles. A single molecule could be amplified into a billion copies in just 30 to 40 cycles. Today a PCR reaction takes around 20 to 90 minutes to complete.

Sensitivity and specificity

One of the dreams of developers and users of diagnostic tools had thus been achieved. Capable of detecting the presence of even a single copy of DNA, PCR takes sensitivity to its ultimate limit. This is the method's 'analytical sensitivity'. (The 'clinical sensitivity' of PCR assays is somewhat more modest because of problems that arise during the preparation of clinical samples.) The point to bear in mind is that, while PCR can multiply a single copy of target DNA, the target first has to be transferred to a reaction tube, and this requires suitable sample preparation.

It soon became apparent that PCR could also deliver on another dream objective in diagnostic

Sunrise over Mushroom Spring, where Thermus aquaticus *was isolated.*

testing: absolute specificity. Today it is possible to develop a diagnostic PCR test that will distinguish between two nucleic acids differing by just one base.

Some technical details

In routine diagnostic practice PCR testing consists of three steps: sample preparation, amplification and detection. The purpose of sample preparation is to isolate the target sequence of nucleic acid (e. g. the DNA of a potential pathogen) from a patient sample. This is done with the help of agents that dissolve viruses or bacteria, thus releasing their nucleic acid. The nucleic acid is then transferred to an amplification tube and frequently has to be concentrated using special techniques. Nucleic acid targets need to be as free as possible of inhibitors that could suppress amplification.

If the DNA or **ribonucleic a**cid (RNA) is double-stranded, the two strands are separated by heating at the start of the second step, amplification. Since the PCR technique requires DNA, not RNA, as a template, RNA samples have to be transcribed into DNA prior to amplification. Reverse transcription of RNA into DNA – which also starts with strand separation if the RNA is double-stranded – is now a relatively straightforward process in molecular biology.

The reaction temperature is then lowered, and the primers anneal (bind) to complementary segments on the strands of target DNA. Annealing is followed by elongation of the primers, in which *Taq* polymerase or another thermostable polymerase attaches one nucleotide building block after another to the primers in an order determined by the nucleotide sequence of the target. Ultimately this produces double-stranded copies of the initial segment which, like the original, then serve as templates for further polymerisation. The end result is an exponential multiplication (chain reaction) yielding millions of copies of the target.

Detecting these millions of copies requires special techniques. Here, incidentally, the analogy of the needle in the haystack fails, since a stack of needles is easy to see with the naked eye, whereas even millions of copies of a DNA molecule remain invisible.

The detection methods in use at the beginning of the PCR era – mainly gel electrophoresis and hybridisation techniques – were laborious and time-consuming. Besides electrophoresis and hybridisation, which are still employed today, automated colorimetric and fluorometric techniques are now also commercially available and provide accurate results relatively simply with the help of photometers.

The biologist **David H. Gelfand** (b. 1944) is Research Director at Roche Molecular Systems, where he and his coworkers are responsible for the discovery, isolation, production, biochemical characterisation and use of thermostable designer DNA polymerases and other proteins needed for nucleic acid amplification. After receiving his PhD from the University of California at San Diego in 1970, he worked for several years as a biochemical research assistant at the University of California at San Francisco before joining Cetus Corporation in 1976. He is the author of numerous scientific articles and book contributions. In the mid-1980s he and Susanne Stoffel (b. 1950) isolated thermostable Taq polymerase from the bacterium Thermus aquaticus. The photograph dates from the same period.

Advances in the automation of PCR have occurred at breathtaking speed. A number of instruments now on the market perform nucleic acid amplification and target detection automatically, and future systems will be able to handle sample preparation as well.

The triumph of PCR

When PCR was introduced for routine diagnostic use in 1992, in the form of a test for detecting the HIV-1 provirus and another for detecting *Chlamydia trachomatis*,[6,7] it did not exactly seem destined to be a resounding success. At the time PCR had to contend with a negative image resulting from early technical teething problems. These included a potentially high risk of contamination and the fact that the first PCR tests could only be performed by scientists with extensive experience in molecular biology. On top of that, the method was initially very labour-intensive and time-consuming. However, these technical deficiencies were soon eliminated. Another obstacle was that PCR did not fill a vacuum in the diagnosis of infectious diseases. On the contrary, it had to assert itself against traditional methods which had the advantage of being recognised and proven. Also, many of the older tests were unbeatably inexpensive, though usually only in terms of the costs of materials, not labour costs. Nevertheless, PCR-based tests soon proved to have advantages that justified switching to the new amplification technology. In most of the examples listed in the table on page 264, PCR has accordingly either replaced traditional routine diagnostic methods or established itself as an important complementary technology.

PCR and diagnostic microbiology

Conventional methods of analysis in microbiology and the diagnosis of infectious diseases are based on certain shared similarities between microorganisms, which means that many of these methods are capable of identifying only a relatively limited group of microorganisms with similar biological properties. This is precisely what most clinicians don't want. They would much rather have systems geared to specific clinical pictures rather than to the biology of pathogens. Let's assume, for example, that a doctor has a patient exhibiting symptoms of meningitis. The first questions the doctor will ask himself are whether the symptoms are due to a microbial infection and, if so, how the infection should be treated. Prompt diagnosis and treatment in this case could be life-saving. And the situation is complicated by the fact that any of a number of very dissimilar microorganisms, including viruses, bacteria, fungi and protozoa (single-celled organisms), might be the culprit. With classical methods, the causative agent can only be identified laboriously by performing tests designed specifically for each pathogen type. Using DNA-based molecular diagnostic methods, it is now possible to amplify the genetic material in a sample and then identify the pathogen very quickly with the aid of multiple probes run in parallel. In lab jargon this is referred to as 'multiplex PCR' or a 'panel test'. Panel tests are designed for specific clinical pictures and in one go provide clinicians with the information on which to base therapeutic decisions.

PCR and HIV

The development of quantitative PCR-based tests for HIV (**h**uman **i**mmunodeficiency **v**irus), the virus responsible for AIDS (**a**cquired **i**mmune **d**eficiency **s**yndrome), is another example of the profound impact that PCR has had on the scientific understanding, diagnosis and treatment of disease. And this story is also a shining example of why scientific creativity should be given free rein to try out new ideas even when no direct application or benefit is obvious. When the idea of developing a quantitative test for HIV was first mooted in the early 1990s, no one really knew what use the test would be. Since manifest AIDS does not develop until years or even decades after infection with HIV, the consensus view was that the virus insinuated itself into a patient's DNA and remained dormant there for long periods, during which the infection was 'clinically silent'. In fact, this is precisely how the lambda bacteriophage behaves after invading its bacterial host, *Escherichia coli*. In addition, it was known that HIV could indeed

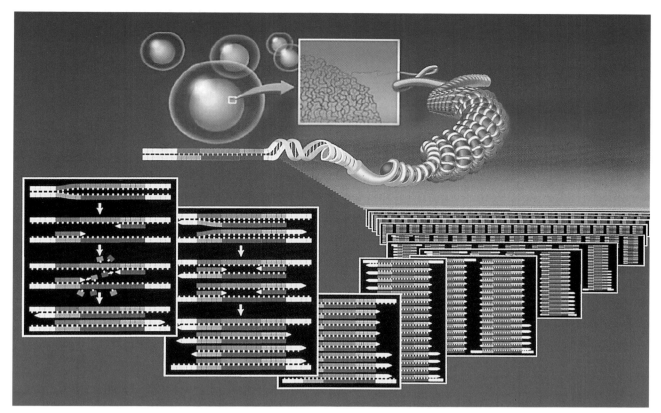

Schematic description of the polymerase chain reaction: Starting with double-stranded deoxyribonucleic acid (DNA) containing the nucleotide sequence of interest (shown in orange and red), millions of copies of the target sequence can be produced by adding nucleic acid building blocks, thermostable polymerase and primers. The primers (shown in blue and green) consist of short strings of nucleic acid building blocks that are complementary to the building blocks at the start of the nucleic acid segment being copied. In the first step the source DNA is separated into single strands by heating to 94 °C. As the DNA cools to 40–60 °C, the primers anneal (bind) to the complementary segments of the single strands. At 72 °C, the temperature at which Thermus aquaticus *feels at home,* Taq *polymerase attaches nucleotide building blocks to the primers with maximum efficiency and in the order dictated by the single-stranded templates. Once assembly of the new strands is complete, producing two copies of the original molecule, the steps are repeated: heating to 94 °C and strand separation; cooling and primer annealing; and assembly of complete double-stranded copies by polymerase at 72 °C. The more temperature cycles are performed, the more copies of the target sequence are obtained.*

insert its genetic material into a host's genome after converting viral RNA into DNA by reverse transcription. According to the prevailing view, AIDS progressed to the acute stage when the dormant virus was reactivated by some as yet unknown process. The therapeutic recommendations of the time accordingly assumed that there was no point in initiating treatment early, since as long as the virus lay dormant in the host's genome it was not susceptible to therapeutic measures. Treatment was not started until reactivation of the virus occurred, this being detectable, for example, by a fall in CD4 T-lymphocyte counts.

When the first quantitative HIV PCR test was used to measure viral concentrations in the blood of HIV-infected patients, it caused quite a stir. The measurements showed that the virus was by no means inactive in clinically normal patients. On the contrary, huge numbers of new virus particles were

being synthesised daily. Patients do not initially develop clinical symptoms because their immune systems are able to neutralise most of the virus. The battle between the virus and a patient's immune system may continue over a number of years, forestalling the onset of any serious symptoms. As the battle progresses, however, the immune system is relentlessly weakened, until viral proliferation eventually gets the upper hand, resulting in the appearance of full-blown AIDS. Quantitative PCR not only overturned received wisdom concerning the course of HIV infection, but also led to a paradigm shift in therapy. Instead of waiting for the CD4 cell count to signal the demise of the immune system, doctors began to initiate highly potent antiviral therapy as early as possible. The success of this approach, known as HAART (**h**ighly **a**ctive **a**nti**r**etroviral **t**herapy), confirmed the correctness of the new view and ultimately resulted in AIDS, though still not a curable disease, ceasing to be an automatic death sentence. Like other chronic diseases, it can now be effectively managed for years, provided patients adhere to their medication regimens. This has substantially extended the survival time of AIDS patients. A test is now available that can detect as few as 50 copies of HIV-1 RNA per millilitre of plasma (c/mL). This astonishing test sensitivity is important for determining the optimum treatment strategy – all the more so as the declared therapeutic goal is to reduce viral loads to below 50 c/mL (i. e. to undetectable levels). Today suitable test methods can detect HIV-1 subtypes A-G of group M. While subtype B HIV-1 viruses predominate in Western countries, studies have clearly shown that infection with non-B subtypes of HIV-1 is on the increase around the world. A test capable of detecting a broader spectrum of genetically distinct variants of the human immunodeficiency virus would therefore be a boon to HIV-positive patients the world over. Work is under way to develop new-generation tests that will also be able to detect newly emergent HIV subtypes.

PCR applications

The use of PCR and similar molecular amplification techniques is by no means limited to clinical microbiology. Another wide-ranging area of potential applications, though still in its infancy, is genetic diagnostic testing – perhaps most interestingly genetic testing for cancers. However, such tests (particularly those for diseases other than cancer) raise a number of ethical issues. For example, is it right to diagnose a disease or predisposition to a disease for which no treatment or means of prevention exists? Ethical questions that need to be discussed and clarified by society are perhaps even more pressing in the case of prenatal diagnostic testing.

By contrast, the use of PCR findings for personal identification in law enforcement and the courts, for example to solve crimes or establish paternity, is widely accepted and routine. PCR was first used in a criminal investigation in 1986, and the first commercial PCR-based forensic test kit was marketed in 1990. Most readers are probably familiar with at least one spectacular story of a criminal who was convicted on the strength of his or her genetic fingerprint, obtained from minute traces of hair, flakes of skin, impressions on a cigarette butt or some other bit of physical evidence collected at the crime scene.

PCR-based genotyping, e.g. HLA typing tests (HLA = **h**uman **l**eukocyte **a**ntigen), has been used to establish associations between specific genetic types and the risk of developing diseases such as diabetes and in population genetic studies. Another major area of application for HLA typing is transplantation medicine, where it is used to determine whether a donated organ has a suitable antigenic pattern for the intended transplant recipient.

In research PCR has given rise to new methods without which modern molecular biology would be

Advantages of PCR over conventional microbiological methods

Problems with conventional methods	Example	Advantages of PCR and similar amplification methods
Microorganisms difficult or impossible to cultivate	Hepatitis C virus: This virus was first discovered with the help of molecular techniques	Work even with pathogens that are impossible to cultivate
Length of time required	Diagnosis of *Mycobacterium tuberculosis* Identification in culture takes 2–4 weeks	Yield results within a day
Unreliable	Diagnosis of *Chlamydia trachomatis*	Highly sensitive and specific
Unreliable in the early phase of infection, when antibodies are not yet detectable	Detection of hepatitis C and HIV in donated blood	Very fast, as they do not depend on antibody production
Do not distinguish between acute and past infections	Hepatitis C, hepatitis B	Can differentiate between past and acute infections, since genetic material from pathogens is present in the blood only in acute infections

unthinkable. An especially impressive example is molecular paleobiology, which makes it possible to establish kinship relationships, and thus answer phylogenetic questions, by analysing the DNA of extinct species. The PCR analysis performed on the famous glacier mummy popularly known as 'Ötzi the Iceman' is worth mentioning, if only as a scientific curiosity. Because the Iceman was found in an area on the border between Austria and Italy, both countries laid claim to his remains. In this case PCR failed to settle the matter, since Ötzi's DNA does not closely resemble that of the modern-day inhabitants of either country. The quarrel was amicably resolved in favour of Italy on the basis of other considerations. Today Ötzi is housed in the South Tyrol Museum of Archaeology in Bolzano.

PCR is also used for microbiological analysis in the food industry. There is strong demand for new and reliable methods for improving quality control of fresh products of animal origin. Because of the perishable nature of these products, conventional methods are often much too slow.

Another application of PCR is in classifying patients on the basis of how they metabolise drugs. The pharmacodynamic behavior of a drug can vary depending on a patient's genetic makeup, i.e. a drug may remain in the body for a longer or shorter period before being excreted, depending on the patient's metabolic type. By adjusting treatment to patient type, it may be possible to enhance positive drug

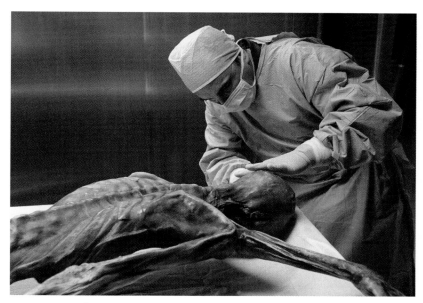

PCR testing of Ötzi found no close genetic kinship between this lone Ice Age wanderer and modern-day inhabitants of Italy or Austria.

effects while reducing side effects. Revival of potent drugs whose development was abandoned because of side effects observed during clinical trials is also conceivable. This would be possible if the side effects occurred only in specific patient types. The drug would then be contraindicated in these patients, while conceivably providing great benefit to others.

As this brief overview indicates, despite all the spectacular successes achieved to date, the exciting new era opened up by PCR is only just beginning.

Friedrich E. Maly

What can genetic tests tell us?

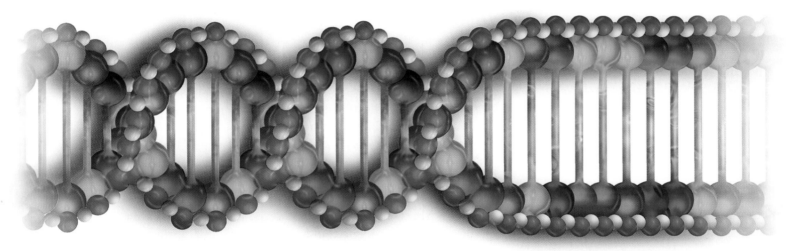

Computer-generated image of DNA.

Each of us possesses a genome, a full complement of genes arranged along chromosomes within the nucleus of each cell of our body. A genome is a plan, or blueprint, containing all the information required for the growth and development of an organism. In the case of buildings, however, we know that how things actually turn out – what a building looks like when it's finished and what sort of condition it will be in a decade or so later – is not determined solely by the plans used on the construction site. The workmanship of the builders, the location, the occupants and the ravages of sun, wind, weather and time all play a role as well. In other words, while the plans for a building may contain all the important structural information, they don't specify every single detail, and external factors – things that aren't in the plans – have a tremendous influence on functionality and appearance. Much the same applies to other types of

'plans', for example the score for a piano concerto or symphony. How the work actually sounds when performed depends greatly on the performers and the venue. To paraphrase the words of Bertolt Brecht: 'Man makes a plan, but a plan is not enough.'

And so it is with the genome. Though we wouldn't exist at all without one, it doesn't determine everything. What we are and what we will become results from the interplay between our genes and the environment – between our genetic blueprint and external factors that aren't 'part of the plan'. This applies just as much to our physical makeup as it does to our intellectual and psychological attributes. For many years, the extent to which individual characteristics such as height and body shape, intelligence, musical talent, illness and health are determined by our genes, and thus are hereditary, was investigated in studies on twins without

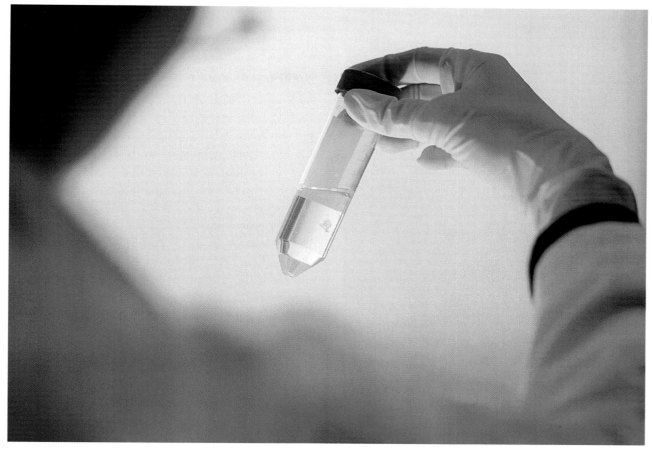

A strand of red blood cell DNA floating in a test tube.

knowing anything about the human genome. While such studies identified traits that were strongly or weakly heritable, they revealed nothing about the underlying genetic blueprint or how to read it.

Unravelled, yes – but really understood?

Identification of **d**eoxyribo**n**ucleic **a**cid (DNA) as the carrier of genetic information and the discovery that DNA consists of a double chain of the nucleotide bases adenine (A), guanine (G), thymine (T) and cytosine (C) on a backbone of phosphorylated sugar have taught us the 'alphabet of life'. According to current knowledge, our genetic blueprint consists exclusively of long strings of these four bases.

The path from the discovery of this universal genetic code – which we share with all living things – to determination of the entire base sequence of the human genome, with its billions of individual 'letters', required great technical advances. Today, as a result of the Human Genome Project, we have a rough draft of the human genome (and of some other genomes as well) in the form AGTTTAGCT-CAGTACTATAGTATACACA…

To understand what these rough drafts mean, it is necessary to understand the basic mechanisms by which genes (segments of DNA) direct production of the building blocks of an organism, notably proteins. At present we know that a part of the genetic blueprint, i.e. a gene, is copied (transcribed) into messenger **r**ibo**n**ucleic **a**cid (RNA), another kind of nucleic acid. This strand of RNA, containing the same genetic information as the strand of DNA from which it was transcribed, is then 'read' by a 'translating machine' known as a ribosome to produce a protein, which performs physiological functions in the cell and the organism as a whole. The genes that code for many proteins have already been identified.

However, the process of unravelling the genome, known technically as sequencing, has also revealed the existence of many genes that we previously knew nothing about and whose function is still a mystery to us. In fact, long segments of DNA, including segments known as 'introns', have been found which are not translated at all. Scientists are busy puzzling over what these segments might be for. And finally – and this is perhaps the most important point here – the genes of different individuals often show small differences, consisting for the most part of single base substitutions, which result in greater or lesser differences in the proteins coded for. Thus, there are an

In the early 1950s the American biochemist **James D. Watson** (b. 1928, left) and the British physicist **Francis C. Crick** (b. 1916) discovered the double-helix structure of DNA while working together at the Cavendish Laboratory in Cambridge. The events that led to elucidation of the structure of nucleic acids are vividly and accessibly described in Watson's book The Double Helix. Watson and Crick's results drew heavily on x-ray crystallographic studies performed at King's College, London, by the physicists Rosalind Franklin (1920–1958) and Maurice Hugh Frederick Wilkins (b. 1916). Watson, Crick and Wilkins shared the 1962 Noble Prize for Medicine.

anisms by which genetic variants and environmental factors jointly bring about specific individual characteristics, and thus also specific diseases.

No different from others, yet special

As long ago as 1909 the Danish botanist Wilhelm Ludwig Johannsen (1857–1927) introduced the important terms 'genotype' and 'phenotype' into genetics. Since then 'genotype' has referred to the entire genetic makeup of an individual, while 'phenotype' refers to the sum of an individual's observable characteristics.

Fifty years ago, in April 1953 to be precise, James Dewey Watson (b. 1928) and Francis Harry Compton Crick (b. 1916) published their description of the double-helix structure of DNA. In so doing they laid the foundation for our understanding of the genetic code. Several decades later, in the early 1980s, the **p**olymerase **c**hain **r**eaction (PCR) was invented, providing a means of amplifying (copying) gene segments hundreds of thousands of times and making the development of genetic tests vastly easier. What, then, are genetic tests? They are laboratory tests that can determine whether particular genetic variants (mutations or polymorphisms) are present at a particular site in the genome or on a particular gene. Some genetic tests are able to determine how a variant differs from the usual base sequence at the site in question. Genetic tests differ from other types of laboratory test – most of which measure concentrations of proteins, hormones, vitamins, antibodies and so on, i. e. concentrations of gene products – in that the object of investigation, the genetic characteristic being tested for, is constant over an individual's lifetime. The genetic variations that occur in cells when they become cancerous are an exception to this rule. If a particular genetic variant is found to be closely associated with a particular disease, a test for the presence of the variant can predict the occurrence of that disease in an individual with a greater or lesser degree of certainty. An example of such a close association is Huntington's chorea, a rare monogenic disorder, i. e. a disorder due to a single gene abnormality. If, as in the case of Huntington's chorea, a disease can be predicted but not treated, detection of a disease-causing gene variant can place a heavy emotional burden on the carrier, even if years or decades are expected to pass before any symptoms appear. Fortunately, gene variants that possess such predictive power, and the hereditary diseases they cause, are rare. It goes without saying that tests whose results are potentially so fateful should be performed only if the individual to be tested has been fully

estimated several million variants of the approximately 30,000 different genes that make up the human genome. And their role? They obviously form the physical basis for differences between individual genomes and thus contribute, together with environmental factors, to making each of us unique. These genetic variants are known as mutations or polymorphisms, depending on their significance. Most mutations are rare and closely associated with a particular disease, whereas polymorphisms are common and show little or no association with specific diseases. The boundary between these two categories of genetic variation is of course a shifting one whose position depends to some extent on the current state of scientific knowledge. Gaining a deep understanding of the genome and how it works will require us to go beyond basic principles and identify the most common and important genetic variants and the ways in which they interact with the environment. It will mean understanding the mech-

informed about the test and will be provided with the necessary medical and psychological follow-up in the event of a positive test result.

And yet, tests whose results can predict survival or otherwise have come to be used more or less routinely in medicine. For example, a diagnosis of HIV infection, which can be made quite simply on the basis of an antibody test available in the form of a test strip, is no less portentous to the person concerned than the result of a genetic test for a fatal disease, and the typical shadow of lung cancer in a chest x-ray film is scarcely less ominous. For that matter, even a simple cholesterol determination can be used – in conjunction with triglyceride and blood glucose levels, age, sex and other basic personal data – to provide a relatively accurate indication of a person's likelihood of suffering a heart attack over the coming years. In each case, what matters is not the technical details of the procedure (whether it be a DNA analysis, an antibody test, a cholesterol determination or an x-ray) but the potential implications of the result. It is these implications which determine what the person undergoing the test will be told and how he or she will subsequently be managed. The physician's responsibilities in this regard have always formed an essential element in the doctor-patient relationship and are expressed in the Hippocratic Oath and the principle of medical confidentiality.

Treatment-relevant genetic tests

Diseases for which an effective form of treatment exists or whose course can be significantly influenced are an entirely different matter. Here predictive genetic tests can be very useful. **M**ultiple **e**ndocrine **n**eoplasia (MEN) is a case in point. Mutations in the MEN-1 gene are strongly correlated with the occurrence of certain tumours of the thyroid gland.[1] When a mutation is identified, usually in an (as yet) unaffected member of an affected family whose members are being screened for the disease, regular determination of calcitonin levels can be performed to detect a tumour at a stage at which thyroidectomy (surgical removal of the thyroid) will cure the disease. Alternatively, it may be decided to perform thyroidectomy immediately, i.e. before any 'biochemical symptoms' appear. The hormonal deficits that result from removal of the thyroid can be corrected by administering thyroid hormones.

The situation is similar for certain rare mutations of the genes BRCA1 and BRCA2. These mutations commonly lead to breast cancer[2] (the designation 'BRCA' derives, incidentally, from the term '**br**east **ca**ncer'). Whether a positive test result is simply a

The Roche LightCycler is used in laboratories to perform a variety of genetic tests that permit rapid decision-making.

cause for increased vigilance and for having the carrier undergo more frequent mammographic screening, or whether breast removal should be performed immediately, is still unclear – both with respect to the relative effectiveness of these options and with respect to patient acceptance. Obviously, patients need to have a major say in decisions like these. Though research on this and similar questions is not yet complete, it is clear that all patients who participate in clinical trials of mammography screening, for example, will be very closely monitored, and this circumstance alone can have a positive influence on health outcomes. Some patients may feel that paying such close attention to a disease that is no more than a possibility may have a detrimental and limiting effect on their quality of life. Such feelings must be taken into account and, if possible, allayed through

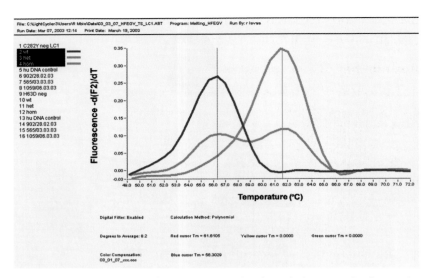

File: C:\LightCycler3\Users\R Mbio\Data\03_03_07_HFEGV_TS_LC1.ABT   Program: Melting_HFEGV   Run By: r lavss
Run Date: Mar 07, 2003 12:14   Print Date: March 19, 2003

1 C282Y neg LC1
2 wt
3 het
4 hom
5 hu DNA control
6 902/28.02.03
7 565/03.03.03
8 1059/06.03.03
9 H63D neg
10 wt
11 het
12 hom
13 hu DNA control
14 902/28.02.03
15 565/03.03.03
16 1059/06.03.03

Digital Filter: Enabled   Calculation Method: Polynomial

Degrees to Average: 8.2   Red cursor Tm = 61.6105   Yellow cursor Tm = 0.0000   Green cursor Tm = 0.0000

Color Compensation: Blue cursor Tm = 56.3029
03_01_07_ccc.ccc

PCR analysis of the HFE gene for the point mutation that substitutes tyrosine for cysteine at amino acid position 282, using the LightCycler and reagents supplied by Genes-4U. If the subject is a homozygous carrier of this mutation, the result shown with a red line will be obtained. The blue line shows the result obtained in homozygous carriers of the 'normal' gene, which codes for the amino acid cysteine at position 282. In heterozygotes (individuals with one mutant and one normal gene) the result shown with the pink line would be obtained. The time required for such a test is less than an hour.

appropriate psychological counselling, and all patients are of course free to decide not to participate in such studies.

Genetic tests have had a particularly profound effect on the diagnosis of metabolic disorders such as hereditary hemochromatosis, an iron storage disease which is one of the most common hereditary metabolic disorders in European populations. Iron, an essential component of many proteins, including the red blood pigment hemoglobin, is absorbed from food by cells present in the wall of the intestine. The amount of iron absorbed is controlled by a protein that normally functions as a brake on iron uptake via the cells of the intestinal wall; by contrast, the body has no mechanisms for controlling the amount of iron that is eliminated. This iron uptake-suppressing protein is the product of the HFE gene.[3] A specific inherited mutation, namely substitution of tyrosine (Y) for cysteine (C) at amino acid position 282 of the HFE protein, blocks this function, with the result that iron is absorbed in uncontrolled fashion and accumulates in the body. Over a period of years, iron overload in the liver, pancreas, joints, skin and other organs can lead to a variety of disorders, including cirrhosis of the liver, diabetes, joint problems and bronze discolouration of the skin. Prior to the identification of the HFE gene in 1996, hemochromatosis was diagnosed by determining the blood levels of

the iron-containing proteins ferritin and transferrin and – if the levels of these proteins were found to be elevated – by determining the amount of iron in a sample (biopsy) of liver tissue. In about 90% of patients with hereditary hemochromatosis the mutation that substitutes tyrosine for cysteine at amino acid position 282 in the HFE protein is found on both the maternal and the paternal chromosome (homozygous C282Y genotype). In individuals with an elevated ferritin level and elevated transferrin saturation, a homozygous C282Y mutation is proof of hereditary hemochromatosis, and patients found to have this mutation no longer require a liver biopsy. Genetic testing for hemochromatosis thus spares many patients the need for a procedure that is not always free of complications, and of course also saves money. Moreover, a genetic diagnosis of iron storage disease permits earlier initiation of the only effective treatment, namely removal of excess iron from the body by phlebotomy (puncture of a vein to remove blood), than would be possible if the diagnosis were made only after the disease had become manifest. However – depending on what studies one looks at – only 10% to 50% of individuals homozygous for the HFE C282Y mutation actually develop iron storage disease. A search is therefore under way for other relevant genetic and environmental factors.

Genetic tests that can demonstrate the presence of variants of the genes that code for the enzymes **m**ethylene **t**etra**h**ydro**f**olate **r**eductase (MTHFR) and **t**hio**p**urine **m**ethyl**t**ransferase (TPMT) are unquestionably useful. These enzymes significantly influence the action of many medications. MTHFR converts the vitamin folic acid into a form required for DNA synthesis, among other things. MTHFR-C677T polymorphism, which occurs frequently, reduces the activity of the enzyme and thereby impairs DNA synthesis. In the absence of any other negative influences on this metabolic pathway, this is of no significance in adults. However, the weakly active homozygous TT MTHFR genotype predisposes carriers to experience adverse events with antifolate drugs such as methotrexate, which are used as cytotoxic agents and inhibit the same metabolic pathway.[4]

The enzyme TPMT is involved in the breakdown of other cytotoxic agents,[5] to mention just one of its important roles. Mutant forms show reduced activity, with the result that cytotoxic agents are broken down more slowly and therefore have a more pronounced action. TPMT*2 (Ala80Pro), *3A (Ala154Thr; Tyr240Cys), *3B (Ala154Thr) and *3C (Tyr240Cys) are the most common (>75%) of the eight mutant alleles of this gene that have been identified to date. In patients with reduced TPMT activity, thiopurine analogues such as azathioprine have to be given at a lower dosage. In such patients the use of cytotoxic agents such as azathioprine and methotrexate at a dosage reduced in accordance with the genetic variant found can decisively reduce the rate of side effects associated with chemotherapeutic agents given for leukemia, rheumatoid arthritis or inflammatory bowel disease, without lessening the therapeutic effect. Pharmacogenetics, the branch of science dealing with the interplay between drugs – which can be regarded as a special kind of environmental factor – and genetic variations is one of the fastest-growing applications of genetic testing.

Is genetic testing the only way to go?

It is important to note, however, that in principle the same information could be obtained without the use of genetic tests, i. e. without tests performed on DNA. After all, mutant genes result in the synthesis of variant proteins, and the abnormal function of these proteins can be detected using nongenetic tests. Though considerably more circuitous and expensive, such an approach would ultimately yield the same information as is provided by genetic tests. Only the route to the information would be different.

Any number of tests possible

Apart from their aura of state-of-the-art modernity, genetic tests do, however, possess one notable peculiarity, namely the fact that the DNA on which they are performed can be stored almost indefinitely and can be reproduced in limitless amounts in a test tube. In principle, therefore, any number of genetic tests can be performed on a single sample of blood, saliva or urine. Accordingly, patients must have the right to limit the number of tests that are done and to have samples destroyed once the information they were intended to provide has been obtained. A public debate about people's right to ownership of their own genetic material, about the right not to know everything and about the nonmedical use of genetic data has already commenced and is sure to intensify. We all have to stand up and be counted. DNA is, after all, our common inheritance. As for physicians, despite all the technical innovations that have transformed medical practice, their primary obligation is the same as it was in Hippocrates' day: *primum non nocere* – 'first, do no harm'.

Michael Tacke

Proteomics targets new disease markers

Same genes, different proteomes. The photographs show two stages in the development of the swallowtail butterfly. The caterpillar and the butterfly have different protein make-ups, but their genomes are identical.

For a long time the study of proteins was a relatively neglected discipline compared with genome research, better known simply as 'genomics'. Then, in the mid-1990s, a new field of protein research called 'proteomics' moved into the scientific limelight, and it has been growing explosively ever since.

The term 'proteome' was coined in 1994 by two Australian researchers, Marc Wilkins and Keith Williams, in analogy to 'genome'. Just as a genome is the full set of genes of an organism, a proteome is the sum total of all the proteins produced by a genome. 'Proteomics' is a collective term for the techniques and technologies used to study proteomes.

While proteomics is still a young science, it is rooted in much older techniques of protein analysis. Unlike these older analytical techniques, however, which characterise proteins one at a time, proteomics has taken protein research into a new dimension by allowing hundreds or even thousands of proteins to be studied in a single experiment. As a result, the full complement of proteins (proteome) in a biological sample can now be investigated systematically. The emergence and continued development of proteomics has been made possible by advances in such fields as mass spectrometry and bioinformatics, and by the gene databases created by genomics research and the (hypothetical) protein sequences derived from genetic sequencing data.

Proteomics has the potential to significantly expand our understanding of physiological and pathological processes. And this increased knowledge could then be used to address unmet diagnostic needs. Later, this chapter discusses some of the ways in which proteomics is being applied in laboratory diagnostics. But first we should look a bit more closely at the genome and proteome themselves

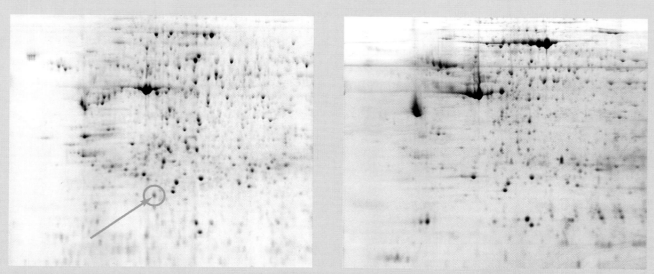

2D gel electrophoresis images. On the left, spot pattern obtained for proteins extracted from tumour tissue; on the right, spot pattern for healthy tissue. Comparison of the images reveals a tumour-associated protein (arrow) on the left which is not present in the healthy control.

2D gel electrophoresis

Two-dimensional (2D) gel electrophoresis was first described in 1975 and since then has been steadily refined. It allows more than a thousand proteins to be separated in one go. The protein mixture of interest is first separated by its isoelectric point (1st dimension) on a roughly 20 cm long strip and then by size (2nd dimension) on a gel measuring roughly 20 x 20 cm. Isoelectric focusing (IEF) exploits the fact that proteins change their net charge according to the pH of the surrounding medium. For each protein, there is a characteristic pH at which the positive (e. g. NH_3^+ group) and negative (e. g. COO^- group) charges will balance, leaving the protein with zero net charge. If the protein sample is exposed to an electric field on a strip with a stable pH gradient, each protein will migrate to the electrode of opposite polarity – e. g. a positively charged protein will migrate towards the negative pole (the cathode) – until it reaches a point where the pH of the strip matches its isoelectric point. There its net charge is zero; the electric field no longer acts on it; and migration ceases. Following IEF, the strip is placed on a polyacrylamide gel, and the proteins are separated by size at right angles to the first dimension of separation. The anionic surfactant sodium dodecyl sulphate is added to confer a negative charge. Another electric field is applied, and the proteins migrate through the pores of the gel at different rates determined by their size. In a final step, staining is used to visualise the proteins in the gel. This produces a characteristic two-dimensional pattern of spots. Ideally, each spot will represent one protein.

and at the most important techniques used in proteomics research.

From genome to proteome

Genomics has made pioneering breakthroughs in recent years. A host of research projects have been carried out in a variety of organisms, resulting in the decoding of a huge number of genes, and even entire genomes. The human genome has been cracked twice – once by the Human Genome Project, supported by government funding from the United States and other countries, and once by the US-based company Celera Genomics. Genomic discoveries contribute greatly to our understanding of cellular processes and events and the underlying mechanisms of disease. But by no means can they provide a complete picture. This is so because, for the most part, genes influence what happens in the cell indirectly, through the proteins they code for. Physiological and pathological processes cannot be fully understood without knowing what proteins are expressed (produced) by cells during these processes and how expressed proteins interact.

The proteome: a snapshot of the genome

While a genome is essentially static, providing a blueprint that changes little, if at all, over the course of an organism's lifetime, no two cell or tissue types express exactly the same proteins, and no cell or tissue expresses the same proteins all the time. The difference between the genome and the proteome is nicely illustrated by the life cycle of the butterfly. A caterpillar and the butterfly it becomes have the same genome but dramatically different phenotypes, i. e.

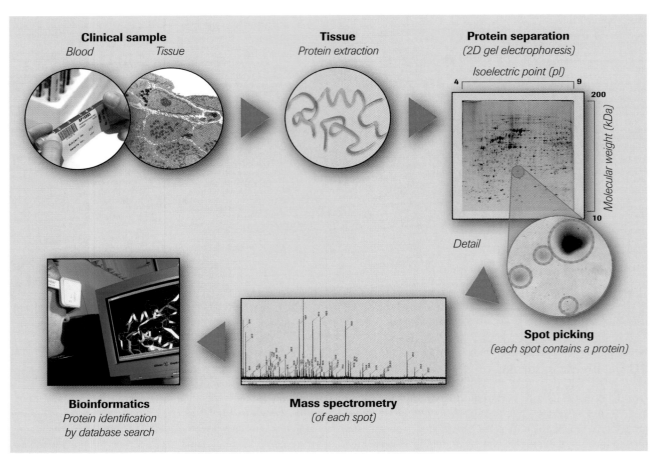

Proteome analysis using 2D gel electrophoresis and MALDI-TOF mass spectrometry. Proteins are extracted from clinical material such as blood or tissue and separated by 2D gel electrophoresis. The resulting protein spots are then cut out of the gel and the proteins are identified by mass spectrometry.

they differ greatly in their physical appearance. These different phenotypes are due solely to differences in protein expression. Similarly, the various types of cell in the body are different because they express different proteins.

A proteome is thus merely a snapshot of all the proteins made by a cell at a given time and under a specific set of environmental conditions. When the conditions change, so does the proteome. The development of disease, for example, invariably involves changes in the protein makeup of the tissues and organs affected. One of the main applications of proteomics is in identifying such changes. Proteins whose occurrence has been found to correlate with a particular disease – a particular cancer, say – can be evaluated as potential diagnostic markers for that disease. But how are marker proteins discovered?

Genes are easy

'Genes were easy', the title of the Human Proteome Project conference held in 2001, tellingly reflects the challenges and complexities of proteome analysis.

One reason why proteome research is so complicated is that a single gene can contribute to the pro-duction of a wide range of proteins, in part because of events that occur after protein biosynthesis, i. e. after DNA has been translated into the amino acid sequence of a protein. Among these post-translational events are such processes as glycosylation and phosphorylation. The tau proteins studied by researchers investigating Alzheimer's disease are a striking case in point. Over 100 variants have been identified, all deriving from a single gene.

As a result of post-translational and other protein modifications, a human being produces hundreds of thousands, or perhaps even millions, of different proteins over the course of a lifetime, numbers that easily dwarf the roughly 30,000 to 40,000 genes of the human genome. In any given type of human cell there are estimated to be at least 10,000 different proteins, at concentrations ranging from 10^2 to 10^6 copies per cell. This huge number of different proteins, each with its own distinct physicochemical properties and present across a large dynamic range of concentrations, poses an enormous challenge to any analytical technique. Unsurprisingly, large-scale proteome analyses would be inconceivable without the help of highly automated techniques. Moreover,

An inside look at a mass spectrometer. The instrument shown here is capable of determining peptide masses that are accurate to up to three decimal places.

given the massive quantities of data that need to be handled and meaningfully analysed, bioinformatics and computer technologies are playing an increasingly critical role alongside sophisticated techniques for protein separation and identification.

Technologies and techniques

A number of techniques are now available for performing proteome analyses. One very widely used approach employs 2D gel electrophoresis for protein separation, followed by mass spectrometry for protein identification.

After separation, the proteins visualised on the 2D gel have to be identified. This is done by first cutting each protein spot out of the gel, a step that is performed by a spot-picking robot. Next, the proteins in the spots are digested (broken up) with protein-splitting enzymes called proteases. The proteases that are used predictably cleave amino acid chains at well-defined sites. The protein-splitting enzyme trypsin, for instance, cleaves after the amino acids arginine and lysine. Enzymatic digestion produces small protein fragments, or peptides, of defined length and mass. A protein's peptide frag-

mentation pattern is as unique as a person's fingerprints – hence the term 'peptide mass fingerprint'.

It is precisely this uniqueness that is exploited in identifying proteins by mass spectrometry. To start with, the peptide mixture from a gel spot is embedded in a suitable matrix and ionised and converted to the gaseous phase by a brief laser pulse. The peptide ions are then accelerated in an electric field and fly two to three metres in a flight tube at speeds that vary with their size. The time to impact on a detector is measured and used to calculate the peptide mass profile. This technique is known as **m**atrix-**a**ssisted **l**aser **d**esorption / **i**onisation **t**ime-**of**-**fl**ight **m**ass **s**pectrometry (MALDI-TOF-MS). The mass profile obtained by MALDI-TOF-MS is then compared with the peptide masses in reference databases.

These databases contain mass fingerprints for all known protein sequences and the fingerprints of all the hypothetical proteins that have been predicted from gene sequences and subjected to theoretical (*in silico*) digestion with site-specific proteases. The experimentally measured peptide profile is compared with the theoretical mass fingerprints stored in databases. This allows most of the 2D-gel protein

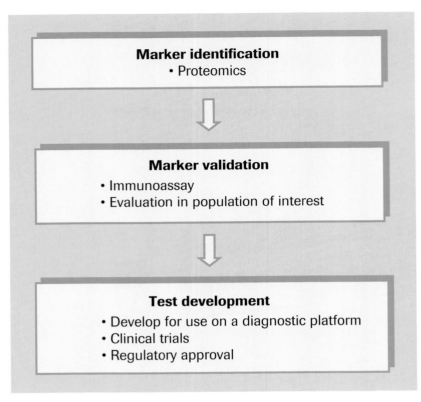

Steps involved in commercialising a new diagnostic marker.

spots to be related to a gene in a database. The ever-increasing number of DNA sequences being fed into databases by genomics research has been critical to the success of this approach to protein identification.

While 2D gel electrophoresis still involves a good deal of laborious manual work, even in sophisticated laboratories, the subsequent steps, from spot picking and protease digestion to mass spectrometry and database analysis, are now largely automated.

Each of the techniques used in proteome analysis has limitations and thus provides only a partial picture of a proteome. For this reason, a number of alternatives to, and variants of, the techniques described above have been devised, and new methods are continually being introduced. Two other techniques currently in wide use are multidimensional chromatography combined with **e**lectro**s**pray **i**onisation **m**ass **s**pectrometry (ESI-MS) and **s**urface-**e**nhanced **l**aser **d**esorption / **i**onisation (SELDI). Different as the various methods are, they can all be used to determine and compare the protein profiles of biological samples.

Applications

Proteome studies are a way of finding out what proteins occur in diseased (e. g. cancer) tissue but not in healthy tissue, or what proteins normally present in a particular tissue disappear in disease. Proteome analysis can also help to elucidate and describe processes of differentiation and regulation, metabolic pathways and entire protein networks. Here we mention just a few examples of the many potential uses for the information provided by proteomics.

A search is under way for proteins whose appearance or disappearance correlates with certain diseases. Such disease-associated proteins could be useful diagnostic markers or provide molecular targets for the development of new therapeutics. Another major application is in studying drugs to determine their mechanisms of action, efficacy and toxicity. Also, biological mechanisms of action can be explored using proteomic techniques, especially through the analysis of protein networks and reaction cascades. The knowledge acquired should shed light on fundamental biological processes and the mechanisms involved in the development and progression of disease. Research is also focusing on the characterisation of metabolic pathways in microorganisms and the identification of key enzymes. Applied to industrial biotechnology, proteomics may lead to improved fermentation processes. And in medicine proteomic studies might make it possible to predict more accurately how new antibiotic compounds will act on pathogens.

Unmet diagnostic needs

Medicine's diagnostic armamentarium is still far from complete in major disease areas ranging from cancer and cardiovascular disease to autoimmune, metabolic and neurodegenerative disorders. For years a wide array of tumour markers have played an important and established role in oncology testing. These markers are used primarily to monitor patients' responses to treatment. Only one of the tumour markers that can currently be tested for, **p**rostate-**s**pecific **a**ntigen (PSA), can provide tumour evidence at a very early stage. The other markers are either not elevated, or occur at elevated concentrations in only a few patients, in the early stages of disease. Yet early detection is often crucial to successful treatment. Many malignancies, including colorectal and breast cancer, are curable if detected while they are still localised, i.e. before they have had a chance to spread from their primary location to other tissues or organs. At a later stage curative treatment is generally not possible.

Cancers can grow for years without producing symptoms, and as a result may go undiscovered until it is too late. That is why mass screening programmes would be so valuable and have been recommended by various cancer associations. For screening to work, people at risk have to be examined at regular intervals and the tests that are used have to provide diagnostically meaningful results. And there's the rub. The non-invasive tests available today for colorectal cancer, for example, are simply not sensitive or specific enough. Endoscopy, by contrast, is excellent at detecting early cancers, but is poorly accepted as a mass screening technique. Many patients are put off by the idea of having an endoscopy because it is an invasive procedure and requires pre-endoscopy bowel cleansing to boot. Screening tests for early biochemical (tumour) markers in the blood could help close the current diagnostic gap by reliably indicating which patients need to be evaluated further by endoscopy. Colorectal cancer is not the only type of malignancy in which early detection remains a problem. There are similar unmet needs in the diagnosis of other cancers.

The search for new markers

The identification of a new marker begins with a careful selection of samples. As a rule, matched samples will have to be taken from patients and healthy individuals. For example, plasma, serum or urine samples will be obtained for comparison from persons with the disease of interest and from healthy controls. Not only must the patients' diagnosis be certain, but care must be taken to ensure that patients and controls are well-matched in terms of age and lifestyle, since otherwise proteome analysis may reveal misleading differences that are totally unrelated to the patients' disease.

Obtaining suitable material of other kinds can be a good deal more difficult. If tumour tissue is to be analysed for tumour-specific proteins, for example, samples of healthy tissue of the cell type that gave rise to the tumour will be required for comparison. Obviously, normal tissue adjacent to a tumour could be used, which would mean removing healthy tissue together with the tumour. The problem is that more extensive or additional surgery for research purposes is ruled out by ethical considerations. And compounding the problem is the fact that the only tissue samples available for study are the ones not needed for diagnosis by the pathologist.

Once suitable specimens have been obtained, proteome analyses are performed using the methods covered earlier. This will provide a list of proteins found in the patient samples but not in the controls, and/or of proteins present at elevated concentrations in the patient samples. These disease-associated proteins are potential marker candidates. However, the road from here to a marketable diagnostic test is a long one.

From marker candidate to diagnostic

All potential marker proteins have to be rigorously checked and validated. One customary way of developing tests for markers in body fluids is to create antibodies that will provide reliable, accurate quantitative measurements of marker concentrations. Once one has got this far, the markers can be tested for diagnostic power in a large, well-characterised collection of clinical samples. At this stage some of the candidates will be found to lack the required sensitivity and specificity, or to be insufficiently robust in the presence of interfering factors.

Once a marker candidate has cleared this first hurdle, the more advanced stages of development can begin. These include adapting the test to the desired diagnostic platform and refining the test itself and the manufacturing processes that will be used to produce it until all the stringent requirements for precision and reproducibility are consistently met. Large-scale clinical trials to validate the marker's intended use will need to be started at the earliest possible point in the development process. Such trials are absolutely essential for gaining regulatory approval of a new test and having it accepted by clinicians.

From single marker to multi-parameter test

There is a growing awareness that tests for multiple markers are needed to diagnose complex, multi-faceted diseases. And in fact there are instances in which diagnostic outcomes have already been improved by testing for a combination of markers rather than just one. The extent and pace of progress on this front will largely depend on the continued development of mathematical algorithms to optimise the analysis and interpretation of the complex data generated by multi-parameter testing.

Recognising the potential of multi-parameter tests, some companies are already developing diagnostic platforms to run them on. Protein chips are expected to enable a whole raft of markers to be measured simultaneously in a single sample. While this may still sound like a distant vision, it is more likely than not that the first systems of this type will be entering clinical laboratories soon.

To sum up, proteomics is a new branch of research that has raised hopes of providing unprecedented insights into physiological and pathological processes. One of its many applications is the search for new and better diagnostic markers. It will be interesting to see how proteomic discoveries shape laboratory diagnosis in years to come – there is good reason to believe their influence will be profound.

Wolfgang J. Fiedler

Near-patient diagnostics

The laboratory goes to the patient

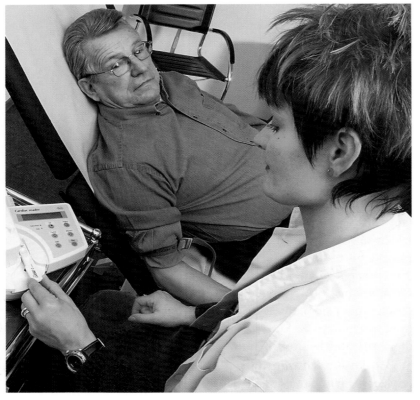

Suspected myocardial damage can be rapidly confirmed or excluded with a near-patient test. A diagnosis of myocardial infarction can then be made on the basis of the patient's signs and symptoms and the ECG findings.

An ambulance is on its way to the nearest accident and emergency department. On board, the emergency team is attending to a patient complaining of severe chest pain, exhaustion and shortness of breath. Dominating the situation and tormenting the patient is the thought: Are these symptoms due to a heart attack (myocardial infarction)? In this situation the presence or absence of a series of

cardiac markers can now be determined in minimum time with a sophisticated near-patient screening test performed on a sample of whole blood. When the patient arrives at the hospital, the test result provides the doctor with crucial information indicating what form of treatment is most appropriate. Because they provide results so rapidly, such **p**oint-**o**f-**c**are **t**esting (POCT) systems are an essential aid to medical decision-making in emergencies of this kind, where any unnecessary delay can result in irreparable damage to the heart muscle. In conjunction with an **e**lectro**c**ardio**g**ram (ECG) and the patient's signs and symptoms, the results of such tests can form the basis for a diagnosis of myocardial infarction.

This basic situation – the transport of a patient with chest pain to a critical care unit – is repeated throughout the world millions of times each year. In a proportion of such cases the test results are negative, and the patient is discharged. The earlier this occurs, the better; not only for the patient but also for the payer.

One of the most important cardiac markers is **c**ardiac **t**roponin **T** (cTnT), a protein released from myocardial tissue in increased amounts in the event of an infarction. Its normal concentration in plasma is extremely low, at about a hundredth of a billionth of a gram per millilitre (0.01 ng/mL). Designing a rapid and reliable, yet simple and compact, test for such a low concentration of a substance is a huge challenge to any test developer. A blood concentration of 0.03 ng/mL or more is suggestive of acute myocardial infarction. Other commonly used markers are cardiac troponin I, creatine kinase MB and myoglobin, each of which can provide diagnostically useful information if determined within an optimal time window after infarction. If they are to influence the choice of treatment, tests for cardiac markers need to have a turnaround time (i.e. the time between ordering the test and receiving the result) of no more than about an hour.

Daily monitoring of blood glucose in diabetes

Considerably less spectacular, though even more common, is the use of near-patient testing in diabetics. Diabetes mellitus has now assumed the proportions of a worldwide epidemic[1], not least as a result of increased life expectancy and changes in lifestyle. Diabetes is a currently incurable chronic disease characterised by disturbed regulation of blood glucose. In healthy individuals the action of endogenous insulin keeps the blood glucose level within certain limits despite the influence of meals and physical exertion. In diabetics this regulation is defective and requires support, e.g. with a suitable diet and administration of carefully calculated doses of insulin at appropriate intervals. Only by regularly testing blood glucose several times each day is it possible to achieve good long-term diabetic control and avoid severe complications such as chronic renal failure, blindness, leg amputations, strokes and myocardial infarction.[2,3] It is scarcely surprising, therefore, that diabetes self-testing products currently account for over half the worldwide POCT market.[4]

From bedroom to battlefield: everyday and extreme settings

The above examples of the use of near-patient **in vitro d**iagnostics (IVD) in acute and chronic diseases illustrate the vast range of settings in which point-of-care tests can be performed: at home in the case of patient self-testing (glucose, cholesterol, blood coagulation time), in the general practitioner's office for routine tests, at the hospital bedside, in the operating room, in the accident and emergency department, in the intensive care unit, in ambulances and rescue helicopters, at accident sites, in disaster areas and even on battlefields, on scientific expeditions, on space flights and at remote, isolated settlements. And it is precisely in extremely out-of-the-way places, far from professional medical services, that POCT systems can play a crucial, and even life-saving, role. The users are mostly professional paramedics with special training in the use of POCT systems. After performing the necessary tests on site they can transmit the results to specialist doctors working in a central office, who can then indicate what actions need to be taken.

Diabetes self-testing accounts for over half of the present market for POCT products.

In order to reduce casualties among combat soldiers, American scientists have combined information technology with the latest medical technology to develop what are known as **m**icroelectrome**c**hanical **s**ystems (MEMS). These are integrated in an interference-free telemedical network. The centrepiece of such systems is a portable unit – known as a **p**ersonal **s**tatus **m**onitor (PSM) – consisting of a communicator, a computer and various sensors which are attached to the soldier's body to monitor parameters such as heart rate, temperature, respiration and movement. An advanced addition to the PSM is the 'smart T-shirt', an undergarment fitted with devices that record the wearer's vital signs. Should the soldier suffer an injury, the array of sensors covering the body can even indicate which parts or organs are most probably affected. Sadly, this is another example – like the introduction of blood substitutes during the Second World War – of how extreme situations such as wars often accelerate the pace of medical progress and lead to breakthroughs.

POCT: saving lives and costs

Among other things, the rapid availability of test results provided by POCT systems satisfies the medical need for rapid diagnosis and prompt initiation of treatment. In emergency situations this is of crucial importance. The short analysis times of between one and five minutes are extremely useful, providing almost real-time measurements. This makes it possible to monitor even parameters that are subject to rapid biotransformation. A particularly sensitive parameter in this respect is glucose,

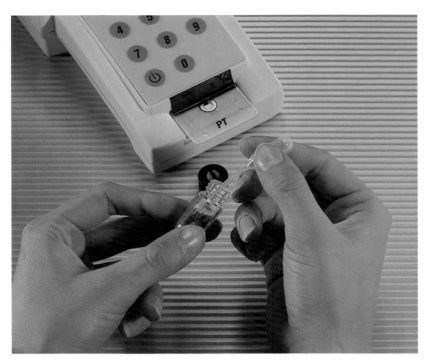

Patients taking drugs that affect blood coagulation have to check their blood coagulation parameters regularly.

whose concentration in whole blood falls by 5–7% per hour. Lactate is broken down even faster, its blood concentration falling by 30–50% within half an hour. If the result is to be of any value, lactate must therefore be measured within five minutes of taking a blood sample. Another extremely 'short-lived' parameter is **p**arathyroid **h**ormone (PTH), whose concentration should be measured before operations on the thyroid gland. Because it is broken down so rapidly, PTH must be measured no later than 15 minutes after the blood sample is taken.

Similarly, measurement of blood gases (oxygen and carbon dioxide) is particularly problematic because of interference by air bubbles present in the sample vessel. In some cases samples are transported in pneumatic tube systems. This causes rapid acceleration and deceleration of the sample vessel, leading to thorough mixing of the blood with any air bubbles present. This results in a falsely high reading for oxygen and a falsely low reading for carbon dioxide. POCT is significantly less subject to this kind of interference.[5]

The rapid availability of test results, e. g. in general practice, often makes it possible for the doctor and patient to discuss treatment options at the same visit at which a test is performed. The anxious wait for results is eliminated. The avoidance of another visit to the doctor also results in cost savings.

The possibility of performing tests with smaller sample volumes is another advantage, particularly in pediatrics and neonatology.

Entrusting these tests to nonspecialist staff, and in some cases even to patients themselves, could help to reduce chronic overburdening of laboratory staff.

In certain indications near-patient diagnostics can result in considerable savings in total treatment cost, i. e. the cost of reliably diagnosing the disease and then providing the most appropriate treatment. Over the next decade economic considerations such as these will further increase the importance of near-patient diagnostics.

What's on the market now?

As compared with highly specialised central laboratories, near-patient or point-of-care testing provides results very rapidly, usually at the place where the sample is obtained and in the presence of the patient. This luxury comes at a price that has to be justified by medical benefit, a consideration underlying much of the debate that currently surrounds near-patient diagnostics.

Parameters that can be determined using POCT systems include blood levels of routine electrolytes (Na^+, K^+, Ca^{2+}, Mg^{2+}, Cl^-), hematocrit (packed-cell volume), blood gases, blood pH, metabolic products such as creatinine, glucose, lactate and urea, and even substances present in extremely small amounts such as pregnancy hormones and cardiac markers.

POCT products now available for home use include systems for measuring blood glucose, cholesterol and coagulation time (e. g. in patients on anticoagulant therapy).

Point-of-care analysers can be divided into three categories on the basis of their size and consequent transportability: large benchtop units that are nevertheless transportable, medium-sized portable devices and hand-held devices.

One of the first POCT devices to be used in home settings – though not an in vitro diagnostic tool – was the clinical thermometer. Over the past few years this has evolved from a fragile glass tube containing a significant amount of mercury into a battery-driven thermocouple and, more recently, into a compact infrared spectrometer that need only be stroked gently across the temple of an infant who would react violently to any more invasive device.[6]

Measurement principles

Measurement may be based on either physical (e. g. optical or electrical) or (bio)chemical principles, and in many cases both physical and chemical techniques are combined.

For example, hematocrit, i.e. the proportion of the whole blood volume accounted for by red blood cells, can be measured on the basis of electrical conductivity. This technique exploits the fact that, unlike the plasma that surrounds them, erythrocytes are nonconductors of electricity. A sample of blood is passed through a narrow channel with electrodes situated at opposite points on its circumference. The conductivity of the whole blood, i.e. erythrocytes plus plasma, is measured. The hematocrit can then be estimated from this figure after determining the concentration of sodium ions, since these are responsible for most of the conductivity of plasma. By contrast, optical methods of determining hematocrit require physical separation of the opaque, light-scattering erythrocytes.

Amperometric test strips permit direct measurement of the concentration of glucose in whole blood. The test strip contains a highly selective enzyme such as glucose oxidase or glucose dehydrogenase. In the case of the Accu-Chek Comfort Curve system a potential is applied via palladium electrodes. The resulting current is measured and the glucose concentration determined by reference to a calibration curve.[7]

No compromise on analytical performance

Lest there be any doubt, it should be stressed at the outset that POCT systems can expect no concessions with regard to their analytical performance. They must meet precisely the same sensitivity[8] and specificity[9] requirements as their 'big brothers', the automated analysers used in central laboratories. If they are to provide highly accurate, usable values, and not meaningless data, they must also have inbuilt quality control mechanisms that detect any malfunction. Only then are they likely to be granted regulatory approval.[10]

Plasma or whole blood?

Some accuracy problems are systematic rather than device-related. For example, values measured in whole blood must be corrected before they can be compared with plasma values. This correction takes account of the different water content of plasma and red cells, but is based on an average hematocrit. If the test subject's hematocrit differs substantially from this average value, the corrected figure will not be accurate. For this reason values measured in whole blood are not always directly comparable with values measured in plasma.

Easy to use, yet robust

An important requirement of any POCT device is that the specified accuracy of measurement must be achievable by a person with no special training in its use. Only if the results it provides are simple to obtain yet reliable will a device be accepted by doctors. In practice, however, the degree of accuracy claimed by the manufacturer is often impossible to achieve without some form of training. A number of studies have therefore pointed to an urgent need for better training of patients in the use of POCT devices.[11, 12, 13] Another requirement that is not always satisfied is regular calibration of devices with calibration solutions.[14]

Integrated technologies

Once the sample fluid is obtained it must be transported to a special measurement site within the device. Numerous components have been developed to provide the necessary 'infrastructure' for this purpose, e.g. capillary systems, pumps, valves, pressure and flow sensors and electrodes. Some promising approaches to the manufacture of POCT products are based on the planar technologies – in some cases combined with moulding techniques – used in the manufacture of integrated electronic circuits. Even silicon has not been excluded as a possible material and in fact has already been used for the manufacture of microneedles.

Mimicking the mosquito

Silicon microneedles the size of a mosquito proboscis make it possible to obtain tiny blood samples of less than a microlitre almost painlessly. Directly attached to a component made entirely of silicon is a microcuvette fitted with a glass cover. Given its cost, silicon did not immediately suggest itself for use in a disposable device. There were also obvious concerns about the strength of silicon as compared with stainless steel, but these have since been dispelled.[15]

Requirements of near-patient testing systems

- Measurement using whole blood
- Small sample volume (10–100 microlitres)
- Result in less than 1–15 minutes
- High accuracy
- Simple operation
- Inbuilt quality control
- Minimal maintenance
- IT interface

Novel sampling module consisting of a lancet with a diameter no greater than that of a mosquito proboscis and a spiral sampling capillary on a 5x5 millimetre silicon wafer.

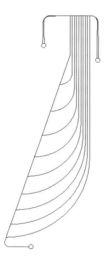

Possible geometric arrangement of individual microchannels for separation of blood cells from plasma.

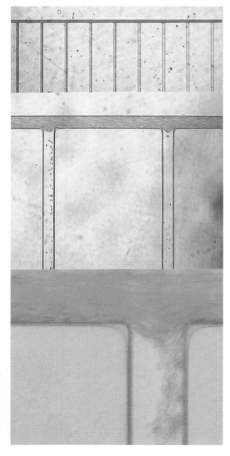

T-microchannel system. The enlarged details show how serial connection of a number of such T-junctions considerably reduces the concentration of cells in the emerging blood plasma.

A particular advantage of integrating the functions of skin puncture and measurement is that the test is performed in a single step and is therefore more user-friendly.

A special kind of propulsion: microfluidics

The fluid-conducting channels required for sample volumes of less than one microlitre have diameters in the range of 10 to 100 micrometres. This is similar to the diameter of human blood capillaries. At these dimensions the special laws of microfluidics apply.

Microchannel systems for blood cell separation

Miniaturised forms of sample preparation, e.g. in microchannel systems, can perform tasks that until now have required a great deal of manual effort. Thus, at present more than half of all samples still need to be centrifuged, e.g. to separate blood cells from plasma. Elimination of this time-consuming and costly step would bring incalculable benefits.

In order to separate blood cells from plasma, microfluidic channel systems were developed. These exploit a phenomenon known as the Zweifach-Fung effect, after its discoverers. In 1968 K. Svanes and Benjamin W. Zweifach (1910–1997) observed that at branching points in very fine blood vessels (capillaries), blood cells tended to enter the branch with less resistance to flow and a higher volumetric flow rate.[16] The really surprising thing about this was that any cells at all entered the (constricted) capillary with the reduced flow rate.[17] It was also found that almost all the red blood cells (erythrocytes) entered the vessel with the greater flow rate if this flow rate was at least 2.5 times that in the other branch. In an article published five years later, Yuan-Cheng Fung reported what seemed at first sight to be an even stranger finding: where a blood capillary branches into two smaller vessels of equal diameter and length, virtually all the erythrocytes flow initially into only one of the two branches.[18] This situation persists until a kind of saturation point is reached, after which the blood cells start to enter the other branch. Once the second branch has been filled to a certain degree, the blood cells once again choose the first branch. The route of the blood cells thus alternates periodically in a kind of random 'switchover mechanism'.

How can this all-or-nothing phenomenon be explained? The direction of movement of erythrocytes at a bifurcation in a capillary appears to be determined by the flow ratio between the two branches. In the design of a microchannel system capable of removing the cellular elements from blood, the ratio of flow rates in the afferent (sample delivery) and efferent (cell removal) capillaries would need to be controlled in similar fashion to that described above. This could be achieved, for example, through differences in the lengths or cross-sectional areas of the efferent capillaries. The art of designing such a separation module consists partly in setting the cross-sectional areas and lengths (depths) of the capillaries to values that ensure that even with multiple serial T-junctions, the flow rates in the efferent channels conducting particle-poor blood are lower by the correct amount than that in the corresponding afferent channel.

Since the flow rate in the afferent channel diminishes from junction to junction, the flow rates in the efferent channels must also diminish correspondingly with increasing distance from the sample inflow point. In this way it is possible to obtain blood plasma with a considerably reduced cell content.[19]

Separation of certain types of blood cell, e. g. leukocytes, is achieved in microfilter systems[20] that exploit differences in size, shape and flexibility. For example, erythrocytes are highly flexible discs with a thickness of about two micrometres and a diameter of about 7.5 micrometres, whereas leuko-cytes are more or less spherical and have a diameter of between 15 and 30 micrometres.

Outlook

A silent revolution is taking place in diagnostic medical devices. In the near future new approaches such as microsystems technology will lead to the development of completely new types of products for the diagnosis of human diseases. There will also be fundamental changes in how, where and by whom these new products are used.

In future, microtechnologies will permit almost continuous monitoring of medically relevant parameters. Portable 'personal laboratories'[21] will not only store results but also provide wireless transmission of data to the doctor, who will then be able to comment on the results and decide on any practical steps to be taken. An age of telemedicine – in which patients will receive care without having to visit a doctor's office – thus lies just around the corner.

Decentralisation of medical diagnostics also means that in future patients will – and will have to – assume greater responsibility for their own treatment. This can increase their self-confidence, since their hand-held 'personal laboratory' will enable them to take control of their disease.[22]

Hamid Emminger and Oliver Mast

Information is our future

Enhancing treatment efficacy with individualised health prognoses

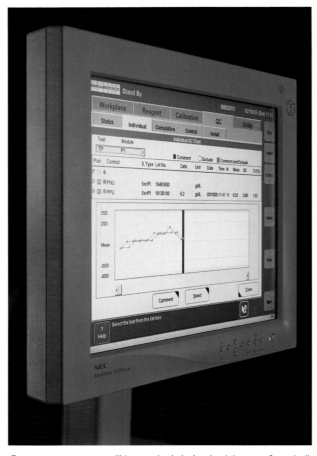

Computer programs will increasingly help physicians perform individual risk analyses and assess the therapeutic potential of alternative interventions.

The technological advances of recent decades have radically transformed the diagnosis of disease: from a part of medical practice based on physiological parameters and the physician's powers of observation to one that relies heavily on sophisticated technology. While the 'diagnostic process' once consisted of measuring physiological variables such as pulse and blood pressure and noting a patient's body odour and 'pulse character', it is now increasingly dominated by physical and biochemical tests employing reagents and devices. As a result, ever-expanding quantities of data are generated in arriving at a diagnosis, leading to an increasingly nuanced understanding of diseases and to treatments that are more finely tailored to individual patients' needs. Apart from indicating statistical normal ranges, however, it has so far remained beyond the capabilities of device-based diagnostics to tell users when findings are pathological or determine what action is required in specific situations. To be able to select the optimum therapy for their patients, physicians must therefore have a clear grasp of an extensive and complex collection of findings when they make therapeutic decisions. 'Optimum' in this context implies taking into account the achievable therapeutic benefits as well as the economic burden placed on the healthcare system.

Diagnosis as a guide to therapy

The welter of data generated by diagnostic tests accordingly does not become a guide to treatment until it has been interpreted by a professional, usually a patient's treating physician or a specialist. Owing to the exponential growth of medical knowledge, interpreting the clinical implications of diagnostic test results is becoming increasingly difficult for physicians who are not involved in research, even in areas of practice where general treatment guidelines are available.

Laboratory findings also pose challenges for patients because of the difficulty of relating them to the ways in which patients subjectively experience illness. Physical signs and symptoms such as pain and fever and the results of imaging procedures are concrete, and their significance is therefore readily appreciated by the layperson. By contrast, it is far more difficult for patients to see elevated levels of cholesterol or the 'blood glucose memory' parameter HbA_{1C} as a sign of disease or a risk factor because findings like these are less 'visibly' related to their potential consequences. Yet helping patients to understand the significance of such findings is an essential part of motivating them to assume a greater role in their own treatment.

Translating diagnostic data into information that will enable physicians and patients to work together towards achieving the best possible treatment outcomes is one of the great technological challenges facing medical diagnostics. What is needed is a transition from descriptive diagnostics to individualised prognostics, i.e. the refinement of data into information that can serve as a basis for action. Advances in medical knowledge – including those brought about by improved diagnostic techniques – are useful only to the extent that they help shape everyday clinical practice in ways that benefit patients. For this reason, new technologies must take into account the ongoing explosion of medical research, the proliferation of treatment standards and guidelines, the growing influence of health insurers and healthcare policy makers, the sovereignty of patients and the trend to patient self-testing.

Explosion of medical research

A burgeoning biomedical research sector is producing a mounting flood of information. After undergoing critical peer review, findings from countless studies are published in journals, conference proceedings and books or are put on the Internet, where they can be accessed from virtually anywhere in the world in seconds. At first blush, this looks entirely positive. But as the flow of new information continues to gather speed, the impossibility of keeping abreast becomes more and more apparent. There is a growing mismatch between the supply of information and the clinician's ability to pick out and absorb what's relevant and apply it in everyday clinical practice. This predicament affects both specialists and general practitioners, who in future will be

Glucometers, already widely used by people with diabetes, are part of a growing trend to patient self-testing.

expected to guide patients through the healthcare maze like skilled pilots.

Proliferation of treatment standards and guidelines

Evidence-based medicine (EBM) has been defined by David L. Sackett (b. 1934) as

the conscientious, explicit, and judicious use of current best evidence in making decisions about the care of individual patients. The practice of evidence based medicine means integrating individual clinical expertise with the best available external clinical evidence from systematic research.[1]

The EBM movement is an expression of the desire to see medical findings implemented quickly in everyday medical practice. Since individual physicians cannot even begin to sift through and assess the mountain of potentially relevant new information in their fields, treatment guidelines and standards have been issued to relieve them of this burden. However, the growing number of guidelines is in itself problematic for the practising physician, who is confronted daily with a variety of diseases and who must also consider a range of concurrent factors that can cause the presenting features of one and the same disease to vary from one patient to the next. The provision of general guidelines for the treatment of individual patients therefore remains a challenge for the future.

Growing influence of healthcare systems

Since health and disease are increasingly economic as well as medical issues, integrated care strategies and disease and patient management systems will soon determine the type of medical care available to a significant number of patients. This will introduce transparency into the medical-care process while at the same time making the quality of treatments measurable and comparable. Because they are essential to optimum healthcare delivery, effective diagnostic practices make a key contribution to quality.

Patient sovereignty

Newspapers, television, the Internet and self-help groups provide people virtually everywhere with ready access to health information, and this is clearly one reason for patients' rising healthcare expectations. Patients are becoming more and more vocal in demanding specific treatment options which they regard (sometimes for good reasons and sometimes not) as best suited to their needs. Patients' expectations regarding physician-patient communication are also rising. Fast, reliable interpretation of medical data based on the latest research evidence and the patient's individual circumstances is increasingly regarded by patients as a basic part of quality care.

Home testing

One of the current trends in medicine is to encourage patients to take greater responsibility for their health. This is done, for example, by involving them more closely in their own treatment and treatment monitoring. Diagnostic devices for patient self-testing have thus become a standard feature in many indications (e.g. in diabetes and asthma and for patients taking anticoagulants). In future such devices will increasingly enable patients to interpret measurements themselves and in some instances will even allow them to adapt their treatment to changing requirements without having to consult their physician.

New technologies

Every new imaging technique or laboratory parameter increases not only the amount but also the complexity of the information that has to be absorbed and applied in diagnostic practice. The analysis and interpretation of the human genome can be expected to generate a host of additional diagnostically relevant data, and one day scientifically established standards of care will dictate that these data be taken into account in assessing a patient's overall situation.

It is easy to see that meeting these challenges is beyond the scope of current healthcare systems. No physician today is able to weigh all the epidemiological and therapeutic evidence that may be relevant to caring for a specific patient and at the same time comply with process- and outcome-based standards. As a result, there is a widespread and legitimate demand that future diagnostic systems should facilitate the process of interpreting rapidly expanding quantities of medical data and deriving evidence-based therapeutic recommendations. Physicians and patients alike are calling for intelligent diagnostic methods that will permit standardised interpretation of data based on comprehensive, up-to-date medical evidence. Moreover, the results need to be intuitively understandable and should be readily accessible anywhere.

Computer-based prognoses in clinical practice

Computers have become the tool of choice for taming immense quantities of data. The question is: Can they also be used to process and interpret diagnostic data in the light of current medical evidence and patients' individual situations? Historically, this has been considered the exclusive preserve of the human mind because of its ability to absorb and evaluate a barrage of information in seconds and then draw specific therapeutic conclusions.

Biometricians, bioinformaticians and mathematicians have been trying for decades to systematically analyse and model these human cognitive skills. 'Artificial intelligence', 'neural networks', 'stochastic models' and 'medical decision analyses' are terms frequently used in this context to describe methodological approaches to dealing with masses of data with the help of automated systems.

A common feature of all these approaches is that they are based on systematic analyses of disease processes and their treatment and use algorithms to give structured descriptions of sequences of events and relationships. Provided the validity of the descriptions is sufficiently general, such approaches can be used to assess prognoses and predict outcomes in individual patients.

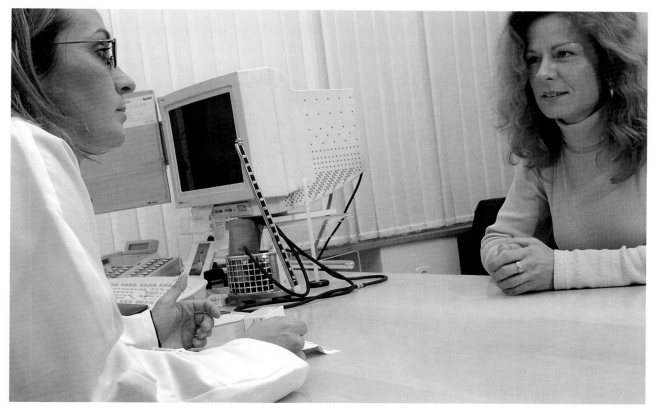

Programs that provide prognostic health information enable doctors to formulate individualised treatment targets for and with their patients.

What a prognostic system has to be able to do

To bring about lasting improvements in routine medical care, computer-based prognostic systems must meet a number of requirements. They must be able to process case-history, diagnostic and treatment data that already exist in electronic form. Based on these data, they should provide prognoses that take into account the medical consequences of various therapeutic options. They should be able to calculate the gain in quality of life and years of life achievable with various therapeutic options and assess the economic consequences of those options. They must be able to evaluate the quality and currency of the underlying medical evidence and take into account all the factors relevant to therapeutic practice, as well as treatment standards and guidelines. They must be available during the consultation and facilitate intuitive use of information by both physician and patient. Finally, they should support medical quality management, and the reliability and quality of their prognoses must be validated and certified.

Modelling in medicine

The method that has been used the longest and most widely for forecasting is stochastic modelling. For example, it is already used routinely in meteorology to construct probability models for forecasting weather events and in asset management to calculate the potential financial performance of stock portfolios. Prognostic models are also already well established in medicine, e.g. for predicting the risk of myocardial infarction[2] based on age, blood pressure, cholesterol levels and other parameters. Regression models permit the prognostic use of findings from individual studies, e.g. from studies on infarction risk. More complex relationships and a broader knowledge base can be described algorithmically and put to prognostic use with the help of Markov models. These depict the progress of a disease as a detailed sequence of events and can be used to assess the consequences of therapeutic interventions. Such models are constructed by systematically reviewing the medical and epidemiological literature on the disease of interest and selecting and evaluating the information relevant for modelling according to criteria of evidence-based medicine.[3]

From data to clinically actionable information

Disease models can be used to accomplish the task (mentioned at the outset) of refining data into information that can form the basis for action. For these models to have an impact on medical practice, they need to be made accessible to clinicians as well as researchers, e. g. via the Internet. Once sufficient epidemiological and clinical information about a disease is available, it can be used to develop a prognostic model. The first systems are already being marketed for the well-researched indication of diabetes mellitus. The Mellibase program, for example, uses patient data to perform individual risk analyses and assess the therapeutic potential of various options. It indicates the probability of specific diabetic complications and quantitatively evaluates the relevance of risk factors associated with them. It also shows the extent to which future complications can be prevented by achieving internationally recommended therapeutic targets. This enables doctors to formulate individual treatment goals for and with their patients – e. g. with regard to smoking status or blood pressure – and immediately calculate and present the expected individual benefits. This analytical tool can thus be used to guide a patient's further treatment. Based on the results of risk analyses, it is also possible to generate a schedule for continuous treatment monitoring, supported by an 'intelligent' warning system programmed to provide recommendations for action.

Other control and warning programs, known as watchdogs, which alert doctors by various means when a dangerous situation arises are already in clinical use. Examples are watchdog systems for monitoring laboratory results, automatically checking vital parameters in intensive care units and performing medication checks. It was demonstrated some time ago, for example, that dangerous elevations of serum creatinine in patients taking nephrotoxic drugs can be detected some 24 hours in advance, and can be countered by dose reduction if doctors are alerted by e-mail. Similarly, the use of watchdog software has been found to significantly improve prescribing practices (assessed as compliance with recognised guidelines) in thrombosis prevention.

Prospects

In the past medical quality, quality of life and cost efficiency have been regarded as separate and distinct quality goals. Future model-based prognostic tools will allow the integrated assessment of multiple quality metrics and provide a decision aid capable of optimising care across all three quality dimensions. Decision support systems will make medical treatment not only more effective and cost-efficient but also simpler and safer.[4] Significant successes have already been reported in real-life clinical settings,[5] e. g. with computerised risk profiles.[6] Physicians are open-minded about such systems, perceiving them as useful additions to their arsenal.[7] Moreover, risk profiles help meet patients' very real need to be well-informed about their health and healthcare options.[8]

There is a need to develop integrated decision support systems that go beyond today's prognostic tools both in terms of the depth of guidance offered and the range of the diseases and applications covered. Future systems should establish direct, context-sensitive links between high-risk profiles and the appropriate medical guideline(s) and/or information in authoritative medical textbooks. Depth will be enhanced by replacing general recommendations such as 'lower blood pressure' with more specific guidance – for example, a detailed overview of an appropriate course of antihypertensive drug therapy which includes dosing recommendations and takes into account any concurrent diseases the patient may have.

For diagnostics companies, medical forecasting offers an opportunity to steadily refine the kinds of data and information their products and services provide. It will also radically change their product landscape (instruments and reagents). While the development of increasingly sensitive diagnostic instruments and novel diagnostic tests will continue, information technology will come increasingly to the fore, bringing about a shift of emphasis from diagnosis to prognosis and treatment support.

This may ultimately lead to advances in pharmacogenomics which will enable physicians to select drug therapies that are not only appropriate for a given diagnosis but are also optimally tailored to a patient's genetic makeup.

Klaus Lindpaintner

Pharmacogenetics:
paving the way to more individualised medicine

Over two hundred years ago Voltaire (1694–1778) complained that physicians put medicines of which they knew little into bodies about which they were equally ignorant. Certainly, in the 18th century scientists did not know what active agents were present in such patently useful and effective medicines as cinchona bark and extract of foxglove. Fortunately, this did not keep physicians from prescribing the medicines available at the time to alleviate the suffering of their patients. Over the course of the 19th century pharmacists, chemists and physicians learned how to analyse, and later how to synthesise, many naturally occurring active substances. Today we know almost everything there is to know about the medicines that we use, and we are learning more and more about the relationships between molecular structure and effect.

Understanding the human body into which medicines are put – to return to Voltaire's critical observation – is a more difficult task. The reason for this is clear: in contrast to the constant structure of every medicine (or at least every synthetic medicine, as opposed to the extracts often favoured by various schools of alternative medicine), all human beings are different. Each and every patient has peculiarities that render him or her unique, and this makes it extremely difficult to standardise treatments. At the beginning of the 20th century the question of how the 'organic individuality' of a person arises could not be answered by scientific argument. What are these differences based on, at the level of an organism's cells and molecules? What structures give rise to the individuality which results in medicines having different effects in different people?

Around the turn of the 20th century physicians became aware that response to medicines differs

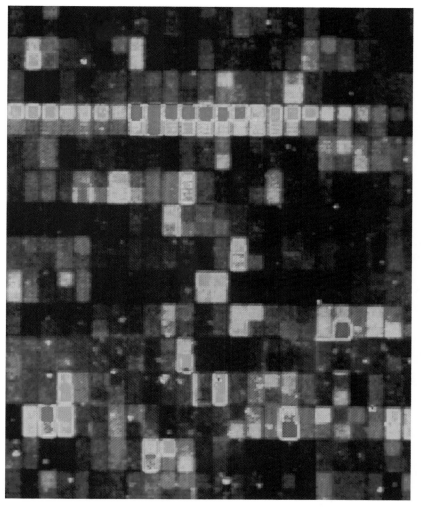

Screenshot of a DNA chip analysis.

from patient to patient. Probably the first to realise this was the British physician Archibald Edward Garrod (1857–1936), who introduced the concept of a patient's 'chemical individuality'. Garrod had observed that the hypnotic agent sulphonal caused acute porphyria, a disorder of liver metabolism, in some patients. This led him to conclude that some mechanism which helped the body to 'detoxify' this drug was inadequately developed in the individuals concerned. He also noted individual differences in susceptibility to infectious diseases and in the success rates of certain medicines. It is to him that we owe the first data on the heritability of these traits. In the first decade of the 20th century Garrod called upon science to direct all its efforts towards identifying the basis of this genetic distinctiveness so that it could be used to improve the health of mankind.

Individuality and genetics

Thanks to today's more detailed understanding of normal and pathological organ and cell function, Garrod's wish is now, around a hundred years later, finally nearing fulfilment. This is due not least to the discoveries and achievements of genome research, the ultimate objective of which is to gain a detailed understanding of the structure, function and interactions of all genes. As a first major step on the road towards this objective, the **H**uman **G**enome **P**roject (HGP) was set up with the aim of determining the sequence of the building blocks that make up the totality of the human genetic material (genome). Thanks to the HGP, we are now able to provide at least a partial description of the chemical individuality of a human being. The results of the HGP describe one 'standard' genome. Knowledge of the primary sequence makes it possible to check this information for constancy or variability between individuals. A key concept in this regard is 'diversity' or – to use a more technical term – 'polymorphism'. This refers to the fact that although all human beings possess the same set of genes, individual genes differ in many small ways from person to person. As a result, people differ in the amount, form and function of the protein molecules that they synthesise on the basis of these genes. Proteins, in turn, act as building blocks and information carriers that determine the form and function of cells and organs. These slight, but in some cases momentous, differences are due mostly to replacement of one of the nucleotide bases – adenine (A), thymine (T), cytosine (C) and guanine (G) – that make up **d**eoxyribo**n**ucleic **a**cid (DNA) with another. They are therefore referred to as **s**ingle **n**ucleotide **p**olymorphisms, or SNPs (pronounced 'snips'). Humans are now estimated to possess between one and five million such polymorphisms. The vast majority of these undoubtedly have no consequences and are irrelevant to a person's health. A small proportion, however, have functional effects and play a crucial role in determining the genetic aspects of our individuality and thus the diversity of the human species. Environmental effects and life's experiences, however, contribute at least as much, with the result that monozygotic twins are very much independent individuals despite being extremely similar in appearance.

Classical hereditary diseases

The existence and influence of relevant individual gene variants has so far been demonstrated primarily in relation to rare classical 'monogenic' diseases, in which changes in a single gene are sufficient to cause the disease in its full-blown form with a high degree of predictability. Cystic fibrosis, a hereditary disorder of airway secretions, and Huntington's chorea, a hereditary neurological disease that progresses inexorably to death, are examples of monogenic diseases in which the affected gene and the changes (mutations) present within it are now known. Patients can thus now be offered far more specific counselling than was previously possible on the basis of family history alone. At the same time, however, the deterministic character of these mutations poses new issues, particularly with regard to the potential psychological impact of learning that one will eventually develop a disease and with regard to the risk of social stigmatisation. This immediately raises additional issues about data protection and the potential for discrimination regarding employment and insurance.

Common, complex diseases

Because of the well-documented familial clustering of most major common diseases, it is assumed that inherited susceptibilities play a role in these entities as well. However, it is considerably more difficult than in the case of monogenic diseases to characterise the genes concerned, identify their disease-relevant molecular variants and elucidate their interplay with the well-known external risk factors for the diseases in question. Such diseases are multifactorial, i.e. no one factor – whether genetic or environmental – overrides the others. This makes it difficult to determine which factors contribute to the occurrence of a disease. An understanding of this complex interplay of factors is nevertheless essential for progress in the treatment and prevention of multifactorial diseases.

Revolution or evolution?

Medicine is a constantly changing field. Are the methods used to treat patients about to undergo radical change in the direction of 'individualised' treatment as a result of the application of molecular genetic technologies? Before speculating about the future, it is often helpful to consider the past and try to see things from a longer-term perspective. Medical progress has, by and large and throughout its history, occurred along two primary trajectories. One of these has been in the area of differential diagnosis, i. e. the ever more specific identificaton of disease variants: the other in the area of prospective risk assessment. The impact of genetics, the study of heredity, and of genomics, the study of the genome of an organism, is very likely to be felt in exactly these same two areas. Conceptually, therefore, nothing radically new is about to happen, though advances in molecular genetics can of course to some extent accelerate the pace at which medical progress occurs.

The central theme of medical progress: differential diagnosis

Throughout history the objective of medical research has been to make medical intervention more successful. This has, in essence, always depended essentially on improving our understanding of diseases and their causes. The history of medicine is characterised by a gradual progression towards this goal, and by our ability to make increasingly accurate and specific differential diagnosis. The level at which diseases are understood, classified and diagnosed has generally been limited by available technologies. Hence the gradual shift from diagnosis based purely on symptoms and signs to an anatomical, then histological and microbiological, description of diseases, and later to an appreciation of the influence of environmental factors on the risk of contracting a disease. Until very recently, however, a fundamental rift remained between the level at which drugs work, i. e. the molecular level, and the level at which we were able to understand, describe and classify illness and the effects of drugs. Thanks to advances in cell biology and biotechnology over the past 30 years, we are now – for the first time – able to understand and diagnose diseases at the same level at which basic disease mechanisms operate and drugs act, namely at the molecular level.

Pharmacogenetics

The molecular mechanisms of drug action and our molecular genetic understanding of 'normal' and abnormal biology come together in pharmacogenetics, the study of the interplay between medicines and inherited characteristics. Strictly speaking, the term 'pharmacogenetics' refers to something far

The British physician and biochemist **Archibald Edward Garrod** (1857–1936) not only proposed the concept of human chemical individuality, but also originated the 'one gene, one enzyme' theory. He was especially interested in hereditary metabolic disorders, which he described as 'metabolic variations' and held to be the biochemical correlates of structural defects. He published a number of articles on metabolic disorders that could be detected by testing the patient's urine. Among other things, he discovered that alkaptonuria is an inherited metabolic disorder rather than bacterial in origin. He also explained albinism – correctly – as a genetic disorder of cellular melanin production.[1]

more specific than the study of patient-to-patient variations in drug response – a description that is almost as common as it is vague. In fact, this field holds out the promise, first, of permitting a more detailed examination of intrinsically normal patient characteristics and, secondly, of diagnosing diseases more accurately, which will translate into more specific, and often more successful treatment.

Pharmacogenetics can be divided into two quite distinct categories: one that may best be referred to as 'classical' pharmacogenetics, since it relates to pharmacokinetic and pharmacodynamic phenomena that have been recognised for quite some time, and another concerned essentially with the identification of pathophysiological subpopulations or molecular differential diagnoses within a broader clinical diagnosis that underlie response, or lack thereof, to particular drugs.

Classical pharmacogenetics

Classical pharmacogenetics deals with gene variants that do not in themselves cause illness of any kind, but rather manifest themselves only when a patient with a variant gene is prescribed a drug whose metabolism (pharmacokinetics) or mechanism of action (pharmacodynamics) are affected by that gene. Classical pharmacogenetics has developed little by little since the middle of the 20th century. It first gained major recognition in the 1950s and 1960s, a time when many new drugs were developed and our biochemical understanding of the metabolic breakdown of drugs increased considerably. More recently, the development of molecular biological and genetic techniques has led to the present, increased interest, as many of the earlier findings can now be explained in molecular terms.

Pharmacokinetics

Pharmacokinetic effects relate to the different response of individual patients to a drug based on differences in absorption, distribution, activation, metabolic breakdown or excretion of the drug. This leads to differences in effective drug concentration at the site of action and thus either to an inadequate effect (if the concentration is too low) or possibly to toxic effects (if the concentration is too high or if the active agent is metabolised to toxic derivatives). Many of the known pharmacokinetic phenomena are linked to variants of the cytochrome P450 enzyme system that cause differences in the breakdown of drugs. Absorption, distribution and elimination may be affected, as may the enzymatic activation of inactive substances, known as 'prodrugs', that undergo conversion to the desired drug only after entering the body. The P450 system comprises a range of enzymes known by abbreviations such as 3C4, 2C19 and 2D6. As a result of genetic variation, each of these exists in several, and in some cases many, different forms possessing different levels of activity. The presence of these enzyme variants affects the metabolism of a substantial number of commonly prescribed drugs. For example, many psychoactive drugs are broken down by enzyme 2D6, which is present in a relatively inactive form in 5–10% of Europeans. This can result in normal doses acting as overdoses and causing corresponding side effects. Patients with this enzyme variant therefore require lower-than-average doses of these drugs. Conversely, the enzyme is present in an overactive form in 1–2% of the population. In these patients the same drugs are broken down so rapidly that at normal doses the drug concentration at the site of action never reaches the level required to bring about the desired effect. These patients therefore require substantially higher doses of the drugs. The 'correct' dose can thus vary by a factor of ten or more between individual patients. Determination of the correct dose for a particular patient is made even more difficult by the impracticality of measuring drug levels and by the fact that many psychoactive drugs take several weeks to exert their full effect. Also, the need to determine more than 30 variants (SNPs) of enzyme 2D6, for example, has so far presented a practical hurdle to implementing diagnostic applications. Use of DNA chips that can test for a large number of SNPs simultaneously may lead to important breakthroughs in this area.

Pharmacodynamics

Pharmacodynamic effects relate to differences in the impact of optimal concentrations of a drug at its site of action. Such differences in response to a drug may be due to DNA-sequence-related molecular variations in the target molecule or other components of the biological pathway targeted. As classical pharmacogenetic phenomena are based on gene variants that themselves do not directly contribute to a particular disease, pharmacodynamic effects occur with drugs that act in a palliative fashion, i.e. that treat the symptoms and effects of disease rather than its causes. Such drugs act on biological pathways of general physiological importance. For example, elevated blood pressure can be reduced very effectively – irrespective of whether its underlying cause is known – by means of drugs that inhibit the basal activity of one of the biological mechanisms known to play a role in determining blood pressure, e.g. the renin-angiotensin system, or the sympathetic nervous system. Examples of such pharmacodynamic phenomena have come to light in the field of asthma therapy. Beta-agonists, which relax the bronchial muscles and thereby dilate the airways in non-specific fashion, are among the most widely used of all drug classes. The beta-2 receptor that they activate occurs in a number of molecular variants. These have no influence on the risk of developing asthma, but can alter the response to beta-agonists by a factor of five.

'Retrospective differential diagnosis'

The situation is quite different in the case of gene variants that are causally related to particular diseases. It is now generally agreed that all common, complex diseases are due to heterogeneous and multifactorial pathological processes that ultimately lead to a constellation of signs and symptoms that we have come to identify as a 'standard' clinical presentation of the disease. We should not expect disease processes that we lump together into a particular clinical diagnosis despite their molecular differences to respond in the same ways to causally acting drugs. Rather, such drugs will benefit only those patients whose disease cause is specifically

Analysis of DNA chips can be used, among other things, to detect variations in genes that code for the synthesis of certain enzymes.

targeted by the particular drug's mechanism of action. The fact that a patient responds to such a drug amounts, therefore, to a 'retrospective differential diagnosis' at the molecular level. What first presented as a pharmacogenetic phenomenon ultimately hinges on whether drugs are prescribed for the correct molecular diagnosis, and thus on recognising molecular differences between etiologically heterogeneous subtypes of a clinically uniform disease process.

Probability of response

Pharmacogenetic effects are a matter of probability. The commonly held view that patients can be divided into two clearly defined groups, responders and non-responders, on the basis of identified pharmacogenetically relevant parameters is naive. Because of the complexity of multifactorial diseases, the presence of a pharmacogenetic effect will always in fact represent two overlapping distributions that cannot be completely separated from each other. The category of 'genotypic responders' will thus always include some clinical non-responders, while that of 'genotypic non-responders' will always include some clinical responders. Determination of an individual's pharmacogenetically relevant

genotype thus only indicates a probability. Rather than labelling individuals as 'responders' or 'non-responders' we should more correctly refer to the greater or lesser probability that an individual will respond to a particular drug.

Ethical and social aspects

The issues that will arise as a result of pharmacogenetic diagnostics are likely to be less controversial than those raised by the diagnosis of classical monogenic hereditary diseases. In the latter case the highly specific predictions as to a person's future that can often be made on the basis of genotyping raise a number of potentially complex personal and family questions, for example, with regard to emotional problems and social issues. Pharmacogenetic diagnoses, by contrast, become significant only in certain circumstances, namely when a person has to take a particular drug. That said, pharmacogenetic data could potentially be used for the purpose of risk management, e. g. in the insurance industry, and this could potentially also raise significant bioethical and social issues. Just like a genetically increased disease risk, a reduced likelihood of response to a particular drug would obviously alter the risk encountered by an insurer or employer, especially if no alternative drug were available. The implications would vary according to the interests of the stakeholder concerned. For example, a low probability of successful treatment for a disease, resulting in earlier death, could have quite different financial implications for a health insurer and a life insurer (i.e. advantageous for the former and disadvantageous for the latter). In the case of chronic diseases in which response or non-response to a drug significantly influences the cost of treatment, the consequences will depend on whether response to the drug in question reduces the long-term cost of treatment or converts an otherwise rapidly fatal condition into a chronic disability with high ongoing health maintenance costs. In the former case the financial risk encountered by the health insurer may be reduced, whereas in the latter case it may be increased. Conflict-of-interest situations of this kind are more likely to occur as a consequence of pharmacogenetic data that identify pathological subpopulations, although we cannot be sure that similar issues will not arise as a result of classical pharmacokinetic and pharmacodynamic stratifications.

Issues such as the ones described above that may be raised by pharmacogenetics or by genetic parameters associated with disease risk are not sufficiently addressed by data protection measures, which are currently being advocated as the principal safeguard against 'information risk'. If they are to be used advantageously, pharmacogenetic data need to be communicated even more clearly than pathogenetic data. In order to provide a secure basis for such use of pharmacogenetic data we will need to establish rules, i.e. guidelines and laws, that permit use of data for the benefit of the patient but not for other purposes. Ultimately, such rules can be formulated only on the basis of public dialogue and consensus.

Challenge of the postgenomic period

To what extent have the achievements of molecular biology and genetics actually influenced medical practice?

On the one hand, these disciplines have already influenced patient treatment in many direct and concrete ways. It is fair to say that, because of the use of recombinant techniques and transgenic animals in biomedical research, every drug developed over the past decade owes its origin directly or indirectly to the achievements of molecular biology and genetics. On the other hand, it is also clear that the expectations raised by the successful sequencing of the human genome, a project whose 'completion'

was seen by many as opening the gates to a flood of biomedical innovations, have proved to be vastly exaggerated. What we now have is raw DNA data that are largely uncharacterised in terms of both function and relevance to health. The achievement that the sequencing of the human genome undoubtedly represents is dwarfed by the challenge of identifying the links between the raw genomic data and biological processes and clinically relevant medical phenomena. A commonly used metaphor is that of a telephone book that initially had only blank pages. So far we have succeeded only in entering all existing telephone numbers into this book in ascending order. The next step is to establish the link between each number and its subscriber. And whereas it took about an hour – based on the entire duration of the Human Genome Project – to sequence a gene of average length, it will take years to arrive at even an approximate description and understanding of the function of each such gene within the complex network of the living organism.

The task that we are now confronted with is daunting in its magnitude. Compared to the sequencing project, which benefited from automation that accelerated the work exponentially, the present task is considerably less likely to be helped along by the use of high-throughput methods.

Links must be established between genomic data and clinical phenomena. The aim of 'genetic epidemiology' is to identify, from among the millions of SNPs present in the human genome, the small proportion – probably a few thousand, at most – that show associations with clearly defined clinical conditions, whether in terms of their incidence (number of new cases occurring in a population over a given period) or prevalence (proportion of a population affected at a given time).

Conclusion

The question of what impact genetics and genomics are likely to have on medicine, and in particular on common, complex diseases, needs to be considered from a number of perspectives.

On the one hand, the approaches and techniques of molecular biology, genetics, genomics and genetic epidemiology have become indispensable to biomedical progress, since this will always depend on increasing our understanding of biology and pathology. On the other hand, we need to be modest and realistic, avoiding overblown expectations about the practical applications of this research and the time frame in which progress will occur. This is not to say that we won't continue to move towards better medicine. But progress will always be incremental, and we will never achieve perfection or find answers to all our questions. Nature will never allow us to unravel all her mysteries. Currently available technologies can to some extent increase the pace of medical progress along established trajectories, i.e. towards improved differential diagnosis and more accurate estimations of risk. However, available therapeutic and preventive measures are not about to undergo a revolution, but rather will continue to evolve at a steady and manageable pace.

Appendix

Emeritus Professor **Monika Barthels,** MD, was born in Göttingen, Germany, in 1934. She received her medical training in Göttingen and Munich and is a pediatrician. In 1968 she spent a scholarship year working with Walter H. Seegers in the Department of Physiology at Wayne State University in the United States, where she studied the influence of phospholipids and bile acids on thrombin formation. After returning to Germany, she headed the central coagulation laboratory and hemostaseology unit (comprising a hemophilia centre and hemostasis clinic) at Hanover University Medical School for 30 years. In 1977 she qualified to lecture in internal medicine, a subject she taught as an associate professor from 1982 until her retirement. She has worked as a freelance science journalist since 1999.

Ralf Bröer, MD, was born in Bad Oeynhausen, Germany, in 1962. He studied medicine in Münster (Westphalia), earning his doctorate there in 1991 under medical historian Wolfgang U. Eckart. After completing his internship, Dr Bröer won a scholarship from the German Research Foundation and the Jung Foundation to work at the institutes of medical history in Hanover and Heidelberg; during this period he also studied history and philosophy. He has been a research associate at the Institute of Medical History in Heidelberg since 1995. His main areas of professional interest are the history of gynecology and obstetrics and the early modern history of medicine. He is the author of numerous books, essays and journal articles on medical history.

Emeritus Professor **Johannes Büttner,** MD, PhD, was born in Giessen, Germany, in 1931. After studying chemistry and medicine in Kiel and Tübingen, he headed the central laboratory at Kiel University's Medical Department I from 1956 to 1969. In 1963 he was certified as a clinical chemist by the German Society of Physiological Chemistry, and in 1964 he completed post-doctoral studies in physiological and clinical chemistry at Kiel University Medical School. He was appointed to a newly created chair of clinical chemistry at Hanover University Medical School in 1969 and in the same year became director of the Institute of Clinical Chemistry I. He was a member of the History of Science Working Group in the Department of History of Pharmacy and Natural Sciences at Braunschweig Technical University from 1978 to 1991. Professor Büttner was president of the German Clinical Chemistry Society from 1972 to 1976 and chairman of the Committee on Standards of the International Federation of Clinical Chemistry from 1970 to 1979. He is the recipient of many awards and distinctions.

Professor **Hans-Joachim Burkardt,** PhD, was born in Mannheim, Germany, in 1946. He studied microbiology at the University of Erlangen in Nuremberg, where he qualified as a university lecturer in 1980 on the basis of post-doctoral work on electron microscopy. Joining Roche in 1984, he headed microbiological diagnostics development and also worked in the PCR business unit. He is currently responsible for the scientific marketing of molecular diagnostic products at Roche Diagnostics in Switzerland.

Thomas Caratsch was born in Winterthur, Switzerland, in 1958. After studying engineering at the Federal Institute of Technology in Zurich, he joined Sodeco Saia in Geneva, where he worked on the development of optical card readers. He later became head of electronics development at Kontron Analytics and held various management positions in which he was involved in developing the PCR instrument business at Roche Molecular Systems in the United States and in Rotkreuz, Switzerland. He was appointed managing director of the Roche Instrument Center in late 1999. He is currently managing director of Disetronic Medical Systems, part of Roche Diabetes Care, in Burgdorf, Switzerland.

Hamid Emminger, MD, PhD, was born in Teheran, Iran, in 1964. He received his medical training in Frankfurt am Main, where he also earned his doctorate under Wolf Singer at the Max Planck Institute for Brain Research. He practiced medicine for two years in the Department of Internal Medicine at St Katharina Hospital in Flörsheim before moving to the Bertelsmann Media Group, where he held a number of managerial positions relating to medicine and the media. He was appointed managing director of the online medical information services Multimedica and Lifeline in Berlin in 1996. Dr Emminger is currently head of New Business at Roche Diagnostics in Mannheim. He is the founder and publisher of a magazine for medical students and has published two medical textbooks.

Professor **Heinz Fiedler,** PhD, MD, was born in Schönfeld, Germany, in 1929. After completing doctorates in medicine and chemistry, he qualified as a university lecturer in 1969 with a post-doctoral thesis on structural changes in fibrinogen. He was chief of the Experimental Division at the Central Diabetes Institute in Karlsburg from 1970 to 1976 and, from 1977, head of the Institute of Clinical Chemistry and Laboratory Diagnostics at Suhl District Hospital. He was a lecturer and later an honorary professor at the Academy for Continuing Medical Education in the German Democratic Republic and is the author of well over 100 papers, lectures and book contributions, mainly on the biochemistry and diagnosis of diabetes mellitus and the development and application of clinical chemistry.

Wolfgang J. Fiedler, PhD, was born in Weingarten, Germany, in 1961 and studied chemistry at Konstanz University. He wrote his doctoral thesis on polyamine alkaloids at Zurich University and subsequently did research in medicinal chemistry at the Medical College of Virginia (Richmond) and at Byk Gulden Lomberg in Konstanz. He is currently working as a consultant in the Diabetes Care/Technology Development Department at Roche Diagnostics in Mannheim. He is also a freelance science editor for the publishing company Wiley-VCH in Weinheim.

Christoph Gradmann, PhD, was born in Marburg/Lahn, Germany, in 1960 and studied history and German in Hanover, Germany, and in Birmingham in the United Kingdom. He was a post-doctoral research associate in the Department of History at Hanover University from 1991 to 1992, and since 1992 he has been working at the Institute of Medical

History at Heidelberg University, where he has been lecturing since 2002. He has published widely on the history of medicine.

Professor **Naotaka Hamasaki,** MD, PhD, was born in Nagasaki, Japan, in 1942 and studied at Kyushu University, Fukuoka, Japan, where he was awarded his MD in 1968 and his PhD in 1972. Since 1992 he has been professor and director of the Department of Clinical Chemistry and Laboratory Medicine at Kyushu University's School of Medical Sciences. He is the author of many scientific and technical publications and has contributed to a number of books.

Erika Keller, MD, was born in Hanover, Germany, in 1940. She studied medicine at the Free University in Berlin and subsequently worked in a bacteriology and serology laboratory attached to a blood bank at Moabit Hospital in Berlin. In 1984 she joined the German Red Cross Blood Service. She has specialist qualifications in laboratory and transfusion medicine.

Emeritus Professor **Elmer W. Koneman,** MD, was born in Denver, Colorado (USA), in 1932. He studied medicine at the Colorado School of Medicine in Denver, where he received his MD in 1957. He worked as a pathologist and microbiologist at the Deaconess Hospital in Billings, Montana (1962–1968), at the Anderson Hospital and Tumor Institute in Houston, Texas (1968–1969), and at the Presbyterian Medical Center in Denver, Colorado (1969–1973). In 1973 he was appointed associate professor of pathology at the University of Colorado School of Medicine and director of clinical pathology at the Rose Medical Center in Denver. He also headed the microbiology laboratory at the Veterans Administration Hospital in Denver from 1989 until he retired in 1998. He has received many awards for his work as a pathologist and microbiologist and for his teaching, including four Excellence in Teaching awards from the University of Colorado. He has published over 150 original papers and numerous popular science articles.

Professor **Klaus Lindpaintner,** MD, was born in Innsbruck, Austria, in 1955 and studied medicine at Innsbruck University. He was awarded his MD in 1979 and then worked as a physician and researcher at various medical institutions in Germany and the United States. He joined the faculty of Harvard Medical School in Boston as an assistant professor in 1993 and was later promoted to an associate professorship there. He became head of preclinical cardiovascular research at Roche Basel in 1997, and in 1998 was appointed head of Roche *Genetics* Europe in Basel. He is the author of numerous scientific and popular science publications.

Professor **Friedrich E. Maly,** MD, was born in Oberhausen, Germany, in 1954. He is head of the Department of Special Analytics and Molecular Diagnostics at Zurich University Hospital's Institute of Clinical Chemistry. He studied medicine in Düsseldorf and Dublin and qualified as a university lecturer in 1991 at Berne University. He then carried out research into the molecular biology of phagocytes at the Scripps Research Institute in La Jolla, California, and pursued further training in medical microbiology and clinical chemistry at Zurich University before qualifying as a specialist in laboratory medicine and laboratory management in 1996. In 1998 he was appointed titular professor at Zurich University. His current research is focused on the development and clinical validation of molecular diagnostic methods.

Oliver Mast was born in Freiburg, Germany, in 1964 and studied medical informatics at Heidelberg University. He then worked as an international market analyst at the Institute of Medical Informatics and Biostatistics in Riehen, Switzerland, and as an international pharmacoeconomics project manager at Roche Basel. He headed the Health Economics/Outcomes Research Department at Bayer Vital GmbH from 1996 to 2002. Since April 2002 he has been head of the Health Information unit at HESTIA HealthCare GmbH, Mannheim, and managing director of the Institute of Medical Informatics and Biostatistics, Basel.

Erika Novotny was born in Wesselburen, Germany, in 1924 and began working with histological methods as a medical laboratory technician in 1948. She remained in this field for 40 years, holding positions in Kiel, Frankfurt am Main, Neustadt (Black Forest), Tübingen and Würzburg, where she was a technician instructor. After she and Gerd Novotny married in 1972, they worked together on developing silver-staining techniques for histological preparations at the Universities in Göttingen and Düsseldorf.

Professor **Gerd E. K. Novotny,** PhD, was born in Vienna, Austria, in 1941. After completing a degree in psychology with a minor in physiology at University College, London, in 1963, he was a visiting

student at the Cecilie and Oskar Vogt Institute of Brain Research in Neustadt (Black Forest), Germany. He then returned to University College to write a doctoral thesis on the effects of ions on electrical activity in the cerebral cortex, for which he was awarded a PhD in 1969. Professor Novotny moved to the Institute of Neuroanatomy at Göttingen University the same year, where he worked on the biochemistry of functional systems in the brain. It was in Göttingen that he and his wife started developing techniques for silver-staining nerve tissue. He qualified as a university lecturer in anatomy in Düsseldorf in 1980 and has been a professor in the Institute of Anatomy at Düsseldorf University since 1982.

Sabine Päuser, PhD, was born in Berlin, Germany, in 1967. She holds a doctorate in biophysical chemistry, awarded in 1993 by Humboldt University in Berlin. After finishing her studies, she spent several years in cancer research at Benjamin Franklin Hospital, Free University of Berlin. She is currently a science editor and writer at Roche Basel. Before joining Roche, she was editor-in-chief of the clinical diagnostics journal *mta Spektrum* in Frankfurt am Main.

Rainer Proetzsch, PhD, was born in Naumburg am Queis, Lower Silesia (then part of Germany), in 1942. After graduating from the University of Bonn with a doctorate in organic chemistry in 1974, he joined Boehringer Mannheim GmbH (now Roche Diagnostics) in 1975, where he held several positions in the Diabetes Care unit and played a leading role in the launch of a number of blood glucose meters. It was at Boehringer that he met Professor Robert Tattersall in the late 1970s. Dr Proetzsch retired in 2003.

Rita Roth, PhD, was born in Basel, Switzerland, in 1951. She has a doctorate in microbiology from Zurich University and has worked as a post-doctoral fellow and research associate in the fields of allergies, immunology and autoimmune diseases at the University of California (La Jolla), Yale University (New Haven, Connecticut) and the Swiss Institute of Allergy and Asthma Research in Davos. She held managerial positions in the diagnostics and life sciences units at Bio-Rad Laboratories and Büchi Labortechnik before joining the Roche Instrument Center in Rotkreuz, Switzerland, as head of Business Development OEM in early 2002.

Leo Schwerzmann was born in Zug, Switzerland, in 1948 and studied engineering at the University of Applied Science in Lucerne. He subsequently pursued post-diploma studies in microelectronics, software and business administration. He worked in process engineering in the chemical industry for several years before joining Tegimenta AG (now the Roche Instrument Center) in Rotkreuz, Switzerland, in 1975, where he played a major role as a systems designer for new laboratory instruments. He is currently head of product portfolio management at the Roche Instrument Center.

Rolf Steinmüller, PhD, was born in Sellingshausen, Germany, in 1963 and studied biology in Giessen, graduating with a doctorate in 1994. He worked as a research associate at several universities before joining BAG-BiologischeAnalysensystemGmbH in Lich, where he is currently product manager for food safety tests. He is the author of many publications, most of them popular science articles.

Peter Stiefelhagen, MD, was born in Dernbach/Westerwald, Germany, in 1951 and is chief physician in the Department of Internal Medicine at the Westerwald Red Cross Hospital. He studied medicine in Freiburg im Breisgau and completed residencies at Citizens' Hospital in Stuttgart and Erlangen University Hospital before being certified as a specialist in internal medicine and cardiology. In addition to his clinical practice, he has been a medical journalist for many years and contributes regularly to numerous medical journals.

Michael Tacke, PhD, was born in Paderborn, Germany, in 1963 and is head of a proteomics department at Roche Diagnostics Germany in Penzberg. After completing a biology degree in Münster, he earned a doctorate in immunobiology from Würzburg University with a thesis on T cell activation. As a post-doctoral researcher at Boehringer Mannheim GmbH (now Roche Diagnostics), he focused on immune responses to the newly discovered hepatitis G virus and the development of a test to detect infection with the virus. From 1997 to 2001 he worked on developing immunoassays for cancer markers at Roche. He is currently involved in the search for new diagnostic markers using proteomics technologies.

Professor Robert Tattersall, MD, was born in London, United Kingdom, in 1943. From 1975 to 1998 he worked at University Hospital, Nottingham, as a consultant physician specialising in diabetes. He is now Special Professor of Metabolic Medicine at the University of Nottingham. Professor Tattersall's work in diabetes research has spanned a wide range of areas, from genetic and psychological factors contributing to diabetes, to insulin therapy, the medico-legal aspects of the disease and, most recently, the history of its diagnosis and treatment. He published the first description of maturity onset diabetes of the young (MODY), an autosomal dominant form of inherited diabetes, in 1974, and he helped usher in the era of glucose self-monitoring in 1978. For his contributions to diabetes research, he was awarded an honorary doctorate by Prague University in 2000.

Professor Dieter J. Vonderschmitt, PhD, was born in Basel, Switzerland, in 1938. After completing a doctorate in chemistry in Basel, he spent three years studying biochemistry and enzymology as a post-doctoral fellow at the Scripps Clinic and Research Foundation in La Jolla, California. He returned to Switzerland in 1967 and worked as a senior research associate, assistant professor and finally associate professor at the Institute of Inorganic and Analytical Chemistry at Neuchâtel University. He was appointed head of the central clinical chemistry laboratory at the Cantonal Hospital in Basel in 1972 and full professor of clinical chemistry at Zurich University in 1980. In September 2001 he took early retirement in order to devote more time to his artistic interests. He also provides management consultancy services to a number of clients.

Burkhard Ziebolz, PhD, was born in Braunschweig-Lamme, Germany, in 1957. He studied biochemistry and microbiology at Braunschweig Technical University, graduating with a doctorate in 1987 for work on new methods of producing glucan. He joined Boehringer Mannheim GmbH (now Roche Diagnostics) in 1989. During his career at Boehringer and Roche he has held a variety of positions. He has been a science communications manager at Roche Diagnostics in Mannheim since 2000. Dr Ziebolz is also a novelist.

Notes and references

From matula to test strip
P 12

1 de Fourcroy AF: *Système des connaissances chimiques, et leur applications aux phénomènes de la nature et de l'art.* Paris: Baudouin, 1801–1802 (an IX-X); 10: 93.

2 Hippocrates; Jones WHS trans. *Hippocrates II.* Loeb Classical Library. London: William Heinemann, 1923: 27.

3 Held W. *Die Urinschau des Mittelalters und die Harnuntersuchung der Gegenwart.* Leipzig: Krüger, 1931: 4.

4 Shakespeare W: *Complete Works. King Henry IV.* Oxford: Oxford University Press, 1987. Reprint of 1905 London ed. Part Two, act I, scene 2.

5 Stahl GE. *Gründliche Abhandlung von Abschaffung des Missbrauchs, so mit Besehung des Urins, und mit der Wahrsagung aus demselben im Schwange gehet...* Coburg: Johann Georg Steinmarck, 1739: 4.

6 Paracelsus. *Opera. Schedula de Urinis. Bücher und Schriften, soviel deren zur Hand gebracht.* Huser J, ed. Strasbourg: Lazarus Zetzner, 1603; 1: 764.

7 Granular degeneration.

8 Heller JF. Unsere heutige Aufgabe. *Archiv für physiologische und pathologische Chemie und Mikroskopie [Neue Folge]* 1852; 5: 1–6. Quotation p 5.

9 Liebig J [v]. *Aus dem Briefwechsel von Justus Liebig mit dem Minister Reinhard Frhn. von Dalwigk.* Darmstadt: A. Bergstraesser'sche Hofbuchhandlung, 1903. Letter from Liebig to von Dalwigk, 6 January 1852.

10 See also: 'Pisse prophets, polarimetry and patient self-monitoring' in this book.

11 See also: 'From hobby to practical science' in this book.

12 Kisskalt K. *Max von Pettenkofer.* In: *Grosse Naturforscher.* Frickhinger HW, ed. Stuttgart: Wissenschaftliche Verlagsgesellschaft, 1948; 4: 26.

Further reading

Bleker J. *Die Geschichte der Nierenkrankheiten.* Mannheim: Boehringer Mannheim GmbH, 1972.

Büttner J, ed. *History of Clinical Chemistry.* Berlin: Walter de Gruyter, 1983.

Büttner J, Habrich C. *Roots of Clinical Chemistry.* Darmstadt: GIT-Verlag, 1987.

Büttner J. Urina ut signum: Zur historischen Entwicklung der Urinuntersuchung. In: Guder WG, Lang H, eds. *Pathobiochemie und Funktionsdiagnostik der Niere.* Deutsche Gesellschaft für Klinische Chemie, Merck-Symposium 1989. Berlin: Springer-Verlag, 1991: 1–21. Contains a comprehensive list of references on chemical urinalysis.

Büttner J. Naturwissenschaftliche Methoden im klinischen Laboratorium des 19. Jahrhunderts und ihr Einfluss auf das klinische Denken. *Berichte zur Wissenschaftsgeschichte* 2002; 25 (2): 93–105.

Ebstein E. *Zur Entwicklung der klinischen Harndiagnostik in chemischer und mikroskopischer Beziehung.* Leipzig: Georg Thieme, 1915.

Foucault M. *Die Geburt der Klinik: Eine Archäologie des ärztlichen Blicks.* Munich: Carl Hanser Verlag, 1973.

Garrod AE. *Garrod's Inborn Errors of Metabolism.* Reprinted with a supplement. Harris E, ed. Oxford: Oxford University Press, 1963.

Gottschalk CW, Berliner RW, Giebisch GH. *Renal Physiology. People and Ideas.* Bethesda, Maryland: American Physiological Society, 1987.

Kutter D. *Schnelltests in der klinischen Diagnostik.* 2nd ed. Munich: Urban und Schwarzenberg, 1983.

Mattelaer JJ. The History of Uroscopy. *de Historia Urologiae Europeae.* Kortrijk, Belgium: European Association of Urology, Historical Committee, 1999; 6: 19–56.

Meites S. *Otto Folin: America's First Clinical Biochemist.* American Association of Clinical Chemistry, 1989.

Pagel W. *Paracelsus. An Introduction to Philosophical Medicine in the Era of the Renaissance.* 2nd ed. Basel: Karger Verlag, 1982.

Rosenfeld L. *Four Centuries of Clinical Chemistry.* Amsterdam: Gordon and Breach Science Publishers, 1999.

Schöner E. *Das Viererschema in der antiken Humoralpathologie.* Wiesbaden: Franz Steiner Verlag, 1964 (*Sudhoffs Archiv,* Beiheft 4).

Szabadváry F. *Geschichte der Analytischen Chemie.* Kerstein G, ed. Braunschweig: F Vieweg u. Sohn, 1966.

Voswinckel P. *Der schwarze Urin: Vom Schrecknis zum Laborparameter; Urina Nigra, Alkaptonurie, Hämoglobinurie, Myoglobinurie, Porphyrinurie, Melanurie.* Berlin: Blackwell Wissenschaft, 1993. Contains a detailed history of urine strip tests.

Wellcome HS. *The evolution of urine analysis. An historical sketch of the clinical examination of urine.* London: Burroughs Wellcome Co, 1911.

Wershub LP. *Urology. From Antiquity to the 20th Century.* St. Louis, Missouri: Warren H Green, 1970.

von Zglinicki F. *Die Uroskopie in der bildenden Kunst: Eine kunst- und medizinhistorische Untersuchung über die Harnschau.* Darmstadt: GIT-Verlag Ernst Giebeler, 1982.

Windows onto the building blocks of tissue
P 27

1 Döderlein G. *Zur Geschichte der Brille.* Tuttlingen: Braun Druck GmbH.

2 Döderlein G. *Zur Geschichte des Mikroskopes.* Tuttlingen: Braun Druck GmbH.

3 Döderlein (ref 1).

4 Harting P; Theile FW, ed. *Das Mikroskop.* Braunschweig: Friedrich Vieweg und Sohn, 1866; 2: 58–120; 3: 79–345.

5 Rossi F. Catalogue, Optisches Museum der Carl-Zeiss-Stiftung, Jena, c. 1980.

6 Rooseboom M. *Microscopium.* Leyden: Rijksmuseum voor de Geschiedenes der Naturwetenschappen, 1956.

7 Nowak HP. *Geschichte des Mikroskops.* Medizinhistorisches Institut, Zurich University. Rothenthurm: published by the author, 1984.

8 Gruber GB. Aus der Historik des Mikroskopes und der Mikroskopie. *Münch med Wochenschr* 1955; 97 (16): 539–541.

9 Ruska E. *Mikroskopie und Zellbiologie in drei Jahrhunderten.* Exhibition catalogue, Second International Congress on Cell Biology; Aug 31– Sep 5 1980, Berlin.

10 Hooke R. *Micrographia.* London: John Martyn and James Allestry, 1665 (facsimile edition, Brussels, 1966).

11 Corrected for two colours.

12 Nowak (ref 7).

13 Döderlein (ref 2).

14 Harting (ref 4).

15 Among those who made major contributions were: Pieter Harting, Anton Dohrn and Paul Mayer, Stephan von Apathy, Charles Minot, Johann Evangelista Purkinje, Martin Heidenhain, and Carl Weigert.

16 Ankel WE. Paul Mayer, Anton Dohrn. In: Freund H, Berg A, eds. *Die Geschichte der Mikroskopie.* Frankfurt am Main: Umschau Verlag, 1963: vol 1.

17 Today's microscopy 'bible' is Romeis's *Mikroskopische Technik,* a textbook initially authored by Alexander Böhm and Albert Oppel and continued after their deaths by the Munich professor Benno Romeis, starting with the 8th edition in 1919. Romeis painstakingly reviewed and, where appropriate, improved on almost all the instructions that had been published on fixation, embedding and staining technique. The last edition by Romeis himself, the 16th, appeared in 1968.

18 Trinkler H. Das Lichtmikroskop und seine Hilfstechniken in der Entwicklung der medizinischen Diagnostik. In: *Labor und Medizin – einst und jetzt. Beiträge zur Geschichte der Labormedizin.* Schweizerischer Fachverband des medizinischtechnischen Laborfachpersonals. Bern: Stämpfli + Cie AG, 1980.

19 Grehn J. 100 Jahre Leitz-Mikrotome. *Leitz Mitteilungen* 1980; suppl 1 (6): 185.

20 Trinkler (ref 18).

21 Trinkler (ref 18).

22 Ackerknecht EH. *Geschichte der Medizin.* 4th ed. Stuttgart: Enke-Verlag, 1979: 129.

23 Kopsch F. *Rauber-Kopsch Lehrbuch und Atlas der Anatomie des Menschen.* 14th ed. Leipzig: Georg Thieme Verlag, 1934: 19–29.

24 Hering E. *Physiologie für Thierärzte.* Stuttgart: Verlag der JB Metzler'schen Buchhandlung, 1832: 38.

25 Schleiden MJ, Schwann T, Schultze M; Jahn I, ed. *Klassische Schriften zur Zellenlehre.* Leipzig: Akademische Verlagsgesellschaft Geest & Portig AG, 1987.

26 Trinkler (ref 18), p 65.

27 Berg A. Karl Ernst von Baer. In: Freund H, Berg A, eds. *Die Geschichte der Mikroskopie.* Frankfurt am Main: Umschau Verlag, 1964; vol 2: 87.

28 Rosner E: Rudolf Virchow. In: Freund H, Berg A, eds. *Die Geschichte der Mikroskopie.* Frankfurt am Main: Umschau Verlag, 1964: vol 2.

29 Pilleri G. Camillo Golgi. In: Freund H, Berg A, eds. *Die Geschichte der Mikroskopie.* Frankfurt am Main: Umschau Verlag, 1964: vol 2.

30 Pilleri G. Santiago Ramón y Cajal. In: Freund H, Berg A, eds. *Die Geschichte der Mikroskopie.* Frankfurt am Main: Umschau Verlag, 1964: vol 2.

31 Trinkler (ref 18).

32 Bauer KF. Joseph von Gerlach. In: Freund H, Berg A, eds. *Die Geschichte der Mikroskopie.* Frankfurt am Main: Umschau Verlag, 1964: vol 2.

33 Berg A. Paul Ehrlich. In: Freund H, Berg A, eds. *Die Geschichte der Mikroskopie.* Frankfurt am Main: Umschau Verlag, 1964: vol 2.

34 Fischer W. Ludwig Aschoff. In: Freund H, Berg A, eds. *Die Geschichte der Mikroskopie.* Frankfurt am Main: Umschau Verlag, 1964: vol 2.

35 Berg A. Martin Heidenhain. In: Freund H, Berg A, eds. *Die Geschichte der Mikroskopie.* Frankfurt am Main: Umschau Verlag, 1964; vol 2: 129.

36 Formal occupational training for medical laboratory technicians was first offered by the Lette Association's School of Photography, founded in Berlin in 1890. In 1912, during the great exhibition 'Women in the Home and at Work', this occupational group was presented to the public as the 'Organisation of Female Scientific Assistants in Medical Institutes'. In 1916, Prof Fränkel's personal assistant, with 20 years of hospital experience behind her, set up a six-month training course in histological technique.

37 Berg (ref 35).

38 It has been overtaken by the modern periodic acid Schiff (PAS) method, which uses periodic acid instead of chromic acid to oxidise the polysaccharide molecule; the resulting aldehyde groups are then stained with the leukofuchsin solution.

39 Klebs 1868, Struve 1872, Ehrlich 1885.

40 Grehn (ref 19), p 1.

41 First described in 1898 by Carl Benda (1857–1932).

42 First described in 1899 by Charles Garnier.

43 The authors wish to thank the following people for providing source materials and illustrations for this chapter: Mrs Götz, Institut für Geschichte der Medizin, Düsseldorf University; Karin Ebert, Optisches Museum der Ernst-Abbe-Stiftung, Jena; Walther Fuchs, Medizinhistorisches Institut und Museum, Zurich University; Prof. Adolf Hopf, Archiv, Cecilie und Oskar Vogt Institut für Hirnforschung, Düsseldorf University; and Mr Stamm, Stadtarchiv, Neuss.

44 Pillerli (ref 29).

Pisse prophets, polarimetry and patient self-monitoring

P 44

1 The original is kept at the University of Leipzig.

2 Mehnert H, Standl E, Usadel KH. *Diabetologie in Klinik und Praxis.* Stuttgart: Georg Thieme Verlag, 1999.

3 Dodu SRA. Diabetes in the Tropics. *Br Med J* 1967; 2: 747–750.

4 Kiefer JH. Uroscopy, the artist's portrayal of the physician. *Bull NY Acad Med* 1964; 40: 759–766.

5 Bush RB. Urine is an Harlot or a Liar. *JAMA* 1969; 208: 131–134.

6 Dobson M. Experiments and Observations on the Urine in Diabetes. *Medical Observations and Enquiries* 1776; 5: 298–316.

7 Home F. *Clinical experiments, histories and dissections.* Edinburgh: William Creech, 1780.

8 Chevreul ME. Note sur le sucre de diabètes. *Ann Chim (Paris)* 1815; 95: 319–320.

9 Roberts W. Certain points in the clinical examination of the urine. Lecture 3 on quantitative sugar testing in the urine. *Lancet* 1862; 1: 535–536.

10 Christian HA. A critical estimate of the fermentation specific gravity method of quantitating sugar in diabetic urine. *Boston Med and Surg J* 1907; 157: 178–181.

11 The polarimeter and saccharometer illustrations and captions are from the manuscript version of the chapter 'From matula to test strip', by Johannes Büttner.

12 Trommer CA. Unterscheidung von Gummi, Dextrin, Traubenzucker und Rohrzucker. *Ann Chem (Heidelberg)* 1841; 39: 360–362.

13 Reiser SJ. *Medicine and the reign of technology – chemical signposts of disease and the birth of the diagnostic laboratory.* Cambridge: Cambridge University Press, 1978: 122–144.

14 Benedict SR. Detection of sugar in urine by use of copper sulphate solution. *JAMA* 1911; 57: 1194.

15 Garrod AE. Lettsomian lectures on glycosuria. *Lancet* 1912; 1: 483–488.

16 Olmsted JMD. *Claude Bernard: Physiologist.* London, 1939. For a short account of Bernard's research on carbohydrate metabolism, see idem, Claude Bernard, 1813–1879. *Diabetes* 1953; 2: 162–164.

17 Whitla Sir W. *A Manual of the Practice and Theory of Medicine.* London: Balliere, Tindall and Cox, 1908; 1: 281.

18 Bang I. *Methoden zur Mikrobestimmung einiger Blutbestandteile.* Wiesbaden: Bergmann, 1916.

19 Jacobsen ATB. Untersuchungen über den Einfluss verschiedener Nahrungsmittel auf den Blutzucker bei normalen, zuckerkranken und graviden Personen. *Biochem Zeitschrift Berlin* 1913; 55: 471–494. Also idem: [The influence of various foodstuffs upon blood sugar in normal, diabetic and pregnant states.] *Hosp-Tid, Københ* 1913, 6: 1550.

20 West KM. Substantial differences in diagnostic criteria used by diabetic experts. *Diabetes* 1975; 24: 641–644.

21 The diagnostic criteria for interpreting oral glucose tolerance have largely been harmonised since the late 1990s. In 1998 a WHO consultation group published new diagnostic values – now standard in most countries except the United States – for oral glucose tolerance tests. If capillary blood is tested, a fasting glucose concentration equal to or greater than 6.1 mmol/L (110 mg/dL) **or** a two-hour value equal to or greater than 11.1 mmol/L (200 mg/dL) is diagnostic for diabetes. In venous blood (VB) and venous plasma (VP) the diagnostic values are: VB: >6.1 mmol/L (110 mg/dL) **or** >10.0 mmol/L (180 mg/dL); VP: >7.0 mmol/L (126 mg/dL) **or** >11.1 mmol/L (200 mg/dL). Source: Alberti KGMM, Zimmet PZ. For the WHO Consultation. Definition, diagnosis of diabetes mellitus and its complications. Part 1: diagnosis and classification of diabetes mellitus. Provisional report of a WHO Consultation. *Diabetic Medicine* 1998; 15: 539–553.

22 Karger-Decker B. Wettlauf mit der Zuckerkrankheit: Insulin. In: *Kräuter, Pillen, Präparate. Abenteuer der Arzneimittelforschung.* Leipzig: Koehler und Amelang, 1981.

23 Päuser S. Lebensrettendes Hormon. *mta* 1999; 14 (2): 86–87.

24 Sanger F. Chemistry of insulin: determination of the structure of insulin opens the way to greater understanding of life processes. *Science* 1959; 129: 1340–1344. A very clear account of Sanger's work is provided by Thompson EOP. The insulin molecule. *Sci Am* 1955; 192: 36–41.

25 Ferry G. *Dorothy Hodgkin. A Life.* Granta Books, 1998.

26 Lawrence, RD. *The Diabetic ABC.* 10th ed. London: HK Lewis, 1952: 17.

27 Sheftel AG. A combined qualitative and quantitative test for sugar in the urine. *M J and Rec* 1927; 126: 663.

28 Compton WA, Treneer JM. Tablet and Method of Dissolving Same. US Patent 2,387,244, October 1945.

29 Williams JR, Humphreys EM. The clinical significance of blood sugar. *Arch Int Med* 1919; 23: 537.

30 Lawrence RD. Cases of diabetes mellitus with a low renal threshold. *Br Med J* 1929; 1: 196.

31 Panel Discussion: What I teach my diabetic patients. *Diabetes* 1956; 5: 55–60.

32 Knight RK, Keen H. Blood sugar by post. *Br Med J* 1961; 1: 1168.

33 Rennie IDB, Keen H, Southon A. Rapid enzyme strip method for estimating blood sugar. *Lancet* 1964; 2: 884–886.

34 Lowy C. Home glucose monitoring, who started it? *Br Med J* 1998; 316: 1467.

35 Sönksen P, Judd S, Lowy C. Home monitoring of blood glucose: method for improving diabetic control. *Lancet* 1978; 1: 729–732.

36 Walford S, Gale EAM, Allison SP, Tattersall RB. Self-monitoring of blood glucose – improvement of diabetic control. *Lancet* 1978; 1: 732–735.

37 Rahbar S. An abnormal hemoglobin in red cells of diabetics. *Clin Chim Acta* 1968; 22: 296–298.

38 Allen DW, Schroder WA, Balog J. Observations on the chromatographic heterogeneity of normal adult and fetal hemoglobin: a study of the effect of crystallization and chromatography on the heterogeneity and isoleucine content. *J Am Chem Soc* 1958; 80: 1628–1633.

39 Trivelli LA, Ranney HM, Tai HAT. Hemoglobin components in patients with diabetes mellitus. *N Engl J Med* 1971; 284: 353–357.

40 Tattersall RB, Pyke DA, Ranney HM, Bruckheimer SM. Hemoglobin components in diabetes mellitus: studies in identical twins. *N Engl J Med* 1975; 293: 1171–1173.

41 Koenig RJ, Peterson CM, Jones RL, Saudek CD, Lehrman M, Cerami A. Correlation of glucose regulation and hemoglobin A1c in diabetes mellitus. *N Engl J Med* 1976; 295: 417–420.

42 The Diabetes Control and Complications Trial Research Group. The effect of intensive treatment of diabetes on the development and progression of long-term complications in insulin-dependent diabetes mellitus. *N Engl J Med* 1993; 329: 977–986.

43 Päuser S. Diabetes im Wandel. Editorial. In: *Neue Ansätze zur Diabetesbekämpfung.* Basel: Roche, 2002.

44 Gamble DR, Taylor KW. Seasonal incidence of diabetes mellitus. *Br Med J* 1969; 3: 631–633.

45 Zimmet P. The Challenge of Diabetes. In: Fischer EP, Möller G, eds. *The Medical Challenge.* Munich: Piper Verlag, 1997.

46 Varela-Calvino R, Sgarbi G, Arif S, Peakman M. T-Cell reactivity to the P2C nonstructural protein of a diabetogenic strain of coxsackievirus B4. *Virology* 2000; 274 (1): 56–64.

47 Varela-Calvino R, Ellis R, Sgarbi G, Dayan CM, Peakman M. Characterization of the T-cell response to coxsackievirus B4: evidence that effector memory cells predominate in patients with type 1 diabetes. *Diabetes* 2002; 51 (6): 1745–1753.

48 Zimmet P, Tuomi T, Mackay IR, Rowley MJ, Knowles W, Cohen M, Lang DA. Latent autoimmune diabetes mellitus in adults (LADA); the role of antibodies to glutamic acid decarboxylase in diagnosis and prediction of insulin dependency. *Diabetic Medicine* 1994; 11: 299–303.

49 Nerup J, Platz P, Andersen OO, Christy M, Lyngsøe J, Poulsen JE, et al. HL-A antigens and diabetes mellitus. *Lancet* 1974; 2: 864.

50 Olmos P, A'Hern R, Heaton DA, et al. The significance of the concordance rate for type 1 (insulin-dependent) diabetes in identical twins. *Diabetologia* 1988; 31: 747–750.

51 Pozzilli P. Prevention of insulin-dependent diabetes mellitus 1998. *Diabetes Metab Rev* 1998; 14: 69–84.

52 Koschinsky T. Subkutanes kontinuierliches Glukosemonitoring – neue Techniken und Therapie-Perspektiven. In: Scherbaum WA, ed. *Symposium zum 70. Geburtstag von Prof. Dr. med. F. Arnold Gries und zum 25-jährigen Bestehen des Deutschen Diabetes-Forschungsinstituts Düsseldorf 2000.* Aachen: Shaker Verlag, 2000.

53 Blood monitoring with the Biostator was an exception. Heparin was added to venous blood samples to prevent clotting.

54 Heinemann L. Minimal-Invasive und Nicht-Invasive Glukose-Sensoren: Stand der Entwicklung. *Spektrum Diabetologie* 2002; 13–21.

55 Päuser S. Auf dem Weg zur künstlichen Bauchspeicheldrüse. In: *Neue Ansätze zur Diabetesbekämpfung.* Basel: Roche, 2002.

56 Following a two-hour warm-up period, the sensors are calibrated with a blood glucose measurement. Glucose levels in interstitial fluid are automatically measured every ten minutes, converted to blood glucose readings and displayed. The readings are about 15 minutes behind the actual blood glucose value. The device has an alarm that sounds if a pre-selected alert level for hypoglycemia or hyperglycemia is reached. At the end of each measurement cycle the polarity of the electrodes is reversed. The device can take continuous readings for up to 13 hours. (All information in this note refers to GlucoWatch G2.)

57 Tierney MJ, Tamada JA, Potts RO, Eastman RC, Pitzer KR, Ackerman NR, Fermi S. The GlucoWatch Biographer: a frequent, automatic and noninvasive glucose monitor. *Ann Int Med* 2000; 32: 632–641.

58 Mastrototaro J. The MiniMed continuous glucose monitoring system (CGMS). *J Pediatr Endocrinol Metab* 1999; 12 (suppl 3): 751–758.

59 Pfeiffer EF. The glucose sensor: The missing link in diabetes therapy. *Horm Metab Res* 1990; 24 (suppl): 154–164.

60 A similar technique now under development is called open-flow microperfusion. Sterile saline solution is continuously perfused into subcutaneous tissues through a catheter with relatively large perforations on its outer surface. The solution mixes with the interstitial fluid, and the perfusate is then pumped out and analysed. The glucose concentration in the interstitial fluid is calculated from the glucose and sodium ion concentrations in the perfusate, with the sodium concentration serving as an index of the percentage concentration of interstitial fluid. The practicability of this technique, developed by Prof. TR Pieber and co-workers at the Department of Internal Medicine, Diabetes and Metabolism Division, University of Graz (Austria), has already been demonstrated in trials.

61 Ungerstedt U, Herrera-Marchintz M, Jungnelius U, Stähle L, Tossmann U, Zetterström T. Dopamine synaptic mechanisms reflected in studies combining behavioral recordings and brain dialysis. In: Kotsiaka M, ed. *Advances in Dopamine Research.* New York: Pergamon Press, 1982: 219–231.

62 Proper calibration is a prerequisite for obtaining accurate glucose readings until the next calibration. To preclude errors, the data manager immediately prompts the user to perform a second capillary blood measurement to confirm the first. If the two measurements produce sufficiently similar results and are close enough to each other in time, the data manager accepts the calibration. Otherwise the calibration procedure has to be repeated.

63 Shichiri M, Kawamori R, Goriya Y, Yamasaki Y, Hakui N, Abe H. Glycaemic control in diabetic patients by a wearable artificial endocrine pancreas with a needle-type glucose sensor. *Diabetologia* 1983; 25: 194. Abstr. 349.

64 Some biographical details are taken from the manuscript version of Johannes Büttner's 'From hobby to practical science'.

65 See note 64.

66 Karger-Decker (ref 22).

Arsenic – detection of a folk poison
P 61

1 Arsenic trioxide, As_2O_3.

2 http://www.wu-wien.ac.at/usr/h96c/h9650434/ARSEN.HTML

3 In 'Von Giftmischern, Erbschleichern und Thronfolgern'(*P.M. History,* 00/5), U Doenike attributes this advance to Jabir ibn Hayyan. According to J Thorwald, *Das Jahrhundert der Detektive* (Munich: Droemersche Verlagsanstalt Th. Knaur Nachf., 1978), the credit goes to a man named Gerber.

4 Also called 'Aqua della Toffina' or 'Agua Toffana' according to *Toxicology: The Basic Science of Poisons;* http://entomology.unl.edu/toxicology/Doull0001.htm

5 See source cited in note 2.

6 See source cited in note 2.

Old scourges and new
P 68

1 Bascomb E. *A History of Epidemic Pestilences from the Earliest Ages.* London: John Churchill, 1851.

2 Marks G, Beatty WK. *Epidemics.* New York: Charles Scribner's Sons, 1976.

3 Shrewsbury JFD. The Plague of Athens. Bull Hist Med XXIV, 1950.

4 Defoe D. A *Journal of the Plague Year.* London: E Nutt, 1722.

5 Account of Bonomo's observation of scabies – Citation to come

6 The chapter on parasitology includes a more detailed account of this discovery.

7 See the chapter on mycology for more details.

8 A turning point in the history of diagnostic microbiology was the discovery of the life cycle of the anthrax bacillus. The French scientist Casimir Joseph Davaine (1812–1882) first discovered anthrax bacilli in the blood of animal victims of the disease, which he could transmit to other animals by injecting the bacteria-laden blood. The unresolved question was how so many animals in epidemic outbreaks could contract the disease in such a short time. Koch provided the answer, recognising that the anthrax agent formed 'resting spores' capable of growing into new bacteria after either short or long periods of rest. When the environmental conditions were right, the multiple spores in the soil proliferated into new cells wreaking havoc on any animal eating the contaminated hay or straw. Hence the high mortality.

9 Lechevalier HA, Solotorovsky M. *Three Centuries of Microbiology.* New York: McGraw Hill, 1965: 129.

10 Brooks J. The sad and tragic life of Typhoid Mary. *Can Med Assoc J* 1996; 154: 915–916.

11 Boccaccio G. *The Decameron.* Translated by John Payne. New York: The Modern Library, 1931: 8–17.

12 Lechevalier HA, Solotorovsky M (ref 9), p 154.

13 Kitasato S. On the tetanus bacillus. *Zeit Hyg Infectionskrankh* 1889; 7: 225–233.

14 Shiga K. Über den Erreger der Dysenterie in Japan. *Centralbl Bakteriol,* etc, I. Abt, 1898.

15 Lechevalier HA, Solotorovsky M (ref 9), pp 162–163.

16 Karger-Decker B. Abgesang der Syphilis. In: *Unsichtbare Feinde.* Leipzig: Koehler und Amelang, 1980: 177.

17 Middlebrook G, Cohn ML. Bacteriology of Tuberculosis: Laboratory Methods. *Am J Pub Health* 1958; 48: 844–853.

18 T'ang FF, Chang HL, Hiang YT, Wang KC. Studies on the etiology of trachoma with special reference to isolation of the virus in chick embryo. *Chin Med J* 1957; 75: 429–447.

19 Jones BR, Collier LH, Smith CH. Isolation of virus from inclusion blenorrhoea. *Lancet* 1959; 1: 902–905.

20 Stamm WE, Tam M, Koester M, Cles L. Detection of *Chlamydia trachomatis* inclusions in McCoy cell cultures with fluorescein-conjugated monoclonal antibodies. *J Clin Microbiol* 1983; 17: 666–668.

21 McDade JE, Shepard CC, Fraser DW, Tsai TR, Redus MA, Dowdle WR. Legionnaires' disease: Isolation of a bacterium and demonstration of its role in other respiratory disease. *N Engl J Med* 1977; 297 (22): 1197–1203.

22 Ogston A. Report upon micro-organisms in surgical diseases. *Br Med J* 1881; I: 369–374.

23 Todd J, Fishaut M. Toxic shock syndrome associated with phage-group-1 staphylococci. *Lancet* 1978; 2: 1116–1118.

24 Shands KN, Schmid GP, Dan BB, Blum D, Guidotti RJ, Hargrett NT, et al. Toxic-shock syndrome in menstruating women: association with tampon use and Staphylococcus aureus and clinical features in 52 cases *N Engl J Med* 1980; 303: 1436–1442.

25 Madigan MT, Martinko JM, Parker J. *Brock Mikrobiologie.* Goebel W, ed. Heidelberg: Spektrum Akademischer Verlag, 2001: 1040.

26 Acute or chronic inflammation of bone marrow and tissue due to the introduction of bacteria (usually *Staphylococcus aureus*).

27 Bergoli MS, Schlievert PM. Toxic shock syndrome toxin. *Lancet* 1984; 2: 691.

28 Warren JR, Marshall B. Unidentified curved bacilli on gastric epithelium in active chronic gastritis. *Lancet* 1983; 1273–1275.

29 Phillips MW, Lee A. The mucosa associated microflora of the rat intestine. *Aust J Exp Biol Med Sci* 1978; 56: 649–662.

30 Päuser S. In einem normalen Magen wachsen keine Bakterien? *mta* 1997; 12 (8): 545.

31 Bauer AW, Kirby WMM, Sherris JC, Turck M. Antibiotic susceptibility testing by the standard single disk method. *J Clin Pathol* 1966; 45: 493–496.

32 A ligand is a substance (or part of a substance) that binds to a receptor. Molecules with ligand properties include substrates, antigens, hormones, proteins and toxins. The corresponding receptors are (in the same order) enzymes, antibodies, receptors, binding proteins and antitoxins.

33 Hörnlimann B, Riesner D, Kretzschmar H. *Prionen und Prionkrankheiten.* Berlin: Walter De-Gruyter, 2001.

34 Yersin Alexandre. La Peste Bubonique à Hong Kong. *Ann Inst Pasteur* 1894; 8: 662–667.

The fungus among us
P 88

1 Ainsworth GC. *Introduction to the History of Mycology.* Cambridge: Cambridge University Press, 1976.

2 Although the same procedures were attempted for amphotericin B, the minimum inhibitory concentration (MIC) breakpoints were within too narrow a range (0.25–1.0 mg/mL), so that clinical correlations were difficult to establish. Host factors seemed to play a larger role in treatment failures than the results obtained from in vitro antifungal susceptibility tests.

Living worms in living flesh
P 94

1 Andry N. *De la génération des vers dans le corps de l'homme.* Amsterdam: Thomas Lombrail, 1701.

2 Foster WD. *A History of Parasitology.* Edinburgh: E&S Livingstone, 1965: 187–192.

3 Bremser JG. *Über lebende Würmer in lebenden Menschen. Nebst einem Anhang über Pseudo-Helminthen.* Vienna: C. Schaumburg et Comp, 1819.

4 Davaine CJ. *Traité des entozoaires et des maladies vermineuses de l'homme et des animaux domestiques.* Paris: JB Baillière, 1860.

5 http://www.m-ww.de/krankheiten/infections-krankheiten/bilharziose.html

6 Foster (ref 2), pp 64–65.

7 Foster (ref 2), p 68.

8 Foster (ref 2), p 92.

9 See chapter 'Windows on the building blocks of tissue' in this book.

10 Millar PS, Gensheimer KF, Addiss DG, Sosin DM, Beckett GA, Houk-Jankowski A, Hudson A. An outbreak of crytosporidiosis from fresh-pressed apple cider. *JAMA* 1994; 272: 1592–1596.

11 Herwaldt BL. Cyclospora cayetanensis: a review, focusing on the outbreaks of cyclosporiasis in the 1990s. *Clin Infect Dis* 2000; 31: 1040–1057.

From hobby to practical science
P 110

1 Fourcroy AF. Chimie. In: *Encyclopédie Méthodique. Chimie, Pharmacie et Métallurgie.* Paris: Agasse, 1796. Tome III: 262–781. Quotation page 738.

2 Fourcroy AF. *Idées sur un nouveau moyen de rechercher la nature des maladies. La Médecine éclairée par les sciences physique.* Paris 1791 (an IV); 1: 142–145.

3 See also 'From matula to test strip' in this book.

4 Beneke R. Johann Christian Reil. Gedächtnis-rede. Halle: Max Niemeyer, 1913, reprint of a report by Reil. Quotation page 55.

5 These included Joseph Louis Gay-Lussac (1778–1850), Louis Jacques Thenard (1777–1857) and Jöns Jacob Berzelius (1779–1848).

6 In the past famous scientists were often honoured for their achievements by being raised to the nobility. A bracketed 'von' or 'de' in a person's name indicates that this honour was conferred after the time described.

7 Ebstein E. Joh[ann] Lucas Schönleins Verdienste um die diagnostische Technik. *Zeitschrift für Klinische Medizin* 1910; 71: 471–477. Quotation from a manuscript of Schönlein's.

8 Virchow R. Über das Bedürfnis und die Richtigkeit einer Medizin vom mechanistischen Standpunkt. *Archiv für pathologische Anatomie und Physiologie und klinische Medizin* 1907; 188: 1–21.

9 Ibid.

10 Scherer JJ. *Chemische und mikroskopische Untersuchungen zur Pathologie angestellt an den Kliniken des Julius-Hospitales zu Würzburg.* Heidelberg: CF Winter, 1843.

11 For a photograph of Heller, see page 21 in 'From matula to test strip'.

12 Gorup-Besanez ECF von. *Anleitung zur qualitativen und quantitativen zoochemischen Analyse.* 1st ed. Nürnberg: JL Schrag, 1850: 223–236.

13 For a photograph of a polarimeter, see page 46 in 'Pisse prophets, polarimetry and patient self-monitoring'.

14 See also 'Windows onto the building blocks of tissue' in this book.

15 See 'Pisse prophets, polarimetry and patient self-monitoring'.

16 Bernard C. *Introduction à l'étude de la médecine expérimentale.* Paris: JB Baillière & Fils, 1865: 394.

17 Bernard C. *Leçons sur le diabète et la glycogénèse animale.* In: Duval M, ed, Paris: JB Baillière & Fils, 1877: 39.

18 Bernard (ref 16), p 236.

19 See reference to Otto Folin's work on urinalysis in 'From matula to test strip'.

20 For a biographical sketch of Prout see 'Pisse prophets, polarimetry and patient self-monitoring'.

21 Prout W. Observations on the application of chemistry to physiology, pathology and practice. *Medical Gazette* 1831; 8: 257–265, 321–327, 385–391. Quotation page 265.

22 See also 'From matula to test strip'.

23 Graves RJ. *Clinical Lectures on the Practice of Medicine.* Vol I, 2nd ed. Dublin: Famin & Co, 1848. Quotation page 32.

24 Lehmann CG. *Lehrbuch der physiologischen Chemie.* Vol 1, 2nd ed. Leipzig: Engelmann, 1850: 21.

25 Rudolf Virchow explained the issues involved at the Meeting of German Naturalists and Physicians in Innsbruck in 1869 in a magnificent lecture that is still worth reading today.

26 Broussais FJV. Leçons du docteur Broussais sur les phlegmasies gastriques, dites fièvres continues essentielles des auteurs, et sur les phlegmasies cutanées aigues. In: de Caignou E, Quemont A, eds. Paris: Méquignon-Marvis, 1819: 1.

27 Physiological Medicine was celebrated by its proponents as an empirical and inductive science. These philosophical terms were intended to convey that the scientist, starting from observation and experimentation, advanced step by step towards general insights. This approach made it possible to apply scientific methods in the hospital. Indeed, Virchow proclaimed self-confidently: 'We define true theoretical scientific medicine as pathological physiology'.

28 Virchow R. Ein alter Bericht über die Gestaltung der pathologischen Anatomie in Deutschland, wie sie ist und wie sie werden muss. *Archiv für pathologische Anatomie und Physiologie und klinische Medizin* 1900; 159: 24–39. Quotation page 39.

29 For a biographical sketch of Frerichs, see 'From matula to test strip'.

30 Flexner A. Medical education in Europe. Carnegie Foundation for the Advancement of Teaching, New York 1912. Report to the Carnegie Foundation for the Advancement of Teaching, Bulletin 6: 161.

31 See also 'From matula to test strip'.

32 See caricature on page 23 in 'From matula to test strip'.

33 See also 'From matula to test strip'.

34 For a biographical sketch of Folin, see 'From matula to test strip'.

35 See 'Windows onto the building blocks of tissue'.

36 The stains used in these methods are eosin (acid), methylene blue (basic) and a degradation product of methylene blue (azure). Azure stains the nuclear matrix of white blood cells dark purple.

37 Naunyn B. *Erinnerungen, Gedanken und Meinungen.* Munich: JF Bergmann, 1925. Quotation page 235 [Naunyn B: Memories, Thoughts and Convictions. Cowen DL, ed. Canton, Mass: Science History Publications, 1994].

38 Naunyn B. Aerzte und Laien. *Deutsche Revue Berlin* 1905; 30: 185–196; 343–355. Quotation page 349.

39 Müller F. Eröffnungsrede. *Verhandlungen des Congresses für Innere Medizin* 1908; 25: 9.

40 Frerichs FT. Eröffnungsrede. *Verhandlungen des Congresses für Innere Medizin* Wiesbaden 1882; 1: 13–17. Quotation page 15.

41 Hopkins FG. The analyst and the medical man. *Analyst* [Cambridge] 1906; 31: 385–404.

42 Peters JP, Van Slyke DD. *Quantitative Clinical Chemistry.* Baltimore: Williams & Wilkins Co, 1931–1932.

43 Drabkin DL. *Thudichum. Chemist of the Brain.* Philadelphia: University of Pennsylvania Press, 1958. Letter page 252.

Motes, protective ferments and hormones

P 129

1 Paullini CF. *Neu-Vermehrte Heylsame Dreck-Apotheke, wie nemlich mit Koth und Urin fast alle, ja auch die schwerste, gifftigste Kranckheiten, und bezauberte Schäden vom Haupt biss zun Füssen, inn- und äusserlich, glücklich curiret worden.* 4th ed. Frankfurt am Main: Friedrich Daniel Knochen, 1734: 260.

2 Reinhard F. Gynäkologie und Geburtshilfe altägyptischer Papyri. *Sudhoffs Archiv* 1916; 9: 315–344, p 331.

3 Kolta KS, Schwarzmann-Schafhauser D. *Die Heilkunde im Alten Ägypten. Magie und Ratio in der Krankheitsvorstellung und therapeutischen Praxis.* Stuttgart: Franz Steiner Verlag, 2000: 30–31.

4 Manniche L. *An Ancient Egyptian Herbal.* London: British Museum Publications, 1989: 107–108.

5 Diepgen P. *Die Frauenheilkunde der Alten Welt.* München: Verlag JF Bergmann, 1937: 50.

6 Fasbender H. *Entwicklungslehre, Geburtshilfe und Gynäkologie in den Hippokratischen Schriften.* Stuttgart; Ferdinand Enke Verlag, 1897: 32.

7 Kühn KG, ed. *Claudii Galeni Opera omnia.* 20 volumes. Leipzig: Karl Knobloch; 1821–1833, Vol 14, p 476.

8 Paullini (ref 1), p 261; Westendorf W. *Erwachen der Heilkunst. Die Medizin im Alten Ägypten.* Zürich: Artemis & Winkler; 1992: 212.

9 Menascha I. Die Geburtshilfe bei den alten Ägyptern. *Archiv für Gynäkologie* 1927; 131: 425–461.

10 Aschheim S. Die Schwangerschaftsdiagnose aus dem Harn durch Nachweis des Hypophysenvorderlappenhormons. II. Praktische und theoretische Ergebnisse aus den Harnuntersuchungen. *Klin Wochenschr* 1928; 7: 1453–1457, p 1454.

11 Schoeller W, Göbel H. Die Wirkung des Follikelhormons auf Pflanzen. *Biochemische Zeitschrift* 1931; 240: 1–11.

12 Manger J. Untersuchungen zum Problem der Geschlechtsdiagnose aus Schwangerenharn. *Dtsch Med Wochenschr* 1933; 59: 885–887.

13 Manger (ref 12), p 887.

14 Hoffmann W. Das Auswachsen des Getreides, speziell der Gerste. PhD thesis, Berlin: University of Heidelberg; 1934.

15 Schwind M. Die Wirkung von Schwangerenharn auf Getreidekörner. MD thesis, Würzburg: University of Heidelberg, Konrad Tiltsch; 1938: 4.

16 Preibsch W, Wagner F. Kritisches über die Verfahren zur Frühschwangerschaftsdiagnose. *Zentralblatt für Gynäkologie* 1967; 89: 1079–1085.

17 Kolta (ref 3), p 165.

18 Kolta (ref 3), p 165–166.

19 Littré E, ed. *Œuvres complètes d'Hippocrate.* 10 volumes. Paris: JB Baillière; 1839–1861; Vol 8: 416.

20 Fasbender (ref 6), p 94; Reinhard (ref 2), pp 331–332; Littré (ref 19), Vol 8: 414.

21 Soranus' Gynecology, translated with an introduction by Owsei Temkin, with the assistance of Nicolson J. Eastman, Ludwig Edelstein, and Alan F. Guttmacher. Baltimore: The Johns Hopkins University Press, 1991; Book 1, XII: 43–44.

22 Rhazes. *Liber Helchauy idest continens artem medicine.* Venice: Locatellus, 1506, fol 403r.

23 Rueff J. *The expert midwife, or an excellent and most necessary treatise of the generation and birth of man.* London: E G[riffin] for S B[urton], 1637: 185.

24 Fischer-Homberger E. *Medizin vor Gericht. Gerichtsmedizin von der Renaissance bis zur Aufklärung.* Bern: Hans Huber, 1983: 222–223.

25 Fidelis F. *De relationibus medicorum libri quatuor.* Palermo; 1602: 420–423.

26 Zacchia P. *Quaestiones medico-legales.* Vol 1. Rome; 1621. Quoted in Zedler JH. *Grosses vollständiges Universal Lexicon aller Wissenschaften und Künste.* Vol 35. Leipzig: Johann Heinrich Zedler, 1743, column 1867.

27 Venette N. *Abhandlung von Erzeugung der Menschen.* Königsberg: Christoph Gottfried Eckart, 1738.

28 Venette (ref 27), p 309.

29 Zedler (ref 26), columns 1864-1879.

30 Zedler (ref 26), column 1866.

31 Zedler (ref 26), column 1868.

32 Lorenz M. *Kriminelle Körper - Gestörte Gemüter. Die Normierung des Individuums in Gerichtsmedizin und Psychiatrie der Aufklärung.* Hamburg: Hamburger Edition, 1999: 134–159.

33 Kergaradec J-A Le Jumeau Vicomte de. *Mémoire sur l'auscultation, appliquée à l'étude de la grossesse.* Paris: 1822.

34 Sonntag E. *Das Hegar'sche Schwangerschaftszeichen.* Leipzig: 1892.

35 Hegar A. Diagnose der frühesten Schwangerschaftsperiode. *Dtsch Med Wochenschr* 1895; 21: 565–567.

36 Hegar (ref 35), p 567.

37 Fasbender H. *Geschichte der Geburtshülfe.* Jena: Fischer, 1906: 489–490.

38 Busch DWH, Moser A, eds. *Handbuch der Geburtskunde in alphabetischer Ordnung.* Vol. 3. Berlin: Friedrich August Herbig, 1842: 20.

39 Ross RS. 'Chemie und Mikroskop am Krankenbette' - Mark Aurel Hoefle (1818–1855) und die frühe Entwicklung der Klinischen Chemie in Heidelberg. *Medizinhistorisches Journal* 1996; 31: 121–146.

40 Hoefle MA. *Chemie und Mikroskop am Krankenbette.* 2nd ed. Erlangen: Enke, 1850: 148.

41 Fasbender (ref 37), p 490.

42 Eulenburg A, ed. *Real-Encyclopädie der gesammten Heilkunde.* 2nd ed. Vol 18. Vienna: Urban & Schwarzenberg, 1889: 50.

43 Fasbender (ref 37), p 487.

44 Multinucleate giant cells produced by the fusion of mononucleate cells.

45 Veit J. Zur Physiologie der Ernährung des Fötus. *Dtsch Med Wochenschr* 1903; 29: 152.

46 Liepmann W. Ueber ein für menschliche Placenta spezifisches Serum. Erste Mitteilung. *Dtsch Med Wochenschr* 1902; 28: 911–912.

47 Liepmann W. Ueber ein für menschliche Placenta spezifisches Serum. Zweite Mitteilung. *Dtsch Med Wochenschr* 1903; 29: 80–81.

48 Opitz E. Zur Biochemie der Schwangerschaft. *Dtsch Med Wochenschr* 1903; 29: 597–601.

49 Freund R. Zur Geschichte der Serodiagnostik der Schwangerschaft. *Münch Med Wochenschr* 1913; 60: 700–701.

50 This was based on polarimetry, in which a polarimeter is used to measure the ability of a substance to rotate the plane of vibration of polarised light.

51 Abderhalden E, Freund R, Pincussohn L. Serologische Untersuchungen mit Hilfe der 'optischen Methode' während der Schwangerschaft und speziell bei Eklampsie. *Praktische Ergebnisse der Geburtshilfe und Gynäkologie* 1910; 2: 367ff.

52 Abderhalden E, Kiutsi M. Biologische Untersuchungen über Schwangerschaft. Die Diagnose der Schwangerschaft mittels der 'optischen Methode' und dem Dialysierverfahren. *Zeitschrift für physiologische Chemie* 1912; 77: 249ff.

53 Abderhalden E. *Schutzfermente des tierischen Organismus: ein Beitrag zur Kenntnis der Abwehrmassregeln des tierischen Organismus gegen körper-, blut- und zellfremde Stoffe.* Berlin: Springer; 1912.

54 Abderhalden E. Diagnose der Schwangerschaft mit Hilfe der optischen Methode und dem Dialysierverfahren. *Münch Med Wochenschr* 1912; 59: 1305–1306.

55 Frewer A. *Medizin und Moral in Weimarer Republik und Nationalsozialismus. Die Zeitschrift 'Ethik' unter Emil Abderhalden.* Frankfurt: Campus Verlag; 2000: 38–46.

56 Deichmann U, Müller-Hill B. The fraud of Abderhalden's enzymes. *Nature* 1998; 393: 109–111.

57 Lindig P. Über Serumfermentwirkungen bei Schwangeren und Tumorkranken. *Münch Med Wochenschr* 1913; 60: 288–290.

58 Abderhalden E. Über Serumfermentwirkung bei Schwangeren und Tumorkranken. Bemerkungen zu der Arbeit von Paul Lindig. *Münch Med Wochenschr* 1913; 60: 411–413.

59 Engelhorn E. Zur biologischen Diagnose der Schwangerschaft. *Münch Med Wochenschr* 1913; 60: 587–588.

60 Freund R, Brahm C. Die Schwangerschaftsdiagnose mittelst der optischen Methode und des Dialysierverfahrens. *Münch Med Wochenschr* 1913; 60: 683–690.

61 Abderhalden E. Bemerkung zur 'Geschichte der Serodiagnostik der Schwangerschaft' von R. Freund. *Münch Med Wochenschr* 1913; 60: 701–702.

62 Michaelis L, von Lagermarck L. Die Abderhaldensche Schwangerschaftsdiagnose. *Dtsch Med Wochenschr* 1914; 40: 316–319.

63 Deichmann (ref 56), p 110.

64 Deichmann (ref 56).

65 Frewer (ref 55), p 179.

66 Aschheim S. *Die Schwangerschaftsdiagnose aus dem Harne.* 2nd ed. Berlin: S. Karger; 1933: 3–5.

67 Schneck P. Selmar Aschheim (1878–1965) und Bernhard Zondek (1891–1966). Zum Schicksal zweier jüdischer Ärzte und Forscher an der Berliner Charité. *Zeitschrift für ärztliche Fortbildung und Qualitätssicherung* 1994; 91: 187–194.

68 Hinz G, Ebert A, Goetze B: Der Exodus: Robert Meyer, Selmar Aschheim und Bernhard Zondek. Drei Namen für Tausende. In: Ebert A, Weitzel HK, eds. *Die Berliner Gesellschaft für Geburtshilfe und Gynäkologie 1844–1994.* Berlin: Walter de Gruyter; 1994: 206–242.

69 Allen E, Doisy EA. An ovarian hormone. Preliminary report on its localization, extraction and partial purification, and action in test animals. *JAMA* 1923; 81: 819–821.

70 Zondek B, Aschheim S. Experimentelle Untersuchungen über die Funktion und das Hormon des Ovariums. *Klin Wochenschr* 1925; 4: 1388–1390.

71 Zondek B, Aschheim S. Ovarialhormon, Wachstum der Genitalien, sexuelle Frühreife. *Klin Wochenschr* 1926; 5: 2199–2202.

72 von Schubert E. Tagungsbericht: Berlin, Gesellschaft für Geburtshilfe und Gynäkologie, 22.1.1926. *Dtsch Med Wochenschr* 1926; 52: 343–344.

73 Zondek B, Aschheim S. Das Hormon des Hypophysenvorderlappens. *Klin Wochenschr* 1927; 6: 248–252.

74 Zondek B, Aschheim S. Das Hormon des Hypophysenvorderlappens. *Klin Wochenschr* 1928; 7: 831–835.

75 Aschheim S, Zondek B. Hypophysenvorderlappenhormon und Ovarialhormon im Harn von Schwangeren. *Klin Wochenschr* 1927; 6: 1322.

76 Aschheim (ref 10).

77 Zondek B. Die Schwangerschaftsdiagnose aus dem Harn durch Nachweis des Hypophysenvorderlappenhormons. I. Grundlagen und Technik der Methode. *Klin Wochenschr* 1928; 7: 1404–1411.

78 Schneck (ref 67), p 192.

79 Aschheim (ref 66), p 62.

80 Schneck (ref 67); Hinz (ref 68).

81 Aschheim (ref 66), p 70–74.

82 Marquart H. 50 Jahre HCG – Nachweis zur Frühdiagnose der Schwangerschaft (Eine medizinhistorische Studie seit der Entdeckung der Aschheim-Zondek-Reaktion). MD thesis, Düsseldorf: 1981, p 24.

83 Kevles DJ. *In the name of eugenics. Genetics and the uses of human heredity.* Berkeley: University of California Press; 1985: 122–128.

84 Wells GP. Lancelot Thomas Hogben. Biographical memoirs of fellows of the Royal Society 1978; 24: 183–221.

85 Marquart (ref 82), pp 24–25.

86 Ruppel G. Erfahrungen mit dem Schwangerschaftstest nach Galli-Mainini von 1952–1960 ausgeführt an der Rana esculenta. MD thesis, Saarbrücken: 1961, p 4.

87 Galli Mainini C. Pregnancy test using male toad. *J Clin Endocrin* 1947; 7: 653–658.

88 Ruppel (ref 86).

89 Bibel DJ. *Milestones in Immunology. A historical exploration.* Madison, Wisc: Science Tech Publ; 1988: 290–293.

90 Got R. Gonadotropine choriale humaine. Isolement et caractérisation. Physical sciences thesis. Paris: 1959.

91 Marquart (ref 82), p 46.

92 Marquart (ref 82), p 45.

93 Bettendorf G. *Zur Geschichte der Endokrinologie und Reproduktionsmedizin. 256 Biographien und Berichte.* Berlin: Springer; 1995: 175.

94 Pfeffer N. *The stork and the syringe. A political history of reproductive medicine.* Cambridge: Polity Press; 1993: 146.

95 Medvei VC. *The history of clinical endocrinology.* 2nd edition, Carnforth: Parthenon Publishing; 1993: 375.

96 Bettendorf (ref 93), p 611.

97 Wide L, Gemzell CA. An immunological pregnancy test. *Acta Endocrinol.* 1960; 37: 261–267.

98 Wide L. An immunological method for assay of human chorionic gonadotrophin. *Acta Endocrinol* 1962; 70 (Suppl): 1–111.

99 Marquart (ref 82), p 63.

100 Vaitukaitis JL, Braunstein GD, Ross GT. A radioimmunoassay which specifically measures human chorionic gonadotrophin in the presence of luteinizing hormone. *Am J Obst Gyn* 1972; 113: 751–758.

101 Research Council. Biologic markers in reproductive toxicology. Washington, DC: National Academy Press; 1989: 188.

102 Böhmer S, Schneider J. Die Entwicklung des diagnostischen Ultraschalls in der geburtshilflichen Medizin. *Der Kinderarzt* 1991; 22: 605–616.

103 Birken S, Canfield RE. Isolation and amino acid sequence of COOH-terminal fragments from the β-subunit of human choriogonadotrophin. *J Biol Chem* 1977; 252: 5386–5392.

Blood lines
P 144

1 Harvey W. *Exercitatio anatomica de motu cordis et sanguinis in animalibus.* Frankfurt am Main: Wilhelm Fitzner, 1628.

2 Landois L. *Transfusion des Blutes.* Leipzig, 1875.

3 Landsteiner K. Über Agglutinationserscheinungen normalen menschlichen Blutes. *Wien klin Wochenschr* 1901; 14 (40): 1132–1134.

4 In the case of the Rh blood group system, which includes about 40 antigens, the lack of uniformity of nomenclature causes even more confusion.

5 Landsteiner was also the first to recognise the importance of the antiglobulin test described by C. Moreschi. This highly sensitive serological method of demonstrating the presence of antibodies was first used for routine blood group testing by R. R. A. Coombs in 1945. Rabbits immunised with human protein (globulin) produce an antihuman globulin antibody. This 'anti-antibody antibody' binds blood group antibodies, thereby causing visible agglutination of the red cells to which they are attached.

6 Landsteiner (ref 3).

7 Crile GW. *Haemorrhage and Transfusion.* D Appleton and company: New York, 1909.

8 Winkler EA. Ernst Unger, 1875–1938, Eine Bibliographie. Inauguraldissertation zur Erlangung der medizinischen Doktorwürde an der Freien Universität Berlin, 1975.

9 Personal communications.

10 Landsteiner K, Wiener AS. Studies on an agglutinogen (Rh) in human blood reacting with anti-Rhesus sera and with human iso-antibodies. *J Exp Med* 1941; 74: 309.

11 Dahr P. Untersuchungen über eine neue agglutinable Blutkörpercheneigenschaft beim Menschen, *Zeitschrift für gesamte Blutforschung* 1942; Band XIX, 181–184.

12 Levine P, Stetson R. An unusual case of intra-group agglutination. *J Am Med Assoc* 1939; 113: 126.

13 Blumberg BS, Sutnick AI, London WT. Hepatitis and leukaemia: Their relation to Australia Antigen, *Bull NY Acad Med* 1968; 44: 1566–1586.

14 Dane DS, Cameron CH, Briggs M. Virus-like particles in serum of patients with Australia-antigen-associated hepatitis. *Lancet* 1970; I: 695–698.

15 In Germany fresh blood used to be classified as a 'custom-made' product the preparation of which was the responsibility of the doctor performing the transfusion. This notion is now obsolete.

16 Speiser P, Smekal FG. *Karl Landsteiner, Entdecker der Blutgruppen und Pionier der Immunologie.* Biographie eines Nobelpreisträgers aus der Wiener Medizinischen Schule. Berlin: Blackwell-Überreuter, 1990.

17 Kunsch K, Kunsch S. *Der Mensch in Zahlen. Eine Datensammlung in Tabellen mit über 20 000 Einzelwerten.* 2nd ed. Heidelberg: Spektrum Akademischer Verlag, 2000.

Cancer signs
P 159

1 Schramm P. Krebs. *Eine Krankheit im Spiegel der Jahrtausende.* Taunusstein: Edition Rarissima, 1987. A discussion of the Edwin Smith Papyrus can be found on the Internet at http://www.eoa.org.eg/oldest.htm. The breast tumours are described just before case 40.

2 Wolff J. *Die Lehre von der Krebskrankheit von den ältesten Zeiten bis zur Gegenwart.* Vol 1. 2nd ed. Jena: Verlag von Gustav Fischer, 1929.

3 Wolff (ref 2).

4 Virchow R. *Die Cellularpathologie in ihrer Begründung auf physiologische und pathologische Gewebelehre.* Berlin: Hirschwald, 1858.

5 In 1846 JC Warren performed the first cancer operation under ether anesthesia.

6 Schridde H. Krebshaare. *Münch Med Wochenschr* 1922; 45: 1565–1566.

7 Frick G, Meduna K. Ueber die Schridde'schen Krebshaare und ihre Bedeutung für die Diagnose von Karzinomen. *Wien Klin Wochenschr* 1936; 3: 76–77.

8 Dietz E. Aus der Steinzeit der Tumordiagnostik. *diagnostica Dialog* 1998; 1: 20–21.

9 Köhler R. *Die Krebs- und Scheinkrebs-Krankheiten des Menschen. Nach den bisherigen Leistungen der Wissenschaft auf dem klinischen Standpunkte bearbeitet.* Stuttgart: JB Müllers Verlagshandlung, 1853: 104.

10 Dietz (ref 8).

11 Boschung U. Labor und Medizin – einst und jetzt: Geräte und Methoden. In: *Labor und Medizin – einst und jetzt. Beiträge zur Geschichte der Labormedizin.* Schweizerischer Fachverband des medizinisch-technischen Laborfachpersonals. Bern: Stämpfli + Cie AG, 1980: 152.

12 Clamp JR. Some aspects of the first recorded case of multiple myeloma. *Lancet* 1967; 23: 1354–1356.

13 Perry MC, Kyle RA. The clinical significance of Bence Jones proteinuria. *Mayo Clin Proc* 1975; 50: 234–238.

14 Bence Jones H. Papers on chemical pathology; prefaced by the Gulstonian Lectures, read at the Royal College of Physicians, 1846. Lecture III. *Lancet* 1847; II: 88–92.

15 Bence Jones H. On a new substance occurring in the urine of a patient with mollities ossium. *Phil Trans Roy Soc London* 1848; 138: 55–62.

16 Boschung (ref 11).

17 Classics in Oncology: Henry Bence Jones (1813–1873). *CA-A Cancer J Clin* 1978; 28 (1): 47–56.

18 Softening and fragility of the bones.

19 Clamp (ref 12).

20 MacIntyre W. Case of mollities and fragilitas ossium, accompanied with urine strongly charged with animal matter. *Med Chir Trans Lond* 1850; 33: 211–232.

21 von Rustizky J. Multiples Myelom. *Dtsch Z Chir* 1873; 3: 162–172.

22 The term 'plasmacytoma', also sometimes used today, was proposed in 1940 by Kurt Apitz (1906–1945).

23 Durie BGM. Multiples Myelom: Eine kurze Übersicht über Krankheit und Behandlungsmöglichkeiten. International Myeloma Foundation. North Hollywood, CA.

24 Ellinger A, Falk F, Henderson LJ, Schulz FN, Spiro K, Wiechowski W, eds. *Analyse des Harns. Zum Gebrauch für Mediziner, Chemiker und Pharmazeuten. Zugleich Elfte Auflage von Neubauer-Huppert's Lehrbuch.* Wiesbaden: CW Kreidels Verlag, 1913: 2nd half, 1184.

25 Ellinger (ref 24).

26 Ellinger (ref 24).

27 Sebastian A. *Dictionary of the History of Medicine.* New York: The Parthenon Publishing Group, 1999: 523.

28 Durie (ref 23).

29 Swazey JP, Reeds K. A crucial experiment of nature: multiple myeloma and the structure of antibodies. In: *Today's Medicine, Tomorrow's Science. Essays on the Paths of Discovery in the Biomedical Sciences.* US Department of Health, Education and Welfare, Public Health Service, National Institutes of Health. DHEW Publication No. (NIH), 1978: 78–244.

30 Edelman GM, Poulik MD. Studies on structural units of the γ-globulins. *J Exp Med* 1961; 113: 861–884.

31 Poulik MD, Edelman GM. Comparison of reduced alkylated derivatives of some myeloma globulins and Bence Jones proteins. *Nature* 1961; 191: 1274–1276.

32 Edelman GM, Gally JA. The nature of Bence Jones protein: chemical similarities to polypeptide chains of myeloma globulins and normal γ-globulins. *J Exp Med* 1962; 116: 207–227.

33 Swazey, Reeds (ref 29).

34 Edelman, Gally (ref 32), p 225.

35 Hilschmann N. Die chemische Struktur von zwei Bence Jones-Proteinen (Roy und Cum) vom χ-Typ. *Hoppe Seyler's Z Physiol Chem* 1967; 348: 1077–1080.

36 Epp O, Colman P, Fehlhammer H, Bode W, Schiffer M, Huber R. Crystal and molecular structure of a dimer composed of the variable portions of the Bence-Jones protein REI. *Eur J Biochem* 1974; 45: 513–524.

37 Cancer of the blood-forming organs.

38 Cancer of the lymphatic tissue.

39 In this disease, first described by Waldenström in 1944, malignant spleen and bone marrow cells produce increased amounts of large immunoglobulins.

40 Boege F. Bence-Jones-Proteine. *J Lab Med* 1999; 23 (9): 477–482.

41 Immunoelectrophoresis was first described in 1953. Grabar P, Williams CA. Méthode permettant l'étude conjuguée des propriétés électrophorétiques et immunochimiques d'un mélange de protéines: application au sérum sanguin. *Biochim Biophys Acta* 1953; 10: 193–194.

42 http://www.vivascience.com/en/faq/faq_bence_jones.shtml

43 Mead GP, Carr-Smith HD, Drayson MT, Bradwell AR. Detection of Bence Jones myeloma and monitoring of myeloma chemotherapy using immunoassays specific for free immunoglobulin light chains. *Clin Lab* 2003; 49: 25–27.

44 Calcitonin in medullary thyroid cancer, insulin in insulinoma, etc.

45 Trinkler H. Das Lichtmikroskop und seine Hilfstechniken in der Entwicklung der medizinischen Diagnostik. In: *Labor und Medizin - einst und jetzt. Beiträge zur Geschichte der Labormedizin.* Schweizerischer Fachverband des medizinisch-technischen Laborfachpersonals. Bern: Stämpfli + Cie AG, 1980.

46 Schramm (ref 1).

47 Trinkler (ref 45).

48 Friedländer C. *Mikroskopische Technik.* Berlin: Fischer, 1883.

49 Simmer H. Die Auffindung eines Zyklus im desquamierten menschlichen Vaginalepithel. In: Habrich C, ed. *Medizinische Diagnostik in Geschichte und Gegenwart.* München: Verlag Werner Fritsch, 1978: 341–356.

50 Trinkler (ref 45).

51 Papanicolaou GN. Note on the diagnosis of the female genital tract. *Proc Race Betterment Conf* 1928; 3: 528–534.

52 Kidd JG. In Memoriam George Nicholas Papanicolaou 1883–1962. *Am J Clin Path* 1963; 39: 400–405.

53 Simmer (ref 49).

54 Papanicolaou GN, Traut HF. *Diagnosis of Uterine Cancer by the Vaginal Smear.* New York: The Commonwealth Fund, 1943.

55 Soost HJ, Baur S. *Gynäkologische Zytodiagnostik. Lehrbuch und Atlas.* 5th ed. Stuttgart: Georg Thieme Verlag, 1990.

56 Streeck RE, Hilfrich R. Papillomavirus-Infektionen: Latente, subklinische oder virulente Erkrankung? Neues Nachweisverfahren erlaubt eine Unterscheidung. *mta Spektrum* 2000; 15 (4): 233–235.

57 Castle PE, Schiffman M, Gravitt PE, Kendall H, Fishman S, Dong H, et al. Comparisons of HPV DNA detection by MY09/11 PCR methods. *J Med Virol* 2002; 68 (3): 417–423.

58 Gutman AB, Gutman EB. An acid phosphatase occurring in the serum of patients with metastasizing carcinoma of the prostate gland. *J Clin Invest* 1938; 17: 473–478.

59 Gold P, Freedman SO. Demonstration of tumor-specific antigens in human colonic carcinomata by immunological tolerance and absorption techniques. *J Exp Med* 1965; 121: 439–445.

60 Maurer A, Müller-Brand J. Verräterische Spuren. *Roche Magazin* 1992; 41: 13–23.

61 Jäger D, Jäger E, Knuth A. Biologische Waffen gegen Tumoren. *mta Spektrum* 2001; 10 (16): 438–440.

62 A method of selectively collecting cells from a sample.

63 Portstmann B. Neue Diagnostika ermöglichen spezifische Krebsbekämpfung In: *Neue Strategien zur Krebsbekämpfung.* Basel: Roche Facetten, 2001.

64 Stieber P. 15 Jahre Tumormarker im klinischen Alltag: ihr Nutzen und ihre Grenzen. *mta Spektrum* 2000; 15 (12): 612–614.

65 http://www4.od.nih.gov/biomarkers/ICDD.htm

66 Portstmann (ref 63).

67 Portstmann (ref 63).

68 Jerónimo C, Usadel H, Henrique R, Silva C, Oliveira J, Lopes C, Sidransky D. Quantitative GSTP1 hypermethylation in bodily fluids of patients with prostate cancer. *Urology* 2002; 60 (6): 1131–1135.

69 Jerónimo C, Varzim G, Henrique R, Oliveira J, Bento MJ, Silva C, Lopes C, Sidransky D. I105V polymorphism and promoter methylation of the GSTP1 gene in prostate adenocarcinoma. *Cancer Epidemiol Biomarkers Prev* 2002; 11 (5): 445–450.

70 Personal communication, Prof. Bärbel Porstmann.

71 Schott H. *Die Chronik der Medizin.* Gütersloh: Chronik Verlag im Bertelsmann Lexikon Verlag, 2000.

72 Wolff (ref 2).

73 Büttner J. Giessener Schüler Justus von Liebigs mit späteren Tätigkeiten in der Medizin. *Giessener Universitätsblätter* 2001/2002; 34/35: 40/41.

74 Bence Jones (ref 14).

75 Manufacturer's product information on the Hydragel 2 IF und Hydragel 4 IF kits for detecting monoclonal proteins in human serum and urine. Fulda: Sebia GmbH, 2003: 16.

76 Carmichael DE. *The PAP Smear: Life of George N. Papanicolaou.* Springfield, Ill: Charles C. Thomas Publisher, 1973.

77 Water fleas of the genus *Daphnia*.

78 Kidd (ref 52).

79 Carmichael (ref 76).

80 Carmichael (ref 76).

81 The illustration was kindly provided by Prof. Elmer Koneman, Colorado, USA.

82 The illustration was kindly provided by Dr Lukas Bubendorf and Dr A Lugli, Institute of Pathology, University of Basel.

83 The illustration was kindly provided by Dr Lukas Bubendorf and Dr A Lugli, Institute of Pathology, University of Basel.

84 The illustration was kindly provided by Dr Lukas Bubendorf and Dr A Lugli, Institute of Pathology, University of Basel.

85 The illustration was kindly provided by Mrs. Martina Mirlacher, Institute of Pathology, University of Basel.

86 A centromere is the site at which the two strands of a chromosome are joined. During cell division it is the site of attachment of the spindle fibres that pull the strands to opposite ends of the dividing cell.

The medium matters

P 172

1 Mochmann H, Köhler W. *Meilensteine der Bakteriologie. Von Entdeckungen und Entdeckern aus den Gründerjahren der Medizinischen Mikrobiologie.* 2nd ed. Frankfurt am Main: Edition Wützel, 1997.

2 Cohn F. *Ueber Bacterien, die kleinsten lebenden Wesen.* Berlin: Lüderitz'sche Verlagsbuchhandlung Carl Habel, 1872.

3 Klebs E. Beiträge zur Kenntnisse der Micrococcen. *Arch Exp Pathol Pharmakol* 1873; 1: 32–64.

4 Lister J. The present position of antiseptic surgery. In: *Verh X. Int med Congr Berlin.* Berlin, 1890: 1891.

5 Klebs (ref 3).

6 Mochmann, Köhler (ref 1).

7 Lister (ref 4).

8 Hitchens AP, Leikind MC. The introduction of agar-agar into bacteriology. *J Bacteriol* 1939; 37: 485–493.

9 Ehrenberg CG: Hr. Ehrenberg übergab eine reichliche Centurie historischer Nachträge zu den blutfarbigen Meteoren und sogenannten Prodigien. In: *Ber Verh Kgl Preuß Akad Wiss.* Berlin, 1850: 215–246.

10 Diodorus Siculus; Welles CB trans. *Library of History. Books XVI.66–XVII.* Cambridge, MA: Harvard University Press, 1963.

11 Curtius Rufus Q; Siebelis J, trans. *Von den Thaten Alexanders des Großen.* 3rd ed. Stuttgart, 1882.

12 Sette V. *Memoria storico-naturale sull'arrossimento stra-ordinare di alcune sostanze alimentose osservato nella provincia di Padova l'anno DCCCXIX.* Venezia: Alvisopoli, 1824.

13 Bizio B. Lettera di Bartolomeo Bizio al chiarissimo canonico Angelo Bellani sopra il fenomena della polenta porporina. *Biblioteca Italiana o sia Giornale di Letteratura, Scienze e Arti* 1823; (VIII) 30: 275–295. (English translation by C Merlino in: *J Bacteriol* 1924; 9: 527–43).

14 Cohn (ref 2).

15 Dixon B. *Power Unseen: How Microbes Rule the World.* Oxford: Oxford University Press, 1994.

16 Ehrenberg CG. Fortsetzung der Beobachtung des sogenannten Blutes im Brode als Monas prodigiosa. In: *Ber Verh Kgl Preuß Akad Wiss* 1848: 354–362.

17 Ehrenberg CG. Hr. Ehrenberg zeigt das seit alter Zeit berühmte Prodigium des Blutes im Brode und auf Speisen als jetzt in Berlin vorhandene Erscheinung in frischem Zustande vor und erläuterte dieselbe als bedingt durch ein bisher unbekanntes monadenartiges Thierchen (Monas? prodigiosa). In: *Ber Verh Kgl Preuß Akad Wiss.* Berlin, 1848: 349–353.

18 Schroeter J. Über einige durch Bakterien gebildete Pigmente. *Beiträge zur Biologie der Pflanzen* 1872; 1: 109–126.

19 Stanier RY, Inngraham JL, Wheelis ML Painter PR. *General Microbiology.* 5th ed. London: MacMillan Education LTD, 1987: 11.

20 Klebs E. Ueber Diphtherie. In: *Verh des Congresses für Innere Med, II. Congress.* Wiesbaden: Bergmann, 1883: 139–154.

21 Hitchens, Leikind (ref 8).

22 Mochmann, Köhler (ref 1).

23 Koch R. Untersuchungen über Bacterien V. Die Aetiologie der Milzbrandkrankheit, begründet auf der Entwicklungsgeschichte des Bacillus Anthracis. *Beiträge zur Biologie der Pflanzen* 1876; 2: 277–310.

24 Vittadini C. Risultato di alcuni esperimenti istituti sul baco da seta e sopra altri insetti; allo scopo di chiarire la vera natura del calcino. *Giornale dell'I.R. Istituto Lombardo di Scienze, Lettere ed Arti* 1850; 2: 305–313.

25 Lister (ref 4).

26 Koch R. Zur Untersuchung von pathogenen Organismen. In: *Mittheillungen aus dem Kaiserlichen Gesundheitsamte* 1, 1–48. Also in: *Gesammelte Werke 1;* 1881: 112–163.

27 Koch R. Die Aetiologie der Tuberculose. Lecture held on 24 March 1882 at a meeting of the Berlin Physiological Society. *Berl Med Wochenschr* 19: 221–230. Also in: *Gesammelte Werke* 1; 1881: 428–445.

28 Mochmann, Köhler (ref 1).

29 Mochmann, Köhler (ref 1).

30 Koch (ref 27).

31 Hesse W. Walther and Angelina Hesse – Early contributions to bacteriology, *ASM News* 1992; 58 (8): 425–428.

32 Hitchens, Leikind (ref 8).

33 Von Gierke E. Zur Einführung des Agar-Agars in die bakteriologische Technik. Ein Gedenkwort für eine deutsche Arztfrau. *Zentralbl Bakteriol* [Orig 1] 1935; 133: 273.

34 Cohn (ref 2).

35 Smith HM. The Seaweed Industries of Japan. *Bull Bureau Fisheries.* Washington, DC: Gov Printing Office, 1905; 24: 133–181.

36 Gildemeister E. Allgemeine, besondere und differentialdiagnostische Nährböden, einschließlich Trocken- und Konservennährböden. In: Kolle W, Kraus R, Uhlenhut P, eds. *W. Kolle und A. v. Wassermann's Handbuch der pathogenen Mikroorganismen.* 3rd ed, vol 9. Jena: G Fischer, 1929: 965.

37 Petri RJ. Eine kleine Modifikation des Koch'schen Plattenverfahrens. *Centralblatt für Bacteriologie und Parasitenkunde* 1887; 1: 279.

38 Hitchens, Leikind (ref 8).

39 The media are (from left to right and from top to bottom): Chocolate agar for selective isolation of *Haemophilus;* CHROMagar combined with colistin-nalidixic agar for isolating uropathogens; Campylosel agar for selective isolation of *Campylobacter;* MacConkey agar, a selective medium for isolating Enterobacteriaceae; a *Legionella*-selective medium; Columbia blood agar, suitable for isolating non-fastidious bacteria; xylose-lysine-deoxycholate agar for isolating enteropathogenic Enterobacteriaceae; Sabouraud maltose medium for isolating fungi; and OFPBL agar, a selective medium for isolating *Burkholderia cepacia.*

Fighting the White Death

P 180

1 Loeffler F. Zum 25jährigen Gedenktage der Entdeckung des Tuberkelbazillus. *Dtsch med Wochenschr* 1907; 33 (12): 449–451, (13): 489–495.

2 Ehrlich P. In: *Frankfurter Zeitung* 2 Jun 1910. Quoted from: Möllers B. *Robert Koch. Persönlichkeit und Lebenswerk 1843–1910.* Hannover: Schmorl und von Seefeld, 1950: 133.

3 Johne A. *Die Geschichte der Tuberkulose mit besonderer Berücksichtigung der Tuberkulose des Rindes und die sich daraus ergebenden medicinal- und veterinärpolizeilichen Consequenzen.* Leipzig: FCW Vogel, 1883.

4 Koch R. Die Aetiologie der Tuberkulose (1882 and 1884). In: Schwalbe J, ed. *Gesammelte Werke von Robert Koch.* Leipzig: Georg Thieme Verlag, 1912; vol 1: 444.

5 Koch (ref 4, 1882).

6 Niemeyer F. *Lehrbuch der speziellen Pathologie und Therapie mit besonderer Rücksicht auf Physiologie und pathologische Anatomie.* Berlin: August Hirschwald, 1863; vol 1: 171.

7 Koch (ref 4,1884), p 472.

8 Koch (ref 4,1882), p 429. Translated by Thomas D Brock in: *Milestones in Microbiology.* Washington, DC: ASM Press, 1999: 110.

9 Koch (ref 4,1882), p 430. Translated by Thomas D Brock in: *Milestones in Microbiology.* Washington, DC: ASM Press, 1999: 110.

10 Brock TD. Robert Koch: *A Life in Medicine and Bacteriology.* Madison, Wisc: Science Tech Publishers, 1988: 119.

11 Koch (ref 4,1882), p 432-433. Translated by Thomas D Brock in: *Milestones in Microbiology.* Washington, DC: ASM Press, 1999: 111.

12 Koch R. Zur Untersuchung von pathogenen Mikroorganismen (1881). In: Schwalbe J, ed. *Gesammelte Werke von Robert Koch.* Leipzig: Georg Thieme Verlag, 1912; vol 1: 122.

13 Koch (ref 4, 1884), p 551.

14 Koch (ref 4, 1884), p 485.

15 Descriptions can be found in Koch (ref 4, 1882), p 431, and Koch (ref 4, 1884), p 491.

16 The gelatin-based culture media used by Koch at the time became liquid at a temperature of over 30 °C, which was required to culture the bacillus.

17 Koch (ref 4, 1884), p 538.

18 Koch (ref 4, 1882), p 438. Emphasis in the original.

19 Koch (ref 4, 1882), p 442. Translated by Thomas D. Brock in: *Milestones in Microbiology.* Washington, DC: ASM Press, 1999: 115.

20 Koch (ref 4, 1884), p 467.

21 Koch (ref 4, 1882), p 442.

22 Koch (ref 4, 1884), p 531.

23 Koch (ref 4, 1884), p 550.

24 Koch (ref 4, 1884), p 469-470. English based on translation by Thomas D. Brock in: *Milestones in Microbiology.* Washington, DC: ASM Press, 1999: 116.

25 Koch (ref 4, 1882), p 444.

26 Koch R. Über bakteriologische Forschung (1890). In: Schwalbe J, ed. *Gesammelte Werke von Robert Koch.* Leipzig: Georg Thieme Verlag, 1912; vol 1: 659.

27 Koch (ref 26).

28 Koch R. Weitere Mitteilungen über ein Heilmittel gegen Tuberkulose (1890). In: Schwalbe J, ed. *Gesammelte Werke von Robert Koch.* Leipzig: Georg Thieme Verlag, 1912; vol 1: 661–668.

29 Koch R. Fortsetzung der Mitteilungen über ein Heilmittel gegen Tuberkulose (1891). In: Schwalbe J, ed. *Gesammelte Werke von Robert Koch.* Leipzig: Georg Thieme Verlag, 1912; vol 1: 669–672.

30 Koch R. Weitere Mitteilung über das Tuberkulin (1891). In: Schwalbe J, ed. *Gesammelte Werke von Robert Koch.* Leipzig: Georg Thieme Verlag, 1912; vol 1: 673–682.

31 Elkeles B. Der 'Tuberkulinrausch' von 1890. *Dtsch Med Wochenschr* 1990; 115: 1729–1732.

32 Letter from Koch to Friedrich Althoff, 5 Dec 1890. Quoted in Gradmann C. Ein Fehlschlag und seine Folgen: Robert Kochs Tuberkulin und die Gründung des Instituts für Infektionskrankheiten in Berlin 1891. In: Gradmann C, Schlich T, eds. *Strategien der Kausalität. Konzepte der Krankheitsverursachung im 19. und 20. Jahrhundert.* Pfaffenweiler: Centaurus, 1999: 29–52.

33 Baumgarten. *Neuere experimentell-pathologische Arbeiten über Tuberculinwirkung.* 1891: 1208.

34 The **B**acille **C**almette **G**uérin vaccine, the first effective tuberculosis vaccine, did not become available until 1924. In 1906 the French bacteriologists Albert Calmette (1863–1933) and Camille Guérin (1872–1961) had already started their experiments to culture attenuated tuberculosis bacteria. The antituberculous drugs still used today for combination chemotherapy were developed between the early 1950s and the mid-1960s. Source: Päuser S. Carpe diem. *mta* 1999; 14 (4): 237.

The analysis of biocatalysts
P 192

1 Rosenfeld L. Clinical chemistry since 1800: growth and development. *Clin Chem* 2002; 48: 186–197.
2 Segel IH. *Enzyme Kinetics.* New York: John Wiley & Sons Inc., 1975.
3 Berzelius JJ. *Jahresbericht über die Fortschritte der Physischen Wissenschaften.* Vol 15. Tübingen: JCB Mohr, 1836.
4 Segel (ref 2).
5 Bernard C. Recherches sur les usages de suc pancréatique dans la digestion. *Pharm Chim (Paris)* 1849; 15: 336–345.
6 Berthelot M. Sur la fermentation glucosique du sucre de canne. *Compt Rend Acad Sci Paris* 1860; 50: 980–984. Cited in: Fruton JS. *Molecules and Life: Historical Essays on the Interplay of Chemistry and Biology.* New York: John Wiley & Sons, Inc., 1972.
7 Fruton JS. *Molecules and Life: Historical Essays on the Interplay of Chemistry and Biology.* New York: John Wiley & Sons Inc., 1972.
8 Segel (ref 2).
9 Segel (ref 2).
10 Segel (ref 2).
11 Buchner E. Alkoholische Gärung ohne Hefezellen. *Berl Chem Ges* 1897; 30: 117–124. Cited in: Fruton JS. *Molecules and Life: Historical Essays on the Interplay of Chemistry and Biology.* New York: John Wiley & Sons, Inc., 1972.
12 Sumner JB. The isolation and crystallization of the enzyme urease. *J Biol Chem* 1926; 69: 435–441.
13 Henri V. *Lois Générales de l'Action des Diastases.* Paris: Hermann, 1903.
14 Michaelis L, Menten ML. Zur Kinetik der Invertinwirkung. *Biochem Z* 1935; 49: 333–369.
15 Briggs GE, Haldane JBS. A note on the kinetics of enzyme action. *Biochem J* 1925; 19: 338–339.
16 Warburg O, Christian W, Griese A. Wasserstoffübertragendes Co-Ferment, seine Zusammensetzung und Wirkungsweise. *Biochem Z* 1935; 282: 157–205.
17 Bergmeyer HU, Gawehn K. *Methods of Enzymatic Analysis.* Weinheim: Verlag Chemie GmbH, 1963.
18 Wohlgemuth J. Beitrag zur funktionellen Diagnostik des Pankreas. *Berl klin Wschr* 1910; 47: 92.
19 Gutman AB, Gutman EB. An 'acid' phosphatase occurring in the serum of patients with metastasizing carcinoma of the prostate gland. *J Clin Invest* 1938; 17: 473–478.
20 Antopol W, Tuchman L, Schifrin A. Decreased cholinesterase activity of serum in jaundice and biliary disease. *Proc Soc Exp Biol Med* 1938; 38: 363–366.
21 Gutman AB, Olson KB, Gutman EB, Flood CA. Effect of disease of liver and biliary tract upon phosphatase activity of serum. *J Clin Invest* 1940; 19: 129–152.
22 Wroblewski F, Jervis G, LaDue JS. The diagnostic, prognostic and epidemiologic significance of serum glutamic oxalacetic transaminase (SGOT) alterations in acute hepatitis. *Ann Intern Med* 1956; 45: 782.
23 LaDue JS, Wroblewski F, Karmen A. Serum glutamic oxalactic transaminase activity in human acute transmural myocardial infarction. *Science* 1954; 120: 497–500.
24 Abderhalden R. Clinical Enzymology. Princeton: D Van Nostrand Company Inc., 1961.
25 Buchner (ref 11).

26 Minakami S, Yoshikawa H. Studies on erythrocyte glycolysis. II. Free energy changes and rate limiting steps in erythrocyte glycolysis. *J Biochem* 1966; 59: 139–150.
27 Rapoport T, Heinrich R, Rapoport SM. The regulatory principles of glycolysis in erythrocytes in vivo and in vitro. A minimal comprehensive model describing steady states, quasi-steady states and time-dependent processes. *Biochem J* 1976; 154: 449–469.
28 Pawson T. Protein modules and signalling networks. *Nature* 1995; 373: 573–580.
29 Markert CL, Møller F. Multiple forms of enzymes: tissue, ontogenetic, and species specific patterns. *Proc Natl Acad Sci USA* 1959; 45: 753–763.
30 The sequence of nucleotides in a nucleic acid or of amino acids in a protein.
31 International Union of Pure and Applied Chemistry and International Union of Biochemistry.
32 Ginsberg HN. Lipoprotein physiology. *Endocrinol Metab Clin North Am* 1998; 27: 503–519.
33 Bertina RM. Genetic approach to thrombophilia. *Thromb Haemost* 2001; 86: 92–103.
34 Protein with antibody function.
35 The author wishes to thank Prof. Sheshadri Narayanan (New York Medical College) and Prof. emeritus Shigeki Minakami (Kyushu University) for critically reviewing the manuscript for this chapter.
36 http://www.thieme.de/dmw/index.html?fr_nav_home.htm&fr_blue.htm&http://www.thieme.de/dmw/inhalt/dmw1998/dmw9825/beitrag/mg282.htm
37 http://www.m-ww.de/persoenlichkeiten/menten.html

The development of coagulation diagnostics: a detective story
P 199

1 Clotting is delayed on rose or other petals due to their non-wettable surface.
2 In hemophiliacs blood can be taken with relative impunity from a skin vein deeply embedded in tissue. The amount of thromboplastin present in tissue is sufficient to seal the minimal wound of needle puncture, but not larger wounds.
3 Blood flow is unimpeded because the inner lining of our blood vessels also forms a non-wettable surface which is additionally protected by local clotting inhibitors. Thrombosis can occur for many reasons, most of which are acquired, e.g. prolonged bedrest, especially after surgery. However, specific contributory genetic defects are identifiable in some 80 % of cases of thrombosis in the young.
4 Sutor AH, Bowie EJ, Owen CA Jr. Effect of cold on bleeding: Hippocrates vindicated. *Lancet* 1970; 2: 1084.
5 Owen CA Jr. A *History of Blood Coagulation.* Rochester, Minnesota: Mayo Foundation for Medical Education and Research, 2001.
6 Buchanan A. Contributions to the physiology and pathology of the animal fluids. *Proceedings of the Glasgow Philosophical Society* 1836: 51–54).
7 Sutor AH. Alexander-Schmidt-Gedächtnisvorlesung: Alexander Schmidts Beitrag zur Blutgerinnungsforschung. In: Heene DL, ed. *Verhandlungsbericht der Deutschen Arbeitsgemeinschaft für Blutgerinnungsforschung 1976.* Stuttgart: Schattauer, 1978: 3–20.

8 Morawitz P. Die Chemie der Blutgerinnung. *Erg Physiol* 1905; 4: 307–422.
9 Owen (ref 5).
10 Howell WH, Holt E. Two new factors in blood coagulation: heparin and pro-antithrombin. *Am J Physiol* 1918; 47: 328–341.
11 Lee RI, White PW. A clinical study of the coagulation time of blood. *Am J Med Sci* 1913; 145: 495–503.
12 Howell WH. Structure of the fibrin-gel and theories of gel-formation. *Am J Physiol* 1916; 40: 526–546.
13 Koller F. Die Blutgerinnung und ihre klinische Bedeutung. *Dtsch Med Wochenschr* 1956; 81: 516–524.
14 Quick AJ. Prothrombin in hemophilia and in obstructive jaundice. *J Biol Chem* 1935; 109: 73–74.
15 Owren PA. Parahaemophilia. Haemorrhagic diathesis due to absence of a previously unknown clotting factor. *Lancet* 1947; 1: 446–448.
16 Ware AG, Guest MM, Seegers WH. Plasma accelerator factor and purified prothrombin activation. *Science* 1947; 106: 41–42.
17 Patek AJ, Taylor FHL. Hemophilia. II. Some properties of a substance obtained from normal human plasma effective in accelerating the coagulation of hemophilic blood. *J Clin Invest* 1937; 16: 113–124.
18 Biggs R, Douglas AS, Macfarlane RG, Dacie JV, Pitney WR, Merskey C, O'Brien JR. Christmas disease: a condition previously mistaken for haemophilia. *Br Med J* 1952; 2: 1378–1382.
19 Biggs R, Douglas AR. The thromboplastin generation test. *J Clin Pathol* 1953; 6: 23–29.
20 Ware AG, Seegers WH. Two stage procedure for the quantitative determination of prothrombin concentration. *Am J Clin Pathol* 1949; 19: 471–472.
21 Owen (ref 5).
22 Alexander B, de Vries A, Goldstein R. A prothrombin conversion accelerator in serum. *Science* 1949; 109: 545.
23 Koller F, Loeliger A, Duckert F. Experiments on a new clotting factor (factor VII). *Acta Haematol* 1951; 6: 1–18.
24 Duckert F, Flückiger P, Matter M, Koller F. Clotting factor X: physiologic and physico-chemical properties. *Proc Soc Exp Biol Med* 1955; 90: 17–22.
25 Jürgens J. *Klinische Methoden der Blutgerinnungsanalyse.* Stuttgart: Georg Thieme Verlag, 1959.
26 Koller (ref 13).
27 Owen (ref 5).
28 Bachmann F, Duckert F, Koller F. The Stuart-Prower factor assay and its clinical significance. *Thromb Diath Haemorrh* 1958; 2: 24–38.
29 Langdell RD, Wagner RH, Brinkhous KM. Effect of antihemophilic factor on one-stage clotting tests. A presumptive test for hemophilia and a simple one-stage antihemophilic factor assay procedure. *J Lab Clin Med* 1953; 41: 637–647.
30 Proctor RR, Rapaport SI. The partial thromboplastin time with kaolin. *Am J Clin Pathol* 1961; 36: 212–219.
31 Rosenthal RL, Dreskin OH, Rosenthal N. New haemophilia-like disease caused by deficiency of a third plasma thromboplastin factor. *Proc Soc Exp Biol Med* 1953; 82: 171–174.
32 Ratnoff OD, Colopy JE. A familial hemorrhagic trait associated with deficiency of clot promoting fraction of plasma. *J Clin Invest* 1955; 34: 602–613.

33 Barthels M, von Depka M. *Das Gerinnungskompendium*. 1st ed. Stuttgart: Thieme, 2002.

34 Jürgens J. Über das Verhalten antithrombotischer Substanzen in der Leber. *Dtsch Arch Klin Med* 1952; 200: 67–85.

35 Duckert F, Jung E, Shmerling DH. A hitherto undescribed congenital haemorrhagic diathesis probably due to fibrin stabilizing factor deficiency. *Thromb Diath Haemorrh* 1960; 5: 179–186.

36 Fickenscher K, Aab A, Stüber W. A photometric assay for blood coagulation factor XIII. *Thromb Haemost* 1991; 65: 535–540.

37 Jürgens (ref 25).

38 von Kaulla KN, von Kaulla E. Thrombin generation in normal subjects. *Circ Res* 1964; 14: 436–446.

39 Hemker HC, Beguin S. Thrombin generation in plasma: its assessment via the endogenous thrombin potential. *Thromb Haemost* 1995; 74: 134–138.

40 Hartert H. Blutgerinnungsstudien mit der Thrombelastographie. *Klin Wochenschr* 1948; 26: 577–583.

41 Seegers WH, Brinkhous KM, Smith HP, Warner ED. The purification of thrombin. *J Biol Chem* 1938; 126: 91–95.

42 Also known as PPSB: prothrombin [factor II], proconvertin [factor VII], Stuart-Prower factor [factor X], and hemophilia B factor [factor IX]), plus protein C and protein S.

43 Owren PA. A quantitative one-stage method for the assay of prothrombin. *Scand J Clin Lab Invest* 1949; 1: 81–83.

44 Biggs R, ed. *Human Blood Coagulation, Haemostasis and Thrombosis*. Oxford: Blackwell Scientific Publications, 1972: 300.

45 Van den Besselaar AMH: The significance of the international normalized ratio (INR) for oral anticoagulant therapy. J Int Fed Clin Chem 1991; 3: 146–153.

46 This story was reported by Dr Hans Wielinger.

47 Information from Dr Hans Wielinger.

48 Clauss A. Rapid physiological coagulation method for the determination of fibrinogen. *Acta Haematol* 1957; 17: 237–246.

49 Lasch HG, Huth K, Heene DL, Müller-Berghaus G, Hörder MH, Janzarik H, Mittermayer C, Sandritter W. Die Klinik der Verbrauchskoagulopathie. *Dtsch Med Wochenschr* 1971; 96: 715–727.

50 A condition in which increased clotting in small blood vessels throughout the body exhausts – 'consumes' – clotting factor reserves, resulting in abnormal bleeding.

51 Laurell CB. Quantitative estimation of proteins by electrophoresis in agarose gel containing antibodies. *Ann Biochem* 1966; 15: 45–52.

52 Nilsson IM, Blombäck M, Jorpes E, Johansson SA. Von Willebrand's disease and its correction with human plasma fraction I-0. *Acta Med Scand* 1957; 159: 179–188.

53 See also: Sadler JE, Mannucci PM, Berntorp E, Bochkov N, Boulyjenkov V, Ginsburg D, et al. Impact, diagnosis and treatment of von Willebrand disease. *Thromb Haemost* 2000; 84: 160–174.

54 Howard MA, Firkin BG. Ristocetin – a new tool in the investigation of platelet aggregation. *Thromb Diath Haemorrh* 1971; 26: 362–369.

55 Moake JL, Rudy CK, Troll JH, Weinstein MJ, et al. Unusually large plasma factor VIII: von Willebrand factor miltimers in chronic relapsing thrombotic thrombocytic purpura. *N Engl J Med* 1982; 307: 1432–1435.

56 Sieber A. Immunochemische Methode zur Bestimmung von Gerinnungsfaktoren mit der Laser-Nephelometrie. *Laboratoriumsmedizin* 1980: 3–8.

57 Egeberg O. Inherited antithrombin III deficiency causing thrombophilia. *Thromb Diath Haemorrh* 1965; 13: 516–530.

58 D-Dimers are mainly the low-molecular-weight end-products of fibrin degradation. But they can also be demonstrated as antigens in higher-molecular-weight breakdown products of fibrin. D-Dimer antigen assays now have extensive diagnostic applications, as they outperform other coagulation activation markers in excluding latent venous thromboembolism: not only are excellent rapid assays available, unlike with other reaction products of coagulation and fibrinolysis, but clinical studies have also shown test sensitivities of 96–98%. However, specificity is only about 60%, in part because D-dimer antigens also accumulate in fresh wounds due to normal fibrin formation. Thus a D-dimer result should only be used to exclude, not demonstrate, venous thromboembolism. Even then it should be borne in mind that the test may fail in some patients.

59 Reviewed in Witt I: Testsysteme mit synthetischen Peptidsubstraten in der Hämostaseologie. *Hämostaseologie* 1988; 8: 47–61.

60 Egeberg (ref 57).

61 Dahlbäck B, Carlsson M, Svensson PJ. Familial thrombophilia due to a previously unrecognized mechanism characterized by poor anticoagulant response to activated protein C: prediction of a cofactor to activated protein C. *Proc Nat Acad Sci* 1993; 90: 1004–1008.

62 Bertina RM, Koeleman BP, Koster T, Rosendaal FR, Dirven RJ, de Ronde H, et al. Mutation in blood coagulation factor V associated with resistance to activated protein C. *Nature* 1994; 369: 64–67.

63 Seligsohn U, Lubetsky A. Genetic susceptibility to venous thrombosis. *N Engl J Med* 2001; 344: 1222–1231.

64 Quick AJ. *The Hemorrhagic Diseases and the Pathology of Hemostasis*. Springfield, Ill: Charles C Thomas Publisher, 1974.

65 Stormorken H. The discovery of factor V: a tricky clotting factor. *J Thromb Haemost* 2003; 1: 206–213.

66 Mammen EF. In memoriam Walter H. Seegers. *Semin Thromb Hemost* 1996; 22: 301–302.

67 Rizza C. Obituary for Rosemary Biggs. Thromb Haemost 2002; 88 (4): XI–XII.

68 Mammen EF. In Memoriam Professor Dr. Hellmut Hartert. *Semin Thromb Hemost* 1995; 21 (suppl 4): 1.

It's a small world
P 212

1 For a detailed discussion of Koch's postulates see the chapter 'Fighting the White Death: Robert Koch, tuberculosis and tuberculin'.

2 Hughes SS. *The Virus – A History of the Concept*. New York: Science History Publications, 1977: 25.

3 Ibid, p 31.

4 Buist JB. *Vaccinia and Variola. A study of their life history*. London: J&A Churchill, 1887

5 Mayer A. Über die Mosaikkrankheit des Tabaks. *Landwn VersStnen* 1886; 32: 451. First published in Dutch, 1885. Translated by J Johnson as Concerning the mosaic disease of tobacco. *Phytopath Class* 1942; 7: 11–24.

6 Hughes (ref 2), p 49.

7 'Every cell originates from another cell.' Virchow R. Cellular-Pathologie. *Archiv für pathologische Anatomie und Physiologie und für klinische Medizin [Berlin]* 1855; 8: 3–39. The quotation is from p 23.

8 Ellerman V, Bang O. Experimental leukemia in hens. *Zentr Bakteriol Parasitenk*. Abt I, Orig. 1908; 26: 595–609.

9 Rous PJ. Transmission of a malignant new growth by means of a cell-free infiltrate. *JAMA* 1911; 56: 198.

10 Lipschütz B. Filtrierbare Infektionserreger. In: Kolle W, von Wasserman A, eds. *Handbuch der pathologen Mikroorganismen*. 2nd ed. Jena: Gustav Fischer, 1913; vol 8: 345–426, 351–353.

11 Goodpasture EW. Cellular inclusions and the etiology of virus diseases. *Arch Path* 1929; 7: 114–132.

12 Stanley WM. Isolation of a crystalline protein possessing the properties of tobacco-mosaic virus. *Science* 1935; 81: 644–645.

13 Bawden FC, Pirie NW. The isolation and some properties of liquid crystalline substances from solanaceous plants infected with three strains of tobacco mosaic virus. *Proc R Soc Bot* 1937; 128: 274–320.

14 Kausche GA, Pfankuch E, Ruska H. Die Sichtbarmachung von pflanzlichem Virus im Übermikroskop. *Naturwissenschaften* 1939; 27: 292–299.

15 Woodruff AM, Goodpasture EW. The susceptibility of the chorio-allantoic membrane of chick embryos to infection with the fowl-pox virus. *Am J Path* 1931; 7: 209–222.

16 Kilbourne ED. *The Influenza Viruses and Influenza*. New York: Academic Press, 1975.

17 Ibid.

18 Krause RM. *Emerging Infections*. San Diego: Academic Press, 1998.

19 Ibid.

20 Koff RS, Grady GF, Chalmers TC, Mosley JW, Swartz BL. Viral hepatitis in a group of Boston hospitals: importance of exposure to shellfish in a nonepidemic period. *N Eng J Med* 1967; 276: 703–710.

21 Parenterally transmitted infections are infections transmitted by a route other than the digestive tract.

22 Lurman A. Eine Icterusepidemie. *Berl Klin Wochenschr* 1885; 22: 20–23.

23 Memorandum prepared by Medical Officers of the Ministry of Health. Homologous serum jaundice. *Lancet* 1943; i: 83–88.

24 MacCallum FO. Homologous serum jaundice. *Lancet* 1947; ii: 691.

25 Hollinger FB, Purcel RH, Gerin JL, Ganem DE, Feinstone SM. *Viral Hepatitis*. Philadelphia: Lippincott Williams & Wilkins, 2002.

26 MacCallum (ref 24).

27 Hollinger, et al (ref 25).

28 Schoub BD. *AIDS and HIV in Perspective – A guide to understanding the virus and its consequences*. Cambridge: Cambridge University Press, 1999.

29 Ibid.

30 Blumberg BS, Alter HJ, Visnich S. A "new" antigen in leukemia sera. *JAMA* 1965; 191: 541–546.

31 Siegert R, Hsin-Lu Shu, Slenczka W, Peters D, Müller G. Zur Ätiologie einer unbekannten, von Affen ausgegangenen menschlichen Infektionskrankheit. *Dtsch Med Wochenschr* 1967; 92: 2341–2343.

32 Transmission from animal to man or from man to animal.

33 Krause (ref 18).

34 Lee H, Lee PW, Johnson KJ. Isolation of the etiologic agent of Korean hemorrhagic fever. *J Infect Dis* 1978; 137: 298–308.

35 Nichol ST, Spiropoulou CF, Morzunov S, Rollin PE, Ksiazek TG, Feldmann H, et al. Genetic identification of a hantavirus associated with an outbreak of acute respiratory illness. *Science* 1993; 262: 914–917.

36 As of early June 2003.

37 WHO: Communicable Disease Surveillance & Response (CSR). Update 69, 29 May 2003.

38 Murphy FA, Peters CJ. Ebola virus: where does it come from and where is it going? In: Krause RM. *Emerging Infections.* Chapter 13. San Diego: Academic Press, 1998: 375–410.

Immunoassays open up new possibilities in diagnostic testing
P 226

1 Berson SA, Yalow RS, Baumann A, Rothschild MA, Newerly K. Insulin-I[131] metabolism in human subjects: Demonstration of insulin binding globulin in the circulation of insulin treated subjects. *J Clin Invest* 1956; 35: 170–190.

2 Ibid.

3 Yalow RS. Radioaktivität im Dienste des Menschen. *Naturwiss Rdsch* 1982; 35: 438–443.

4 Yalow RS, Berson SA. Assay of plasma insulin in human subjects by immunological methods. *Nature* 1959; 219: 1648–1649.

5 Adolf Butenandt (1903–1995), Edward Adelbert Doisy (1893–1986), Tadeus Reichstein (1897–1996) and Edward Calvin Kendall (1886–1972).

6 A ligand is a substance or part of a substance that binds to a receptor (docking molecule). Molecules with ligand properties include substrates, antigens, hormones, proteins and toxins. The corresponding receptors (in the same order) are enzymes, antibodies, receptors, binding proteins and antitoxins.

7 Köhler G, Milstein C. Continuous cultures of fused cells secreting antibody of predefined specificity. *Nature* 1975; 256: 495–497.

8 Sevier ED, David GS, Martinis J, Desmond WJ, Bartholomew RM, Wang R. Monoclonal antibodies in clinical immunology. *Clin Chem* 1981; 27: 1797–1808.

9 Engvall E, Perlmann P. Enzyme-linked immunosorbent assay (ELISA). Quantitative assay of immunoglobulin G. *Immunochemistry* 1971; 8: 871–874.

10 Van Weemen BK, Schuurs AHWM. Immunoassay using antigen-enzyme conjugates. *FEBS Lett* 1971; 15: 232–236.

11 Ritchie RF. A simple, direct, and sensitive technique for measurement of specific protein in dilute solution. *J Lab Clin Med* 1967; 70: 512–517.

12 Eckman I, Robbins JB, van den Hamer CJA, Leutz J, Scheinberg IH. Automation of a quantitative immunochemical microanalysis of human serum transferrin. A model system. *Clin Chem* 1970; 16: 558–561.

13 Addison GM, Hales CN. The immunoradiometric assay. In: Kirkham KE, Hunter WM, eds. *Radioimmunoassay Methods.* Edinburgh: Churchill Livingstone, 1970: 447–461.

14 Jenkins SH. Homogenous enzyme immunoassay. *J Immun Methods* 1992; 150: 91–97.

15 Samuels A. Immunoenzymology reaction processes, kinetics and the role of conformational alteration. *Ann NY Acad Sci* 1963; 103: 858–898.

16 Henderson DR, Friedman SB, Harris JB. 'CEDIA', a new homogeneous immunoassay system. *Clin Chem* 1986; 32: 1637–1641.

17 Dandliker WB, Feigen GA. Quantification of the antigen-antibody reaction by the polarization of fluorescence. *Biochem Biophys Res Commun* 1961; 5: 299–304.

18 Anderson RR, Lee TT, Saewart DC, Sowden KM, Valkirs GE. Internally referenced immuno concentration assays. *Clin Chem* 1986; 32: 1692–1695.

19 Melchers F. Auf der Suche nach dem Immunsystem. In: Drews J, Melchers F, eds. *Forschung bei Roche/Research at Roche.* Basel: Editiones Roche, 1989: 179–196.

20 Ibid, p 189.

21 Aumiller J. Nobelpreis für Medizin 1984. *Hexagon Roche.*

22 Borgmann W. Für die Freiheit gestritten, Umwege zu gehen. Zum Tod des Freiburger Medizin-Nobelpreisträgers Georges Köhler. *Stuttgarter Zeitung,* 3 Mar 1995.

The rise of automation
P 236

1 Asper R, Vonderschmitt DJ. Laboratory Mechanization and Automation. In: Vonderschmitt DJ, ed. *Laboratory Organization, Automation.* Berlin: Walter de Gruyter, 1991.

2 Haeckel R. Mechanization and Automation in Clinical Chemistry. In: Bergmeyer HU, ed. *Methods in Automatic Analysis.* 4th ed. Weinheim: Verlag Chemie, 1982: 450–481.

3 Nitzan D, Barrouil C, Cheeseman P, Smith R. Use of sensors in robot systems. *Proc 1983 Int Conf Adv Robotics.* Tokyo, 1983: 123–132.

4 Minder EI, Vonderschmitt DJ. Robotized preparation of fecal samples for analysis of endogenous substances. *Chemom Intell Lab Syst* 1992; 17: 119–122.

5 Skeggs LT. An automatic method for colorimetric analysis. *Am J Clin Pathol* 1957; 28: 311–322.

6 Bissé E, Scholer A, Vonderschmitt DJ. Continuous-flow analysis for glucose with use of glucose dehydrogenase immobilized in glass tubes. *Clin Chem* 1985; 31: 137–139.

7 Bierens de Haan J. In: Curtius HC, Roth M, editors. *Clinical Biochemistry. Principles and Methods.* 2 vols. Berlin: Walter de Gruyter, 1974: 491.

8 Bücher T, Kreli H, Lusch G. Molar extinction coefficient of NADH and NADPH at Hg spectral lines. *J Clin Chem Clin Biochem* 1985; 12: 239–240.

9 Furman WB. *Continuous Flow Analysis. Theory and Practice.* New York: Dekker, 1976.

10 Vonderschmitt D. Wirtschaftliche und menschliche Grenzen der Medizintechnik aus der Sicht des Laboratoriums. *Schweizer Spital* 1980; 1: 30–35.

11 Coakley WA. *Handbook of Automated Analysis. Continuous Flow Techniques.* New York: Dekker, 1981.

12 Lutz RA. Batch Analyzer. In: Vonderschmitt DJ, ed. *Laboratory Organization, Automation.* Berlin: Walter de Gruyter, 1991.

13 Haenseler E. Random Access Analyzers. In: Vonderschmitt DJ, ed. *Laboratory Organization, Automation.* Berlin: Walter de Gruyter, 1991: 454–455.

14 Aliquots are portions of equal size.

15 Anderson NG. Analytical techniques for cell fractions: XII. A multiple-cuvet rotor for a new microanalytical system. *Anal Biochem* 1969; 28: 545–562.

16 Aellig A, Frei J. Centrifugal Analyzers. In: Vonderschmitt DJ, ed. *Laboratory Organization, Automation.* Berlin: Walter de Gruyter, 1991.

17 Eisenwiener HG, Keller M. Absorbance measurement in cuvettes lying longitudinal to the light beam. *Clin Chem* 1979; 25: 117–121.

18 Anderson (ref 15).

19 Frei J, Brechbühler T. *Histoire de la Société Suisse de Chimie Clinique.* Schweizerische Gesellschaft für Klinische Chemie, 1996: chapter 3.

20 Keller H. *Klinisch-chemische Labordiagnostik für die Praxis.* 2nd ed. Stuttgart: Georg Thieme, 1991: 56.

21 Haeckel R. Ektachem, ein neues Analysensystem. *GIT Labor-Medizin* 1979; 2: 201–205.

22 Sonntag O. *Trockenchemie. Analytik mit trägergebundenen Reagenzien.* Stuttgart: Gustav-Fischer, 1988.

23 Greyson J. Problems and possibilities of chemistry on dry reagent carriers. *J Aut Chem* 1981; 3: 357–372.

24 Keller H. Das Vision-System: Ein Evaluationsbericht. *Lab Med* 1987; 11: 7–19.

25 Haenseler (ref 13).

26 Dati F, Sauder K. Immunchemische Methoden im klinischen Labor. *GIT Labor-Medizin* 1990; 13: 357–372.

27 Pal SB. *Enzyme-labelled Immunoassays of Hormones and Drugs.* Berlin: Walter de Gruyter, 1978.

28 Dandliker WB, Kelly RJ, Dandliker J, Farquhar J, Levin J. Fluorescence polarization immunoassay, theory and experimental method. *Immunochemistry* 1973; 10: 219–227.

29 Popelka SR, Miller DM, Holen JT, Kelso DM. Fluorescence polarization immunoassay. II. Analyzer for rapid, precise measurement of fluorescence polarization with use of disposable cuvette. *Clin Chem* 1981; 27: 1198–1201.

30 Cammann K. *Das Arbeiten mit ionenselektiven Elektroden.* Berlin: Springer, 1977.

31 Külpmann WR. Determination of sodium with ion-selective electrodes: A new method or a new quantity? *J Clin Chem Clin Biochem* 1990; 28: 813–815.

32 Maas AHJ, Siggaard-Anderson O, Weisberg HF, Zijlstra WG. Ion-selective electrodes for sodium and potassium. A new problem of what is measured and what should be reported. *Clin Chem* 1985; 31: 412–415.

33 Keller (ref 20), pp 209–217.

34 Vonderschmitt DJ, Siegrist HP. *Die Führung medizinischer Laboratorien.* Rotkreuz: Labolife Verlagsgemeinschaft, 2001: 21–26.

35 Libeer JC. Solid phase chemistry in clinical laboratory tests: A literature review. *J Clin Chem Clin Biochem* 1985; 23: 645–655.

36 Keller H. Solid Phase Analysis. State of the Art, Advantages and Disadvantages. In: Vonderschmitt DJ, ed. *Laboratory Organization, Automation.* Berlin: Walter de Gruyter, 1991.

37 Vonderschmitt DJ, Hänseler E. Sinnvolle Prä-senzanalytik in der Praxis. Der informierte Arzt, *Gazette Médicale* (separatum) 1993; 16: 1139–1142.

Matters of the heart
P 248

1 Kunsch K, Kunsch S. *Der Mensch in Zahlen. Eine Datensammlung in Tabellen mit über 20 000 Einzelwerten.* 2nd ed. Heidelberg: Spektrum Akademischer Verlag, 2000: 56.

2 Auenbrugger L. *Inventum novum ex percussione thoracis humani ut signo abstrusos interni pectoris morbos detegendi.* Vindobonae (Vienna): JT Trattner, 1761. English translation: *On percussion of the chest; being a translation of Auenbrugger's original treatise entitled Inventum novum ex percussione thoracis humani et signo abstrusos interni pectoris morbos detegendi.* Translated by J Forbes in: *Original Cases With Dissections and Observations Selected from Auenbrugger, Corvisart, Laennec and Others.* London, 1824. (Subsequent English editions of *Inventum novum:* Willius FA, Keys TE. *Cardiac Classics.* St Louis, MO, 1941: 193–213; Camac CN. *Classics of Medicine and Surgery.* New York, 1959: 120–147; *Bull Hist Med* 1936; 4: 373–403, with an introduction by Henry E Sigerist).

3 Schott H. *Die Chronik der Medizin.* Gütersloh: Chronik-Verlag, 1993: 225.

4 Herrick JB. Clinical features of sudden obstruction of the coronary arteries. *JAMA* 1912; 59: 2015–2020.

5 LaDue JS, Wróblewski F, Karmen A. Serum glutamic oxaloacetic transaminase activity in human acute transmural myocardial infarction. *Science* 1954; 120: 497–500.

6 Wacker WEC, Ulmer DD, Valle BL. Metal isoenzymes and myocardial infarction, malic and lactic dehydrogenase activities and zinc concentrations in serum. *N Engl J Med* 1956; 255: 449–456.

7 Ebashi S, Toyokura Y, Momoi H, Sugita H. High creatine phosphokinase activity of sera of progressive muscular dystrophy. *J Biochem* 1959; 46: 103–104.

8 Gässler N. Isoformen der Kreatinkinase. *mta* 1999; 14 (1): 4–7.

9 Wróblewski F, Ross C, Gregory K. Isoenzymes of myocardial infarction. *N Engl J Med* 1960; 263: 531–536.

10 World Health Organization. Report of Joint International Society and Federation of Cardiology / World Health Organization Task Force on Standardization of Clinical Nomenclature. Nomenclature and criteria for diagnosis of ischemic heart disease. *Circulation* 1979; 59: 607–609.

11 Chan DW, Taylor E, Frye T, Blitzer RL. Immuno-enzymatic assay for creatine kinase MB with subunit specific monoclonal antibodies compared with an immunochemical method and electrophoresis. *Clin Chem* 1985; 31: 465–469.

12 Katus HA, Remppis A, Looser S, Hallermeier K, Scheffold T, Kubler W. Enzyme-linked immunoassay of cardiac troponin T for the detection of acute myocardial infarction in patients. *J Mol Cell Cardiol* 1989; 21: 1349–1353.

13 Henry JP, Gauer ON, Reeves JL. Evidence on the atrial location of receptors influencing urine flow. *Circ Res* 1956; 5: 85–90.

14 de Bold AJ, Borenstein HB, Veress AT, Sonnenberg H. A rapid and potent natriuretic response to intravenous injection of atrial myocardial extract in rats. *Life Sci* 1981; 28: 89–94.

15 de Bold AJ. Atrial natriuretic factor: polypeptide hormone produced by the heart. *Science* 1985; 230: 767–770.

16 Renin is released into the blood from the walls of the renal arteries. Release is increased in the presence of inadequate renal blood flow and sodium deficiency. Renin is an enzyme responsible for producing angiotensin I, which is converted by the **a**ngiotensin **c**onverting **e**nzyme (ACE) to angiotensin II, the most potent vasopressor yet identified and the stimulus to aldosterone production.

17 Aldosterone controls sodium chloride reabsorption and potassium excretion. Vasopressin – released from the posterior lobe of the pituitary gland under the effect of aldosterone – and angiotensin are antidiuretic peptide hormones. The hormonal action of vasopressin is mediated by hypothalamic osmoreceptors which control the osmotic pressure of the blood, and also by atrial blood volume receptors. Its release is inhibited by natriuretic peptides.

18 Sudoh T, Kangawa K, Minamino N, Matsuo H. A new natriuretic peptide in porcine brain. *Nature* 1988; 332: 78–81.

19 Sugawa A, Nakao K, Morii N, Sakamoto M, Suda M, Shimokura M, et al. Alpha human natriuretic polypeptide is released from the heart and circulates in the body. *Biochem Biophys Res Commun* 1985; 129: 439–446.

20 McDowell G, Shaw C, Buchanan D, Nicholls DP. The natriuretic peptide family. *Eur J Clin Invest* 1995; 25: 291.

21 I. e. the prohormone fragment terminating in a COOH group.

22 I. e. the prohormone fragment terminating in an NH₂ group.

23 Hunt PJ, Richards AM, Nicholls MG, Yandle TG, Doughty RN, Espiner EA. Immunoreactive amino-terminal pro-brain natriuretic peptide (NT-proBNP): a new marker of cardiac impairment. *Clin Endocrinol* 1997; 47: 287–296.

24 The authors wish to thank Dr Bhuwnesh Agrawal for critically reviewing the manuscript and for his many useful comments.

25 From the Greek *stethos* 'chest' or 'heart' and *skopeou* 'look at'.

26 Eckart WU, Gradmann C. *Ärztelexikon: Von der Antike bis zum 20. Jahrhundert.* Munich: CH Beck'sche Verlagsbuchhandlung, 1995, pp. 224–225. Interested readers are also referred to: Duffin J. *To See with a Better Eye: A Life of RTH Laennec.* Princeton: Princeton University Press, 1998.

27 Schott (ref 3), p 224. English translation by B. Alexander: *On the Seats and Causes of Diseases as Investigated by Anatomy.* London: 1769.

28 Heberden W. *Commentaries on the History and Cure of Diseases.* London: T Payne, Newsgate, 1802 (Pectoris dolor, chapter 70, pp 362–368).

The dawning of a new era
P 258

1 Mullis KB. *Robert-Koch-Stiftung e.V. Beiträge und Mitteilungen* 1993; 17 (Apr): 18–21.

2 Päuser S. Genius und Zufall. *mta Spektrum* 2001; 16 (3): 97.

3 Rabinow P. *Making PCR. A Story of Biotechnology.* Chicago: The University of Chicago Press, 1996.

4 Groß M. *Exzentriker des Lebens. Zellen zwischen Hitzeschock und Kältestress.* Heidelberg: Spektrum Akademischer Verlag, 1997: 165.

5 Ibid.

6 *Chlamydia trachomatis* is a sexually transmitted bacterium that can cause unpleasant infections of the urogenital tract.

7 These tests were developed by Roche and marketed under the Amplicor trademark.

8 Mullis KB. The unusual origin of the polymerase chain reaction. *Sci Am* Apr 1990: 56.

9 http://www.nobel.se/chemistry/laureates/1993/press.html

10 http://www.karymullis.com/

What can genetic tests tell us?
P 266

1 Zarnegar R, Brunaud L, Clark OH. Multiple endocrine neoplasia type I. *Curr Treat Options Oncol* 2002; 3 (4): 335–348.

2 Venkitaraman A. Cancer susceptibility and the functions of BRCA1 and BRCA2. *Cell* 2002; 108 (2): 171–182.

3 Bomford A. Genetics of haemochromatosis. *Lancet* 2002; 360: 1673–1681.

4 Innocenti F, Ratain MJ. Update on pharmacogenetics in cancer chemotherapy. *Eur J Cancer* 2002; 38 (5): 639–644.

5 McLeod HL, Siva C. The thiopurine S-methyltransferase gene locus – implications for clinical pharmacogenomics. *Pharmacogenomics* 2002; 3 (1): 89–98.

Proteomics targets new disease markers
P 272

Further reading

Ezzell C. Proteins rule. *Sci Am* 2002; 286 (4): 26–33.

Tyers M, Mann M. From genomics to proteomics. *Nature* 2003; 422: 193–197.

Hanash S. Disease proteomics. *Nature* 2003; 422: 226–232.

Martin DB, Nelson PS. From genomics to proteomics: techniques and applications in cancer research. *Trends Cell Biol* 2001; 11: S60–S65.

Wulfkuhle JD, Liotta LA, Petricoin EF. Proteomics applications for the early detection of cancer. *Nat Rev Canc* 2003; 3: 267–275.

Hochstrasser DF, Sanchez JC, Appel RD. Proteomics and its trends facing nature's complexity. *Proteomics* 2002; 2: 807–812.

Near-patient diagnostics
P 278

1 At present about 151 million people worldwide suffer from diabetes.
2 The Diabetes Control and Complications Trial Research Group. The effect of intensive treatment of diabetes on the development and progression of long-term complications in insulin-dependent diabetes mellitus. *New Engl J Med* 1993; 329: 977–986.
3 Adler AI, Stevens RJ, Manley SE, Bilous RW, Cull CA, Holman RR. Development and progression of nephropathy in type 2 diabetes: The United Kingdom Prospective Diabetes Study (UKPDS 64). Kidney Int 2003; 63: 225–232. *See also* other UKPDS studies.
4 Diabetes Control and Complications Trial Group (ref 2) and Adler, Stevens, Manley, et al (ref 3).
5 Zaman Z, Demedt M. Blood gas analysis: POCT versus central laboratory on samples sent by a pneumatic tube system. *Clin Chim Acta* 2001; 307: 101–106.
6 Beeler I, Szucs T, Gutzwiller F. Ist das Praxislabor medizinisch und wirtschaftlich sinnvoll? *Praxis* 2001; 90: 887–896.
7 Frost SJ, Firth GB. A year's experience of the Roche Advantage II glucose test strip. *Clin Chim Acta* 2001; 307: 69–73.
8 Number of true positive test results divided by the number of test subjects who actually have the disease, i.e. the proportion of individuals with the disease who are correctly identified as such.
9 Number of true negative test results divided by the number of test subjects who do not have the disease, i.e. the proportion of disease-free individuals who are correctly identified as such.
10 Fraser CG. Optimal analytical performance for point of care testing. *Clin Chim Acta* 2001; 307: 37–43.
11 Alto WA, Meyer D, Schneid J, Bryson P, Kindig J. Assuring the accuracy of home glucose monitoring. *J Am Board Fam Pract* 2002; 15: 1–6.
12 Bergenstal R, Pearson J, Cembrowski GS, Bina D, Davidson J, List S. Identifying variables associated with inaccurate self-monitoring of blood glucose: proposed guidelines to improve accuracy. *Diabetes Educ* 2002; 26: 981–989.
13 Skeie S, Thue G, Nerhus K, Sandberg S. Instruments for self-monitoring of blood glucose: comparisons of testing quality achieved by patients and a technician. *Clin Chem* 2002; 48: 994–1003.
14 Yuoh C, Tarek Elghetany M, Petersen JR, Mohammad A, Okorodudu AO. Accuracy and precision of point-of-care testing for glucose and prothrombin time at the critical care units. *Clin Chim Acta* 2001; 307: 119–123.
15 Smart WH, Subramanian K. The use of silicon microfabrication technology in painless blood glucose monitoring. *Diab Tech Ther* 2000; 2: 549–559.
16 Svanes K, Zweifach BW. Variations in small blood vessel hematocrits produced in hypothermic rats by micro-occlusion. *Microvasc Res* 1968; 1: 210–220.
17 Fung YC. Stochastic flow in capillary blood vessels. *Microvasc Res* 1973; 5: 34–48.
18 Yen RT, Fung YC. Effect of velocity distribution on red cell distribution in capillary blood vessels. *Am J Physiol* 1978; 253 (Heart Circ Physiol 4): H251–H257.
19 Päuser S. Major advances via miniaturisation. In: *Innovation – our key to success.* Basel: Roche, 2002.
20 Wilding P, Kricka LJ, Cheng J, Hvichia G, Shoffner MA, Fortina P. Integrated cell isolation and polymerase chain reaction analysis using silicon microfilter chambers. *Anal Biochem* 1998; 257: 95–100.
21 Kricka LJ. Microchips, microarrays, biochips and nanochips: personal laboratories for the 21st century. *Clin Chim Acta* 2001; 307: 219–223.
22 The author wishes to thank Dr Carlo Effenhauser for his many helpful comments and for critically reviewing the manuscript.

Information is our future
P 284

1 Sackett DL, Rosenberg WMC, Gray JAM, Haynes RB, Richardson WS. Evidence-based medicine: what it is and what it isn't. *BMJ* 1996; 312: 71–72.
2 http://www.intmed.mcw.edu/clincalc/heartrisk. htm, 19-Mar-03.
3 Haynes B, Glasziou P. Definition of evidence-based medicine. In: *EBM Online.* BMJ Publishing Group, 2002.
4 Bates DW, Cohen M, Leape LL, Overhage JM, Shabot MM, Sheridan T. Reducing the frequency of errors in medicine using information technology. *J Am Med Inform Assoc* 2001; 8: 299–308.
5 Evans RS, Pestotnik SL, Classen DC, Clemmer TP, Weaver LK, Orme JF, et al. A computer-assisted management program for antibiotics and other antiinfective agents. *N Engl J Med* 1998; 338: 232–238.
6 Lowensteyn I, Joseph L, Levinton C, Abrahamowicz M, Steinert Y, Grover S. Can computerized risk profiles help patients improve their coronary risk? The result of the Coronary Health Assessment Study (CHAS). *Prev Med* 1998; 27: 730–737.
7 Grätzel von Grätz P. *DocCheck Scientific Newsletter* Antwerpes AG, vol 7, 2001.
8 *Diabetics; a representative survey of 201 respondents with type 2 diabetes on their interest in and understanding of risk information concerning diabetic complications* [in German]. An unpublished survey conducted by TNS EMNID on behalf of HESTIA Health Care, 2002.

Pharmacogenetics: paving the way to more individualised medicine
P 289

1 Schott H. *Chronik der Medizin.* Gütersloh: Chronik Verlag im Bertelsmann Lexikon Verlag, 2000.

Further reading
Lindpaintner K. The impact of pharmacogenetics and pharmacogenomics on drug discovery. *Nat Rev Drug Discov* 2002; 1 (6): 463–469.
Ross A. Pharmacogenetics and future drug development and delivery. *Lancet* 2000; 355: 1358–1361.
Diasio RB, Johnson MR. The role of pharmacogenetics and pharmacogenomics in cancer chemotherapy with 5-fluorouracil. *Pharmacology* 2000; 61 (3): 199–203.
Jornvall H, Hoog JO, Persson B, Pares X. Pharmacogenetics of the alcohol dehydrogenase system. *Pharmacology* 2000; 61 (3): 184–191.
Weber WW. Pharmacogenetics. Oxford: Oxford University Press, 1997.
De Boer JG. Mutations and the genetic code. In: *Nature Encyclopedia of Life Sciences.* London: Nature Publishing Group, 2001. http://www.els. net/[doi:10.1038/npg.els.0000823]
La Du BN. Pharmacogenetics. In: *Nature Encyclopedia of Life Sciences.* London: Nature Publishing Group, 2001. http://www.els.net/[doi:10.1038 /npg.els.0002012]

Personal name index

Subject index

Illustration acknowledgements

Fortune tellers, true observations and honest efforts
Diagnostic methods with histories dating from before 1840

11: Wellcome Library, London. **12:** Woodcut from: Joannes Actuarios. *De urinis libri VII.* Basel: A Cratander, 1529. **13 (l):** Adapted from: Ackerknecht E. *Kurze Geschichte der Medizin.* 2nd German ed. Stuttgart: F Enke Verlag, 1975. **13 (r):** Frontispiece from: Henricus Martinius. *Anatomia urinae galenospagyrica.* Frankfurt: G Fickwirt, 1658. **14:** Johannes de Ketham. The *Fasciculus Medicinae of Johannes de Ketham Alemanus. Facsimile of the First (Venetian) Edition of 1491.* Monumenta Medica, vol 1. Sigerist HE, ed. Milan: R Lier & Co, 1924: plate I. **15 (l):** Institut für Geschichte der Arabisch-Islamischen Wissenschaften, University of Frankfurt am Main (Prof F Sezgin). **15 (r):** Dornaeus G. Anatomi / das ist Zerlegung der lebendigen Körper. Oder von distillierung des harns. In: Theophrastus Paracelsus. *Chirurgische Bücher und Schrifften.* Johannes Huser, ed. Strasbourg: Zetzner, 1605: Appendix, 58–70. **16 (t):** Hooke R. *Micrographia.* London: John Martyn, 1665: plate VI. **16 (b):** Dornaeus, *loc. cit.* **17 (t):** Oil painting by Anicet Charles Gabriel Lemonnier (1743–1824). Musée d'Histoire de la Médecine, Université René Descartes, Paris. **17 (b):** Marcet A. *An Essay on the Chemical History and Medical Treatment of Calculous Disorders.* 2nd ed. London: Longman Hurst Rees Orme Brown, 1819. **18:** Bowman W. On the structure and use of the Malpighian bodies of the kidney, with observations on the circulation through that gland. *Proceedings of the Royal Society (London)* 1842; 132: 57–80. **19 (t):** Oil painting of Otto Folin by Emil Pollak-Ottendorff (c.1934) commissioned by Folin's students to mark his retirement, on display at Harvard Medical School. Photograph kindly provided by Folin's biographer, Dr Samuel Meites, Columbus, Ohio. **19 (b):** Simon F. Pathologisch-chemische Untersuchungen. I. Einige Ergebnisse aus der Schönlein'schen Klinik. *Beiträge zur Physiologischen und Pathologischen Chemie und Mikroskopie* 1843–1844: 100–123, plate. **20 (l):** Stenbeck T. Eine neue Methode für die mikroskopische Untersuchung der geformten Bestandtheile des Harns und einiger anderen Secrete und Excrete. *Zeitschrift für Klinische Medizin* 1892; 20: 457–475. **20 (r):** Instrument on left: Methe JH. *De Urinarum Natura Ac Diversitate.* Medical Dissertation. University of Marburg: Philipp Casimir Müller, 1727: 23. Instrument in centre: Heller JF. Die pathologisch-chemische und mikroskopische Untersuchung zur medizinischen Diagnose. In: Gustav von Gaal. *Physikalische Diagnostik und deren Anwendung in der Medizin, Chirurgie, Oculistik, Otriatik und Geburtshilfe.* Vienna: Braumüller & Seidel; 1846: 531–646. Instrument on right: Schotten C. *Kurzes Lehrbuch der Analyse des Harns.* Leipzig and Vienna: F. Deuticke, 1888. **21 (l):** Österreichische National-

bibliothek, Vienna. **21 (m):** Heller JF. Ueber Erkennung des Albumins, der Urate, der Knochenerde und einer eigenthümlichen Proteïnverbindung im Harn. *Archiv für physiologische und pathologische Chemie und Mikroskopie* 1852; 5: 161–171. **21 (r):** Lithograph by H Monath, after an 1839 painting by Carl Engel (1817–1870). **22 (t):** Mitchell C. *Modern Urinology.* Philadelphia: Boericke & Tafel, 1912. **22 (b):** Sachse M. *Praktische Harnuntersuchungen und ihre diagnostische Verwertung.* Radebeul: Dr Madaus u. Co, 1929. **23 (tr):** Anonymous pencil drawing. Private collection. Photo: Deutsches Museum, Munich. Reproduced from: *An das Licht gebracht – Diagnostik durch Farben.* Exhibition catalogue. Habrich C, ed. Deutsches Medizinhistorisches Museum Ingolstadt. Ingolstadt: Max Reindl, 1999. **23 (tl):** Lithograph by P Rohrbach, from a photograph by G Schauer. Bildarchiv Preussischer Kulturbesitz, Berlin. **23 (b):** Ultzmann R, Hofmann KB, *Atlas der physiologischen und pathologischen Harnsedimente.* Wiesbaden: W. Braumüller, 1871: plate XVI. **24:** Carl Zeiss Jena, Optische Messinstrumente: Jena; 1942. **25/26:** Roche. **27:** Catalogue, Optisches Museum der Carl-Zeiss-Stiftung, Jena. **29 (l):** Roche. **29 (r):** Hooke R. *Micrographia.* London: John Martyn, 1665. **30:** Optisches Museum der Carl-Zeiss-Stiftung, Jena. **31:** Harting P. *Das Mikroskop.* First German edition. Braunschweig: Verlag Friedrich Vieweg und Sohn, 1866; 2: 58, 59, 66. **32:** Photographic Archive, Cecilie und Oskar Vogt Institut für Hirnforschung, Düsseldorf University. **33:** Stadtarchiv, Neuss, Germany. **34:** Private collection of E and G Novotny. **36:** Roche. **37–43:** Private collection of E and G Novotny. **44:** Wellcome Library, London. **45 (l):** Roche. **45 (r):** Wellcome Library, London. **46 (l):** Keystone. **46 (m):** Portrait by HM Page, after a portrait by John Hayes, c.1830. Royal College of Physicians, London. **46 (r):** Institute für Geschichte der Medizin, University of Vienna. **47 (l):** Einhorn M. Fermentation as a practical qualitative and quantitative test for sugar in urine. *Medical Record* 1887; 31: 91–94. Picture, p.94. **47 (r):** Duval M. L'œuvre de Claude Bernard. Paris: JB Baillière & Fils, 1881: frontispiece. **49/50:** Prof. Robert Tattersall. **51 (l):** Wellcome Library, London. **51 (r):** Roche. **52:** Prof. Robert Tattersall. **53 (l):** Institut für Diabetes-Technologie, University of Ulm. **53 (r):** Dr Hans Wielinger. **54:** Prof. Robert Tattersall. **55/57:** Roche. **58:** Institut für Diabetes-Technologie, University of Ulm. **59/60:** Roche. **61:** Vincent WT. *The Records of the Woolwich District.* Woolwich: JP Jackson; London: JS Virtue & Co., c 1890. **63:** Thorwald J. *Das Jahrhundert der Detektive,* vol. III, *Handbuch für Giftmörder.* Munich: Droemer-Knaur. **65:** National Library of Medicine. **66:** Thorwald J. *Das Jahrhundert der Detektive,* vol. III, *Handbuch für Giftmörder.* Munich: Droemer-Knaur. **67:** Roche. **69:** Schreiber W, Mathys FK. *Infectio.* Basel: Editiones Roche, 1987: 18–19. **70/71:** Bulloch W. *The History of Bacteriology.* London: Oxford University Press, 1938. **72/73:** Prof. EW Koneman. **75:** Schreiber W, Mathys FK. *Infectio.* Basel: Editiones Roche, 1987: 30. **76 (t):** Medizinhistorisches Institut und Museum, University of Zurich. **76 (b):** Prof. EW Koneman. **77:** Schreiber W, Mathys FK. *Infectio.* Basel: Editiones Roche, 1987: 69. **78 (t):** Prof. EW Koneman. **78 (m/b):** Washington C. Winn, Jr. **79–81:** Keystone. **82 (l):** Reproduced from: Blazer MJ. *Campylobacter pylori in Gastritis and Peptic Ulcer Disease.* New York and Tokyo: Igaku-Shoin, 1989. **82 (r):** Weyant RS, et al. *Identification of Unusual Pathogenic Gram-Negative Aerobic and Facultatively Anaerobic Bacteria.* 2nd ed. Centers for Disease Control. Baltimore: Williams

and Wilkins, 1996. **83–86:** Prof. EW Koneman. **87:** Keystone. **88:** Prof. EW Koneman. **89:** Ainsworth GC. *Introduction to the History of Mycology.* Cambridge: Cambridge University Press, 1976: 164 and 169. **91–93:** Prof. EW Koneman. **94:** Roche. **95:** Foster WD. *A History of Parasitology.* Edinburgh: E&S Livingstone, 1965. **96–97 (l):** Prof. EW Koneman. **97 (r):** Foster WD. *A History of Parasitology.* Edinburgh: E&S Livingstone, 1965. **98–105:** Prof. EW Koneman.

From hobby horse to applied science
The emergence of routine diagnostic laboratories (from 1840 on)

109: Pasteur in his laboratory. Oil painting (1885) by Albert Edelfelt (1854–1905). Musée National du Château de Versailles. picture-alliance / akg-images. **111:** Oil painting by Jacques Louis David (1788), The Metropolitan Museum of Art. 1977 gift purchased by Mr and Mrs Charles Wrightsman in honour of Everett Fahy (1977.10). Photograph © 1989 The Metropolitan Museum of Art. **112:** Grimaux É: *Lavoisier 1743–1794 d'apres sa correspondance, ses manuscrits, ses papiers de famille et d'autres documents inédits.* Paris: Ancienne Librairie Germer Baillière, 1888: plate p. 128. **113 (l):** Oil by Johann Friedrich August Tischbein ('Leipzig Tischbein', 1750–1812). Reproduced from: Masner K, Hintze E, eds. *Die Historische Ausstellung zur Jahrhundertfeier der Freiheitskriege.* Breslau, 1913. **113 (r):** Ebstein E, ed: *Deutsche Ärztereden aus dem 19. Jahrhundert.* Berlin: Julius Springer; 1926: plate p. 6. **114 (l):** Rabl M, ed. *Rudolf Virchow. Briefe an seine Eltern 1839–1864.* 2nd ed. Leipzig: W Engelmann, 1907: frontispiece. **114 (r):** Title page of Johann Franz Simon's main work, 1840. **115:** Österreichische Nationalbibliothek, Vienna. **116:** Gorup-Besanez ECF von. *Anleitung zur qualitativen und quantitativen zoochemischen Analyse.* 1st ed. Nuremberg: JL Schrag, 1850: 235. **117:** Autograph sketch from a handwritten application by Wilhelm Heintz, 1847. Source: Geheimes Staatsarchiv Preußischer Kulturbesitz; I. Hauptarchiv Ministerium der geistlichen Unterrichts- und Medizinalangelegenheiten: VIII D, no. 76, fol 124. **118:** Thudichum JLW. *Briefe über die öffentliche Gesundheitspflege, ihre bisherigen Leistungen und heutigen Aufgaben.* Tübingen: F. Pietzker, 1898. **119:** Garrod AB. On the blood and effused fluids of gout, rheumatism and Bright's disease: Second communication. *Medico-chirurgical Transactions* 1854; 37: 49–59 with plate. **121:** Baumann E, Kossel A. Zur Erinnerung an Felix Hoppe-Seyler. *Hoppe-Seyler's Zeitschrift für Physiologische Chemie* 1895; 21: 1–61. Photograph by E Fuchs, Strasbourg. **122:** Riegel F. Die klinischen Neubauten in Gießen. *Klinisches Jahrbuch* 1894; 5: 126–137 with plates. **123 (t):** Prof. U Boschung, Institut für Geschichte der Medizin, University of Bern, Switzerland. **123 (b):** Kirchhoff G, Bunsen R. Chemische Analyse durch Spectralbeobachtungen. *Annalen der Physik und Chemie* 1860; 110: 161–189, plate VI, fig 1. **124 (t):** MacMunn CA. *The spectroscope in medicine.* London: J & A Churchill, 1880: chart I (facing p.63), detail. **124 (b):** Thudichum JLW. Report on researches intended to promote an improved chemical identification of disease. *Tenth report of the Medical Officer of the Privy Council and Local Government [London]* 1867; Appendix 7: 152–294. **125 (l):** Ehrlich P, Lazarus A, Pinkus F. Leukaemie. Pseudoleukaemie, Haemoglobinaemie. In Nothnagel H, ed. *Specielle Pathologie und Therapie.* 1st ed. Vienna: Alfred Hölder, 1901: vol VIII, part

I, no. 3. Colour plate II. **125 (r):** Deutsches Medizin-historisches Museum Ingolstadt, Germany. **126 (l):** Gowers WR. An apparatus for the clinical estimation of haemoglobin. *Transactions of the Clinical Society of London* 1879; 12: 64–67. **126 (tr):** *Spektral-Apparate. Preisliste Nr. 27.* Hamburg: A Krüss Optisch-Mechanische Werkstätten, 1909: 7. **126 (br):** Vierordt K von. *Die Anwendung des Spectralapparates zur Photometrie der Absorptions-spectren und zur quantitativen chemischen Analyse.* Tübingen: H Laupp, 1873: plate I, fig 1a (lithographed plate). **127:** Marquardt M. *Paul Ehrlich als Mensch und Arbeiter: Erinnerungen aus dreizehn Jahren seines Lebens (1902–1915).* Stuttgart: Deutsche Verlagsanstalt, 1924: frontispiece. **128:** Hastings AB. Donald Dexter Van Slyke 1883–1971. *Journal of Biological Chemistry* 1972; 247: 1635–1640. **129:** Wreszinski W. *Der große Medizinische Papyrus des Berliner Museums.* Leipzig: Hinrich, 1909: Appendix. **130:** Title page from: Paullini CF. *Heilsame Dreck-Apotheke.* 1734. **131:** Sournia, JC, ed. *Illustrierte Geschichte der Medizin.* Salzburg: Andreas und Andreas, 1983: 8; 2853. **132/133:** Fischer-Homberger E. *Medizin vor Gericht.* Bern: Verlag Hans Huber, 1983: 185. **134:** Beck L. *Zur Geschichte der Gynäkologie und Geburtshilfe.* Berlin: Springer, 1986: 121. **135:** Hegar A. Diagnose der frühesten Schwangerschaftsperiode. *Dtsch med Wochenschr* 1895; 21: 566–567. **136:** Eulner HH. Hallesche Straßennamen als Denkmäler. *Hallesche Monatshefte* 1958; 5: 408. Rep 40A2. **137:** Ebert A, Weitzel HK, eds. *Die Berliner Gesellschaft für Geburtshilfe und Gynäkologie 1844–1994.* Berlin: Walter de Gruyter GmbH und Co KG, 1994: 138 and 220. **138:** Beck L. *Zur Geschichte der Gynäkologie und Geburtshilfe.* Berlin: Springer, 1986: 228. **139 (l):** Aschheim S, Zondek B. Schwangerschaftsdiagnose aus dem Harn. *Klin Wochenschr* 1928: 1407. **139 (r):** Aschheim S. *Die Schwangerschaftsdiagnose aus dem Harne.* 2nd ed. Berlin: S Karger, 1933. **140:** *Biographical Memoirs of Fellows of the Royal Society* 1978; 24: 182. **141:** *Grzimeks Tierleben.* Augsburg: Bechtermünz Verlag (now © Droemer Verlag, Munich), 1979/80; 5: 375. **142:** Bettendorf G. *Zur Geschichte der Endokrinologie und Reproduktionsmedizin.* Berlin: Springer, 1995: 611. **144:** Keystone. **146:** *Wien klin Wochenschr* 1901; 40. **147:** Roche. **148:** Archiv Berndt-Karger-Decker. **149/150:** Medizinhistorisches Institut und Museum, University of Zurich. **152/155:** Roche. Photographed with kind permission from Mrs Santoro and Dr Stebler-Gysi of the Swiss Red Cross Blood Donation Centre, Basel. **157:** Roche. **159:** Lyons AS, Petrucelli II RJ. Die Geschichte der Medizin im Spiegel der Kunst. Köln: DuMont Buchverlag, 1980: plate p. 209 (top left). **160:** The Royal Institution, London, UK / The Bridgeman Art Library. **161:** Prof. R Lamerz, Medical Dept II, Ludwig Maximilian University Hospital, Großhadern, Germany. **162:** Riedler GF, Graswinckel JV. *Blut unter dem Mikroskop.* Basel: Editiones Roche; 1978. **163 (l):** Roche. **163 (r):** Ellinger A, Falk F, Henderson LJ, Schulz FN, Spiro K, Wiechowski W, eds. *Analyse des Harns. Zum Gebrauch für Mediziner, Chemiker und Pharmazeuten. Zugleich Elfte Auflage von Neubauer-Huppert's Lehrbuch.* Wiesbaden: CW Kreidels Verlag, 1913: 2nd half, 1184. **164 (l):** Prof. R Huber. **164 (r):** Roche. **165:** National Library of Medicine. **166 (t):** Prof. EW Koneman. **166 (b) / 167:** Dr L Bubendorf, Dr A Lugli. **168:** Dr L Bubendorf. **169:** Genentech. **170:** M Mirlacher, Molecular Pathology Division, Institute of Pathology, University of Basel. **171–173:** Roche. **174:** Photographed courtesy of Ms Heckendorn, Bacteriology

Laboratory, Central Laboratory, Basel Cantonal Hospital. **175:** Koch R. Die Aetiologie der Tuberkulose. In: Schwalbe J, ed. *Gesammelte Werke von Robert Koch.* Leipzig: Georg Thieme, 1912: vol 1, plate XXVII. **177:** Medizinhistorisches Institut und Museum, University of Zurich. **178/179:** Roche. **180–182:** Robert Koch Institute (RKI), Berlin. **183:** Koch R. Die Aetiologie der Tuberkulose (1882 and 1884). In: Schwalbe J, ed. *Gesammelte Werke von Robert Koch.* Leipzig: Georg Thieme, 1912; vol 1: plate XXVII. **184:** Koch R. Verfahren zur Untersuchung, zum Konservieren und Photographieren der Bakterien, 1877. **185 (l):** Koch R. Die Aetiologie der Tuberkulose (1882 and 1884). In: Schwalbe J, ed. *Gesammelte Werke von Robert Koch.* Leipzig: Georg Thieme, 1912. **185 (r):** RKI. **186:** Koch R. Die Aetiologie der Tuberkulose (1882 and 1884). In: Schwalbe J, ed. *Gesammelte Werke von Robert Koch.* Leipzig: Georg Thieme, 1912, **187:** RKI. **188 (t):** *Ulk.* Supplement to the *Vossische Zeitung,* 14 Nov 1890. **188 (b):** Aus der Welt der unendlich Kleinen. Supplement to *Kladderadatsch,* 23 Nov 1890. **189:** *Ulk.* Supplement to the *Vossische Zeitung* 16 Jan 1891. **190:** RKI. **192/193:** Keystone. **194:** National Library of Medicine. **195:** Roche. **197:** Prof. N Hamasaki. **198:** Keystone. **200:** Medizinhistorisches Institut und Museum, University of Zurich. **201:** Prof. M Barthels. **202 (l):** National Library of Medicine. **202 (m):** *Scand J Clin Lab Invest* 1965. 17 (suppl 84): cover photograph. **202 (r):** Prof. M Barthels. **203:** Rizza C. Obituary for Rosemary Biggs. *Thromb Haemost* 2002; 88 (4): XI–XII. **207:** Elisabeth Hartert. **208:** Heike Sichmann. **210:** *Lebende Mikrowelt / The Living Microcosm / Microcosme Vivant.* Basel: Editiones Roche, 1991: 43. **211:** Roche. **212:** Hughes SS. *The Virus – A History of the Concept.* New York: Science History Publications, 1977. Original photograph reproduced courtesy of VM Zhdanov, DI Ivanovsky Institute of Virology, Moscow. **213:** Hughes SS. *The Virus – A History of the Concept.* New York: Science History Publications, 1977. **214/216:** Prof. EW Koneman. **217:** Roche. **219:** Keystone. **220:** Fischer EP. *Images & Imagination.* Basel: Editiones Roche, 2001: plate p. 133. **222:** Roche.

The laboratory revolution
The rise of automation and antibody techniques (from 1960 on)

225–226: Roche. **227:** picture-alliance / dpa. **228–233:** Roche. **234:** Dr O Mundigl, H Seul, Dept of Cell Biology, Roche Penzberg. **236–247:** Roche. **248:** Keystone. **249 (t):** Medizinhistorisches Institut und Museum, University of Zurich. **249 (b):** Photographed courtesy of the Medizinhistorisches Institut und Museum, University of Zurich. **250 (l):** Roche. **250 (r):** National Library of Medicine. **251:** Prof. HA Katus. **252 (l):** Keystone. **252 (r):** Roche. **253:** Institute of Physiology, Free University of Berlin. **254:** Roche **255:** Johny Syversen, Scanpix A/S, Oslo.

The human genome and the road ahead
Nucleic acid amplification and chip technologies expand the frontiers of diagnosis (advances since 1983)

257–259: Roche. **260 (t):** DH Gelfand, Roche. **260 (b):** Thomas Brock, University of Wisconsin-Madison. **261/262:** DH Gelfand, Roche. **263:** Roche. **265:** © Photo Archive, South Tyrol Museum

of Archaeology, Bolzano, Italy, *www.iceman.it.* Photo by Augustin Ochsenreiter, Marco Samadelli and/or Josef Pernter. **266/267:** Roche. **268:** Keystone. **269:** Roche. **270:** Prof. FE Maly. **272:** picture-alliance / dpa / Keystone. **273–289:** Roche. **291:** Keystone. **293:** Roche.

Concept	Roche Corporate Communications, Basel
Design, typesetting and printing	Gissler Druck AG, Allschwil
Lithos	Lithoteam AG, Allschwil
Binding	Grollimund AG, Reinach

7000627

F. Hoffmann-La Roche Ltd
CH-4070 Basel, Switzerland

© 2004, *Editiones Roche*

ISBN 3-907770-89-7